The Psychology of Reading

The MIT Press   Cambridge, Massachusetts, and London, England

The Psychology of Reading

Eleanor J. Gibson and Harry Levin

WB

Fourth printing, 1985

This book was set in Monotype Baskerville.
It was printed on R & E Book
and bound by The Murray Printing Company
in the United States of America.

Library of Congress Cataloging in Publication Data

Gibson, Eleanor Jack.
    The psychology of reading.

    Includes bibliographical references.
    1. Reading, Psychology of. I. Levin, Harry,
1925–   joint author. II. Title.
BF456.R2G46   418   74–9810
ISBN 0-262-07063-4 (hard)
ISBN 0-262-57052-1 (paper)

8/31/04

For Jimmy and Debbie

Contents

Preface

In this book are merged the result of fresh interests, fourteen years of research, and a fruitful collaboration. In 1960, with colleagues from various disciplines, we were invited to initiate a program of theoretically based research on reading—a totally new field of research for us all. Experimental psychologists had shunned this vital field for nearly sixty years. It is true that when Woodworth's classic edition of *Experimental Psychology* appeared in 1938, it contained a brilliant chapter on reading. But S-R psychology won the day, and when the 1954 edition by Woodworth and Schlosberg appeared, reading was out. Few experimental psychologists had touched it in the interval, and there was nothing new to say.

It was a surprise, then, when an invitation came from a government organization to recruit a research group from experimental psychology, developmental psychology, and linguistics to undertake a fresh assault on the learning processes involved in reading. We considered the opportunity for some time. Did we want to give up or put off the research we were individually pursuing? More important, were we intellectually (and motivationally) prepared to generate new, interesting, worthwhile research on the reading process? Could we do research that would, in the end, help children learn to read? (That question is still unanswered.)

As experimental psychologists, we were intrigued by the fact that no one had proposed a good theory of how one learns to read; there were many theories of how paired associates are learned, stored, retrieved, and so on. But were any of them productive for a theory of reading? We thought not, and so we decided to invest our time and anguish on the problem.

The original group of colleagues existed as a loose confederation, each of us doing his own research but meeting at intervals to learn from and criticize one another. We were generously supported by the United States Office of Education for three years, and the present authors later enjoyed support of research grants and conferences from the U.S.O.E. and also the National Institutes of Health (NIMH and NICHHD).

The plan of this book evolved in a seminar in the spring of 1972, and serious writing began in the fall of 1972. A fellowship from the John Simon Guggenheim Memorial Foundation made it possible for one of us, Eleanor Gibson, to take the academic year of 1972–73 off from teaching to work on the book. The William R. Kenan Charitable Trust provided a term's leave for Harry Levin. The Department of Psychology at the Massachusetts Institute of Technology, under the chairmanship of Professor Hans Leukas Teuber, made us welcome and provided offices, secretarial and library assistance, and, best of all, warm friendship and encouragement. It is hard to express adequate thanks to the group there.

A number of students from two seminars have read first drafts of chapters of the book and have contributed enormously to its quality. Carol Bishop generously read and criticized all the chapters, to their enduring benefit. We acknowledge deep gratitude to our friends who were willing to commit themselves on paper, so eloquently, about how they read something—Roger Brown, William M. Gibson, and David Pettijohn. Ann Buckler helped prepare the references and the indexes. Finally, because we want their names remembered, we thank Carol Kannus and Ann Smith, who not only typed the manuscript handsomely but corrected our many lapses and errors.

Ithaca, New York
May 1974

I

Concepts Underlying the Study of Reading

1

Introduction

Reading has received more attention than any other aspect of education. The ability to read well is the basis for success in school and later, so there is small wonder that instruction in the early grades is organized around learning to read. Methods of teaching reading have their loyal and vocal advocates, and partisanship in methods has a history in America as far back as Colonial times. An observer of American education cannot avoid the impression that prescriptions for teaching children to read are fads.

We do not intend an exhaustive examination of reading programs, but their range is vast. The McGuffey Readers, widely used at the turn of the century, have had a recent vogue, as though the moral injunctions of the McGuffey stories might firm up the will of the young reader to learn. Reform of the English writing system appears over and over with the assumption that a tighter correspondence between the speech sounds and writing will be helpful. Most recently, the initial teaching alphabet (ITA) had large-scale use in Great Britain and modest tryouts in the United States. Specially colored words to mark relationships with speech have been tried. Some educators advocated a regimen of physical exercises for the prereading child. Others suggested a program of drugs to facilitate neurological processes in the brain. There are computer programs for reading instruction and even on-line computer-guided instruction. Each new method is widely trumpeted, vociferously defended, and then abandoned except by a few faithful acolytes. Educators and laymen alike seem bemused with the hope that a formula for instant excellence in reading will be discovered, but the history of research on reading should not make us hopeful that a magic key will appear.

There have been two lines of research on reading, one of which is the subject of this book, but it is useful to compare it with the other approach to reading research. Among psychologists and educators, research on reading has had an interesting and perplexing history. Starting around the turn of the century and until about 1925, an attempt to understand the process of reading was an important problem for experimental and educational psychology and generated many experiments based on carefully thought out theoretical positions. The list of psychologists who were involved reads like a *Who's Who* of early experimental psychology: Cattell, Huey, Buswell,

Judd, Thorndike, Dodge, Woodworth, among others. Edmund Burke Huey deserves special mention. His book, *The Psychology and Pedagogy of Reading*, was published in 1908. Over sixty years ago, he raised many of the basic problems that concern us today and many that we will treat in this book. His theories and experiments are surprisingly up-to-date, and we are poorer for the fact that his analysis of the reading process did not have the influence on psychological and educational research that it merited.

Around 1920, the focus of research changed in a dramatic way. The research became oriented toward curricula. That is, rather than asking questions about the process of reading ("How do we read?"), the questions had to do with comparisons of the value of one method of teaching reading over another. The reason for this reorientation of reading research appears to stem from the extreme and vocal advocacy of one method over another. It was the beginning of the fruitless "phonics" versus "whole word" debate. For the time being, theory-based research on how a child learns to read or how we can understand the skilled reading process decreased. Curriculum research was the rule almost exclusively from 1920 to 1960 and continues today, though theory-based research is again coming into its own. Regretfully, it seems fair to say that the results of these 40 years of research test out poorly. We are in no better position to say that one method is superior to another. For every study that indicated the efficacy of one method, an equal number of studies reported results in favor of some contrasting method. The results tended to be interpreted with statements like "It all depends on the teacher."

There is today great dissatisfaction about the outcomes of teaching children to read. As many as 25% of school children read more poorly than their grade levels would predict. In turn, these failures to read are distributed unevenly in the population, since the preponderance of failures occurs among poor children in urban schools. The economic and social consequences are obvious. And, although there is much concern with new methods and programs to increase both child and adult literacy, the solutions are not imminent.

Curriculum research compares methods of teaching reading. The aims and methods of theory-based research on reading are quite different. For one, the concern is with the process of reading rather than the outcomes of a method. Further, the investigation of processes is guided by theories which apply not only to reading but more generally to perceptual learning and to cognitive and linguistic development.

The first part of this book provides the theoretical background that we need to understand reading. Theory-based research often, but not always, involves laboratory experiments. For example, the theory of perceptual learning described in Chapter 2 has been the basis for many experiments concerning children's use of orthographic rules in recognizing words. Theories are necessary guides not only to research but also to fruitful observation of children who are learning to read. In this case, theory-based observations provide the foundation for ordering the complex events that occur in the classroom, and in turn the observations themselves often enrich and expand the theory.

What Is Reading?

Compared with the massive efforts to find practical solutions to educational problems, there have been in psychology only comparatively modest attempts to understand the process of reading. What is reading? What are the relationships between spoken language and reading? How do we recognize letters, words? How does the grammar of a language influence the process of reading? How do we get meaning from written texts? Is there more than one kind of reading?

First, what do we mean by reading? *Reading is extracting information from text.* We have construed the word *text* very broadly, to mean not only the printed page but also combinations of text and pictures, diagrams, graphs, illustrated instructions, and so on. The first guiding principle for our research is that there is more than one process of reading. And if this is true, there is likely to be more than a single efficient way of giving instruction in this process. Consider the range of skill from a child reading a picture book to the mature reader extracting information from highly specialized texts in mathematics, or logic, or physics. Consider the illustrations in Figure 1–1 of three kinds of text. Reading is not simply the decoding of written symbols to sound. Advocates of ultrasimple phonetic writing systems (like Pittman shorthand, for instance) often try to give the public this impression, but fortunately no one has been fooled so far—for very long, at least. Literacy does not consist of being able to give a name or a sound upon presentation of a written character. Neither is it passive acquisition of an image somewhere in the head that a written word can then be matched to. Reading is an active process, self-directed by the reader in many ways and for many purposes.

A Fire

Jim lived on a farm. He had horses and cows in a big barn on his farm.

Once Jim saw a fire burning near his barn. He did not want his horses and cows to be burned. Jim ran to see what was burning. When he reached the fire, he saw that it was burning dried grass and weeds.

First, he ran into the barn to save his horses and cows. He led them to a safer part of the farm.

burn

48

Figure 1–1. Samples of three widely varying kinds of text. (a) A child's picture book. From McCracken and Walcutt, 1963.

UNIT 4
collar and facings

a—Machine-baste interfacing to WRONG side of one collar section 1/2'' from raw edges.
Trim interfacing close to stitching.

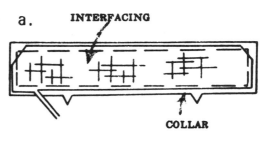

a. INTERFACING

COLLAR

b—Clip dress neck edge to stay-stitching.
With RIGHT sides together, pin collar to dress, matching centers back and small dots.
Baste. Stitch.
Trim seam; clip curve.
Press seam open.

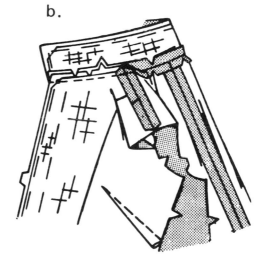

b.

(b) Instructions for following a dress pattern.

Hotels are both expensive and depressing.
Some hotels are shabby.
Therefore some expensive things are shabby.

This argument, for all its obvious validity, is not amenable to the traditional sort of analysis. True enough, it can be expressed in terms of A and I propositions by using the symbols "Hx," "Bx," "Sx," and "Ex" to abbreviate the propositional functions "x is a hotel," "x is both expensive and depressing," "x is shabby," and "x is expensive," respectively. Using these abbreviations, the argument can be symbolized as:

$$(x) [Hx \supset Bx]$$
$$(\exists x) [Hx \cdot Sx]$$
$$\therefore (\exists x) [Ex \cdot Sx]$$

But forcing the argument into the strait jacket of the traditional A and I forms in this way obscures its validity. The argument in symbols is invalid, although the original argument is perfectly valid. The notation here obscures the logical connection between "Bx" and "Ex." A more adequate analysis is obtained by using "Hx," "Sx," and "Ex," as explained above, plus "Dx" as an abbreviation for "x is depressing." Using these symbols, the original argument can be translated as:

1. $(x) [Hx \supset (Ex \cdot Dx)]$
2. $(\exists x) [Hx \cdot Sx] / \therefore (\exists x) [Ex \cdot Sx]$

So formulated, a demonstration of its validity is easily constructed. One such demonstration proceeds:

3. $Hw \cdot Sw$	2, EI
4. $Hw \supset (Ew \cdot Dw)$	1, UI
5. Hw	3, Simp.
6. $Ew \cdot Dw$	4,5, M.P.
7. Ew	6, Simp.
8. $Sw \cdot Hw$	3, Com.
9. Sw	8, Simp.
10. $Ew \cdot Sw$	7,9, Conj.
11. $(\exists x) [Ex \cdot Sx]$	10, EG

(c) A logical proof. From Copi, 1961. © The Macmillan Co., 1961.

Reading for Many Purposes

What do we read for? Perhaps the earliest instigation to generate a writing system was the need to retain accurate information that surpassed anyone's powers of recall. According to an old Chinese proverb, "The palest ink is better than the best memory." Archaeologists who dig up stone tablets chiseled with orderly marks frequently discover, if they can decipher them, that they are accounts of sales or some form of invoice. Certainly a business would not survive long if no one could keep or read the books. One can tie a string around his finger to remind him to buy a quart of milk on the way home, but if he needs bread, meat, eggs, salt, baby food, scouring powder, paper towels, dog food, etc., there are not enough fingers to go around, even if he could remember what item each one represented. We no longer have a few bards or scribes whom society relies on to remember its sagas or write its letters—there are just too many people and too much information. So the mnemonic function of writing and reading is a primary one and one that any child can easily be made aware of.

Reading and writing for the purpose of communication is also obvious to a child. A letter from Grandma is a prize joyfully awaited and may be full of interesting news like an imminent visit or a gift on the way. This is not even written the same way as a grocery list but has its own traditions and varying styles that we adapt for different occasions and receive with varied emotions.

It is true that adults usually gain a kind of "functional autonomy" in reading; it happens without special motivation sometimes when one has no intention of using the information. Sitting in a subway, it is almost impossible not to read the ads, as any adman knows. We read the backs of breakfast cereal cartons absentmindedly, without remembering the description of the contents. But this is the exception. We read mainly because we need to. True literacy depends on being able to extract information for innumerable reasons.

It is frequently assumed in schools that one needs to read primarily in order to learn things from books, like geometry and history and psychology and physiology. This can lead to attempts to "gild the philosophic pill," to borrow a phrase from Gilbert and Sullivan. Children are seldom deceived by this. It seems important to show them at once that you can read for pure unadulterated enjoyment, that reading a story or a poem by yourself and for yourself is sheer pleasure. Reading aloud to young children or letting them watch you absorbed in reading a novel is the obvious means of imparting this knowledge, but it should go on in school, too. Teachers should read "fun" books to children for a treat as long as the mechanics of the skill are still giving them problems. And of course, letting children read to themselves as soon as they can and whatever they want is equally important.

Reading to learn is an essential and entirely different activity from reading a poem or a novel for pleasure. It is a doubtful tactic to try to get across the functions of reading by sugar-coating the real lesson in ways that are actually irrelevant to the information that must be extracted. This is sometimes done on television programs and in overdecorated textbooks and may have the effect of preventing the child from learning to direct his own reading activity in different ways depending on his purpose.

The Plan of This Book

This book is divided into three parts, each designed for a unique purpose. Part I is devoted to psychological and linguistic principles that provide the basis for understanding the reading process. We feel that a number of books on reading have failed in what should be an important function, that of providing the psychological and linguistic concepts that will give the student of reading insight into the learning process and what it is that must be learned to be a good reader. Advice about instruction or comparison of programs, or prescriptions about what to do with retarded readers, cannot take the place of giving the potential teacher the intellectual tools to think for himself when problems arise. There is no such thing as a pedagogical panacea. Problems will arise, new ones, because children are different and environments are different. The teacher must be able to accommodate to them independently by providing the environment and the materials that the child's particular needs demand. We believe that we can be most helpful to teachers and others concerned with the teaching of reading by giving them insights into the process of reading rather than dogma. The aim is to help them solve problems, not to provide a cookbook approach. In line with this aim, we shall favor rather than eschew theory, for as a great educator once said, there is nothing so practical as a good theory.

Besides this introduction, there are six chapters in Part 1. The next two are devoted to psychological principles relevant to reading. Chapter 2 is a theory of perceptual learning and a demonstration of its relevance for understanding the reading process. Reading is a high-order perceptual skill, and the principles described in this chapter will be utilized throughout the book although we shall stress the point that reading is a highly complex cognitive process involving much more than perceptual skill.

Chapter 3 is concerned with the development of cognitive strategies. Reading is not memorizing paired associates. It requires much more complex psychological processes of strategic search, organization for remembering, use of natural units in problem solving, the discovery of rules and order, and the economical use of them. Above all, it requires the ability to transfer knowledge of rules and economical strategies to new material, something a child has to learn to do for himself.

Chapter 4 contains some essential linguistic concepts for understanding reading, such as the nature of phonetics and phonemics, parts of speech, how to analyze sentences, and various approaches to grammar.

Chapter 5 takes up the development of language in the child—a vital preliminary in all three of its aspects. How and when the child gains knowledge of phonology, meanings, and the grammatical rules of the language that he hears are covered here.

In Chapter 6, we turn to the nature of written language. The writing system that is used to represent the ideas to be conveyed can be of several kinds. The kind employed for writing the child's native language (or the one he is going to learn to read) will determine what kind of initial training procedures are optimal. The representation of the information system and the processes for extracting information must be happily matched.

Finally, Chapter 7 deals with the perception of words and will apply many of the basic concepts so far presented. It defines the properties of a word and summarizes the results of a large number of experiments on word recognition—how features of a word affect its perception under controlled conditions.

Part II is devoted to the acquisition of reading skill, beginning in Chapter 8 with development of prereading skills. These include development of graphic discrimination and its differentiation from pictorial perception, the early development of writing, and specific kinds of pretraining which have been thought to promote readiness to read, such as analysis of speech into units like words and syllables and practice in visual perceptual skills.

Learning to "decode," what has so often been thought of as the heart of learning to read, is treated in Chapter 9. We do not propose an ideal program, since we consider that this must vary with the students and the situation, but we consider the major psychological and pedagogical problems that arise, such as the child's motivation, the unit for initial decoding practice, the nature of early reading errors (they tell us what the child is doing), the teaching of spelling patterns, and the use of regularities within words.

Chapter 10 takes up the transition to skilled reading. There is no clean break anywhere along the line, but at some point the mechanics of reading must smooth out. Eye movements and subvocalizing come in here, as does progressive ability to extract meaning. We will consider especially progress in the use of grammatical structure and larger patterns for processing text in more economical ways.

Learning from reading and studies of how it can be enhanced are the subjects of Chapter 11. New and sophisticated research relating reading to comprehension and to analyses of style and discourse is considered.

The subject of the last chapter of this section is the currently much-argued question of models for reading. A recent survey sponsored by the U.S. Office of Education (Davis, 1972) lists and compares more than 30 so-called models. We consider two major classes of them, information processing models and analysis by synthesis, and attempt an evaluation of the model controversy. We conclude with a set of principles about reading, illustrated by some case studies, which we believe that any theory of reading must take into account.

Part III is called "Questions People Ask about Reading." There is no educational topic that has been so burdened with folklore, anecdotes, and dubious diagnoses as reading. But a number of the questions examined by popular writers in Sunday supplements and argued at teachers' meetings are legitimate and important ones, such as the question of a difference in dialect between the child and the teacher, or between the child and the text. Unfortunately, there is no objective answer at the moment to many of these questions. We discuss some of them, including the dialect question, the nature of dyslexia, and cross-national comparisons of reading, and present what evidence there is and what appears at the moment to be the most dispassionate and sensible view. But our aim throughout this book is to avoid "hot air" and pat answers that may turn out to be wrong.

2

A Theory of Perceptual Learning and Its Relevance for Understanding Reading

What is perceptual learning, and how is it different from other kinds of learning? To answer this question, we have to think first about what perception is. A functional definition of perception will serve us best. Perception is the process of extracting information from stimulation emanating from the objects, places, and events in the world around us. This information is vast, especially when one considers that it occurs over time as well as space. A newborn infant probably takes in very little of it (more than we used to think, however). Perceptual learning is learning to extract the relevant information from the manifold available stimulation, that is, the invariant information that specifies the permanent layout of the environment, the distinctive features of things that populate and furnish the environment, and invariants of events that enable us to predict outcomes and detect causes.

Much of this learning goes on at an early age, along with maturation of attentive behaviors, and then we speak of perceptual development of the individual. Early development of perceptual constancy is an example, that is, developing the ability to perceive things in their true sizes, shapes, and locations despite everchanging stimulation due to movements of things or of the observer himself. Perceptual learning goes on in the young scholar too, especially when he is learning to read. And it goes on in the adult when he learns professional skills like differentiating rock formations or bird songs or how to spot forgeries.

Perceptual learning is different from some other kinds of learning. It is not response learning, for instance, like increasing the probability of a rat's pressing a bar when an appropriate schedule of reinforcement is provided. It is not association of a response with a stimulus, like associating a name with a newly introduced person's face. It is not problem solving or inference from premises like working out an algebraic proof. In short, it is not *adding on* of anything. It is, rather, an increase of specificity of discrimination to stimulus input, an increase in differentiation of stimulus information. It is extraction or "pulling out" rather than adding on. The modification is in *what* is perceived.

Perceptual learning (and development) can be characterized in four important ways. It is *adaptive* to the needs of the person. For instance, we learn to see where it is safe to walk and to drive; to differentiate things that are edible from things that aren't; to differentiate telephone numbers so we can call friends; and to differentiate their names in the telephone book so we can find the number. Second, it is *active*. We use our receptor systems —our hands, eyes, and ears—to explore, to search for the useful information. Part of the basis of perceptual learning is an improvement in economical patterns of search behavior, such as increased skill in scanning for wanted information in reading something like a newspaper. Perceptual learning, third, is *selective*. Not all the potential information in stimulation is effective. The information is rich; we learn to extract what has utility for reducing uncertainty for our way of life. A species is adapted, in fact, with the means for doing this in characteristic ways. Man is a nearsighted creature; he can fixate his eyes on one focal point, unlike a horse; he can move his eyes in their orbits and point both them and his head; and he has excellent optical resolution. If it were not for these provisions, he could not learn to read fine print and differentiate the graphic symbols of our writing systems.

Finally, in accord with its definition, perceptual learning progresses toward better and better *differentiation*. What may be originally amorphous or confusible with something else comes to be perceived as structured and more specific, in closer correspondence with information in stimulation. The child's learning to perceive fine differentiations between confusible letters is one example; his discovery of orthographic structure such as spelling patterns is another, acquired much later. Both will be considered in detail further on.

The definition and theory of perceptual learning will be developed under three major headings. First, we shall consider *what is learned*. Next, we shall consider what *processes* are involved in perceptual learning. And finally, we shall describe some *trends* that can be observed in perceptual development.

What Is Learned

The exposition of any theory must begin with a description of what it is trying to explain. For a learning theory, this means describing what it is that is learned. What is learned in perceptual learning can be usefully divided into three classes of modification.

Distinctive Features

The people and objects and symbols that furnish the world differ from one another in characteristic ways that we must learn to distinguish if we are to perceive and ultimately behave adaptively. There are sets of things that differ from other sets. There are sets of people, sets of plants, sets of rocks, sets of playing cards—material objects of all kinds. There are also sets of coded items, like words and written symbols Things belonging to a set share common features that serve to distinguish that set from other sets. The set of animate things shares features like plasticity, growth, and motility that distinguish it from inanimate things. But sets can be divided further; there are alternatives within them. In order to identify something as unique, we must know its alternatives—what it might have been, but isn't quite. Things come in finite sets, and there are feature contrasts within the set that are shared in different degrees by the members of the set. We shall refer to these as "distinctive features," which permit specification with respect to a set of alternatives. This specification is one aspect of meaning.

Distinctive features are relational, not absolute like building blocks or elements. They are contrastive, as sharp or blunt, or straight or curved are contrastive. An object (or a symbol) is characterized by a pattern of distinctive features that is unique for that object, but members of a set may differ by few or many features—that is, features are shared within the set to different extents. One more qualification: distinctive features must be invariant over a number of transformations which are irrelevant or noncritical for differentiating the objects, or symbols, such as speech and writing.

The concept of distinctive features was elaborated by Roman Jakobson (Jakobson and Halle, 1956), who applied it to the phonemes of human speech. A small set of feature contrasts, like voiced-voiceless or consonantal-nonconsonantal, are sufficient to distinguish all the phonemes of all the languages of the world and render each one unique, because the set can be combined in so many ways. They are, furthermore, invariant when produced by different voices or even by a machine. This fact, as well as the contrastive relations, makes clear that they are not elements, but attributes. Jakobson also thought the features developed in the child's production (and presumably also in perception) by a process of differentiation or splitting, beginning with just one broad distinction (consonant-vowel) and progressing in a hierarchy of successive divisions over time to use of the full set of features employed by his native language.

The letters of an alphabet form a set, and differ from one another by one or more of the distinctive features that differentiate within the set. Since we are interested in reading, it is worth pursuing this example, both to illustrate the concept of distinctive feature and because knowledge of the features is potentially useful in understanding a child's progression in attaining reading skill.

Alphabets and writing systems are different for different languages, as we shall see in a later chapter, and it is not clear as yet whether there is a universal set of potential distinctive features as there appears to be for phonemes. There could well be, although of course if this is the case they are drawn on selectively by different systems. Some alphabets, like Hebrew and Arabic, make much more use of diacritical marks, for instance, than others. We shall confine the discussion here to the Roman alphabet and the uppercase capital letters, since a body of pertinent research is available for them.

This research began with the intuitive construction of a possible feature chart, to see whether it might at least be possible to find an economical set of contrastive descriptive features that would provide a unique pattern for each of the 26 letters. An example of such a chart is shown in Figure 2-1. The list of features is by no means definitive. We shall arrive at that only by research which will eventually provide an objectively obtained set of features which are really used in distinguishing one letter from another.

Features	A	E	F	H	I	L	T	K	M	N	V	W	X	Y	Z	B	C	D	G	J	O	P	R	Q	S	U
Straight																										
horizontal	+	+	+	+		+	+								+			+								
vertical		+	+	+	+	+	+	+	+	+					+	+		+				+	+			
diagonal /	+							+	+		+	+	+	+												
diagonal \	+							+	+	+	+	+	+	+									+	+		
Curve																										
closed																+		+			+	+	+	+		
open V																				+						+
open H																	+		+						+	
Intersection	+	+	+	+		+	+						+			+						+	+	+		
Redundancy																										
cyclic change		+							+			+													+	
symmetry	+	+		+	+		+	+	+		+	+	+	+		+	+	+			+					+
Discontinuity																										
vertical	+		+	+	+		+	+	+	+					+							+	+			
horizontal			+	+	+	+									+											

Figure 2-1. A possible feature chart for Roman capital letters. From Gibson., 1969, p. 88, by permission of Prentice-Hall.

The method for pursuing this research consists of seeing what letters people most often confuse with one another, or sort together into classes. Because different features are shared by pairs of letters to varying extents, we can use the probability of confusing two letters to form a confusion matrix, which we can then analyze mathematically to discover the dimensions that describe it. One of the first attempts to obtain such a matrix (Gibson, Osser, Schiff, and Smith, 1963) used a method of matching judgments, with four-year-old children as subjects. Very few of the children knew any letter names as yet, with the occasional exception of their own initials, so it was assumed that any incorrect matches they made were caused by visual rather than acoustic similarities.

The child was shown one letter, presented as a standard, in the window of a memory drum. It was followed, one second later, by a multiple-choice set of six letters, one of them the correct match. The letters in the choice set were randomly selected, but the sets were arranged so that every letter appeared an equal number of times in the choice sets for every standard. A balanced block design was employed, so that any one child judged only a fraction of the total number of displays. The children's errors were combined to form a confusion matrix. Significantly high confusions were M and W, N and M, Q and O, E and F, P and R, K and X. Many letters were never confused at all. This fact, plus the fact that the children actually made very few errors, limited the possibilities of analyzing the matrix. The number of errors for pairs of letters was correlated with a crude prediction made from the number of features they shared according to the feature chart. Some high correlations resulted, but also some low ones. The latter occurred especially when there was a low error rate for all the pairs for a given letter—too little variance. Another method which promised to give a more refined indication of similarity was then turned to.

The experiment (Gibson, Schapiro, and Yonas, 1968) employed a same-different judgment of two letters exposed simultaneously by projection on a small screen. If the subject thought they were identical, he pressed one button; if he thought they were different, he pressed another. His latency—the time he took to respond—was the index used, as well as the few errors that were made. Since all the possible combinations of different pairs and an equal number of same pairs (to prevent a response bias toward saying "different") required too many judgments, two sets of nine letters each were used, each with a different group of subjects. The sets were C, E, F, G, M, N, P, R, W; and A, D, K, H, O, Q, S, T, X. A set of nine artificial characters made up by the experimenters was also tested. The subjects were college students and seven-year-old children.

The results yielded a wide range of latencies. The mean latency for adults for the dissimilar pairs GW and WT were very short, 458 msec and 472 msec, respectively. The mean latencies for similar pairs were much longer; for PR, for instance, 571 msec and for OQ, 593 msec. The errors and the latencies were correlated very significantly, so the latency measure has validity. The mean latencies for judging pairs of artificial graphemes were the same as those for the familiar letters. Since the artificial characters had no names, it was concluded that the subjects were not naming the letters, but comparing them visually.

For each set of nine letters, a hierarchical cluster analysis (Johnson, 1967) was performed on both the latency data and the errors. This analysis essentially looks at the space in which the letters are grouped by the data and finds the shortest distances between the members. The process is re-iterated, yielding larger and larger sets until it finishes up with just one set. One can then plot the successive stages of the process in a tree structure (see Figure 2-2). By looking at the nodes in this structure, that is, the points where divisions occur, it is possible to infer what attribute was critical for the differentiation, and thus arrive objectively at distinctive features that are actually used.

In Figure 2-2, for adults, the first division is clearly attributable to a straight-curved contrast. All the letters with curves are grouped on the left branch, and the others, which as it happens all contain diagonals, on the right. At the next node, the round letters are differentiated from those with an intersection at the center. The tree structure for errors was very similar. The features used by children in Figure 2-2 look quite similar to

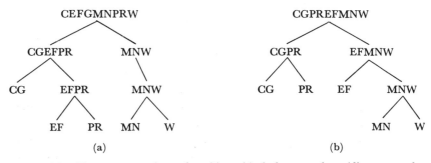

Figure 2-2. Tree structures drawn from hierarchical cluster analyses (diameter method) of same-different judgments of letter pairs by adults (a) and seven-year-old children (b). From Gibson, Schapiro, and Yonas, 1968.

those used by adults, but the first straight-curved split groups horizontals, verticals, and diagonals together. Diagonality splits off later, and intersection also seems a less prominent feature than for adults, who clustered at one node on that property.

A sorting method was tried out later by Gregory Lehne, since it was desirable to check whether the features located by the nodes have generality over different procedures. The subjects were simply told to sort the letters into piles so that the ones that "were alike" were together. The probability that a letter would appear in a pile with another was then calculated. Lehne found that third-grade children sorting the same nine letters shown in Figure 2-2 were using the same features found before, since a cluster analysis of his data yielded the identical structure. Lehne also had a group of children sort all 26 letters. A cluster analysis of the data appears in Figure 2-3. It is clear again that straight-curved is the first contrast. The round letters without intersection are separated off at the second node, and the curved letters with intersection at the third. Diagonality begins to

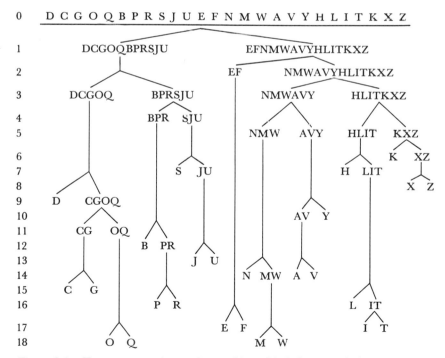

Figure 2-3. Tree structure drawn from a hierarchical cluster analysis generated by sorting of 26 letters by third-grade subjects using the diameter method. Data and diagram courtesy of Gregory Lehne.

be separated off on the right branching by the third node, but again this feature does not seem to have as high a priority in the hierarchy as it does for adults, since K, X, and Z do not separate off from horizontal-vertical letters until the fourth node.

Distinctive features also serve to differentiate more complex reading materials than letters, but they are harder to get at and define. We shall discuss the distinctive features of words in a later chapter.

Invariants of Events

What is learned includes not only distinctive features of things that are static, but also invariant relations of events that occur over time. Events—happenings in the world—are part of the infant's experience from the beginning. The appearance of an adult, with a face coming closer and looming over him, for instance, is one of the earliest events displayed to him, recurring very frequently. It has been demonstrated that a very young infant perceives looming, that is, something approaching him. Ball and Tronick (1971) have in fact shown that even a 20-day-old infant responds adaptively to a looming object. An event like looming specifies an outcome with adaptive significance or meaning: imminent collision if the acceleration of magnification increases rapidly.

Real events, like appearance, disappearance, and reappearance, begin to have meaning for a child long before he can talk about them. Rulelike invariants are discovered by the child in early observations of events and manipulations of things. The constancies are good examples of such learning. The face fills more and more of the child's field of view as it comes toward him, and less and less as it withdraws, but the reversibility of this event is perceived before long and provides the information for discovery of an invariant property. When a child can manipulate an object with his own hands, move it to and fro and turn it over, he can provide himself with information about constant properties of things like their shapes and sizes.

Meaning (the aspect of it which we refer to as adaptive significance) is rooted in the perceptual learning provided by these experiences. They give information about contingencies, invariants, and causal relations. The specification of invariants is of the greatest possible adaptive significance. There is a long road from perception of the meaning of an ongoing event to perception of meaning in words printed on a page that one is reading, but the beginning is here.

Invariant properties of speech and writing are themselves learned through observations of events, or by performance. An adult reads most letters correctly even though they are written in many different handwritings. It seems very likely that a child's attempts at making letters himself— a highly observable and interesting event—contributes greatly to his learning the critical features that distinguish one letter from another and must be present if a letter produced by just anyone is to be read and the irrelevant irregularities, awkwardnesses, and flourishes disregarded.

Higher-Order Variables

Both static things and events have not only irreducible invariant properties, like a distinctive feature of a letter, or the accelerated magnification of the event of approaching; they also belong to superordinate structures. Finding the relations between distinctive features or between events is learning about higher-order structure, a third aspect of meaning. Relations can be thought of as superordinate or embedded, so there are two ways of thinking about structure: the whole formed by the relations of subordinate features, or the part in its relation to the whole. But in any case, perceiving higher-order structure is the third kind of modification that we need to consider under what is learned. A thing or an event can be specified within a system or a hierarchy of sets, each with features contrasting with another set. A man belongs to a set of animate things. Approach belongs to the set of movements in space.

Two notes played on a musical instrument yield an event with invariant irreducible relations—a temporal pattern or a rising or falling frequency pattern, in the latter case a "glissando." Repetitions of the same event yield the kind of structure called a "run" (Restle and Brown, 1970). These may further be embedded within a melody or a complex musical composition like a symphony. Simple structures like runs are easily picked up (Restle and Brown, 1970). Children like musical patterns with runs composed of glissandos, like "Three Blind Mice," but the ability to appreciate more complex musical structures requires time to develop (Werner, 1948, 1961, pp. 124 ff). Rhythm is another kind of event which has irreducible relational invariants combined into more complex structures, with analogies to speech. Martin (1972) has presented convincing evidence for rhythmic patterning in speech, showing that the patterning carries a heavy information load in ordinary connected speech. He proposed a hypothesis of preset timing, that "since the accented elements dominate the temporal organization of an utterance, they must in some sense be planned first.

Intervening, lower-level syllables then are planned subsequently in hierarchical fashion, by (metaphorically) reading the rhythm tree, level by level, from the top down" (Martin, 1972, p. 199). The quotation refers to production, but Martin has also made it clear that rhythmic information contributes to intelligibility, to "decisions about syntax, morphology and meaning," which are themselves structured and perceived as events.

Lashley (1951) stressed that the serial organization of behavior involves complex, hierarchically organized systems. This is particularly true of language, spoken or written. As perception develops, more complex orders of structure in the hierarchy are learned and processed. Lashley argued persuasively* that these structures could not be the result of associative connections between elements. Learning to perceive them, in that case, cannot be adequately explained as a process of association.

Learning to perceive higher-order structure is especially important for comprehending language, both spoken and written. We are not conscious (unless we are required to be) of differentiating phonemes; we hear words and sentences and intended meanings which are often even rather badly produced. The structure that creates these higher-order variables can be thought of as a set of rule systems, phonological, syntactic, and semantic, that describes the organization of the subordinate relations. We will consider them in detail in a later chapter.

Written language obviously has information for a hierarchy of structures. Letters have patterns of distinctive features, so they are themselves higher-order structures. But a word is a pattern of letters and is a still higher-order structure. The vocabulary of a language in written form contains many repetitive patterns and constraints that constitute orthographic rules. "Spelling patterns," as they were called by Fries (1962), have, in addition, contrastive features that relate in regular fashion to the way they are sounded. For example (Fries, 1962, p. 201):

> The reader must learn through great practice to respond automatically to the contrastive features that separate these three patterns each of which contains a large number of words.

---

*"The word 'right,' for example, is noun, adjective, adverb, and verb, and has four spellings and at least ten meanings. In such a sentence as 'The millwright on my right thinks it right that some conventional rite should symbolize the right of every man to write as he pleases,' word arrangement is obviously not due to any direct associations of the word 'right' itself with other words, but to meanings which are determined by some broader relations" (Lashley, 1951, p. 509).

MAN	MANE	MEAN
DAN	DANE	DEAN
BAN	BANE	BEAN
HAT	HATE	HEAT
FAT	FATE	FEAT
MAT	MATE	MEAT

Written words, like spoken ones, are of course combined into still higher-order structures, like phrases and sentences and paragraphs. Higher-order structures, once detected by the learner, provide him with larger units of information that he may be able to process as wholes or "chunks," a very great cognitive economy. We are going to suggest and elaborate as we proceed the proposition that *the reader processes the largest structural unit that he is capable of perceiving and that is adaptive (has utility) for the task he is engaged in.*

Processes and Principles

Once we have defined what it is that is learned, we can tackle the question of the processes involved. How does learning take place? Can we formulate any principles for guiding and enhancing the learning process? The answer to these questions seemed obvious to learning theorists, both lay and professional, for centuries. The learning process, it was thought, consisted of associating one thing with another. The elements to be associated varied occasionally—sometimes they were sensations, sometimes ideas, and of course for the past 50 years or more they were thought to be stimuli and responses. But this simple and ancient notion does not work for perceptual learning, because what is learned is not addition of something but rather extraction of something. What processes could yield extraction of a distinctive feature or an invariant from the surrounding ongoing stimulation, or differentiation of a contrast?

Differentiation by Abstraction

In thinking about how concepts are developed, we are accustomed to refer to a process of abstraction. Something invariant over instances is perceived and pulled out, so to speak, from the accompanying variable context. It is, to quote William James, a process of *dissociation from varying concomitants.* Something like this happens when a distinctive feature is differentiated, but it is a perceived contrast, not an idea, that is abstracted.

Consider the case of a child's differentiating the distinctive features of phonemes. In learning to distinguish the voiced-voiceless contrast or the aspirated-nonaspirated, for instance, does he associate something to a stimulus? He hears his parents, baby-sitter, and others talking and is exposed to numerous examples of these feature contrasts. But obviously he is never exposed to one feature alone as a stimulus, and there is no response that could be attached to it because he does not articulate phonemes yet. The contrast must be abstracted from the speech flow, and even over different voices.

An associative theory, furthermore, does not explain the ordered, hierarchical differentiation of features. But hierarchical differentiation is entirely consistent with the notion of systematic abstraction of relations, with the grossest contrast, consonant-vowel, coming first, followed by progressive abstraction toward the more subtle features.

Another point in favor of the view that feature contrast is abstracted as a relation is the fact that discovery of this relation as evidenced by one instance is at the same time generalized to all other possible instances. The evidence for this point necessarily comes from production, but is nevertheless convincing. When the child produces the contrast accurately in one case, he is able to do so in all the other applicable cases without practice. This is a beautiful example at the perceptual level of what has been called "generalizing abstraction."

A good example of this systematic generalization comes from Velten (1943), a linguist who observed his own child's language development. At an early stage of speech production, the child did not use the voiced-voiceless feature contrastively (e.g., *p-b, t-d, s-z* were not consistently given the proper feature value). But when one pair was learned, so were the others. The abstract contrastive relation was applied systematically to all the relevant classes, obviously not by practicing an associated response in each case.*

The notion of a process of abstraction at a perceptual level is not a new one. Werner (1948, 1961), for example, presented evidence for a process of "primitive abstraction" or "concrete abstraction," analogous to the conceptual abstraction that emerged at a later genetic level. Relationships are brought forth which do not stand out in isolation. Here is his report of an earlier instructive experiment by Russel, who investigated the "apprehension" of relationship in children from one year, seven months, to five years old.

---

*See Slobin (1971, pp. 64 ff.) for a clear and simple discussion of this case.

Once these children had learned that by touching one of two figures which exhibited contrast in form or size a bell would ring, they were able to adjust their choice to a variation in these figures (provided that the figural relationship itself remained the same). Having grasped the fact that it was the larger with respect to the smaller, or the round with respect to the angular, or the symmetrical with respect to the asymmetrical, which was the "ringing figure," they made a correct choice even when presented with variations of these contrasting pairs. The child understands and is able to transpose diverse opposites: outline vs. solid, symmetrical vs. asymmetrical, thick vs. thin, small vs. large, round vs. angular, etc. (Werner, 1961, p. 219)

Invariants characterizing ongoing events are abstracted in a somewhat different sense. A relation is discovered over a variable transformation in time. The perspective transformations that occur when an object is rotated away from the perceiver and back again give information about the object's shape. One could formulate this as a mathematical rule, although the developing infant learning about constant shapes of things obviously does not. It is an abstraction, nevertheless, of a relational property given by the reversibility of the event.

If we want to facilitate abstraction of a relation (and we often do in educational situations), we can draw attention to it by enhancing the feature contrast, or by providing uncluttered examples of the invariant property. An old experiment on concept learning by Hull (1920) required subjects to learn to call by the same name sets of Chinese characters which could be classified by containing a common radical. The radicals were not easy to abstract from the complex characters, but when they were drawn in red and the rest of the strokes in black, learning was facilitated.

Ways of enhancing or making salient a relation depend on what it is that must be abstracted from the context, of course. Starting with the maximum contrast and progressing toward smaller ones suggests itself as a second way of defining the relation clearly, and there is some research to support the efficacy of this method (Lashley, 1938; Gibson, 1969, pp. 99 ff).

Introducing already salient properties and making them redundant (correlated) with the relation to be abstracted has often been tried (as in the Hull example above), but ability to use redundancy develops slowly. The child may notice only the salient property, defeating the instructor's purpose. An experiment by Gibson and Shepela (1968) illustrates this point. A group of children in a Head Start class were taught, over a period of days, to name nine letters of the alphabet. Some had the letters presented all in black. Others had them divided into three groups of different colors, one color going with a set of three letters having rhyming names (e.g., A, K, and J were printed in red). After rather lengthy training, all the children were tested on the letters printed in black. The number of letters identified successfully was disappointingly small, in both cases. Although the children who had seen the colored letters were surprisingly good at remembering what color they had been when they were shown the black versions, this did not facilitate learning the names of the letters.

Older children (third grade) given artificial letters in three colors quickly learned to identify them by an arbitrary name, and did not remember the colors better than chance would predict. This finding leads us to a second process in perceptual learning, learning to ignore irrelevant information.

Ignoring Irrelevant Information
It is a common observation of teachers and parents that young children's attention wanders, that they tend to be extremely distractible. Along with this has gone the notion that ability to ignore the irrelevant and to process only wanted information increases with age. The distinctive features and invariants are extracted from stimulation and the variable, noisy context is ignored—doesn't get through the gate, so to speak.

Is there an inhibition of irrelevant stimulation so that, although present, it is not perceived, or perceived only minimally without complete processing? And does such a process improve with age? There has been a good deal of research on this problem in recent years, since it is of educational as well as theoretical interest. Results of this research at present are not very consistent, tending to vary with the task and the age range considered. This is not surprising, really, for the child must have learned the relevant distinctive features and differentiated them from the irrelevant before he could ignore the irrelevant; and what is critical information for one task is not necessarily for another. Perception, as we pointed out earlier, is adaptive for the task, as well as actively selective in abstracting and differentiating distinctive features.

Consider the following experiment by Lehman (1972), which shows that the development of ability to ignore the irrelevant depends on the task and the features to be selected or ignored. Lehman gave children from three age groups (kindergarten, second, and fourth grades) objects differing in shape or texture and asked them to match one of a pair differing in one of the two properties to a standard. The children explored the objects (concealed from sight) by touch, and their hand movements were photographically recorded. Only one of the variables was relevant for making the match, so the other could be ignored. For instance, if texture (sandpaper, fur, etc.) was the critical feature distinguishing the objects, the child did not need to examine the outlines of the object. When the children were told beforehand what variable was relevant, over 80% of their search was confined to the relevant feature. There was some improvement with age in ignoring the irrelevant feature, but all performed well. The younger children were better at ignoring shape than texture, which appeared to be more salient for them.

On the other hand, when the experimenter did not tell the children what the distinguishing variable was, although it remained the same from trial to trial (the shapes in a trial, for instance, were always alike, while the texture varied) there was a very significant age difference. Kindergarten children showed no improvement in ignoring the irrelevant variable. Second graders improved on the texture problems, where shape could be ignored, but not on the shape problems. Only fourth graders showed a significant improvement in ignoring whichever one was irrelevant. Thus when the relevant distinguishing property had to be discovered, and then the irrelevant one ignored, the economical strategy did not appear until about eight years and was still not perfect. The older children showed a better ordered, more systematic search, as well. Thus selective attention in the sense of extracting and noticing the distinguishing variable and ignoring the irrelevant can appear early under some conditions, but takes longer to develop under others.

A method of studying selective attention much used in recent years is the so-called dichotic listening experiment. Through earphones, one message can be presented to one ear and a different one to the other. The listener can be asked to "shadow" (pay attention to and report) what comes in one ear and to ignore the message coming to the other. It is also possible to present two messages at once to both ears, with some differential feature distinguishing the messages, like different voices (e.g., a man's and a woman's), and to ask the subject to attend to one and ignore the other. Adults are quite good at this task and generally remember little or nothing of the message to be ignored.

Maccoby (1967) performed experiments of this type, somewhat simplified, on children from kindergarten, second grade and fourth grade. In a typical experiment, the child heard a man's and a woman's voice each speaking a word (but a different one) at the same time. The child was asked to report the word spoken by only one of the voices. There was improvement with age in the ability to report correctly the word spoken by the asked-for voice and a progressive decline in the number of intrusion errors, that is, reporting the word spoken by the voice that was to be ignored. A number of factors effect performance in this task. Greater familiarity of a target-word or phrase, in relation to the nontarget one, affects the number of correct reports. The nature of the process is still a problem for research, but it is nevertheless true that ability to ignore irrelevant information improves with age as well as ability to select out and use distinctive features.

We can pretty safely surmise that "attention" must be accompanied by "inattention." One implies the other. But inattention can be of two kinds. It can be a nonintentional failure to attend—just not paying attention. What mother has not sometimes said, "Sally, you're not listening to me," when Sally was daydreaming or watching television. But there is also *active inattention*. Again, it can be of two kinds. It can be a sense-organ adjustment, such as turning the head and eyes away from the television set so as to dampen its stimulus input and facilitate hearing what mother is saying. Or it can be a covert shutting out, perhaps a neural inhibition, such as occurs when listening to two voices at once and ignoring information coming from one of them. It is the latter process that is not well understood, but it is the one of developmental interest, since it involves awareness of what is wanted and not wanted, with active cognitive direction.

Optimally adaptive perception must consist of some balance between heightened attention to information required by task demands and some incidental exploration of other potential input. Rigid orientation, especially of the receptor systems, does not seem adaptive, leading us to consideration of the third process in perceptual learning, the peripheral mechanisms of attention.

Peripheral Mechanisms of Attention

The filtering process we have just discussed, especially in the listening experiments, must be conceived of (however little we know about it) as a central attentive process that selects or rejects. But we can make sense organ adjustments that literally expose us optimally to wanted information, like fixating a word, or cocking an ear, or thumping a wheezy patient's chest in suitable places while listening through a stethoscope. Such activities can be thought of as attentive mechanisms, but they are peripheral ones, not central. We can observe scanning movements of the eyes, head turning, and palpating, and their selective function is obvious. We can "filter out" unwanted visual information easily by closing our eyes, but we do not refer to this process as filtering—it is a literal shutting out.

Exposing the receptors to needed aspects of potential stimulation is the result of an exploratory process, one that is highly susceptible to learning and development. Exploring the array of available stimulation facilitates discovery of critical features of the world. It is adaptive, for it changes with the task, becoming selective for a given task as practice continues. Yet rigid selectivity in the orientation of receptor mechanisms is not optimal, for the unexpected can occur. The observing responses (Atkinson, 1961; Wyckoff, 1952) that are specifically conditioned in a given situation are selective but not flexible and are thus not suited to discovery of new information.

Development of skill in the exploratory use of peripheral sensory systems has been emphasized by many psychologists (Gibson, 1969; Piaget and Inhelder, 1956; Zaporozhets, 1965). Studies of the development of exploratory skill in identifying objects by touch have without exception found a progression from a "clutch" or global contact which is not exploratory to a planned search for distinctive features in which the two hands play different roles and the fingers obtain different information as they move over the contours and raised or indented surfaces of the object (see J. J. Gibson, 1962). One finger may dominate the exploration, with the others playing different roles, sometimes indicating "where to feel next," much like information obtained from a peripheral retinal area when the gaze is fixated elsewhere.

Searching by touch is active and skill in search increases developmentally, becoming more flexible and more adaptive for the task, which can vary from appraising a surface texture, as in wool grading, to making fine measurements or of course identifying objects. It also becomes more systematic for a given task, often following an ordered program. These same developmental trends appear in visual exploration and search, which is of special interest to us here. Visual attention in the young infant is a little like the clutching grasp; it is not active search but appears to be drawn involuntarily to certain salient properties of a visual display, such as high brightness contrast or motion of an object. But it increases in activity and flexibility with age, and this increase in exploratory looking is correlated with discovery of distinctive features of the world of things.

Piaget (1963, 1970) has described the development of what he refers to as the "perceptual mechanisms" in looking behavior. Some processes that develop, according to him, are decentration, visual transport, relating, and visually placing in reference. All of these suggest development of exploratory activity suitable for the detection of distinctive features. Piaget has applied these concepts mainly to the study of illusions, not our present concern, but he emphasizes that the perceptual learning which occurs is "dependent on autoregulations" and "is not reinforced, since the subject does not know the error in his estimate" (1970, p. 719). We shall return to this point shortly.

Most of the laboratory studies of the development of looking behavior with age have used pictures as stimuli, while photographing the subject's eye movements (see, for example, Mackworth and Bruner, 1970; Vurpillot, 1968; Zinchenko et al., 1963). Suffice it to say here that children make many more small eye movements than adults; they do not adequately cover the display; they do not select the informative areas for fixation; they do not make long eye movements toward such an area; and they do not alter the eye movements appropriately when the display is represented. Systematic comparison and planned search increase progressively with development.

Nodine (Nodine and Evans, 1969; Nodine and Lang, 1971) has studied the looking behavior of prereading (kindergarten) and reading (third-grade) children while they compared two strings of letters in order to decide whether they were the same or different. The children's eye movements were photographed as they made the judgment. The number of letters fixated, the length of fixation, where the children mainly looked, and the number of paired comparisons between similarly placed letters in the two words were compared for the two age groups.

The displays shown the children were pairs of four-letter nonsense strings, half of the pairs the same and half different. A same pair might be EROI—EROI; a corresponding different pair might be EROI—EORI. The difference in the strings always consisted of a juxtaposition of the two medial letters, so there was an appropriate target spot for concentrating fixations. Furthermore, half the pairs contained middle letters that were highly confusable (e.g., OEFU), while the other half had middle letters of low confusability (e.g., OFWS). If the high-confusability "different" strings were fixated longer in the target area, it could be concluded that the child was giving specific visual attention to an examination of the distinctive features of the letters.

The third-grade children scanned much more efficiently in differentiating the words. Kindergarten subjects required an average of four more fixations and spent on the average 1.25 seconds longer for each matching test than third-grade subjects. The third-grade subjects exhibited significantly more paired comparisons, that is, systematic scans from one word to the other comparing the corresponding letters in the sequence. Both groups of subjects spent more fixations on target-letter positions than on non-target-letter positions, but the older group spent relatively more time on target letters than the younger. The frequency of a scan from target to target was equal to the frequency of a scan from target to nontarget for kindergarten subjects, but the frequency of a scan from target to target was double that of a scan from target to nontarget for third graders. The kindergarten children scanned more within words than between. Thus the quality of the visual scanning increased in specificity and economy, the older children attending selectively to informative details in the display and tending to ignore irrelevant and redundant ones.

A later experiment by Nodine and Stuerle (1973) confirmed these findings. Both first-grade and third-grade children required fewer fixations, less fixation time, and fewer cross-comparisons than kindergarten children to judge sameness or difference of pairs of letters of varying degrees of confusability (see Figure 2-4). In addition, the fixation patterns of the older children were qualitatively more attuned to informative features of the letters. An experiment (Nodine and Simmons, in press) with large letterlike symbols, in which pairs of symbols might differ on one of four dimensions, again found that third-grade children made many fewer fixations per pair to reach a judgment of same or different. Fixations on the areas of presumed feature contrast exceeded chance for both kindergarten and third-grade children. Although the third-grade children made many fewer fixations, a higher proportion of them (.41) were on distinctive feature areas than for kindergarten children (.36).

Causal relationships are hard to analyze here; the reader must know where the information is in order to use his eyes most effectively in a comparison. There must be at least two steps in effective peripheral attention: first, location of the informative areas of the display, and then comparison of distinctive features, whether by systematic active manipulation of the receptor mechanisms or some internal attentive process.

Reinforcement and Motivation in Perceptual Learning
Since the time of Edward Thorndike (and earlier, if we trace the history), it has been assumed by most psychologists and educators that what is learned is selected by external reinforcement—a reward or punishment generally applied by the experimenter or the parent or the teacher. The reward could be relief from hunger or a token of some desirable kind, or at a later stage simply "that's right," or "good." Punishment could be something physically aversive, but at a later stage it could be "no," or "that's wrong." Along with such a notion of reinforcement went the notion that the subject's motivation is based on physiological needs or on some sort of pleasure principle (Thorndike used the term "satisfaction").

For reinforcement to be applied by another person, it is necessary, obviously, for that person to have knowledge of what the learner is doing or thinking or perceiving. When a child is learning to differentiate the

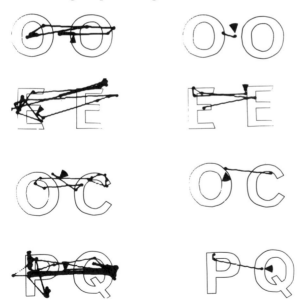

Figure 2-4. Eye movements made by kindergarten (left column) and third-grade children (right column) deciding whether pairs of letters were the same or different. Note the enormous increase of economy in looking with age. Photographs courtesy of Dr. Calvin Nodine.

distinctive features of the speech he hears, or of the letters that he is comparing, or the rules that govern perspective changes in shape as he turns an object in his hand, the "other one," parent or teacher, cannot know what he is perceiving. What is learned in perceptual learning cannot depend on externally applied reinforcement because an external agent cannot have knowledge of the learner's knowledge until the learner is ready to inform him of it—and then he has learned. The learning, as Piaget said, is autoregulated. Others have remarked this too, of course (see Gibson, 1969, Chapter 7). It must occur through reduction of uncertainty by the child getting his own information.

Along with this interesting fact about perceptual learning goes another concerning the learner's *motivation*. Why does the child look around the world and explore the effect of turning the object in his hand? To obtain a material reward? Hardly. He appears to be innately curious about things and happenings in the world, to have an *intrinsic motive to get information about things and people and places and events*. Even Pavlov, the spiritual father of the behaviorists, stressed this, calling the need to get information about the world the "what-is-it" reflex.

It is scarcely rated high enough—this reflex that one might call the investigatory reflex, or, as I call it, the "What-is-it?" reflex; this is . . . one of the fundamental reflexes. Both we and the animals, at the slightest environmental variation, dispose the appropriate receptor apparatus in the direction of the agent of the variation. The biological significance of this reflex is enormous. If the animal lacked this reflex, then its life would every moment hang by a thread. And for us this reflex goes a very long way indeed, appearing finally in the form of that curiosity which creates science and gives and promises us supreme, unlimited orientation in the surrounding world. (Elkonin, 1957, p. 55)

A related kind of motivation was studied in a series of experiments begun in the late 1940s in the primate laboratory of Harry Harlow. In a typical experiment (Harlow, Harlow, and Meyer, 1950) dubbed "learning motivated by a manipulation drive," monkeys were given mechanical puzzles which could be taken apart. They remained in the animals' living cages for 12 days and were reset at intervals. After 12 days, these monkeys and some naive ones were observed in a test period with the assembled puzzle. All of the monkeys given the previous opportunity to manipulate the puzzle performed successfully at once, but the naive monkeys were not successful during the test period. Manipulation of the puzzle had evidently interested the monkeys and been its own reward. "Curiosity" seems to us a better term than "manipulation drive," since the monkeys didn't just manipulate, they learned something.

Butler (1953, 1965) carried these experiments farther, showing that a drive to explore visually, even when no manipulation is possible, is strong and persistent. When monkeys were placed in a chamber with a small window that could be opened to provide a glimpse of the outside world (merely the laboratory or objects like other monkeys or a moving toy train), they not only opened the window and looked out, but even learned a discrimination problem for the reward of looking out the window.

Human primates, as well as monkeys, have strong motives to explore their environment. Berlyne (1960, 1966) has investigated looking behavior in a large number of preference experiments, showing that subjects prefer to look at displays with a certain degree of complexity (novelty, hetero-geneity, incongruity, etc.). Human infants have been shown, in any number of experiments, to look more at a heterogeneous display than a homo-geneous one. It is possible (Brennen, Ames, and Moore, 1966) that the degree of preferred complexity increases with age. An interesting fact about these experiments with infants is that habituation sets in after a long look, and a fresh display will then win attention. There is good evidence that this habituation is not some form of sensory fatigue, but "getting to know" the display (Friedman, 1972; McCall and Melson, 1970).

To return to the problem of reinforcement of learning, is there no rein-forcement in perceptual learning in the absence of external reinforcement? Or is there a different kind of reinforcement that goes along with intrinsic motivation? Berlyne thought that reduction of subjective uncertainty through exploratory behavior reinforces an instrumental response. We agree that there is an important insight here and that reduction of un-certainty may be reinforcing for perceptual learning (and perhaps all cognitive learning). But there need not be specific responses involved. The S-R formula does not apply to perceptual learning because it is not a re-sponse that is learned but a distinctive feature, an invariant, or a structure that makes order out of chaos and reduces information. Collating of features, finding permanent, invariant attributes of things and places and predictable relations in events, is adaptive and achieves cognitive eco-nomy. These are the things that are learned, and no outside agent can reinforce them. Whether this achievement is "rewarding" in the sense of giving satisfaction, and whether strategies leading to perception of structure and invariant relations tend to be repeated are other questions, calling for research.

Even in infancy, finding a predictable relation seems to have a high reinforcing value and to result in repetition of the activity. Experiments using the technique of "nonnutritive sucking" (e.g., Eimas et al., 1971) are one example of this. A nipple is placed in an infant's mouth, not attached to a bottle of milk, but to a long empty tube. Sucking by the infant results in change of pressure in the tube and through a transducer can trigger a contingent event, such as a buzzer sounding or a recorded human voice saying something. Finding the contingent relation between sucking and production of the event seems to be inherently reinforcing, for the infant learns to repeat the procedure almost instantly, with appropriate modifications when the contingent event is modified or repeated too often without change and loses his interest.

"Contingency awareness" was the subject of an article by Watson (1966), who showed that learning occurred with no other reward than observing a predictable event in the world. Watson played a game with his two-month-old son. He held out his arms when the child was watching him, and when his eyes turned toward one of them, Watson closed his fist, and then opened it again. When the infant turned away and then looked back, the fist closing and opening was repeated. This contingency was soon learned and behavior producing it increased. The contingency game was continued with other and more complex events. Piaget (1952, 1963) has reported a number of illustrative examples of an infant's interest in contingent events and pleasure in producing them. He speaks of this as "trying to make the interesting spectacle last" (1963, pp. 200 ff). When one thinks of the richness of causal and contingent relationships to be observed in the world even of the infant, and his early demonstration of knowing something about contingent relations, the reinforcing value of discovery of order and predictability is hard to doubt.

Is discovery of structure and reduction of uncertainty reinforcing by the time a child reaches school? There is reason to think so (unless society has weakened this natural source of reinforcement by stressing tangible rewards), but there exists little experimental evidence, only common-sense observation. There is a natural reward for reading. One finds out something. Getting wanted information from the marks on the page is an obvious motivation for learning to read, and every effort should be made to encourage and take advantage of it. Its role will be examined in Chapter 8.

Trends in Perceptual Development

The two preceding sections were devoted to the consideration of perceptual learning—what is learned and the processes that might be involved. Because we are interested in the development of reading skill from its beginning to the apex of mature reading, it is important to know whether there are trends in perceptual development that should be manifested in the normal attainment of reading skill. Three major trends in perceptual development will be distinguished and illustrated.

Increasing Specificity

As the child grows and has increasing encounters with the world of stimulation, his perceptions become progressively more differentiated and in more specific correspondence with stimulus information. The classic literature of experimental psychology supports this trend in two well-known phenomena. Primary generalization to new stimuli after a response has been conditioned to a given stimulus is far greater in children than in adults; it decreases progressively with age. If the stimuli vary along a band or continuum, the range responded to by children as the same as the originally conditioned stimulus is significantly wider than that responded to by adults (e.g., Mednick and Lehtinen, 1957). The "generalization gradient" does not drop off as sharply.

The second case is the intrasubject variability found in experiments calling for psychophysical judgments. The younger the subject, the greater the variability, whether he is judging by adjustment of a pointer or making relative judgments, such as more-less or higher-lower or same-different (see Gibson, 1969, Chapter 20). Even when the mean error or average constant error, for instance in discrimination of horizontal and vertical lines, is no greater than in adults, younger children nevertheless show greater variability (Volkmann and Pufall, 1972).

In the case of graphic shapes differing in a small number of features, an increase in specificity of correspondence between discrimination and stimulus information is critical for the development of reading skill. Gibson, Gibson, Pick, and Osser (1962) examined the development of discrimination of letterlike forms in children from four through eight years.

First a set of graphic forms was constructed which were comparable to the Roman capital letters, embodying as nearly as possible the distinctive features that characterize these letters and giving special attention to kinds of transformation that have been thought to give children either much or only a little trouble. There were transformations of straight to curved; of rotation and reversal; of perspective or foreshortening, such as occur when a book is tilted back or to one side away from the line of sight; and a transformation from broken (an opening) to closed or vice versa. Some of these transformations (e.g., straight into curved, open into closed) are critical for distinguishing letters. Some, like foreshortening, are not, since one must be able to read a book at many slants, ignoring small perspective changes in the letters. For the straight-curved transformation, there were three degrees of change, so that the effect of amount of change in this important contrast could be measured. Two examples are shown in Figure 2-5.

The forms were drawn on small cards and covered with transparent plastic. The task given the children was to compare a standard form with each of its transformations (12 in all) and copies of itself, and to select and hand to the experimenter only the exact copies of the standard. The cards were presented on a lectern-shaped stand containing five slotted rows (see Figure 2-6). The standard for a given trial was centered, alone, in the top row. All transformations and copies of a particular standard were arranged randomly in one row. The standard was removed and a new one inserted in the top row when a row (trial) was completed. The children matched for 12 different standards, each with all 12 transformations.

The number of errors (choosing as "same" an item that did not exactly match the standard) was obtained for each child. Errors did indeed decline with age from a large number at age four to only a few at age eight. The degree of change, as represented by the number of straight-curved transformations, was an important variable. A single transformation was

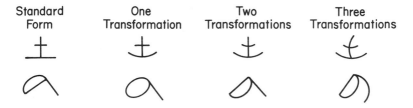

| Standard Form | One Transformation | Two Transformations | Three Transformations |

Figure 2-5. Transformations in straight-curved feature of a letterlike form.

hard to detect and elicited many errors at four years, but three such changes were easily differentiated even then. The older children rarely made an error when this contrast, so important for letters, was the variable.

The children were thus progressively increasing the specificity of their discrimination in accordance with stimulus changes. But it is particularly interesting to examine the rate of improvement of differentiation in relation to the type of change. The errors were grouped into four classes, pooling types of transformation within a class, to yield an age curve for perspective transformations, for transformations of rotation and reversal, for straight-curved transformations, and for open-closed transformations. The errors thus grouped are plotted by age in Figure 2-7.

The perspective transformations are hard to detect at all ages, and although there is a decrease with age, it is not striking. Foreshortening of a letter, unless excessive, is irrelevant for reading, and it is tolerated by the reader. Rotations and reversals, as commonly noted by teachers of young children, are responsible for many errors at four and five years. It is actually incorrect to think of these confusions as "errors" at this age, for children learn early in life that real objects can be rotated and reversed. Although

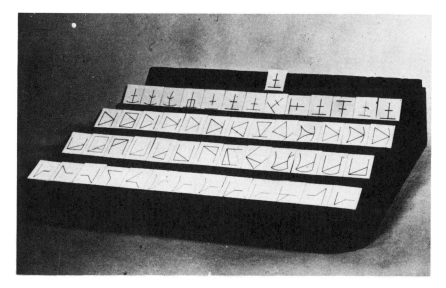

Figure 2-6.   Stand containing arrangement of letterlike forms, with standard to be matched at the top. From Gibson, Gibson, Pick, and Osser, 1962, p. 899. Copyright 1962 by the American Psychological Association. Reprinted by permission.

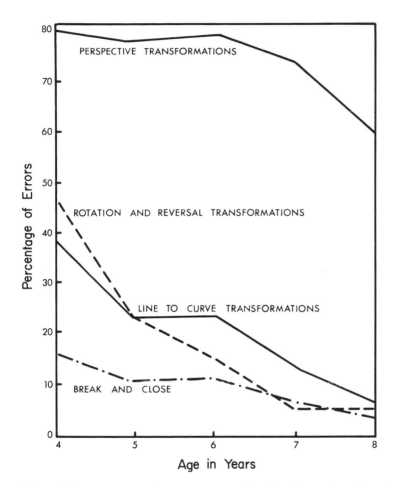

Figure 2-7. Developmental error curves as a function of type of tranformation. From Gibson, Gibson, Pick, and Osser, 1962, p. 899. Copyright 1962 by the American Psychological Association. Reprinted by permission.

such manipulation produces a family of visible transformations, the object nevertheless remains the same. This is not true for a line drawing on a piece of paper, but it is only to be expected that a child will have to learn that what is a completely reversible transformation yielding constancy for a solid object becames a nonreversible one for characters written on a piece of paper. These "errors" dropped to a very small number by eight years, when most children had successfully learned to discriminate reversals.

The open-closed transformations produced few errors even at four years. They are critical features for differentiating solid, rigid objects, and there is no transition between them. They are referred to as "topological" transformations by Piaget and Inhelder (1956). The difference is discriminated early with objects, and it carries over to symbols drawn on paper. An O and a C are similar, but the contrasting distinguishing feature is easy to detect.

It is interesting that the discriminations studied in this task are associated with and predict achievement in the early school years.* We might speculate that a child long before he begins school needs ample experience in detecting invariants over transformations and discovering what transformations are critical ones.

Adults usually have the impression that a strange alphabet, such as Arabic or Hebrew or Hindi, is an unusually difficult one to discriminate. It is more likely, however, that the set of distinctive features characterizing the strange alphabet does not overlap completely with his familiar one and he simply has not done the requisite perceptual learning. One is easily convinced by a few weeks of study that a set of graphic items changes perceptually from a confusable assemblage to unique, easily discriminable units.

The developmental trend of increasing specificity is relevant for reading in other ways than discrimination of graphic features, and we shall have many occasions to refer to it. It is prominent in hearing and producing phonemic differences, achievements which are basic to learning a phonetically based writing system. It is prominent too in extraction of word meanings, which we will consider in a later chapter.

Optimization of Attention
A second important trend in perceptual development is the optimization of attention. We already had a good deal to say about this in discussing the

---

*Personal communication from Harold Stevenson.

ignoring of irrelevant information and the active strategic use of peripheral sensory systems, such as systematic scanning movements of the eyes and touching and palpating with the finger tips.

A study of poor and good readers among sixth-grade boys (Willows and Mackinnon, 1973) and another by Willows (1974) used a technique of Neisser's (1969) to examine deployment of attention while reading aloud. The subjects were given a multiple-choice test for comprehension after reading a passage of text printed in black. In an experimental condition (the "selective-reading condition") the same black passages were employed, but a text of red words was typed between the lines. The boys were told to read and remember the black story so they would be able to answer questions about it. They were also told to ignore the red words, which were only there to distract them. The red lines each contained one wrong answer to the questions that would follow the story in the multiple-choice test. A sample story is printed below. The red lines are indicated by *x*s.

One morning a big poster outside of Oak
xxxxx a rummage sale folding tables
School told people about a basement bargain
xxxxx volunteers new textbooks volunteers
sale. Inside were long counters on which
xxxxx folding tables new textbooks a rum-
things collected by the children were displayed.
xxxxx mage sale folding tables a rummage sale
Price tags were fastened to all articles. Most
xxxxx new textbooks volunteers new textbooks
of the customers bought old but useful furniture.
xxxxx folding tables a rummage sale volunteers a
The sale was a huge success, and the money was
xxxxx rummage sale new textbooks volunteers
used to purchase library books.
xxxxx folding tables volunteers.

Multiple-Choice Questions Following Story

1. What was going on in the basement of Oak School?
   a craft display, a basement sale
   a rummage sale, a bazaar
   an open house, a tea
2. Who had collected the things for the sale?
   volunteers, boy scouts
   friends, parents
   teachers, children
3. On what were the things displayed?
   old furniture, work benches

    bookshelves, a row of desks
    long counters, folding tables
4. What was purchased with the money that was made?
    a new library van, new textbooks
    library books, story books for poor children
    kindergarden books, library furniture

When good and poor readers were compared on oral reading for errors, the poor readers made more errors and took longer in the selective reading condition than in the control condition; but the good readers performed equally well under both conditions. On the multiple-choice test, poor readers made more errors of comprehension than good readers in *both* the selective reading and control conditions. But good readers in the selective reading condition made more comprehension errors that were *intrusions* from the red lines than did poor readers. This may seem surprising, but it will be noticed that the material in the red lines was relevant to the topic. Neisser (1969) found that his adult subjects were normally quite able to ignore the material in the red lines. But they nevertheless noticed their own names if they appeared in the red print. The good readers in the Willows experiment were better at selecting the relevant lines and reading the words correctly—the outward orienting of attention—in the selective reading. They were also reading more effectively for meaning, which requires covert attention, since they made fewer overall errors of comprehension than poor readers.

Why did the better readers make more intrusion errors? The answer is that good and poor readers were affected in different ways by the irrelevant lines. The poor readers were affected by the physical presence of the lines, as shown by marked deterioration of their oral reading. They were little affected, however, by their verbal content, that is, relevant meanings. Good readers were unaffected in the mechanics of oral reading, but their understanding of the content of the relevant lines was affected by the interlinear material. They were reading for meaning, and there were competing meanings in the text before them.

It remains to be emphasized once more that optimal attending is a skill that develops in the child from "capture" at the earliest stages to flexible, adaptive, controlled exploration in the adult. Strategies of search, selective pickup of wanted information, and progressive ability to use the most relevant information depending on the task will be discussed in Chapter 3, where we shall examine development of cognitive strategies that are essential for good reading.

Increasing Economy of Information Pickup

The third trend in perceptual development is increasing economy of information pickup. Children develop progressively the ability to process information more efficiently by detecting order and structure present in the available stimulus information. Economical processing can move in two ways: toward using the smallest distinction in criterion that suffices for a decision, or toward pickup of the largest units that carry structured information. Human beings (and other animals) tend to perform, even in perceiving, in the most economical way of which they are capable. Capacity for economical adaptive perception increases with development, most obviously in the ability to take advantage of rules and structural redundancies in the information presented. In reading, there is almost no end to the development of this trend. Size of the units sampled during fixation increases as skill increases, redundant portions of the text are skimmed, and the structure provided by grammatical relations and meaning is used to process whole phrases and sentences as a unit.

An excellent example of use of the most economical distinctive feature for making a perceptual decision is an experiment by Yonas (1969). The subjects were both children and adults. They took part in a discrimination reaction time experiment in which they had to decide whether a letter projected on a small screen before them belonged to a "positive" set which had been previously defined for them. If it did, they pressed a key and their reaction time was recorded. The experiment had three conditions. In Condition I, only one letter belonged to the positive set. Eight others were projected one at a time in a random order, with the positive letter interspersed. In Condition II, three of the nine letters chosen at random were positive, thus increasing the positive set and leaving six in the negative set. In Condition III, there were again three letters in the positive set and six in the negative, but the positive and negative sets were so chosen that a single feature contrast (presence or absence of diagonality) sufficed to differentiate all the positive from all the negative letters. Testing for this single feature was sufficient for a decision.

All the subjects took part in the three conditions, in counterbalanced order. For each condition, the reaction times were averaged for blocks of 30 trials, yielding five blocks with increasing practice. Condition I was fastest throughout. Conditions II and III had slower and equal latency in the first block of trials. But Condition III, where only a single feature need be processed, dropped rapidly over the blocks of trials, outstripping Condition II in speed of decision and approaching Condition I in latency. Even second-grade children showed this trend toward economical processing, although their latency overall was far greater than that for sixth-grade children or adults.

The ability to perceive order and abstract a simple rule develops over the preschool ages in the well-known oddity problem. The subject is given a series of single problems with varying stimulus objects or varying properties of similar objects and must learn to choose the odd object from a set of three, whatever the nature of the variation. The question is whether the child will perform without error on a new problem, operating with a rule that covers all problems, despite changes in absolute properties of the stimuli. Children improve on this type of problem from three years to third grade (Gollin and Shirk, 1966; Lipsitt and Serunian, 1963). In an experiment by Keeney, Jenkins, and Jenkins (1969), oddity was made redundant with the shape of a target item in a training task. Three-year-old children responded on the basis of the shape alone and did not transfer the redundant oddity principle to a standard oddity problem. But a significant proportion of four- and five-year-olds responded correctly on the first two trials of the transfer task, transferring the oddity principle immediately. They had noticed the redundant, relational property and were able to use it when the opportunity occurred.

Ability to perceive and use redundancy in an economical way increases generally with intellectual development. Spitz, Goettler, and Webreck (1972) studied the ability to discover and utilize redundancy in a digit-span task, comparing subjects from third grade, seventh grade, and college, as well as a group of educable retardates. They were shown strings of digits of varying lengths (4 to 10) and asked to recall them immediately. The strings of digits were selected at random, or else contained either of two types of redundancy: repetition redundancy (e.g., 5, 2, 8, 5, 2, 8) or couplet redundancy (5, 5, 2, 2, 8, 8). When the strings of digits were as long as 6 or more, the use of couplet redundancy went steadily up with developmental age. Repetition redundancy had little effect in facilitating recall for the two lower mental age groups (retardates and third graders) but it was effective as compared with the nonredundant series for seventh graders and especially college students. Strategies of recall were observed by noting pauses between digits. The college students more often matched response to input grouping with the repetition series than did the other age groups. The two lower mental age groups generally failed to recognize the presence of repetition redundancy.

When the presence of repetition redundancy in an eight-digit series was externally enhanced by spatial separation and underlining, performance improved and so did subjective grouping during recall. Retardates and third graders still did not perform as well as on just four nonredundant digits, but equality was achieved by seventh graders. Thus, making the redundant feature salient caused the subject to notice it and take advantage of it. It is not clear from these experiments, however, that the younger subjects would transfer the ability to new digit series without enhancement by external separation and underlining, and be able to generate the economical process for themselves.

It can be concluded that as mental age increases, there is an increasing capacity to discover organization present in verbal material and to use it economically. Structure such as repetition redundancy is one kind of organization to be taken advantage of in reading, as in spelling patterns, for instance (see p. 22). We shall turn to the subject of developing and transferring economical cognitive strategies in the next chapter.

Summary

This chapter presented an overall view of perceptual learning and development, considering three problems: what is learned, what processes may be involved, and some trends in perceptual development. What is learned includes distinctive features of things and coded symbolic material, invariant relations in events, and structure, both superordinate and subordinate, which may also be thought of as higher-order relations and rules. Processes involved include abstraction of relations, ignoring irrelevant information, adaptive use of peripheral sense-organ adjustments, and perhaps reinforcement by discovery of structure and reduction of uncertainty. There are three outstanding trends in perceptual development: increasing differentiation or specificity of correspondence between stimulus information and discrimination, optimization of attention, and increasing economy of information pickup. All of these have implications for reading and will be drawn upon as we discuss the acquisition of reading skill and the behavior of the mature reader.

3
The Development of Cognitive Strategies

The task of perception is the search for invariants: for the permanent features that distinguish things, the order and structure in stimulus information, and the predictable relationships within events. A child's ability to discover these invariant properties of the world develops for many years, as the world offers him the material for his spontaneous exploration to exploit. Natural structure must be present and extracted for organization to be perceived as useful and for economical strategies to develop their own autonomy. Thus perception of invariants and ordered relations must precede self-directed strategic use of them.

But the psychological processes characterizing mature reading go far beyond perception, to remembering and problem solving and organization of conceptual knowledge for better extraction of meaning. There are good and poor strategies of making use of organization in all intellectual activity, from the simplest to the most complex. Research on development of strategies of dealing with cognitive tasks should help us to understand reading, the epitome of them all. We shall consider developmental research on cognitive strategies in five kinds of intellectual tasks, and then go on to the question of transfer of effective strategies to new activities. Can we train a child to organize his behavior in efficient ways and expect these ways to function autonomously thereafter? Finally we shall look briefly at conceptual development and meaning, since transfer and use of higher-order structure in reading depend on them.

Strategies of Organization in Intellectual Tasks

Focusing Attention in a Simple Decision

Evidence for evolution of attention in children was presented in the last chapter. Let us consider this evidence once more in the framework of efficient cognitive functioning in a very simple task of deciding whether two things are the same or different in some respect. The experiment chosen is one by Pick, Christy, and Frankel (1972). Second graders and sixth graders were asked to decide whether two objects briefly presented to them were the same in any of three features, their color, shape, or size. The objects were colored wooden animal shapes one-half inch thick mounted on a neutral plywood background. There were six animals, six colors, and two sizes (small and large). All the feature differences were easily distinguishable. A number of the possible pairs were selected for judgment. Color or shape was always the relevant aspect, with size sometimes varying but irrelevant. The child's decision of same or different was timed.

The main variable of the experiment was whether or not the child was informed prior to exposure of the pair what aspect was to be the relevant variable. In one condition he was told before each trial to decide whether the color was the same, or whether the animal was the same. In a second condition, the child was told as the exposure was concluded that he was to judge whether animal or color was the same or different.

The question was whether the difference in reaction times between the conditions would be greater for one age group than for the other. Knowing what to look for ahead of time should make for a more efficient decision. It did, in fact, for both groups, but significantly more for the older group. In other words, the older children were better able to exercise selectivity of attention before the display was presented, either by skill in focusing or skill in ignoring the irrelevant features.

Making efficient decisions by looking for just what is wanted is important in learning from reading, and a set for what is relevant is characteristic of the skilled reader. Such alertness can be encouraged, although we do not know at present whether it can be "trained."

Efficiency of Search

Systematic exploration for a wanted target is another cognitive task that appears in many forms and occurs under many conditions. "Find the picture that matches this one," or "find the E" are exercises often given children. An old laboratory version of this task was to search through a page of randomly arranged type, canceling out all tokens of one letter or number. A more recent version is the scanning task (Neisser, 1963). A list of letters, numbers, or words is presented behind a half-silvered mirror, and when a light goes on the subject sees the list and scans down it from top to bottom to find a target letter or word embedded somewhere in the list. Over many trials, the target is embedded at random in the rows of the list, so as to cover all the possible positions. To find a rate of scan, it is essential that the subject scan systematically from top to bottom and he is told to do so. This task was employed by Gibson and Yonas (1966a and b) with children and adults varying such factors as number of targets, similarity of contextual to target items, and auditory distraction. The children were from second, fourth, and fifth grades, and the adults were college sophomores.

Although scanning speed was slower the younger the age group, second-grade children were able to scan nearly as systematically as adults, and showed, relatively, no greater deterioration from searching for two targets rather than one or from auditory distraction. This task is not feasible for first-grade children because they do not as yet scan systematically enough. But within a year the task has become possible. During the year they have been trained to scan from left to right. But given instruction and a few practice trials, they can scan systematically downward. A planned strategy even when not specifically pretrained has become possible.

Organizing pictorial and verbal information for effective search was the subject of a developmental investigation by Westman (1971). She asked whether children would, progressively, perceive and utilize taxonomic structure available for organization to facilitate a search task. The child was presented with either a set of colored photographs of common objects or their corresponding printed verbal labels. He was instructed to place them on a grid in front of him in a manner which would allow him to find any one of them as easily as possible. The 36 items for each type of display (photographs or labels) belonged to six categories: animals, body parts, clothing, eating utensils, fruits, and tools. All had been pretested on second graders and selected as known categories. Subjects from second, fourth, and sixth grades were compared. The subject was given the shuffled stack of 3 × 3 inch photographs or words typed on 3 × 3 inch squares and asked to arrange them on a grid with a 13 × 13 square array, so as not to covary exactly with the number of categories. The subject arranged the material on the grid so as to "find any item as easily as possible." After ordering them once, he was given an opportunity to rearrange them if he could see a better way.

The quality of ordering was assessed by means of a scale constructed from pilot data, and then the subject was given a specific target item to locate. Twenty-five items were searched for, and search time was recorded after each block of five.

The quality of the ordering of both types of items increased with age, especially between second and fourth grades. Less time was spent arranging the photographs than arranging the words, but the quality was not significantly different in the two modes, although the words permitted a consistent alphabetical arrangement as well as ordering by category. The number of children who used the alphabetic principle increased with age, but it was not used as often as the category structure in any group. Time to search for and locate an item decreased with age, particularly between second and fourth grades. Search time was shorter with photographs than words for all three age groups. The correlation between quality of the ordering and the search time was significant (r = .546) for all three age groups. The quality of the ordering did not lose its influence on search time throughout the entire 25 search trials.

This study makes it clear that ability to perceive and to make effective use of categorical structure improves with age, but especially between second and fourth grades. The ability undoubtedly depends heavily on knowledge of the categories and instances selected.

Westman also gave children interpolated training between the initial ordering of the picture or word material and a later opportunity to order. The training in one condition was simply the search for targets, as already described. In the second condition, it was a verbal discussion about categories with the material at the same time visible to the children. Ordering was in many cases improved after these experiences, but more so by the verbal discussion and particularly for sixth graders, where 95% of the children produced an improved ordering. It is interesting that children who had used the alphabetic rule in initial ordering did not give it up, despite the nature of the discussion, and a few even used it after the discussion although they had not before. They had independently found a new strategy during the interval and realized its efficiency despite the experimenter's talk.

Discovery and Use of Natural Structure
Inhelder and Piaget (1964), in tracing the early development of logical thinking in children, made distinctions between different kinds of relational structure. The kind of structure in the material used by Westman (1971), simple class membership, they called additive. Children can make use of such structure, when their knowledge of the category is sufficient, by second grade in tasks like ordering, search, and sorting. Its use calls for recognition of similarities or common features, and properties that mark a class off from other complementary classes. However, the ability to reduce a collection of items to a class and the ability to use this membership rela-

tion economically and spontaneously when it has utility for some task do not necessarily go hand in hand. We shall return to this point later when we consider transfer, but it should be emphasized now that perceiving relations and natural structure on the one hand and using them strategically are not the same. The distinction is akin to what Flavell and others have called "production deficiency" and "mediation deficiency" (Flavell, 1970). A child may fail in a task because he does not yet comprehend relations that are needed for it; but he may fail despite having attained this information because he is still unable to perceive their usefulness. In the Westman experiment, the children in general understood the categorical relations and were progressively more able to use them for ordering and search.

A more difficult kind of relation exists when a set of things can be classified in two interlocking ways at once. Inhelder and Piaget refer to this as multiplicative classification or cross-classification. It is exemplified graphically in matrices, such as the Raven *Colored Progressive Matrices*, which are used as an intelligence test. According to Inhelder and Piaget, multiplicative classification and additive classification are mastered around the same time, about seven to eight years, but that may be, they say, because the multiplicative classification can be represented graphically, so the child can perceive the structure of the matrix although he may not yet understand the logic of it. A representation could initially make the classification possible because the similarities and differences and the twofold symmetry are directly perceptible, as in Figure 3-1.

Children ranging in age from four to eight were given the problems shown in Figure 3-1. The multiple choices on the right were presented one by one on small cards and the child was allowed to try each of them in the empty cell of the left-hand figure. He had to choose the correct picture, justify his choice, and then state when asked whether one or two of the other pictures might not fit as well. In the case of items with two attributes (items 1 through 4), the younger children often made the correct choice, but they usually could not justify it and would give in to a suggestion for changing it. The correct choice must then have been due, according to Inhelder and Piaget, to perception of graphic symmetry rather than to abstraction of the dimensional properties and intersectional relations within the matrix. A child of seven, however, presented with problem 6, chose the green bird, correctly. When asked why it was best, she answered, "There's a blue fish and a green fish, and then a blue bird and a green

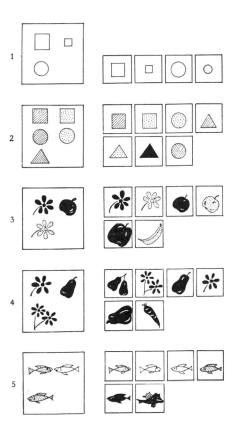

Figure 3-1. (a) Matrix problems presented to young children by Inhelder and Piaget. From Inhelder and Piaget, 1964. New York: The Humanities Press.

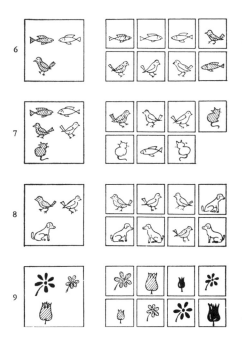

(b) From Inhelder and Piaget, 1964, pp. 160–161.

bird. They are turned in opposite ways on top, so they ought to be turned in opposite ways at the bottom as well."

Ability to perceive the graphic structure of the matrix thus seems to precede ability to abstract and describe the relations. The complexity of the matrix (number of dimensions) is of course a factor determining how early the regularities are perceived. There have been several experiments in which children were given training in solving multiple classification problems, as these are generally referred to, with some attendant success in detecting the structure when new problems were given (Caruso and Resnick, 1972; Jacobs and Vandeventer, 1971a, b). One such experiment will be described, since it suggests that at about first-grade level the pickup of natural order can be fostered and within limits transferred as a general skill.

Parker, Rieff, and Sperr (1971) gave children of three age levels ($4\frac{1}{2}$, 6, and $7\frac{1}{2}$) training based on a task analysis of multiple classification (Resnick, 1967). The children were of roughly equivalent ability in the multiple classification skill at the beginning. Children in an experimental group received a pretest, training, and a posttest. Children in a control group received a pretest, played a game with the experimenter, and then received the posttest. For the pretest, five of the matrices from Inhelder and Piaget (see Figure 3-1) were selected. The posttest consisted of these same five matrices plus nine transfer ones. Of these, ones presenting the same dimension on which the subject was trained were criteria for the subject's performance. Others contained one or more new dimensions not used in training.

The elaborate training program was divided into 13 steps, progressing in difficulty. The subject was not advanced to a new step until he had mastered the previous one. Training began with a 3 × 3 matrix, instead of a 2 × 2 one, since a common attribute (color or form throughout the training) is easier to perceive when there are more examples of the shared attribute. The items were real objects at the start, rather than pictures. The subject filled in the rows and columns according to common colors, common forms, etc., and was questioned frequently by the experimenter as to what belonged in a critical cell and asked to justify his choice. The procedure attempted to make clear the principle of cross-classification and required the subject to show stability of choice. The posttest was administered one to three days later.

Results on the posttest showed significant effects of treatment (training or no training), age, and an age by treatment interaction. The interaction showed that the training increased in effectiveness with the age of the child. It was, in fact, completely *ineffective* with the youngest group, but the oldest group performed correctly on four out of the five criterion matrices following training. Scores also improved on the transfer matrices, relative to the control group, except for the 4½-year-old children. The oldest group surpassed both younger groups on "far transfer" tests, that is, two new dimensions. In fact, they performed as well on these as on the criterion and moderate transfer tasks. The authors speculated that the training program might not have been adequate for the youngest group (it was an arduous one, lasting 60 minutes and divided into two sessions). It seems possible, however, that one simply cannot teach intersectional relations between dimensions at this age. Dimensions as such are abstracted much later than simple contrastive distinctive features. The training program employed names referring to dimensions, such as "shape" and "color," terms which may not yet have class inclusion status for four-year-olds, even though they can use the words.

We can conclude that finding order at the level of intersecting dimensions develops between four and seven years and that ability to transfer a strategy of using it is not immediately spontaneous. Something like this is required in generalizing contrastive spelling patterns (see Chapter 9, p. 294).

Problem Solving with Verbal Material

Discovery of structural relations and use of them in the problems considered above is a basic skill that develops during the child's early school years. Now we turn to the development of strategies in solving a verbal problem, one requiring knowledge of words, the constituent relationships of letters in words, and categories. A task employed to study this was anagram solution, in an experiment by Gibson, Tenney, and Sharabany (1971). The purpose was to investigate children's strategies of solving anagrams—discovering a word in a set of jumbled letters—and in particular to see whether children in third and fourth grades could use some form of structure in a set of anagram problems to facilitate solution. Adults have been shown to use categorical relations between the anagrams of a set to reach a solution (Rees and Israel, 1935; Safren, 1962). Children of third- and fourth-grade level were chosen, since they would presumably have mastered the initial mechanics of reading skill by this time and would recognize words well enough to permit study of their ability to use meaning effectively. Would they perceive the meaningful relationships embedded in the material presented, and could they use them if they did?

Two experiments were performed, using two types of meaningful relation. The first, done with children who had just completed third grade, employed sentence meaning in a set of five anagrams. There were six sets of anagrams, each set capable of being organized as a sentence. A set of five anagrams was presented to the child on a board constructed of metal. The letters forming the anagrams were taken from a magnetized Scrabble game, so that they would stay in place on the board, but could be manipulated during solution. The five anagrams were arranged one above the other. When a board was presented, the anagrams were covered with red sticky ribbons which stripped off easily to reveal the anagram. The child pulled off one ribbon at a time and attempted to solve the anagram. His time was recorded. If he did not discover the solution in 60 seconds, the experimenter arranged it so he could see the solution, and he went on to the next.

There were three experimental conditions. In Condition S (structure) the anagrams on all six boards were arranged to yield a sentence when they were solved (see Figure 3-2). In Condition NS, the same anagrams were scrambled so that they did not yield an ordered sentence when solved. In Condition S-NS, the first four sets of anagrams, when solved, yielded a sentence. The last two, however, were scrambled as in Condition NS. The expectation was that if the child discovered the sentence structure in the first four sets and used it effectively, he would search for it again, and when it was *not* present, show impaired solution of the problem.

Pretesting made it clear that children of this age were slow in finding the sentence structure, if they did at all. Consequently, the S-NS group was given help in finding it by asking the child to read the words in order each time he completed one of the anagrams. This procedure did help to reveal the structure, for mean solution times for the three groups on the first four boards was shortest for Group S-NS, who had the hint. It was next shortest for Group S and longest for Group NS, as expected. But only the difference between S-NS and the other two was significant. The children in Group S, who had structure present but no help, were so busy with the mechanics of solving individual anagrams that the sentence structure in most cases either was not noticed or not taken advantage of.

Perhaps sentence structure is not intrinsically appropriate for this task, where even an adult subject attacks the anagram as an individual problem, concentrating on letter clusters and constraints within the word. But adults do develop a "set" and use categorical relations in solving anagrams belonging to a common taxonomic class (Rees and Israel, 1935; Safren, 1962). Would children do this? Fourth-grade children (second term) were chosen as subjects, on the assumption that they would be freer

Condition S		Condition NS	
Presolution	Solved	Presolution	Solved
IJLL	JILL	CLNEA	CLEAN
EHLPS	HELPS	MMO	MOM
MMO	MOM	IJLL	JILL
CLNEA	CLEAN	EHLPS	HELPS
EHOSU	HOUSE	EHOSU	HOUSE

Figure 3-2. Arrangement of anagrams before and after solution, with sentence order present or absent. From Gibson, Tenney, and Sharabany, 1971.

by this time for pickup of higher-order meaningful relations. Again there were six sets of anagrams. In one of two conditions (S), structure in the form of taxonomic class membership was present on each board. The categories were fruit, drinks, animals, utensils, colors, and furniture. Pretests showed that these were all familiar classes for children of this age and that they could give examples of them. In the second condition (NS), each board of five anagrams consisted of items drawn randomly from the total pool of 30 used in Condition S. The mean solution time was calculated for subjects in the two groups. A subject was stopped after 75 seconds if he had not solved the anagram, and the solution was arranged for him by the experimenter, as before.

The categorical structure in this experiment was discovered and used by the children. As Figure 3-3 shows, the solution time for the group provided with taxonomic relations within a set was shorter than that for the other group on every set. When anagrams within a set were considered,

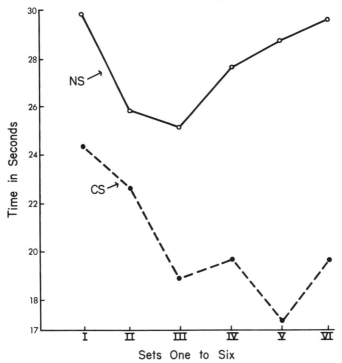

Figure 3-3.   Solution times for anagrams presented in sets containing categorical relations versus randomly drawn sets. From Gibson, Tenney, and Sharabany, 1971.

the advantage for Group S appeared on Trial 3 and increased through the fifth anagram. Error data (failure to solve) showed the same trends.

Were the children in this experiment really aware of class inclusion, or did they come up with free associations after the first two words and simply try them out? In other words, what strategies for solution were they using? Some of them commented on the class membership, especially an easy class like colors. For example, "Oh, these are colors!" or "I just saw blue and red and knew that all the rest must be colors." Not all the subjects were so verbal about the categories, and some of the comments revealed the operation of association rather than class inclusion or use of lexical features. For instance, one child who had *knife* and *fork* as the first two instances said, "I'm trying to think of another silverware, but I can't." He had stopped manipulating the letters (as the children typically did, in an apparently trial-and-error fashion), and was simply associating in a semicontrolled fashion.

Strategies of solution on the anagram task can tell us a great deal about the child's level of progress in pickup of higher-order information for reading. A sophisticated adult does not simply manually or mentally manipulate the letters by trial and error. He makes use of his knowledge of sequential probabilities, and especially of constrained clusters (Boykin, 1972; Mayzner and Tresselt, 1962). He frequently "sounds out" combinations. In Boykin's experiment, the selection by subjects of high-probability vowel and consonant clusters led to the greatest number of correct responses. Consider a hypothetical example, the scrambled letters of the word *prawn*. A sophisticated subject knows that *WN* is a common final consonant cluster but impossible as an initial one, that *PR* never ends an English word, and that *A* is a common medial vowel. This knowledge is internalized even though seldom verbalized, and the word, seemingly automatically, pops out. But is it an "animal" word, which Boykin's subjects were told to find? For an adult, words have lexical features like class membership, and he knows at once that this is the word he wants. We do not know how immediately a child's category awareness would be accessed in this situation, but the long process of becoming literate involves problem-solving strategies at various levels that do not come all at once. Perhaps they can be fostered by providing the relevant information at the right time.

Development of Strategies for Remembering

Are strategies for remembering important as processes underlying reading skill? It might seem not, for none of us thinks that learning to read is simply a matter of memorizing—learning by rote. Yet learning to read and learning from reading necessitate remembering a lot of things. It is important to realize, therefore, that a good memory does not imply a good rubber stamp, but instead involves good organization of material for recall, and searching for meaningful relations in whatever it is that must be remembered even when it is first perceived. Young children are not automatically aware of the difference between perceiving something and actively doing something with it so that they can easily recall it later. There is, of course, incidental learning that results in remembering without any special intention to do so, but research on incidental and intentional learning has consistently shown better recall when there is an intention to remember. An intention to learn and awareness of good ways of remembering develop with age.

Experiments by Appel, Cooper, McCarrell, Sims-Knight, Yessen, and Flavell (1972) tested the hypothesis that memorizing and perceiving are undifferentiated for the young child, with deliberate plans for remembering only gradually emerging as a distinctive kind of cognitive activity, dependent upon perception but going beyond it, cognitively speaking. Effective remembering involves various cognitive abilities, such as rehearsing, classifying, giving names to things so they can be verbally rehearsed, calling up images when words are the data given, and relating the data, perhaps in such ways as sentence elaboration. Appropriate mnemonic devices vary with the task. What do children do when they are instructed to memorize items for future recall? Does it differ from what they do when they are simply told to "look at" the same things?

Appel et al. tested children of three age groups (preschoolers, first graders, and fifth graders) under two sets of instructions, once when they were told to memorize a set of items for future recall and once when they were told merely to look at a similar set of items with no hint that a recall test would ensue. The items in each set were 15 pictures of common objects that could be categorized into five sets of three each. They were presented to the child in a random arrangement for study for $1\frac{1}{2}$ minutes, during which he was allowed to manipulate them in any way he chose. The child's behavior was recorded during this interval and four potential mnemonic strategies were analyzed: *sequential naming* of two or more; *sequential pointing* at two or more; *rehearsal*—naming while not looking at them (silent lip movements were observed); and *categorizing*—rearranging pictures in groups of category members.

Fifth graders generally recalled more than the younger children. The difference between amount recalled in the look and memory conditions was significant only for the fifth graders. What about "study" activities? Naming the items occurred more frequently in the younger children than in the fifth graders. For the youngest, it occurred equally often in the two conditions. Pointing was also more common in the younger children and was not related to condition. Rehearsal was engaged in significantly more often by the fifth graders and more often in the memory condition. However, it did *not* improve recall, and it was negatively related to clustering (grouping by category) in recall. Rehearsal was not the most effective strategy, since it apparently inhibited categorization, an appropriate activity for the task. Fifth graders categorized significantly more than younger children and more in the memory condition, suggesting that it was a deliberate memory strategy. Preschool children thus do not differentiate by study strategy between looking and recalling instructions in this task.

The basic idea of intentional remembering seems to develop before appropriate specialized cognitive activities do. The preschoolers had not yet developed either the basic idea or the ability to engage in different appropriate activities, but first graders in some experiments have shown evidence of possessing the basic idea. Russian research (Smirnov and Zinchenko, 1969) provides evidence for three developmental levels:

1. A first stage in which children exhibit no purposeful behavior in remembering. "It seems less a matter of the children's recalling material than the material presents itself to them for recall" (p. 476).
2. A second level in which recall operates as purposeful behavior, although the child lacks appropriate and flexible means to carry out his purpose.
3. A third stage in which the child possesses methods that will facilitate recall, although his stock of methods is slim. His earliest mnemonic activity is naming and repetition. Meaningful grouping evolves later.

There is a rapidly growing body of experimental literature on the development of mnemonic strategies in children, both in this country and in the Soviet Union. The reader is referred to Flavell (1970), Smirnov and

Zinchenko (1969), and Meacham (1972) for detailed reviews of this litera-' ture.*

Rehearsal is an obvious strategy for any adult who anticipates making a speech, conducting a ceremony, or being examined on something like driving regulations. He studies awhile and then tests himself, with some knowledge of when he is ready. It has been known since the time of Ebbinghaus that active rehearsal is a good strategy for remembering something, either by rote or just the topical essentials. Do children know this? A large literature† exists showing that young children do not spontaneously rehearse but tend to do so increasingly as they grow older, perhaps influenced by what happens in school or prompting by an adult in the role of either instructor or model. The interesting thing about this progression, however, is the way the strategy develops, becoming more purposive and more "conscious." It is obvious how important awareness of the task and selective repetition and self-testing are for the mature reader. Two experiments tell us something about how he achieves this maturity.

Flavell, Beach, and Chinsky (1966) gave children (kindergarteners, second graders, and fifth graders) a memory task which is virtually certain to elicit verbal rehearsal in adults. Seven pictures of objects (easily recognizable as well as ones with names producing highly observable mouth movements when pronounced) were spread before the child. The experimenter slowly pointed to some of them and then asked the child to point to the same objects in the same order as the experimenter had, after rearrangement of the pictures. Over a number of such trials an observer lipread the child's covert verbalizations, and finally the child was asked how he had tried to remember the pictures. Few of the kindergarten children (two out of twenty) showed any detectable verbalization but all of the fifth graders did. A later experiment by Keeney, Canizzo, and Flavell (1967) showed that spontaneous rehearsal resulted in better recall. They also found that nonrehearsers could be induced to rehearse by instruction and practice, with subsequent improvement in recall, although some of them, when not reminded, abandoned the strategy. Naming of objects, rehearsing when they are present, and rehearsing when they are absent are progressively more mature strategies, and development in this order has been observed.

*See also *Human Development,* 1971, *14,* no. 4 for a symposium on these issues.
†See, for example, Flavell, Beach, and Chinsky (1966); Bernbach (1967); Kingsley and Hagen (1969); Haith (1971); Meacham (1972).

It seems clear from these studies that simply appealing to "verbal mediation" as a strategy for remembering is woefully inadequate. Rehearsal and self-testing are something very different from the young child's labeling. A child's growing awareness of potentially useful strategies and efficient self-monitoring of them is an impressive aspect of development—it is as if he is becoming a little psychologist, aware of his own processes. Why not? To anticipate a bit, something analogous happens with language, a development of "linguistic awareness" which is deeply involved in a child's facility in learning to read.

Conceptual organization, the most effective strategy for remembering, almost invariably shows improvement with age,* but a conceivable difficulty with studies of it is the possibility that the relations and instances embedded in the task by the experimenter are difficult ones for children to discover, or to comprehend even if they are pointed out. An experiment by Tenney (1973 and in press) circumvented this problem by giving children an opportunity to generate their own relations and instances for efficient recall. Subjects were drawn from kindergarten and third and sixth grades. There were three conditions for generating related material: *categorical,* in which the experimenter gave the child a category name and presented him with one instance, e.g., "Blue is the name of a color you will be asked to remember. Tell me three other colors that will be easy for you to remember along with blue"; *self-planned,* in which the child was given the key word *blue* and told, "Tell me three other words that will be easy to remember along with *blue*"; and *free association,* in which the child was told, "Tell me the first three words you think of when I say the word *blue*." Twelve key words were presented, all belonging to easy categories (e.g., food, days of the week). Out of the 48 words that resulted, 12 were selected to yield a personalized list for recall, either with clustering possible or mixed so that it was not possible. At a second session, the list was read to the child, followed by a recall test. A child took part in only one of the experimental conditions.

The novel aspect of the results was what the children did in the self-planned condition. Rather than generate words related by meaning or category the kindergarten children showed a strong tendency to generate rhymes (e.g., to *blue* one gave *boo, clue,* and *glue*). They were likely to do this in the free-association condition as well. They seemed to have no idea

*See, for example, Appel et al., 1972; Moely et al., 1969; Neimark et al., 1971; Westman, 1971.

what kind of material would be easy to remember. By third grade, children were able to generate a useful structure of their own, and by sixth grade self-planned categorical structure was general. Recall for this condition reflected the nature of the structure selected and rose steadily with age. For the sixth-grade children, clustering in recall was significantly better after self-planning than it was when the experimenter suggested a category to them.

Two other interesting points were found. When a category was suggested to them, the kindergarten children responded appropriately and had greatly improved recall compared with other conditions. Clustering in this condition, in fact, did not differ across age levels (see Figure 3-4). Free association resulted in no significant clustering at any age level. It was no aid to amount recalled, compared to groups given nonclusterable lists. Why not? Lists are evidently not remembered by processes of association that are akin to free association. Only one subject clustered completely using his free association structure, due almost certainly to the nature of his associations. Associations themselves tend to shift with age toward con-

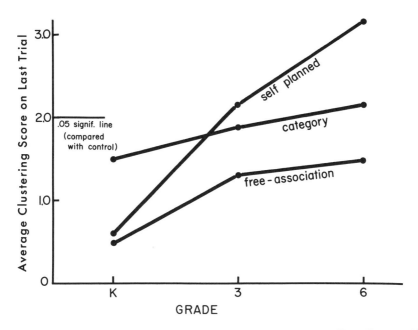

Figure 3-4.   Clustering in recall with three kinds of list structure. From Tenney, 1973, p. 57.

trol by semantic features, as we shall see. What seems to be lacking in the kindergarten children is *awareness* of the advantage of organization by semantic features in this task. It goes along with a shift in the salience of features of words from acoustic to semantic.

Finally, an experiment by Scribner and Cole (1972) is of interest, because training was introduced in the use of semantic structure as a mnemonic aid. Children from second, fourth, and sixth grades were subjects. Lists of 20 words, divisible into four categories of 5 items each, were read to the child. In a "cued" condition, the experimenter told him the four category names before reading the list and reminded him of them again before recall. In a "constrained" condition, the children were not only given the category names, but were required to recall words belonging to a category together (e.g., "Tell me all the tools you can remember"). A recall trial giving children of both groups only category names followed, and then a transfer trial plus recall was given with a new list under the cued condition. Children in the constrained condition were superior to those in the cued condition at all grade levels, so simply providing information about an economical rule does not assure its use. Some children in the cued condition ignored the categories altogether. Training in using the rule was more effective. Nevertheless, there was a marked drop-off in all measures of organization when the training procedure was terminated and the children were left to direct their own recall. This result agrees with many others in finding that attempts to induce the use of new cognitive structures and strategies by brief experimental intervention are likely to have only a short-lived (if any) effect in promoting efficiency in use of a higher-order structure. Insightful understanding of the utility of the strategy appears to be lacking. We shall consider this point in the next section on transfer of effective strategies.

Transfer in Cognitive Tasks

What Is Transfer and What Is It That Transfers?

"Transfer" is a term employed by learning psychologists and by educators with the rather loose implication that something learned in one situation will affect, either beneficially or adversely, learning in another situation. The word itself is used metaphorically, since its dictionary meaning is "to convey, carry, remove or send from one person, place, or position to another" (*Webster's New World Dictionary of the American Language,* 1958).

The term was introduced into psychology rather late. It cannot be found in the index of any of the earlier histories of psychology. The earliest use of it that we have found in a book is in Thorndike's first *Educational Psychology*, published in 1903. It is used occasionally in the classic experimental paper by Thorndike and Woodworth in 1901. About the same time in Germany (1900), G. E. Müller, in a paper with Pilzecker, proposed a "substitution hypothesis": that "active substitution" occurs when idea *a* was connected with idea *b* and idea *A*, similar to *a*, also produces *b*. Their experiments were done as paired associate learning, with nonsense syllables for material. Thorndike's theory of transfer was formulated in strict opposition to the old educational doctrine of "formal discipline" based on the notion that the mind had faculties, such as memory, that could be strengthened quite generally by exercise with any kind of subject matter. The teaching of Latin and geometry and the use of rote memorizing as a learning technique were often defended by proponents of the doctrine of formal discipline on the basis that they trained the "reason," ability to think clearly and to remember accurately.

Thorndike's theory of learning underlies his concept of transfer. Learning, for Thorndike, consisted of forming a "bond" or "associative connection" between a "sense impression" and a response. It was an elementaristic theory, referrred to by Hilgard (1956) as the doctrine of specificity of connections, or connectionism. Learning was always specific, never general. Transfer depended on the presence of identical elements in the original learning and the new learning which it facilitated. What were the identical elements? "By identical elements are meant mental processes which have the same cell action in the brain as their physical correlate" (Thorndike, 1913, p. 359). Some of these processes he conceived of rather broadly—attitudes, for instance. But they had to be specifically describable and specifically applicable in another task for transfer to occur. Thorndike, it might be noted, had a specificity doctrine of intelligence, as well as transfer.

The Gestalt psychologists did not make use of the term *transfer*, but did emphatically recognize generalization via common principles or awareness of common relationships. "Insight" and perception of relationships became part of the system of knowledge and were assumed to be used appropriately and nonspecifically. Piaget likewise (so far as we have been able to discover) has never used the term *transfer*, but assumes that knowledge once assimilated in "schemata" is at the general disposal of its possessor.

Vygotsky took pains to argue that specific training was valueless and that only relations fully understood by the learner were effective for further spontaneous application.

Practical experience also shows that direct teaching of concepts is impossible and fruitless. A teacher who tries to do this usually accomplishes nothing but empty verbalism, a parrotlike repetition of words by the child, simulating a knowledge of corresponding concepts but actually covering up a vacuum. (Vygotsky, 1962, p. 83)

Vygotsky criticized Thorndike's attack on formal discipline on the grounds that he experimented with the narrowest, most specialized and most elementary functions, commenting that

Thorndike's work merely makes it appear likely that there are two kinds of instruction: the narrowly specialized training in some skill, such as typing, involving habit formation and exercise and more often found in trade schools for adults, and the kind of instruction of school children, which activates large areas of consciousness. The idea of formal discipline may have little to do with the first kind but may well prove to be valid for the second. It stands to reason that in the higher processes emerging during the cultural development of the child, formal discipline must play a role that it does not play in the more elementary processes: All the higher functions have in common awareness, abstraction, and control. In line with Thorndike's theoretical conceptions, the qualitative differences between the lower and the higher functions are ignored in his studies of the transfer of training. (Vygotsky, 1962, p. 97)

If we examine Thorndike's evidence for the theory of identical elements as the basis of transfer, Vygotsky appears on the whole to be justified. Thorndike's well-known experiments with Woodworth (Thorndike and Woodworth, 1901) are typical and led them to reject the doctrine of formal discipline. They chose two tasks involving observation and judgment, gave the subjects practice in the tasks, and tested them before and afterward in similar tasks. One task required estimation of the area of small rectangles varying in size from ten to one hundred square centimeters. Afterward the subject was tested in estimating areas of rectangles of other sizes and also figures of different shape. There was improvement in estimation of the training shapes: five of the six subjects improved in estimation of the rectangles of different areas, and four of the six improved in estimating areas of different shape. There was, then, a carry-over of something they had learned. What was it? The authors commented that one gets "more accurate mental standards and more delicacy in judging different magnitudes by them. In the case of estimations of magnitudes in terms of unfamiliar standards such as grams or centimeters, the acquistion of the mere idea of what a gram or centimeter is, makes a tremendous difference in all judgments" (Thorndike and Woodworth, 1901, p. 344). So it was a concept that was learned and could be generalized to new figures. The only thing wrong with this notion, to the present authors, is calling a concept an "identical element." This is repugnant because a concept is not an element. "Element" suggests something primitive, meaningless, and irreducible rather than an abstraction from a number of examples. Concepts and rules, both abstract, can be applied to new situations, but they are relational and therefore are not elements.

In other experiments, Thorndike and Woodworth gave their subjects cancellation tests. They canceled all the words containing es and os in a number of pages of print. Then they were tested for canceling words containing other pairs of letters (i and t, s and t, e and a, e and r). The subjects were actually slower at canceling words containing the new pairs after long practice with the first pair. If one recalls the scanning experiments described in the preceding chapter, it seems clear that during practice the subjects were learning a very economical technique of searching for the minimal distinctive features characterizing an e-o word as different from others, and learning to ignore all the other letters and potential letters. Given a new pair, attention had to be redirected to a new set of features.

Other evidence cited in Thorndike's *Educational Psychology* of 1913 includes transfer experiments on "cross education" (e.g., striking a target with one hand, then the other), memorizing (memorizing French vocabulary and noting its effect on memorizing other material such as chemical formulas), the effect of card sorting on typing, the effect of training in learning habits of neatness in arithmetical work, etc. (see Thorndike, 1913, Chapter 12 for a lengthy summary). When improvement in a second task did occur, some presumably specific bit of learning was always cited, as in the case of estimation of lines and squares (see above), where transfer to lines of different length and previously unpracticed rectangles was said to be due to learning the concept of a centimeter.

In one study cited, by Scholckow and Judd (Judd, 1908), there is evidence of positive transfer by way of comprehension of a general principle. In this classic experiment, boys in grades five and six practiced throwing darts at a target under twelve inches of water. Half of the boys were first given a full explanation of the principle of refraction. During practice, the group given the explanation did not excell over the other group. All the boys had to learn how to use the dart, and practice was essential. But when the twelve inches of water were reduced to four, there was a striking difference between the two groups. The boys who understood the principle adjusted rapidly to the new condition, while the other group showed no benefit from their previous practice and made many errors.

Thorndike performed some in-school research as well, to evaluate transfer from school subjects. Thorndike (1924) and Brolyer, Thorndike, and Woodyard (1927) examined the effect of different high school curricula on intelligence test scores. Intelligence tests were given at the beginning of the year to very large numbers of high school students, all of whom were retested at the end of the year. The question was whether students who had studied Latin, mathematics, physics, and chemistry showed larger gains in their intelligence test scores than those who took commercial and manual training courses. They did, by seven points, but the interpretation of such a result is extremely ambiguous. In any case, it does not seem to constitute an argument against the value of formal discipline, although it had an effect on changing school curricula.

As we see it, the issue of "formal discipline" as against the doctrine of specificity of training is, or should be, a dead issue by the present time. No one would accept either doctrine. The question is whether we are justified in the continuing use of the term *transfer* at all, since it originated in an elementaristic, narrowly associative kind of theory. It seems to us wisest (though we may prove to be wrong) to retain the term while attempting to erase the stigma of its elementaristic origins. We are not interested in training specific acts in school. The whole goal of learning, in school or outside, is adaptability and flexibility. In retaining the term *transfer* in the following pages, we will mean by it the generalizability of knowledge.

In Chapter 2 we considered what is learned in perceptual learning. Now we are concerned with what is transferable, in the sense of generalizable, in both perceptual and cognitive learning. Broadly speaking, what is generalizable is *knowledge*. Consider the following quotation from Thorndike (1913):

The only thing that can "develop" or "strengthen" the faculties or the mind is knowledge, and all real knowledge is science. The effect of this on the mind is to furnish it with something. It constitutes its contents, and, as we have seen, the power, value, and real character of mind depend upon its contents. Without knowledge, the mind, however capable, is impotent and worthless. (L. F. Ward, quoted by Thorndike, 1913, p. 433)

The shortcoming of this quotation is that it says nothing about the nature of the contents—they could even be collections of specific associations, as Thorndike thought. We amplify it, therefore, and say that knowledge is relational and only in that sense transferable. Distinctive features are relational, and they make possible the discrimination of new members of a set that can be distinguished by already familiar features (Pick, 1965; Gibson, Schapiro, and Yonas, 1968). Orthographic rules are relational and can be transferrred to the reading of hitherto unseen words or pseudowords (see Chapter 7); all kinds of principles, order, and concepts are relational, and this chapter and nearly all the others contain examples of their ubiquity and broad applicability. Woodworth (1938), in his famous chapter on transfer of training, admitted that principles might transfer to a new situation. But he saved what remnants he could of his original declarations with Thorndike as follows:

We think of principles as "abstract." But if they are embodied in words they are concrete bits of behavior and their transfer from one situation to another creates no difficulty for the theory of identical components. Any idea that can be recalled, or any attitude that can be reinstated, is concrete enough to qualify. Perhaps anything that can be learned can be transferred. But does not everything that can be learned have the concrete character of an act or way of acting? (Woodworth, 1938, p. 207)

Our answer is "No." Principles can operate without being embodied in words. A child speaks grammatically, employing principles of syntax long before he can verbalize a rule. The principle of seriation is discovered by a child and applied to new series before he can verbalize the principle (Sinclair de-Zwart, 1967, 1969). Attempts to teach seriation or conservation by verbal methods were not successful in her experiments.

Cognitive, attentional strategies were particularly considered in this chapter. Such attentional strategies as grouping and clustering by concept or by order have been examined with the question in mind whether they can be explicitly taught. Can one "teach for transfer"? If so, what, when, and how? One must ask whether the knowledge one wishes to be transferred—the feature, the concept, the strategy—is appropriate for the changed task. One must also ask if the pupil will perceive its utility. Providing training in what are sometimes referred to as the subroutines, however carefully the task has been analyzed by the psychologist, does not ensure their use.

To sum up, what is meant by transfer? Not literal carrying over to a new situation of an "identical element." Not strengthening a presumed "faculty" by exercise. But rather, the application of knowledge to a hitherto unexperienced situation. To be transferable, the knowledge *must* be relational, or it could not be applied to a situation with new content. Invariants, rules, and strategies are all relational and can (if the learner perceives their utility) be applied to new content. Rehearsal is a good strategy for remembering lists of things, and a child who has once discovered the utility of this strategy will probably apply it when entirely new material is presented for learning. Strategies of organization are even better for remembering, and a child of ten or so can generalize this principle so far as to invent idiosyncratic relations within new content. The possibility of transferring relational knowledge to new situations does not mean that it will automatically happen, however. The knowledge must be possessed *and* its utility perceived for transfer to occur.

Transfer by Rule

Transfer of rules or principles has been of great interest in educational research, especially to those involved in the teaching of mathematics. Learning a rule obviously does not guarantee its spontaneous application in a new but appropriate situation. Practice in application, as all mathematics teachers know, is imperative as well as comprehension of the rule. A rule sometimes given by teachers to their pupils goes: "When two vowels go walking, the first one is talking." The efficacy of this kind of rule simply presented as a prescription seems extremely dubious. Mechanical memorization of a jingle does not bring about comprehension, whereas explanation of a principle may, if it happens at the right time. Explanation or telling may not be the best method, however, of training for comprehension and use of a principle. Telling the principle followed by drilling might lead to frustrating attempts to apply a formula when it is no longer appropriate. There is a considerable educational literature on the issue of the relative value of the "tell-and-drill" method versus "heuristic" methods (often referred to as the "discovery" method).* In the latter case, the student is typically given concrete data and assisted in making inferences from the data himself, rather than the teacher stating the generalization to him. The principal argument for this approach is the

*For a discussion of the issue see Henderson (1963); Ausubel (1961); Shulman and Keislar, 1966.

higher probability of appropriate transfer to a new situation.

We might think of this process as analogous to Piaget's process of "assimilation," a self-regulatory process of acquiring and ordering information present in stimulation that is for Piaget the key learning process, without which transfer cannot occur. To quote him, "I shall define assimilation as the integration of any sort of reality into a structure, and it is this assimilation which seems to me fundamental in learning" (Piaget, 1964, p. 18). Assimilation must be active. Thus "the goal in education is not to increase the amount of knowledge, but to create the possibilities for a child to invent and discover" (p. 3). It was emphasized in Chapter 2 that active search for invariants (order and structure in the information present in stimulation) is the essence of perceptual learning. Hearing or reading a rule is not learning in this sense, and to quote Piaget once more, "Words are probably not a short cut to a better understanding. . . . The level of understanding seems to modify the language that is used, rather than vice versa. . . . Mainly language serves to translate what is already understood. . . . (p. 5)

It is worth pointing out here that getting the student to arrive at a generalization on his own has value in addition to its transferability, and that is its motivational value. Discovery of structure (reduction of uncertainty) is reinforcing. Montessori emphasized this point as well. After recounting several episodes of children learning through their own efforts, Montessori remarked, "I think my never-to-be-forgotten impression was that joy experienced by one who has made a discovery" (Shulman and Kieslar, 1966, p. 41).

Teaching Strategies for Transfer

Can one teach strategies and expect them to be used spontaneously thereafter in appropriate situations? There has been great interest in this question in recent years on the part of two groups of researchers. One group consists of professionals who work with the educable mentally retarded—children who can learn, but who do not pick up concepts and economical strategies naturally and easily for one reason or another. The other group includes a number of Soviet psychologists, who are interested in the question for philosophical as well as practical reasons.

Consider briefly an example of the Soviet work, much of which is devoted to training mnemonic strategies of the kind we have just been considering. The purpose of this work is stated as that of "accelerating" the development of organizational skills. Samokhvalova (reported in Smirnov, Istomina, Mal'Tseva, and Samokhvalova, 1971–1972) worked with second-, fourth-, and sixth-grade pupils on the use of conceptual classification as a memorizing technique. The sixth graders were found to employ conceptual classification on their own initiative, so instruction was confined to the younger groups. The technique introduced several stages of training, each with substages. The first was instruction in conceptual classification as an independent act. Cards bearing words or pictures were presented simultaneously and sorted into classes. Then the cards were classified during sequential presentation. Finally, the reverse ability (finding exemplars) was practiced. The second step was using classification for remembering. An "algorithm of actions" was practiced for acquiring this technique, proceeding through five steps, with all the operations practiced to mastery before advancing. According to the authors, the pupils acquired "voluntary control" over the process, presumably implying that the strategy was thereafter at the service of the pupil for new problems. Some of the pupils did not require training in all the steps, but some apparently needed very extended practice.

Emphasis on the need for a long-term training sequence for transfer has been made also by researchers in this country working with disadvantaged children, slow learners, and the educable mentally retarded. Unfortunately, residual transfer some time after the immediate conclusion of the experimental training has seldom been measured, except by very crude methods such as giving an IQ test a year later (the way Head Start programs have tended to be evaluated). It will be profitable, nevertheless, to look at a few experiments in training strategies.

A group of psychologists in the Department of Special Education at the University of Minnesota have done a great deal of work with educable mentally retarded children and underachieving children in inner city schools, attempting to train them in skills of learning and remembering. In a typical experiment (Taylor and Whitely, 1972) subjects were given lists of paired associates to learn and were encouraged to generate "elaborations," such as sentences relating the pair, to facilitate learning. Earlier studies had shown that the successful learners tended to verbalize their elaborations overtly. In this study, overt verbalization was encouraged in an experimental group to enhance training and was then prohibited in an ensuing transfer condition with a new list. The subjects in this group were told to "make a picture in their minds" connecting the two words (a real picture was shown first with a practice pair) and then required to describe the image to the experimenter. In the transfer condition, they were told to do the same thing, but "keep their images a secret." Comparison with suitable control groups showed that their gain from the training was maintained in the transfer task despite only covert elaboration.

Whether the effectiveness of a twenty-minute training period of this type would be maintained permanently and also transfer to nonexperimental situations is a question worth considering. Long-term special training, however, has been shown to persist and to generalize widely in an experiment by Ross (1970a). She conducted a nine-month game program with educable mentally retarded children. The children in her experimental group spent 100 minutes per week playing group games that required the manipulation of numbers. There was a wide variety of games, and in each session the game controller (a young adult) introduced many beginning number concepts incidentally within the game context, but made no attempt to teach these concepts directly. Each game required the use of two or three kinds of number knowledge. The control group was taught the same concepts intentionally in the normal classroom situation. Pre- and posttests on a number knowledge test gave strong support for the efficacy of the long-term game training program. The experimental group excelled over the control group, obtaining higher scores on all measures. Furthermore, their number knowledge was exhibited spontaneously outside the experimental setting in the classroom, at home and in free play.

Variability of Training Conditions

It has often been observed that learning may be very specific to the context or situation where it has taken place. Varying contexts and material with practice in a skill may slow down progress at the time, but it is usually essential for effective transfer. If variability is going to be pretty much the rule in operating with a skill, should it not be introduced during learning? A demonstration of this principle in learning to read was provided by Levin and his colleagues (Levin, Baum, and Bostwick, 1963; Levin and Watson, 1963a, b) in experiments training subjects in a "set for diversity." Their hypothesis was that since English orthography does not have a simple one-to-one correspondence between letter and sound, children should not be encouraged to think that it does. The experiments simulated children's early learning using adult subjects and pairing strings of artificial graphemes with familiar words. A list of such pairs was presented for learning with correspondences within the pairs either constant or variable as to repeated elements. A trigram of three artificial graphemes might be paired, for instance, with the word *his*. Other trigrams contained the same medial grapheme. In the "constant" lists, this medial grapheme was always paired with a sound comparable to the medial vowel in *his* (words like *hit*, *sit*, etc.). In the "variable" lists, there were two or three vowel sounds, but they were all represented by a single written symbol.

Transfer lists of new pairs followed learning of the first list. For some groups, the transfer list was a variable list, and for some a constant list. For original learning, there was little difference in difficulty of learning the variable versus the constant list. But when the transfer findings were compared, the group whose variable list was preceded by an original variable list was at an advantage. The authors concluded that a set for diversity was engendered by the first list and transferred as a general set to learning the second list.

This experiment was repeated (Levin and Watson, 1963b) with variable versus constant correspondences in the initial position of the word with similar results. Most efficient learning of the second list occurred when a variable list was preceded by a different variable one. These results suggest that teaching children initially to expect one-to-one constant mappings of letters to sounds is not an effective way to promote transfer in decoding at later stages of learning to read. The nature of the correspondence system should be revealed as soon as possible if transfer is to be optimized. The nature of this correspondence will be discussed in Chapter 6 when we consider the system of English orthography.

Learning Sets

A "learning set" procedure for facilitating learning and effecting interproblem transfer was developed by Harlow (1959) while studying the capacity for discrimination learning in nonhuman primates, but the procedure has been shown to be applicable with human children. Interproblem transfer from an easy to a hard discrimination may make the hard one possible when it might otherwise not have been. Learning sets are not formed easily in young or retarded children, but interproblem transfer has been shown to occur with them (House and Zeaman, 1963). The children received pretraining with objects differing multidimensionally ("junk" objects), learning for any one problem which of two objects would be rewarded when selected consistently. Then four objects were selected and paired with one another in all possible ways so as to yield 12 problems. The subjects learned one problem after another. Half the subjects were allowed to correct wrong choices and half were not. The question was whether a subject's speed of learning a new problem would increase over blocks of problems. There was interproblem improvement with the non-correction procedure, but not with correction. It will be noted that in this experiment a rewarded object in one problem would at some point be the unrewarded one in another, introducing the possibility of negative transfer. A learning set procedure can be used with new material appearing on each problem, without reversals, as would normally be appropriate in educational situations. Such a procedure is essentially *giving practice in transfer*, but no specific "bond" or item of information is literally "transferred."

Developmental Readiness and Transfer
Learning for transfer requires that the child be ready, developmentally, for a new strategy or processing of a more complex structure in order to generalize it spontaneously. He may be able to use the more complex structure with help and instruction, but be unable to take advantage of it on his own if underlying preparatory skills have not yet been fully mastered. For many tasks there are levels of cognitive activity which have a subordinate relation to others, some achievements necessarily preceding others. Chapter 8, on prereading skills, will concentrate on this issue, for it is simply not true that one can teach anyone anything at any time.

One example will illustrate the stage concept in an attempt to "restructure" a child's behavior in classifying a set of objects. Children progress in classifying sets of objects from "heaps" or graphic collections based on spatial characteristics to hierarchical, nested classification based on properties of class inclusion and exclusion (Inhelder and Piaget, 1964). Kuhn (1972) attempted to advance children's level of classificatory behavior by letting them observe a model who performed a task of classifying a set of objects at a level lower or higher than that just exhibited by the child himself. The child was given a set of 12 wooden forms of four shapes and three colors and told to "put together the ones that go together." His sorting was photographed, he was asked to explain it, and he was then assigned to one of six stages of classification performance. A week later, he witnessed an adult model sort two similar sets of objects at one of the six stage levels and give her reasons for the sorting. The child then sorted several sets of objects in a posttest, and a week afterward sorted again in a second posttest. The sorting by the model was done at one of four levels: — 1 (below the child's quality of performance), 0 (same level as the child's), + 1 (one level higher), + 2 (two levels above the child's). The subjects ranged from four to eight years old. The posttest sortings were rated for changes in the model's direction. The greatest change occurred in the + 1 condition, where the model's level of classification was just one stage superior to the child's. Children in a control condition did not change to a higher level. The pattern of change was especially interesting. Children who witnessed a + 1 model often showed a delayed change (in the second posttest), but if the change appeared earlier, it was sustained. Children who witnessed a + 2 model and showed a change to that level on the first posttest reverted to a + 1 level on the second posttest, although they had not witnessed that type of sorting. The children did not simply imitate, since the least change occurred for the — 1 subjects, who had witnessed a poorer level of sorting than they were developmentally capable of copying but could improve on by themselves.

It would seem that progression under some circumstances can be stimulated by a model, but only to the modest extent that the child is ready for. Kuhn concluded that "mental operations can be reorganized only gradually, over a period of time, through their continuing exercise and application." It is the child's own understanding that must change if what he learns is to be transferable. Ability to take advantage of higher-order structure needs time and opportunity for assimilation, and short-term intervention at a level beyond the child's comprehension is of little value. That is why the frequent suggestion of "Why not just tell him how to do it?" is psychologically unsound.

Learning by Observation

In the experiment just described, most of the subjects learned something (limited, to be sure, but something) from observing the slightly superior performance of someone else. How is it that they learned anything when they were not engaged in doing direct practice themselves? It has always been assumed, by parents, teachers, and producers of television programs like "Sesame Street" that children do learn something from observation. They watch the clown in "Sesame Street" make mistakes in spelling a word before succeeding (accompanied by applause) and may learn vicariously to avoid those errors and spell it correctly themselves. Parents and teachers demonstrate to the child how to write his name and expect him to profit by it in some way. What is the truth of the matter? Is there transfer from watching someone else do something or learn something? Can one learn by observation?

In the first place, the answer is "Yes." Certainly we learn things by observation. In fact, even young kittens can learn to solve a problem faster by watching a demonstration cat perform the problem. Facilitation is still greater if they watch the demonstrator learn the problem, committing errors in the early stages of performance. It is not necessarily essential to go through the motor maneuvers. Observational learning, if it occurs, is perceptual learning. Perceptual learning is not response learning, but this does not mean that active attention, a kind of participation, is not essential. Observation can be as effective a source of information as trial-and-error performance for some problems, as recent experiments on observational learning have shown. An experiment by Zimmerman and Bell (1972) studied observation as a method of rule learning in a visually presented problem. The subjects (fifth graders) learned from observing a model, transferred the rule without further tuition, and, when the rule was systematic (not an arbitrary one), recalled and used it equally well three weeks later.

Observational learning by young nonhuman primates has frequently been reported. Is that just because monkeys are born imitators? Observational learning is probably seldom mere imitation. In Kuhn's experiment, the children were not simply imitating because they did not revert to a more primitive stage of classifying after witnessing the model. The kittens that solved the problem faster after watching a demonstrator cat did not imitate the demonstrator's errors.

Must observational learning be "intentional" learning? We think that observational learning occurs even when nonintentional in young children. This does not mean that it is unmotivated, only that it is not intentional in the sense of instructions being given or a deliberate decision to learn on the child's part. There is intrinsic motivation to extract information, and incidental learning is typical of the young child or animal before attention has come under as conscious self-control as it will later. It is selective just the same, and even the learning as a result of incidental observation is certainly not adequately described as imitation. The two examples par excellence are perceptual learning about the world through looking at it in the young infant who has no other way of exploring it, and learning to comprehend and produce language in the slightly older child. Imitation is obviously impossible in learning to differentiate faces from objects, one object from another, or one simple event sequence from another when an infant is a few months old. But learning occurs. Language acquisition is not taught the child, but happens mainly through observation. We shall consider it in Chapter 5, where evidence will be presented to show that imitation is not a sufficient description of how language is learned, whereas opportunity to hear and observe is essential. Intention and deliberate practice may come in at some stage, but then something has already been learned that can be practiced.

By the time a child is seven or eight, his spontaneous propensity for incidental learning is less obvious. He has become better able to direct and sustain attention and to ignore what is currently irrelevant. But that does not mean that observational learning is "out." Considerable research has centered recently on learning by observation of some special type of model. A new kind of transfer is implied here—the kind referred to by Freud as "transference." Transference occurs, presumably, if the child identifies himself with the model. If he tries to put himself in the model's place and wants to do as the model does, his motivation might be subtly manipulated and his attention and interest drawn to some desired event. (Kuhn's model was an attractive young adult.) Models can be used for reverse effects, too. Ross (1970a) used "dumb stooges" who committed errors that the children were having trouble eliminating. The stooge was corrected and even occasionally chided by the children with apparently useful vicarious effects. We shall return to the role of models in reading when we consider motivation in the initial stages of reading. Where intrinsic cognitive motivation is lacking, "transference" from a model may be a possibility.

Development of Concepts and Meaning

There is a good reason for including a discussion of conceptual development in a book on the psychology of reading. Development of the ability to classify, to generalize, and to think in relational terms is essential to the growth of cognitive economy and to transfer as we understand it. This progression is closely related to meaning and to the semantic aspect of the structure of language. Language acquisition is the topic of Chapter 5, but meaning is a psychological concept which precedes language. Meaning begins with the real things in the world, their distinctive features, and events that have observable and predictable relations between things and people and actions. Although children are aware of meanings in a real environmental context at an early age, before speech has developed to any great extent, it is a long time before they generalize meanings in a systematic way to the semantic aspect of language, both spoken and written.

The problem of meaning has been a puzzle to psychologists and philosophers for centuries, so we do not hope to solve it here. But before taking up language and growth of linguistic meaning, usually referred to as "semantics," it seems important to stress that linguistic meanings have their origins in perception of things and events in the world—in fact, in perceptual learning. We described a three-way classification of what is learned in perceptual learning in Chapter 2. Consider briefly what each class has to do with meanings in the world, in our view.

We learn *distinctive features* of things, which permit unique specification of something with respect to a set of alternatives. These are features that characterize something as different from something else. Water and sand are both substances, both have surfaces; but water is wet and sand is dry, water is transparent but sand is opaque, both are shapeless in the sense that they can be made to fit the shape of a container, but sand has visible particles and water does not, so that one is potentially textureless while the other has a grainy texture, and so on. These are real properties that differentiate the two substances. One can also point to adaptive distinguishing properties (a relation between the survival of the perceiver and the substance). Water is consumable, but sand is not, so learning this differentiating feature is of utility to an organism, as is the fact that sand can be walked upon, but water cannot.

We learn, second, *invariant properties of events*. Invariants of events may be described in terms of features, but the most important properties of events are ones that specify their adaptive significance. "Looming" can be described as a motion of approach, a change of location of some object with respect to the spatial layout and the observer. It is reflexive and not controlled by the perceiver. But the important property is that it specifies imminent collision. Retreat, on the other hand, is also a change of location, contrasting with looming or approach, but it specifies loss or deprivation of something. Consider the example of imprinting: Retreat of an object from the newborn precocial chick or duckling specifies maternal deprivation, and the chick runs after the retreating object. Depth downward (an event, because looking and head motion are involved) specifies stepping or falling off; depth upward may specify to a bird a safe place to fly. The adaptive specification of these properties of events is sometimes inborn (e.g., imprinting, response to looming), or it may be discovered through observation or experience. But the meaning, as in the case of distinctive features, begins to be learned or picked up in a concrete situation, before language means anything to the young creature (if it ever does). It progresses, certainly, to something more conceptual as more contrasting features and invariant properties are experienced and assimilated. This advance toward conceptual knowledge about the real world seems the essence of meaning and the foundation for language.

But are these meanings unstructured, added on one after another as experiences multiply? No, because perceptual learning also includes the pickup of structure, of higher-order variables. A thing or an event can be specified within a system or a hierarchy of *sets*, each with properties contrasting with another set. A man belongs to a set of animate things, to the set of humans rather than nonhumans, to the set of males rather than females. Letters are inanimate; they belong to a set of graphic items, rather than solid three-dimensional objects; they are arbitrary designs, rather than pictorial; and so on.

The same point can be made for events. Approach and retreat belong to the set of motions in space. They are directional, reflexive, have velocity, take place in a medium, etc. An important fact about these systems of relationships (superordinate and subordinate) is that they are not as rooted in a concrete experience as distinctive features and properties of a particular event. They are *systems of relations*, and one cannot represent them by anything specific. Their degree of abstractness as concepts (although all concepts are abstract) is very great, and when they are considered all in relation to one another, as a system of knowledge, structure overshadows the specific. To go back to an earlier point, transfer (if we choose to use the term) implies travel within this highly complex and abstract system, not transport of a specific element, however the element is defined.

Language has words to express all these classes of meaning. A nice example, parallel to invariant properties of events, is Miller's (1972) classification of verbs of motion. He has 12 "primitive concepts" that taken together distinguish 217 different verbs. All of these are rooted originally in perceptually describable events. Some research on early development of several aspects of conceptual meaning will extend this discussion and lead up to semantic development in language, considered in Chapter 5.

Acoustic and Semantic Generalization in Development

The term "generalization," unfortunately, has two meanings, which we must be careful to distinguish. At an early age, before the many sets of things, distinctive features that differentiate the sets, and the features that distinguish members of a set from one another have been learned, children confuse things, especially when they are alike in a number of very salient properties. Babies do not distinguish between their own caretakers and others until six months or so. This contrasts with generalization at a high level, which is based on recognition of common properties that define a class rather than failure to discriminate. There is a trend toward specificity in perceptual development because for a long time things continue to be progressively differentiated as unique. Early generalization—better termed "primary generalization"—is the same thing as failure of differentiation.

Of special relevance to us is the kind of primary generalization that happens with words. Under experimental conditions that allow mistaking one word for another, younger children are, first of all, more likely to confuse *any* word with another than older children (Cramer, 1972); but when this overall excessive rate of confusion is taken account of, it turns out that acoustic similarities of words are associated with the majority of confusions. Later on, only well into the school years, meaningful relations between words take over and eventually exceed acoustic confusions in determining mistaken recognitions. Acoustic confusions are often referred to as "clang" confusions. A child of five is far more likely to mistake or substitute *fountain* for *mountain* than *hill* for *mountain*. Children are not aware, consciously, of the basis for doing this—that they are using rhyme as a common property—they are simply failing to distinguish between two like-sounding words. Given a real event context, combined with a sentence context, they rarely do this. But a number of experiments conducted under more impoverished conditions have shown a developmental progression away from acoustic generalization toward semantic generalization.

Riess (1946), with a conditioning technique, found greater generalization at eight years of age to homonyms than to synonyms, but by adolescence the situation was reversed and semantic similarity became more effective. Perhaps the younger subjects simply had less knowledge of similarity of meaning. Rice and DiVesta (1965) controlled for this in an experiment using a paired associates method, making sure that the homonyms, synonyms, and antonyms they used were recognized as such by the subjects. In the younger children (third and fifth grades) generalization occurred as a result of phonetic but not semantic similarity. But semantic generalization became increasingly apparent in older age groups. Felzen and Anisfeld (1970) confirmed these findings using a continuous recognition method. Children in third and sixth grades listened to a list of words and judged for each word whether it had appeared before on the list. False recognition of phonetically related (rhyming) words was more frequent for third graders than false recognition of semantically related words, but semantic similarity was more effective in producing errors for sixth graders. Luria and Vinogradova (1959) also demonstrated a correlation between increasing mental age and a change from generalization over clang relations to generalization over meaningful similarity.

Cramer (1972) controlled for the overall greater error rate in younger children (the subjects were from first and fifth grades) and found more acoustic than semantic generalization in both age groups in a recognition memory experiment. The words were presented acoustically, and in list format, possibly enhancing the salience of sound resemblances. But when instructions were given to think about the meanings of the words so as to remember them exactly, while errors were not reduced in first graders, they were for fifth graders (both synonym and rhyming errors). When instructions to pay careful attention to sound were given, errors were reduced in first graders (due to a decrease in synonym errors, however). These results strengthen the evidence that the relations between words are perceived differently at these two age levels.

One implication for reading instruction that follows from these results is the importance of helping the first grader to hear the difference between words like *town* and *down* when they are presented out of context, because the child needs to do some phonemic analysis, with awareness of what he is doing, in order to discover correspondences between spoken and written language. There is also the strong implication that early reading instruction cannot simply assume that the semantic system is fully developed and will just "take care of itself" when the child manages to articulate the words on the page.

Concrete to Abstract or Vice Versa?
Primary generalization, as referred to above, is primitive in the sense that it is a failure to differentiate. But there is another level of verbal gener-

alization, attained only when semantic features of words are recognized and differentiated. This kind of generalization depends on the ability to classify words by abstracting common features from sets of words. Useful transfer in a verbal medium depends on this kind of generalization.

We said in Chapter 2 that there is a trend toward specificity in perceptual development. Is that not belied by the fact that children abstract semantic features of words rather late? Is it not, in fact, the other way around, a trend away from specificity to generality? One often hears the argument that children's thinking is "concrete" and progresses toward "abstract" thinking. There is, in fact, a great deal of evidence to justify this proposition. The point is that the concrete-abstract distinction is not the same as the issue of generalization vs. specificity. Primitive generalization—lack of discrimination—is a fact. But there is progression toward another kind of high-level generalization, which does coincide with increasing ability to abstract features and properties of things and events.

There is no contradiction here; differentiation of features (progressive specificity) goes hand in hand with the ability to abstract that is required by "secondary" or high-level generalization. For instance, one cannot perceive the likeness between two things unless he can at the same time perceive that they are different. Recognition of similarity is not the same thing as failure to discriminate (Gibson, 1959).

A similar point has been made by other authors. Inhelder and Piaget (1964), in their study of the early growth of logic in the child, define a class as the set of properties common to the members of the class, together with the set of differences which distinguish them from another class (p. 7 ff). But things can belong to more than one class. Children do not master the difference between *some* and *all* until age seven or so, and tend to say *all* when *some* would be correct, not taking account of two variables at once. The principle of class inclusion requires differentiating the properties common to the class from the set of differences distinguishing it from another class; failure to do this results from "lack of differentiation between class and object" (p. 99). In other words, objects, features of objects, and differences from other objects must be appreciated before true classification—generalizing abstraction—is possible. When this is possible, the child is on the way to achieving "hierarchical" classifications. He can say that all the yellow flowers are primulas, whereas all the pink ones are petunias, but they are all flowers; none of them are trees, but trees and flowers are all plants. Order relations of classes are very important for understanding meanings, including the lexical features of the words we read.

Brown (1958, Chapter 8, pp. 264 ff.) has an excellent discussion of the difference between concreteness and specificity or differentiatedness. Children do indeed have more concrete terms in their vocabulary, because it is learned in very concrete situations. But this does not mean that the terms are applied with perfect discrimination. Anecdotes abound about the young child's use of *Daddy* for men who are not his father, or *bow-wow* for all four-legged animals. Such anecdotes are not only ubiquitous but are also supported by observation from diaries about infants kept by psychologists and linguists. To quote Brown,

The assumption is that discrimination is primitive and that one must learn to overlook differences, to *abstract from* unique situations so as to categorize them together. All the evidence on animals, primitives, and children argues that one might better make the opposite assumption. Mind begins with the absence of differentiation. (p. 280)

Further, "The ability to appreciate a situation in its unique concreteness is a late development, a product of much learning, rather than the primitive state of mind" (p. 281). And finally,

It is redundant to say that abstraction of this sort will be acquired later than their subordinates. The abstraction implies the differentiation of subordinates. Before differentiation there can only be the abstraction that is a failure of discrimination. However, there remains an empirical form of the thesis of a concrete-abstract progression. It may be that as one moves from animals, to primitive men, children, and civilized adults one finds abstractions of advancing level. The level is now measured by the number of differentiated subordinates rather than by the range of the category. (p. 286)

There still remains the question of the difference between "concrete" and "abstract." The difference is not at all the same as that between "distinct" and "abstract." An abstract meaning can be very distinct, in the sense that an abstract term can be quite specifically differentiated from another one—in mathematics, for instance. "Concrete" is usually taken by psychologists to mean "picturable" or representable in some literal, reproducible form. Objects are concrete, and sculptures are concrete and so are other kinds of representations. Words themselves, when written or spoken, are concrete. That is not to say that all of these may not have an abstract meaning. But, as Brown says, "picturability decreases with increasing abstraction"; and development of abstract meanings increases with age.

Syntagmatic versus Paradigmatic Associations

How are words related for children, if not abstractly? Is there a way they are typically related to one another that changes with development of the ability to think categorically? A time-honored method of studying interword relations is the collection of so-called free associations to a word presented to the subject. The developmental comparison of free associations has revealed some interesting differences between children and adults. These differences appear to be the result of the growth of conceptual structure toward a systematic organization of meaningful and syntactic features, as opposed to an organization based on experienced frequency of one word following another, or acoustic similarity such as rhyme.

As early as 1916 it was observed by Woodrow and Lowell that younger children tend to produce associations based on contiguity, whereas adults produce associations based on similarity of grammatical class, semantic relationship (such as being superordinate), or contrast. This finding has been replicated many times (Brown and Berko, 1960; Entwisle, 1966; Entwisle, Forsyth, and Muuss, 1964; Francis, 1972; Lippman, 1971; Mc-Neill, 1966; Palermo, 1971), although interpretations of the change have differed. Ervin (1961) introduced the term "syntagmatic-paradigmatic shift" to designate the change, and suggested that the younger children's responses were syntagmatic because the words often had been heard contiguously in a sentence where syntax had placed them in relation (e.g., *green* → *grass*; *go* → *home*). The words would ordinarily be of different grammatical classes such as adjective → noun or verb → noun in such associations. But older children (beginning around eight years) and adults are apt to give associations belonging to the same grammatical class, designated by Ervin as paradigmatic (e.g., *green* → *red*; *go* → *come*).

Associations like *green* → *red* are clearly not determined by frequent contiguity in sentences. We never say "The grass is green red." No one ever spoke a sentence in which *come* followed *go*. McNeill (1966) considered the proposition that the shift to this type of paradigmatic "association" was caused by learning implicit grammatical rules about classes of words. He rejected the idea on the basis that children produce grammatical sentences well before the age of the shift toward paradigmatic associations, and suggested instead that words are classified by assigning features to them, both grammatical and meaningful (cf. Katz and Fodor, 1963). The word *man* is not just a noun, but is characterized also by the features animate, human, male, etc. Children younger than seven or eight do not have featural properties defining classes organized hierarchically. Hierarchical arrangement of features results in a kind of tree organization in which one winds up with a pair of alternatives which are distinguished by a single bipolar contrast (e.g., male-female, in the example above). McNeill thought that such a cognitive organization of verbal features would tend toward producing a paradigmatic response that formed a minimal contrast with the stimulus word (e.g., *black-white, boy-girl*). Minimal contrast responses of this sort do indeed increase with age, as do superordinate responses (e.g, *man → human*), which also support a hierarchical feature-analysis theory of word meanings.

The control of association by contrastive features fits the hypothesis that features of things and events are *perceived* as contrastive relations. It makes sense that verbal meanings should, as development progresses, become organized conceptually in ways consistent with extraction of perceptual information and its development. That features should be organized in some systematic way makes sense, as we saw in the case of the distinctive features of phonemes or graphemes. Experience and learning are required for development of systematic organization of word meanings.

Francis (1972) recently suggested that young children's so-called syntagmatic associations are not the result of associative frequency, but are the result of making some kind of functional or descriptive sense, like the possibility of combination in a meaningful sentence. Young children, she thought, "organize the lexicon and construct sentences according to a system of functional relations between words."

The paradigmatic shift comes only gradually, as a result of learning to segment sentences and make comparisons. Her hypothesis is

that the syntagmatic-paradigmatic shift is caused by a lengthy reorganization of the mental filing system of the preschool child based on abilities to isolate words from sentences and to make comparisons across related constituents. Preschool associations are based on making sense together in possible functional or descriptive sentences wherein the semantic relations between referents are the glue. Later, paradigmatic associations come to include those based on thoughtful operations of comparison and inclusion. McNeill's hypothesis of semantic feature system learning would be subsumed, for this must be based on experienced degrees of commonality between sets of predicates: but also included must be a hypothesis of form class learning based on comparisons of semantic relations between constituent phrases. (pp. 956–957)

The syntagmatic-paradigmatic shift seems therefore to show that children's conceptual development advances, not by adding associations or progressively collecting statistical distributions resulting in categorization of form classes, but by segmenting sentences into meaningful constituents (words) which by comparison and constrast develop into a system of meanings. The structural relationships of meanings make possible the development of lexical features, which will be discussed in Chapter 5.

Summary

This chapter continued the survey of cognitive development that began with perceptual development in Chapter 2. The first section dealt with the development of strategies of organization in different intellectual tasks, including simple decision making; search, discovery, and use of structure present in the material presented; solution of problems involving words; and finally remembering, where varied strategies like rehearsal, subjective organization, and clustering by categorical features can be used for greater economy. Efficient strategy for all these tasks improves with development, but something else happens too. As his economy of processing increases, so does the child become more aware of what he is doing, how he is controlling his own intellectual processes in an autoregulatory fashion. He is learning, in short, how to learn on his own.

In the next section, the nature of transfer and its value were discussed. A child cannot be supplied with ready-made responses suitable for any occasion. That is why it is so important that we help the child to learn on his own, but what has utility for future application and learning must be relational, rather than specific "elements" in Thorndike's sense. Can we assist self-regulatory learning by facilitating understanding of invariant features, rules, and strategies? To some extent, it seems so. Varied training conditions, use of learning set procedures, and encouragement of spontaneous observation and search for invariants may all help.

The third section dealt with the course of conceptual development from about age five on. If we want to know what opportunities can be provided that will result in effective progress in economical self-processing of relevant information, we must know something about the child's potential for comprehension at the time. This is particularly true for reading. Developing a system of meanings, both for real events and for words, is part of learning to read. We cannot supply this growth for the child, but we can try to understand how it progresses and foster it.

4

Linguistic Concepts Necessary to Study Reading

The first part of this book, as we stated in Chapter 1, is designed to discuss the psychological, developmental, linguistic, and even historical (in origins of writing systems) concepts which we found necessary to introduce the psychology of reading. This chapter will review those linguistic concepts which we found necessary in the subsequent exposition. We do not plan a formal, systematic discussion of linguistics. There are many excellent introductions to linguistics (e.g., Hockett, 1958; Gleason, 1961; Langacker, 1973; Bolinger, 1968; Elgin, 1973). Rather, our purpose is to select from the discipline of linguistics those concepts which we needed to interpret the research on reading, to theorize about reading, and to design and carry out research on reading. This is a chapter of the type accompanied by the caveat to the reader "If you are familiar with introductory linguistics, you may safely skip this chapter."

During the past several decades, linguistics has been a discipline rich in theory, revisions, and debate. As psychologists concerned with the reading process we have not found it necessary to involve ourselves in the arcane matter of linguistics. Rather, we have found the fundamental concepts sufficient and so have not needed to take up theoretical cudgels for one or another point of view. We have been eclectic and opportunistic, borrowing those concepts and theories which helped us with the task of understanding the reading process. Finally, this chapter differs in a fundamental way from the other chapters in this book. In them we have attempted to select, interpret, and evaluate research literature. In this chapter we set forth definitions and concepts which are useful in research but are not primarily the subject of research.

Linguistics has been concerned principally with the analysis of speech, though texts often give passing mention to writing systems and incidentally reading (e.g., Gleason, 1961; Hockett, 1958; Bloomfield, 1933; Langacker, 1973). This neglect is somewhat surprising, since there are some obvious parallels between hearing-speaking and reading-writing, as diagrammed in Figure 4-1.

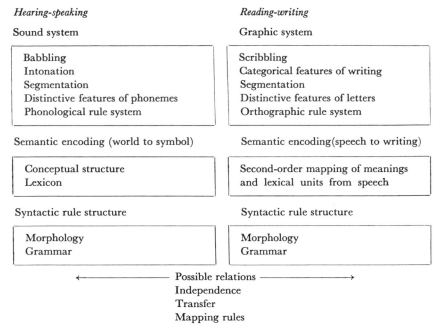

Hearing-speaking	*Reading-writing*
Sound system	Graphic system

Babbling Intonation Segmentation Distinctive features of phonemes Phonological rule system	Scribbling Categorical features of writing Segmentation Distinctive features of letters Orthographic rule system

Semantic encoding (world to symbol)	Semantic encoding(speech to writing)

Conceptual structure Lexicon	Second-order mapping of meanings and lexical units from speech

Syntactic rule structure	Syntactic rule structure

Morphology Grammar	Morphology Grammar

←————————— Possible relations —————————→
Independence
Transfer
Mapping rules

Figure 4-1. Some parallels between hearing-speaking and reading-writing. From Gibson, 1972, p. 9.

Phonology

Phonetic versus Phonemic Units of Speech Analysis

Descriptive linguistics, tied as it was to anthropological field methods, had the difficult task of noting every speech sound that a speaker utters. The motive was the need for the anthropologist who was studying a language, usually unrelated to any languages he knew, to preserve the sounds of that language. The task was probably an impossible one. "Phoneticians at one time set as their goal the exact and detailed description of every sound" (Gleason, 1961, p. 239). Such an analysis is *phonetic* and has as its purpose the description and analysis of every sound in the language. The unit of the analysis in phonetics is the *phone*. In theory, a detailed phonetic record would permit a skilled phonetician to "read off" the language, somewhat like reading music. The International Phonetic Alphabet (IPA) is still much in use and is usually the pronunciation guide that one finds in dictionaries.

Every language has a finite number of sound contrasts which serve to keep words separate and unconfused. This inventory of sounds is substantially smaller than all the phones that a speaker may potentially utter. Such sound units which actually distinguish between utterances are *phonemes*. In English, there are about forty phonemes which serve to make up, in various combinations, the sound system of the language. The phoneme (the study of which is called *phonemics*) is a class of contrastive sounds. For example, one phoneme is the consonant /k/. If you listen carefully to this sound in the words *keep* and *cool* you can tell that the articulation patterns, particularly the position of the tongue, is different for these two items in the class /k/. But this difference in articulation is not phonemic in English, though it is conceivable that the two /k/ sounds which we group into a single class may be contrastive in another language and would be classified as two different phonemes.

The simplest way to identify phonemes is through a series of minimal contrasts:

bit
hit
sit
lit

The *it* cluster is constant, but since we understand these as separate words we infer that /b, h, s, l/ are phonemic in English. Pretend that you would respond the same way to *hit* and *sit*. We would then have no basis for two phoneme classes /h/ and /s/ and could group these into a single phoneme class. In Japanese, for example, /l/ and /r/ are not contrastive and both sounds are categorized as a single class. Phonemes, in other words, are sounds that make a difference in speaking and understanding a language. Phones, as the two articulation and sound patterns for /k/ indicate, may or may not serve the function of contrasting utterances.

For some linguists, the phoneme can be profitably analyzed into bundles of distinctive features, as described in Chapter 2 (Chomsky and Halle, 1968). In the next chapter, we point out that the child's acquisition of the phonemic system of his language involves successive contrasts in the distinctive features which describe particular phonemes.

Syllables

We will have occasion to refer to syllables as units in language development, as higher-order units in word perception, and as initial units of reading instruction in the discussion of syllabic writing systems. Wardhaugh (1969) points out that teachers' concern with syllabification is usually a part of phonics programs, but that the linguistic rules for the syllable are complex and children are really taught the conventions of hyphenation.

There is surprisingly little discussion of syllables in standard works on linguistics.* Two current definitions of the syllable are the breath group conception and the vocalic center definition. The first is used by Hockett (1958, p. 64): "The force of pushing (of air by the lungs) varies rhythmically, in a way which correlates with the successive units we call *syllables* in English and certain other languages." Gleason (1961) assumes that we know what a syllable is and defines vowels as syllable nuclei.

Whorf's (1956) formula for the English monosyllable which is taken up in detail in Chapter 6 builds the syllable around a vowel which may or may not be followed by specific consonants and consonant clusters. The formula provides a precise statement about what consonants or consonant clusters may surround the vowel to produce phonologically legal English monosyllables.

Syllabification, it appears to us, has been more a matter of style and spelling conventions than of linguistic theory. More discussion of syllables occurs in prefaces to dictionaries than in linguistics works (cf. *Webster's Third New International Dictionary*, 1966), and there is far from complete agreement among lexicographers and publishers about the nature of syllable boundaries. For example, "When two identical consonants occur medially, a division is made between the consonants (as in *col-lie, mil-lion, camel-lia*)" (p. 22a, Vol. 1), and such rules go on in fine print for pages.† Many readers will empathize with the hours spent in school on "where to put the hyphen."

In contrast to the dearth of linguistic concern with the syllable, there has been increasing psychological research on the syllable as a perceptual unit. Although many of these studies are discussed elsewhere in this book, they merit at least brief mention here to show that serious thinking about the linguistic nature of the syllable is overdue.

Savin and Bever (1970) reported that reaction times to whole syllables

---

*An early study by Trager and Bloch (1941) is a sophisticated discussion of the phonological constraints provided by syllables.
†A common convention in multimorphemic words is to maintain the morpheme boundaries in syllabification.

were faster than reaction times to initial phonemes of the syllable. Recently, Foss and Swinney (1973) demonstrated that reaction times—times for pushing a button when the target was heard—were fastest for two-syllable words, next for initial syllables, and longest for the identification of initial phonemes. Presumably, these investigators used the dictionary syllabifications as their source of syllables, although Foss and Swinney indicate an awareness of the phonological rules for syllable formation by mentioning that "no syllable can begin with the sequence /kt/ since the rules of syllable structure forbid it" (p. 253).

When the task is the naming of one- and two-syllable words presented tachistoscopically, the evidence for the perceptual unity of the syllable is less clear than when the subjects are measured for motor reaction times to auditory stimuli (Spoehr and Smith, 1973). For pronouncing the word, Spoehr and Smith found the notion of *vocalic center groups* (VCGs) more predictive of their results than syllables. VCGs are based on speech production data from the Haskins Laboratories and have been used by Hansen and Rodgers (1968) to form instructional materials for children learning to read. Hansen and Rodgers propose an algorithm, shown below, for grouping consonants and vowels in mono- and polysyllabic words. The vowels and consonants that are implicated in the vocalic center group are printed in capital letters and the other letters of the word are in lowercase. The term V stands for a single vowel which may be spelled by a single letter or by digraph or trigraph spellings; e.g., *oo* in *door* or *eau* in *beauty*.

(1)	VCV	V + CV	*mATIng*	*mA + TIng*
(2)	VCCV	VC + CV	*mATTIng*	*mAT + TIng*
(3)	VCCCV	VC + CCV	*thIRSTY*	*thIR + STY*

We present the Hansen and Rodgers research as another way of "parsing" words into syllablelike units, not as a hypothesis about word recognition. In fact, the assumptions underlying their hypothesis are unlikely because it assumes that a reader inspects the word first for the presence of vowels and consonants, then identifies the letters, and finally tests a pronunciation for the word. As will be seen in Chapter 7, the weight of the evidence on word perception contradicts such assumptions.

Spoehr and Smith concluded that this algorithm, without the possibilities for recycling that Hansen and Rodgers also propose, was sufficient to account for the perceptual units in their task. It should be pointed out that Spoehr and Smith found the units useful without necessarily accepting the Hansen and Rodgers word recognition model. The comparisons of these various studies are further evidence of the conclusion that we will return to many times: The nature of the task determines the nature of the perceptual unit.

McNeill and Lindig (1973) reported an important study concerning the "psychological reality" of various linguistic units which place the previous findings in a very sensible perspective. From earlier studies (Savin and Bever, 1970; etc.), it might be inferred that subjects respond faster to larger units so that syllables are identified more rapidly than phonemes, words more rapidly than syllables, sentences faster than words, etc. McNeill and Lindig found these results perplexing, since they could lead to counterintuitive assumptions if the size of the linguistic units were continually enlarged. Further, they objected to the interpretation that rapid reaction times imply psychological reality and slow reaction times, nonreality.

McNeill and Lindig tested the hypothesis that the rapidity of search is a function of the nature of the list in which the target is embedded. That is, phonemes should be identified more easily in a list of phonemes than in a syllable list, syllables should profit from a syllable list, etc. The results clearly confirm their hypothesis: In the conditions where there was a match between the target and the list, reaction times were fast. When there were mismatches between targets and lists, their subjects took longer to respond to the target. "Listeners respond more quickly when the target and the search list are on the same linguistic level compared to when they are on different levels" (p. 424).

Generally, reaction times were shorter for lower linguistic levels, but this finding has few implications for the perceptual reality of those levels and is likely due to the shorter size of the target units. The researchers conclude that what is "real" is what subjects pay attention to. These findings do not mean that syllables or even phonemes may not be efficient perceptual units, but that one linguistic level is not intrinsically more real than another. We point out in the next chapter that it is difficult for young children to segment, that is, pay attention to phonemes, but they can with training attend to units at that level. Similarly, syllables appear to be more available than phonemes under certain task requirements. The important conclusion to be drawn from this research is that there are no natural perceptual priorities among linguistic units: One must take into account the nature of the task and the competence of the subjects.

Morphology

Morphemics

In this book we will have occasion to refer to morphology in our discussions of language acquisition, word perception, and early reading skills. Morphemes are discovered in a language by contrasting units of content rather than minimal contrasts of sound. The morpheme is the smallest meaning-bearing unit in the language. Loosely speaking, a morpheme is a word, although a word can be made up of more than one morpheme. We might speak of words as being mono- or polymorphemic. Morphemes are phonemes which have content.

Morphology is best made clear by examples. Consider the word *chair* compared to *chair(s)*. In the singular form, the word is a single unbound morpheme. It can be understood as a meaning-bearing unit which cannot be further subdivided into meaningful elements. *Ch* standing alone has no meaning, nor does *air* have any meaningful relationship to the word *chair*. The plural *chairs* contains two meaningful elements, *chair* and *s*, the letter of which marks (means) more than one. We may say then that *chairs* contains two morphemes: the first, *chair*, free or unbound (because it has meaning by itself) and the second, *s*, a bound form which means "more than one" and cannot stand alone, but only as a suffix to nouns (hence the "bound" categorization).

Words may be decomposed into their morphemes. Further examples from Langacker (1973) may be useful. "*Telephones* then has three morphemes, while *telephone* contains two and *phone* just one. A morpheme usually has a fairly clear and constant meaning in all its uses, although it is easy to find exceptions" (p. 71).

English has a reasonably simple morphological system. The five inflectional morphemes are the suffixes, given in their written rather than phonemic forms: *s* (plural or possessive or third person singular verbs), *ed* (past), and *ing* (progressive verb forms). The English-speaking student who is learning a foreign language and is overwhelmed by the many declensions and conjugations of that language may take solace in the reported difficulty of acquiring English as a second language, though the difficulty in English is *not* its inflectional morphology.

Another part of English morphology is its *derivational morphological* system, which is rather complicated and performs a different function than the inflectional suffixes just mentioned. If we add the suffix *ly* to *quick* we change the part of speech from an adjective to an adverb. Unfaithfulness is morphologically *un* + *faith* + *ful* + *ness* and serves to turn the root form *faith* (a noun) to *faithful* (an adjective) to *faithfulness* (a noun). Notice that *un* can make *faithful* negative, but we cannot say *unfaith*. Derivational morphology, then, serves by means of prefixes and suffixes to change a word from one to another part of speech. We will see in the next chapter that the inflectional and derivational systems differ in their rate of acquisition by children.

Morphophonemics

In later chapters, especially when we discuss the orthographic (spelling) rules of English, we often refer to a "morphophonemic" level of analysis. It should be clear from the previous sections that both phonemes and morphemes are analyzed not in isolation but as significant contrasts in the language. By "significant contrasts" we mean simply that if the contrast were not made, the utterance would not be understood. If English did not make the contrast between /l/ and /r/, the sentence, "The right cake batter is light" would be ambiguous. Likewise, we need the bound morphemes *ed* and *s* to make sense out of the contrasts in the following sentence:

Yesterday he wanted to go home but today he wants to stay. The reader might try interchanging the inflections to realize the necessity for these morphemic contrasts.

Morphemes which we group as having the same meaning may vary in their phonemic shape. The most common example is that the graphic *s* of the plural may be pronounced /s/, /z/, or /ɨz/ depending on the sounds preceding the suffix. To take an example from Francis (1958, p. 209), phonemes as different from the three plurals as the /en/ suffix in *oxen* may share the same morphemic category as the *s* plurals. Conversely, two completely different morphemes may share identical phonemic shapes: *meet* and *meat* (Hockett, 1958, p. 135).

According to Francis (1958), the field of morphophonemics is complex and not yet fully worked out in English. For our purposes we may think of this branch of linguistics as concerning the influence of the morpheme or word on the nature of the phonemes making up that word. We shall see in Chapter 6 that use of a morphophonemic level of analysis helps to regularize the English orthographic system when compared to the consideration of phonemes (or letters) without reference to their morphemic environments.

Syntax

According to Fries (1952), there are more than two hundred different definitions of the sentence. Many of us remember the common school definition that a "sentence expresses a complete thought." The exceptions are obvious.

(4)   Today is Monday.

(5)   But not today.

Sentence (4) qualifies for the pedagogical definition; (5) obviously does not. If we adopt the graphic definition that a sentence is set off by periods, we gain little in understanding the nature of sentences. In fact, many writing systems do not set off sentences by periods and spaces.

Listeners are not accurate unitizers of the sentences in the speech stream because although a period and space might lead us to expect pauses at the ends of sentences, there are often intrasentence pauses that last longer than those between sentences. In speech, sentences may by marked by the intonation contours. So we recognize a question by a falling intonation, a statement by level intonation, a command by the pattern of stress and rising intonation.

Nevertheless, in descriptive linguistics the nature of a sentence was assumed, and the influence of the famous American linguist, Leonard Bloomfield (1933), was such that questions about the speaker's intentions or the meanings which may underlie sentences were not addressed. Rather, there were techniques for analyzing the phonological patterns as uttered or written. This type of grammatical analysis is called an *immediate constituent analysis* and has as its purpose the division of a sentence as heard or read into the elements that make up the sentence, that is, the constituents of the sentence. The outcome of an immediate constituent (IC) grammatical analysis is to group the morphemes that form units, that is, that go together. Take the sentence "The window is open." Most readers would agree that this simple sentence has two constituents: a subject and a predicate.

(6)

The window   is open

Any juxtaposition of the words would not make sense, like putting *the* alone and combining *window is*. To take a sentence that is a bit more complex: "The boy reads the book."

(7)

The boy   reads the book

reads the book

Phrase Structure Rules*

In both examples above, the sentences had two main parts, and in the second, the predicate could be further subdivided between the verb and the direct object. Said another way,

S → NP + VP (a sentence may be rewritten as a noun phrase and a verb phrase).

"The learned boy reads the book" would be diagramed like this:

(8)

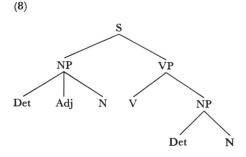

But complications mount as we ask more questions. Surely we are not really interested in this sentence or that, but in all the sentences of this type. And what constitutes this "type"? As we look at the tree diagram (8) we see that it implies that certain words are more closely related to some words than they are to others. The determiner *the* is more closely related to the noun *boy* than it is to the verb *reads*. It is this grammatical structural relationship between not only words, but the structures made

*We are indebted to Prof. Charles Elliott for his suggested introduction to transformational grammar.

up out of words, that we want to examine and to understand. Thus, the tree diagram (8) is a generalization about "The learned boy reads the book," and "The fat lout spilled the soup," and "The jolly fellow brought the presents" and all other English sentences of the same structure.

There are, however, many other English sentences with a somewhat different structure. For example, consider (9):

(9) The cake that she made won the prize.

By substituting elements one at a time, we can find other sentences of equivalent structure. For instance, "She won the prize," "He got it," are in some ways similar, in that *she* can be substituted for *the cake that she made* without changing the grammatical relationship between subject and predicate.

So far we have two types of noun phrases: one like *the learned boy* and the other like *the cake that she made*. The tree diagram in (8) can also be written as a "rule": NP → Det + Adj + N. This rule says that a noun phrase may be rewritten as a determiner + adjective + noun. And we can also specify the composition of the other noun phrase by a rule: NP → NP + S, that is, that a noun phrase may be rewritten as a noun phrase + sentence. These are two generalizations about English. Now if we could somehow combine them we would have a generalization which would be much more far-reaching than either of the separate ones.

By using notation which allows for optional categories, we can combine these rules as follows:

$$NP \rightarrow \begin{Bmatrix} NP & S \\ (Det) & (Adj) & N \end{Bmatrix}$$

The curly brackets mean that the speaker may make a choice between the top and the bottom line, but must take one. The parentheses mean that what is enclosed is optional. Notice that by using this rule we can make different phrase structure trees. This is a *phrase structure* rule, and it is a generalization about a number of different English structures, any one of which could be shown in a phrase structure tree.

But there is a problem here, as we shall see. If we perform an immediate constituent analysis of (9), that is, if we show the relationships between the words and phrases of (9), we will have (10):

(10) The cake that she made won the prize.

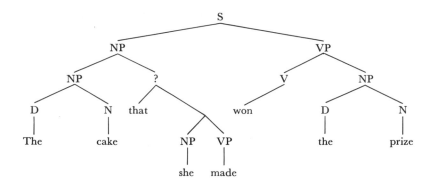

The phrases *the cake* and *that she made* are in a grammatical relationship with one another, and taken both together are the noun phrase *the cake that she made*. And the relationship between *won* and *the prize* is apparent. But what about the verb *made*? Doesn't it really have an object? We know that *she* made something. We even know from this very sentence what it was she made. It was a cake. So isn't the verb *made* in a grammatical relationship with the noun phrase *the cake*? If we only allow ourselves to look at the words and phrases of a sentence as they appear, we certainly will miss that relationship, a very real relationship which is definitely there.

If we use the top line of our NP rule, that is, NP + S, we can make another tree:

(11) The cake that she made won the prize.

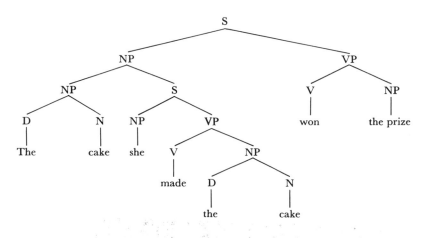

Now we have expressed the grammatical relationship between *made* and *the cake*. But if we now read this off, we would have to say "The cake she made the cake won the prize," and that is clearly not English.

Transformational Grammar*

We need, then, something to adjust this expression of grammatical relationships, both overt and covert, so that it will end up as a proper grammatical English sentence. There is another type of rule that does just this, and it is called a *transformation*. A transformation contains a "structural description." If a structure matches this, the transformation takes effect and alters that structure. It may add certain structural words (like *that*); it may delete certain structures (like *the cake*), or it may change the positions of structures.

There are several important ideas to be examined here. Phrase structure rules are generalizations about possible structures in the language. By realizing one or another of these possible structures, one can "generate" a phrase structure tree, and that tree will be an expression of the grammatical relationships of a particular sentence; at that stage in our progress we have a *deep structure*, a level of structure at which all grammatical relationships, covert or overt, are represented. But this may not yet be a grammatical sentence, and so transformations are required. Transformations operating on a deep structure produce a *surface structure*, one in which all grammatical relationships may not be directly represented, but which is a grammatical sentence for the language.

Here are some of the advantages gained by taking this view:

(a) An immediate constituent analysis, operating only on surface structures, would find it quite difficult to account for discontinuous structures. From this viewpoint, such structures are simply the result of a transformation moving part of one constituent away from another part. For example:

(12) Did he go to the store?

(13) He looked the case up.

*A detailed discussion of transformational rules and generative grammar is beyond the scope of this chapter. Interested readers may find the following references useful: for a general introduction to Chomsky's thinking, Lyons (1970); for Chomsky's own writings, which require considerable linguistic knowledge, Chomsky (1957, 1965). Greene (1972) discusses Chomsky's influence on psychology and Chomsky's own readable statement on his theory and cognitive psychology (Chomsky, 1968). A simplified version of transformational grammar is presented by Jacobs and Rosenbaum (1968) and by Elgin (1973).

In (12) clearly *did* is part of the verb phrase *did go,* and in (13) *up* is clearly part of *looked up.*

(b) Ambiguous sentences cannot be understood by a surface structure analysis. To use some of Chomsky's favorite examples:

(14) Flying planes can be dangerous.

(15) Visiting relatives can be tedious.

It is clear that (14) is paraphrased by "To fly planes can be dangerous" or "Planes which are flying can be dangerous," while (13) has similar paraphrases. Our viewpoint accounts for or explains this similarity in surface structure by proposing that each of the two readings represented a different deep structure, and that the transformations which applied to the two different structures accidentally produced identical surface structures.

(c) Sentences which are obviously related may appear to have widely different surface structures. The transformational viewpoint accounts for this by saying that these sentences have very similar deep structures, but that different transformations have been applied to form different surface structures. For instance, consider (16)–(18):

(16) The boy batted the ball.

(17) The ball was batted by the boy.

(18) Did the boy bat the ball?

In all cases the grammatical relationship between the verb *batted* and the noun phrase *the ball* remains unchanged; likewise the relationship between the verb and the noun phrase *the boy.*

(d) Perfectly grammatical English sentences have implicit elements and relationships which we know are there, but which do not appear in surface structures, as we have already noted in the sentence "The cake she made won the prize," or in imperative sentences like "Jump!", where *you* is understood.

Parts of Speech

We have freely used terms like *noun, verb, adjective,* etc., assuming that most readers will accept and find adequate the common, intuitive definitions of parts of speech, or *form classes,* to give them their technical designation. Descriptive linguistics was much concerned with parts of speech and the criteria for assigning words to one or another class (cf. Francis, 1958, for an excellent chapter on parts of speech in this tradition). We should note also that there is a recent trend in the study of languages which takes up the semantic organization of words in a person's lexicon (cf. Fillenbaum and Rapaport, 1971; Miller, 1972).

The school definitions of form classes seem quaintly simple, e.g., "A noun is the name of a person, place, or thing" or "The subject of a sentence is a noun." But how do we handle "To err is human, to forgive, divine," where the infinitive phrase acts as the NP or subject and the transformational rules which generated that sentence are numerous and complicated: pronominalization, pronoun deletion, coordination, coordinate deletion, verb deletion, etc. Parts of speech can be defined, but the task is more cumbersome and sophisticated than ". . . name of a person. . . ."

Parts of speech are grouped into two broad categories: *function* words and *content* words. Function words are a small set that function to order other words; they lack content of their own but determine the meanings of other words. Some examples of function words are *the, and, by, to, but, why.* They are the words that are left out in a telegram. Content words (nouns, verbs, adjectives, adverbs, etc.) make up the rest of the vocabulary and are so named because they *contain* meaning. When we take apart the NP *the leaf,* the determiner *the* functions to inform the reader that we are referring to a particular leaf as compared to the indefinite article in *a leaf.*

How do we know that *leaf* is a noun rather than a verb, as in *to leaf through the book?* Francis (1958) gives five criteria for a word to be classified as a noun.

1. The commonest noun marker is that it is preceded by a determiner, as in our example above. There may be modifiers between the determiner and the noun, but they may be left out without torturing the meaning of the structure: e.g., *a thin, spidery leaf.*
2. Nouns can take two inflections, the plural *s* or *es* and the possessive *'s.*
3. Nouns are formed by certain derivational suffixes: break*age,* draft*ee,* consisten*cy,* violin*ist,* etc. The form of the derivational suffix depends on whether a verb or adjective or another noun is being changed to a noun form.
4. Position in the sentence is a possible, but not reliable noun marker. Nouns usually precede verbs.
5. Stress patterns distinguish identically spelled words that occupy different form classes. *Réfuse* is distinguished from *refúse* by the primary and secondary stress on the two syllables of the noun and stress only on the second syllable in the verb form.

In general, parts of speech are defined not by the word in isolation, which is highly unreliable, but by the part that the word plays in a larger grammatical structure. Similar functional analyses may be made for other parts of speech: verbs, adjectives, adverbs, prepositions, etc.

Modern grammars do not explicitly define parts of speech but make the same assumption: Constituents of a sentence are labeled consistently, e.g., as an NP, because their main element is a noun and this type of phrase behaves consistently from sentence to sentence. Alternatively, the environment of a noun is determined by phrase structure rules:

NP → (Det) N	The girl
NP → (Det) (Adj) N,	The pretty girl
but not	
NP → N (Det)	*Girl the.

Case Grammar

To the psychologist working with linguistics, the distinction between syntax and semantics often seems arbitrary and difficult to understand. In future chapters we will have occasion to see that readers respond primarily to the meaning of a sentence rather than to its formal grammatical or formal phonological features.

Fillmore (1968) has elaborated the theory of a case grammar in English which imaginatively combines syntactic and semantic features of the language. "I shall adopt . . . the term *case* to identify the underlying syntactic-semantic relationship . . ." (p. 21).

The case notions comprise a set of universal, presumably innate concepts which identify certain types of judgments human beings are capable of making about the events that are going on around them, judgments about such matters as who did it, who it happened to, and what got changed. (Fillmore, 1968, p. 24)

Brown's (1973) summary of Fillmore's first and basic set of case relations is given in Table 4-1. Brown has found Fillmore's case grammar useful for understanding the first stages of children's language development. Presumably, the reason Brown and we also find case grammar theoretically congenial is that the first set of cases Fillmore proposes deals with perceptual invariants which every listener-reader experiences.

Latin and many other languages mark case relations by affixation on the base form of the noun. As can be seen from the examples in Table 4-1,

It is a linguistic convention to mark ungrammatical forms with an asterisk.

Table 4–1 Fillmore's Case Concepts Defined and Exemplified

Case Name	Definition	Example (Italicized noun is in designated case)
Agentive (A)	The typically animate, perceived instigator of action	*John* opened the door. The door was opened by *John*.
Instrumental (I)	The inanimate force or object causally involved in the state or action named by the verb	The *key* opened the door. John opened the door with the *key*.
Dative (D)	The animate being affected by the state or action named by the verb	*Adam* sees Eve. *John* murdered *Bill*. John gave the book to *Bill*. *Daddy* has a study.
Factive (F)	The object or being resulting from the state or action named by the verb	God created *woman*. John built a *table*.
Locative (L)	The location or spatial orientation of the state or action named by the verb	The sweater is on the *chair*. *Chicago* is windy. John walked to *school*.
Objective (O)	The semantically most neutral case: anything representable by a noun whose role in the state or action named by the verb depends on the meaning of the verb itself	Adam sees *Eve*. The *sweater* is on the chair. John opened the *door*.

Source: Brown, 1973, p. 133. (Adapted from Fillmore, 1968.)

in English, case relations are marked by prepositions or by word order. Further, the ubiquitous concern in the study of foreign languages with whether a noun is "masculine, feminine, or neuter" is paralleled in Fillmore's theory by the ecologically real semantic distinction between animateness and inanimateness. "Agentive and Dative cases require nouns that have animate reference" (Brown, 1973, p. 135).

One of the powers of case grammar is that the case frames provide a means for classifying verbs. To take an example used by both Fillmore and Brown, the verb *open* may appear in the following frame (Fillmore, p. 27):

[——— O (I) (A)]

which means that *open* is obligated to appear in a sentence with a noun in the objective case and the sentence may also contain elements in the agentive and instrumental cases. The following sentences illustrate the case constraints which a verb like *open* places on the nouns in the sentence. Sentence

(19) illustrates the meshing of case and transformational grammar because an underlying sentence "Someone or something opened the door" is assumed, with the agent deleted.

(19) The door opened. [————O]

(20) John opened the door. [————O + A]

(21) The wind opened the door. [————O + I]

(22) John opened the door with a chisel. [————O + I + A]

Fillmore regards the six cases so far discussed as a basic minimum and suggests others that may be useful to a more complete case grammar: benefactive (B), as in "John did it for *Mary*"; comitative (C), as in "Adam walked home with *Mommy*"; temporal (T), as in "They arrived at noon" (Brown, p. 133).

Fillmore's treatment of the possessive shows clearly that his grammar is intricately involved with the semantic features of the lexicon. He makes the distinction between alienable and inalienable possession. For example, *his brother's face* is an example of inalienable possession since this particular face is inseparable from its owner, whereas *his brothers' car* is alienable in that the possessor and the possessed may be separated.

In summary, case grammar is useful because it is a semantically based system congruent in many respects with the experiences of the speaker, writer, or reader. The distinction between syntax and meaning is blurred so that case analyses of sentences use an amalgam of both types of information. It provides a classification for verbs according to the case environments they may take. The residual case, objective, is, it is true, somewhat of a catchall in that its meaning is neutral and depends on the meaning of the verb.

Suprasegmental Features

Written language is often considered a pale reflection of speech. After all, speech involves a range of variations in pause, stress, pitch—variables generally called the intonation contours of speech. Some of these speech behaviors are communicated by punctuation, but the few punctuation marks available to the writer are meager substitutes for the range of variation available to the voice. In truth, there are some things we can write but not say (see Chapter 6), but the balance tips strongly in the direction of the richness of speech over print. Skilled authors are able to capture some of the speech qualities in writing, but most of us must be content with jerry-built substitutes like underlining, rows of exclamation marks, dashes, etc.

We have heard teachers admonish their pupils to "Read with expression." Reading aloud in the early grades probably has little justification other than to give the teacher some insight into the child's progress. Does he pause at appropriate places in the text? Does he drop his voice at the end of sentences and raise it slightly when beginning the next sentence? Does he stress each word equally so that it sounds as if he is reading a list, or does he distribute and modulate his stresses so that he seems to understand the text and the interrelationships between words, phrases, sentences, etc.? In technical terms, the teacher is listening for *juncture, pitch,* and *stress.* Our discussion of these variables relies heavily on Gleason (1961).

Juncture refers to the pauses in speech. Gleason contrasts the words *night + rate* and *nitrate.* The first has a pause between the two words—called open juncture, which usually occurs within or between words. Closed juncture is a long pause between sentences or phrases (in writing sometimes indicated by a period or comma). The designations of juncture in print are not reliable, however. Open juncture may occur between syllables within words, e.g., *un + known.*

English has four stresses, roughly heard as varying degrees of loudness on the syllable. Monosyllables when said in isolation have *primary* stress on the vowel /´/. *Weak* stress is marked /˘/, and *tertiary* stress is marked /`/. To a skilled phonetician another stress level, called *secondary* and marked /ˆ/, may be heard. A common comparison is the words *black bird* and *blackbird.* The first has primary stress on *black* and secondary on *bird,* meaning a bird that is black. The species of birds named by their color has a pattern of primary and tertiary stress. The noun and verb forms of the word *permit* are distinguished by their stress patterns (as well as changes in the vowel): *pérmit* (as a noun); *permít* (as a verb). Since the stress arrangements serve to separate utterances otherwise alike, stress is considered to be phonemic in English.

We have seen that juncture may be open or closed and that there are four stress levels, primary, secondary, tertiary, and weak. To complicate matters further, English has four *pitch* levels. Pitch level 2, called *mid,* is the normal pitch of the voice. Pitch 1, *low,* is lower than 2, and 3, *high,* is as much above 2 as 1 is below 2. An *extra high,* 4, is infrequent. The most common pitch arrangement in English is 2 3 1. Another designation for pitch is more pictorial than the system of numbers.

I'm ²going ‖ho‖me.

A monotone consists of extension of pitch level 2 over a large part of the utterance, with little variation in pitch levels.

The intonation variables have been well studied in speech. It seems to us that there is an oral reading style which is quite different from intonation patterns in spontaneous speech. Imagine hearing someone in the next room. We think that it would be easy to decide whether the sounds were conversation or someone reading aloud. The definitive clues are likely to be the patterning of suprasegmental information, though, so far as we know, no one has worked out the details of the comparison.

Clay and Imlach (1971) have studied intonation variables in oral reading. They used juncture, pitch, and stress to appraise the reading behavior of 103 children who were on the average 7½ years old and who had been in school for about 2½ years. Each child read aloud four stories which varied in difficulty; the fourth story challenged even the most skilled readers. The investigators analyzed the tapes of the readings for (a) three levels of juncture (length of pauses); (b) four levels of pitch; and (c) four levels of stress (essentially judgments of loudness). Children were assigned to four groups on the basis of the speed and accuracy with which they read the stories.

The most skilled readers paused briefly at punctuation and read, on the average, 7.4 words between pauses, whereas the lowest group read only 1.3 words between pauses. The skilled readers showed more variability in pitch, that is, they read with "expression," but for all groups the most common style was to continue the same pitch level on both sides of a period. The researchers expected a drop in pitch at the end of sentences, with the new sentence beginning with the next higher pitch level. But the same pitch level across sentence boundaries occurred in the skilled and unskilled readers for different reasons: the high group because they were reading rapidly, the low group because they read in a monotone.

It will be recalled that the normal pitch midpoint in speech is level 2, while in reading level 3 was most frequent. Clay and Imlach do not make this point, but one of the characteristics of what we have called a reading style may be higher than normal pitch.

The most proficient reading group stressed one word for every 4.7 words which was appropriate for the phrasing, but the lower groups were pausing after almost every word and often emitting more than one stress per word. The poorer readers, that is, were reading continuous text as though it were a list of unrelated words. In general, for the good readers weak stress was more common than in ordinary speech, which may be another distinction between reading and speaking styles. The investigators interpret these results as indicating that proficient readers are using higher-order grammatical and semantic information in their reading rather than a stereotyped word-by-word or phrase-by-phrase strategy. In their words:

One is tempted to suggest that the best readers can work through a sequence of possibilities guided by story, intersentence, and sentence cues, and can drop to the levels of phrase, word and letter possibilities if necessary, whereas the other groups work at best on the two- and three-word phrase and more usually at the word, syllable and letter level. (pp. 138–139)

This description of skilled reading fits well with our own conception, and the acquisition of the multiple skills will be the concern of Part II of this book.

Summary

It was not our intention in this chapter to provide a complete picture of linguistics. Rather, we have selected for defintion those concepts which we have found necessary to understand the reading process and its acquisition. Our needs have not forced us to support one of many competing linguistic traditions. We have taken as freely from descriptive as from generative linguistics.

The phonological concepts of phonetics and phonemics were described and compared. Morphophonemics plays a large part in subsequent chapters and so was defined, as were inflectional and derivational morphology. The syllable is treated more extensively in psychological than linguistic research. In grammar, we introduced the notions of deep and surface structures and phrase structure grammar and gave examples of transformational rules and immediate constituent analysis of sentences. We discussed parts of speech. We indulged in a lengthier discussion of case grammar than its present formulation warrants because we are impressed with its links to semantics and to the ecologically valid observations of occurrences, events, and states. Finally, we took up the suprasegmental variables, juncture, pitch, and stress, because we believe that these provide guides to the analysis of oral reading skills and to the yet-to-be-researched stylistic differences between speech and oral reading.

5

Language Development

Children, it is often asserted, are linguistically mature by the time they start to learn to read. They have mastered the phonological system of their language, except perhaps for a few hard-to-articulate sounds. They can say and understand all of the sentences which the grammar of their language allows, except for rare and complicated sentences. They are able to communicate and to extract meanings, although their vocabularies will continue to grow and there will be refinements in word meanings. These later developments may themselves be consequences of literacy. In this chapter we will review the nature of language development, paying special attention to the status of the child in the period of roughly five to seven years, when he is beginning to read.

The assumption of linguistic maturity at age six implies a theory about the acquisition of reading skills. Learning to read is said to entail only one unique process, decoding or translating text to sound. Once the child can do this, so goes the line of speculation, reading simply involves hitching the consequences of decoding to the language the child already has. For example, since the child understands spoken language as well as he ever will, his ability to make sound from text is grafted onto his ability to understand language, so that the comprehension of text is ipso facto explained. We believe that this conception of reading is an oversimplification, and the theme of the later parts of this book will be to offer alternative formulations of the reading process.

Language development has been more actively studied during the past decade than any other problem in the psychology of language. Most attention has been given to the acquisition of the grammatical system, including important observations across languages. There has been some, but too little, work on phonological development. Recently, promising research on the acquisition of meaning, or semantic development, has begun both with adults and children. The wealth of research and theory of language development presents us with problems of selection. We will take as a guideline for the review of language acquisition those aspects which are most relevant to understanding the process of learning to read. However, it is often impossible to present a complete picture of the six-year-old without reference to how he arrived at that period in his development.

We call the reader's attention to a number of books about language development that provide a more thorough treatment than is possible in this chapter: Brown, 1973; McNeill, 1970; Menyuk, 1969, 1971; Slobin, 1971.

Phonological Development

By the time children start to read, mastery of the sound system of their language, both in perception and production, is very good. There are a few children whose articulation and receptive discrimination of some sounds are not perfect, but by and large the phonological aspect of language is set. What has been the course of phonological development? When it is still imperfect at ages five to six, how do we describe these points of late development?

Jakobson (1968; Jakobson, Fant, and Halle, 1963) has provided a powerful theory of phonological development, at least in its productive aspects. The theory claims to chart the emergence of various sounds in all languages, making the strong claim that the order of emergence of sounds is universal. Since all languages do not use the same phonemic contrasts, exposure to a particular language will guide the later course of development, but the first abstractions from the sounds of a child's language will be those attributes of sound which are common to all languages. As McNeill (1970) says, Jakobson's theory has provided us with the rare case when we have a powerful, precise, and reasonable theory for which we have little firm data.

The keystone to Jakobson's theory is the notion of *distinctive features* which we have defined in Chapter 2. It may be useful to repeat part of that discussion.

Things come in finite sets, and there are feature contrasts within the set that are shared in different degrees by the members of the set. We shall refer to these as "distinctive features."
Distinctive features are relational, not absolute like building blocks or elements. They are contrastive, as sharp or blunt, or straight or curved are contrastive. An object (or a symbol) is characterized by a bundle or pattern of distinctive features that is unique for that object, but members of a set may differ by few or many features—that is, features are shared within the set to different extents.

The concept of distinctive features was first applied to phonemes. Jakobson devised an economical set of contrasts or features so that every phoneme of every language could be characterized by a pattern of the presence or absence of those features. A segment of sound has phonemic function in the language if it differs from all other sounds by at least one distinctive feature. Figure 5-1 presents a set of features and the values of each phoneme with respect to those features. For example, /b/ and /p/ have the same values on all features except one, voicing (tense-lax in the figure). Of course, phonemes may differ in the number of features that they share; for example, /p/ and /d/ differ in three features. A feature matrix provides a theoretical basis for predicting those sounds which will be confused with one another in speech recognition and the sound substitutions in misarticulation. In general, the phonemes that share many features are more confusable than sounds that have few features in common. These hypotheses assume that all features have equal weight, and the refinement of feature theory involves research that assigns varying importance to different features in tasks like discrimination among phonemes.

At about eleven months, according to Jakobson, children babble less, as though they were attending to the speech around them without the interruptions of their own vocalizations. First, children produce contrasts in sound which represent the extremes of a feature, and further sound contrasts successively define other features. Moreover, the early sounds which a child produces have features that are common to many languages, hence the claim for the interlanguage universality of the sequence which children exhibit.

Perhaps this theory of phonological development will be clearer if we go through several steps of the developmental sequence. The initial sounds are /p/ and /a/, and early phonemic development consists in differentiating the features represented by these two sounds. The phonemes /p/ and /a/ are as different as speech sounds can be: /p/ is a consonant—the vocal tract is closed, there is no acoustic energy; /a/ is a vowel—the tract is open and acoustic energy is at a maximum. The basis of phonological development is the child's saying the syllable *pa* or the repetition *papa*. The first phonemic distinction occurs on the consonants when the child says *ma* or *mama*. The consonants are divided thereby into oral and nasal categories. Next the oral consonants are divided into the contrasts *pa* and *ta*. The feature which distinguishes /p/ and /t/ Jakobson calls "grave-acute."

The next division occurs among the vowels with the addition of the narrow vowel /i/, so that narrow and wide vowels are set apart, or the feature compact-diffuse begins to be filled in. These divisions go on successively.

Distinctive-feature pattern of English phonemes

	o	a	e	u	ə	i	l	ŋ	ʃ/ĵ/ĉ	k	ʒ	ĝ	g	m	f	p	v	b	n	s	θ	t	z	ð	d	h	#
1. Vocalic/ nonvocalic	+	+	+	+	+	+	+	−	−	−	−	−	−	−	−	−	−	−	−	−	−	−	−	−	−	−	−
2. Consonan-tal/noncon-sonantal	−	−	−	−	−	−	+	+	+	+	+	+	+	+	+	+	+	+	+	+	+	+	+	+	+	−	−
3. Compact/ diffuse	+	+	+			−		+	+	+	+	+	+													+	
4. Grave/ acute	+	+	−	+	+	−		+					+	+	+	+	+	+									
5. Flat/plain	+	−		+	−																						
6. Nasal/oral								+						+					+								
7. Tense/lax									+	+	−	−	−		+	+	−	−		+	+	+	−	−	−		
8. Continu-ant/inter-rupted									+	−	+	−	−		+	−	+	−		+	+	−	+	+	−	+	
9. Strident/ mellow									+		+	+			+		+			+	−		+	−			

Key to phonemic transcription: /o/ - pot, /a/ - pat, /e/ - pet, /u/ - put, /ə/ - putt, /i/ - pit, /l/-lull, /ŋ/ - lung, /ʃ/ - ship, /ʃ̂/ - chip, /k/ - kip, /ʒ/ - azure, /ĝ/ - juice, /g/ - goose, /m/ - mill, /f/ - fill, /p/ - pill, /v/ - vim, /b/ - bill, /n/ - nil, /s/ - sill, /θ/ - thill, /t/ - till, /z/ - zip, /ð/ - this, /d/ - dill, /h/ - hill, /#/ - ill.

Figure 5-1. Phonemes and their feature values. From Jakobson, Fant, and Halle, 1963, p. 43.

In each case a further phonemic contrast serves to indicate that the child has added new distinctive features to his repertoire. For our purposes, it is important to note that phonological development involves a hierarchical differentiation of higher-order invariants into more and more refined contrasts.

The kindergarten-aged child has made most of these differentiations. Late-appearing phonemes are rare in all languages and involve many feature differences from the sound segments which the child already uses productively. In English, for example, /θ/, as in *thing*, appears late. In a study of phonological development among the Quechua, Solberg (1971) confirmed that rare sounds among the world's languages had complex feature characteristics and appeared late in development.

Jakobson's is a theory of the production of speech after the period of babbling, that is, when the child begins to acquire a linguistic system. It seems reasonable to think of the formulation also as a theory of language perception, again in the same age period. Distinctive feature analysis has proved useful in studying children's discrimination of language sounds well before the first year of age. Voicing appears to be discriminated by infants as young as one month (Eimas et al., 1971), and studies have been undertaken on infants' sensitivities to other features (e.g., McCaffrey, 1971).

The few attempts to confirm Jakobson's theorized sequence of speech production have not found a point-by-point match between data and theory, though the overall model of successive differentiation appears to be true (Velten, 1943; Leopold, 1939–1949). Strong evidence comes from the fact that errors of mispronunciation are sounds based on failure of feature differentiation just prior to the feature distinction that would yield a correct pronunciation (Solberg, 1971). To take an unlikely example, before the differentiation of vowels on the compact-diffuse axis, the child might say *fat* instead of *fit*. The dearth of empirical data is undoubtedly due to the difficulty of performing the appropriate studies. The research would have to be longitudinal, with detailed observations collected on each child. In fact, almost all of the studies on spontaneous speech production have been diary accounts of single children kept by linguistically trained parents (Velten, 1943; Leopold, 1939).

We would expect that errors of mispronunciation and speech recognition would involve sound segments (phonemes) that are relatively complex in their distinctive feature description compared to the sounds with which children have no difficulties. These late-developing aspects of phonology are potentially significant for the child who is learning to read. Menyuk (1971) has summarized those studies of sounds that were mastered early and late by children. Irwin (1947) recorded the spontaneous production of sounds by children aged 29–30 months. Wellman's data (cited in Menyuk, 1971; see Table 5-1) show the sounds mastered before and after the age of four. Snow's (1963) study is most relevant to the reading age and indicates the sounds produced with few and with many errors.

There is substantial agreement among the three studies. Stops (b, d, g, p, t, k), nasals (m, n) and glides (w, y, h) are mastered early. The feature voiced-unvoiced is an acquired distinction by the age of four (Menyuk, 1971). In fact, recent evidence indicates that voicing is discriminated in perception of speech sounds perhaps as early as one month of age and certainly by six months (Eimas et al., 1971). The later acquisitions, the even-numbered columns in Table 5-1, are mainly continuants (s, z, š, ž, v, e, ð, l, r) or sounds that have a gradual release (c, j).

In general, though there are less data on speech perception than on production by children, the features which predict both are similar. The stops /p/, /t/, /k/ are acquired early. These sounds can be identified only within

Table 5-1 Rank Ordering of Usage of Sounds, Mastery of Sounds, and Accuracy in Production

Irwin's Data		Wellman's Data		Snow's Data	
1	2	3	4	5	6
Greater than Adult Usage	Less than Adult usage	Mastered by 4	Mastered after 4	From 1 to 91 Errors	From 100 to 1067 Errors
d	y	w	t	n	l
h	s	h	z	p	ŋ
b	ž	m	v	m	j
m	š	n	s	b	č
k	θ	b	š	w	š
g	ŋ	f	ž	h	s
p	f	p	č	d	v
w	č	d	r	t	r
t	n	k	v	k	z
	z	g	j	y	ð
	ð	l	θ	f	θ
	r	y	ð	g	z

Source: Menyuk, 1971, p. 76.

the context of an adjoining vowel because the syllable determines both the nature of the sound and the way it is articulated. Notice the differences in the formation of the mouth and the resulting sound for the initial phonemes in the words *keep cool*. To say that both are forms of the phoneme /k/ obscures the fact that the anticipation of the vowel sounds determines the articulation of /k/ and the consequent perceptible acoustic differences between the two.

One hypothesis about speech production is that early and late sounds differ in the specificity of their articulatory movements, or articulatory gestures, to use the more technical term. The distinction between labial /p/, lingual /l/, and velar /k/ forms involves the formation of sounds from the front to the back of the mouth. There are clearly marked places of articulation for these early sounds. For the later sounds, mainly continuants, the articulatory gestures require further differentiation of the basic gestures. The target points in the articulatory apparatus are not so clear. Said more simply, those sounds produced by easy motor gestures are produced early. The sounds whose motor articulations are more complicated appear later in development.

Menyuk (1971) has laid out the Jakobsonian course of feature differentiation in a tree diagram (see Figure 5-2). This shows that the first distinction occurs on the feature vowel-consonant. Vowels are differentiated on the feature narrow-wide, consonants on oral-nasal. The readers's attention is called to Figures 2-1 and 2-2, which diagramed the hierarchical organization of Roman capital letters. Though the two domains subjected to a distinctive feature analysis—sounds and letters—are different, it is important to notice that the general model for analysis is the same and the general forms of the outcomes are similar.

In summary, the acquisition of the sound system of a language can be best understood by a theory of distinctive features. Significant sounds in a language are each unique bundles of a reasonably small inventory of features. Development involves the abstraction and use of the set of features. This development is hierarchical, which means that a general feature such as consonant-vowel is used first, then is differentiated into another feature contrast, like oral-nasal, which is further differentiated and so forth. The school-aged child has mastered some distinctions more reliably than others. The vowel-consonant feature appears early. Within the consonants, those that are most easily identified appear earlier than less

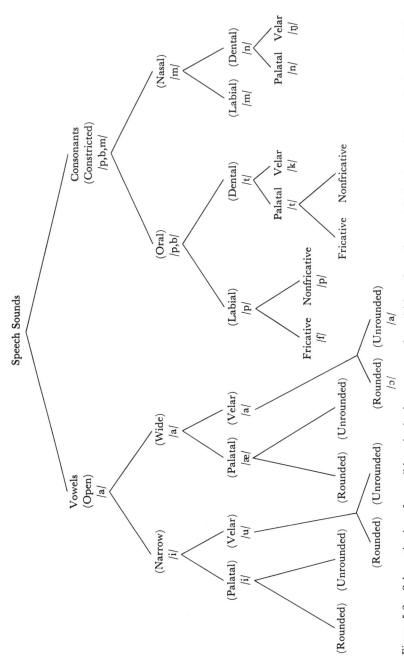

Figure 5-2. Schematization of a possible order in the sequence of acquisition of speech sound distinctions with examples from English. Examples are given below figures. From Menyuk, 1971, p. 74.

easily identified sounds. Likewise, easily produced sounds, in terms of the motor articulatory gestures involved, are mastered earlier than sounds made by more complex motor articulations.

The Acquisition of Phonological Rules

In any language, the order of sounds which are put together to form an utterance is rule governed. That is, certain sounds may occur in sequence, others may not. Further, the legality of sounds depends upon their position in words as well as upon morpheme and syllable boundaries. For example, the phoneme /ŋ/, as in *thing*, is a common terminal sound in English words, but it cannot begin a word. The sequence of phonemes /km/ cannot occur together unless separated by a morpheme boundary: *milkmaid*. Whorf (1956) argues that the phonological rule system is an example of the quasi-mathematical precision of at least one aspect of linguistics. He has developed a formula for the English monosyllable whose violation under natural conditions does not occur. He avers, with no formal evidence but nevertheless probably correctly, that the language of speakers of English is governed by these phonological rules by the age of six. Mispronunciations mostly follow the legal sequences of sound. Made-up words, like *slithy toves,* do not violate these phonological rules. (See Chapter 6 for a more detailed discussion of Whorf and of phonological and orthographic rules.)

A number of studies agree with Whorf's claim that at least by kindergarten age, children are under the influence of the phonological rule system of their language. Messer (1967) tested nursery school children, ages 3;1 to 4;5 for their implicit knowledge of phonology. He created pairs of "words," one of which could be generated by Whorf's formula and the other not, e.g., *klek* vs. *dlek.* The nongenerable member of some pairs violated the initial consonant cluster; that of others contained impossible clusters in both the initial and terminal positions. The child judged which of each pair sounded more like a word.

By a large margin, these preschool children chose the words that conformed to English phonological rules. Further, words that violated both the initial and terminal constraints were usually rejected; that is, their correct counterparts were chosen more frequently than when only the initial cluster was illegal.

Messer also analyzed the mispronunciations of the children's choices.

Illegal words were mispronounced more often than permissible words. Ninety-one percent of the impossible words became more like English as a result of the mispronunciations. And, interestingly, this drift toward English was accomplished very economically by a shift of one distinctive feature, so that *škib* became *skib*, for example.

Several other studies converge on the generalization that children have abstracted the phonological rule system which precisely governs their perception and production of language. Menyuk (1968) tested the ability of preschool, kindergarten, first-, and second-grade children to imitate nonsense words of the form CCVC when the words contained legal or illegal initial consonant clusters. Children at all grade levels repeated the English-like words more correctly than the illegal forms. For both types of pseudowords children tended to get better with age, though the age effect was not very strong. Apparently, by preschool the effects of phonological rules are nearly as strong as they are going to be, at least with respect to the imitation of wordlike sounds. These children repeated real words perfectly. Whether a wordlike sequence sounds like English is important for the child's reproduction of the sequence, but it is still a feeble effect when compared to the ease of pronouncing real words that convey meanings.

Morehead (1971) looked not only at the influence of phonologically legal versus illegal words on imitation, but also at the degree of legality, that is, how close the pseudoword was to complete obedience to English phonological rules. Perfect compliance with the rules does not necessarily generate a real English word, but the nonword *could* be a word, e.g., *trong*.

Morehead studied four groups with mean ages of 4;2, 5;4, 7;0, and 20 years. They imitated six CCVC sequences that varied in their closeness to English phonology. The imitation conditions are complicated but do not change the relevance to this discussion of phonological development. Overall, the word was imitated more correctly the closer it was to English, though the relationship between correct imitation and distance from English was linear only for adults. Adults made more exact imitations. The children introduced more phonetic changes, but these changes, as in Menyuk's study, were in the direction of making the sequence more like English. Some of the phonetic changes created meaningful words, called "semantic changes" by the author. Four-year-olds made more phonetic changes, seven-year-olds more semantic changes. Semantic changes increased with age except for the adults, who imitated with greater fidelity.

Like Messer, Morehead reports that the changes in the direction of the phonological rules were efficient in terms of the number of phonemic distinctive features involved.

We may assume from this research that by about four years children have abstracted a phonological rule system which has potent consequences in the child's reception and production of language. He is able to distinguish English from non-English phonological rules, and he will assimilate his productions toward those rules. Further, around age seven he tries to assimilate violations of the rules not only in the direction of permissible sounds, which four-year-olds will do, but in the direction of meaningful words.

Segmentation into Phonemes and Syllables

Language can be analyzed into various linguistic segments: sentences, phrases, words, syllables, and phonemes. Similarly, written text may also be analyzed into these levels, with the exception that the phoneme is a segment of spoken language whereas letters and letter clusters are corresponding orthographic units. Since an early task in learning to read is to learn the correspondences between the spoken and written forms of language, we may ask whether children at the ages when they learn to read have extracted the units which will be appropriate for learning to read. For example, if the child has not abstracted that set of features which in various combinations make up the phonemes of his language, then the strategy for teaching him the correspondences between letters and the phonemes they represent will be impossible. That is, can beginning readers as part of their phonological development segment speech into phonemes, syllables, or words? In this section, we will review children's abilities to segment. Discussion of programs designed to teach children to segment as prereading training will be taken up in Chapter 8.

Psycholinguists have been interested in the "reality" of the phoneme (see, for example, Savin and Bever, 1970; Warren, 1971).* There is no doubt that the phoneme is naturally real since even a child makes use of minimal contrasts, e.g., *pit-bit*, in his production and perception of language. Likewise, the presence of alphabets, rhymes, spoonerisms, etc., point to the phoneme as a natural unit of language. Only when the subject is asked to consciously abstract and use the phoneme for some task does the

*See Chapter 4 for a critique of these studies as showing the psychological reality of phonemes or other linguistic units, especially the study by McNeill and Lindig (1973).

segment of this size seem unavailable to the child, and even to the adult it is available only with some difficulty and is less available than higher-order segments like the syllable.

Savin and Bever's (1970) experiments with adults are a good example of research on the reality of phonemes. Subjects listened to tapes on which had been recorded sequences of monosyllabic nonsense words. One group of subjects was required to identify words that began with a target phoneme; another group was given syllables to identify that contained the other group's target phonemes. These experiments tested /b/ (*barg* was one of the syllables), /s/ (*sarg*), and /æ/ (*bælg*). In every case, the time to identify the syllable was shorter than the time to recognize the phoneme. Adults could recognize phonemes, but it took longer than recognizing syllables. The experimenters concluded

that phonemes are primarily neither perceptual nor articulatory entities. Rather, they are psychological entities of a nonsensory, nonmotor kind, related by complex rules to stimuli and to articulatory movements, but they are not a unique part of either system of directly observable speech processes. In short, phonemes are *abstract*. (p. 301)

If this characterization of the phoneme is true, it is unlikely that pre-reading children have analyzed the stream of speech into units as small as the phoneme. In fact, the evidence is unequivocal that children do not come to school with the ability to segment speech at this level although this is not to say that they cannot be taught to recognize phonemes (see Chapter 8).

Savin (1972), based on his informal observations of inner-city children who were having difficulty learning to read, says that these children were not able to break speech into phoneme segments. Children were not able to learn pig Latin, for example. This common children's language game requires the speaker to detach the initial phoneme or cluster, move it to the end of the word, and add a constant syllable, usually /ay/. So *run* becomes *unray*; *shoot, ootshay*; *grin, ingray*; etc. Incidentally, learning pig Latin seems like a useful experimental task to study segmentation at the levels of words, phonemes, and clusters. Segmentation into syllables, by comparison, was easy for these children. He thought that syllables were unanalyzed entities to the children, so that *hot, sit, run*, etc., were the basic units in their language. On that basis, Savin recommends that reading be taught as though English were a syllabic writing system, with no attempts, at least initially, to analyze the phonological and the orthographic syllables into their constituent elements.

In a large test battery of prereading skills, Calfee, Chapman, and Venezky (1972) studied the ability of kindergarten children to segment common CVC words. The procedure involved training, testing, and a transfer task, and since it involves prereading training this line of research will be more fully developed in Chapter 8. Suffice it to say here that kindergarten children can learn to separate the VC portion of the CVC word. So if the child is presented with *hat* he can learn to say *at*, or *it* to *sit*, or *op* to *top*. However, if the response required of the child was in itself a meaningful English syllable, as *at* or *it*, these children did more poorly on subsequent nonsense materials. It is as though the children in the first sequence learned that the required response made sense and so abstracted a semantic rather than a phonological generalization which interfered with subsequent task requirements that destroyed the semantic information. We will see that the abstraction of semantic information has high priority in children's language development.

In the same battery of tests, the kindergarteners were asked to tell whether a word began with a certain sound (phoneme). "The word *look*, does it begin with l-l-l? *Morse*, does it begin with m-m-m?" Notice that this task can be done only with continuants where the consonant can be said without a succeeding vowel. The children could perform this task at only a chance level.

Bruce (1964) studied children's ability to analyze words into their constituent phonemic segments. His subjects were 5 to $7\frac{1}{2}$ years old. The children were given a series of words and asked to delete a given sound in each and to pronounce the resulting word. For example: *stand* − *t* = *sand*. Only children with a mental age of seven or higher had some success with this task. Up to six years, they were not able to delete component segments of the original word. At a mental age of six they could delete a phoneme, but it was often not the directed sound, and they could not recombine the remaining phonemes to create the new word.

Russian psychologists have carried out research on various levels of segmentation: sentences, words, and phonemes. In fact, an important part of Russian prereading training involves the segmentation of words into phonemes (Elkonin, 1963). The extensive program of research is summarized by Zaporozhets and Elkonin (1971, pp. 169 ff). Elkonin's pedagogical programs are based on the findings of Zhurova (1963) and others that children have considerable difficulty in analyzing words into sounds. Zhurova devised some ingenious queries and tasks to study children's ability to segment words into phonemes. To a child named Igor,

(Is your name Gor?)

No, Igor.

(What have I left out?)

Igor.

(But what have I left out, Gor)

I-I-I-Igor. (for a three- or four-year-old)

Other variations involved omitting the first phonemes in the word for an animal, as a sort of password in a game, etc. Similar observations were made for terminal phonemes.

Children aged 3 to 6 indicated that they understood the task but could only pronounce the phoneme within the context of the whole word or syllable. So Igor, it will be noted, could not say "I-I-I" in isolation, though he could say "I-I-I-Igor." According to Zhurova, young children can say the isolated phoneme but only after extensive training. By about seven years, prereading children are able to segment initial phonemes, and with more difficulty terminal phonemes, after a few examples from the experimenter.

Liberman (1973) compared the ability of four-, five-, and six-year-old children to segment spoken words into phonemes and into syllables. The child was asked to repeat a word or sound and to tap out the number of segments (phonemes or syllables) that he heard. Four-year-olds could not segment into phonemes, but about half of them could identify the number of syllables. Only 17% of the five-year-olds could segment phonemes, but by the age of six 70% could identify the number of phonemes and 90% tapped out the correct number of syllables.

Using a third-grade group, Liberman asked the children to read monosyllables and counted the errors on the initial and final consonants. Although the overall error rate was low, there were twice as many errors on the initial than on the final consonants. She also looked at errors in reading vowels and found that there were more errors on vowels than consonants and that the error rate of vowels was independent of position in the word; that is, the children misread the vowels just as often whether the vowel was in the initial, medial, or terminal position in the word. Liberman attributes the consonant difficulties to failures in phonemic segmentation but suspects that the results on the vowels are due to the complex spelling-to-sound correspondences which vowels represent in English. In general, children at the ages when they usually start to read cannot easily segment words into phonemes. They are able, though, to analyze words into syllables with apparent ease.

Segmentation into Words

Huttenlocher (1964) studied the abilities of children ($4\frac{1}{2}$ to 5 years) to segment and to reverse pairs of words, as well as two pairs of digits and one pair of letters. The items are reproduced in Table 5-2. One group of 33 children was given the task of reversing the pairs. A second group of 33, in order to study their ability to separate words without reversing, was asked to give the first item, tap with a pencil, and give the second item. Overall, these are difficult tasks for children of this age. Thirteen children were unable to do any reversals; ten were not able to segment the pairs.

When the pair forms a common English sequence, e.g., *man-runs; I-do,* children have the most difficulty dividing and reversing them. It is as though a meaning-bearing sequence has a unitizing force which is difficult for the child to fracture. We will shortly say more about the compelling effects of meaning on children's ability to segment sequences of language.

Karpova (1955) had preschool children count the number of words in a sequence of unconnected nouns, which they were able to do with little difficulty. However, if other categories of words, e.g., adjectives and verbs, were added to the list of nouns, children aged 3 to 6 had difficulty counting the number of words. Seven-year-olds tended to succeed at this task. A list made up of various parts of speech more nearly approximates the natural language than does a list of nouns, so it may be that when the sequence has some structure younger children cannot divide it into word segments.

Karpova also tested her subjects' ability to segment words in sentences. She proposed three stages in the analysis of sentences. In the first stage,

Table 5-2   Pairs of Items in Each of Five Categories

Category	Pairs
i	5-2; D-S; 3-7
ii	*black-white; child-lady; foot-hand*
iii	*man-runs; red-apple; she-went*
iv	*do-I; you-are; it-is*
v	*table-goes; house-did; orange-cow*

Source: Huttenlocher, 1964, p. 264. Copyright 1964 by the American Association for the Advancement of Science.

the child considers the meaning of a sentence independent of its actual structure. When asked the first word in a sentence, the child describes a reasonable first event.

Sasha G. (3;6):

The children have already had dinner.

(What's the first word?)
They were sitting at the table.
(The second one?)
They ate.
(The third one?)
I don't know.

In the second stage, the child divides the sentences into meaning units, most commonly nouns.

Ira K. (4;3):

The boy will read the verses.

(What's the first word?)
boy.
(The second one?)
verses.

Later in stage 2, the child segments sentences into subject and predicate groups.

Galja N. (6;3):

The children will let the snake out.

(What's the first word?)
The children.
The second one?)
Will let the snake out.

In the third stage, the child identifies almost all words, though he may still have difficulty with prepositions and conjunctions.

Holden and MacGinitie (1972) repeated some parts of Karpova's research with English-speaking kindergarten children. The subjects repeated sentences while pointing to a poker chip for each word that they said. The authors report that the rhythm of sentences in some instances determined how the children segmented the sentences. A pervasive finding was that the children grouped function words with either preceding or succeeding content words. For example, *you/have/to/go/home* and less frequently, *you /have/to go/home*; also, *houses/were/built/by/the men* (p. 554). Contrary to Karpova, these researchers did not find a consistent subject-predicate break, since some words were joined across phrase boundaries. In general, the main basis for segmenting a spoken sentence correctly into words depended on the frequency of words with lexical meaning compared to the incidence of small function words.

What can we say now about children's abilities to segment speech? There is no doubt that in speaking and understanding language, preschool-aged children can automatically discriminate units as small as the distinctive features of the phoneme. They do not confuse *pat* and *bat*, for example. In natural language use, however, there is no reason for the child to attend to the details of phonology. He listens for meanings and communicates meanings. These are the first units he abstracts, and as Huttenlocher and Karpova found, meaning units take priority in the child's analysis of speech. Sequences of words composing a meaningful utterance are difficult for the child to analyze into lower-order units.

When the experimental task requires the analysis of phonology, the syllable unit is availabe to the child, perhaps because the syllable has characteristics like the presence of stressed vowels and intersyllabic pauses which facilitate its abstraction from the speech stream. For children, and to some extent for adults, phonemic analysis is unnatural and difficult. Under natural language conditions, it is hard to conjure up a situation in which the child has to analyze speech at the phonemic level. As will be seen in Chapter 8, children can learn to analyze language in phonemic segments, but usually only after training.

Morphological Development

Compared to languages that conjugate verbs elaborately or mark the cases of nouns and their adjectival modifiers, English has a reasonably simple system of inflectional morphology. The five morphemes which occur in the suffix position are the *s* of the third person singular verbs (*he runs*), *s* of the plural (*several girls*), *s* marking possession (*the boy's gloves*), *ed* in the past tense of verbs (*she wanted*), and *ing* forming the progressive form of verbs (*he is running*). There are three orthographic forms of inflectional morphemes, but each *s* may be pronounced various ways depending on its phonological environment. The phonological details will be discussed below. There are in addition irregular morphological forms in which the plural and past tense are marked by sound changes rather than by suffixation, for example, *men, children, geese,* the zero morpheme of *sheep* (that is, the singular and plural forms are the same), and in verbs, *ran, went, brought.* These forms are called morphophonemic because morphological information is signaled by phonemic variations. As will be seen, children's extensions of morphological rules to the irregular instances provide us with information about their knowledge of the regular rules. Some common examples are *sheeps, runned, goed.*

Besides the simple system of inflectional morphemes, English has a more elaborate system of derivational morphemes, which are the sounds and spellings that derive one part of speech from another: *happy-happiness, relax-relaxation, admit-admittedly, refúse-réfuse, large-larger,* etc.

Berko's (1958) is the classic study on the acquisition of morphology. She tested two groups of children, preschoolers and first graders, for their knowledge of the rules of inflectional morphology as well as the derivational forms for the diminutive *y,* comparative *er* and superlative *est,* and the agentive pattern (*er* as in *manager*). Each child was shown cartoonlike drawings and asked the following kinds of questions (see Figure 5-3):

This is a wug.
Now there is another one.
There are two of them.
There are two————.

First-grade children did better than preschoolers on about half of the inflectional items. Although plurals are written *s* or *es,* the phonological forms of English may be /s/, /z/, or /ɨz/, and the particular sound is conditioned by the preceding phonemes. The same environmental sound conditioning is true for the possessives and third person singulars. If the stem ends in /s, z, š, ž, č, j,/ the morpheme is /ɨz/, e.g., *glasses, watches.* If the stem ends in /b, d, g, v, ð, m, n, ŋ, r/, a vowel, or a semivowel, the morpheme is /z/, e.g., *rings, runs.* If the stem ends in /p, t, k, f, θ/, the morpheme is /s/, e.g., *hops, hits.*

First graders control the phonological rules so far as /s/ and /z/ are concerned, responding correctly more than 90% of the time. There appears to be an increase in ability between preschool and first grade, since the younger children reply correctly with these two forms in about 75% of the

This is a Wug.

Now there is another one .
There are two of them.
There are two _____ .

Figure 5-3.   Cartoonlike drawings used to test children's knowledge of inflectional morphology. From Berko, 1958, p. 154. Reprinted by permission of the Johnson Reprint Corp.

instances. However, neither group appears to have mastered the /iz/ form, although some children did provide this correct plural to the nonsense stem. On the other hand, both groups accurately pluralized the real word *glass*, which suggests that *glasses* was a single word in their vocabulary rather than base form + suffix.

Newfield and Schlanger (1968) found the same order of difficulty using real words as Berko did with nonsense materials. With real words, though, children supplied many more correct plurals, for example, 81% correct versus 39% for the /iz/ plural. Anisfeld and Tucker (1967) replicated Berko's findings regarding pluralization by six-year-olds using nonsense stems. They found, however, that when the task was to recognize rather than to produce the appropriate plural, the children performed about equally well on the /s/, /z/, and /iz/ allomorphs.

The past tense *ed* has three allomorphs /t, d, id/ which are conditioned by the final phoneme in the base form. After /t, d/, the morpheme is /id/

as in *melted*. After /p, k, c, f, θ, s/, the morpheme is /t/ as in *hoped*. After stems ending in voiced sounds except /d/, the morpheme is /d/ as in *played*. Both groups of children supplied the /t/ and /d/ forms accurately, but they did not appear to control the morphophonemic rule for /ɨd/, although as with the plurals they were able to give the past tense of the real word *melt* as *melted*. Neither group of children knew the irregular past for the real word *ring*; *rang* was given by only 17% of the children.

The progressive morpheme *ing* is not phonologically dependent on preceding sounds and was used appropriately by 90% of the children. The third person singular provided the same results as the plurals, with /ɨz/ correctly formed by about 50% of the subjects.

Possessives provide one interesting comparison. When the word ends in an *s* or *es* spelling, the plural possessive is formed by adding nothing, the so-called zero morpheme. Both groups of children could form this plural possessive with a high degree of accuracy, probably because they had only to repeat back the nonsense form. Finally, very few of the children gave any evidence of knowing how to form derivations. They could not answer with the comparative *er* or the superlative *est*. They solved the diminutive by saying not *wuglet* or *wuggie*, but *baby wug* or *teeny wug*.

What can we say about children's knowledge of morphological rules at the ages of five to six, when they usually start to read? For the morphemes that are spelled *s*, the child knows the phonological rules that yield the allomorphes /s/ and /z/. For /ɨz/ he uses the base form alone as its plural or possessive or third person singular. Since /ɨz/ follows sibilants (e.g., *glasses, churches*), children are prepared to take a word ending in a sibilant as the inflected form.

The notion that terminal sibilants signal plurals to young children has been tested directly (Anisfeld, Barlow, and Frail, 1968). First- and second-grade children were given pseudowords of the form CVC and asked to choose between two artificial plurals *(Narf-Nark)*. The children preferred the phonemes /f/, /v/, and /ts/ as plurals. These segments share the distinctive features + continuant and + strident. Berko's "sibilants," which take the plural allomorph /ɨz/ also end their base forms with sound segments that may, in almost every case, be described as having the features + continuant, + strident. It seems reasonable, therefore, to think that morphemes terminating in sounds with these two distinctive features are interpreted as plurals by young children. These findings also make reasonable the observation that young children naturally abstract distinctive features from segments of speech sounds.

Vocabulary Development

For about the first fifty years of this century, a favorite occupation of child psychologists was to estimate the sizes of children's vocabularies. Although at first glance it would seem that counting the number of words that a child knows is a straightforward task, there are many problems of method and definition that make the studies difficult to compare and to understand (McCarthy, 1954). Some studies counted the words children used; others, the words they understood; and still others combined these sources of vocabulary. Spontaneous verbalizations were used as well as vocabulary tests, standardized to various degrees. Counts made from written productions exist. Studies vary on what constituted different words; for example, should *amuse* and *amusement* used by the same child add one or two words to his vocabulary score?

Nevertheless, an obvious generalization seems warranted. The size of children's vocabulary increases exponentially between one and six years. An early study by Smith (1926) based on a test of recall and of word recognition is still widely quoted, and there is no reason to question the overall form of the results today (see Table 5-3). The major increase in vocabulary size occurs around $2\frac{1}{2}$ to 3 years. As we will discuss later in this chapter, children's utterances become longer and grammatically more complex

Table 5-3   Increase in Size of Vocabulary in Relation to Age

Age			Average	Number	
Years	Months	N	IQ	of Words	Gain
	8	13		0	
	10	17		1	1
1	0	52		3	2
1	3	19		19	16
1	6	14		22	3
1	9	14		118	96
2	0	25		272	154
2	6	14		446	174
3	0	20	109	896	450
3	6	26	106	1222	326
4	0	26	109	1540	318
4	6	32	109	1870	330
5	0	20	108	2072	202
5	6	27	110	2280	217
6	0	9	108	2562	273

Source: M. E. Smith, 1926.

during this same age period. The artificiality of counting number of words irrespective of what else is happening in the child's language seems obvious. He is talking in longer and more complicated sentences, which means that he is using more words. The interpretation can be read both ways, of course. But it is unlikely that the grammatical structure of his language is a result of his expanding vocabulary.

Even though children have substantial receptive and productive vocabularies they tend to use a reasonably small corpus of words over and over. To some extent, this tendency is determined by the nature of the language. English has few articles—*a, the*—which are frequently used so that in conversation they represent 7% of the total number of words employed (Zyve, 1927). The high incidence of a small subset of a child's vocabulary appears to be one justification for the limited vocabulary in children's readers. It is important to note that the child knows vastly more words than the repeated ones, so there is no reason to constrain his reading materials drastically.

A number of useful manuals of the frequency of words used by children have been compiled, which are invaluable in constructing experimental materials and in creating reading materials and spelling lists. One Thorndike and Lorge (1944) count is based on children's books. Horn's (1926, 1927) International Kindergarten Union List is based on preschool children's speech. Fitzgerald's (1934) list is based on children's correspondence, and Rinsland (1945) tabulated over 25,000 words used by children both in conversations and compositions. A recent list (Carroll, Davies, and Richman, 1971) is a computerized count of various textual sources.

Several early vocabulary studies classified words according to their part of speech. Without the context, either verbal or situational, it is often impossible to assign a word to its part of speech; e.g., bit *dog, dog* his steps, *dog* days, in which the same word is a noun, verb, and adjective. Children around two years of age utter words that are preponderantly classified as nouns, roughly 60% (McCarthy, 1954). This figure may be misleading. These children are emitting one- or two-word utterances which usually reflect objects or events immediately available to the child in his surroundings. Also, at that age many children are occupied with what Brown calls "The Naming Game," which is requests for the names of objects around them. However, without more contextual information we cannot tell how often the child uses a noun as another part of speech, with the meaning carried by intonation and by the situation.

After this noun-ful period, only about 20% of a child's conversation will consist of nouns. The change is also understandable in terms of the grammatical constraints of sentences. As language matures from one- or two-word sequences to adultlike sentences, nouns have specific and limited functions in the sentences. The sentences require articles, verbs, adjectives, prepositions, adverbs, etc., which inevitably reduce the overall proportion of nouns. As we have said, vocabulary development is best understood in the context of language development, overall.

Perhaps the most important aspect of vocabulary development is the acquisition of the meanings of words. This is the substance of a later discussion of semantic development.

Grammatical Development

Somewhere around their first year children start to say single understandable words. Around 18 months, they put two words together so that their language consists of one- and two-word utterances. Gradually, over the next three or four months, there are more two- than one-word sayings; then, an occasional three-word group. And then the size of sentences, a word we use advisedly, explodes. The growth is traced by a steep rising curve, as can be seen in Figure 5-4. The similarity in the stages of the curves is impressive. Though children may start the process of language development at different chronological ages, the nature of growth is similar. In fact, the best index to a child's linguistic maturity is the mean length of his utterance measured in morphemes.

The period of single-word utterances is called the *holophrastic* period, which implies that the word functions as a phrase or sentence (DeLaguna, 1927), although Bloom (1971) questions this interpretation. Recording the single word is easy enough but interpreting it is difficult. Mothers seem to know what the child means, though, and it would be interesting to study the cues they use to interpret the word and whether they are indeed often correct. When the child says, "Milk!" and the mother gives him some, she likely makes her interpretation from many kinds of contextual and historical evidence. The child has just been crying, it is four hours since he was fed, the word is uttered with imperative emphasis, etc. At another time, responding to other subtleties, she may decide that the baby means, "The milk spilled on the floor," or that he is joyously dabbling his fingers in it.

DeLaguna (1927) believes that children add the second word in order

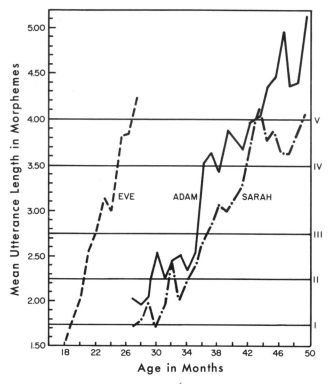

Figure 5-4. Development of length of children's utterances. From Brown, Cazden, and Bellugi-Klima, 1969, p. 29. © 1969 University of Minnesota.

to form a predicate or to say something about the first word which acted as a subject. This interpretation is unlikely. Holophrases do not simply name objects or events, though many words may do just that. But the child who says "Baby," presumably meaning, "Pick me up," is using the word as a predicate in the implied sentence, "You pick me up." Besides, as we shall see, the second word often does not predicate and may simply modify the first word, as in "pretty baby." Bloom (1971) does not think that there is a relationship between the one-word and multiple-word utterances. Grammatical development begins, she thinks, with two words, and in a sense this may be so by definition since grammar is defined as the rules by which words are put together to form sentences. The question is still an open one, and the direction of research has recently been almost exclusively focused on the acquisition of language involving two or more words.

About ten years ago there was an exciting consensus of findings on the nature of two-word utterances from three different laboratories (Brown and Bellugi, 1964; Miller and Ervin, 1964; Braine, 1963). Each group had a research program which involved the frequent recording of the language of a small group of children. The ways in which the masses of observations were reduced and summarized can be understood only in terms of the dominant linguistic theory ten years ago. Linguistics was descriptive and nontheoretical. Regularities in language were induced from a devoutly empirical what-goes-with-what? strategy. Grammars were based on the "privilege of occurrence" of forms with each other. Adjectives, for example were defined as those words which could follow an article or another adjective or be followed by an adjective or a noun.

Two-word utterances arrange themselves into a neat and simple pattern. One class has fewer words and usually precedes the larger class. The first has been called *pivot* (P) words and the second, *open* (O) class words. Children add words to the open class more rapidly than they increase the number of pivot words. Examples of two-word combinations are given in Table 5-4. The rudimentary children's grammar may be written:

(1) S → P + O

That is, a sentence consists of a pivot word and an open class word. Although this is the modal form, other permutations were observed in the two-word utterance stage:

Table 5-4   Fragment of Pivot Grammar of One Child

Pivot Words	Open Class Words
allgone	boy
byebye	sock
big	boat
more	fan
pretty	milk
my	plane
see	shoe
night-night	vitamins
hi	hot
	Mommy
	Daddy
	.
	.
	.

Source: McNeill, 1966, p. 22.

(2) S → O + P

(3) S → O + O

In fact, Bloom (1970) observed occasional sentences of the form

(4) S → P + P

which vitiates any serious attempt to consider this a grammar, because the generalization now is essentially that any two words may be said together, and that is hardly a predictive, rule-governed statement such as a grammar requires.

McNeill (1970) has made an elaborate case that the adult form of the grammar involves a process of successive differentiation of the P and O classes. His model of how parts of speech serving the same function as the P class may evolve from pivot words is illustrated in Figure 5-5. The hierarchical development is not unlike the successive differentiation of distinctive features in phonology. At time 1, there is an undifferentiated P_1 class of words. By time 2, articles and demonstratives have split off from the initial P class, leaving a residual P_2 class, which later divides into adjectives, possessives, and a P_3 residual, etc. This analysis is purely grammatical and speculative.

Recently, these same two-word sentences have been analyzed from a totally new point of view and in a framework which we find more congenial to our thinking about perceptual development and language. Bloom (1970) gives several informative examples from her own observation of a 21-month-old child.

Time

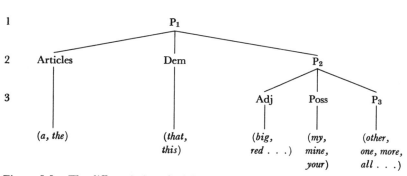

Figure 5-5. The differentiation of adult grammatical classes from a single pivot class. From McNeill, 1970, p. 59.

(5) Mommy sock

occurred in two separate contexts, as follows:

(i)   Kathryn picked up her mother's sock;

(ii) Mommy putting Kathryn's sock on Kathryn. (p. 5)

And another example later:

(6) No dirty soap

could be interpreted:

(i) There is no dirty soap.

(ii) The soap is not dirty.

(iii) That isn't dirty soap.

(iv) I don't want the dirty soap. (p. 6)

A descriptive statement about sentences (5) and (6) tells us nothing about the context in which the child spoke, what the child probably meant, or what the child intended to communicate. Without information about the situation, about the child's previous utterances and inferences about what she was trying to communicate, the several P + O forms would be classed together. It seems that the reorientation to a concern with the perceptual and communicative function of language leads to a richer and more productive understanding of language. The child talks about objects and events that are going on. Incidentally, these communications take certain forms which can be described grammatically. But the important point is that children speak about experiences that have meaning for them. The preoccupation with form (or grammar) obscured, it seems to us, the experiential focus of language.

When this point of view gained some cogency, the existing two-word corpuses were reanalyzed by Bloom (1970), Brown (1973), and Schlesinger (1971). Although the categories of intent varied somewhat among these investigators, the categories of meanings which young children were communicating were of the following sorts. Bloom (1970, pp. 62 ff) assigned noun-noun constructions to the following categories:

1. Conjunction

2. Attributive

3. Subject-object

4. Genitive

5. Locative

Schlesinger (1971, pp. 73–78) allocates two-word utterances to these categories (where X is any word):

1. Agent + action *(mail come)*

2. Action + direct object *(see sock)*

3. Agent + direct object *(Eve lunch)*

4. Modifier + head *(pretty boat)*

5. Negation + X *(no wet)*

6. X + dative *(throw Daddy)*

7. Introducer + X (ostension) *(see boy)*

8. X + locative *(sat wall)*

When two-word utterances are put into categories such as these, it is clear that children are not simply putting words together but are actually saying things that are meaningful to them. Our theory of language development emphasizes the primacy of the semantic component, or meaning, in the production and comprehension of language. Before language, in fact from birth, children attend to and differentiate their world. The process is one of perceptual and cognitive learning, discussed in Chapters 2 and 3. They extract distinctive features and invariants from their experiences, group objects and events that share features, and classify on the basis of similar and different features. The distinctive, permanent features of objects are extracted and serve to differentiate objects and their class memberships. Events are perceived and discriminated from one another. Children learn that people do things to objects that cause their relocation in space. Observing the transformations and the event provides information for constancy and the notion of causality. People approach the child, retreat, and disappear. Objects are in view and out and then again in view: information for appearance, disappearance, and reappearance. Objects that reappear maintain the features they possessed before disappearance.

Objects have names, often taught to the child by adults playing endless naming games. Objects are associated with certain people, giving rise to the rudimentary idea of possession. Objects have locations. We could go on to ever longer lists of the knowledge about the world which even the prelinguistic child has extracted.

In other words, before he speaks the child is semantically wise. The task of language acquisition, then, is to relate language to his existing perceptions and cognitions. The functional classifications of early language refer specifically to those objects, events, and relationships that the child knows about and typically occur in their actual context. Since those aspects of reality are meaningful to him, his motivation is strong to abstract the relevant language. He talks early about attribution: *that car, that doll, that chair.* About possession: *Mommy sock, baby chair.* About location: *sweater chair, truck floor.*

More important, he indicates agent-action-object relationships, which are the most pervasive yet simple relationships in language. Modern linguistic theory, in fact, takes this simplest sentence, which is the expression of the simplest relational events in the child's world, as the foundation for the most complex sentences imaginable.

Children necessarily begin to talk about the things that they already know exist. They attend to the language which has to do with what they already know. As they become epistemologically more sophisticated, so does their language. Once a child controls language, it undoubtedly plays a part in subsequent perceptual and cognitive development. When the child can ask questions or talk about things not in view or guide his actions and thinking by language, his mental development is accelerated.

If children's semantic development is so much ahead of language production, why doesn't the child use sentences whose complexity matches his prelinguistic knowledge? Apparently, children are limited in the number of morphemes they can say in a single sentence because of cognitive or processing limits. Still, as can be seen in Figure 5-4, the limits are not long lasting. After the period of two-word utterances, the number of morphemes the child can use in a single utterance increases very rapidly.

One final point. The developmental processes of abstracting features and economically grouping information operate on language as they do on nonlinguistic aspects of the world. Children extract invariant relations of grammar and semantics as features of language as they do features of shape or of permanence-impermanence. Our point is that the basis of knowledge is reality and eventually language qua language is another reality that children learn about.

The ways children learn negation is a good example of the interplay between semantics and grammar. Bloom (1970, pp. 170 ff) identified three meanings of negation in the language of children she observed: (a) *nonexistence,* indicating that the referent was not in the context; (b) *rejection,* not wanting something, and (c) *denial,* when a statement was not the case. McNeill and McNeill (1968) describe the semantics of negation in Japanese in roughly the same terms. Whereas Japanese marks these semantic variations morphologically, English does not, so the various meanings must be judged from the context. Bloom thinks that the three meanings of negation develop in the order given above, a sequence that does not seem unreasonable in relation to the perceptual development of children. Nonexistence depends on the child's knowing that an object has permanence regardless of its immediate physical availability, what we have called the perceptual events of appearance and disappearance. Rejection is not so clear and seems tied to the motivational and emotional needs of the child. It is not surpising that denial appears developmentally latest of the three meanings because the child is denying the truth of a verbal statement rather than of an event, as "Here is an apple" or "That not a apple."

The various meanings of negation are expressed in similar grammatical forms, so without extralinguistic information it is not possible to separate the meanings. Bellugi (1967) has done the most elaborate description of the syntax, as opposed to the semantics, of negation. The developmental course of negative utterances looks like this (from McNeill, 1970):

First stage:

No . . . . wipe finger
More . . . . no
Not a teddy bear

Second stage:

(two to four months after Stage 1)
I can't catch you.
We can't talk.
I don't like him.
Don't leave me.
He no bite you.

Third stage:

(two to six months later)
Paul can't have one.
I didn't did it.
You don't want some supper.
I not crying.

The syntax of negation in English is complex and beyond the scope of this discussion. The developmental course represents a combination of increasingly adult forms as well as instances of earlier forms. The important point is that the various meanings of negation are learned early, but the grammatical forms in which the meanings are clothed take a longer developmental course.

We may expect that more complex grammatical structures will be mastered only by older children, and in fact that some may be so complex that many adults do not understand them. What makes a sentence complex? As we have seen earlier in this chapter, the child uses over and over only a small set of the vocabulary that he knows. Analogously, the grammar constructed from children's spontaneous verbalizations may underestimate the nature of the rule system that he uses to construct and to understand language. To get at the more complex aspects of grammar, it may be futile to wait for the spontaneous occurrence of the structure. The child will have to be confronted with these kinds of sentences and the degree of his comprehension observed.

As a first approximation to the selection of complex sentences, C. Chomsky (1969) sought ones "which deviate from a widely established pattern in the language, or whose surface structure is relatively inexplicit with respect to grammatical relationships, or even simply those which the linguist finds particularly difficult to incorporate into a thorough discription" (p. 4). According to these general criteria for complex or late-to-be-understood structures, Chomsky selected four types for empirical investigation. We will summarize two of these.

Chomsky hypothesized that if the structure associated with a single word is at variance with a general pattern in the language, that deviant structure should appear late. The assumption seems to be that the child has abstracted the general pattern which he extends to the odd instance. With linguistic maturity, the older child makes the appropriate distinctions between the more and less common patterns. It is difficult to see how this case is an example of linguistic complexity. Rather, it appears to be predictable from theories of rule formation and categorization (see Chapter 3). For many cognitive tasks, children will extend a functional rule to inappropriate instances until they learn the distinguishing features between the two categories.

Consider the following sentences (after Chomsky, pp. 10, 11):

a. John wanted Bill to leave.

b. John begged Bill to leave.

c. John expected Bill to leave.

d. John asked Bill to leave.

e. John liked Bill to be on time.

f. John preferred Bill to be on time.

g. John chose Bill to bell the cat.

h. John promised Bill to leave.

In sentences a–g, *Bill* is the subject of the infinitive verb, that is, Bill will do the leaving, being on time, etc. Said more formally, the implicit subject of the complement verb is the first preceding NP. This has been called the "minimal distance principle" (MDP). But notice in sentence h that John will do the leaving, and since *John* is the more remote NP, sentences with the word *promise* violate the MDP. Does this exception to a general pattern lead to late comprehension of the exceptional case?

There are a number of features that might serve to distinguish *promise* from the verbs which concur with the MDP. The verbs that make up the major class are commands and requests (though the request category is a bit complicated). Consequently, the distinction might be on semantic grounds: commands and requests vs. *promise*. The other verbs can be paraphrased as imperatives:

Leave!
Bell the cat!

Promise sentences cannot be so paraphrased.

Do children act as though *promise* falls under the MDP and, if so, does the tendency decrease with age? Chomsky used an elaborate interview procedure to get at this and similar questions. For example,

Donald tells Bozo to lie down. Make him do it.

Donald promises Bozo to lie down. Make him do it.

Twenty-one of 40 children made the correct interpretation of *tell* and *promise*. Most of the 19 children who did not answer all questions correctly did use the MDP for *tell*, but tended to use it inappropriately for *promise* or at least to give mixed answers to *promise*. There was no relationship between the ages of the children and the ability to use the MDP or to appropriately avoid it with *promise*. Some five-year-olds could form this subtle distinction; some nine-year-olds still had not made the appropriate distinction.

Another source of complexity, according to Chomsky, is the congruence between the surface structure of a sentence and its underlying meaning. We can reasonably assume that simple sentences of the form "John sees Mary," a subject-verb-object construction, are easiest for children to understand. If this form does not reflect the real SVO relationships, then the task for the listener is more difficult. The examples are familiar in the linguistic literature:

(7) John is eager to see.

(8) John is easy to see.

Sentence (7) should be easy to understand since John is the subject of *eager* and of the complement *to see*. In (8) John is only the superficial subject, since the sentence can be rewritten several ways to show that *John* is the real object of the sentence: "To see John is easy," "Someone finds John easy to see," "It is easy to see John."

Is there a developmental course between the ages of five and ten in how these sentences are understood? At the youngest ages of this sample, children construe the sentences in the usual SVO order, so that they think John is doing the seeing in both sentences. Older children, nine-and ten-year-olds, invariably interpret the sentences correctly. The ages between yield variable results, so we are able to conclude that this source of sentence complexity affects younger children and not older ones, but the transition between five and ten years presents an unclear picture.

One of Chomsky's final tests, having to do with pronominal reference, will be summarized. The problem can be seen in the following three sentences:

(9) He found out that Mickey won the race.

(10) After he got the candy, Mickey left.

(11) Pluto thinks he knows everything.

In sentence (9) the pronoun must refer to someone outside of the sentence. The pronouns in (10) and (11) may refer to someone either in or out of the sentence. The age 5;6 is the approximate cutoff point for mastering this complexity. Children younger than that age do not understand the distinctions between (9) and (10), (11); children older than 5;6 invariably see the various possible interpretations.

Chomsky's (1969) research is one of the few that looked specifically at grammatical competences of children during the elementary school years. Even difficult structures cannot be said to vary consistently with age. For some of the grammatical forms that she tested, some five-year-old children could interpret them whereas some ten-year-olds could not. The most we can say is that there are some grammatical constructions which are still in the course of mastery during the period five to ten years. The statement that a child has completely mastered the grammar by five or six years is patently untrue.

From Chomsky's data, it does appear that children interpret sentences in the form SVO even if the surface form of the sentence does not invite this interpretation. The SVO form, although not universal among the world's languages, is nevertheless the most common (Greenberg, 1962). It follows from our previous discussion on cognitive development and the perceptual and cognitive bases of language that this sequence is natural. The perceptual regularities in the real world upon which children base their conception of the world are made up of events in which somebody does something to recipients of action: mothers pick up babies, children eat food, children ask for objects, children push toys, etc. The child's world is a perceptually available universe of agents-actions-objects. The child's notions of causality are based on such ubiquitous observations. Language that reflects the natural sequence should be easier to understand than word orders that are incongruous with children's inferences from real events.

In this section we shall review children's acquisition of word order in their language. The most obvious well-formed exception to the SVO sequences is the English passive sentence:

(12) John was hit by the ball.

(13) Mary was eaten by the dragon.

If our notions about the ease of understanding a construction are due to the match between the sequences of events in reality and the sequence in language, passive sentences should appear later than actives and be more difficult to understand. Children should interpret (12) and (13) as John doing the hitting and Mary doing the eating.

This simple model for language comprehension assumes that the children use the algorithm SVO, that is, that they apply a semantic rather than a syntactic strategy to understanding sentences. For active sentences, the semantic and syntactic strategies yield the same results; for passive sentences, they do not and the semantic strategy wins out. Another assumption must be added to the model for comprehension: The sentence has to make sense.

(14) John was carried by the train.

The initial semantic step, interpret the first noun as subject and the second as object, yields

(15) John carried the train,

which is not sensible. In such cases, the child must give up the semantic strategy and employ the syntactic information to intercpret the sentence, if he can. Sentences (12) and (13) are called *reversible* passives; (14) is a *nonreversible* passive. We expect on these grounds that passives will be understood at a later age than actives and that nonreversible passives will be interpreted before the reversible forms.

In one way or another these variables have been looked at by a number of investigators. Slobin (1966) had children in kindergarten, second, fourth, and sixth grades and adults respond to the truth or falseness of sentences describing pictures. The sentences were simple actives, passives, negatives, and negative passives. If the subjects were responding to the grammatical complexity, the order of difficulty should be actives < negatives < passives < negative passives. In fact, the evident order of difficulty was actives < passives < negatives < negative passives, that is, the interpretation of the passives was easier than the negatives. This finding was true mainly for nonreversible passives. Therefore, children seemed to respond to the truth value, that is, to the semantic content of the fact that only one word could be an agent and the other an object. Nonreversibility removed the problem of which is the agent and which the object in the passives. The grammatical system explored in this study was known by the six-year-olds, though the latencies in responding to reversible and nonreversible sentences decrease from six to ten years and remain steady thereafter. Said another way, response to the meaning aspects of these sentences improves between six and ten years, after which the subjects are as good as they are going to be.

Turner and Rommetveit (1967) investigated the abilities of children, preschool through third grade, to imitate, understand, and produce active and passive sentences, each of which had a reversible and nonreversible form. All children could imitate all sentences about equally well, suggesting that imitation for short sentences is an echoic process. Comprehension and production involved real understanding, and the results were quite different. Active sentences were processed more accurately than passives, and nonreversible sentences were better than reversible ones, until the third grade, where there was little variation due to sentence types. Children handle sentences best in which the grammatical and semantic form is the same, as in active sentences. Where the semantic subject and object violate the common SVO order, children impose the active, more natural order and understand the first noun to be the actor. When that early strategy yields anomalous sentences for nonreversible forms, e.g., *the flowers are watered by the girl,* the children use syntactic information to interpret sentences. However, when children are about eight or nine years old, they use the grammatical information adequately.

A great deal of evidence was adduced by Bever (1970) to show that children below five use a semantic strategy to understand. He replicated in his data the reversible-nonreversible findings discussed above. Bever, however, did not take the full step of relating early language use to the child's knowledge of real events and relationships but only to the child's perception of sentences. The perception of sentences, we maintain, must be understood on the basis of the child's extralinguistic as well as linguistic experiences.

To young children, language is a medium for communicating messages. The medium of grammar, like phonology, is opaque. There is no reason why he should be aware of language itself as an object of inquiry or perusal. Does the child ever stand off and look at his and others' language, like a linguist? Does he become aware that the structure of language as well as its content is a proper subject for study? This is not to say that children do not use grammatical rules when they produce and understand language.

The rules are acquired because they order the child's language in ways that are congruent with reality. Purely semantic interpretation of language can lead to errors, as in the passives. The evidence is that the priorities of meaning are not overridden by the demands of grammatical structure until the child is eight or nine years of age. Can we say that the child now knows the rules of grammar? An explication of what we mean by "knowing the rules" is not obvious (Gleitman, Gleitman, and Shipley, 1972). Certainly the child speaks as though he is following the rules. But following rules is different from knowing them. Knowing rules implies an extension of the rules to novel and appropriate situations, and children obviously can show that they are following the rules. At the most sophisticated level, however, knowing grammatical rules means the ability to reflect on language and to state the rules. This is a demanding criterion. Not even trained linguists can state all of the rules for all of their utterances. Rules have not even been formulated for some utterances. But the ability to take a metalinguistic attitude has been studied. Gleitman et al. (1972) extensively interviewed a small group of bright, articulate children, aged five to seven, about their knowledge of grammar. The children talked about anomalous sentences spoken to them by an adult. Here is one example:

(1) I saw the queen and you saw one.

(2) I saw Mrs. Jones and you saw one.

The four younger children accept (1) without question which is consistent with their tendency *not to notice syntactic deviance when no semantic anomaly arises* [italics ours]. On the other hand, all of the subjects rejected (2). (p. 153)

It sounds funny cause *You saw Mrs. Jones* is okay, but *I saw one*—it should mean something like *I saw—You saw a tree and I saw one too.* You can't say it with a name. [So what's the problem?] Because you have to say something like *You saw a tree and I saw one.* But you can't say something like *You saw Mrs Jones and I saw one.* You have to say *You saw Mrs. Jones and I saw her, too.*

On the whole, these child-informants responded first to the meaning of the statement. They were able, though, to correct syntax in some sentences where the meanings were reasonably preserved, as *John and Jim is a brother.* Often syntactic deviance obscures the meaning of a sentence so that it is not possible to make a distinction between syntax and semantics. Also, there is not, as these authors imply, an either-or response to semantics or syntax. There is a developmental order, as their own data show, for children to respond earlier to meaning anomalies than to grammatical errors. But, by the early elementary grades, at least bright children do not merely follow grammatical and semantic rules but have some awareness of the rules and are able to talk about them.

Is the child linguistically mature at five or six years when he learns to read? Certainly, he appears to control the bulk of adultlike grammar. C. Chomsky (1969) demonstrated that some complex forms were not understood by elementary school children, but we will turn shortly to a discussion of whether children did not know the grammatical rules or did not know the meaning of the sentences. A survey of children's use of common syntactic constructions indicated a rise in the variety of constructions used at the first grade and at the seventh. There was no evidence of substantial increments of new forms between these grades. Also, written forms indicated somewhat greater maturity than spoken language, but that is not surprising since the child can monitor his language more easily when writing than when speaking. Differences in vernacular and literary styles appear early, but there is unfortunately very little evidence on this important aspect of literacy (O'Donnell, Griffin, and Norris, 1967).

The Development of Word Meanings

If there are universal characteristics to early child language, their source lies in the universal perceptual and cognitive experiences of childhood. As we have indicated in the previous section, the semantic knowledge of children is prior to grammar and is reflected in grammar. In this section, we extend the same point of view to the child's acquisition of the meanings of words.

The meaning of a word may be defined by a bundle of semantic features which differentiate that word from others (Katz and Fodor, 1963). Semantic features can be thought of as similar to phonological distinctive features, which act to characterize speech segments and whose patterns distinguish among sound segments or phonemes. The basis for Jakobson's distinctive features was reasonably clear: the articulatory gestures which produce the sounds, the physical characteristics of sound, and the perceptual qualities of the sounds. The concept of semantic features is considerably less developed, but we will discuss some perceptual basis for arriving at a primitive set of meaning features. There is still much to be done in deriving a minimal and efficient set of semantic features. They should serve to group words into concepts; their patterns should predict the learning of words and the confusions among them; the features should be amenable to a theory of acquisition of meanings; etc. Several researchers have attempted to show how the organization of subjective lexicons might be derived from a small number of semantic features (Fillenbaum and Rapoport, 1971; Collins and Quillian, 1969; Miller, 1969). Further, words confused in memory are usually ones that share a number of features (Felzen and Anisfeld, 1970). At this time, the study of meaning using a semantic feature strategy is gaining currency and appears to be very promising.

An example of semantic features applied to kinship terms might look like the following:

	mother	father	son	daughter
Animate	+	+	+	+
Human	+	+	+	+
Male	−	+	+	−
Female	+	−	−	+
Adult	+	+	?	?
Child	−	−	?	?

Another example (from Clark, 1971, p. 19):

	before	after
Time	+	+
Simultaneous	−	−
Prior	+	−

These two examples illustrate the ad hoc nature of the array of usable features which seem to be chosen to differentiate the specific corpus of words whose relationships are being considered.

We have found the discussion of the development of word meanings by E. Clark (1973) congenial with our thinking about the relationships between perceptual development and language development, so that much of what follows is based on her work.

The Semantic Feature Hypothesis states that when the child first begins to use identifiable words, he does not know their full (adult) meaning: he only has partial entries for them in his lexicon, such that these partials correspond in some way to some of the features or components of meaning that would be present in the entries for the same words in the adult's lexicon. (p. 12)

For the child the meaning of a word involves only a few features, so that the development of meaning involves the differentiation of more specific features. If the child's word names a category, then since his definitions have sparse features we expect that the category of which the word is a member will be overextended. This means that he will admit more words to a category than would the adult whose words are defined by more features so that admission to a category is more highly restricted. We take exception to Clark's belief that when a child initially learns the meaning of a word he learns a matrix of semantic features which define that word. More likely, the word *dog* is first an attribute of the object being named. The object *dog* has an infinite number of characteristics or features, and the child has no basis for choosing some group of these features to serve as criteria for *dog*. The word *dog* is simply another characteristic of a familiar object. If, however, the child extends the word *dog* to a cow and learns the error, he has a basis for abstracting the semantic features which distinguish a dog from a cow. *Features are contrastive.* It will be recalled that in acquiring phonological distinctive features, the child is motivated to distinguish features that in some combinations are phonemic, that is, serve to contrast sound segments. Feature matrices both in phonology and semantics are useful insofar as they put into a single category those sounds and objects or events that are similar and distinguish this category from another whose feature values are both similar and different. In one of the above examples, *mother* and *father* differ on at least one feature, sex. Features are not an arbitrary choice of characteristics that can be assigned to an object, but a set of characteristics that permit contrast between the meanings of objects, events, or relationships. In fact, the bulk of Clark's discussion concerns the meanings of relational concepts whose distinctions are based on semantic contrasts that are often subtle: more-less, above-below, before-after, etc.

Two questions are important. What are the bases for the choice of features, and in what order do they enter into the child's system of word meanings? The first semantic features are the perceptual attributes of the referents which the child is naming; e.g., barking for dogs, meowing for cats. Theoretically, every perceptual feature has as ready access to the inventory of lexical features as any other, so that pointed ears, barking, spots, etc., may be selected as semantic features. Perhaps certain features may be more salient perceptually and therefore acquire lexical status early, but we do not have the evidence to make this statement with confidence. For example, Jarvella and Sinnott (1972) found that for nine- to twelve-year-old children as well as for adults, nouns which completed sentence frames were almost all concrete. Animacy appeard to be a salient feature because 80% of the subject nouns and 50% of object nouns were animate, and almost all animate nouns were human.

Semantic features may be constrained to sets that serve to distinguish categories. But at this stage in our study of meaning, features are opportunistic lists that do the job of defining categories.

Semantic features are derived from perceptual abstractions: abstractions, because if four-leggedness is a feature defining the category animal, we ignore whether the legs are as long as a giraffe's or as short as a bassett hound's, whether they move like a gaited horse's or like a running dog's. Semantic features are themselves abstractions. *Animate* is an inference based on growth, breathing, animate motion (compared to rigid motion, for example), etc. We may hypothesize that for children the distinctive perceptual feature constrasts will form the initial inventories of features. Anglin (1970) has argued that definitions occur from the bottom up, from the concrete to the abstract. His data are unconvincing, however, and may be due to the limited store of words he used, the kinds of tasks he gave his nine-year-old subjects, and the nature of the categories. His most abstract category was the form class *noun*, which children could not use as a categorizing feature but with which they were certainly functionally familiar in their everyday language.

Clark prefers the interpretation that word meanings start with the general features and develop in a general-to-specific fashion. The development from nondifferentiated to specific is the process of perceptual learning that we have discussed in Chapters 2 and 3. However, since perceptual learning precedes the use of features in linguistic meaning, there is no necessary constraint in the order in which the available perceptual information is used in assigning meanings to words. As one example of a hierarchical order of features, notice the way that Clark defined *before* and *after* (see p. 147). The three features defining the comparative terms are successive differentiations from top to bottom. The formulation is neat and the examples are convincing, but we must leave this as a question open to additional theory and research.

It would be an oversimplification, writes Clark (1973), to assume that all features of meaning are perceptually based, since functional, social, or cultural factors frequently determine word meanings (p. 74), especially, we would add, as the child grows older. We described earlier Chomsky's (1969) finding that school-age children define *promise* as though it were a member of the class of verbs containing *tell, say, assert,* etc. Chomsky's explanation was syntactic. Yet Clark points out that the incorrect interpretation of *promise* occurs because children have not learned the social role features of *promise,* that the person doing the promising always will carry out the promised act, as in "John promised Mary to carry her books."

The problem of meaning has occupied psychologists, linguists, and philosophers at least since the time of Aristotle. Empirical work is in its infancy, however. The approach using semantic features is attractive, but an appraisal of the eventual value of this line of theory and research awaits many years of research.

Theories of Language Development

Almost every child, except under extreme conditions of individual or social pathology, learns to speak and to understand the language of his community. The task would seem to be formidably complicated. Even young children are able to say things that they have never said before and to understand utterances which they hear for the first time. The reader may note that he probably has never read a sentence exactly like the previous one, yet he has no difficulty understanding it. Language is a creative process. Its hallmark is novelty, yet the uniqueness of any single utterance is taken in stride and the speaker is hardly aware that almost any string of language contains novel and unique elements. We must admit, in all fairness, that a completely satisfactory theory of language acquisition and language use does not exist.

To the man in the street the question, "How does a child learn language?" must seem an empty philosophical conundrum. He learns by imitating the language he hears, of course, and in fact respectable linguistic accounts of ten or fifteen years ago dismissed the acquisition problem with the imitation explanation (see, e.g., Hockett, 1958). But imitation raises more questions than it answers. How does a child imitate? Why doesn't he imitate everything he hears? What are the conditions under which imitation occurs? Besides, the early utterances of children are unlikely to be things they have heard: all gone sock, all gone truck, daddy bye-bye, here baby, here toy, etc. Moreover, when the young child is given the task of imitating an adult's sentence, he comes out with systematic though unadultlike variations on the adult's sayings to him (from McNeill, 1970, p. 106).

Adult: Oh, that's a big one
Child: big one
Adult: But, he was much bigger than Perro
Child: big a Pcrro
Adult: Salad dressing
Child: Salad dressing
Adult: That's not a screw
Child: dat not a screw
Adult: Are they all there?
Child: all dere?

The child seems to extract the meaning of the adult's sentences, but he by no means gives a point-by-point rendition of what he hears. Finally, there is substantial evidence that a child cannot imitate what he does not understand (Slobin and Welch, in press). And if the imitation explanation needs a further coup de grâce, children regularize nongrammatical pause patterns that they hear (Ford, 1970):

Adult: The   sheep jump   over the   ditch.
Child, regularizing the pause pattern:
          The sheep   jump over   the ditch.

S-R Theory and Reinforcement
In keeping with the most pervasive paradigm in American psychology, some theorists try to explain language acquisition as the consequence of the reinforcement of stimulus and response connections (cf. Staats and Staats, 1963) or the operant reinforcement of utterances that a child emits (cf. Skinner, 1957). However, these theories bear the burden of explaining what is reinforced and whether the course of acquisition follows the rules of reinforcement. It is unlikely that parents reinforce well-formed sentences and ignore or punish unacceptable utterances. From an adult's point of

view, which among the child's two- or three-word utterances merit rein-forcement? And when the child begins to use sentences that approach the adult model, parents respond *not* to the form of the sentence but to its truth value. "Mommy hided the doll" may be perfectly plausible to the parent, whereas a well-formed "Mommy doesn't like me" will be corrected because Mommy does like him—the utterance is grammatical but untrue.

On the face of it, the picture of parents as skilled dispensers of rein-forcements for grammaticality is unlikely. The child at an early level of competence, e.g., with a mean length utterance of 2.0 morphemes, cannot approach adult competence regardless of the parent's intervention. Never-theless, the early utterances are rule governed and not incorrect from the child's point of view.

Further, the frequency of reinforced behavior usually shows a gradual increase as a function of the pattern of reinforcement. Early language be-havior does not work like that. A form appears suddenly and is used widely and even overextended. When the child begins to use the third person of irregular verbs (e.g., *went*, *grew*) he will adapt the weak form to the gram-matical forms that he already knows, so that one hears *wented*, *grewed*, and finally the two forms are separated. Reinforcement theory has a hard time explaining the sudden extensive occurrence of new forms and the loss of the correct (presumably reinforced) forms to another pattern. There is no evidence of a positively accelerating curve. Forms once they appear come into the child's language with a rush.

Even the acquisition of vocabulary is difficult to explain via reinforce-ment. The child learns at about the same time "Hit the ball!", "Get a hit," "That's a hit tune," etc. Each use of *hit* would take a different set of reinforcements. A more sophisticated S-R theory says that the child learns the form class membership of words and puts together an utterance by fitting words into their appropriate slots in the sentence (Jenkins and Pa-lermo, 1964). The various form class memberships of the same word in-dicate the unlikelihood of such a process.

In fact, the obvious difficulties of explaining the complexities of lan-guage acquisition by popular extant theories have forced us to develop new theoretical approaches to account for behavior as ubiquitous yet as re-calcitrant to simple explanation as language.

Language Acquisition as Rule Learning

From all kinds of language around them and without any systematic external guidance, children extract a language. Language is a system of rules of various degrees of complexity and abstractness. The process of language acquisition is the course of learning these rules. To take a simple example we have used before, the child shows that he knows the morphological rule for plurals when he says *sheeps* or *gooses*. He of course cannot state the rules, but he acts as though he is following them. Some children (Gleitman et al., 1972) are aware of language and can talk about language as an object. The rules to be learned must be abstract. They are not simply the surface form of the language because at about seven a child can tell you that "The boy blows the whistle" and "The whistle was blown by the boy" have the same underlying meaning.

Admittedly, we do not have a completely satisfactory conceptualization of the structure of languages nor how the rules are acquired. Since all languages at an abstract level have certain universal characteristics and since acquisition is universal, some theorists postulate a biological basis for language. According to this point of view, the human mind is uniquely designed to detect the underlying rules of languages and to use them within the context of specific languages (Lenneberg, 1967; Chomsky, 1965; McNeill, 1970). This is a strong hypothesis and its proof can only be inferential: a sort of "Well, how else would you explain language development?" Lenneberg (1967) has pointed out the similarities between other biologically based developments of children and their language development.

The Perceptual and Cognitive Bases of Language
There is an alternative to the hypothesis of a genetically determined propensity for language acquisition, and it is a point of view which is congenial with our own theoretical orientation. All children, regardless of the circumstances of their early lives, have some universal perceptual experiences. They abstract the invariant relations of their worlds: objects, events, and the spatial layout. Even prior to language, they acquire elaborate and complex meanings. They are, of course, unable to talk about them in adultlike terms. Nevertheless, as we have pointed out, children's early language reflects their knowledge of reality. It is small wonder that the basic sentences, even in rudimentary form, show an abstract conception of subject-verb-object which is the most common inference from many events which every child sees or hears or feels. From this point of view, language is the coding of meanings which the child already has gained. Language development may be universal not in a unique way but because it is part and parcel of universal perceptual and cognitive knowledge. One may draw analogies between cognitive development and language (Sinclair

de-Zwart, 1967) in ways similar to Lenneberg's (1967) correlations between biological growth and language. This is a task yet to be done. Still, such an approach to language development does not make the untenable assumptions of imitation and S-R theory and maintains the obvious requirement that the explanation of language must come to grips with the rulelike nature of language behavior. Said another way, we entertain the hope that the principles of perceptual learning and cognitive development, elaborated in Chapters 2 and 3, are general enough and powerful enough to explain language acquisition as well as the later accomplishment of learning to read.

Summary

This chapter reviewed the nature of language development, paying particular attention to the ages when instruction in reading usually begins. By and large, children have mastered the production and recognition of the sound aspects of their language. Late articulations are those sounds formed by motor acts which are less precise than sounds acquired earlier. A Jakobsonian analysis of sound reproduction by successive differentiation of distinctive features was advanced as being the most heuristic theory and as yet most congruent with existing data.

Considerable attention was paid to children's ability to segment speech into various units, since segmentation is considered a precursor to learning to read. Breaking the stream of speech into phoneme-sized segments is very difficult for children around the age of six. Less difficult, but still requiring training, is segmentation into syllables and words.

Children near the age of four indicate their awareness of the phonological rule structure of English. They are able, for instance, to discriminate between English-like pseudowords and sounds that violate the rules of the language. Inflectional morphology at the preschool period has been mastered except for the /iz/ form of the plural and possessive. Derivational morphology is still in nascent form.

Early grammatical forms were treated as reflections of meanings which the child has abstracted from real-world experiences. The apparent primacy of the sentence form subject-verb-object was discussed as an abstraction from many events which the prelinguistic child has experienced. There is evidence that school-age children still do not understand complex grammatical constructions as, for example, sentences which distinguish between *tell* and *promise*, although such later developments are open to either grammatical or semantic interpretations of children's knowledge.

The emergence of word meanings was treated in terms of the differentiation of semantic features and the categorization of objects, events, and relationships by the refinement of features which function to differentiate objects and to include or exclude them from categories.

Finally, theories of language acquisition that depended on imitation or the reinforcement of stimulus-response connections were rejected as inconsistent with the natural phenomena of language development. We preferred a theory of perceptual learning and development by which language and children's comprehension of reality were explained by the same assumptions and constructs. However, it is fair to say that an adequate theory of language acquisition does not yet exist.

To return to our original question, the prereading child is indeed a reasonably mature language user, although substantial development in segmentation, morphology, grammar, and meaning takes place during the course of learning to read and probably is influenced by the acquisition of literacy.

6
Writing Systems

The History of Writing

Spoken language, we suppose, is as old as the history of social man. Written language, on the other hand, is young. Modern writing systems can be traced back five or six thousand years. If we consider protowriting, which was usually a form of picturing, the origins are at the most twenty thousand years ago. This span of time is, in Van Loon's terms, but a day in eternity.

The history of writing is a fascinating reconstruction of archaeological evidence. Apparently the first motivations to write were mundane and prosaic. People had to record the contents of warehouses or inventories of shipped goods or the ordnances of war. These are just the meaningless lists without organization that tax the memory. Although it is not the purpose of this chapter to review the history of writing in any detail, we call the reader's attention to an excellent book by Gelb (1952). The alphabetic writing system, as we know it in English and most other modern languages, had its origins in the Middle East about four thousand years ago. Figure 6-1 summarizes the history of writing and the forerunners of the alphabet. The evolution of writing from pictures to logograms and then to a sound-based system seems a reasonable solution to an obvious problem.

It is to the Sumerians that we are indebted for having taken the important step leading to a fully developed writing. The organization of the Sumerian state and economy made imperative the keeping of records of goods transferred from the country to the cities and vice versa. Records were kept in concise ledger form of the type "5 sheep" or with a personal name, "10 bows, X." The choice of one sign for one word resulted in the origin of a logographic system which soon expanded into a phonographic system through the necessity of expressing personal names in an exact way to prevent confusion in the records. (Gelb, 1952, p. 194)

For the Middle Eastern languages the syllabary was a reasonable representation of the spoken languages, which contained a limited number of consonant and vowel (CV) sequences. The transition between syllabaries and alphabets is interesting. West Semitic syllabaries (Phoenician, Hebrew, etc.) indicated that monosyllables ended in vowels, but none developed a full system for noting vowels.

No Writing: *Pictures*

Forerunners of Writing: *Semasiography*

1. Descriptive-Representational Device

2. Identifying-Mnemonic Device

Full Writing: *Phonography*

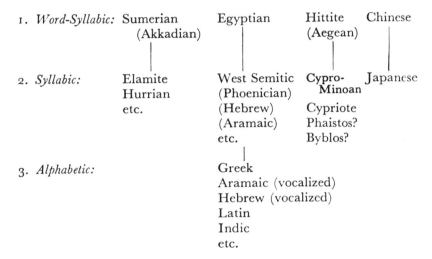

1. *Word-Syllabic:*	Sumerian (Akkadian)	Egyptian	Hittite (Aegean)	Chinese
2. *Syllabic:*	Elamite Hurrian etc.	West Semitic (Phoenician) (Hebrew) (Aramaic) etc.	Cypro-Minoan Cypriote Phaistos? Byblos?	Japanese
3. *Alphabetic:*		Greek Aramaic (vocalized) Hebrew (vocalized) Latin Indic etc.		

Figure 6-1. Stages of the development of writing. From Gelb, 1952, p. 191. Copyright © 1952 in the International Copyright Union. All rights reserved.

The question may now be legitimately asked: If these early Semitic writings were not alphabets what, then, is the alphabet? The answer is clear. If by the word "alphabet" we understand a writing which expresses the simple sounds of a language, then the first alphabet was formed by the Greeks (Gelb, p. 197). Hundreds of alphabets throughout the world different as they may be in outer form, all use the principles first and last established in the Greek writing. (Gelb, p. 198)

In Gelb's terms, it is unfair to say that the Greeks actually invented the alphabet. Historical changes in writing were unidirectional with changes occurring as modifications of previously existing forms rather than the introduction de novo of a form, e.g., the notion of the alphabet independent of a consonant syllabary. The evolution of writing was in every case from logograms to syllabaries to alphabets. There are no examples of a syllabary growing out of an alphabet.

Types of Writing Systems

As can be seen in Figure 6-1, Gelb divides the evolution of writing into two basic stages: *prewriting*, in which messages are conveyed by arrangements of pictures, and *full writing*, which exists in three forms: (1) word-syllabic, (2) syllabic, and (3) alphabetic. Our concern is with full writing, or what Gelb calls "phonography," because the writing is related in various ways and at various levels to spoken language. None of the forms of writing is found in a pure state. English, which is written alphabetically, contains word elements such as the logogram " + ," which can be read as "plus," "added to," "the sum of," etc. English also has occasional syllabic written forms: the syllable *ten* in 10th.

Our major discussion will concern alphabets, especially English. However, it is interesting to compare the alphabetic with the other writing systems: the word-syllabic Chinese, the Japanese syllabaries, and the character-syllabary combinations used to write Japanese.

Chinese Logographs

An excellent summary of nonalphabetic writing schemes, namely, Chinese, Japanese, and Korean, is given by Martin (1972). Chinese writing is *logographic*, or in Gelb's terms, *word-syllabic*. Generally, a character stands for an object or an idea or an event. When the writing system was devised, spoken Chinese lent itself well to such a system, since Chinese words are usually single morphemes which are monosyllables. The grammar, like English, contains few inflectional morphemes. To the reader of an alphabetic system, the job of memorizing thousands of characters seems overwhelming. There may be a total of 50,000 Chinese characters. "Today it is estimated that a thousand common characters will account for 90 percent of the text occurrences in popular publications on the mainland" (Alleton, 1970, p. 47, cited by Martin).

According to Martin, there are five principal categories of Chinese graphs:

1. *Pictographs* are direct iconic representations, as for the sun, a tree, etc.
2. *Simple ideographs* depict an idea: a pointer above or below a line to depict up or down.
3. *Compound ideographs* combine simple graphs: Two trees mean "grove"; three trees represent the word for "forest."

4. *Phonetic loans* borrow a graph to represent a word with the same or similar sounds.

5. *Phonetic compounds* contain an element, called the *radical*, that hints at the meaning and an element, the *phonetic*, that hints at the sound. (pp. 83–84)

Radicals are a kind of semantic classification system. Chinese uses about 200 radicals, considerably fewer than the number of available characters. Further, the character may be analyzed into constituent elements, or features, in ways that are analogous to the features of letters or words. However, the comparison is an inexact one since the features of characters are graphic features (strokes) and of radicals, semantic features.

Japanese Syllabaries and Logographs

When the Japanese borrowed the Chinese writing system they may have done themselves a disservice, since the history of Japanese writing is a series of attempts to bring the logographic system into line with the nature of spoken Japanese. Japanese differs from Chinese in two important ways that have influenced its writing. Japanese is composed of about 100 CV syllables which in combinations make up Japanese phonology. Further, the grammar of Japanese is polysynthetic, which means that it is richly inflected at the ends of words.

To add to the borrowed Chinese logograms, the Japanese developed two syllabaries: *hiragana* and *katakana* (see Figure 6-2). The first is used mainly for grammatical suffixes and the second for words borrowed into Japanese. It is possible to write Japanese using only the syllabaries, but this has not caught on. Most commonly, in newspapers and books a combination of Chinese-originated characters, called *kanji*, and the syllabaries are used together. Kanji provide the base forms of the morphemes and hiragana the grammatical addenda. Loan words and new words, like scientific terms, are written in katakana.

To readers of alphabetic writing systems, a character or logographic system appears overwhelming in the number of characters that have to be memorized. Of course, as we saw above, a reasonably small subset of all the possible characters suffices for most writing. Still, in China and Japan there have been extensive attempts to revise the writing system. The up-down, right-to-left direction of Japanese text is giving way to left-to-right linear writing. The characters have been simplified, the numbers

This is the Hiragana Chart:

COLUMN / LINE	A	I	U	E	O
SINGLE VOWEL	あ A	い I	う U	え E	お O
K	か KA	き KI	く KU	け KE	こ KO
S	さ SA	し SHI	す SU	せ SE	そ SO
T	た TA	ち CHI	つ TSU	て TE	と TO
N	な NA	に NI	ぬ NU	ね NE	の NO
H	は HA	ひ HI	ふ HU	へ HE	ほ HO
M	ま MA	み MI	む MU	め ME	も MO
Y	や YA		ゆ YU		よ YO
R	ら RA	り RI	る RU	れ RE	ろ RO
W	わ WA		ん N		を O

Figure 6-2.   The Japanese syllabaries, hiragana and katakana. From Walsh, 1969, pp. 156–157. Charles E. Tuttle Co.

This is the Katakana Chart :

COLUMN / LINE	A	I	U	E	O
SINGLE VOWEL	ア A	イ I	ウ U	エ E	オ O
K	カ KA	キ KI	ク KU	ケ KE	コ KO
S	サ SA	シ SHI	ス SU	セ SE	ソ SO
T	タ TA	チ CHI	ツ TSU	テ TE	ト TO
N	ナ NA	ニ NI	ヌ NU	ネ NE	ノ NO
H	ハ HA	ヒ HI	フ HU	ヘ HE	ホ HO
M	マ MA	ミ MI	ム MU	メ ME	モ MO
Y	ヤ YA		ユ YU		ヨ YO
R	ラ RA	リ RI	ル RU	レ RE	ロ RO
W	ワ WA		ン N		ヲ O

Figure 6-2 (cont.)

of strokes reduced to about five per character, and the characters, as might be expected from the need to create type faces for the characters, have been simplified and stylized and so made more standard. There is a Romanization of Japanese, but this seems to be used mainly by readers of Roman alphabets who are learning Japanese.

The iconic origins of Japanese kanji are often recognizable even though the characters have been simplified and stylized. Insofar as they are picturelike, their meanings are apparent and provide a mnemonic for memorizing the characters. We have chosen several illustrations that caught our fancy from a book designed to give English-speaking tourists a rapid introduction to reading Japanese (Walsh, 1969).

To sell 賣 speaking 言 means *to read*. The new character, 讀 is pronounced YOMU by itself and DOKU in compounds. (p. 83)

The Chinese put a *woman* 女 under a *roof* 宀 and made *peace* 安. (p. 101)

A picture of a man bending over the edge of a cliff looking 厃 for his friend who has just toppled over and lies below 㔾 forms the character for *dangerous* 危. (p. 124)

Recent reports from China stress as a long-term goal the reform of writing to be based on the sound system of the language(s) and the use of the Roman alphabet. Chairman Mao Tse-tung is quoted as saying "The written language must be reformed. It is necessary to take the road of phoneticization which is commonly adopted by other languages in the world" (*New York Times*, October 15, 1972).

A particular cost to China in introducing a sound-based writing system will be the loss of mutual intelligibility of ideographic writing among the 1800 languages and dialects spoken in China. The present writing in spite of its problems can be read in all of China, although the oral rendition or paraphrase will differ from one spoken language to another.

The tradition of educational research is very strong in Japan so that there is a great deal of information about reading, especially on the unique combinations of writing systems. The two syllabaries, hiragana and katakana, each have 46 characters. In a study in Tokyo, children entering school knew the sound values of all hiragana characters. Children learn hiragana before the first grade, and it is reported to be acquired quickly (Muraishi, 1972). Katakana begins in the second half of the first grade and is finished by the second grade. Kanji characters are introduced gradually: 46 in the first grade, 105 in the second, 187 in the third, etc. According to a recent plan of the Japanese Ministry of Education, 966 kanji will be mastered in elementary school (Sakamoto and Makita, 1973).

A writing system which combines ideographic, or meaning elements, with a syllabary, or sound-correlated elements, suggests many interesting observations. There have been a number of clinical reports by neurologists on the effects of brain lesions on reading. The studies tend to agree that with injury to the left hemisphere of the brain, the ability to read kana is lost before kanji (Sakamoto and Makita, 1973). This sequence may be attributed to the nature of the correspondence or to the fact that kanji is learned later, more slowly, and by different kinds of practice than the sound-related writing. Geschwind (1972) recently reported some findings by the Japanese neurologists which indicate that the nature of the writing system is directly responsible for these findings. Injuries to Broca's area of the left hemisphere of the brain result in the loss of the ability to read the syllabic system. Injury to Wernicke's area leads to difficulty with kanji. The tradition of neurological research has distingusihed those two areas as controlling different aspects of language behavior. Broca's area relates to the sound-producing functions in language, Wernicke's area to comprehension or meaning-related functions of language. So far as one can generalize from neurological case reports, the two parts of the writing system—the sound- and the meaning-correlated elements—are affected in different ways that are reasonable from what we know about the localization of language functions in the brain.

Are there differences in how efficiently ideographic or syllabic or combined writing can be read compared to alphabetic systems? A Chinese ideogram may translate to a word or a phrase in English. A syllabic sign corresponds to a larger phonological unit than a letter. Martin (1972) has the impression, apparently shared by other Japanese experts, "that the same content takes up less space in printed Japanese than it does in English" (p. 101). Further, does the combined Japanese writing using an amalgam of meaning and sound correspondences present problems compared, for example, to syllabic-phonological writing alone? Reading efficiency usually has been measured by speed of reading or by patterns of eye movements. The research has been done with adult, skilled readers.

Combined kanji and hiragana is reported to be easier to read than the syllabary alone, presumably because the ideographs serve to create salient graphic units in the text. They are the clues for dividing the text into word or meaning units, since Japanese is written without interword spaces.

The question may be raised as to why the Japanese use the Kanji-Hiragana combination in spite of the fact that they could communicate with Hiragana only—it is a simpler writing system. The answer is that this combination can be read more quickly and more accurately. Takahiko Sakamoto photographed the eye movements of college students when they were reading short sentences of identical meaning but written in one condition all in Hiragana only and in the other condition in the Kanji-Hiragana combination. The reading of the all-Hiragana sentences required twice as much time as the other. Also, in the case of the all-Hiragana sentences, a shorter perception span, more frequent fixations, longer fixation pauses, and more regressions were recorded in comparison with the Kanji-Hiragana combination. (Sakamoto and Makita, 1973, p. 443)

Clark (1972, unpublished paper) measured the eye-voice span in reading Japanese written as a combination of kanji and katakana or katakana alone. Her subjects were advanced students of Japanese whose native language was English. The eye-voice span technique will be described in detail in Chapter 10. Basically, it is a measure of unitizing in reading based on the number of words that the eye is ahead of the voice when reading aloud (cf. Buswell, 1920; Schlesinger, 1968; Levin and Kaplan, 1970). Clark's hypothesis was that since more information per graphic character existed in the normal, mixed writing form, the span should be longer for that method of writing. In fact, the eye-voice span was the same for the various writing systems whether measured by the number of words or by the number of graphic characters. She found, as have other researchers using this technique with alphabetic writing, that meaningful texts yielded longer spans than did unconnected word lists. It would be interesting to have the results of this technique with native speaker-readers of Japanese.

Shen (1927) compared the reading rates of Chinese and American students enrolled in an American university. The Chinese read about six Chinese words per second, Americans, five English words per second. Reading rate seems to be determined by units signaling the meaning (words in this case) rather than by the graphic nature of the print. This finding fits well with Clark's results. Also, Shen found that the fixations of the eyes were closer together in reading Chinese than in English. The graphic layout of Chinese—more squat characters, taking up about two lines compared to English, which is more spread out horizontally—likely accounts for this finding.

In general, though the evidence is meager, there are few aspects of reading which can be attributed to the graphic characteristics of writing systems. This speculation echoes Gray's (1956) conclusions from his cross-national study of reading for UNESCO. He found reading skills to be remarkably similar regardless of the language being read. These findings do not mean that the process of reading is not influenced by the nature of the writing system, but that the outcomes are alike. It seems reasonable that different writing systems which relate to language at different levels will involve attention to and abstraction of different aspects of the orthographic system. Readers of a syllabary must search for invariances at one level, readers of an alphabetic system, at another level. But the skilled readers of one system are able to read as efficiently as skilled readers of another. Evidence for this conclusion is discussed in Part III.

Design Characteristics of Writing

In looking at an encyclopedia's illustration of scripts of many different languages there was no doubt that they were all examples of writing in spite of the obvious differences of Roman compared to Arabic scripts, for example. What are the graphic characteristics of writing compared to line drawings, to take one basis for comparison, that give the impression of similarity? We will present evidence in Chapter 8 that even children who have not yet learned to read are able to discriminate writing from pictures.

The design characteristics of writing systems are tentative. With the vast number of scripts as well as those that existed historically but are no longer used, an exception can be found to any characteristic. Taken as a set, though, these characteristics describe writing and, what is more important, distinguish writing from drawing or painting. They characterize writing at the *graphic level* only and should be considered to describe the graphic display without considering the relationships of the graphs to sound or to other characteristics of the spoken language.

1. Writing is formed by tracings on a surface. These tracings may add to the surface, like ink or dye, or like a chisel, can carve out a tracing. Taken alone, this feature obviously does not distinguish between writing and drawing.

2. Writing is rectilinear. It is composed of lines of print which are parallel to each other. The parallel lines may be vertical (Chinese) or horizontal. There are historical instances of curved lines; e.g., the Phaistos disk (Gelb,

1952, pp. 156–157). Writing on statues or engravings which is not rectilinear but follows the contours of the surface does not preclude rectilinearity, but may be thought of as a decorative or artistic variant.

3. Writing is unidirectional. Current writing systems are predominantly left to right, less frequently right to left, and only occasionally top to bottom. The starting point for each line is fixed. It is true that the extinct Greek boustrophedon was read on alternate lines from left to right and from right to left.

4. Writing has a fixed orientation. The elements of the writing system cannot be transformed relative to each other. For example the letters AB retain their orientations wherever they appear in the text, so that a variation like Aᗺ does not occur.

5. Writing is patterned. That is, a small inventory of basic units can be combined to form a practically infinite number of graphic patterns. Graphic distinctive features—vertical, horizonatal, diagonal, curved, open-closed—combine to form letters which in turn form clusters, syllables, words, phrases, sentences, paragraphs, etc.

6. Writing has gaps (or spaces) in the graphic display. These gaps mark graphic units. We advance as a hypothesis, which may turn out to be limited to the Roman alphabet, that the size of the gap is related to the size of the unit. The smallest gaps separate letters, larger ones, words; then sentences, and largest are paragraphs, which involve a gap at the end of a line and an indentation at the beginning of the succeeding line. Gaps mark syllables as units in syllabary writing schemes but not in alphabetic ones, though we do have the convention that when words must be separated, as at the ends of lines, the gap occurs at the syllable boundary.

Graphic units may be marked in other ways than by spaces. Hebrew, Arabic, and German have letter forms which occupy terminal positions in words; another form of the letter is used in initial and medial positions. An interesting writing system is Devanagari, used in India. The letters appear to hang from a horizontal line whose length defines the length of the word so both the line and the spaces mark word boundaries.

7. Written units are roughly equal in size. Different letters occupy about the same area and words are more or less similar in size. This makes writing appear regular with more or less equal black and white spaces. The quality is staccato. Even Chinese logographic writing is designed to occupy an ideal square regardless of the number of elements in the character complex. This means that the constituent characters are proportionately sized

so that the total characters occupy equal spaces, regardless of their internal complexity.

8. Writing has various forms that are not usually mixed. A text may be handwritten, typed, printed, cursive, capitals and lowercase, etc. Not all writing systems have the same variations. Styles are mixed only for conventional reasons, as capitals at the beginnings of sentences.

A comic-strip device involves the violation of the last design characteristic of writing as well as several earlier ones.

Л Ǝ ∧ d

The message we get is that the writer is either a child learning to write or a semiliterate adult. Notice that this graphic display violates design characteristics numbers 4, 7, and 8.

It is possible to lay out an inventory of characteristics which taken together discriminate writing from all other graphic displays. Even simple line drawings involve so many features in rich and complex combinations that a feature analysis, though feasible, is very difficult. Why should this be? Compared to other graphic products, writing was a deliberate invention. The designers of writing set out to create efficient systems. These systems have evolved over 5,000 years to be even more efficient so that there has obviously been a historical convergence on a limited set of graphic features that are the universal attributes of writing.

Anthropologists, linguists, and missionaries designed writing systems for nonliterate groups, especially for American Indian languages in the nineteenth century. The specifications for these writing systems usually combined graphic with phonological and morphological characteristics of the language being written.

An interesting writing system which fits none of the standard classifications was invented early in this century by Silas John, an Apache shaman (Basso and Anderson, 1973). The system contains symbols, some of which can stand alone and others of which can enter into compounds. Each symbol corresponds "to a single line of prayer which may consist of a word, a phrase, or one or more sentences" (p. 1015). Some symbols may give directions for nonverbal ritual actions as well as words for the prayers. Silas John's invention is clearly a memory aid, since it clues the small number of specialists to speak and act out the religious rituals in a precise, undeviating fashion. This Apache script may be classified as phonetic-semantic, since the reader renders each character into memorized Apache speech.

Venezky (1970c), for example, believes that orthographies should facilitate:

1. Discrimination of letters and linking them to sounds.
2. Pronunciation of words, either in isolation or in phrases or sentences.
3. Reading aloud connected discourse.
4. Acquisition of a sight vocabulary—high frequency function words.
5. Silent reading for comprehension.

These demands on an orthography can be solved in various ways. From the point of view of the graphic nature of writing, the units (letters, syllabic items, or logograms) should be easily discriminable from one another. Graphic units could be more discriminable at the expense of adding distinctive features to the basic array. In fact, Moorhouse (1953, p. 151) reports that at one point Arabic writing became so cursive and ornamental that it was difficult to discriminate among letters. Arabic then added diacritics and other marks to distinguish letters.

The Effects of Graphic Characteristics on Reading

Size of Type

In this section we shall survey briefly how factors such as type faces, interlinear spacing, direction of the writing (left-to-right vs. right-to-left; vertical vs. horizontal) influence reading. Also, we will look at the research on the most informative parts of the printed text.

The printer's measure for size of type is the *point*, as in 8-point or 14-point type. A point is roughly equal to 1/72 inch, measured vertically. Line length is measured in *picas*, about 1/6 inch, so that a 30-pica line is about five inches. *Leading* is the space between lines, so that two-point leading is 2/72 of an inch (Tinker, 1965).

Tinker and his coworkers carried out an elaborate research program to investigate the influence of such physical characteristics of the text on legibility. The most common method for measuring legibility was speed of reading. The subject was given a set of paragraphs in which one word spoils the meaning. He was to cross out that word. For skilled readers, the accuracy was almost 100%, so there is no question that the subject was reading for meaning rather than running his eyes over the text. The score was the number of paragraphs read during a fixed time—usually a brief period of $1\frac{1}{2}$ to $1\frac{3}{4}$ minutes.

Lowercase texts are more legible than texts printed all in capitals. Tinker attributes this finding to the variety of word shapes that ascending and descending lowercase letters create compared to the regular, rectangular outlines of block capitals. The evidence for this hypothesis will be taken up in Chapter 7.

Eleven-point type is most legible as measured by speed of reading and by patterns of eye movements. "To obtain satisfactory legibility the printer of materials for adult reading may employ 9, 10, 11, or 12 point type, provided he employs an optimal line width and leading" (Tinker, 1965, p. 141). Optimal leading is two points, with which line widths from 14 to 31 picas are equally legible.

For children, factors like size of type, length of line, and space between lines do not seem to be clearly implicated in ease of reading. In an extensive study by McNamara, Paterson, and Tinker (1953), type sizes over the range of 8 to 24 points had no effects in the first and lower second grades; in the upper second, 14-point had a slight advantage; in the third grade there was also a small advantage for 14-point, although 10- and 12-point were almost equally good. Likewise, line length or leading showed no consistent results.

Apparently, for young children who are reading slowly with a great deal of attention to the details of the text, physical features of the textual display are only peripherally important. Adults whose reading is practiced and automatic do find certain type sizes and layouts easier to read.

Horizontal vs. Vertical
Chinese and Japanese print texts from top to bottom and from right to left. Even these vertical arrangements are in transition. Writing reforms in both China and Japan are advocating horizontal, left-to-right printing. Sakamoto (1961) reported that eye movements for meaningless patterns are smoother for horizontal than for vertical arrangements. However, on real text, Japanese readers moved their eyes more efficiently along vertical lines of print, obviously indicating that readers do best what they are accustomed to.

Research by the Japanese Language Research Institute (cited by Martin, 1972) found that in horizontal printing, horizontal rectangular characters are easiest to read, followed by squares, and vertical rectangular characters are most difficult. Word-separated printing is read most efficiently, but it is not clear whether these results compare vertical with horizontal printing or whether the comparisons are among arrangements in the horizontal format.

Left-to-Right vs. Right-to-Left

Semitic languages are written right to left; most others are written in the opposite direction. There is no reason to believe that one direction is more "natural" than another. Feitelson (1966) raises this question and reports that research at the Hebrew University showed that one direction is as easily acquired as another, presumably for the first language that the person is learning to read.

If the direction of writing has little to do with initial acquisition, directional reading habits do affect the recognition of textual materials. In a study which was the first of a large body of research that is now difficult to summarize in any simple fashion, Miskin and Forgays (1952) presented English words and Yiddish words (written right to left) at very brief durations of exposure to one or another side of a central fixation point. The study was extended by Orbach (1953). English recognition was superior if the material was to the right of the fixation point; Yiddish, if it was to the left. These results are presumably explained by the scanning habits which have developed from reading these languages and are attributable to the direction in which these languages are written. Since the exposures were too brief for actual scanning, it is more reasonable to assume that the writing systems led to habitual attention patterns in the readers.

Other Characteristics of Type

In English, the first, leftmost, parts of words carry more graphic information than the final parts. The following example is taken from Huey (pp. 97–98):

f	is	es	ɔt	eal	o	ɔu
I	th	do	nc	app	t	yc

A final point about the graphic characteristics of texts. If the text is mutilated so that only the top half or the bottom half is visible, it is reasonably easy to read the top and very difficult to read the bottom (see Figure 6-3). The preponderance of distinctive features exist in the tops of the letters. According to Huey (1908), Javal decided that the reader's eyes move along a line between the middle and the top of the line of print.

Everybody knows the story of Mary and her little lamb; but not every one knows that Mary E. Sawyer, who was born in Worcester county, was the heroine of the poem.

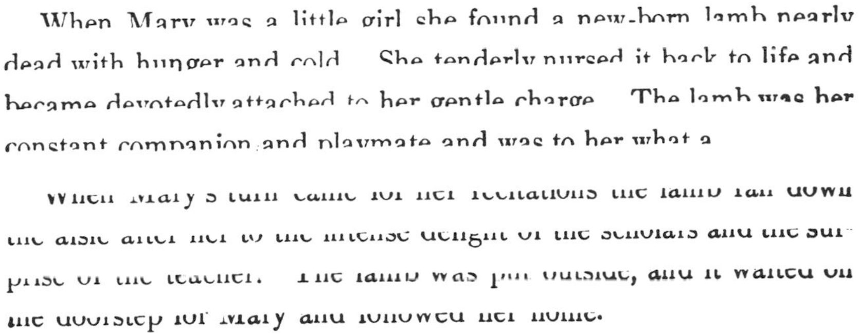

When Mary was a little girl she found a new-born lamb nearly dead with hunger and cold. She tenderly nursed it back to life and became devotedly attached to her gentle charge. The lamb was her constant companion and playmate and was to her what a

When Mary's turn came for her recitations the lamb ran down the aisle after her to the intense delight of the scholars and the surprise of the teacher. The lamb was put outside, and it waited on the doorstep for Mary and followed her home.

Figure 6-3. A comparison of text mutilated by removal of top or bottom halves of letters. From Huey, 1908, p. 99.

However, this may evolve as a strategy to take advantage of the distinctive features of print rather than creating the locus of the distinctive features.

What Writing Can Do that Speech Cannot

Compared to the richness of speech, writing is a meager system. A speaker uses stress, pitch, rate, pauses, voice qualities, and a host of other sound patterns not even vaguely defined to communicate a message as well as attitudes and feelings about what he is saying. Writing can barely achieve such a repertoire. We use "quotes" for sarcasm and underlining for emphasis, which in effect exhausts the written conventions for emotion. Stress patterns disambiguate utterances that sound alike, though notice in the first example that the graphic convention of capitalizing makes the references clear: White House vs. white house.

There are some occasions when writing can communicate information that speech cannot. Foremost are *homophones*, words that sound alike but are spelled differently. It is commonly reported that Japanese speakers, because the language has a large number of homophones, write characters in the air to make themselves clear to each other.

Consider the homophones *principle* and *principal*. In isolated speech, the two words are indiscriminable, although in conversation one assumes that the context would keep their separate meanings clear. When the words are written, there is no problem about the different meanings of the two words. In a loose sense, the terminal *le* and *al* function as ideographic rather than phonological elements which correspond to the meanings rather than to the sounds of the words (Carroll, 1972b).

One of the most famous sentences in the psychological literature is Lashley's (1951) "Rapid righting with his uninjured hand saved from loss the contents of the capsized canoe." The ambiguity that Lashley wanted to illustrate exists only in speech, not in writing.

Bolinger (1946) calls meaning units that are specific to writing "visual morphemes." He describes several classes. Iconic signs or conventionalized figures are used as international traffic markers. The horizontal diameter in a circle to mean Do Not Enter has a vaguely universal symbolic quality. A car on two wheels trailing skid marks seems to represent a slippery road directly, at least to a driver.

Other examples of spellings rather than drawings appear to take on their visual morphemic character from connotations that go with spelling patterns. For example, the *or* suffix is a visual morpheme of prestige: *advisor, realtor, expeditor,* as are the prestige spellings *Bettye, Murphee, Alyce, Smythe,* etc. (Bolinger, 1946, p. 336).

Orthographic Rules of English

Glurck is not an English word, but it could be. It looks like a word and can be readily pronounced. *Ckurlg* is not an English word and could never be one. It contains sequences of letters that do not occur in English, and though it can be pronounced with difficulty, few readers would provide the same sequences of sound. In both speech and writing, the concatenation of sounds and of graphic units is not random. English, like every other language, has permissible or legal sequences. Czech seems, to the English speaker, to be full of tongue-twisting consonant clusters: *strc, prst, skrz, krk.* Italian seems "liquid" perhaps because of the frequency of vowels and vowel sounds: *amore, bella, stanza.* The permissible sound structure of a language is analyzed into *phonological rules.* Children as young as four years are able to discriminate English from non-English phonology (Messer, 1967). The nature of these rules behaves like a higher-order invariant in the language. We are able to recognize when passers-by are speaking English or another language without understanding anything that they are saying.

Likewise, in writing, *orthographic rules* govern what sequence of letters and groups of letters may be put together to form words. Everyone knows that the letter *q* is followed by *u* and that the cluster of the two letters is pronounced /kw/. The cluster *km* is not permitted, unless it crosses a morpheme boundary: *milkmaid*. A few consonant clusters may appear at both the beginnings and ends of words: *sk—skunk, risk*; *sh—shop, rush*. In far more cases, a consonant cluster is restricted to the beginnings or endings of words: *tr, bl, ck, ng, rt*, etc. In this section we will describe the orthographic rule system of English and several ways to conceptualize this system. How readers use and acquire orthographic rules is discussed in Chapters 7 and 9.

In English orthography there are two separable issues which are often confused. The first is the orthographic rule system: the legal letter sequences. The second is the relationships or correspondences between these written sequences and the spoken language. One often hears that English letter-to-sound correspondences are "chaotic." We can cite the anguish of educators and spelling reformers to show that almost all letters in English have various pronunciations and that sounds can be spelled in various ways. We will describe the analyses of the correspondences to show that the systems are related in complex (though not chaotic) ways, depending on the units and the levels of analysis.

Old English, we are told, had a regular letter-to-phoneme correspondence system (Francis, 1965). The spoken language changed in many ways while writing adapted to these changes slowly, if at all. There were massive infusions of French, Latin, and Greek to the Germanic base of English so that the modern English lexicon is less than fifty percent Germanic. The writing system, in a sense deliberately, abandoned regular spelling-to-sound correspondences to indicate the differences in the meanings of homophones: *principal* vs. *principle*. Spellings showed the origins of words: *cord* to mean a piece of string; *chord* to show the Greek etymology of the word and its meaning in geometry. Printing essentially froze the writing system even though the spoken language has changed and continues to change. Deliberate attempts to "reform" English spelling have been unsuccessful, leaving aside for the moment the question of whether such reforms are sensible (see pp. 183–186).

Alphabetic writing systems vary in the directness and simplicity of their correspondence to spoken language. Gaelic is more complicated than English. Finnish is simple and direct. Spanish and Italian fall in between though closer to the one-to-one end of the scale, if one developed a ranking across the world's languages. Does the nature of the correspondence make any difference? It seems reasonable that the nature of the match will influence early teaching (see Chapter 9). From what evidence we have about learning to read languages other than English, children learn early to decode languages that closely match sound to writing (Elkonin, 1963; Feitelson, 1966; Mikita, 1968; Venezky, 1972b). After instruction begins these children are able to decode, that is, to read aloud words or any sequence of letters that follow the orthographic rules of their language. One of the authors had the experience in Italy of informally testing first-grade children some three months after they had started to learn to read. The children could read aloud any pseudoword which followed Italian orthographic rules.

However, this early advantage in learning to decode does not guarantee later proficiency in reading. By about the fourth grade, regardless of a language's correspondence system, children vary in reading ability. The reasons for this will be discussed later when we take up the changes from early to skilled reading (Chapter 10).

The inclination to search for a point-to-point correspondence between written and spoken English has frustrated these searchers. Hall (1961) documents the perverseness of English by listing the many spellings that sounds may have. Bloomfield (1942) asked educators to pretend that the correspondence system was regular and simple by selecting for early instruction only cases of words which maintain simple, regular correspondences. The most popular spelling reform, ITA, increased the size of the alphabet to reduce what these researchers believed to be chaos.

Some Facts of English Orthography

Several investigators have done the unglamorous but useful job of counting and describing some characteristics of English orthography. Even unadorned frequencies point to parameters that any description of orthographic rules must account for. A manual was prepared by Zettersten (1969), who analyzed different types of English prose. The main findings are summarized in Table 6-1. Since only the most frequent clusters in text were counted, many permissible clusters are not included in the table.

Four of the five most frequent letters are vowels. In fact, for sample after sample of running text, there are almost precisely 6.5 vowel letters for every 10 consonants (Zettersten, p. 47). Taken with the fact that there

Table 6-1   Rank Orders (Frequency) of Letters and Consonant Clusters in Word-Initial and Word-Final Positions

Rank	Letters	Initial	Final
1	E	TH	N
2	T	H	S
3	A	W	R
4	O	T	D
5	I	B	T
6	N	M	F
7	S	S	ND
8	R	C	NG
9	H	F	L
10	L	D	M
11	D	R	NT
12	C	L	LL
13	U	P	ST
14	M	N	TH
15	F	WH	RS
16	P	PR	W
17	G	G	LD
18	W	ST	NS
19	Y	SH	CH
20	B	FR	SS
21	V	V	P
22	K	CH	C
23	X	J	TS
24	J	TR	GHT
25	Q	GR	RD
26	Z	PL	CK
27		BR	RT
28		CL	NTS
29		SK	CT
30		K	WN

Source: Zettersten, 1969, pp. 21, 24, 26.

are about four times as many consonants as vowels in the alphabet, the orthographic pattern of vowels and consonants may be anticipated to be mutually constraining.

English words, on the whole, are more likely to start with single consonants than with consonant clusters; they more usually terminate with clusters. Individual consonants are as likely to be in final as in initial positions. Quite a different picture obtains when consonant *clusters* are compared. The clusters *th*, *st*, and *ch* appear in either position. But most initial consonant clusters do not appear in final position, and vice versa. Even this superficial description of orthography suggests that orthographic rules must take into account the sequence of vowels and consonants and the position in the word occupied by the letter or cluster.

Whorf's Formula for the English Monosyllable

Benjamin Lee Whorf, most famous for his writings on linguistic relativity, developed the formula for the English spoken monosyllable as an example of the precision with which linguistic rules can be formulated (1956, pp. 220 ff). Although the formula is designed to show the phonological rules which govern the monosyllables, both in its general form and in many details it is applicable to orthographic rules. The changes are slight. For example, the phonemic /kw/ is written *qu*, or the terminal /a/ may be written *aw*.

Every English syllable contains at least one vowel. Words may begin with a vowel. Also, words may begin with any single consonant, except the sound that is spelled *ng*. As we saw above, this digraph spelling of the phoneme is common at the ends of words: *sing, lung, bang, tang*, etc. Words may also end with vowels. In fact, all vowel spellings except *u* may appear in the final position of monosyllables: *ma, me, to, hi*. The word may end in any single consonant except *h* or *q*. Finally, the clusters which frequently end words are constrained so that *l* may be joined by *b, m, f; s* with *p, k*, and *t*, etc.

This discussion of Whorf's formula for the English monosyllable is deliberately a condensed summary. The model permits one to go from left to right to generate any and all permissible monosyllables around the vocalic nucleus. Many monosyllables devised by following the formula do not occur in English. But they all are potentially legal words since the formula is a guide to English phonological and (with appropriate transformations) orthographic rules. These rules govern the constraints or the conditional redundancies in English spelling.

The syllable, then, is a higher-order unit that regulates the nature of its constituent parts, that is, letters and letter clusters. Further, a syllable boundary may also be a morpheme boundary although morphemes may be polysyllabic. There has been surprisingly little linguistic analysis of the syllable (Clare, 1969). Whorf's rules for the formation of English syllables may be concatenated to form polysyllabic and polymorphemic words. Orthographically and phonologically, the syllable is constructed around a vocalic nucleus, and the orthographic rule system specifies the nature of the consonants and consonant clusters that may precede or succeed the vowel, including a rule that in some cases there may be no consonants before or after the vowel.

There is little research on orthographic boundaries at the levels of clusters, syllables, or morphemes. Relevant and applicable research has come from phonology, however. MacKay (1972) analyzed corpuses of German and English synonymic intrusions. These are errors in speech when a speaker inadvertently combines two words or phrases having roughly the same meaning. For example, "Don't shell" is a synonymic intrusion of "don't shout" and "don't yell" (Hockett, 1967). Inspection of the points at which the breaks occur can tell us about the unitary character of clusters, of syllables, and of morphemes.

Breaks rarely occur within consonant clusters. Breaks do occur more often than expected by chance at the syllable boundaries. Excluding consonant clusters, when breaks occurred within the syllable, they most often preceded the vowel, so that the group was V + C or V + CC. Further, morphological boundaries had a strong effect. For those morphemes which were composed of more than one syllable, the intrusions were inspected to see whether the breaks occurred at the morpheme boundary or at the syllable boundaries which were intramorphemic. Breaks tended to fall at the morpheme boundaries. Further, in affixed words showing morphological breaks, the majority of the intrusions split after the prefix rather than before the suffix of the word.

As least for phonology, and there is no reason not to extend the findings to orthography, the hierarchy of units appears to be consonant clusters → syllables → morphemes.

Orthographically, words are letter strings bound by spaces. There is ample evidence (discussed in Chapter 4) that young children sometimes are unaware of word boundaries in both their production and reception of speech. Even adults do not recognize junctures between words when they are ambiguous. Consider the following pairs:

more ice / more rice
great ape / gray tape
grade *A* / gray day

The preponderance of errors occurs when the first word ends in a consonant and the second begins with a vowel. "To plague Ames" had about six times as many errors of recognition as "to play games" (O'Connor and Tooley, 1964). The speaker probably becomes more acute about words as units *after* he becomes literate.

Venezky's Analysis of Spelling-to-Sound Correspondences
Venezky's (1967, 1970a, 1970b) purpose in analyzing a large, 20,000-word corpus was to extract empirically the correspondences between spelling and sound. It is obvious that single letter-to-phoneme relationships do not take us very far in English, although many individual initial consonants do relate simply and regularly to sound. Since there are more than twenty-six graphic units, Venezky first had to define the functional spelling units before the next step of mapping the spelling units to sound. Some clusters are obviously important: *th, ch, oo*. Others are intuitively less significant: *tch, ck*, and *dg*, for example. Further, Venezky needed a procedure for handling that mainstay of teacher's rules, the final, silent *e*, as in *rove*. Several solutions are possilbe: the unit is the discontinuous *o . . . e*, or it is part of the unit *ve*, or it is a unit by itself. Venezky anticipates a solution when he points out that it is too simple to label the final *b* in *bomb* as silent, since in certain morphological forms it is not—*bombard* and *bombardier*— though *b* is silent before suffixes—*bombing, bombs, bombed*. The inductive rule, at this point, is that *b* is silent in word-terminal positions and before certain suffixes.

Venezky's major inference from his analysis is that "spelling [graphemic] units are not related directly to sound, but to an intermediate (morphophonemic) level first and then to sound" (p. 84). Gillooly (1971) diagrams Venezky's model in this way (pp. 7–27):

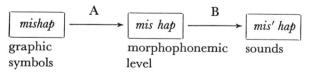

graphic symbols   morphophonemic level   sounds

The correspondence which is truly implicated in reading is A, from the graphic display to the morphophonemic level. Correspondence B from the morphophonemic level to sound is an automatic ability of speakers of the language. Phonological rather than orthographic rules are implicated in B; the converse is true for A. That is, the reader must make the judgment that *sh* does not form a cluster in *mishap* because the two letters are separated by a morpheme boundary and so have their independent values (compared to *ship* or *smash,* for instance).

Venezky calls graphic units which predict sound *functional units,* of which there are two classes, *relational units* and *markers. Ch* is a relational unit because its morphophoneme /č/ is not predictable from *c* and *h*. Markers are usually letters which map to zero morphophonemes, that is, that are not themselves pronounced but indicate the pronunciation of other letters. Most common is the final e: *mate, base,* etc. However, the *i* in *city* can be thought of as a marker since it marks the sound value of *c* as /s/.

An analysis of orthography has two parts: the abstraction of the important graphic units and their interrelationships, and the correspondences between the graphic units and sound, that is, the way that graphic units are pronounced. Venezky lists the following factors as conditioning the correspondence between spelling and sound:

1. Graphemic environment of the unit. The unit *c* corresponds to /s/ before *e, i,* or *y* plus a consonant or juncture.

2. Position in the word. Initial *gh,* as in *ghost, gherkin, ghoul,* corresponds to /g/.

3. Stress. Intervocalic *x* may be pronounced /ks/ or /gz/ depending on the main stress in the word: *axiom, exercise* vs. *examine, exist.*

4. Morpheme boundaries. For, example, *mishap* vs. *ship; phase* vs. *shepherd.* This influence on pronunciation is probably the most important, since the sound correspondence of clusters holds only within morphemes and within syllables. The reader must make the decision that the cluster either does or does not straddle a morphemic or syllabic boundary before he can arrive at the appropriate pronunciation. Usually, the pronunciation across the boundary involves the sound values of each of the letters forming the cluster.

5. Form class. A knowledge of both morpheme identity and part of speech is necessary for the pronunciation of *ate* at the ends of words. In adjectives and nouns, this letter group is pronounced as in *duplicate, frigate, syndicate;* in verbs, the same letters take the following form: *deflate, duplicate, integrate.*

6. Phonological influences. Certain sound sequences are not allowed in English. When a string of disallowed phonemes is signaled by the spelling, one or another of the sounds must be dropped. For example, /bp/ and /pb/ do not occur as adjacent sounds in English words, so that words like *subpoena* and *clapboard* retain the pronunciation of only the second consonant.

Chomsky and Lexical Representation

A more recent approach is exemplified by Chomsky. Flying in the face of years of apparent consensus, he argued that English orthography is near optimal for writing the English language (Chomsky, 1970). This point of view is so dramatic that it deserves careful attention. Francis (1970) introduces the new analysis of orthographic rules this way:

> . . . the three writers represented here [Chomsky, Reed, and Venezky] start from the premise that writing is systematic in its own right and that standard orthographies are not phonemic transcriptions *manqué* but representations of linguistic structures at a somewhat deeper level, bearing a rather complicated relationship to any given acoustic-auditory phenomenon, which must in turn be considered merely an alternative representation of the same underlying structure. (pp. 44–45)

It will be recalled that in Chapter 4 we described the transformational analysis of a sentence in the following way. A deep structure representation of the sentence is postulated, to which is applied transformational rules whose outcome is the surface structure of the sentence. Finally, phonological rules bring the sentence to its palpable, auditory form. To understand Chomsky's analysis of orthography requires that this model be somewhat expanded. At the surface structure level, decisions about the specific words, or lexical items, are made. It is at this stage that the grammatical skeleton is fleshed out with meaning-bearing elements or words of the sentence. So far as meaning is concerned, Chomsky is called a "lexicalist," since the focus of semantics, in his theory, involves the choice of words that have meaning in the framework or context of the sentence's grammatical form. His theory of lexical choice, which applies equally to written or spoken language, led him to believe that English orthography is near optimal.

Chomsky postulates an abstract form, the *lexical representation* of the word, at a point between the surface structure and the phonological end point of the sentence. Lexical representations are abstract in the sense that the speaker-reader is aware of them only intuitively, but their criterion as a construct makes clear certain aspects of word choice and the similarities among words. Further, since lexical representations are selected after the surface structure, the grammatical forms of the word are specified; that is, the speaker knows that the word is a noun, *courage*, not its adjectival form, *courageous*.

Lexical representations contain only that information not predictable from the surface structure or the phonological rules of the language. Although the phonological rules are complex (cf. Chomsky and Halle, 1968) they are perfectly automatic to the mature language user.

Thus the lexical representation of the common item of *histor-y, histor-ical, histor-ian*, or *anxi-ous, anxi-ety*, or of *courage, courage-ous*, or of *tele-graph, tele-graph-ic, tele-graph-y*, and so on must be selected so as to contain just what is not predictable in the variant phonetic realizations of these items. (Chomsky, 1970, pp. 6–7)

The correspondence of letter to sound segment for the lexical representation is presumably very close. Further, the realization of the overt form from the lexical representation involves automatic rules such as the placement of stress. The advantages to the reader of the spelling-to-sound correspondences in the underlying forms are:

1. The semantic similarity of related words are preserved graphically; for example, *anxious* and *anxiety* appear alike to the reader, who can go directly from the appearance of the word to its meaning without attention to redundant phonetic information.

2. Lexical representations are resistant to change and persist over long historical periods.

3. Lexical representations are common to a wide range of dialects.

There is no necessary direct correspondence between the phonological and the orthographic rule systems when there can be mediation by the abstract lexical representations. The systems might be diagramed this way:

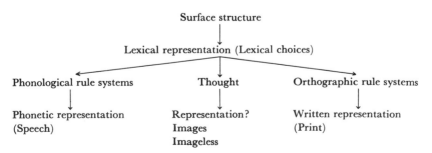

Reading aloud: conversion of print to lexical representation and lexical representation to phonetic.

Reading silently: conversion of print to lexical representation and lexical representation to thought.

Taking dictation: conversion of phonetic representation to lexical representation to written representation.

Chomsky's theory provides an important new perspective on the nature of orthography. It points out the possible futility of the attempts to discover useful sound-to-spelling correspondences at the surface level. The system is regular only by reference to a more abstract level where the spelling preserves the similarity of meanings among words whose sounds are varied. However, these phonological variations are rule governed and presumably automatically available to speakers of English. To build these phonological redundancies into the orthographic system would be inefficient and might actually distract from the skilled reader's ability to derive meaning directly from the text.

This view of orthography assumes a skilled speaker-reader of English who has had enough linguistic experience for the phonological rules to become automatic and has read enough to acquire intuitions about an underlying representation of the orthographic system. Chomsky says, "The sound system that corresponds to orthography may be a late intellectual product" (1970, p. 17). The implications for teaching reading consequently are not apparent. One suggestion by C. Chomsky (1970) is that vocabulary enrichment might provide the appropriate background for readers to take advantage of the abstract basis of English orthography.

Comparison of Chomsky and Venezky

There is a superficial similarity in the analysis of orthography by the two investigators Chomsky and Venezky. Both posit an underlying, more abstract level of words in order to read them. They differ, however, in what they mean by reading, so that the underlying level has different purposes in their models. Chomsky's lexical representation gives the reader direct access to the meaning of the word. Pronunciation of the word is trivial. Given the speaker's automatic control of his language, he can go from the lexical representation to saying the word.

Venezky, by comparison, wanted to build an efficient system for predicting from spelling to sound. His approach was nontheoretical and empirical. The orthographic units were determined on the basis of frequency, with the observation that to ignore clusters and insist on single letters as units would not take advantage of the patterns in the data. To take the next step, the mapping of the sound values to the graphic units, Venezky found it useful to take advantage of the morphophonemics of English. This is not an abstract representation of words, but a level which provides information about the internal structure of the word, namely, its morphemic (and therefore syllabic) boundaries.

Chomsky assumed this information about the morphology and form class membership of the word since the lexical representation occurs between the surface structure of the sentence and sound, at the stage of lexical choice. Most important, both writers indicated that we need to know more about a word than its surface orthographic structure in order to pronounce it or to understand it.

Spelling Reform

As far back as the year 1200 there were attempts to renovate English spelling to bring it into closer correspondence with the spoken language (Zachrisson, 1931). There was a splurge of activity in the seventeenth century, and since the middle of the nineteenth century the activities of reformers, though hardly successful, have been continuous. George Bernard Shaw was probably the most famous advocate of English spelling reform. Figure 6-4 presents a page of his play, *Androcles and the Lion,* printed both in traditional orthography and in his version of the new English spelling. Recently, a transitional alphabet to be used in the early stages of learning to read, the ITA or initial teaching alphabet, was tested extensively in Great Britain and to a lesser extent in the United States. This alphabet is reproduced in Figure 6-5.

Spelling reform is based on the premise that single letter-to-sound correspondences would make it easier to read English. When they speak of reading, reformers inevitably mean pronunciation. Zachrisson's (1931, p. 3) comment is typical: ". . .it [English] has an orthography which is a disguise rather than a guide to the pronunciation." Since the alphabet has 26 letters and there are about 40 phonemes in the spoken language, the revised alphabets add letterlike forms or restrict letters and clusters to single, invariant pronunciations. We doubt that writing systems which bring English to a strict letter-to-phoneme correspondence would be useful, for the following reasons:

ANDROCLES AND THE LION

ANDROCLES [*scrambling up in the greatest agitation*] Oh, please dont say that. This is dreadful. You mean so kindly by me that it seems quite horrible to disoblige you. If you could arrange for me to sacrifice when theres nobody looking, I shouldnt mind. But I must go into the arena with the rest. My honor, you know.

THE EDITOR. Honor! The honor of a tailor?

ANDROCLES [*apologetically*] Well, perhaps honor is too strong an expression. Still, you know, I couldnt allow the tailors to get a bad name through me.

THE EDITOR. How much will you remember of all that when you smell the beast's breath and see his jaws opening to tear out your throat?

SPINTHO [*rising with a yell of terror*] I cant bear it. Wheres the altar? I'll sacrifice.

FERROVIUS. Dog of an apostate. Iscariot!

SPINTHO. I'll repent afterwards. I fully mean to die in the arena: I'll die a martyr and go to heaven; but not this time, not now, not until my nerves are better. Besides, I'm too young: I want to have just one more good time. [*The gladiators laugh at him*]. Oh, will no one tell me where the altar is? [*He dashes into the passage and vanishes*].

ANDROCLES [*to the Editor, pointing after Spintho*] Brother: I cant do that, not even to oblige you. Dont ask me.

Figure 6-4. A page from Shaw's *Androcles and the Lion* comparing traditional orthography and Shaw's reformed spelling. From George Bernard Shaw, *Androcles and the Lion*, pp. 90–91. The Society of Authors on behalf of the George Bernard Shaw Estate.

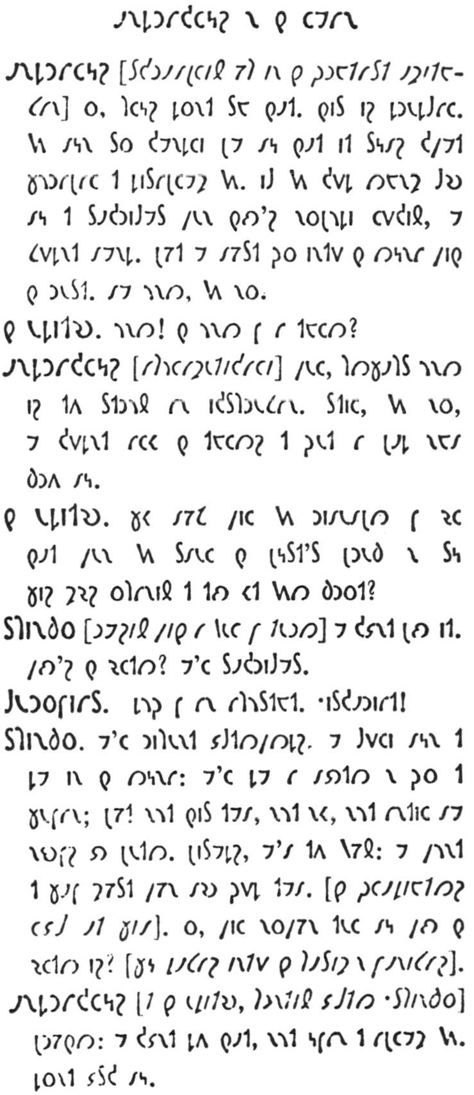

Figure 6-4 (cont.)

THE INITIAL TEACHING ALPHABET

Number	Character	Name	Example	Traditional spelling
1	æ	ae	ræt	rate
2	b	bee	big	big
3	c	kee	cat	cat
4	d	dee	dog	dog
5	ce	ee	meet	meet
6	f	ef	fill	fill
7	g	gae	gun	gun
8	h	hae	hat	hat
9	ie	ie	tie	tie
10	j	jae	jelly	jelly
11	k	kae	kit	kit
12	l	el	lamp	lamp
13	m	em	man	man
14	n	en	net	net
15	œ	oe	tœ	toe
16	p	pee	pig	pig
17	r	rae	run	run
18	s	ess	sad	sad
19	t	tee	tap	tap
20	ue	ue	due	due
21	v	vee	van	van
22	w	wae	will	will
23	y	i-ae	yell	yell
24	z	zed or zee	fizz	fizz
25	ʒ	zess	houses	houses
26	wh	whae	when	when
27	ch	chae	chick	chick
28	th	ith	thaut	thought
29	th	thee	the	the
30	ſh	ish	ſhip	ship
31	ʒ	zhee	meʒuer	measure
32	ŋ	ing	siŋ	sing
33	a	ah	far	far
34	au	au	autum	autumn
35	a	at	appl	apple
36	e	et	egg	egg
37	i	it	dip	dip
38	o	ot	hot	hot
39	u	ut	ugly	ugly
40	ω	oot	bωk	book
41	ꞷ	oo	mꞷn	moon
42	ou	ow	bou	bough
43	oi	oi	toi	toy

Figure 6-5. The initial teaching alphabet (ITA). From Downing, 1965, p. 71. Copyright © 1965 by Scott, Foresman and Co. Reprinted by permission of the author.

1. The principal basis for the efficient recognition of words is the intra-word conditional redundancies generated by orthographic rules (see Chapter 7). Phonetically precise spelling would remove these important clues to efficient word perception.
2. Current English spelling preserves the morphological similarity of words: *telegraph, telegrapher.* Reformed spelling does away with this more abstract representation of words.
3. Traditional orthography distinguishes the various meaning of homophones: *principal-principle, cord-chord.*
4. English spelling occasionally shows the etymology of words. For example, the *ph* spelling for /f/ indicates Greek origin: *philosophy, sphere.*

On balance, though reformed spelling may simplify the pronunciation of words, the cost would be high to skilled readers who get grammatical and semantic information about words from their orthographic forms. The reformers operate on the implicit but mistaken assumption that to read is to pronounce. For children learning to read, easy pronunciation may be helpful, but even then only during the initial phases of reading (see Chapter 9). Adults learning to read English as a second language report that the task is easy, probably because they are able to use the higher-order information provided by English orthography (Halle, 1969).

Summary

This chapter was concerned with the nature of writing. Writing systems came after picturing about 5,000 years ago and evolved in Asia Minor from logographic writing to syllabaries to true alphabets in Greece. Today most languages are written alphabetically, though logographic writing is still used in China and syllabaries in Japan. On the whole, the efficiency with which skilled readers can extract information from the type of text they have mastered is about equal for the various writing systems.

Eight design characteristics of writing were postualted which, taken together, distinguish writing from other tracings, like drawings or paintings. For example, writing is patterned, in that a small inventory of basic units can be combined to form a practically infinite number of graphic patterns. Other characteristics are that writing is unidirectional and written units are roughly equal in size.

Size of type and spaces between lines appear to make some difference in the efficiency with which adults read. These factors have little influence on children's reading. There are several occasions when writing is more informative than speech, especially in making clear the meanings of homophones, words that are pronounced alike but differ in spelling and meaning.

The major part of the chapter was concerned with English orthographic rules, that is, the systematic order of letters and letter clusters in words. A second and independent problem has to do with the correspondences between orthography and the spoken language. Some empirical information about the incidence of letters and clusters at the beginnings and ends of words was presented. Venezky, in an analysis of spelling-to-sound correspondences, found that reference to the morphophonemic level of English simplified the rules for pronouncing English written words. Chomsky postulates an abstract lexical representation of the word which contains information about a word not predictable from its grammatical form or from the automatic rules for its pronunciation. Chomsky argues that English orthography is optimal for reading since it maintains the meaning-bearing characteristics of the word.

Finally, a brief review of spelling reform indicated that a strict correspondence between single letters and phonemes may simplify pronunciation but may make it more difficult for skilled readers to extract meaning from text.

7
On the Perception of Words:
An Application of Some Basic Concepts

A word is a microcosm of human consciousness.

Vygotsky

Why Words?

A Classic Experiment

The body of research which this chapter will examine and try to interpret deals with the perception or recognition of single words, or parts of them. But we normally read text arranged in sentences and any single word is embedded in a context of other words. Can we learn anything, then, from research on the perception of a word? Classic experiments performed by Cattell in 1885 and 1886 convinced psychologists that we could. Cattell used a tachistoscope, a device for very fast exposure of a visual display, and found that with an exposure of 10 msec only three to four unconnected letters could be read, whereas two unconnected words could be read and as many as four connected short words. Even more impressive, perhaps, when single words were briefly exposed they were recognized as quickly as single letters, and in fact it took longer (measuring reaction time) to name letters than to name words. He concluded from these results that words are read as wholes, not letter by letter. These results have been confirmed many times, in 1898 by Erdman and Dodge, who also showed that the eye movements in reading are quick jumps (saccades) from one fixation to the next and that the information is extracted almost, if not entirely, during the fixation. This seemed to many psychologists to tell us something so important about how we read that experiments on word recognition multiplied, their authors seeking to discover what it is that makes it possible to read a whole word (or even a phrase) as a unit. Cattell attributed the effect primarily to meaningfulness, but as it has turned out, many other factors may play a role in conferring on a word its apparent unity.

The validity of studies of single-word perception has often been queried, but it is an interesting body of research in its own right, and gives us some answers about the formation (or extraction) of higher-order units. The economy of reading in units at least as large as words is too obvious to need discussion. Furthermore, the word alone carries more burden of information in reading than it does in speech. Speech has many redundancies that are absent in reading. The speaker's intonation, facial expression, lip movements, and above all the environmental situation in which the speaker is communicating something to the listener carry so much meaning that single words can be omitted or not heard with little loss. There is redundancy in written text, however, of two kinds. There is interword redundancy given by the verbal context—meaning and syntactic relations of the same kind that are present in speech. But there is also intraword redundancy in the written word of a kind that is not available in speech. It has been estimated (Garner, 1962) that intraword redundancy is higher than contextual redundancy; that is, letters are more constrained and thus more predictable than words. Information about letter constraints reduces uncertainty and facilitates reading the word. These constraints—conditional rules about position of consonant clusters, number of vowels that can follow one another, etc.—were described in the previous chapter. The experiments on single-word perception presumably tell us a great deal about the role these rules play in reading.

One may ask, at this point, whether ability to read larger units tachistoscopically correlates with the development of reading skill, a different, but

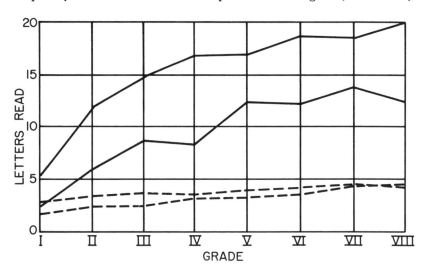

Figure 7-1.   The increase with age in number of letters read correctly with tachistoscopic presentation of unconnected consonants, nonsense syllables, unfamiliar words, and familiar words. Data from Hoffman, 1927; figure from Woodworth, 1938, p. 738.

very pertinent question. There is evidence that it does. Hoffmann (1927) measured the increase in tachistoscopic span for unconnected consonants, nonsense syllables, and unfamiliar and familiar words with advance in school grade, looking at pupils in the upper and lower quarters of academic ability. The number of letters read correctly was least for groups of consonants and greatest for familiar words (although there was little difference for the lowest group in first grade). From the first grade to the eighth there was a barely discernible rise in the span for randomly selected consonants, but there was a large increase for familiar words (see Figure 7-1). For the upper quarter of the pupils, the gain was from 5 to 20 letters in words during these years, and for the lower quarter from 3 to 12. The lower quarter never achieved the span reached by the upper quarter by the third grade. The rise in both cases is most rapid from first to third grades, a fact that coincides with other more recent findings in the experiments described below.

Recent work with patterned (legal) and nonpatterned nonsense words exposed tachistoscopically found that legal letter patterns were read with significantly more facilitation by good than by poor readers (Goldberg, personal communication).

Methods of Studying Word Perception

A majority of the studies of word perception and the factors that facilitate or hinder it have used the tachistoscope. But there are a number of possible methodological variations. Since they can make a vital difference in the results obtained, they must be described briefly. The tachistoscope itself can be used in various ways. It can be set for a fixed exposure time, with a fixed contrast between the target displayed and the background, and the subject's hits or errors simply counted. Or it can be set at an exposure time too fast for the subject to see anything but a blur, and then repeated exposures given with ascending duration until the subject's threshold is reached—the point where he can make an accurate report. Rather than a hit or error score, he is scored on the number of repetitions required or the duration of exposure required for correct recognition (Postman and Adis-Castro, 1957).

Another method of measuring a recognition threshold is to present the display with a fixed exposure duration, beginning with a very low brightness contrast between target and background and progressing by fixed steps to higher contrast until the subject reports the target word or letters correctly (Gibson, Bishop, Schiff, and Smith, 1964). Results are reported as number of steps required or as some measure of contrast at the threshold. A crude but still effective informal method of getting a threshold is to present the target at a distance too far for the subject to read it accurately, and then move it slowly towards him until he makes an accurate report. This method is obviously not very useful except for intraindividual comparisons.

Cattell (1886) used reaction time as well as tachistoscopic exposure and made some interesting discoveries by this method. How long it takes to read something involves not only the perceptual decision, however, but also the time for articulation, which can vary widely with aspects of the material that may not be of interest. Latency has been used successfully in several experiments (Rubenstein, Garfield, and Millikan, 1970; Rubenstein, Lewis, and Rubenstein, 1971a, 1971b) recently to make a decision that avoids the motor confounding. In these experiments, the subject was asked to observe a projected display of letters and to decide whether it was a word or not. If yes, he pressed one key; if not, he pressed another. The displays can be varied in interesting ways that reveal, by how long it takes to make the decision, some of the features that characterize "wordness." Latency measures can also be taken in a same-different classification task, varying aspects of the letter display (Barron and Pittenger, 1973).

A method with many variants involves detection of some feature within an exposed word or set of letters. Pillsbury (1897) presented tachistoscopically words containing misspellings or misprintings and noted what the subject read. The subjects seldom detected the errors at fast exposures and reported some word, allowing Pillsbury to infer some of the factors that affect word perception. Other experimenters have asked the subject to detect which letter was printed upside down, or whether a particular letter was present in the display or not (generally referred to as a "probe" technique). Detection of the presence of something, rather than identifying a word or group of letters, is quite a different task, and one cannot safely generalize conclusions from one to the other. A detection task, furthermore, seems intuitively less closely related to reading.

One other method, more closely allied to detection than to identification, should be mentioned. This is the method of scanning through a word list for a target (Neisser, 1964). The subject is given a target word or letter to search for. The target is embedded in a list of other words or alphanumeric characters of some sort. Time to locate the target can be related to features of the target, or features of the context in which it is embedded, or more particularly to the relations between the two. The experimenter can manipulate any of the features of the words or characters and look for those that facilitate or interfere with search. Again, one must be careful about generalizing to reading from this task, because it is not clear that the subject's decision depends on what is generally thought of as recognition. We shall return to this point later.

What Is a Word?

Words as Feature Complexes

If we are to present the array of facts about word recognition in a useful way, we must consider first what a word is. It is not just a "stimulus" or a "response," nor is it enough to call it a "verbal stimulus" or a "symbol." It is a composite of many things and can be described in many ways, all important. A word can be described graphically (see Chapter 6). In our writing system it is composed of letters, ranging from one to many, sequentially spaced from left to right with small spaces between letters and larger spaces at either end of the word. It can be described phonologically and can be analyzed into phonemic units which are combined sequentially according to a rule system characteristic of any given language. These rules are relevant for the topic of this chapter, for they are intraword redundancies that do not cross word boundaries. A word can be described orthographically (see Chapter 6). There are orthographic constraints peculiar to a language that constitute a rule system comparable (and often confused with) the phonological constraints. They are also intraword redundancies and do not cross word boundaries.

A word can also be described as a morpheme or a combination of morphemes—units of meaning. While meaning is given in additional ways, a word nevertheless conveys some meaning by itself. A word can finally be described as a unit of syntax. Linguistic analysis commonly begins with the sentence as a unit, but analysis reaches down to words, which can be described as parts of speech, that is, verbs, nouns, and so on, which may also possess inflections that provide morphological information.

These multiple descriptions of a word are all valid and important for us as students of the reading process. We see that a word possesses many kinds of information, features of the word itself, which may or may not be extracted in the perceptual process. To capture this notion, a word will be defined as a *complex of features*, a composite representation of five classes of information: graphic, phonological, orthographic, semantic, and syntactic. The notion of a word as a complex of features is not new (see Bower, 1967; Fillenbaum, 1969; Gibson, 1971; Katz and Fodor, 1963; Perfetti, 1972). The notion has most often included only lexical meaning or semantic features of words; however, we shall broaden it to include all the five classes of descriptors named.

Each class of features can be broken down further into subclasses. Semantic features can be subdivided in various ways, such as pleasant-unpleasant, animate-inanimate, concrete-abstract, mass-count, and into taxonomic categories which can be arranged hierarchically with subordinate-superordinate relationships (e.g., apple → fruit → vegetable → edible). Full recognition of a word depends on extraction of all of these kinds of information. It should be emphasized again that they are features of the word itself, whether they are extracted by the perceiver or not. The fact that there is similarity of features within a class that may give rise to confusion errors in an experimental setup is a witness to the objectivity of this information. Errors due to graphic similarities, phonological similarities, and so on all occur in predictable ways. But there are other kinds of error in experiments on word recognition that are not due to features of the word itself. They are the result of subjective variables that interact in recognition experiments with the word's features. We shall endeavor to consider these two types of variable separately.

Frequency, Familiarity, and Expectation
Other variables that are often manipulated in experiments on word perception are word frequency, familiarity of the observer with the word, and a number of factors which will be lumped for convenience under the term "expectation." These variables are not necessarily features of the word, but depend more upon the experience of the observer, and are thus separable from the features of the word.

The foregoing statement does not apply to word frequency, which is usually considered an objective variable, measurable by counting the number of tokens of the word's occurrence in samples of text such as newspapers or magazines. The Thorndike-Lorge count of word frequency is often employed as an objective index of a word's frequency. Counts of frequency exist for children's literature as well. In addition to the objective interpretation of frequency, there is the subjective one dependent on how often a reader has actually been exposed to a word. The term "familiarity" is used to make this distinction when it is the observer's experience that is stressed. Another variable not easily classified is set size, that is, the number of alternatives within a class of words being used in an experiment. Set size can of course be objectively defined by the experimenter, but it may or may not be known to the subject.

Variables included under the heading of expectation—the subject's understanding of the task, biases that he brings to it, and context-induced expectations—seem to be clear examples of internal subjective variables. The experiments below will be organized according to objective variables of the word, and then internal subjective variables.

Experimental Studies of Word Perception

Graphic Features
One of the earliest classes of variables studied in experiments on word recognition was the graphic feature. Type font, external configuration of the word (word shape), position of letters in the words, and features of individual letters have been examined. Type style was discussed in the previous chapter and research on it will not be summarized here, since within reasonable limits different type styles do not appear to play a very great role in legibility (Paterson and Tinker, 1940; Tinker, 1965). A reader must be prepared for irrelevant transformations in specimens of letters, as long as the distinctive features remain constant, and it would appear that we learn to do this remarkably well for printed letters and even cursive writing. Consider the accompanying illustration from Chapanis (Figure 7-2). However different individual handwritings, they evidently preserve the critical features of the letters if they are legible at all. The reader is able to filter out a lot of "noise" and of course does this more readily as he becomes practiced in reading any particular handwriting.

The difference between upper- and lowercase type, on the other hand, has usually been thought to play a role in speed of reading (Starch, 1914; Tinker, 1955), lowercase being faster. Children are generally started out with lowercase, the reasoning based mainly on the apparent salience of the ascending and descending letters. It must be remembered, however, that absolute legibility of a single letter is not what matters; it is relative confusability with other letters that is important. Among lowercase letters, *c* and *e* are easily confused, for instance (Sanford, 1888).

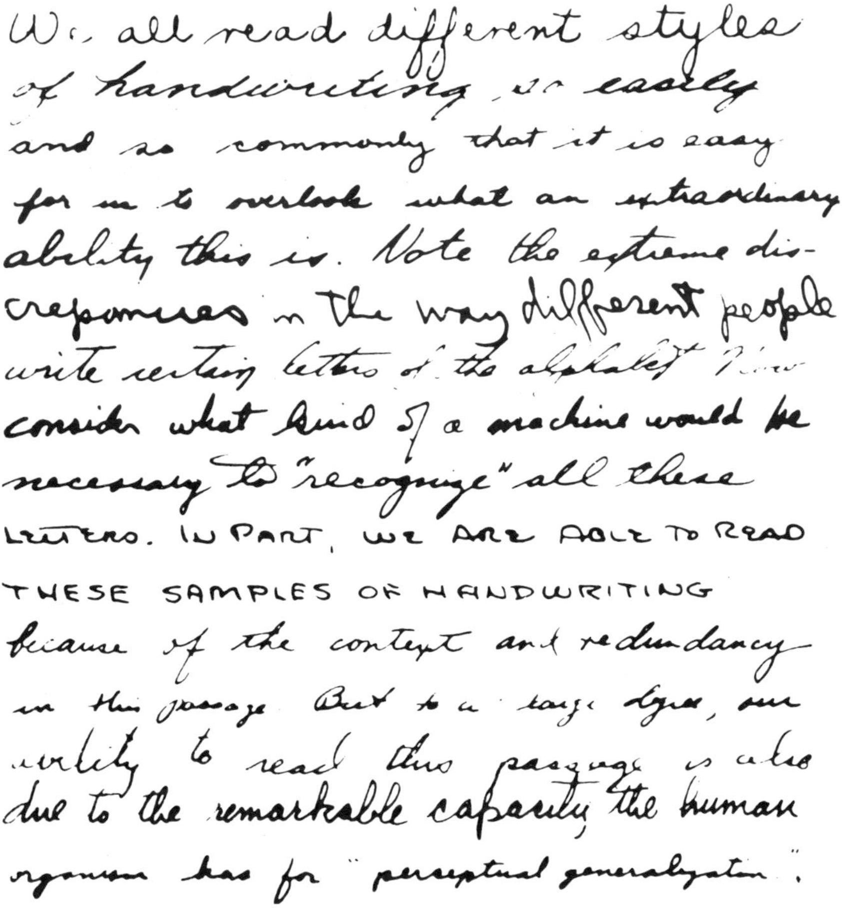

Figure 7-2. Variations in handwriting. From Chapanis, 1965. Copyright © 1965 by Wadsworth Publishing Company, Inc. Reproduced by permission of the publisher, Brooks/Cole Publishing Company, Monterey, California.

Ascending and descending letters contribute to inhomogeneities in what is referred to as total word form or word contour. It has often been speculated that words are recognized on the basis of their outlines or contours, as indicated in the diagram:

This speculation resulted partly from Cattell's finding that adults typically read in units of words. Recent research on the effectiveness of global form or contour as a basis for recognition of the word has consistently tended to refute the idea (Edelman, 1963; F. Smith, 1969a). Overall word shape is not a good enough differentiator, and children (as well as adults) do not use it. Not only is differentiation poor without internal analysis, but without such analysis there would be no basis for transfer to new words.

What are the principal graphic cues to word recognition? Dominant letters (Zeitler, 1900), such as capitals, have been suggested, but except for capitalization, it is not clear what a dominant letter is. There is ample research that shows, however, that the beginnings and ends of words are especially salient, particularly the beginnings (Broerse and Zwaan, 1966; Bruner and O'Dowd, 1958; Horowitz, White, and Atwood, 1968; Marchbanks and Levin, 1965; Nelson, Peebles, and Pancotto, 1970; Oléron and Danset, 1963). Since results of these experiments are in agreement, despite some variations in methodology, it will be sufficient to describe one experiment. Oléron and Danset presented their subjects with nine-letter words, exposed tachistoscopically, and recorded reaction times as well as accuracy. The word display was impoverished by blurring all but three letters at the beginning, the middle, or the end. Four degrees of blur were employed, with nine words each presented once in all of the three versions in random order balanced across subjects. For all levels of blur, the order of accuracy was the same: initial letters intact was best (65%); final letters intact next (54%); medial letters intact least (43%). Reaction times gave the same order of performance.

There are several reasons for this very reliable finding. When the subject is allowed only one rather fast look, the letters in the center may undergo a masking effect; perception of the letters on either side of them will reduce their visibility. The letters on the ends are not equally susceptible to this effect, because they have a white space rather than another letter on one side of them. Thus, one finds the effect with children who do not yet read well (Marchbanks and Levin, 1965), and even with nonsense words (Wagner, 1918). But for the adult reader of actual words (as in the experiment described) there is a further reason. The beginning of the word provides more information for its identification than either the middle or the end. Knowing the beginning, the rest of the word is more predictable. Why should the end get more attention than the middle? Oléron and Danset suggest that dependent probabilities are bidirectional, from the end back as well as from the beginning. The ends give gender, number, and often part of speech. Among the words they used were *commencer, opération, réligieux*, for instance. Inflections at the end are informative, as are constrained letter clusters even when they are not suffixes (see Chapter 6). The skilled reader attends to this information, as we shall see below. Spelling errors are influenced in a similar way, tending to occur primarily in the middle of words (Jensen, 1962).

Length of a word has sometimes been considered an important variable for recognition, but length is apt to be confounded with frequency (which will be considered later) and thus is not necessarily a uniquely graphic feature.

We discussed the distinctive features of individual letters in Chapter 2. These are obviously graphic features within the word and of course play a role in word recognition, since it is clear that words are not recognized graphically by general outline or contour. Smith, Lott, and Cronnell (1969) presented words for recognition that were printed in a mixture of upper- and lowercase and in different type sizes as well as in the usual style. A search task was used in which the subject had to find given target words embedded in traditionally printed text or in one of the mixtures of type. When case (upper and lower) was alternated but size of type held constant, as many target words were identified in a fixed time ($2\frac{1}{2}$ min) as when both were constant. Size differences, however, did interfere with target identification. These experienced readers thus adjusted quite easily to shifts of type, suggesting that they were relying on great familiarity with the sets of distinctive features of letters.

The set of graphic features characterizing handwriting, however, may be a different subset than ones differentiating either lower- or uppercase types, despite a reader's tolerance of variation in different handwritings. Corcoran and Rouse (1970) presented words tachistoscopically for recognition in three experiments. In Experiment I words were either typed or handwritten. In one condition the two kinds of material were presented in separate lists, but in another they were presented in a mixed list. The mixed condition resulted in poorer performance. In Experiment II, two handwritings were employed, and in Experiment III upper- and lowercase type were used. Mixing the two kinds of material had no effect in these experiments. Handwriting and type apparently have different characteristics and require different procedures of feature extraction. But within either set tolerance for idiosyncrasies exists. Upper- and lowercase type do not have identical feature descriptions for a given letter, in many cases, but the skilled reader presumably has had considerable experience in reading them in combination.

One other physical display characteristic is of great importance for word recognition by the adult reader. It is not precisely correct to call it a graphic feature, but it belongs with the set of physical features of the visual display. It is simultaneous versus sequential presentation of the letters displayed. If one reads letter by letter, from left to right, it should make little difference whether the letters are presented one at a time in a sequence, or whether the whole display is present simultaneously for the reader to scan. But experiments have made it clear that it does make a difference. Kolers and Katzman (1966) presented subjects with sequences of six letters presented serially so that each letter fell upon the same part of the viewing screen as every other one. Various kinds of words were presented, with varying lengths of letter duration. The subject's task was to name the word. For a subject to name the word correctly 90% of the time, the mean duration per letter had to be as long as 375 msec. This is at least three times as long as the exposure duration necessary to recognize a familiar six-letter word displayed as a whole. This poor performance was not due to inability to read the single letters, since the subjects could name the letters correctly at shorter durations. They could spell the word correctly while unable to name it correctly.

Newman (1966) performed an experiment in which a set of one to ten letters was presented on a screen so that with each successive presentation the letters were moved one space to the left, the first letter dropped off, and a new one added. The appearance was of a continuous band of text moving across a screen behind a window that could be adjusted for the reader to see a given number of letters simultaneously. Six lengths of span (letters visible simultaneously) were used. The subject was asked to read the text, a passage roughly 100 words in length, aloud. The percent of words read correctly when new letters were added at a rate of one per sec rose from 9.53% when the span of letters visible simultaneously was 1 to 96.51% when it was 8. The lack of context letters radically reduced the speed at which the material could be read.

These experiments employed adult skilled readers as subjects and rather rapid rates of presentation. Wolfe (1939), with much slower rates of presentation, found little difference between sequential presentation and simultaneous presentation with nine-year-old children (both normal and retarded readers). However, the children were shown all the words with whole-word presentation first, and the same words were presented afterward sequentially. It might be, though, that these children had not yet internalized the knowledge of intraword regularities that is automatically available to good adult readers. It is time to consider how these regularities affect word recognition.

Intraword Redundancy

Meaning vs. rules Single words are characterized by two kinds of redundancy within the word, described by phonological and orthographic rules, as discussed previously. Is there evidence that these are used in word recognition for the efficient extraction of units larger than the letter? Cattell's experiments might appear to answer this question positively, but they could be (and were) interpreted as being an advantage caused by the word's meaning or familiarity. A number of experiments have appeared in recent years showing that a letter is recognized more readily (by a competent reader) when it is embedded in a word than when it is displayed alone or embedded in a random collection of letters or meaningless symbols (Krueger, 1970; Lott and Smith, 1970; Novik and Katz, 1971; Reicher, 1969; F. Smith, 1969b; Wheeler, 1970). Reicher's experiment, the first of this group, required a forced choice by the subject (was a given letter present or not?) when the exposed letter was presented alone or as part of a word. The subject could not simply guess from seeing the first of the word, since it was chosen so that either the target letter or a different one could be present and in both cases constitute an actual word (e.g., if the target letter was *t*, the word could be either *mat* or *map*). Reicher attributed the superiority of the word display to meaningfulness, but a later experiment by Krueger (1970) found a similar small effect with third-order nonsense words which had spelling approximating English (see p. 207), but no meaningful reference, so the ascription of the effect to meaning alone is dubious.

The superior ease of recognizing a target letter embedded in a word has been referred to recently as the "word-superiority" effect, a phrase which tacitly attributes the effect to the meaningfulness and familiarity of the word. Baron and Thurston (1973) questioned this interpretation and performed experiments comparable to Reicher's (1969) and Wheeler's (1970), embedding target letters in pronounceable and unpronounceable nonwords as well as real words. The word and pronounceable nonword conditions were both superior to the unpronounceable nonword condition and did not differ from one another, so it was concluded that the so-called word-superiority effect could be accounted for entirely by "pronounceability." Evidence was also presented to show that pronounceability is not effective merely because it increases the subject's ability to remember the critical items. They also presented some evidence to show that pronounceability as such (as opposed to knowledge of orthographic rules) is unlikely to be the main cause of the word-superiority effect.

Pronounceability vs. orthography   The role of pronounceability in tachistoscopic word recognition has been studied in a number of experiments. What, exactly, is pronounceability? The coincidence of phonological and orthographic rule systems tends to confound them experimentally. Furthermore, it is possible that phonological and orthographic units within the word larger than the letter have correspondence rules that serve to carve out segments such as syllables, or letter clusters that in a given environment within the word map to a constant pronunciation, yielding subunits larger than single letters. This latter possibility was the basis for an experiment by Gibson, Pick, Osser, and Hammond (1962). A series of nonsense words that were orthographically legal were constructed by placing typical English initial consonants or consonant clusters at the beginnings and similarly constrained consonants at the end, with a vowel or vowel cluster in the middle. A list of 25 such monosyllables, ranging from four to eight letters in length, resulted. They were pronounceable, orthographically correct, and had constrained letter clusters placed in environments that made their pronunciation predictable. A control list was constructed by inverting the consonant clusters in each of the pseudowords to yield an unpronounceable, orthographically illegal string of letters (for example, *sland* vs. *ndasl*).

The two lists of words labeled "pronounceable" and "unpronounceable" were mixed and presented to subjects tachistoscopically at five expo-

sure durations, beginning at 30 msec and increasing to 250. The subjects
were college students. As Figure 7-3 shows, the percentage of pronounceable words read correctly was greater for all exposure durations. When
the written reproductions of the words were scored for accuracy of initial
and final consonant spellings separately, more errors occurred on the final
clusters, but the difference between pronounceable and unpronounceable
words was still present at a high level of significance. The clusters as such
were not merely subunits created by high bigraph frequency; it was a cluster in its legal place in a word that facilitated recognition.

Could it be that a more frequently *emitted* verbal response is favored,
simply because it is more available as a response? In an attempt to answer
this, the experiment was repeated asking the subject to make a different
judgment, merely to indicate a choice of one of four responses presented
to him (the letters that had been actually exposed and three more sets that
were the most frequent errors in the first experiment). The results confirmed the previous experiment, suggesting that the pronounceable words
were indeed perceived more accurately. Phonological and orthographic

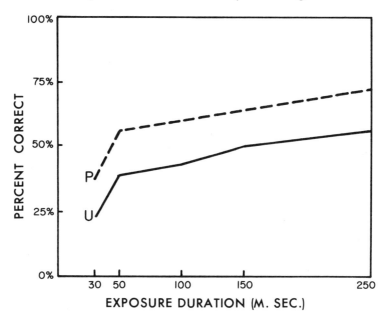

Figure 7-3.   Percentage of pronounceable and unpronounceable words read correctly
at five exposure durations. From Gibson, Pick, Osser, and Hammond, 1962, p. 562.

regularity are thus effective in facilitating recognition of units of word size when meaning and familiarity are absent.

When do these rule systems begin to be effective in creating units for the reader? Biemiller and Levin (1968) displayed the same nonsense words to third- and fourth-grade children, and found they took longer to read the less pronounceable words. Unfamiliar patterns of articulation could have been responsible for this time difference. But other evidence, with time for articulation ruled out, suggests that children are able to make use of intraword redundancies to some extent at about the third-grade level. Gibson, Osser, and Pick (1963) compared children who had just completed first and third grades on three-letter strings presented tachisto-scopically. They included real familiar words, pronounceable nonsense words, and unpronounceable nonsense words (e.g., *ran*, *nar*, and *rna*). Some of the four- and five-letter strings used in the experiment described above were also included. The first graders read (and spelled out) most accurately the familiar three-letter words, and also read the pronounce-able trigrams significantly better than the unpronounceable ones. But the longer pseudowords were seldom read accurately and were not differen-tiated by pronounceability. The third-grade girls read all the three-letter combinations with high and about equal accuracy, but showed differen-tiation on the longer nonsense words; the pronounceable four- and five-letter nonsense words were more often perceived and spelled out correctly than their unpronounceable counterparts. The simple and characteristic CVC pattern of the three-letter pronounceable nonsense words was pre-sumably a kind of structure already familiar to the younger group, but the longer words, containing consonant clusters with conditional constraints, were not yet recognized as legal or illegal structures.

Rosinski and Wheeler (1972) compared children in first, third, and fifth grades (toward the end of October) on 20 sets of nonsense words taken from the above experiments and varying from three to six letters in length. The judgment did not involve a fast exposure of limited duration. The child was shown a pair of words typed on cards in uppercase and asked to point to the one that "was more like a real word." One of each pair was pronounceable, the other not. Word length was matched in a pair, but otherwise the two sets of words were randomly paired. The first-grade children performed at chance level, even on the three-letter combinations. The other two groups both performed better than chance, "correct" choices ranging between 70% and 80%. Length (up to six letters, at least) did not seem to affect accuracy.

Golinkoff (1974) replicated this experiment with a number of modifications. Her subjects were chosen from first and second grades (late in the year). Pairs of words contained the same letters, but one member was phonologically and orthographically legal, whereas the other was not. There were three conditions of word presentation: visual alone, auditory alone, and redundant visual and auditory. The results revealed an interaction of age with condition. First-grade children performed only slightly better than chance with visual or auditory presentation alone, but significantly better (72% correct) when presentation was bimodal. But the second graders were significantly better with visual presentation alone (82.5% correct, as compared with 65% for auditory presentation and 70% for bimodal presentation). Thus combining auditory and visual presentation appeared to help in beginning stages of learning to read, but toward the end of second grade, visual information for wordlikeness had become of predominant importance. Golinkoff correlated performance on the wordlikeness test with reading scores on the Metropolitan Achievement Test (given at the end of the year) and found a significant relationship ($r = .50$). Ability to generalize knowledge of English orthography does thus reflect reading ability measured in other ways.

We conclude that at least some children toward the end of second grade, given unlimited time for decision, can discriminate structure in letter strings that involves quite complex conditional rules. This knowledge of regularities is generalized to new items, as the last several experiments show. The children must do a lot of the rule induction for themselves, since it is seldom explicitly taught. In fact, we have only limited information as yet as to what the important regularities are that generalize to produce facilitation, or how they do it.

The advantage of pronounceable, orthographically correct items as targets in a search task has been demonstrated by Clare (1969). Orthographically correct, pronounceable items in the context of the search task in which a target letter is embedded do not appear to facilitate search, however (Gibson, Tenney, Barron, and Zaslow, 1972; James and Smith, 1970). A single-letter target may be inappropriate for the contextual advantage of orthographic structure to be useful. Zaslow (1972) has shown that when constrained consonant clusters (initial clusters alone or final clusters alone) are targets in a search task, adult subjects locate them faster when they are in the appropriate constrained position even when the containing string is not a word.

In all the above experiments, a word's pronounceability and its orthographic legality have been confounded. Is the phonological legality of a word (its pronounceability, for short) important in reading a word? Is it, in fact, the reason why orthographic legality is effective—because the subject "says it to himself" and it sounds right? Since these two sources of intraword redundancy are themselves redundant, it is hard to separate them. It is possible that pronounceability plays an important role early in learning to read and then is superseded by orthographic information (see Golinkoff, 1974). However, it is not essential for learning to make use of orthographic redundancy. Gibson, Shurcliff, and Yonas (1970) investigated the recognition of pronounceable and unpronounceable nonsense words in congenitally deaf subjects. If pronounceability, as such, is what facilitates reading the unfamiliar but rulelike items, we should find an interaction with the ability to speak and hear them. But the deaf subjects profited just as much in reading the so-called pronounceable combinations as hearing subjects did. For them, the two types of nonsense words must have been differentiated by orthographic structure alone.

Independent effects of both pronounceability and orthographic patterning were demonstrated in a recall experiment by Nelson (1969) using artificial materials, but orthographic patterning was a more significant variable. Congruency of spelling pattern and pronounceability, comparable to the kind of redundancy found in real words, was the most effective factor in facilitating recall, and strengthens the middle-of-the-road hypothesis that both phonological and orthographic redundancy are important variables in word recognition. An experiment with children by Thomas (1968) exposed tachistoscopically two types of trigrams, both pronounceable, one in a CVC arrangement (e.g., *ruf*) and one in CCV arrangement (e.g., *fru*), and found the CVC arrangement superior for recognition. Since English three-letter words are more commonly of this type, the effectiveness of orthographic structure apart from pronounceability appears to be supported.

Some models of reading (to be discussed in Chapter 11) hypothesize a stage in processing in which the visual input is transformed to a phonetic representation. In a study by Rubenstein, Lewis, and Rubenstein (1971) such a stage is referred to as "phonemic recoding." They hypothesized that even when a word is seen, not heard, a "search through the internal lexicon" is carried out in the "phonemic code." They performed an experiment using a reaction-time measure in which the subjects (adults) decided whether a string of letters visually displayed to them was a word or not. They presented four kinds of material: real words, legal nonsense words (orthographically and phonologically correct), and two types of illegal nonsense words, one which was both orthographically and phonologically illegal (e.g., *tritv, codg*), and one which was illegal but considered by the authors to be pronounceable (e.g., *fuzg, topk*). It was argued that a speedier decision for the third category than for the last would be evidence for phonemic recoding. They found that real, familiar words yielded the shortest latencies, legal nonsense words the longest, and the two illegal categories were in between. The illegal but presumably prononunceable words took slightly longer (15 msec) than the illegal nonpronounceable ones.* Why? Because, the authors thought, the unpronounceable ones deviated to a greater extent from phonological well-formedness. The biggest difference, however, was between legal and illegal nonsense words, so our tentative conclusion that both phonological and orthographic legalities can play a role in word recognition is still tenable.

Baron and Thurston (1973) dismissed pronounceability as a source of facilitation on the basis of an experiment involving homophones. Three types of words were compared in an experiment using a detection technique (a single word was exposed, followed by a mask, and then the subject had to decide which of a pair of alternatives had been exposed). Three types of words were exposed: 1. homophones (e.g., *fore* and *four*); 2. pronounceable nonhomophones (e.g., *sore* and *sour*); 3. unpronounceable nonwords (e.g., *fcre* and *fcur*). The argument was that Condition 1 should have no advantage over Condition 3 if sound was a crucial variable, since the two alternatives were phonetically identical. But if information about pronunciation were uninfluential in the word superiority effect, performance on the homophones should be better than on the unpronounceable controls (Condition 3) and as good as on the pronounceable controls (Condition 2). The latter results were obtained, and the conclusion was drawn that the sound of the word was not an effective variable. Baron (1973) drew a similar conclusion, namely, that meaning in reading can be derived from visual analysis of text without the use of an intermediate phonemic code.

*A recalculation of the significance of this difference by a probably more valid method (Clark, 1973) did not yield a significant difference.

For a number of reasons the "pronounceability" versus legal orthography issue is still unsettled. Sound may play a role at some stage of learning and drop out, as we saw. Even more important, some techniques of measuring word superiority may correlate with actual reading and some may not. Different measures have yielded different results. Some probably reduce the role of phonetic processing compared to others.

Probability of letter sequences We have been referring to legal or rulelike nonsense words as a way of identifying nonreal words that have kinds of internal redundancy that are characteristic of a real word. What are the correct ways of describing internal redundancy? That there were such redundancies was recognized some years ago, and investigation of them was greatly influenced by communication theory, new and much in vogue at the time. A measure known as "approximation to English" was devised and tested with word recognition techniques. "Order of approximation" refers to the number of letters given before a succeeding one is supplied as being likely to come next in the sequence. Given three letters, say *ver*, the fourth can be supplied by searching through text for the next letter that follows this triad, or it can be supplied by subjects via guessing procedures. One then takes the new triad of the last three letters and reiterates the procedure until the desired length is achieved. Some examples of eight-letter strings of fourth-order approximation to English are *vernalit* and *ricaning*. These strings obviously resemble English words; they are easily divided into syllables and are of course pronounceable. A zero-order approximation is obtained by randomly drawing a letter at a time. Examples are *yrulpzox* and *dlegqmnw*. Miller, Bruner, and Postman (1954) exposed tachistoscopically strings of letters having four orders of approximation to English. Accuracy of recognition was greater as order of approximation increased. A similar experiment was performed by Wallach (1963) with fifth-grade children. There was improvement in recognition, comparing zero-order and fourth-order approximation, but it ranged widely in degree over individual children. The degree of improvement was found to correlate significantly with scores on a spelling test.

A recent experiment by Lefton, Spragins, and Byrnes (in press) confirms Wallach's results with children, using a guessing technique. Pseudowords of seven letters each were presented with one letter missing. The pseudowords were either first-order or fourth-order approximations to English.

Subjects were children from first, third, and fifth grades. A missing letter was replaced with a dash and the child was given as long as he wished to fill it in with "the name of the letter he felt would belong there." There were strong effects of grade level. For grade 1, there was no difference in correctness of guessing between the two orders of approximation. Third-grade children showed a great increase in accuracy for fourth- as compared with first-order approximations, and fifth-grade children's results were almost identical with those of adults. In a second experiment, Lefton (in press) varied duration of viewing time from 50 msec up to 10,000 msec, using adult subjects, and found no significant effect due to increased viewing time. He concluded that the "familiarity effect" was more direct than "guessing" from context.

Such results, during the sixties, were interpreted as based on knowledge of the transitional probabilities for sequences of letters—what letter most often follows a given one. Redundant sequences (three letters, say, taken from a real word) were followed up by successful guessing at what was most likely to come next.

An experiment by Mewhort (1966), however, makes this interpretation of letter-by-letter predictability seem greatly oversimplified. He presented fourth-order and zero-order approximations of words to subjects with different extents of spaces between letters. With normal spacing, he obtained the expected increase in recognition with higher approximation to English. But when the spacing was increased, recognition of the fourth-order approximations was impaired, whereas recognition of the zero-order approximations was not. In other words, increasing the spacing between letters disrupted the ability of the subjects to use the redundancy in the higher-order sequences. There is no reason why this interaction with order of approximation should have occurred if the subjects were simply operating on a guessing basis. It seems far more likely that larger structural segments were perceived as units when spacing allowed perception of letter context.

Summed bigram or trigram frequency has been used as an alternative procedure for quantifying intraword redundancy, and has also generally carried with it the implication that sequential prediction of letter probability accounted for any results in which higher summed frequencies predicted higher recognition scores (Anisfeld, 1964). Simply on the face of it, this idea is not very attractive if one considers mapping correspondences from spelling to sound. The trigram *ati*, for instance, occurs with high frequency, but it is an unlikely unit for reading because it is pronounced

differently depending on its context in a word (e.g., *relation* vs. *relative*);
ign, again, is a rather high-frequency trigram, but consider how it is read
in *sign* vs. *signify*. This does not mean that there are not subunits within a
word, of course, but rather that this is a poor way of defining them, especially for a child learning to read. Gibson, Shurcliff, and Yonas (1970)
summed both bigram and trigram frequencies in an experiment on tachistoscopic recognition of pronounceable and unpronounceable pseudowords
and did not find either of them good predictors. In a stepwise regression
analysis, word length and "pronounceability" accounted for 87% of the
variance and the counts added only one point to the prediction of errors.

Inference vs. unitization If the sequential probability of one letter
following another is an inadequate description of what kind of redundancy
underlies the "word-superiority" effect and the generalization of knowledge of legal orthography to pseudowords, what concepts shall we substitute? It must be emphasized again (see Chapter 6) that in English orthography, pronunciation cannot be predicted via single letters. Conditional rules for clusters, underlying morphemic information, and morphology must be taken into account, so it makes sense that these same
variables must be important also in accounting for the word-superiority
effect.

Smith and Haviland (1972) attempted to compare two hypothetical
processes, which they termed "inference" and "unitization." The "inference hypothesis" holds that "for any letter string the unit of analysis is always a single letter" but "when a word is expected, the subject's knowledge of the redundancy of English enables him to use the letters he analyzed first to make inferences about the remaining letters" (p. 59). (It will
be noted that the subject is assumed to expect a word for inference to work,
and this has by no means always been the case in experiments demonstrat-
ing generalization of the effect to legal pseudowords.) The "unitization
hypothesis" holds that "words are perceived more readily than nonwords
because the unit of analysis is larger in the former case then in the latter."
In other words, the subject segments the presented string into perceptual
units larger than single letters, which "correspond to pronounceable English sequences, and then analyzes these units." Fewer units to be processed
would be more economical. This was the view of Gibson et al. (1962), but
in view of more recent findings, some of them already discussed, it is no
longer so plausible.

Smith and Haviland attempted to compare the two hypotheses by equating redundancy for words and nonwords, thus presumably equating the opportunity to use inference. The words were pronounceable, the nonwords not. A forced-choice test of a single letter (following tachistoscopic exposure) was required. The words were three-letter items of high frequency (e.g., *bug*); the nonwords were trigrams varying in the middle letter, always a consonant (e.g., *bdg*). Only two medial letters were used for a set of eight items, *a* and *u* or *s* and *d*. The subject was presented, in Part I of the experiment, with one of the three-letter items for 30 msec and then given a choice card containing three dashes and two alternative letters, above and below one of the dashes, from which to select the letter that had appeared in that position. In Part II the subject learned the rules for generating the items, thus presumably equating the words and nonwords for redundancy. In other words, he knew the population of items. In Part III, he was tested again with the same probe technique used in Part I. The percentage of correct choices jumped 10% from Part I to Part III for both words and nonwords; words exceeded nonwords in both parts by 7%. The authors concluded that the unitization process was favored by these results—that the words were segmented into larger units, whereas the nonwords were not. It is not immediately apparent what the larger units would be within three-letter words such as *rag* or *bug*, or how the larger units were formed in the first place if not by rule (excluding inference, if one can by virtue of these results, does not exclude use of rules). A second experiment with extended practice still obtained the word-superiority effect after 500 trials. This experiment would have been more convincing if both sets of items had been nonwords, half pronounceable and half unpronounceable, since meaning and long familiarity were present in the words.

Let us consider once more what kind of orthographic redundancy is present in a word. It may indeed possess high probability of one letter following another, as in the experiments using counts of approximation to English. This has been referred to as "correlational redundancy," that is, a sequence of two letters, one following the other with some degree of predictability. But as we saw in Chapter 6, English monosyllables have structural redundancies that can be described in other ways: They must contain a vowel, and they may contain consonants and consonant clusters that are highly constrained as to position. This "conditional redundancy" seems to us a better description of what can or cannot constitute an actual word.

A comparison of correlational and conditional redundancy in trigrams presented at threshold durations for recognition was performed by Cole-gate and Eriksen (1972). Correlational redundancy was defined as an exactly predictable sequence of two letters. It existed within a list of trigrams such as *had, hag, han, pod, pog, pon, rud, rug, run.* Conditional redundancy existed when letters in any two positions were uncorrelated with each other, but any two positions taken jointly determined the third. Such a list consisted of *han, hug, hod, pad, pun, pog, rag, rud, ron.* For instance, if the viewer perceives the two letters *ha,* the third has to be *n.* If he perceives the second two, *an,* the first has to be *h,* and if he perceives *h* and *n,* the third has to be *a.* An important form of spelling redundancy in English, it has been suggested, consists of conditional rules like *"ck* can end a syllable but cannot begin it" (see Chapter 6). In the Colegate and Eriksen experiment, the subjects were given lists of the sets to learn, and then tested with both the redundant forms of trigrams and a nonredundant control set. Both redundant sets were discriminated better than the nonredundant control, but the number of trials on which all three letters were correctly reported was significantly greater for trigram sets with conditional redundancy. Thus conditional redundancy increased the frequency of responding with the letter pattern as a whole. The authors concluded, with appropriate reservations about tachistoscopic exposure, that the form of redundancy found in actual words is functional for rapid reading, where brief fixations are followed by short saccadic movements during which perception is minimal.

The experiment by Zaslow mentioned earlier is another attestation of the effectiveness of conditional redundancy. Constrained consonant clusters placed correctly in pseudowords significantly facilitated their discovery, as compared with the same clusters in the incorrect location. More well-controlled research on the forms of intraword redundancy that the reader actually uses to increase his efficiency is badly needed.

Syllabification and word recognition A series of familiar syllables, whether it forms a real word or not, is particularly easy to read (Zeitler, 1900). If a long pseudoword is invented and given to someone to read, he invariably segments it into syllables. Try *provelogicamencular,* or even a real word like *hyperlipoproteinemics.* The syllable is a higher-order unit than the letter. Segmentation is determined partly by morphemic constituents (e.g., *hyper, lipo, protein,* etc.) but there are rules governing the structure of a syllable (see Chapter 4), whether or not it is a morpheme.

Shaffer and Hardwick (1969) performed an interesting study with a group of very experienced typists. The typists were given lists of words to transcribe on the typewriter as fast as possible while maintaining accuracy. There were four kinds of text: *real words*; *syllabic items* constructed from the real words by shuffling letters to make a nonsense word having syllabic structure; *high approximation to English,* items constructed with the letter probabilities of written English; and *zero-order approximation,* items constructed randomly with all letters equally likely to occur. Mean times per symbol were calculated for the four kinds of text. Means for long word were as follows: Real words were shortest (178 msec); syllabic items next (219 msec); high approximation next (274 msec); and of course zero-order worst (371 msec). The interesting thing about these comparisons is the superiority of the syllabic nonsense text over the higher-order approximation. The syllable is a good unit and facilitates transcription better than high sequential probability of single letters succeeding one another.

Spoehr and Smith (1973) investigated the role of syllables in perceptual processing using accuracy of tachistoscopic report as a measure. One and two-syllable words, each one five letters long, were presented (e.g., *paint* and *paper*). They were equated for frequency and initial letters. Significantly more letters in the one-syllable words were reported correctly, so the syllable appeared to be functional as a higher-order unit. Spoehr and Smith argued that if this were true, accuracy for neighboring letters within the syllable should be highly correlated. (This is a prediction about correlational redundancy, as Colegate and Eriksen termed it.) On the other hand, for a two-syllable word, one would not expect a high correlation for the letters on either side of a syllable boundary. For instance, if one compares the correlation between two letters at syllable boundaries (e.g., the second and third letters in *paper*) it should be less than the correlation between the second and third letters in its one-syllable mate (e.g., *paint*). Such a comparison was carried out for each of the matched pairs of words, but the difference was not significant.

Spoehr and Smith proposed that the correct higher-order unit was not, therefore, the syllable, but a "vocalic center group" (see Chapter 4). They applied an algorithm for segmenting their two-syllable words into vocalic center groups, and using the boundaries thus determined, recomputed the comparison made between one- and two-syllable words. The difference now was significant, leading them to conclude that the vocalic center group was the true higher-order unit, rather than the syllable. It is obvious, however, that this conclusion depends on how a syllable is defined. Rules for segmentation into syllables are somewhat arbitrary (compare two dictionaries), and we do not know how Spoehr and Smith carried out their first syllable segmentation.

The experiment was repeated using a probe technique (which of two letters was correct in a given position) and the previous effect confirmed, so the authors concluded that the effect was perceptual and not the result of inference. But it follows then, from their own research and from their own reasoning, that word perception makes use of rules.

The correlational technique used by Spoehr and Smith is analogous to a comparison made by Baron and Thurston (1973) within real words and pronounceable and unpronounceable pseudowords. They looked for a correlation between accuracy of perceiving two critical letters in the three word types (always the same letters for the two types) and found a correlation for word and pronounceable nonword items but not for unpronounceable ones. The two critical letters in their experiments were separated—either in positions one and three or one and four. It appears, therefore, that perceiving one letter can facilitate perceiving another in pronounceable items even when the letters are not neighbors, a finding in keeping with Colegate and Eriksen's results with conditional redundancy.

Frequency

A factor that has consistently and repeatedly been shown to enhance ease of recognition is a word's frequeny of usage in the language. Frequency is usually measured objectively by a word count through magazines or newspapers. The most commonly used source is the Thorndike-Lorge count (Thorndike and Lorge, 1944). Other measures have been used, such as the frequency of the word's emission by a given population, or its "familiarity" as rated by a given population. It is a pretty safe generalization that frequency by any of these measures, and with nearly all the experimental methods—thresholds of recognition, latency, number of items correct with a short exposure, judgments of "is it a word?"—is a good predictor of single-word recognition. The experiments are too numerous to summarize in detail. For typical studies, the reader is referred to Howes and Solomon (1951), Solomon and Postman (1952), Rosenzweig (1956), Rosenzweig and Postman (1958), McGinnies, Comer, and Lacey (1952), King-Ellison and Jenkins (1954), Baker and Feldman (1956). In some of these experiments (e.g., Solomon and Postman, 1952) the frequency was built-in in the course of the experiment by giving variable amounts of practice with nonsense words before testing for recognition. These experiments have generally found recognition to be a function of the number of exposures of the word in the pretraining task. One exception to this was the finding of Postman and Rosenzweig (1956) that pretraining which varied spoken frequency before testing visual recognition was ineffective (written frequency was effective, as in the other experiments). Simply hearing a word frequently, then, does not affect its threshold for visual recognition. This finding was replicated by Sprague (1959).

A variable which seems to cut across the word frequency effect is that of set size. For spoken language, a listener can identify words more accurately if he knows the list from which the words will be chosen, and the shorter the list, the more intelligible the words will be (Miller, Heise, and Lichten, 1941). The same effect appears to hold for visual recognition thresholds (Fraisse and Blancheteau, 1962). Pierce (1963) showed that the word-frequency effect dropped out completely when the subject was given a list of the words to be exposed, so that he knew the set in advance. Pierce interpreted this finding as supporting an explanation of the word frequency effect as "response bias"—a function of the subject's tendency to guess frequent rather than infrequent words to fill in fragmentary percepts.

The effect of word frequency on recognition thresholds has often been interpreted as due to response bias, a reflection of a subject's tendency to guess when he doesn't actually perceive the word, and to guess a word that is frequent in the language that he hears (Goldiamond and Hawkins, 1958; Goldstein and Ratliff, 1961). Evidence for the response bias interpretation commonly turns up strongly in experiments where subjects are forced to say something, to guess, if they did not perceive clearly. The word frequency effect may be in part attributed to response bias, in line with guessing hypotheses. But there is also evidence that perceptual information extracted from the display contributes to the word frequency effect (Newbigging, 1961; Smock and Kanfer, 1961). It is not clear that the effects have ever been cleanly separated or exactly what is supposed to be happening when a so-called response bias operates.

This discussion of the interpretation of the word frequency effect may seem a trifle academic for our purposes, but it gives us reason to be cautious in drawing morals for teaching reading. If sheer repetition (frequency of exposure) leads to nothing but predictable guessing behavior, it is not apparent how useful it is. Such an extreme view is undoubtedly wrong, however, for frequent exposure is necessary for opportunities to extract and internalize the useful intraword redundancies. It is also likely that very frequent words like *the* and *and* come to have unique graphic features that describe them, in combination, as well as conditional rules for subordinate segments, such as the *nd* cluster.

Meaning

Cattell, as we saw, invoked meaning of a word (and familiarity with its meaning) to interpret his results. But it is now clear that the meaning of a word is confounded with the variables we have referred to in the section above as intraword redundancy, as well as familiarity. Does meaning as such contribute to ease of recognizing a word? There are many kinds of meaning, or meaningful features, of course, that can characterize a word or a string of letters, and there have been several attempts at quantifying a word's meaning. A few experiments will be described which provide evidence pro or con for how some aspect or measure of meaning relates to recognition.

One experiment by Gibson, Bishop, Schiff, and Smith (1964) attempted to separate referential meaning from pronounceability in a test of recognition (using a measure of threshold contrast) and in tests of remembering. Trigrams were chosen which could be arranged to form (1) items (initials) with semantic reference, (2) a pronounceable item with no referential meaning, and (3) an item that was unpronounceable and also meaningless (e.g., IBM, MIB, and MBI). Perceptual thresholds were significantly lower for both the pronounceable and the meaningful items than for the control ones, but lowest for the pronounceable items. Retention, on the other hand, was facilitated more for the meaningful items.

Further evidence has been provided recently that meaning affects recognition. Henderson (in press), using a same-different judgment, compared meaningful abbreviations (e.g., VD, FBI, RSVP) with nonabbreviations (random letter strings of comparable length). None of the abbreviations was orthographically regular. Pairs shown for comparison were of three types: both meaningful items, both nonmeaningful, or mixed. Meaningfulness was a significant variable, resulting in a lowered reaction time. With long practice, the effect held up for "same" responses, but disappeared with "different" responses. Henderson concluded that "an appeal to meaningfulness implies access to the lexicon which may be faster than grapheme-by-grapheme analysis"—in other words, that semantic processing might be direct or might occur in parallel with orthographic processing.

Another recent experiment (Barron and Pittenger, in press) used a same-different judgment to compare reaction times to pairs of high-frequency real words, orthographically acceptable nonwords, and orthographically illegal nonwords. For "same" judgments, there were significant differences among the three: Real words were faster than pseudowords, and legal nonwords were faster than illegal ones. Meaning did thus appear to play a role, in addition to orthographic acceptability, in contrast to Baron and Thurston's (1973) findings. The "different" responses, however, did not show these differences after early practice. Why "different" judgments were not affected is not easily explained, but it is clear that current technical and methodological differences prevent an unequivocal conclusion about the role of meaning in the perception of single words or pairs of words.

Other experiments found negative results for referential meaning. Taylor (1958) paired nonsense items with pictures of familiar objects, thus giving the subjects an opportunity to learn referential meanings to the verbal items. Control items were presented with equal frequency but without pictorial referents. Recognition thresholds were not lowered by learning pictorial associations. Postman and Rosenzweig (1956) found that familiar English words with referents (e.g., *bun* and *pen*) were not recognized any sooner than familiar syllables (e.g., *est* and *ing*). Clare (1969) used a training procedure to establish referential meaning for nonsense words and tested recognizability as target items in a search task. There was no effect as compared with control items.

Other definitions or measures of meaning have shown some effect. Kristofferson (1957) found a significant correlation between meaning (*m* as scaled by Noble, 1952) and threshold for word recognition. However, meaning covaried with familiarity, which may have been the effective variable. Johnson and Zara (1964) found an effect of *m* on recognition threshold, but it interacted with word frequency. The threshold ratio of high to low *m* words decreased as word frequencies increased. Hershenson and Haber (1965) compared English words with Turkish words, increasing exposure duration until the subject could report all the letters of the word. English words were always easier to perceive than Turkish words, but repeated exposure facilitated both.

The elusive effect of meaning in the recognition of individual words has led to investigation of another semantic aspect of words, their concreteness or abstractness. Again, the dimension is apt to be confounded with word frequency, without careful controls. Two experiments (Riegel and Riegel,

1961; Spreen, Borkowski, and Benton, 1967) found lower recognition thresholds for words with concrete as opposed to abstract meanings. The Spreen et al. experiment tested only auditory recognition, so its relevance is doubtful for our purposes. Riegel and Riegel presented words tachistoscopically, obtaining a threshold measure with 16-year-old subjects. Fifty words that could be classified in various ways were presented. The variables for classification included (among 40 in all) number of letters, number of syllables, presence of prefix or suffix, frequency of first syllable, transitional probabilities, word frequency, and being concrete vs. nonconcrete. "Concrete" was defined as having a physical referent (e.g., *bird* vs. *pity*). These variables were correlated with recognition thresholds, and the highest correlation obtained was for concreteness ($r = .66$). Word frequency yielded a high correlation ($r = .50$). Transitional probabilities yielded a correlation of .44. A rare first syllable, as opposed to a prefix, is an aid compared to a very common prefix, which does little to reduce the alternatives for what the rest of the word might be (a very common situation in German, the language in which the experiment was conducted). Intercorrelations among some of the variables was high (between concreteness and absence of a prefix, for instance), so there was confounding of the variables, but the superiority of the concreteness dimension was rather striking.

Unfortunately, Winnick and Kressel (1965) investigated the concreteness dimension with tachistoscopic recognition and obtained negative results. Concrete and abstract words of both low and high frequency were used. The mean threshold for concrete words was identical with abstract, but there was an effect of frequency. The main contribution to this effect came from the concrete words. In a retention experiment, the same authors found that degree of abstractness did have an effect on free recall. Two other experiments bear on the issue. Paivio and O'Neill (1970) varied frequency, imagery concreteness, and meaningfulness as measured by associations (Noble's m) in an experiment on recognition thresholds. Ratings of familiarity were also obtained to supplement the frequency measure. When familiarity and m were controlled, concreteness (defined by imagery ratings) was unrelated to recognition thresholds. Threshold was most strongly related to frequency and familiarity, and only slightly to m. Rubenstein, Garfield, and Millikan (1970) also failed to find an effect of concreteness when subjects had to judge whether a display of letters was a word or not.

The comparison of speed of recognition of homographs with nonhomographs yields one more fact pertinent to this rather ambiguous picture of the effect of meaning on word recognition. Two studies (Rubenstein, Garfield, and Millikan, 1970; Rubenstein, Lewis, and Rubenstein, 1971a) found that homographs have a lower recognition threshold than nonhomographs. The words *yard, chest,* and *bulb,* for instance, had lower recognition thresholds than nonhomographs, with word frequency held constant. This finding held when the two meanings were equiprobable, but not when one was rare. The authors suggested that the lower recognition time for a homograph as compared with a nonhomograph is due to the greater number of lexical entries for the homograph. This might be thought of as a form of redundancy. Normally, with a single word, there is no redundancy of meaning. There is contextual redundancy of meaning in phrases and sentences that contributes to the recognition of words, but meaning has not always turned out to be a crucial factor in recognition of isolated words. The small but fairly often found effect of m may also be attributable to the fact that m is actually a measure of redundancy of meaning (the number of associations a word calls up). The real effectiveness of meaning for creating economical units in reading is probably less attributable to the single word than to sentence context where meaning interacts with grammar.

Grammatical Variables
It seems even less likely that grammatical features of a word, such as its part of speech, would affect single-word recognition than that meaning does. Syntax operates over words; morphology operates by way of inflections, giving cases, tense, and so on. A sentence is usually considered the appropriate unit for analysis of grammar (see Chapter 4), and there are subunits, clauses and phrases, that are larger units than the word. But we do differentiate between word classes like nouns and verbs that play different grammatical roles. There has been speculation by linguists (Chafe, 1970) that the verb is the "heart" of the sentence and implies much of the rest of it. If that were the case, it might conceivably be supposed that verbs should have lower recognition thresholds than other parts of speech because they carry such a burden of information, and have therefore been more strongly focused on. There appears to be almost no research on this question. A paper by Schlosberg (1965) reports a little comparative data for recognition of nouns and verbs. His method consisted of presenting

three short, three-letter words in sequence (one at a time), varying the interstimulus interval. At the interstimulus interval which gave the largest differences between kinds of words, about 60 msec, nouns had the advantage over verbs when they were presented first in the sequence. Verbs had the advantage over nouns when they were presented second. For the third position in the sequence, overall the most favorable for recognizing anything, nouns and verbs were equivalent and yielded essentially identical scores. Schlosberg interpreted the interaction of part of speech with position for the first two words as due to the subject's expectation of parts of speech, based on customary sentence order. For the third position, which might be considered relatively neutral in this respect, we find no relationship between noun or verb and ease of recognition. This result probably tells us that, like meaning, helpful redundancies of syntax operate mainly over units larger than the word.

Inflections of a word, on the other hand, have been shown in the case of verb tense to affect recognition, though not in the sense of lowering the threshold. Gibson and Guinet (1971) studied pickup of morphological transformations (verb inflections) in third- and fifth-grade children and college sophomores. Words were exposed briefly one at a time on a screen for the subject to read and record. There were three types of base words (real words, pronounceable nonsense words, and unpronounceable nonsense words) varying in length from four to seven letters. There were four versions of each one: the base word alone, the third person singular (*s* was added to the base word), the past tense (*ed* was added), and the progressive (*ing* was added). The questions asked were whether the verb ending functioned as a subunit of the word, resisting errors and permitting a longer word to be read, and whether such a tendency, if present, was learned by third grade or only later.

As in earlier experiments, the real words were read with fewest errors and the pronounceable nonsense words with next fewest. A base word lengthened by an inflectional suffix was not read more correctly than a word of equivalent length that did not contain a suffix. But the inflectional endings themselves were read with fewer errors than noninflectional endings on words of equivalent length. Furthermore, if an error was made on the inflected ending, there was a tendency to substitute one of the other inflections (for example, *ing* for *ed*). Both these latter tendencies increased from third to fifth grades. Thus, inflectional endings tend to be processed as unitary word features and this is done increasingly as reading skill develops. They can therefore serve as clues to structure of a phrase or a sentence. But they add another kind of information (morphological) to the base word. Their presence does not, therefore, facilitate recognition of the word as a whole, since an additional feature must be processed. The base word is marked with a feature that says "present tense" or "past tense" or "progressive," and it seems to be processed separately, albeit unitarily.

Subjective Variables

All the variables so far discussed can be considered, in some sense, features of the word itself that may or may not be extracted or known to the reader. But recognition of single words may also be affected by subjective variables that are contributed by the reader and that vary from one occasion to another and from person to person. Being hungry or not hungry, having special personal interests or values, or being set to expect something are all examples of such variables, and they can interact with the information in the word itself to affect the reading process by setting priorities for features or giving different values to features. These variables are often responsible for errors, ones consistent with the nature of the subjective variable. They increase recognizability only when the word's actual features happen to coincide with the subjective variable. For that reason, a lengthy study of them would not add greatly to our understanding of the reading process, but it is worth giving a few examples of experiments with such variables to show how they interact with information in the text.

Physiological needs have often been thought to be the strongest class of internal variables—needs like thirst and hunger. Do such needs affect one's perception of immediately present stimulation? Do they even affect the accuracy and speed with which a word is perceived? They would undoubtedly have little or no effect if the stimulus display was of high contrast and ample duration. Studies investigating the question have therefore typically used low contrast or very brief presentations. Wispé and Drambarean (1953) hypothesized that with increasing physiological need the recognition thresholds for need-relevant verbal stimuli would be lowered: that hungry and thirsty subjects would report food and water words more rapidly than neutral words. Would a hungry person see *waffle* at a lower threshold than *waddle,* for instance? Or a thirsty person see *lemonade* at a lower threshold than *serenade?* The authors varied word frequency, as well as membership or nonmembership in a relevant category. Subjects were deprived of food and water for one of three periods: 0 to 2 hours, 10 hours, or 24 hours. The words were exposed very briefly and then exposure duration was increased by short intervals until the correct word was reported. The subjects were encouraged to guess. There was a significant interaction between need-relevant versus neutral words and the three periods of deprivation. At the zero (shortest) period of deprivation, there was no difference between the need and the neutral words, while after longer intervals of deprivation the need-word thresholds were lower than the neutral-word thresholds.

The question arises as to the importance of this variable. Does it account for more of the variance than word frequency? The answer was definitely "No." Word-commonness was the more important factor. But the motivational variable was nevertheless effective in itself, perhaps not very surprising considering the instruction given the subjects to guess when they could not see clearly.

Another internal subjective variable that has been investigated frequently in studies of word recognition is the subject's system of personal values. Values for these studies were typically defined and measured by a scale deriving from the Allport-Vernon Study of Values (1931). A questionnaire investigated the relative priority of a subject's interests relative to six general areas: theoretical, economic, aesthetic, social, political, and religious. The first of these experiments (Postman, Bruner, and McGinnies, 1948) hypothesized that words representing the areas of interest that a subject valued highly would lead to short mean duration thresholds of recognition because the subjects would be selectively sensitized to them. Subjects were ranked for strength of interest in the six areas and words relevant to all six areas were exposed to them. There was a slight tendency for words representing highly valued interests to have lower thresholds than those representing less valued areas. This finding was challenged by other psychologists, especially by Solomon and Howes (1951), who felt that the superiority of recognition in the subjects' areas of high interest could be accounted for by their greater familiarity with words in that area. They repeated the Bruner et al. experiment with low- and high-frequency words from the various areas and found word frequency to be the most significant main variable. The subject-by-frequency interaction was significant also, lending support to their hypothesis that values operate to build familiarity with words in any person's life history and thus affect recognition. The subject is more apt to be familiar with the words in his field of interest, and this will show up especially when the less frequent words are presented and he is compared with people having different value systems. The word value effect on recognition, they thought, was dependent on building individual frequencies of exposure linked to personal interests. The effect of motivation could operate, as a consequence, by making a child attend to the structure and information in words that interest him and thus enhance the learning process. Teachers typically capitalize on this possibility by letting the child choose words he wants to know.

Another measure of value of words is obtained by ratings on Osgood's "semantic differential." Johnson, Thomson, and Frinke (1960) and Johnson, Frinke, and Martin (1961) selected words rated differentially as good or bad by students on the good-bad dimension of the semantic differential and compared them for differences in visual duration threshold. Even with frequency controlled, the good words were reported at slightly lower thresholds than the bad words. However, they found that good words had higher m values than bad words even with frequency controlled, so whether goodness as such has any control over a word's perceptibility is unclear. In any case, there is no apparent lesson to be drawn for reading, since *danger* is rated as a bad word although it is obviously one for which a low threshold of recognition would be desirable.

One other subjective factor that has an extremely strong effect on word recognition should be mentioned here for completeness, although it will be reserved for full treatment in a later section. That is the subject's expectation. Expectation can be induced in many ways, for instance by instruction. A classical demonstration of the effect of instructions on perception is to tell a group of subjects that a list of words will be flashed on a screen, all of them belonging to some category, like animals or food. If ambiguous words are then flashed on the screen, the viewer is apt to record more words belonging to the category suggested to him than neutral words or words belonging to a nonsuggested category.

An example of such an experiment is one by Samuels (1968a) with both college students and fourth graders as subjects. They were presented with very short exposures of word pairs. The pairs on one condition consisted of an adjective followed by a noun with an obvious semantic relevance (e.g., *dark night*). The subjects were familiarized with the pairs before testing. Other pairs provided controls without such relevance, or pairs with which the subject had not been familiarized beforehand. The nouns were also presented singly, with and without previous familiarization. Appropriate associations within pairs had a strong facilitative effect on recognizing the noun target for both adults and children. Children showed more interference than adults when an inappropriate adjective preceded a noun (e.g., *dark noise*). Children also showed a much stronger tendency than adults to guess from a previously familiarized list. The adults set themselves a higher criterion of confidence for actually perceived information than the children.

Context is both useful and effective in reading, as we shall see in Chapter 10. But the children's extreme willingness to guess was not an asset for accuracy of report, and trapped them into many errors.

Summary

This chapter considered in some detail the factors that influence recognition of words. Although we seldom read single words, but rather connected text, these studies do tell us a good deal about a number of variables that appear to influence the speed or accuracy of perceiving a word. Perceiving a word obviously has something to do with reading, even though information usually comes in larger segments. A word was defined as a composite of features, classified as graphic, orthographic, phonological, semantic, and syntactic. Another feature of a word which may be considered as having an objective aspect (but also a subjective one) is its frequency of occurrence in the language (paralleled, to some extent at least, by its familiarity to the reader). There are also subjective variables, internal and individual rather than belonging to the word, that affect how easily a word or what word is perceived.

Any or all of these variables might affect a word's recognizability. Evidence for the effectiveness or noneffectiveness of all of them was considered. Features of a word may be given different priorities depending on the task or on a subject's expectations. Indeed, the subjective variables interact with those in the word by setting priorities for extraction of information, and often lead to errors because other informational features go unexamined.

Within the word itself, when it is not part of a larger context, facilitation of correct recognition may be the result of some type of redundancy that produces economy either because it can be used selectively (e.g., the two meanings of a homograph) or because it reduces information. The prime example of the latter is the conditional constraints imposed on a word by the rules of orthography and phonology. Only certain combinations of letters or sounds *can* be a word. Knowledge of these rules even in the skilled reader is tacit rather than explicit, but it is there and has been shown to be used to great advantage. Children acquire this knowledge slowly, partly perhaps because it is implicit, but it is crucial for reading programs to provide the kinds of experience that will permit maximal extraction of the conditional relations in English orthography.

II

The Study of Reading

8

The Development of Prereading Skills

With our study of the basic psychological and linguistic principles that underlie reading completed, we shall turn to the process of learning to read. But learning to read does not begin with associating a written word with a spoken one. A number of subordinate skills must have developed to some level of maturity before a child can benefit from actual reading instruction. Schools have long recognized this and generally administer tests of "reading readiness" to children at the end of kindergarten or the beginning of first grade. What is it that a child must know in order to make easy progress in learning to read? There has been keen interest in this question in recent years since attention has been drawn to the "disadvantaged" child who is presumably going to have some problems when he enters school. Since reading is a language skill, it seems obvious that a good knowledge of his mother tongue should be at his command when he is about to read and write it. The difficulty of learning to read for the deaf child is legendary, and there seems no doubt that it is his lack of knowledge of the language that is responsible. But what about the hearing child? Speech is ordinarily very well developed by six years, when children are frequently dubbed "chatterboxes" and certainly seem to have little or no trouble in communicating with adults or other children. Is there any need to worry about the linguistic foundation for reading?

The Perception of Speech Sounds

Just how precise is a child's perception of the sounds of speech? What is the specificity of correspondence between the stimulus information and what the six-year-old listener extracts from it? The earlier chapters stressed that the speech stimulus contains three classes of information: meaning, grammar, and sound. The third of these, the phonetic information that can be analyzed and discriminated at a number of levels, receives little attention in ordinary communication. In listening to the speaker's message, we attend to his meaning, what he intends to tell us, not the sound (unless he is speaking too loudly or not loud enough). We simply are not aware, normally, of the phonological aspects of speech despite the fact that we can produce them ourselves.

It has become very clear in recent years, however, that rather specific discrimination of aspects of the phonetic stream is important for learning to read, and that these discriminations are not necessarily at the automatic disposal of even an accomplished speaker. Any system of writing with a phonetic basis, whether syllabic or alphabetic, demands some perceptual analysis of the speech stream in order to match it to the written code.

What units of speech does a child hear? Speech consists of an infinite number of combinations of a quite small number of components (see Chapter 4). Fragmentation and recombination of sounds appear to be essential for mastery of the speech system and for decoding it to written symbols. It is this fragmentation and recombination in innovative utterances that so far seems to be beyond the ability of any animal but man. The child must develop the ability to hear *segmentation* in what is spoken to him before we can reasonably expect him to learn to map the written code to speech or vice versa. To quote Savin (1972, p. 319),

Practically all discussions of learning to read assume that the child already perceives speech as a sequence of phonemes and that the heart of learning to read (at least at the beginning, in the *cat-rat-hat* stage) is quite simply learning which letters of the alphabet correspond with which phonemes.

But as Chapter 5 made clear, young children do not automatically analyze the phonemic information in speech. Before five or so, they do not even always hear words as subordinate units. Japanese children who begin learning to read with a syllabary are taught to analyze speech into syllables before they learn the written symbols for them and this accomplishment is a necessary precursor (Muraishi, 1972). Analysis to a level as fine as the phonemes, with any awareness of it at least, certainly cannot be taken for granted, as we saw. But to quote Savin again, "In the present author's experience everyone who has failed to learn to read even the simplest prose by the end of first grade has been unable to analyze syllables into phonemes, as shown by the following observations: They are insensitive to rhyme" (p. 321). He gives the example of a child who was read aloud the *hat-cat-fat* list and then asked whether *bicycle* belonged to the same family. The child responded "Yes."

Exactly what are the facts here? It seems as if children must hear rhymes, because they generalize (make confusion errors) on the basis of sound similarities (see Chapter 3). Furthermore, they make "clang" associations on free association tests. In fact, Entwisle (1966a and b) found that the percentage of rhymes produced as free associations by children was high in kindergarten and then dropped steadily through third grade. But these errors and spontaneous associations are evidently not the result of acoustic analysis and conscious awareness of the similarity.

An extensive test of the rhyming abilities of two samples of kindergarten children, aged about $5\frac{1}{2}$ years, has been reported by Calfee, Chapman, and Venezky (1970; also in Gregg, 1972). The child was asked whether or not two words "sounded the same at the end." He was first given a pretraining series with corrective feedback. None of the children did better than chance. In another test, the child was asked to produce a rhyme. First, the experimenter gave two rhymes for each word spoken by the child in a picture-naming task. Then the child was asked to give a rhyme to a word pronounced by the experimenter as the name of a picture. He was given feedback and two rhymes when he failed. The percentage of rhymes produced was 39%. The distribution of the children's scores was bimodal; some were quite good at the task and even gave nonsensical rhymes. But a number of children failed on every item. It appeared that these children simply did not have the concept of phonetic similarity, or that the task given did not succeed in tapping the skill. Later testing of a group of Israeli children (Venezky, Shiloah, and Calfee, 1972) with three versions of a rhyming task confirmed these findings. Success on a rhyming task was also found to correlate very significantly with scores on a test of reading achievement at the end of first grade. Ability to recognize and produce rhyme thus seems to indicate ability to deal with sounds as abstractions. Kindergarten children tested for rhyming in the spring surpassed those tested in the fall, and first graders, as a group, surpassed both.

The ability to perceive the rhyming likeness is important for later acquisition of spelling patterns, so time spent in any activity that promotes it is not wasted. Children can learn to play rhyming games and abstract the concept of rhyme in this way. One such game is "stinky-pinky." The listener is given a simple definition of a two-word phrase whose components rhyme, for instance, "an overweight animal that meows." He is supposed to guess the answer (*fat cat*), and then he can have a turn asking someone else to guess. Several simple instances (e.g., *pretty kitty, dumb thumb, funny bunny*) usually suffice to teach the game to children of six, or whenever they become able to produce a simple definition (or even a partial one).

The evidence on development of ability to analyze speech into segments has already been presented in Chapter 5, but we shall return to the topic at the end of this chapter when some empirical studies and programs for teaching segmentation will be briefly summarized.

Early Development of Graphic Discrimination and Writing

Scribbling and Spontaneous Writing

We have considered the early genesis of speech in Chapter 5 in some detail. Just as sound making has a long development, so does graphic production. Sound production begins spontaneously in young infants as babbling. Graphic production, if the child is given an appropriate tool and a surface for marking, begins spontaneously also, although somewhat later than babbling. In Cattell's scale of infant intelligence (1960), the normal age for a child to scribble spontaneously when given pencil and paper is 18 months. Given a demonstration, he will produce scribbles even earlier. Why does he do this? It has sometimes been claimed that he does it merely for the sake of exercising his arms and hands. J. Gibson and P. Yonas (1968) demonstrated that this is by no means the case. The child is interested in looking at the traces he is making and will cease at once if he cannot see his production. "The making of traces on a surface, the controlling of the displayed trace, and the seeing of these new display variables were assumed to motivate the act of scribbling, not the transient feedback from the activity itself" (Gibson and Yonas, p. 355).

Fourteen children, ranging in age from 15 to 38 months (mean age 28 months) were studied in their homes in a free-play situation. The experimenter simply presented the child with a paper attached to a board, and one of two tools, identical except that one left a trace whereas the other did not. Each child was given a session with both tools, and his intervals of scribbling were timed. For all the subjects, elimination of the trace significantly reduced scribbling activity. The infants often called attention to the scribbles by pointing or naming, but this behavior did not occur when the tool left no trace. One 16-month-old subject had had no previous experience with trace-making tools. She was first handed the nontracing tool, but did not scribble. When given the tracing tool, she at first waved it, then fortuitously struck the paper, saw the mark left on it and began scribbling with great interest and increasing control. She had discovered what the authors refer to as the "fundamental graphic act." The act of trace making helps the child to distinguish the variables of graphic information

—straightness, curvature, tilt, continuity, closedness, intersection, and so on—variables that he must be able to distinguish and use as a feature set when he learns to read. Scribbling seems to be its own reward, and furthermore it furnishes an unparalleled opportunity for learning the relations between the finger movements that guide the tool and the resulting visual feedback.

Children perceive and comprehend pictures long before they learn to read. Lines on paper can correspond to the edges of surfaces in the world and can be thought of as representing them. A photograph of a tree or a line drawing of a tree has an iconic or projective likeness to it which is understood without learning (Hochberg and Brooks, 1962). For writing this is not the case, but for the human species, at least, the making of nonpictorial graphs is nevertheless interesting and has a genetic development which seems to be to some extent self-directed, as two classic studies tell us.

Hildreth (1936) and Legrün (1932) studied children's early productions of "writing" and classified them into stages or levels. Hildreth observed the writing behavior of children between three and six at a private school in Manhattan. The children were given materials and requested to write their names or any letters or numbers they could make. If they demurred, they were told "just to pretend they could write." She set a zero level, a scribble, below three years. Level 1 was "something beyond aimless scribbling . . . [with] considerable tendency toward the horizontal and some systematic 'up and down' scratching" (p. 294). Level 2 was a more regular form of level 1 with consistent linearity. A contrast between straight lines and curves, opposite diagonals, and intersections can be observed in some of the samples at level 3, that is, a greater variety of features used contrastively. Level 4 has well-marked units and real or approximations to real letters. The levels are illustrated in Figure 8-1. These children were all classified as prereaders. Their parents had not encouraged the children to write, they said, leading Hildreth to conclude that "writing" improves from ages three to six without any direct instruction.

Legrün's observations resulted in five stages, also illustrated in Figure 8-1. These stages were:
1. Unorganized scribbles.
2. Zig-zag lines without much variation in form.
3. Better-articulated forms showing some variation of structure but not broken up into parts.

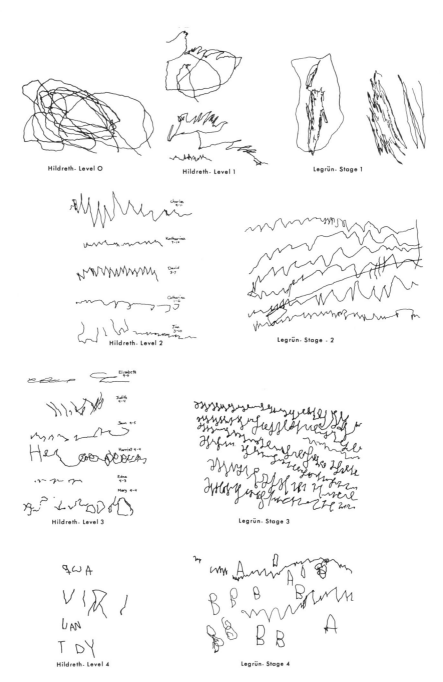

Figure 8-1. Representative samples of "writing" in its early stages of development. From the Society for Research in Child Development, Inc. © 1936 by the Society for Research in Child Development.

4. Increased differentiation of forms with linear arrangement of elements divided up to look like words.
5. Further differentiation with occasional interpositions of true letters and figures.

Lavine (1972), in summarizing these results, commented that as early as age three many children are producing "forms that contain features that are characteristic of writing and not of pictures—linearity and horizontal orientation. Many at this age also produce variation of height" (p. 25). There is thus some early, painless, and apparently self-motivated learning about the writing system for the school to build on later. Durkin (1966) found that children who read early had a strong interest in printing prior to or simultaneous with learning to read. Described as "pencil and paper kids," they moved in sequence from scribbling and drawing to copying letters, to questions about spelling, to learning to read.

A prereading program can easily furnish opportunities for children to produce writing and present models, thus capitalizing on their spontaneous motivation. Such an informal preschool program was undertaken by Ginsburg, Wheeler, and Tulis (1970) and the results followed up in a thesis by Wheeler (1971). No attempt was made to teach reading or letter-sound correspondences, nor was there formal instruction of any kind. The setting was an open classroom in a public-school kindergarten. The children were given notebooks and told to do their writing in them, but they were free to choose and to take part in a number of other activities. Models, including alphabet and word charts, were present in the room from which they could copy if they wished. The children did spend a fair amount of time in some form of graphic activity, varying from scribbling to (later in the year) writing some words and phrases.

Wheeler (1971) analyzed the children's productions, dividing the school year into 15 ten-day periods, to see if the spontaneous graphic activity showed any developmental trends. The productions were coded as scribbles, designs, pictures, letters, numbers, words, sequences of related words, sentences, and symbols (e.g., a " + " sign). There appeared to be a sequence in the frequency of these categories, with scribbles occurring most often early in the year, and the following order as the year progressed: designs, pictures, letters, words in isolation, word phrases, words in sentences, and finally symbols. The main conclusion was that the quality of the output improved over the year, apparently by spontaneous self-correction since no teacher or adult intervened to correct errors. The children varied greatly in the number of letters produced, but they all produced some, with increasing frequency. The letters were analyzed for errors, with the finding that errors decreased as the year went on; at the end of the year, most of the errors appeared to be attributable to confusion with another letter (e.g., *h* for *n*). Errors in production were found to correspond well with errors in discrimination (by comparison with data of Gibson, Schapiro, and Yonas, 1968). Figure 8-2, from Wheeler (1971), shows the change in context of the letters produced over the year. Letters in isolation gave way to letters in words.

Children did, then, progress in writing with purely spontaneous motivation and without specific instruction. It must be remembered, however, that much of the graphic activity as the child increased his output of letters and words was the result of copying, so in a sense it is not true writing. Does a child learn to read by engaging in spontaneous graphic activity? Not as indicated by this experiment, for the children could apparently read very little of what they had produced by the end of the year. But as a prereading activity which provides opportunities for learning the visual

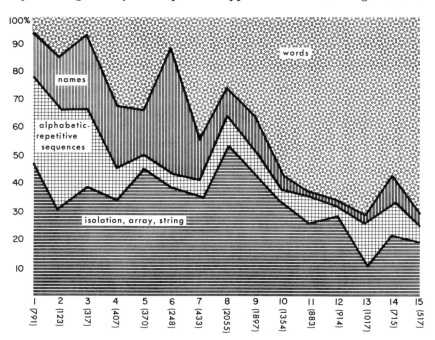

Figure 8-2.   Percentage of letters produced in isolation, in repetitive strings, in names, and in words from beginning to end of a kindergarten year. From Wheeler, p. 76.

characteristics of letters, the features that distinguish them, it may be a very effective exercise. We shall turn now to the perception (as opposed to production) of graphic displays.

Differentiation of Writing from Pictures

Both pictorial representations and writing develop from the "fundamental graphic act," taking diverse courses. How early does a child perceive the difference between a pictorial representation and a non-pictorial graph? How early does he perceive writing as writing? Since perception very often precedes production (in language comprehension, for instance) it is possible that children recognize writing not only as different from pictures but as writing before they are able to read or produce a letter or word. Lavine (1972) investigated this question with children between the ages of 3 and $6\frac{1}{2}$ years who had not yet been taught to read. Her essential method was to show a number of graphic displays to children, to see whether they could classify them as pictures or writing, and then to ask them what they were, getting more precise information about their ability to identify both.

The variables of her study were the child's age, his cultural background, and most importantly, differences built into the stimulus displays. In generating the displays, she attempted to locate and provide examples of characteristics emerging in the historical development of writing systems (see Chapter 6). What features do children settle upon as criteria for writing? How early do they do it? Must they know how to read a letter in order to know that it is a letter? Do they learn the distinctive features that characterize letters as a set before differentiating individual letters?

The variables chosen by Lavine for investigation were iconicity (pictorial representativeness), multiplicity of units, linearity, variety of units, and graphic characteristics of individual writing systems, such as the Roman alphabet, cursive writing, Hebrew writing, and Chinese characters. These variables were contrasted in separate displays and also combined in various ways, such as a presentation of a linear, multiple-unit, iconic display. Variety of units, multiplicity of units, and units arranged linearly in a string were thought of as intuitively universal descriptive characteristics of writing. Variety was defined as no more than two contiguous identical units in a string. The displays could also be classified in three other ways: as conventional writing actually present in the child's own environment,

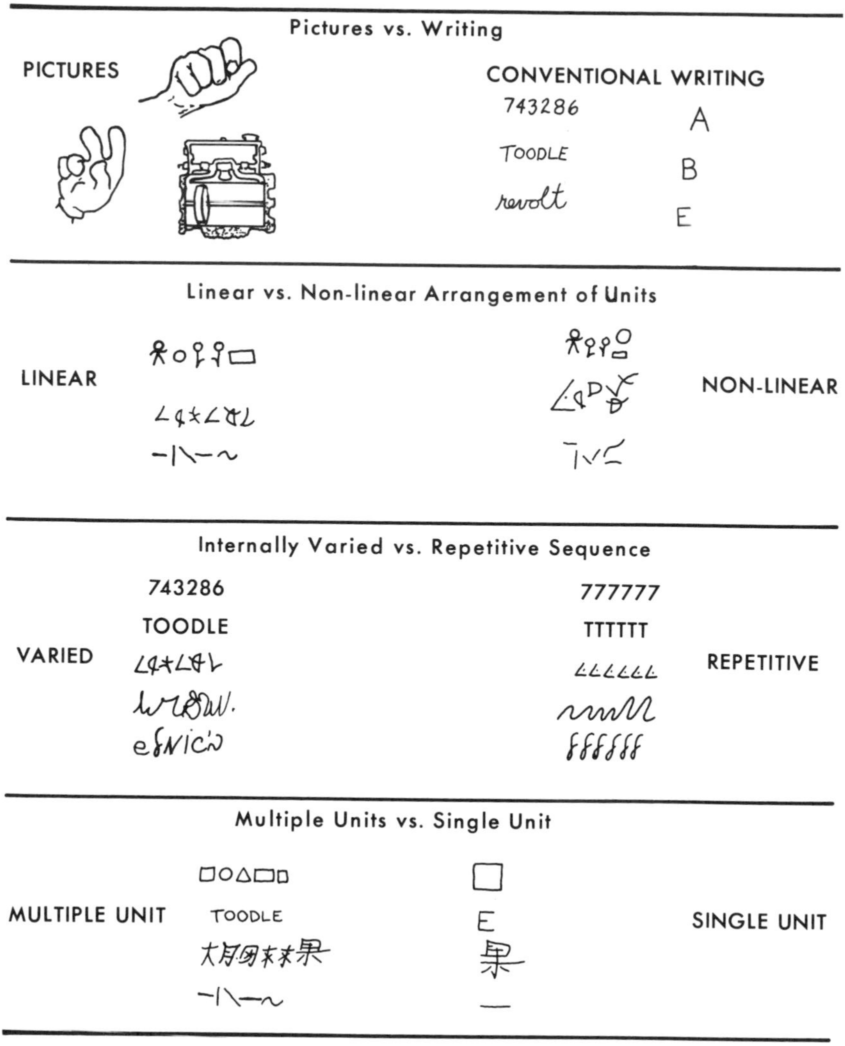

Figure 8-3. Displays contrasting categorical features and nonfeatures of writing as characterized by Lavine. From Lavine, 1972.

as similar in features to conventional writing but not present in the child's environment, and as neither truly similar to conventional writing nor present in the environment but having some characteristics of writing, like linearity in nonrepetitive designs. Some of the displays used are presented in Figure 8-3.

The displays were prepared on plastic-coated cards so that the child could handle them and sort them into two appropriate receptacles, one for writing (a mailbox) and one for nonwriting (a cylindrical wallpaper-covered receptacle). The child's verbal responses were recorded verbatim and later coded as (1) writing (any term commonly used to denote writing or a form of writing, such as "letters" or a specific letter name), (2) alien writing (writing mentioned, but unconventionality indicated), (3) object label, (4) name of abstract form, like "square," (5) don't know.

Three single letters, A, B, and E, were included among the displays. Children from a middle-class neighborhood in Ithaca, New York, when asked to name them showed an increasing ability with age to name one or more. Of the three-year-olds, 27% could name two; of the four- to five-year-olds, 47% could name two; and of the five- and six-year-olds, 67% could name two. None could read any of the words. When responses to iconic displays were compared with noniconic, the iconic displays were always given object labels, never called writing. The samples of true writing were labeled in some way as writing by 86% of the three-year-olds, 90% of the four-year-olds, and 96% of the oldest age group. It is clear that even three-year-olds distinguish between graphic displays depicting objects and those containing letters (single letters or a word), whether or not they are able to name the letter or read the word.

What are the criteria used by the child to recognize a display as writing? Separate analysis of the variables showed that linear arrangement played a role, but not a heavy one when the units of the display were not actually letters. Variety (nonrepetitiveness of units) was definitely a factor influencing the child's categorization of the display as writing and showed a tendency to increase with age. Multiple-unit displays were more often responded to as writing than single-unit displays, but the difference was absent for the two older groups when the displays were actually letters. The important information for them was in the features of the letters themselves, not in some more global feature of the string.

A similar but less marked increasing sensitivity to familiar features of

Table 8-1 Percentage of Subjects Responding "Writing" to Displays Varying in
Alienness

		Age 3	Age 4	Age 5
Roman	TOODLE	87%	93%	100%
Cursive	*revolt*	87%	93%	87%
Artificial Characters	∠ ٩ ت∠ ʁ ⊦	93%	93%	73%
Hebrew	e ʃ N i c ᴎ	87%	100%	100%
Mayan Design	‖ ᴔ‖ ⌐ˀ 日	27%	0%	7%
Chinese	大 月 夕 禾 禾 果	40%	13%	20%

Source: Lavine, 1972.

real letters is indicated in Table 8-1, where displays varying in similarity
to the print or script actually present in the child's surroundings are
compared. The real printed word in Roman type is responded to as writing
100% of the time by five-year-olds (though none could read it), but the
artificial characters in line three of the table only 73% of the time. The
Hebrew characters got a 100% response of writing, doubtless because they
are real letters making use of many of the same distinctive features as
Roman characters. The design and the string of Chinese characters, although linear and varied, differ from both Roman and Hebrew script in
internal features, and only the youngest group showed much tendency to
call them writing. Knowledge of the pattern of features (unique structure)
of each letter was obviously still incomplete, judging from the absence of
a difference in responses to Roman script and Hebrew.

What have the children learned that permits them to classify writing so
accurately before they can read, when they can name few letters, if any,
and do not know the unique shape of each letter? It seems that they have
learned the set of internal contrastive features used for writing and some of
the global characteristics, like variety of elements and multiple units, although the component feature contrasts seem to be the most salient
criteria. Yet the children do not learn individual shapes first and then
later induce the component features. It would seem that the features must
be abstracted first, followed by the differentiation of individual letters as
unique shapes. A very interesting thing about these results is that the children do this learning spontaneously, painlessly, and without formal in-

struction. Since they differentiate letters as writing without knowing their names and without having them identified in each case by even a class name (witness the high response to Hebrew writing, which few had ever seen) one cannot appeal to labeling explanations via learning either individual or category names. The case is one of pure perceptual learning. Children seem to develop tremendous sensitivity to differences in graphic materials simply by having plenty of graphic displays around to look at.

The necessity of everyday exposure to written material for this learning to occur was apparent in other results obtained by Lavine when the same tests were given two groups of children in Yucatan, Mexico, one in a city in a fair stage of technological advancement (Merida) and one in a remote rural village where reading matter and print were rare. The children growing up in the culture that provided a very limited exposure to print were by no means as knowledgeable about writing as the Ithaca group we have described. Cultural setting was at least as significant a variable as age. It is interesting, though, that children from all three environments distinguished pictures from writing at three years.

Development of Graphic Discrimination

The research just reviewed tells us that children in a middle-class environment with ample exposure to print have come a long way toward the visual discrimination of letters before reading instruction is begun. But in general, it is the contrastive features that define the set as writing that have been learned rather than the unique shape of each letter as a separate entity. Children do continue to progress in discrimination of letterlike forms up to the age of eight, as research described in Chapter 2 (pp. 36 ff.) showed, although by seven years changes in features important for writing (straight vs. curved, orientation, open vs. closed) are usually detected, even in artificial, unfamiliar material. Even left-right reversals, the bugaboo of teachers, yield less than 10% errors.

How much trouble does visual discrimination of one letter from another actually give children at the beginning of first grade? They do not ordinarily confuse many letters, even at four years (see discussion of confusion matrices for letters in Chapter 2). Features used to discriminate letters fall into a pattern much like an adult's, as cluster analyses described in Chapter 2 demonstrated. Calfee, Chapman, and Venezky (1970) tested two samples of kindergarten children on matching letters at various levels of difficulty. When single letters were presented for matching to a choice series of five letters, the error rate was quite low (83% and 87% correct matches overall), even though the letters had been especially chosen to be confusing, as in the samples below:

G—C Q G D O   r—n m w r u
b—h d b f k

The major source of error was the right-left mirror image transformation (e.g., *b* vs. *d*). Errors on these items were high (around 40%), but otherwise there were almost no errors.

When letter groups were tested, the error rate increased sharply. A typical example of a bigram group was:

CQ—OQ OC QC CQ CO

Note that there is an order reversal, as well as letters with high visual confusability in the matching set. Correct choices fell to 36% and 48%. Choices of reverse order accounted for most of the errors. For groups of three and four letters, the percent correct dropped to 30% and 35%. When the child had to match from memory, with the standard removed before the matching series was presented, his performance was no worse, but reversal and order errors still prevailed.

The fact that matching was essentially perfect with single letters except for reversals agrees with anecdotal and empirical results from many sources. Estimations agree that more than half of all kindergarteners make these errors. It was suggested in Chapter 2 that this is an obvious and only-to-be-expected error, since from the child's point of view up to the time of reaching school, it is not an error: Objects are many-sided and shape is perceived as constant. For most children, the error is corrected in a reasonable length of time. Shankweiler and Liberman (1972) tested a large number of third-grade children with word lists (60 real-word monosyllables) containing a number of potentially reversible letters, having them read the words aloud. Reversals of single letters accounted for only a small proportion of the errors, even for the poorest readers (10% for a selected group of very poor readers). Taking account of opportunities for error, they occurred less frequently than other consonant errors. After the first grade, even children who have made little progress in learning to read have little difficulty in visually identifying single letters (Shankweiler and Liberman, 1972; Shankweiler, 1964).

Sequence reversal and order mistakes in letter strings and real words are another matter. Word matching and matching letter strings are difficult for kindergarteners (Calfee et al., 1970) and are still a prime source of difficulty for third graders who read poorly (Shankweiler and Liberman, 1972). Experienced readers (see Chapter 7) recognize words via orthographic patterns larger than the letter (subordinate units like constrained clusters and syllables), but beginning readers do not process words this way and information about order in the letter string is lost. Errors of order in matching a string of letters or reading a word are not necessarily reversals. "Permutation confusions are common and although there is little systematic research on the problem, right-left order-reversal confusions appear to occur frequently in word matching but not so exclusively as right-left mirror-image confusions in single-letter matching" (Calfee et al., 1970, p. 13).

When matching tests for single-letter orientation, letter order (with a reversal distractor), and letter-string detail (a distractor with a similar letter substituted in a group of three) were given to three kindergarten populations of different socioeconomic status in the early fall, significant differences were apparent. Test performance improved as the socioeconomic status of the school population increased. But retests given in February showed much less variance due to socioeconomic status. The figures in Table 8-2 are taken from a report by Chapman (1971) and show only small differences between the populations. The children had learned something and the groups were evening up. Exactly what or how they had learned is not obvious.

Besides the ability to discriminate between letters and between letter strings (skills somewhat analogous to the ability to recognize similarities

Table 8-2   Percentage Correct for Tests of Visual Matching Given to Three Kindergarten Groups of Different Socioeconomic Status in February (Wisconsin Basic Prereading Skills Project)

	High SES	Middle SES	Low SES
Orientation	88.0%	88.5%	79.0%
Letter Order	81.5%	80.5%	75.0%
Letter String Detail	86.5%	83.0%	79.5%

and differences between phonetic units of various sizes), there is also a segmentation ability required of the beginning reader, but one by no means as serious a source of difficulty as phonemic segmentation. Children do not automatically understand the different units of visual text such as a letter, a word, a phrase, or a sentence. Beginning first graders do not perceive the boundaries of written words as such, in many cases (Meltzer and Herse, 1969). When asked to point out words, a child may indicate letters or whole lines of text. Since words are actually separated by spaces greater than those between letters, the information on the page should be fairly easy to distinguish once the child has the concept of a graphic word. The fact that words are units of speech and also units in a printed text and as such correspond is obviously a basic concept to get across early in the game.

Discrimination Training
Despite the fact that frequency of visual confusions of letters at ages five and six seems in the past to have been exaggerated, there are still many children in kindergartens who make some confusions, especially of mirror-reversal letters and of order within letter strings. Training children to make the necessary discriminations has been the subject of considerable research, often generated by a theory of perceptual learning.

One of the earliest theories to find favor was espoused by Fernald (1943), who was concerned with remedial techniques for helping retarded readers. She emphasized the value of motor practice in learning to distinguish confusable letters and words, assuming rather like the Soviet "motor copy" theorists of perceptual development that the activity of producing the shape would contribute to development of a "schema" or image that would form the basis of correct discrimination. But tracing an outline or copying (motor pretraining) was not found to be particularly effective for developing recognition of letters (Williams, 1969). Practice in discriminating "hard" pairs, without motor reproduction of them, was more effective.

Although motor pretraining is not particularly effective as training for recognition, it is possible that such training might help in forming an arbitrary association, such as a letter with its name. Levin, Watson, and Feldman (1963) investigated this possibility, using artificial graphemes arranged in a string, each grapheme paired with a sound. Pretraining conditions included tracing the graphemes, copying them, just observing them, etc. A small amount of motor pretraining before learning the verbal response was totally ineffective. Repeated tracing of an initial grapheme gave only slight facilitation for later association of the grapheme string and the verbal response. Tracing a medial or a terminal grapheme was actually worse than no tracing at all.

There seems to be no clear evidence that motor practice such as tracing or copying will facilitate learning a verbal naming response to the visually-presented graphic stimulus or even recognition of it. Still, very retarded children may get some benefit from motor pretraining that does not show up in the normal child who has little trouble with discrimination. Remedial workers often claim to have found this to be the case, and Montessori preschool classes emphasize modality—redundant presentation of letter shapes (tracing, coloring, cutouts, touching letters cut out of sandpaper, etc.)—but the effectiveness of such presentations has not been empirically documented.

A theory of perceptual learning rather similar to motor pretraining, though without the "copy" notion, goes by the name of "acquired distinctiveness of cues." The hypothesis holds that two initially confusable visual displays can be rendered perceptually more discrete by teaching a distinct and different response to each one. Hendrickson and Muehl (1962) tested this hypothesis with the letters *b* and *d*, requiring three groups of kindergarten children to learn names for them. One group (the attention-consistent motor group) was pretrained by making consistent directional motor responses, pushing a handle with the left hand to *d* and with the right hand to *b*. Arrows below the letters pointed to the left and right. (The arrow on the subject's left always pointed left for a left motor response and the opposite for a right motor response.) A second group, the attention-inconsistent motor group) differed in the placement of the arrows in relation to the motor response. Half the arrows pointed inward and half outward. The subject found the arrow that pointed the same way as the letter, sometimes on his left and sometimes on his right and pushed the handle with the hand on the same side as that arrow. Thus the motor responses to the two letters were inconsistent, half with the left hand and half with the right hand for both letters. A control group had irrelevant pretraining, matching color stimuli. The transfer task was learning the names of the two letters. The two groups that had motor pretraining did not differ significantly by any measure on learning the letter names. They both excelled the control group. The conclusion is inescapable that the nature of the motor response in relation to the letter's shape was of no importance.

Another pretraining experiment deriving from an S-R theoretical approach was performed by Staats and Staats (1962). Two groups of kindergarten children were given discrimination training and then had the task of associating the spoken version of the word to each of four visually presented words (a task referred to by the authors as "texting" behavior, which they consider "the operant conditioning of a vocal response under the control of a visual verbal stimulus"). In accordance with the theory, reinforcement (tokens exchangeable for toys) was "made contingent upon the emission of the correct vocal operants in both discrimination and texting training." One group had discrimination training with the words which were later used in the transfer task. The procedure was an oddity task in which three words were presented on a card, two identical and one different. The other group was pretrained with the 12 lower-case letters which were to be used in various combinations to form the four words in the transfer task. Three letters were presented on a card and the subject chose the odd one.

A control group received no discrimination pretraining. The transfer task was paired-associate learning with the subject trying to anticipate the correct response. Subjects who had had word-discrimination pretraining had more correct responses over the blocks of learning trials than did the other two groups. Seeing the actual words was somewhat more useful than seeing individual letters. An interesting finding of this experiment was the lack of a significant correlation between success in discrimination training and success in the paired-associate learning task. Insofar as Staats and Staats' learning task simulates early reading training, success on visual discrimination cannot be assumed to be a good predictor of reading achievement. Different processes are involved. It is noteworthy that many reading readiness tests, including the Frostig test, which is supposed to assess perceptual ability, are poor predictors of reading achievement (Rosen, 1966; Rosen and Ohnmacht, 1968; Pick, 1970). Two carefully prepared readiness testing programs that have been evaluated will be presented at the end of the chapter.

Whether or not success on discrimination training predicts association of written with spoken words and actual reading, the learner obviously has to be able to differentiate the written symbols in order to progress any further in learning to read. In that case, where discrimination training is needed, the question of how best to do it is not trivial. Another way of looking at discrimination training was proposed by Pick (1965), who investigated the effects of pretraining in a discrimination task on what children had actually learned by presenting them with different transfer tasks. Three groups of kindergarten children were given practice in discriminating transformations (three types) of some standard forms. All received the same practice on a matching task until they made no errors. Then they went on to a transfer task. For one group, the transfer task had the same standard forms as before but new transformations (called the *prototype* group). This group should have found the transfer task easy if they had constructed a schematic prototype of the standard forms. A second group, the *distinctive feature* group, had new standard forms, but their variants were made by performing the same transformation used in the training task. This group should have found the transfer task easy if they had learned the distinctive ways in which the transformations varied from the standard and from each other. A third group had both new standards and new transformations in the transfer task.

The distinctive feature group made fewest errors on the transfer task, the prototype group next, and the group with all new material most. Pick concluded that as children improve in their ability to discriminate among letter shapes, they are learning to attend to differences among the shapes rather than simply learning each letter as a structure. Pick's results were replicated by Odom, McIntyre, and Neale (1971), who found also that feature differences were learned most characteristically by reflective rather than impulsive children.

If children do learn to discriminate letter shapes by features, then the best instructional technique, if training is needed, would be to emphasize feature differences. Samuels (1970a) varied pretraining of kindergarten children before they learned the letter names for *b, d, p,* and *q.* One group was trained to note distinctive features of the letters; one was given visual discrimination training on the letters but not on their distinctive features. The first group surpassed the second in learning the letter names, but the second was no better than a control group with no pretraining. Emphasis on contrastive features that distinguish confusable letters would thus appear to have value, but providing the emphasis by adding some redundant characteristic like color is a dubious practice because children may come to rely on the redundant feature instead of the critical one, as they did in the experiment by Gibson and Shepela (1968) described in Chapter 2. (See also Samuels, 1968b.) Redundancy is useful when it combines with other information to form an economical rule or pattern. When it is simply an alternative that can be selected to the neglect of other information, it can hinder rather than help, depending on the task. Enhancing a feature difference with color and then gradually fading it out by use of a screen tinting process was found effective by Egeland, Braggins, and Powalski (1973).

Some of Piaget's notions of perceptual development have been applied to reading by Elkind (1967), especially Piaget's concept of "decentration." Decentration is presumed to increase developmentally as the child becomes more able to direct his own activity, freeing him from being "stimulus bound," or controlled by field effects produced by the stimulus display. Elkind and Deblinger (1969) gave a group of disadvantaged children training in "perceptual reorganization" (by, for instance, having them solve simple anagrams) and later compared their reading achievement with a comparable group of children who had not had the training. It is not clear that the training actually increased reading skill, nor is it clear why it should (see Pick, 1970, for a critique of this study).

We can summarize this section with the conclusion that letter discrimination normally proceeds quite well spontaneously and that confusion of single letters is seldom an important source of difficulty in learning to read, at least with the Roman alphabet. There is some reason to think that with certain alphabets, such as Hebrew (Feitelson, 1965), drill on visual letter discrimination is an important preparation for learning to read. If drill is given, it should not be on irrelevant material which will provide little or no transfer (as is true of some of the material in the Frostig program, for instance), and it should emphasize the distinctive features that account for the differences between letters. When letter strings are to be discriminated in a training situation, it seems wise to borrow a finding from research on perceptual learning of other problems and follow a progression from easily discriminated letters and words to more difficult ones.

Intermodal Matching and Association

Studies of Intermodal Matching
It has often been assumed that because reading involves decoding graphic symbols to sounds, some ability is required to match visual to auditory input, or to "integrate" the two. It has also been assumed that individual differences in such an ability can be tested and will predict reading achievement and even that training in such a matching task will be a good prereading task and will transfer to early reading achievement. All of these assumptions are doubtful, since there is no underlying similarity in the

auditory and visual input in speech and reading except at a high level where grammar and meaning are involved. The decoding mapping system is arbitrary as regards the physical units of the two modes, as examination of alternative writing systems shows (see Chapter 6). Nor is initial learning to read merely a matching task.

As Pick pointed out (1970), the tasks given to children to investigate intermodal matching, usually sequences of lights or dots and tones, are so unlike any aspect of the reading task that it seems implausible that the same processes are involved. Yet research in this area continues to multiply and it seems wise to scrutinize it critically. Birch and Belmont (1964, 1965) tapped out auditory patterns with a pencil, which were matched to spatially arranged dot patterns by 5- to 11-year-old children. Retarded readers were poorer at this task than normal ones, and the authors concluded that the retarded readers were deficient in auditory-visual integration. Over all children, there was improvement with age, but it leveled off, the greatest increase occurring between kindergarten and second grade. Scores correlated with reading achievement in first grade at a $< .001$ level of significance, in second grade at $< .05$, and after that there was no relationship. The correlation between IQ and reading, on the other hand, went up with age. The authors concluded that "perceptual factors" were most important for initial acquisition of reading skill but that "factors more closely associated with IQ are more important in its elaboration." This is a rather tempting conclusion, since reading skill certainly changes as it develops, but there is no reason to think that perceptual factors drop out or that matching dots and auditory patterns are representative perceptual factors.

Birch and Belmont's study has been criticized many times for confounding several important variables, for instance, sequential presentation of the auditory pattern and simultaneous spatial presentation of the dot pattern. Furthermore, the auditory pattern was always presented first. Even more critical for their interpretation (that it is the development of intermodal relations that is responsible for the correlation with reading skill) is the absence of intramodal controls. Later investigators have attempted to remedy these deficiencies in a number of experiments. The first of these (Blank and Bridger, 1966) presented visual stimuli sequentially. They compared a group of retarded readers and a group of normal readers. Members of the groups were matched on intelligence scores. They were given three tasks. One was a visual-visual task in which dot patterns similar to Birch and Belmont's were to be matched to temporally separated visual flashes, with long and short intervals between flashes made analogous to spatial separation of the dots. The temporal pattern was always given first. The retarded readers did significantly more poorly than the normal readers, despite the absence of an intermodal variable. In a second task, a standard dot pattern was shown, removed, and then a set of three dot patterns presented for the subject to select a match. There was no difference between retarded and normal readers on this task. In a third task, the children were shown a temporal sequence of light flashes and asked to give a verbal description of the sequence they had seen. The retarded readers performed worse than the normal ones; they had difficulty reporting both the number of lights and the placement of the pauses, and if one was reported accurately, the other tended not to be. The authors thought the retarded readers had difficulty applying conceptual categories to temporal sequences of stimuli. The measure is a rather peculiar one, however; it is possible that they could not have described the dot patterns either, although they matched them adequately. The subjects in this experiment were between nine and ten years old, and it is possible that quite different factors were at work than for Birch and Belmont's first graders.

Muehl and Kremenak (1966) also provided intramodal controls for Birch and Belmont's intermodal comparison, including the intermodal comparison as well. The visual task was a spatially presented dot-dash pattern (e.g., •—•). The auditory task was a patterned sequence of long and short sounds. There were four tasks, visual-visual, visual-auditory, auditory-visual, and auditory-auditory. The judgment was same-different; the subjects first graders. They were tested at the beginning of the year and reading achievement was assessed at the end. The visual-visual task was easiest, the auditory-auditory hardest. At the end of the year, the poorest 23% of the readers were compared with the best 22%. A multiple regression analysis was done with the four matching tasks. Only the two intermodal tasks contributed to the final prediction. The authors then performed a second regression analysis putting in scores from seven reading readiness subtests plus the four matching tests. Now only letter naming (one of the reading readiness tests) accounted for a significant portion of the variance. The two intermodal matching tasks correlated fairly significantly with letter naming. The conclusion was again drawn that reading involves ability to integrate auditory and visual information, but later studies throw further doubt on the interpretation.

Sterritt, Martin, and Rudnick (1969) combined all the possibilities of matching (auditory sequential, visual spatial, and visual sequential) in nine separate same-different matching tasks and gave them to third-grade children. They found that intelligence test scores predicted reading achievement very well, but the matching tests did not. Even a combined score from the nine tests showed very low correlations (r = .25 with phonics analysis and .23 with comprehension). Intramodal sequential matches related as well to reading as intermodal ones. None of the tests, in any case, seemed specifically related to reading at the third-grade level. Bryden (1972) also gave all the nine possible combinations of tests to pupils selected as poor and as good readers from the sixth grade. They were matched for IQ. All subjects took all tests. In an analysis of variance, the good readers were superior to the poor readers in overall performance (but only at the .05 level of significance). The deficit appeared on all tasks, no one of them showing a clearer relation to good or poor reading than another. Poor readers were deficient whether or not a visual-auditory transformation was required. There was thus no evidence that poor reading in sixth grade was related to a specific deficit in intermodal integration. When the poor readers and the good readers were separated, there was a fairly high correlation within the group of poor readers (.60) but a very low one (.14) within the group of good readers. Thus, at the sixth-grade level, matching performance is a predictor of reading ability only in poor readers. Bryden thought coding the sequential patterns and retaining them over the 10-second interstimulus interval might be the important factor for the poor readers, but another experiment by Vande Voort, Senf, and Benton (1972) makes this interpretation unlikely.

Vande Voort et al. gave two intramodal matching tasks, visual-visual (simultaneous dot patterns), auditory-auditory, and one intermodal task, auditory-visual, to two age groups of retarded readers and to control groups of normal readers of approximately the same mean age and IQ. Control subjects performed better than retarded readers. There was not a significant interaction with the intermodal task, the poor reading group performing worse on all three matching tasks (comparable to Bryden's results). The control groups improved with age on all three tasks, but the retarded readers did not improve with age on any of them. The results looked as though the retarded readers failed to develop some skill required by intramodal as well as intermodal matching. Vande Voort et al. thought possibly the retarded readers were deficient in remembering the patterns over the interstimulus interval, so all the groups were given the auditory-visual task simultaneously; that is, the auditory pattern was played at the same time the corresponding visual stimulus was shown. Both groups improved, but the difference scores did not change for the retarded readers. They still performed significantly worse than controls.

Taken together, the results of these experiments plus others too numerous to summarize fail to support the hypothesis that intermodal integration is a developmental skill uniquely related to reading, at least beyond the first grade. But poor readers apparently do not continue to improve with age (after eight years, at least) on these matching tasks, and the matching tasks do seem to show some relation to reading deficiency (not reading *proficiency*, because the correlation disappeared within the group of good readers, even though there was still variability among them). Does this mean that reading at some presumably early stage of skill is simply a matching task? Not at all. But it may imply that some process involved in these pattern matching tasks is similar to that required for getting some of the information necessary for initial reading success. If so, it is not obvious what this process is, but it seems likely that it involves extraction of structure of patterned information, the relations between subordinate units, both over time and space and within and across modalities. Both analyzing a pattern and perceiving the structure of a pattern are necessary for reading. This dual process does not seem to come as easily to some children as others. We will consider the question of analysis and extraction of higher-order structure in the next chapter.

Learning Letter Names

One of the studies above reported a typical finding (see Chall, 1967, pp. 141 ff.) that preknowledge of letter names by beginning readers is a good predictor of reading achievement. It even correlates to some extent with the matching tasks, but that does not mean, of course, that they are tapping the same process. There may well be a third factor associated with both, but different from both. In any case, the question of whether children should be taught the names of letters of the alphabet in kindergarten is a persistent one. The same argument has recurred every decade or two, as Chall points out, and the same or almost the same research is done over again. We will consider a few recent studies to see if they shed any fresh light on the controversy. We are not questioning the ubiquitous finding that there is a correlation between knowledge of letter names before entering first grade and the child's ensuing reading achievement. The question is whether a child should be required to memorize the names of the letters as a useful prereading skill. It is possible that untaught knowledge (or reasonably spontaneous learning) of the names of letters is simply a symptom of a child's awareness of linguistic concepts or of his interest in language and reading, and not in itself something to build on.

Although the correlational studies of knowledge of letter names found a positive relation with reading achievement, experimental studies in the classroom have not. Ohnmacht (1969) gave early training in letter names to all the children in one classroom, training in both letter names and letter sounds in another, and neither in a third. The group trained on names and sounds was superior to the other groups, but the group that was taught only the letter names was no better than the group without pre-training. R. J. Johnson (1970) also found that classroom training on letter names did not provide an advantage in reading achievement compared to a control group. Elkonin (1973) reported that teaching of letter names in the Soviet Union in fact interfered with learning to read. He found that children who knew the names of many letters tried to read by putting together the names of letters and had to be retaught. Samuels (1972) performed a laboratory experiment to see if learning names for four artificial letters would facilitate later learning of two-letter words constructed from these letters. Different groups of first-grade children received one of three kinds of pretraining. One had visual discrimination training with the letters. One learned names for the letters (the names were names of real letters). A third group learned names for pictures of dogs. When they were compared on the word-learning task, no significant differences were found.

An interesting paper by Venezky (1971) discusses some of the issues involved in this ancient controversy. Advocates of teaching letter names have sometimes argued that in the process, visual letter discrimination is improved. But we have seen that letters are discriminated quite well by first grade, and learning alphabet names for many children is a very slow and painful process. It has also been argued that it is a method of introducing the child to letter sounds, because letter names are based upon the acrophonic principle, the sound assigned to the letter being the first sound of the letter's name. But Venezky showed that only 16 English letters follow this principle, and further that the sounds first taught for some letters (e.g., *c* and *g*) are not consistent with the acrophonic principle, leaving only 9 letters whose names begin with the sound used in initial reading. Many other letter names have the sound embedded in them (e.g. *s*, *m*, *n*) at the end. But the child would have to segment the name to reach the desired phoneme in most cases (e.g., in *b*, *d*, *t*, or *k*, *j*), and we have seen that this is an extremely difficult task at five or six years. Knowing the sounds of letters is presumably of value, but Venezky suggests that there are easier ways of teaching it.

A paper by Read (1971) analyzed twenty cases of children who had taught themselves some form of spelling. The spelling was in every case based on a phonetic principle, and the phoneme-letter correspondences hit upon appeared almost invariably to be derived from the child's knowledge of the letter's name. The children categorized the sounds of English in a highly abstract way, but it did not result in the representation of speech that is learned in school—the standard English spelling pattern. (Read thought the children's spontaneous categorizations revealed the child's conception of English phonology, and thus the ways in which it differs from adult phonology and the abstractions inherent in the spelling system of English.) These children's original spelling systems began before they were able to read and usually persisted well into first grade. "Writing" consisted of spelling words or messages with alphabet blocks or movable letters and eventuated in actual writing.

The invented spellings, while often looking very implausible to parents and teachers were roughly the same system for all the children, according to Read. They abstracted phonetic categories and collapsed what were for them allophones within them according to a rule or principle (common to the children) that revealed aspects of their phonological system. To give a few examples:

1. Front vowels were simply represented with the letter's name, as in the following spellings:*

DA	*day*
LADE	*lady*
FEL	*feel*
MI	*my*

2. Lax vowels presented a problem. The children solved it by simply contrasting them phonetically with tense vowels, e.g.,

FES	*fish*
FALL	*fell*
ALRVATA	*elevator*
PANSEL	*pencil*

The organization appears to be based on place of articulation, and the relationships were adhered to very consistently.

*Note that the sound even here generally has to be abstracted from the letter's name (D, for instance), so these unusual children had to be capable of phonemic segmentation.

Some homography, as Read puts it, is required by the lack of symbols, since the names of so many letters do not contain their sounds, and in any case there are not enough letters to go around. But the children solved this by using very general phonetic relations and did not demand distinct representations for every distinct sound, as alphabet reformers might have predicted. Instead they abstracted on the basis of front-back, tense-lax, syllabicity, and other phonetic differences (place of articulation being particularly important), collapsing sometimes into rather broad categories. Obviously they could not invent lexical derivations since their knowledge of lexical features was incomplete, so in a transformation like *divine divinity* the second *i* was rendered *i* in the first case and *e* in the second.

The case with consonants is complex, but again was phonetically derived. The invented spelling of *t* before *r* was *ch*, e.g.,

AS CHRAY *ash tray*

The *t* is actually affricated in English before *r* and the children perceived this. It is also possible that they were not completely aware of the word segmentation. Other details of the system would require too much space to describe. Read summarizes his finding in the following generalization: "The fact that children's spontaneous spelling is already systematically abstract suggests that it is chiefly the facts of English, rather than the principle of spelling, that they have yet to learn" (p. 16). His evidence, he feels "supports the view that spelling is 'rule-governed behavior'—that is, spellings need not be learned one-by-one, but rather that what is learned is a principle."

Read felt that these children did distinguish the letter names from the sounds that the letters represent, using a letter to spell only a segment of its name, e.g., the use of *d* in DA *(day)*. It seems to the writers that this is a rather unusual accomplishment and that these were not run-of-the-mill children. It is obvious, however, that the spellings are abstracted from phonetic contrasts. Whether this impedes or facilitates learning to read is not obvious. Addition of morphological and lexical information when learning to read in school later may convert the system to adult spelling without difficulty. Read says: "The development from phonetic to morphophonemic is not a direct move from phonetic to adult spelling; rather, there is a dramatic change in the type of (non-adult) spelling the child creates" (p. 27).

These spontaneous spellers were not corrected by their parents unless they asked to be. The parents accepted the child's own spelling efforts and provided writing materials. Some parents refuse to do this, for fear the child may acquire "bad habits," but if learning to spell is not a process of acquiring habits but rather abstraction of principles, such parental refusal is a mistake. The phonetic abstractions that the children made were not wrong, but analysis of the sound system had to be extended and related to lexical knowledge. Because phonemic segmentation is so difficult for many children, spontaneous attempts to do it and apply it should be encouraged. Since he has shown he is capable of abstraction, a child should not find it hard to accept a further abstraction, that the written form of a word corresponds to an abstract lexical form, that is, corresponds to what he hears not literally but by way of a more extensive rule system.

Cognitive Factors

It is obvious that ability to discriminate both the sounds of speech and the distinctive features of visually presented symbols, and to make some associations or learn correspondences between them, are not all that is needed for a child to learn to read quickly and easily. Deeper cognitive abilities—perceptual, attentional, conceptual, and linguistic—are basic and essential. The development of these abilities was treated at length in the earlier chapters, so we need only be reminded of them here. To make use of the rule systems available in written text, the child must be able to perceive and make use of redundancy to reduce the information. We discussed the development of this ability in Chapter 2. It will become clear in the next two chapters that economical processing of spelling patterns, abstraction of conditional rules in spelling, and use of syntax and hierarchical feature order to extract meaning are high-level perceptual and cognitive abilities needed for attainment of skilled reading.

In Chapter 3, cognitive strategies for learning and remembering were described. A child literally learns how to learn. He does not realize, at first, that there is something he can do besides passive observation. Awareness of these strategies does occur with development. We know little as yet about whether and how they can be taught, but a few experiments cited in Chapter 3 suggest that there may be ways. "Linguistic awareness" (see Mattingly, 1972) too seems to be important—whether the child can think about language objectively, with the knowledge that it is different from things and events but represents them, that there is an arbitrary assignment of symbols, for instance, and that a word is not a feature of an object.

A child needs to be aware of this arbitrary symbolism (it can be different in different languages) to comprehend the nature of the writing system. If he can reflect upon the language that he speaks, he will find it easier to understand parallels where they exist between the spoken and the written code; and where they do not, he will discover this too and search better for alternative solutions, new cues, and new types of redundancy.

Children are often given word games to play (finding rhymes, pig Latin, etc.) to increase their ability to reflect about language. Anagrams can be used at a considerably later stage (Elkind and Deblinger, 1969). The notion of a code can be introduced in games (Levin and Mitchell, 1969) and may enrich the child's concept of what language and reading are all about. It is important that the child have certain concepts very clear before formal reading instruction is begun. Obvious ones are *word, letter, sentence,* and *sound.* In addition to these, a child may need some help in understanding the meanings of *same* and *different* or *alike* and *not alike.* Adults take these meanings for granted (as well differentiated), but children of four, or even five, frequently do not and are even confused (Donaldson and Wales, 1970). Since prereading exercises frequently require children to choose the two pictures, or the two letters, or the two sounds that are the same or alike, the meaning of the words must be made clear to them.

Programs for Teaching Prereading Skills

Preparing children for learning to read in kindergarten, Head Start programs and even television programs are the order of the day. Ready-made programs are available with lessons all planned out for the teacher. In the past, a justifiable concern with choosing some program and sticking slavishly to it was the lack of research on and evaluation of the program. Thorough empirical tests are now being made of some programs, two of which deserve particular mention as illustrations of what is being done.

The Wisconsin Prereading Skills Program

A prereading skills program has been developed over the past five years at the Wisconsin Research and Development Center for Cognitive Learning (Venezky, 1971a; Chapman, 1971). The basic assumption was that reading is not a single skill, but a complex of skills which can be divided into simpler, component skills. The plan behind the project was that two stages should be provided: a test of the component skills that would reveal deficiencies in individual children, and an instructional program to be used during the kindergarten year in either group or individual activities to remedy these deficiencies. Five skills were selected for test and inclusion in the instructional program. The skills were included on the basis of two criteria, namely, relating directly to learning to read, and showing a high partial correlation with reading. Tests chosen for the battery under study in 1971 included letter orientation, letter order, letter string detail, sound matching (e.g., /š/ in *shoe*), sound blending, segmentation learning (eliminating the initial sound from a word), and picture-sound association learning. The last test required the child to say a simple sound in response to a picture of something that might make that sound (e.g., /š/ to a picture of a child holding his finger upright before closed lips).

Since tryouts with several versions of the tests on several samples of children showed that varying numbers of children were deficient in some of these skills, a program was devised consisting of instructional songs and games (often given names like "hot potato," "battle," "letter lotto"). The main objectives were to develop skill in matching letter strings and words taking orientation and order into account, matching words on the basis of constituent sounds, and blending sounds into real words, using letters or pictures to elicit the sounds. Instruction was aimed at developing transfer of the skills.

The Wisconsin group has performed a number of experiments on instructional techniques used in the program, chiefly aimed at sound segmentation and single-sound production, which consistently gave the most trouble. One (Wilder, 1972) was a replication of an experiment by Elkonin (1963), which was described in Chapter 5. One group of kindergarten children received all three phases of training used by Elkonin (giving the name of a picture; placing plastic tokens in a row of squares representing the number of sounds in the word, then tokens alone; and finally segmentation of the word without any props). A control group had speech training alone without props. Transfer tests were administered after training. There were no differences between the groups. Although both averaged high on tests of the training words, there was no transfer to new words. The authors speculated that younger children might have shown a difference between the two techniques, but neither group, with five 20-minute training sessions, acquired a transferable skill.

More encouraging results were obtained in an experiment on teaching children individual speech sounds (Venezky and Shiloah, 1972). Picture-sound pairs were taught by several different procedures to kindergarten children. Cards with line drawings of pictures having some plausible connection with a sound were shown the child and the sound produced for him. Sometimes it was introduced simply as a paired associate; otherwise it was introduced (with the picture) as part of a story. In another procedure, children were taught songs built around the sound, as well as shown the picture and told the story. The children learned with apparent ease to produce the sounds and to recognize them and to choose the appropriate picture. Group instruction was superior to individual instruction. The importance of the experiment, to the authors, was that children could be taught to manipulate single speech sounds in isolation—an important fact if single letter-sound correspondences were going to be taught as such.

A program including some of the tests developed at Wisconsin was administered by Calfee (1972) to a number of children just beginning first grade and compared later with measures of reading achievement at the end of first grade. Tests included were visual word matching, phoneme identification, phonetic segmentation, alphabet recognition, and vocabulary recognition. Multiple regression analyses with several samples of children consistently revealed the primary importance of phonetic segmentation and identification. Vocabulary was also high in priority. It is very possible that IQ underlies both these skills and reading achievement. One should not exaggerate the importance of these tests for predicting learning to read, however, for even as multiple predictors they accounted for only 30% of the variance in first-grade reading achievement.

The Pittsburgh Perceptual Skills Curriculum
For several years work has proceeded at the Learning Research and Development Center at the University of Pittsburgh on training in perceptual skills considered basic for school progress. The project has four goals:

1. To identify perceptual skills directly related to reading and arithmetic at the primary level.
2. To determine whether these skills can be trained effectively.
3. To determine whether the training would transfer to "classroom behaviors."
4. Given the first three, to prepare a curriculum suitable for use in a school classroom.

The method was mainly that of empirical validation of intuitions about potentially basic skills, followed by constructing and administering tests and evaluating them against other data.

The program, in its 1972 version, included visual-motor skills development, auditory-motor skills development, general motor skills development, and learning to name and print (from left to right) the letters of the alphabet and numbers. Two tests, the Visual Analysis Test and the Auditory Analysis Test, will be described briefly and the follow-up work on them summarized. The general motor skills program seems entirely irrelevant to reading; no evidence was presented to link it up, and it is common and pertinent knowledge that clumsy people and even people badly handicapped by cerebral palsy have often achieved the highest degree of literacy. As for the alphabet training, it is neither innovative nor of unquestionable value for reading pretraining.

The visual analysis test This test consists of a number of copying tasks. A model (a geometric configuration) is provided and the child is required to reproduce the model in a square frame alongside it. The test items increase in difficulty by increasing the number of elements in the design, by increasing complexity of the configurational relationships, and by reducing the number of aids (in the form of dot matrices) in the space where the model is to be reproduced. An easy and a difficult item are shown in Figure 8-4. This test was administered to a large number of kindergarten, first-grade, and second-grade children. Scores were related to grade level and to another drawing test. Scores for the first- and second-grade children were correlated with achievement tests of reading and arithmetic. The correlation with reading words was .40 in first grade and .36 in second grade. Correlations with arithmetic were higher (.55 and .58), not surprising in view of the fact that counting seems almost essential for most of the more difficult items. Variation in IQ could be responsible for these correlations. A training program intended to teach copying skills (the Design Board Program, Rosner, 1971a) was given to a number of four-year-olds, preceded and followed by a drawing test. The test scores improved. But an older group of kindergarten children had equivalent scores, so the ability might have matured without the training. Another training experiment with the Design Board Program extended over six months and showed a difference (.05 level) between the trained group and a control group on a copying task with test items different from the train-

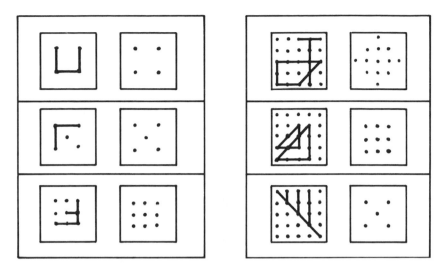

Figure 8-4.   Easy (left) and hard items (right) on the visual analysis test. From the Pittsburgh Perceptual Skills Curriculum; see Rosner, 1971a.

ing items. The training program is a progressive one requiring mastery of simple tasks before proceeding to more complex ones. Progression to higher levels as each in turn was mastered definitely occurred. Unfortunately, we have no evidence that the training would facilitate learning to read.

The auditory analysis test   An auditory analysis test (Rosner and Simon, 1971) was constructed by the same group. This test also increases in difficulty as it progresses from item to item. It calls for ability to segment sounds within a word. The method requires the child to repeat a word given to him by the examiner, and then delete a sound from it. For example, he repeats *cowboy* and then is asked to delete the *boy* ("Say it again but don't say *boy*"). The test progresses to longer items and smaller units for segmentation, e.g., *er* to be deleted from *offering* or *l* to be deleted from *clutter*). This test was administered to children ranging from first through sixth grades. Scores were correlated with the language arts subtests of an achievement test and showed good correlations, especially in third grade (.84). First-grade children had a correlation of .53 on the test with word reading, second-grade children, .49.

An experiment was conducted (Rosner, 1971b) to see whether auditory perceptual skills could be trained. A group of nonreaders entering first grade was given auditory analysis training, as well as the customary reading instruction, while a control group received only reading instruction. They were matched for IQ and scores on the test when instruction began. On a posttest, the experimental group significantly excelled over the control group (a gain of nearly 10 points for the experimental group, but only 3 for the control group). However, a group of children who entered first grade with some knowledge of reading also increased their scores on the test (nearly 13 points) without any special auditory training.

The children in the experimental and control groups were asked, after the training of the experimental group, to read simple words. Some of the words were taken from instructional materials which they had covered and some were new "transfer" words. There was a marked contrast between the two groups, the experimental group excelling on both sets of words. A replication with children who had already had three months of reading instruction yielded similar results, with an especially striking difference on transfer words.

It seems clear from these studies and the Wisconsin ones that auditory perceptual analysis of words is an important skill for learning to read and that training in it helps and does show transfer, at least at initial stages of learning to read. The training program devised by the Pittsburgh group is again a progressive one, beginning with nonverbal sounds, then segmenting in turn phrases, words, syllables, and finally single phonemic sounds. Clapping for each unit, marking (with dashes), deleting sounds, producing omitted sounds, and substituting sounds are successive stages of training, with apparently successful results in kindergarten and first grade.

In concluding this section, we must warn that the answers to "reading readiness" are by no means all in. Mastery of the skills described above as components of reading does not necessarily ensure instant success in learning to read, so far as we know at present. Teachers often ask whether, once a child has knowledge of components a and b and c and d, reading problems are effectively prevented. Our present judgment is that we cannot answer with a confident "Yes." It is true that job analysis has proved a useful tool in industrial psychology. Task analysis may be equally useful in educational psychology. But an intellectual task is not simply a sum of components—especially reading, which is more than one task and differs with the material and the reader's purpose. Even if it were, one could miss an essential component. Something is missing in these analyses. They do not as currently presented reach toward adaptive cognitive strategies of extraction of higher-order structure or the development of independent analysis and organization.

The most important of the components identified was phonetic segmentation and identification, that is, the ability to analyze an initially impenetrable complex acoustic structure. This is an interesting and reliable finding. Certainly a child deficient in this ability should be helped to develop it, and it seems from the research now available that he can. But we cannot agree with Calfee (1972) that effective teaching is primarily "remediation" or even "preventive maintenance," as he suggests. This approach of identifying and remedying (if necessary) component skills must not be allowed to take its place in the long history of panaceas. The people who do the research would not think of it as one, but school systems that buy "curriculum packages" might easily do so.

Summary

This chapter examined the development of prereading skills, including the analysis of speech sounds, early production and discrimination of writing, intermodal relations, and cognitive factors. Auditory analysis of the sounds of speech, when it must be done deliberately with attention to the phonetic stream or to production of isolated sounds, is poorly developed in most children of kindergarten age. They know how to speak, but phonetic analysis does not always develop spontaneously. On the other hand, graphic production occurs very early, excites great interest in young children, and shows a sequence of development, given the opportunity, from scribbling to drawing to attempts at copying letters to production of names and words (not necessarily read as words). Perhaps because traces on paper are permanent objective things, they seem to be much easier for a child to analyze into graphic features than are phonetic displays.

Children in a culture replete with graphic displays, both pictorial and written, learn with no instruction to differentiate writing from pictures. They learn a great deal about features of writing such as linearity and variety of units that can be recombined in many ways, and by five years or so many children can identify a letter as a letter even though they do not know its name. More than that, sorting and matching studies (see Chapter 2) have shown that preschool and kindergarten children differentiate letters by features very like those used by adults, though of course they have not been taught to do so (adults, in fact, could not tell you exactly what features they use).

The inscrutability of the physical aspect of the phonetic message as contrasted with the accessibility of the physical aspect of the graphic one is fascinating in view of the apparent ease of learning the spoken language and the difficulty (in many cases, at least) of learning the written version. One reason for this, speculative we admit, is that speech carries meaning for the child and is used for communication from the start. The physical (phonetic) aspect is not noticed and is too ephemeral to be observed at length. Writing, on the other hand, carries no meaning in the sense of a message when it is begun spontaneously. There may be a moral here: that the semantic, communicative function of writing should be introduced in a simple way even before real written words are controlled by the child.

In line with the early spontaneously acquired knowledge of features of writing and of letters, development of graphic discrimination does not usually present much of a problem except when order within a string is involved. Now something akin to a grammar enters in, and the child does not know the rules. Literal memorization of order in a letter string is hard. It would be difficult for an adult with an unfamiliar set of graphic symbols. It is not clear to what extent drill in matching letter strings will help a child before he knows that words can be written and that there are rules for combining letters. Once he is onto the rule system he does not have to match or remember order—he can generate it. There is some evidence of improvement in kindergarteners in matching letter strings between early fall and February (Chapman, 1971). Perhaps exposure to words in proper orthographic order yields some perceptual learning, but it seems more likely that an attentional factor is involved, since as we shall see, spelling patterns are not learned easily. For children who need training in learning to differentiate letters, it appears that emphasis on contrastive features that distinguish confusable letters is the best technique. For learning to discriminate order in two-letter strings, it may be best to begin with easily distinguished strings and progress to more confusable ones, a principle borrowed from other research on perceptual learning.

Many studies of intermodal and intramodal matching of sequential visual and auditory patterns and dot patterns have sought to relate these skills to reading achievement. Poor readers do seem generally to be deficient in all of these tasks (not only intermodal matching) as contrasted with good readers, but differences in grade level and selection of subjects make the results hard to interpret. It was speculated that extraction of structure of patterned information may be a process common to these tasks and to reading.

Studies teaching children names of the letters of the alphabet as groundwork for learning to read have not found the task useful for learning to read (though it might be for teacher-child communication) despite the fact that knowing the names before entering school is a good predictor of reading achievement. There is no reason to discourage children from learning them on their own, however, since children who invented their own spelling systems, using letter names for the sounds, became aware of the alphabetic principle and used it. However unconventional their orthography, they succeeded on their own in phonemic abstraction, a real and useful achievement.

Cognitive factors in prereading skill were treated only briefly, since they were discussed extensively in Part I. Awareness of learning strategies, ability to think about language objectively, and understanding that writing carries meaning and information are all important factors.

Two prereading skills programs were described briefly. Research is still continuing on these programs, so they are presented only as examples. Both programs operate by analyzing reading into component skills, testing these skills, and constructing training programs to remedy deficiencies. Auditory skills (phonetic analysis) stand out as high-priority ones and also as ones that may require training. It was emphasized that, however good the training provided, it cannot be assumed that the reading process is simply a sum of component skills.

9
Beginning to Read

In the beginning was the Word.

John 1:1

Despite all the current emphasis on literacy, the wealth of programs commercially available, the "learning specialists" who have set up in shopping centers, and the arguments over phonics or whole-word methods, it is the beginning phase of learning to read that we seem to know least about. All the talk is of what the teacher does or should do and not of what happens or should happen in the child. This is a very peculiar situation. There is presumably a learning process going on, but it is a rare psychologist who studies it. The approach to beginning reading has most often been how to program the teacher or the computer or the curriculum package, or how to remedy things when the program hasn't worked and the child didn't learn.

Little as we know about how the spoken language is learned, there seems to be more interest in how that happens than in the learning process for reading. Learning to read should be more accessible to study than learning spoken language, since it happens later. Why is there so little investigation of the learning process? Partly, we think it is because it has been taken for granted by most psychologists that this is an educator's problem, purely applied, not theirs. Partly, it is because too many people (both psychologists and educators) have taken it for granted that the process must be one of association, either association of a letter with a sound or of a whole printed word with a spoken one, with some right-or-wrong type of reinforcement thrown in by the teacher, and so there is no theoretical problem.

We take exception to both these views. We think the investigation of learning to read should focus on what is happening in the child. This chapter will therefore not be program oriented, although several experimental programs will be described briefly at the end. It will be focused, instead, on the learning process: what the child learns, what the process might be like, and some important variables that can affect it. Second, we shall depart from the traditional associationist view. We think that reading is rule governed. As a consequence, the learning process is better viewed as abstraction of principles. Finding the invariants (patterns and order) and inducing the rules have proved to be useful concepts for understanding acquisition of speech. It is time to try this approach on learning to read.

Because a learning process that involves abstraction of invariants or inducing rules is of necessity largely internally regulated, the question of motivation and reinforcement becomes very important. If the child must essentially "do it himself," what will make him do it, keep him at it, and tell him when he has perceived a useful relation? Because of its central importance, we shall start with this question.

Motivation for Learning to Read

Intrinsic Motivation

There is no question that spontaneous motivation for learning is both effective and ubiquitous. From the moment of birth, children are learning about their world, the surfaces and places and walls and sky around them, the objects contained in or on them and the relations between them, the kind of events that can take place in relation to these and to themselves (you can't put your hand through a solid door or walk where there is no supporting surface), predictable relations of all kinds with reference to objects and actions, and predictable relations involving one's own actions and the probable consequences for the behavior of other people (if a baby cries his mother will come to see what's troubling him). An infant learns these things entirely on his own. No one has to tell him to do it. From six weeks or so, he is looking, looking at everything that happens around him, especially anything unfamiliar, as a large body of experimental evidence now attests. He has become extraordinarily knowledgeable about all these things by the time he is a year old.

It has been accepted by psychologists for at least a decade that there is "intrinsic motivation" to know, to find things out, to get what is ambiguous, clear; what is amorphous, orderly (Day, Berlyne, and Hunt, 1971). Probably most people have always taken this for granted. To quote Bruner (1966), writing about the "will to learn":

Almost all children possess what have come to be called "intrinsic" motives for learning. An intrinsic motive is one that does not depend upon reward that lies outside the activity it impels. Reward inheres in the successful termination of that activity or even in the activity itself.

Curiosity is almost a prototype of the intrinsic motive. Our attention is attracted to something that is unclear, unfinished, or uncertain. We sustain our attention until the matter in hand becomes clear, finished, or certain. The achievement of clarity or merely the search for it is what satisfies. (p. 114)

Intrinsic motivation is as persistent and as effective for learning language as it is for learning about the world of places and things and happenings. In Chapter 5 we discussed the process of acquiring language and made it clear that the child's urge to understand language and to communicate is entirely spontaneous. He even practices on his own, when there is nobody there to talk to or to correct him. Ruth Weir (1962) discovered that her $2\frac{1}{2}$-year-old son Anthony talked to himself in his crib after he had been put to bed at night before falling to sleep. She put a microphone above his crib and recorded his soliloquies, which were not actually monologues, but a "dialogue with imaginary interlocutors." These soliloquies might be of the following playful form:

Daddy
Daddy bucket please
Another book please
Donkey
Fix the donkey
And the blue box and the big box (p. 80)

The soliloquies often took the form of sequences that give the impression, most convincingly, that the child was practicing aspects of sentence structure, such as the following transformational and morphological exercises:

There's a hat
There's another
There's hat
There's another hat
That's a hat (p. 111)

There is the light
Where is the light
Here is the light (p. 112)

Bobo go take off the hat
Bobo took off the hat (p. 112)

Bobo's not throwing
Bobo can throw
Bobo can throw it
Bobo can throw (p. 120)

There were even frequent examples of phonological practice. The conclusion is inescapable that the child was highly motivated to learn on his own.

In the last chapter we reviewed research showing that children, given the tools and proper surroundings, will scribble, draw, and print spontaneously, improving their writing activity without formal instruction. They also learn to differentiate pictorial graphic information from writing and learn the distinctive features used in writing on their own. This is learning for its own sake, motivated intrinsically and by the desire to extract information. Some children (Read, 1971; see also Chapter 8) even invent their own spelling systems. All these activities can be described as play, although few people agree on the definition of play. O. K. Moore (Moore and Anderson, 1968) devised what he termed an "autotelic" system, one which assumes that the primary motivation is the child's natural curiosity and desire to learn to read. A "talking" electric typewriter, simply made available to the child, gave him the means of discovering what a letter "said." There are problems with this method (financial, among others), but the motivational emphasis is a healthy one.

It seems as if we should be able to draw on the child's well of curiosity, to appeal to an urge to know what it says on the printed page. To extract the information that is there (as in speech) would appear to be a natural motive, and a child should be set going on his own as soon as possible. Opportunity to look at any book he chooses, whether he literally "reads" it or not, seems essential. If the books interest him enough (say, comic books), he is almost certain to ask for words and make some progress on his own. Note the following anecdote:

Peter loved books as soon as he could handle them. He would sit on the floor and ritualistically take books from the shelves, open them, turn pages, close them, replace them and examine others. Once he said to me, "Words, words, words."
He began to read in a curious way. The World Almanac fascinated him. He fixed upon the list of nations, so the first word he ever read was "Afghanistan." When he was 5, he would entertain us with a recital of the countries he was working on, with figures of their area and population. (I must ask him some day if he remembers the area of Bulgaria.)*

Desire to ascertain the information in the text makes the content or theme of what is taught an important consideration. Sylvia Ashton-Warner (1963) asked children what words they would like to learn to read or

*From "Aunterly Love" by Ruth Block, *New York Times Magazine*, October 1, 1972.

print and taught them these, however exotic or unconventional their choices. Miller (1969a) gives an appreciative description of her method:

Mummy, daddy, kiss, frightened, ghost, their own names—these are the words children ask for, words that are bound up with their own loves and fears. She writes each child's word on a large, tough card and gives it to him. If a child wants words like police, butcher, knife, kill, jail, and bomb, he gets them. And he learns to read them almost immediately. It is *his* word, and each morning he retrieves his own words from the pile collected each night by the teacher. These are not dead words of an expert's choosing, but words that live in a child's own experience. Given this start, children begin to write, using their own words, and from there the teaching of reading follows naturally. Under this regimen, a word is not an imposed task to be learned with reinforcements borrowed from some external source of motivation. Learning the word is itself reinforcing; it gives the child something he wants, a new way to cope with a desire or fear. Each child decides where he wants to start, and each child receives something whose value he can recognize. (Miller, 1969, p. 1073)

Probably items like *zowie, whee!, bicycle,* and *birthday cake* are just as good vehicles for learning about letter-sound correspondences as *see baby*. One classroom program (Levin and Mitchell, 1969) encouraged children to invent their own stories and taught them the words so they could print them in a notebook, illustrate the stories themselves, and take them home to read to their families.

One hears that children from culturally impoverished home backgrounds seem to have some of their natural curiosity and desire to explore stifled (though one wonders if observation of this has been limited to the school situation). People working with inner-city families have often characterized the family environment as disorganized and lacking in structure (Deutsch, 1967). As one researcher put it, "Life environments that are disorganized, threatening, or amorphous, in this way, are likely to depress exploratory behavior, the clarity of the child's self-image, his perception of effective adults, and his grasp of logic and order in the world" (Minuchin, 1971, p. 941). Under these conditions, intrinsic motivation for learning might be low, since the child would have experienced little of the satisfaction that comes from resolving apparent contradictions and learning about a predictable, orderly world.

Minuchin studied the correlates of curiosity and exploratory behavior in a group of 18 four-year-old black children in a Head Start program. She took a number of measures of curiosity and exploration; one, for instance, was a coded recording of the children's behavior in new natural situations (trips to the harbor, etc.). Other measures were taken of the children's self-image, perceptions of adults and the environment, and concept formation. The children varied widely on the measures of curiosity and exploration. There was a strong positive correlation between degrees of curiosity and exploration and some of the cognitive and emotional variables. There were six children in the sample who Minuchin thought "projected an environment characterized by sustained crisis, little coherence, ineffective and poorly defined adults; and whose conceptual grasp of order in the physical environment and of the relationships among objects tended to be poor. These children also showed limited curiosity or exploratory behavior" (p. 948). Minuchin cautions, rightly, that there was no first-hand evidence of the actual home environment of the children. Assuming that disorder generally reigns in homes of disadvantaged children is certainly unjustified. The wide variability in Minuchin's group cannot be overemphasized, and we do not know what results a middle-class sample of children would have yielded. But if there are children whose lives have not presented orderly and consistent patterns, and if an expectation of finding order is required for maintaining a motive for active exploration, intrinsic motivation to learn might sometimes need nourishment. It may be useful to prepare experiences of finding order and predictability in simple preschool situations to revive a dormant motive to search for invariants in the world.

Achievement Motivation

In many societies, achieving something, mastering a task, surpassing someone else in completing it, or simply acquiring competence is, or is assumed to be, a strong motive (McClelland, 1961). We give grades in school to rouse this motive, presumably. (There can be no other reason from the learner's point of view, for a grade is an entirely nonspecific knowledge of results and could not contribute to learning.) A motive to acquire competence, even without an emphasis on competition, is not at all the same as a desire to "know what it says," to extract the information. It is based on a need to deal with the environment in a competent way, rather than to understand.

The desirability of appealing to or trying to make use of such a motive has frequently been questioned. It can lead to feelings of anxiety or failure, and nothing is more devastating to a child's motivation than feeling that he has failed. But our society, on the whole, takes it for granted that it is a good thing to know how to read well, although subcultures within it vary in the value they place on it. Children growing up in Harlem may view achievement in sports as more important than reading. Fathers in a middle-class suburb may think it more important for their children to make the little-league baseball team than to get an A in reading. The value placed by their peers and parents on any activity is obviously going to make a difference in the extent to which children's natural motivation is channeled into it. Teachers in our culture expect girls to excel in reading as compared to boys, and they do, at least until sixth grade, when the difference tends to diminish. But a study by Johnson (1972) of sex differences in reading in four English-speaking nations (Canada, U.S.A., England, and Nigeria) found that in grades 2 through 6, girls excelled in Canada and the U.S., but the difference was exactly reversed in England and Nigeria. The early superiority of girls in our society is apparently the result of cultural factors rather than genetic or maturational ones. Reading ability of boys is more highly valued in England and Nigeria than it is in North America. In Nigeria, in fact, schooling has a very low priority for girls and most of the teachers are men. Sex differences in favor of boys even increased from second to sixth grades in Nigeria and England.

It is not being suggested that an achievement motive for reading should be "harnessed," so to speak. But it is important to remember that social values instilled in the child at an early age can affect his natural motivation to learn one thing rather than another.

Role Models

Social psychologists make use of a concept referred to as a "role model"—someone who presents a character and a set of values with whom another person can identify. In Chapter 3, learning from observation was discussed and we recalled Freud's concept of "transference." If a child can identify himself with a model who commands his respect, he may adopt as his own the motives of the model. Teachers are often supposed to provide the model for the child. The teacher reads, presumably likes to, and encourages the child to. But if one considers this idea seriously for a few minutes, it seems obvious that in many cases—perhaps even most of them— the teacher as a model for the child is a mismatch. The teacher in the early grades in our society is nearly always a woman, often middle-aged, and for some children not easy to identify with. The teacher is nearly always white and the children are often black. Yet we cannot afford to lose this source of influencing the child's value system, since Bandura (1969) has shown it to be extraordinarily effective for learning (not learning to read, to be sure, but there is every reason to think the findings are generalizable to other intellectual activities). Ross (1970a, b), as cited in Chapter 3, has shown that use of models facilitates learning of number concepts by retarded children in game situations.

Parents and older siblings present models for the child and surely do influence their values outside the school, but not all families value learning. A system tried recently in a number of schools may have enormous potential for strengthening the motivation to learn in children whose family background has not encouraged it, that is, letting older children in the school work with younger ones in pairs (Hagen and Moeller, 1971; Lippitt and Lippitt, 1968). A child old enough to command respect but not too old to identify with, of the same sex and racial background, who enjoys learning and can provide some help and encouragement to the younger child, should be an ideal model and a potentially successful tutor. There are few hard evaluations of this type of tutoring, as yet, but generally enthusiastic responses abound. There is some evidence that a tutor who experienced difficulties at an earlier stage himself is especially sympathetic and helpful. The experience, in the cases we are acquainted with, is generally mutually rewarding, as well. There is nothing like teaching someone yourself to find out what you need to learn and to strengthen your urge to do it.

External Incentives and Reinforcers

The era of behaviorism extolled the value of external incentives and reinforcers in establishing "control" of behavior. The notion has been widely applied to learning to read as well as to a rat pressing a bar. The operant approach to reading was recently summarized by R. D. Bloom (1971), who considers that the mechanism by which a reading response is connected to a particular textual cue is reinforcement.

It is argued that the use of environmentally attractive features as reinforcers, when made accessible to the learner, *contingent* upon the occurrence of specific reading behavior, will provide a powerful basis for particularly establishing and motivating early reading efforts. (R. D. Bloom, 1971, p. 7–6)

The view was elaborated originally by Staats and Staats (Staats, 1968; Staats and Staats, 1962; Staats, Staats, Schutz, and Wolf, 1962), who emphasized the importance of "extrinsic" reinforcers, such as candy and trinkets. They felt that the "sources of reinforcement" typically depended upon in classroom situations were inadequate in supporting the reading behavior of many children. Tangible reinforcement, as opposed to only the knowledge of being correct, was considered especially important for socially disadvantaged children.

Dependence on grades as a reward for learning they felt to be thoroughly inadequate, both because of its nonspecificity and because of the delay in feedback. Application of operant principles is assumed to involve the "gradual shaping" of reading behavior with very explicit sequencing of instruction in a progressive hierarchy of subskills. "Such component reading skills can serve as the focus of reading instruction involving the application of consistent and adequate reinforcement contingencies by which these behaviors may be gradually strengthened" (Bloom, 1971, p. 7–8).

A typical experiment based on the operant reinforcement principle makes use of tokens contingent upon the occurrence of appropriate responses. The tokens are exchangeable for such prizes as candy, toys, or money. Generally a schedule of reinforcement is used so that a specified number of correct responses must occur before a token is earned. Contingent token reinforcement has been used with flash cards requiring recognition of phonemes, letters, words, and larger units consisting of single sentences or paragraphs. Extensive programs have been based on this reinforcement principle. The systems have been elaborated in some cases to provide "token economies," in which tokens of different values can be earned to purchase items selected by the learner (Staats and Butterfield, 1965), or a system permitting students to select interesting events (depicted by stick figures and referred to as the "reinforcement menu") to engage in after successfully completing a defined task (Addison and Homme, 1965).

Of the various experiments undertaken in this milieu, two will be described to illustrate the general method and some variations on it. An experiment by Staats et al. (1962) presented six four-year-old children with a "textual program" consisting of 26 words arranged so the word stimuli could be gradually combined into sentences and then into short storylike sets of sentences. Equipment included words typed on cards, a picture board that included a small picture of each of the verbal stimuli that could be pictured, a word board that could hold three rows of three words and a small picture of an animal, and some discrimination cards holding several words that could not be pictured. The child began with picture matching, progressed to word matching, and then learning some words (at first illustrated with the picture), and after the first five words relevant sentences were introduced using them. The procedure of introducing words and sentences was reiterated and stories introduced. There were eight 45-minute sessions. The children were divided into two groups and received extrinsic reinforcements. For a correct response, they received either a tangible reward such as candy or a small toy, or a red token which was inserted in a "token board." The tokens could be exchanged, when the board was filled, for a "secret surprise." Each child earned about 100 reinforcers per session. One group of children began with no reinforcement other than social and was switched to tangible reinforcement when the child wanted to stop. The other group began with tangible reinforcement for two days. Reinforcement was then discontinued, but reinstated when the child indicated that he wanted to stop.

The children who began with no tangible reinforcement indicated during the first or second session that they wanted to stop. After reinforcement was introduced they showed cumulative curves of progress, learning totals of about 17 "texts." The children who began with tangible reinforcement and then had it withdrawn all asked to leave the program after the fifth or six day. One returned and made a little progress after reintroduction of the rewards. It is hard to interpret these results other than to say that the prizes kept four-year-olds at what must have been a long (to them) and rather tedious task (there were many trials on each "textual stimulus"). The authors comment, "This was, perhaps, the primary value of the reinforcers: i.e., they strengthened the behaviors of staying in the situation and working" (p. 39).

An experiment by Holt (1971) was done with first graders, using reinforcement "menus" in combination with a programmed text which resulted in a large increase in reading productivity (defined as the number of words read) during a seven-week program. Experimental sessions lasted 50 minutes, five times a week. The first 15 sessions were used to determine a baseline rate of response and no reinforcement was given. Beginning with the sixteenth session, the subject was placed under reinforcement contingencies and was allowed to participate for five minutes in his selected activity if he successfully completed a fixed number of pages in the programmed text. The specified number of pages increased from 10 to 40 (indicated on the graph in Figure 9-1 as FR10, FR16, etc.). Sessions 36 and 37 were not reinforced. The last two sessions were again reinforced at FR40. The results are presented in Figure 9-1. The rise with reinforcement is shown between days 16 and 35. When reinforcement was dropped on days 36 and 37, the rate dropped nearly (but not quite) to the original baseline rate.

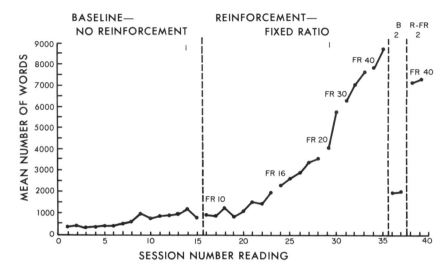

Figure 9-1. Number of pages read depending on reinforcement contingencies. From Holt, 1971, p. 366.

When reinforcement was reinstated, it rose again, though not to its highest level. Holt reports that there was a significant gain in reading proficiency on a pre- and postreading achievement test, and that the children could work with good comprehension and retention over long time spans when a chosen activity followed. There was no control group in this experiment, and one would expect some increase in tested reading achievement over seven weeks in any case, but the reward of a period of self-selected activity did keep the children productively at the task for long periods.

What can we conclude about "extrinsic reinforcers," whether in the form of candy, money, prizes, or free play? They keep the child at the task. When they are withdrawn, the rate of activity at the task drops immediately and sharply. When the reinforcers are discontinued the learner seems to have no motivational basis for continuing. The progenitors of this technique argue that if continued long enough, the activity would gain secondary reinforcement value on its own, but we doubt that this would happen unless sufficient skill had been attained for the content of the text to rouse the subject's interest if the behavior was contingent on the props before.

A recent study (Lepper, Greene, and Nisbett, 1973) warns that discretion in the use of extrinsic rewards is essential, because they found evidence that when children already had an intrinsic interest in an activity, presenting the activity within a system of extrinsic incentives had the effect of undermining the intrinsic interest. They presented a novel activity (drawing with colored felt pens) to a nursery school population during three free play periods when other activities could be chosen. Two unseen observers recorded the time each child spent working with the target materials and selected the highest-ranking children for an experiment, dividing them into three groups. One group was a "no-award" group, one was an "expected-award" group, and a third was an "unexpected-award" group. These children were taken individually to a separate room, told a study was to be made of the pictures children drew with the magic markers, and presented with the material. The no-award and the unexpected-award groups received no further instructions, but the expected-award group was told that they might win a "good player award" for their work. The award, a certificate bearing a red ribbon, a large gold star, and a place for the child's name, was shown them. After six minutes of drawing, the no-award group was dismissed with thanks, whereas the other two groups received the awards, had their names written on them, etc. A week to two weeks later, the magic markers were again introduced during the free play period and the time spent by the children on the activity recorded as before. The no-award and the unexpected-award groups showed no decline in interest compared with their preexperimental behavior, but the expected-award group manifested a significant decrease, spending significantly less time (half or less) on the activity than the other two groups. Ratings by three "blind" observers of the quality of the pictures drawn were significantly lower for the expected-award group than for the other two. Introduction of an expected reward thus had a detrimental effect on both motivation and quality of work. While one should not generalize too broadly from this limited evidence, it is clear that the effect of extrinsic incentives when intrinsic interest is already present can be deleterious.

It may be useful to maintain the practice of populations of children who seem to have little or no intrinsic motivation to learn to read at the task with planned rewards in the hope that exposure to reading material will develop an intrinsic interest. But as R. D. Bloom (1971) concludes, "There is surprisingly little clear-cut evidence dealing with the ability of operant techniques to alter such covert features of reading as comprehension or the formation of inference" (p. 7–10). We know of none and expect none, for a schedule of external reinforcement cannot even be imposed on, let alone produce, comprehension or inference. They must come from within the learner. To quote Bloom once more, the goal of the operant reading model is "control" over the process, whereas that of a cognitive model is understanding the process.

Selective Reinforcement by Reduction of Uncertainty

If extrinsic reinforcers do not affect comprehension or inference, does anything, or does anything need to? The notion of reinforcement comes from S-R psychology, and it may be that it is time to abandon it in considering how a cognitive skill like reading is learned. We can give a child knowledge of results, tell him when he reads something right or doesn't, test his comprehension, and try to correct it. But it seems as if the rest has to come from within. One cannot "emit" comprehension until he has it and then have it stick by itself. A powerful selective factor for learning, however, is reduction of uncertainty (see Chapter 2). Furthermore, finding order, a pattern, a higher-order structure, or a rule is powerfully effective for cognitive economy. Autoregulation of the cognitive processes—perceptual, memorial, and conceptual—seems to seek economy; the invariant, the best structuring principle, and the most comprehensive rule are automatically preferred and retained. Progression from chaos or disorder to order is rewarding.

Reduction of uncertainty and the trend toward economy in processing information was considered at length earlier, so a reminder is enough at this point. Presentation of material so that a child can be led to find structure and use it is the principle to keep in mind.

Learning to Read Words

What Is to Be Learned?

As always, the first thing to consider is what it is that must be learned; our problem in this chapter is what must be learned in the early stages of acquiring reading skill. The reader may object at once, why words? Don't we want children to read sentences and paragraphs and stories and notes mother left about letting the dog out? Of course we do, and we do begin with them, but they must be analyzed into words and some information extracted from the word. According to Shankweiler and Liberman (1972), the major barrier to reading acquisition is not in reading connected text but rather "in dealing with words and their components." Reading with little comprehension, they say, is a consequence of reading words poorly, not the other way around.

How is this done? The child must learn to attend, first, to the graphic information on the page in addition to the meaning it conveys. Studies of early reading errors, we shall see, make it clear that this combination of foci for attention is not automatically attained. Second, the child must learn the correspondence rules that link the phonological to the orthographic system. Since English does not simply represent one letter with one sound directly and uniquely, the two systems are related at a more complex level. The unit for "decoding," as some call it, presents a problem to be discussed below, and its solution requires learning to deal with units at more than one level. Intraword relations must be analyzed if transfer to new words is to occur, and this does not happen automatically in many children. Finally, structures of words are related; there are "families" of them, knowledge of which provides enormous economy of processing. Research on learning these relations will be presented.

What about meanings of the words? Can we assume that meaning comes automatically with "decoding" to sound, since the child has already progressed a long way in developing his semantic system for speech? It is a current, often expressed view that the meaning is there, transferred directly, as the child produces the "phonetic transcription." For instance,

The relationship between LAD ["Language Acquisition Device"] and reading consists in the fact that the brain function involved in understanding representational auditory stimuli is the same as that required in the reading process after the sound is decoded from the visual symbols of language; that is, as the child recognizes the words in a sentence he gets their meaning in terms of sound values just as he does in spoken language. It is often not appreciated that once the child has decoded the sound, he then utilizes this ability which is acquired spontaneously through the facilitation of LAD. (Callaway, 1970, p. 6)

This notion seems to us entirely too simplistic. It is true that meanings of words have great saliency for children—they attend to them rather than the word's phonetic features, or graphic features when they begin to read. But that does not mean that a child has an instant program for extracting meaning from the written word. The following section on early reading errors will clarify the way in which children actually do use or try to use meaning when reading instruction is begun.

Development of Attention to Graphic Information as Reflected in Early Reading Errors

Typically, when children learn to read they are required to read aloud so that teachers can monitor their progress. There has been much discussion about the advisability of silent versus oral reading, since the mature reader usually reads to himself and the question has been raised whether reading aloud tells us much about the eventual transfer to efficient silent reading. Nevertheless, oral reading does make public the process of reading and can provide teachers with insights about the child's progress. Reading errors, especially if they are analyzed in ways other than a simple categorization of correct-incorrect, can provide information about children's strategies in reading and reveal the sorts of information that the reader exploits or is learning to exploit (Weber, 1968, p. 98). Errors in behavior provide insights about the strategies and processes that the learners are implicitly using. We may hark back to our discussion of grammatical development, where we saw that the child knew the common pluralization rules when he said *gooses* or *mans*. Such examples can be multiplied many times over in the development of complex skills.

In this section we shall consider evidence about learning to read based on the errors that children make. The substantial literature on this topic has recently been reviewed by Weber (1968). First she raises the question about the relationships between oral and silent reading. Many standardized tests of reading achievement contain subtests on oral reading (Shankweiler and Liberman, 1972). Eye-movement patterns differ in the two modes of reading. In silent reading there are fewer eye fixations, shorter pauses, and fewer regressions (see Chapter 10 for a detailed discussion of eye movements). For adults there is generally substantial correlation in comprehension of materials read aloud and silently. Some investigators believe that for beginning readers, silent reading is the more demanding task. For our purposes, however, the particular argument is largely irrelevant, since we are interested in the strategies used in reading which we can glean from oral reading regardless of whether the two modes tap exactly the same skills.

Weber found that until recently the various schemes for classifying reading errors focused on the letters and words, so that the role of errors in the sentence or discourse was largely ignored. Further, the classifications differed from each other, making comparisons across studies almost impossible. There is general agreement that most reading errors are *substitutions*, that is, that the child reads a word different from the printed one. Yet, until recently, the graphic relationships between the printed word and the word read were not analyzed. It seems reasonable that if the graphic display is *three* and the child says *there,* he is telling us something different about his reading process than if he says *yesterday* to *three*. The response *four* to the printed *three* gives us still different information about the child's reading strategies.

It was to such questions that Weber (1968) turned in studying errors within the context of the sentences that first-grade children were reading. In her words:

Inaccurate responses have tended to be handled as isolated units rather than as elements in grammatical constructions that are hierarchically related to one another in order to form sentences. Inaccurate responses are usually considered indications of perceptual inaccuracies or evidence of a poor sight vocabulary rather than responses based on reader's expectations based on his knowledge of the constraints imposed by grammatical structure. (p. 113)

Weber (1970) studied the errors of two classes of first-grade children. Whole words which were misread were categorized according to the scheme in Table 9-1, and the frequencies of the error types are given in Table 9-2. By far the most common error was the substitution of a word for the one actually printed in the text. The sentences were analyzed for their grammaticality and their preservation of meaning, although not necessarily the meaning intended by the author, *up to the point of the error.* For both classes, the sentences with the errors were grammatical around 90% of the time, and what is more, this attention to the preceding context varied little with the reading abilities of the children.

These findings, then, do not support the characterization of the relatively low achiever as a word-by-word reader. Rather, they suggest that children—no matter what their potential for acquiring literacy skills—bring to the task a fundamental linguistic ability, which in its rigidity shapes their reading responses into familiar language structure. (Weber, 1970, pp. 153–154)

The question can now be asked how the powerful pull of generating a meaningful sentence interacts with the graphic display. The sentence "Spot can help me" may be read to the point of the errors "Spot can hear" or "Spot can see." In both cases the context is acceptable, but in the first error example the graphic similarity between *help* and *hear* is obviously closer than between *help* and *see*. Weber constructed a graphic similarity index taking into account shared letters, number of letters, positions of similar letters in the printed and error versions, etc.

It will be recalled that about 90% of the substitutions were grammatic-

Table 9-1   Types of Reading Errors

Type	Printed Word/Response
1. Substitution	funny/family
2. Omission	the *black* umbrella/the umbrella
3. Insertion	down the creek/down *to* the creek
4. Scramble	In went the animals/In they all went

Source: Weber, 1970, p. 151.

Table 9-2   Percentage and Frequency of Error Types

Class		Substitution	Omission	Insertion	Scramble	Total
1	%	79.9	8.5	9.2	2.4	100
	N	(856)	(91)	(99)	(26)	(1072)
2	%	93.9	3.2	2.6	.2	99.9
	N	(818)	(28)	(23)	(2)	(871)

Source: Weber, 1970, p. 151.

cally acceptable, leaving only a small number of errors whose graphic similarity could be compared to the grammatical errors. In both classrooms
and among the various ability groups, the ungrammatical errors were
graphically more similar to the printed text than the errors which maintained the meanings of the sentences to the point of the error. The two
tasks seem for these first-grade children to be incompatible. The pull for
meaning was strong, but entailed little attention to the printed word. Attention to the graphic nature of the word—much rarer—resulted in errors
that violated grammaticality. Children used only one of the two sources of
information about the word. The developmental course of the integration
of the two kinds of information will be taken up later.

Errors which yield acceptable sentences up to the point of the error may
or may not be meaningful as the child continues the sentence.

Printed sentence: He said, "Can I help you?"
Reading: He said, "Come/I help you?" (Weber, 1970, p. 154)

If the error did not upset the meaningfulness of the sentence to its end, children tended to disregard the error, though 30% of the children did go back
to correct their original errors. Although Weber does not say so, these chil-

dren must have been using information from the discourse outside the sentence, since the sentence itself, error and all, was perfectly acceptable. When the error eventually created an ungrammatical sentence, some 60% of the errors were reread and corrected; 39% of the ungrammatical sentences were tolerated without correction. At this point and for the first time in Weber's data, good and poor readers differed. About twice as many errors were corrected by more able readers when the error by the end of the sentence yielded a meaningless sentence.

Weber's results indicate, therefore, that children in the early course of their reading are sensitive to the structures of the sentences they produce. Meaningful, grammatical sentences are powerful considerations for young readers, who operate under the assumption that sentences they read should make sense. Further, this belief about reading is held by both good and poor readers. The actual graphic display takes second place to grammatical acceptability.

Reasonable as this might be as a tactic for the young reader, he must sooner or later read what is actually written rather than what he invents. Biemiller (1970), working with the same children that Weber studied, detected a developmental sequence in learning to read that showed a progression from invention, to attention to and constraint by the actual graphic display, to an integration of the two strategies.

Biemiller noticed that at some point in the first grade most children stop and say nothing when they come to a word they cannot read. By the nature of her study, Weber ignored these *nonresponse* errors. A few children start to read with this strategy; many more act as Weber described—they say something reasonable though unrelated to the printed word. Children enter this nonresponse period at various points in the first grade and remain nonresponders for longer or briefer periods. Biemiller defined the nonresponse period as one in which more than 50% of the errors were silent perusals by the child. In simplistic terms, the beginning reader starts with the strategy that any word that yields a sensible sentence can be said; then he gets the idea that what he says must have some relationship to the text, but he is unable to decode the text and so keeps silent; finally, with increased decoding skills he reads a word that has some relation to the graphic display. Errors at this point require the child to be quite sophisticated. He has to say a word that *both* makes sense in the context of the sentence *and* resembles the graphic constraints of the printed word.

In general Biemiller's hypotheses were confirmed. He compared the three periods: *pre–no response, no response,* and *post–no response.* Since the no response period was set at 50% of such errors, there were still substantial errors of commission to analyze during this period. In all three periods, contextual errors of the types Weber described were the most frequent. Still, the number of graphic substitutions, that is, evidence that the children were paying attention to the graphic display, increased across the three periods. Quite dramatically, "over 70 per cent of graphically similar substitutions made by children in the post–no response stage were contextually constrained. . . . In the post–no response phase, however, the biggest shift is in the direction of making substitution errors that are both contextually and graphically constrained" (p. 89). That is, children were now paying attention to both the context of the sentence and to the spelling of the words. Interestingly, about 90% of the substitutions were words that the children had encountered elsewhere in their reading. The tactic seemed to be, if you are going to guess, try a word you have seen before. Could this be due to the frequent repetitions of a small vocabulary in first-grade reading books?

Biemiller's phases undoubtedly are influenced by the type of reading instruction that the children are receiving. In both his classrooms, the teachers emphasized the meaning as well as the decoding aspects of reading. Scottish children who received more analytic training than American children made more errors that changed the meaning of sentences; that is, they did not exploit contextual information as much as American children (Elder, 1966). Ilg and Ames (1950) report results that on the surface contradict Biemiller's. Substitution errors were related to the graphic display through age seven but by age nine meaningful substitutions outnumbered them. It is difficult to reconcile these findings without knowing the details of reading instruction which the children received. Biemiller was dealing with six-year-olds, and though errors based on graphic similarity increased toward the end of the year, contextual errors overall were still the most frequent.

Biemiller's results have certain practical diagnostic values. Children who enter the no response phase early are more successful readers at the end of the first grade. Many children start school with the notion that reading is speaking with books open in front of them. The speech is not nonsensical. Still, the earlier the realization by the child that what he says must be determined by what is printed, the better is the prognosis for early reading achievement.

Reading connected discourse yields errors which preserve the meaning of the sentence to the point of the error. It is also useful to ask about the nature of errors on words presented in lists. For instance, do children reverse letters or words? Even in a list of words, reversals of letters like *b* and *d* may result in nonsense forms and we have seen the strong pull of meaningful substitutions. Reversible words, like *saw* and *was, raw* and *war,* etc., may yield errors that make sense, and so errors might be likely to occur in the initial or terminal parts of such words. A further consideration is that medial parts of words are vowels, which may be more error prone than consonants. Shankweiler and Liberman (1972) tested these notions with elementary school children in the second and third grades. Reversals were reported to account for only a small proportion of the total errors. Further, reversal errors were not reliable, that is, a child could not be characterized as consistently high or low on reversal errors, which brings into question the hypothesis that reading disability is generally due to persistent tendencies for the retarded reader to reverse letters or letters in word order. Finally, errors on reversible letters occurred less frequently when the letters were presented singly with a short exposure duration than in words.

When children were given words to read, fewest errors were made on initial consonants, next on final consonants, and most on medial vowels. The sequence initial-terminal-medial in frequency of misreadings has been elaborately documented (see Chapter 7). Except for a group of children whose reading was problematic enough to refer them to clinics, the locus of errors was reasonably independent of the child's reading ability. A later study by Liberman was reported in Chapter 5. It is important to note that children who made errors on word lists almost without exception substituted a real word rather than a nonword.

Although there is no gainsaying that much can be learned about the process of reading by studying the ways children and adults read individual words, the normal reading process is extracting information from connected discourse. The ability to read words may under certain circumstances predict the quality of reading discourse (Shankweiler and Liberman, 1972; Weber, 1968). Still, meaningful prose in a passage provides the readers with many kinds of information that may make the words available when children could not read them in isolation. First-, second-, and third-grade children could read many more words in prose passages than the same words in lists (Goodman, 1965), and this ability increased with grade level. The third graders were constrained by the graphic nature of the words. Like Weber's (1970) subjects, if errors resulted in ungrammatical sentences, the children corrected their previous reading to bring the sentence into a meaningful form. One of the few cases in which Goodman failed to find correction was when the child concentrated on decoding a word that was difficult for him and lost the meaning of the passage. Goodman's views, it must be mentioned, are strongly influenced by his aversion to a heavy tuitional emphasis on decoding.

In summary, the important lesson we have learned from the study of early reading errors is that young children find it difficult to attend to syntactic-sematic and graphic information at the same time.

Correspondence Rules and Decoding
It has often been said that the alphabet is a cipher on the phonemes of the sounds of speech. In that case, should it not follow that reading is simply decoding to speech and that learning to read is simply a matter of learning which letter goes with which sound? Reading has often been defined as decoding; it has been said that if children at six years were aware of phonetic segmentation, there would be nothing to teach them except letter-phoneme pairings. For example, consider the two following statements from Bloomfield (1942):

> In order to read alphabetic writing one must have an ingrained habit of producing the sounds of one's language when one sees the written marks which conventionally represent the phonemes. (p. 128)
> The letters of the alphabet are signs which direct us to produce sounds of our language. (p. 129)

Also note the following statement from Fries (1962):

> The process of learning to read in one's native language is *the process of transfer* from the auditory signs for language signals, which the child has already learned, to the new visual signs for the same signals. (p. 120)

A more moderate expression of what seems to us still a decoding view is found in Venezky (1972a): "Reading is the translation from writing to a form of language from which the reader is already able to derive meaning" (p. 1). Venezky warns that simply decoding from writing to speech is not in itself reading, for one could learn to pronounce texts in a foreign language without understanding it. This view, though deemphasizing mere decoding, is still not satisfactory to us since it seems to imply, despite the warning, that the learning process does not involve meaningful relations, that, whether one calls it decoding or not, it is nevertheless a kind of mechanical transduction. It is only a step from this notion to the assumption that an S-R formula can be applied: The written letters are stimuli, the sounds are responses, and they are arbitrarily connected by a process of memorizing. (Venezky, we should say, did not make this leap; no particular learning theory was implied.)

Since we have eschewed an S-R point of view, we shall not talk about graphic stimuli and spoken responses being associated with one another. A better view, we think, is that linguistic information can be represented in two ways, phonetically and graphically. These systems map to one another (both ways), not necessarily in a one-to-one fashion, but by correspondence rules. English spelling does not map to sound by way of single letters representing single phonemes, as we saw in Chapter 6. Nor can a spoken word often be spelled correctly by the use of a simple phonetic code. That is why we must speak of mapping rules, which are often conditional and usually involve units larger than the letter and the single phoneme (which cannot be pronounced independently). What does a child do, then, when he begins to read?

We have seen, from a study of early errors, that children are aware of meanings and use context to guess at a word, often producing one that bears no graphic resemblance to the word in the text. Later on, errors are often based on graphic similarity, whether they make sense or not, showing that the child has learned to focus attention on the graphic information—a phase he must go through at some point, even though he does not yet have the capacity to process graphic and semantic-syntactic features in parallel. We do not want the child to be "stuck" at the phase of handling only the graphic information and simply emit speech, even if he can do it with facility. We are speculating that the manner of teaching the mapping system could influence the outcome, and we are going to argue for a multilevel approach, possibly not the fastest to get results at first, but we want the one that yields most transfer to new material and aims for parallel processing of a word's informational features—graphic detail, graphic structure, semantic content, and so on. How do we start?

Samuels (1970c, 1971) has elaborated on the conventional view that paired associate learning is the basic process involved in early acquisition of reading skill. As he put it,

In the beginning stages of learning to read, there are several types of skills which the child is called upon to master which, in essence, are paired-associate learning tasks. For example, the child may be required to learn letter names, letter sounds, grapheme cluster sounds and oral responses for whole words. In each of these tasks, the student is given a printed verbal stimulus to which he must learn to associate a verbal response. (Samuels, 1971, p. 1)

When the cue and the appropriate response are hooked up, we can say the learner is able to read or recognize the word, i.e., upon stimulus presentation he can say the correct word. (Samuels, 1970c, p. 25)

The latter is referred to as the "hookup or associative stage." Samuels emphasized that paired-associate learning was not a simple, single-stage process, but involved attention to distinctive graphic features, perceptual learning, visual and auditory memory, and mediational stages. He also emphasized the role of "memory strategies such as being able to note relevant feature differences among stimuli and the ability to encode these . . . in visual memory" (Samuels, 1971, p. 7). The importance of improving strategies of recognition for learning the relevant paired associates was stressed, since he considered the ability to recognize a stimulus as one that was presented before to be essential for paired-associate learning. When the learner focuses attention on the relevant stimulus information, "hookup" with the response (provided the response can already be produced) should be rapid.

Most of this argument rests on respectable experimental evidence. It might be added that the response should not only be one the learner can "emit," but one that he understands. Teaching him to respond with the appropriate sound when shown the letter cluster *sh* may make little sense to him, and in that case it will not be retained or applied in a new situation.

So far, we may feel we can go along with this, provided the S-R terminology is jettisoned and the notion of mapping from one system of representation to another made to replace it. But there are some serious problems to be faced. What are the distinctive features that we want the learner to focus on? How do we get his "attentional strategies" into play? What level of unit of stimulus information (and corresponding mapping) are we going to choose to focus on—letters, words, sentences? In other words, what level of unit do we want the child to deal with in learning mapping rules for the written and spoken language? The first decision must be this one, for the informational features are different at different levels of segmentation, and so then must the appropriate attentional strategies be different.

In previous chapters, the various levels at which written and spoken language could be mapped were reviewed, from discourse to sentence to phrase to word to morphemic units and syllables within the word. In English, it was pointed out that single letters do not map perfectly to sound, even if one could sound out a single phoneme (and in the case of most consonants, one cannot). There are subunits within the syllable, in particular, the many constrained consonant clusters that characterize English orthography. The constraints correspond to phonological constraints, but the relations are best described as conditional or rulelike, rather than as matching one element to another. Where do we plug into this system of correspondences?

The old whole-word versus phonics controversy made (superficially at least) the assumption that one unit must be chosen for emphasis. Proponents of a whole-word method argued that meaning was lost by reducing the learning process (paired associates, of course) to smaller units. Proponents of phonics argued that learning by words resulted in no transfer

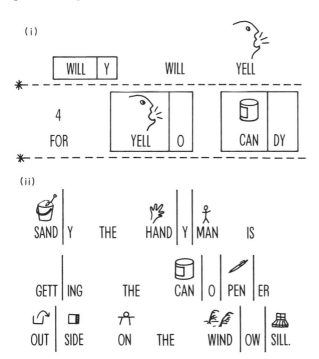

Figure 9-2. Sample of a rebus syllabary used with kindergarten classes in the Philadelphia area. From Gleitman and Rozin, 1973, pp. 467, 471. Reprinted with permission of the authors and the International Reading Association.

to new words, that learning whole words was essentially logographic and the benefits of an alphabetic writing system lost. Thus, one should teach letter-sound correspondences and get the child to "blend" them into a word. But one cannot make three single phonemes for *b-a-t*: It comes out as five, and how can one blend that into bat?

Some languages, notably Japanese (see Chapter 6), segment perfectly into a small number of syllables. Syllables can be pronounced as a unit. Segmenting into syllables, one could teach via a phonetic method. Children learn fairly easily to segment words into syllables. They could presumably learn that orthography is phonetically related to speech by syllabic analysis of the written and spoken words. Syllables recur in a number of words, so there would also be some basis for transfer (though not much in English, since the number of syllables is around 4000). Gleitman and Rozin (1973) carried out a lengthy instructional experiment teaching American children beginning reading with a syllabic method. They reasoned that the fundamental conceptual problem in reading acquisition is "awareness of phonological segmentation," as well as attending to the *sound* of language as a cue to meaning. Both these problems could be simplified for the child, they thought, by beginning with sound units that are easy to segment from a word and are, in reverse, easy to combine to form a word.

Gleitman and Rozin prepared a syllabary of 60 syllables. The syllables were combined with pictures (pictographs) on a rebus principle, letting the sound of the picture's name stand for a syllable, such as a picture of a bee representing the word *be*. Figure 9-2 shows a sample of writing in the rebus syllabary, which was introduced to kindergarten classes in the Philadelphia area. The children were taught to break words into syllables, shown pictures of words that are simple syllables (e.g., *can*), shown some

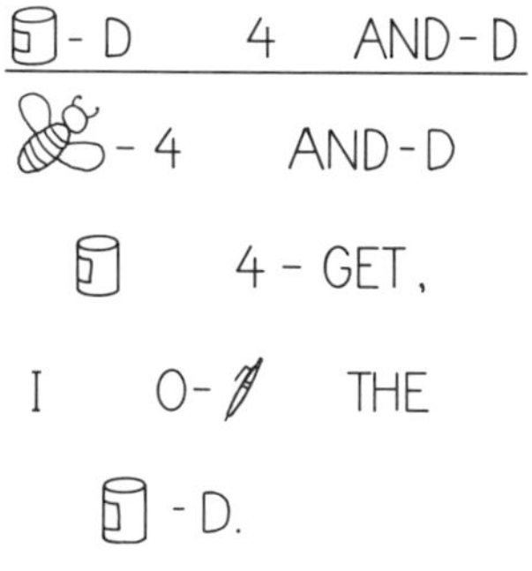

Figure 9-2   (cont.)

short one-syllable words spelled out (e.g., *the*); the cards were placed in a row, and a sentence was "read." Redundant presentation of a picture and the printed syllable was used when possible. This procedure was reported to be learned very quickly by the children.

Gleitman and Rozin considered the procedure only an introductory approach to teaching children that the writing system "tracks the sound stream," for English has far too many syllables to be learned as a syllabary, and the alphabetic principle, they agreed, must eventually be learned. They felt that learning to "blend" phonological entities like syllables would make it easier to learn a phonemic principle, possibly by spontaneous induction from the syllabic base. As they put it,

Our approach is to ease this process by, as it were, recapitulating the historical development of writing in the process of teaching it: we begin (as did early man) with pictorial representations, and proceed by steps to rebus and syllable before introducing the highly abstract alphabetic notation. (1973, p. 481)

A particular advantage of their method is that the child succeeds early in "reading" something. Whether it transfers to phonemic analysis and facilitates learning of it is not known; this experiment provides no evidence. Certainly it has no transfer value in itself for reading longer monosyllabic words like *strong* or *church* or *quaint*, although the syllable undoubtedly has psychological reality as a unit of a polysyllabic word (see Chapters 4 and 7).

Given the objections to words, letters, and even syllables as proper units for introducing the child to reading, what unit are we going to settle on? The sentence? Certainly sentences must be introduced at once because there is too little information in a single word to let the child know that he can find out something interesting from reading. But we also know that the difficulties come in reading words. The conclusion we have arrived at is that the problem of finding an ideal segment and concentrating on it in beginning to learn to read is a false one. A *multilevel* approach is essential. What the child reads must make sense. At the same time, it must not be so hard that he fails. Whatever the segment, it must be the most economical one that he is capable of processing. Practice with it must yield transfer to new words. A child might be able to read a sentence with little practice simply by noting only the first letters of the words that make it up (a child, or anyone else for that matter, will use the minimal cue that works), but there would be no transfer to any other words or sentences. We want to present real information in real sentences—start with it and end with it—

but in between we try for some analysis on the child's part. So learning to read at the beginning must involve sentences, even if the child does some guessing. It must also include learning to segment words. Words included in the sentence should often be polysyllabic, since syllabic segmentation is easy and may get across the idea of analysis. They could well be words like *cowboy* and *Sunday*, so the child will learn about intraword morphemic segments. The latter is important, because English orthography is morphophonemic, not just phonemic. And there must be intrasyllable analysis, at some point, not just letter by letter, but by way of constrained letter rules and patterns. Whatever the lesson of the day, it must, we think, finish with something meaningful at the end (see the discussion of the Project Literacy experimental program at the end of the chapter).

Analysis of Intraword Relations

There is good evidence that there must be analysis of intraword relations for transfer to new words to occur. Bishop (1964) worked on this problem, using college sophomores as subjects in simulated learning-to-read situations. Different groups of subjects were given training by a whole-word method or by a component-letter method, with Arabic words, letters, and appropriate word and phoneme pronunciation. After training, new words made by recombining the already presented components were presented for the subjects to learn to read. Figure 9-3 shows training and transfer words and indicates their pronunciation. Compared with a control condition, the component training group showed very significant transfer.

Training words	Phonetic symbols	Transfer words	Phonetic symbols
و ر ا ف	fa:ru:	ى ر ى م	mi:ri:
ى د ا ف	fa:di:	و ت و م	mu:tu:
ا ف ى ت	ti:fa:	ا ش و ك	ko:sa:
ى ن و ت	tu:ni:	ى ف ا ك	ka:fi:
ا ش ى ش	si:sa:	ا ف ى ن	ni:fa:
ى م ى ش	si:mi:	ى د ا ن	na:di:
ى ف ا د	da:fi:	ا ش ى ر	ri:sa:
و ك و د	do:ko:	ى ف ى ر	ri:fi:

Figure 9-3. Training and transfer words used in a simulated learning to read experiment. From Bishop, 1964, p. 216.

The whole-word group also showed some. The subjects were examined at the end for knowledge of component grapheme-phoneme correspondences. It turned out that *all* the transfer in the whole-word group was accounted for by those subjects (12 out of 20) who had induced the component correspondences for themselves without teaching. Although more than half of the subjects in Bishop's experiment induced the subordinate correspondences for themselves, it cannot be assumed that children would do so. In fact, there is evidence (Bowden, 1911) that many children do not.

An experiment similar to Bishop's was conducted by Jeffrey and Samuels (1967) with six-year-old children, using artificial graphemes and CV English words, again with the result that transfer only occurred when training with component correspondences had been provided. The children were given training in "phonic blending" as well. Almost no component correspondences were induced by the word-trained group. It must be remembered, however, that the training took place in a single short session. A third study (Marsh and Sherman, 1970) with younger children found transfer from learning "sounded-out words" to learning both isolated letter-sounds and whole words, but little if any transfer between the two latter tasks.

Accepting the fact that the average child cannot be expected to induce component letter-sound correspondences from whole words automatically when he is introduced to reading, and that there are few one-letter to one-sound correspondences in English anyway, what has been tried to help them learn, and what have been the results? The most frequent attempt has been to try to get the child to produce individual phonemes and "blend" them, when presented with a string of letters (the *b-a-t* paradigm).* But we have already indicated the problems inherent in this method, which are summed up neatly by Venezky (1972a):

> . . . we have no explanation for how a fused unit emerges from independent units, given that the independent units can be articulated separately, and that the articulatory instructions for some fused forms are significantly different from those for the independent units which form them. That is, even if the separate units could be articulated with zero pause between them, the result would not be a fused unit. (p. 17)

*A study of auditory blending by Chall, Roswell, and Blumenthal (1963) found that auditory blending ability in first through fourth grades is positively correlated with oral and silent reading ability, especially oral. The examiner sounded the "component parts of the word" (e.g., *m-a-p*) and asked the child to say the word he heard. The positive correlation with tests of reading achievement (around .60) is impressive and interesting, but there is no evidence of a causal relation. We can only conclude that the better readers apparently understood the principle of phonetic analysis.

The task, in short, is a highly artificial one, and if the child grasps the idea at all he is probably capable of inducing letter-sound relations for himself. As Gleitman and Rozin (1973) put it: "When the teacher asks the child to blend such units (to pronounce the sounds in such a way as to obliterate the demarcation line between them), this is in some ways tantamount to asking the child to 'know how to read' " (p. 457).

Acquisition of "letter-sound generalizations" of the single letter-sound variety is thus difficult to teach and of dubious value given the nature of English orthography. Bloomfield (1942) urged that only "regular" letter-sound correspondences be taught first, moving on later to "irregular" ones. The Bloomfield-Barnhart program (Bloomfield and Barnhart, 1963) is organized insofar as possible according to this system. It is clearly not entirely possible if the child is to read sentences or stories, for words like *the* and *to* are essential. The child does not acquire a set for variability, he is not introduced to the morphophonemic principles of English orthography, nor its conditional rule system until later. Might it not be better, in the long run, for him to be introduced to the system as it really is?

If a child is going to learn specific letter-sound correspondences and generalize them to new words, must he memorize them by a paired associate method? Is there not some hope that he can induce them if given sets of words constructed so as to facilitate abstraction of a relation, that is, to isolate a conceptual invariant from a variable context? Silberman(1964) prepared an iterative reading program designed to teach children to read aloud combinations of four initial consonants (*f, r, s,* and *n*) and four vowel-consonant word endings (*an, it, at,* and *in*). It was expected that children would automatically induce the internal correspondences if given enough contrastive practice with a sample of the possible combinations (e.g., *fan-fin, sat-fat, ran-fan,* etc). He should be able to transfer the induced mapping invariant to a novel combination that had not been taught (e.g., *rat*). The children in the experiment were in the lowest quartile in reading readiness in the low first grade in a culturally deprived neighborhood. They did not show automatic transfer until they had specific practice in decoding novel words *within* the training program. Teaching sounds independently, and then "blending" was not successful. They needed practice in *generalizing the decoding skill*. This procedure finally proved effective for reading new words. The children did eventually succeed in generalizing the relation to a new word, but practice in the transfer strategy itself was required.

A relational strategy was compared with two nonrelational ones by Skailand (1971). Like Silberman, she chose her subjects from families of very low economic status. They were enrolled in kindergarten. She taught 28 words and syllables to four groups of children with different types of presentation. There were two lessons of 15 minutes per week, over a period of ten weeks. Two to four of the words or syllables were presented in a training period, with some review. One group, the whole word or "sight" group, always had two words displayed on a card, with the words paired so that they had no letters in common (e.g., *tap* and *rub*). The experimenter pronounced the words for them and they also pronounced them, either simultaneously or following her. A second group had the "grapheme-phoneme" treatment. They saw the same cards as the sight group, but the sounds of the letters were given them, followed by "blending" of the letter into the word or syllable. The subjects tried to pronounce the sounds and words with or following the experimenter.

The other two treatments presented the words as patterns. In the third, words were paired by similarity of spelling patterns (e.g., *tap* and *nap*). The subjects pronounced the first word with or following the experimenter and attempted to identify the second word. If they were unable to, it was pronounced for them. In the fourth group, contrastive predictable spelling patterns were presented in pairs (i.e., *tap* and *tape*). The same patterns recurred with other words (i.e., *hat* and *hate*). The children were again encouraged to attempt the identification of the second word.

Two posttests were given after completing the 20 periods of instruction. One was a recall test for all the words and syllables that had been taught, and the other was a transfer test in which the children were asked to pronounce 26 new words and syllables containing the same correspondences as the words and syllables that had been taught, but each differing in one letter.

The recall test showed a clear difference. The two groups that had had the words presented in a relational pattern, either similar or contrastive, significantly excelled over the other two groups, remembering twice as many on the average. The pattern treatments did not differ from one another. On the transfer test, there was overall very little transfer. The children taught with patterns were somewhat better than the other two groups, but the difference was not statistically significant.

Although there was little evidence of spontaneous induction or transfer in these two experiments, the value of emphasizing relational spelling patterns and rulelike internal structure of words does seem indicated, rather than sight-word or letter-by-letter paired-associate learning. The training periods were short, the children very young, and the subjects drawn from specially disadvantaged groups. We will turn now to some work with older children emphasizing learning of rules and patterns.

Learning Word Structures

Analysis of intraword relations can be looked at from another angle, the learning of word structures: The word may be taken as the unit, with emphasis on the rulelike relations within it (and between it and other words) that make it a higher-order unit that is more than just an arbitrary string of letters. Orthography is a kind of grammar, as we saw in Chapter 6. It has rules that are highly generalizable, aside from single letter-to-sound correspondences. Can children learn them, how early, and how do they do it?

Venezky, who studied English orthography and its correspondence with pronunciation (Venezky, 1970a), and his colleagues have performed a series of tests of ability to generalize predictable correspondence rules. They constructed a set of synthetic words (pseudowords made up of letter strings without meaning), some of which incorporated regular spelling-to-sound correspondence rules but some of which did not have regular correspondences (Calfee, Venezky, and Chapman, 1969). The regular patterns chosen included the final (marker) *e* pattern, the initial *c* pattern, and other less frequent ones. The synthetic words *cabe*, for instance, tests both rules, as does the synthetic word *cipe*. The marker *e* tells the reader that the vowel is "long"; the *c* before an *a* tells him that the *c* is to be pronounced /k/; and the *c* before *i* tells him that the *c* is to be pronounced /s/. A number of vowel digraphs were tested, some with fairly regular correspondences (e.g., *neem*) and some with irregular ones (e.g., *houm*). The 40 synthetic words were presented to third-grade chilrden, fifth-grade children, high school students (eleventh and twelfth grades) and college students to be pronounced. Good readers and poor readers were identified by other measures in all four groups.

Analysis of the pronunciations of predictable patterns showed that the percentage of appropriate pronunciations increased from third grade to high school, that better readers in third and sixth grades were consistently more likely than poorer readers to give appropriate responses to predictable patterns, that good and poor readers continued to differ in the final *e* pattern even through college; and that certain predictable patterns were not totally mastered by even the better, older readers. Figures 9-4a, b, and c show the age-related relationships and contrast the good and poor readers for three patterns.

Correlations between pronunciation and reading level were high in third graders (.66 and .52) and lower in sixth graders (.16 and .46), whereas correlations between IQ and reading increased from third grade to sixth grade, where IQ was a better prediction of reading than the pronunciation score (r = .49 and .35 in third grade, increasing to .77 and .82 in sixth grade). What predicts successful reading, as measured by the tests, at least, changes from early to later grades. But for at least one pattern (the final *e* pattern) there is still a significant difference between good and poor readers at the college level.

Inappropriate responses were analyzed into ones that would have been appropriate for that letter in a different environment ("plausible" ones) and "wild" ones (e.g., pronunciation of *c* as /m/). Poor readers gave twice as many wild responses as good readers, especially in the youngest group. Although the correlation between pronunciation score and reading rank decreases at higher grades, readers continue to increase their mastery of predictable letter-sound correspondences through high school, long after formal reading training has ceased. The data from this study are correlational and do not tell us whether instruction on specific patterns would produce good readers, or whether a good reader automatically picks them up for himself. The question is obviously an important one. Several bits of evidence (Venezky, 1972a) suggest that examples are more influential than verbalization of rules. A strong bias toward pronouncing *c* as /k/ (either correctly or incorrectly) can be related to the very small number of words included in introductory readers in which *c* is followed by *e, i,* or *y*.

Another study with synthetic words (Venezky and Johnson, 1972) found high correlations between knowledge of letter-sound correspondences and comprehension in first grade (r = .76) and third grade (r = .69). They suggested that children who learn to read with phonics programs are heavily dependent on letter-sound correspondences at the primary levels for comprehending written discourse. As letter-sound generalizations become more readily available, other factors such as context come into play and the correlation with comprehension drops. An interesting finding in this study was the difference between handling of an initial *ce* (as in *cent*) and a final one (as in *face*). The /k/ pronunciation so favored in initial position was not present in final position, suggesting (quite rightly, we think)

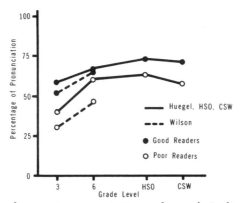

a. Percentage of correct pronunciations of vowels in final -e patterns.

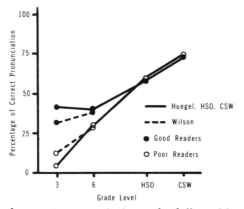

b. Percentage of correct pronunciations of c followed by e or i.

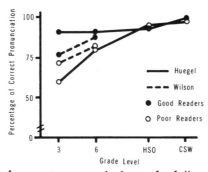

c. Percentage of correct pronunciations of c followed by a, o. or u.

Figure 9-4. Development of ability to pronounce synthetic words appropriately. From Calfee, Venezky, and Chapman, 1969, p. 42, and the Wisconsin Research and Development Center for Cognitive Learning.

that the *ce* is not only treated as a unit, but that conditional rules (a letter-by-position interaction) are also influential. Later work with a more extensive sampling of patterns (Venezky, Chapman, and Calfee, 1972) strengthened this generalization, since position of the letter in the word turned out to be an important factor in the responses to almost all patterns. These authors emphasized the importance of introducing real-word examples for each pattern in reading programs within the early period of instruction, before incorrect biases generated by frequent examples of a single letter with a single pronunciation could take over. We wish to emphasize the evidence in these studies supporting the importance of structure within the word and getting the child to notice it. Good readers do this, processing letters in clusters and relational contexts.

Alphabet reformers have always assumed that the necessity of processing word structure, that is, conditional information beyond the letter, was a hindrance to reading. The assumption actually rests on little or no evidence. Venezky (1972b) investigated this question with Finnish children from grades 1 through 3. (Finnish is considered by many linguists to have the most regular single letter-to-sound correspondence of any language.) Synthetic words constructed to look like Finnish words were given the children to read aloud, as in the studies reported above. Finnish children begin school at seven years of age, and only 19 letters and one superscript are required for Finnish spelling, so comparisons with the studies above must be cautious. There was, indeed, a high level of mastery of letter-sound correspondences by the end of first grade (nearly 80% correct). The reading score received by each child at the end of the year was correlated with the pronunciation score for the synthetic words. The correlations ranged from .508 (Grade 1), to .528 (Grade 2), to .487 (Grade 3). The correlations account for only about 25% of the variance, despite the great regularity (one-to-one letter-sound correspondence) of the language. High letter-sound ability by itself thus does not guarantee high reading ability or even decoding ability. "Irregularity" of orthography is not the root of all reading problems, and reading failures are by no means unheard of in Finland, according to Venezky. Highly educated Finns who are fluent in English as a second language have in several cases known to us reported that they read faster in English than in Finnish. The redundancy of the conditional rule system of English makes this report plausible even if anecdotal. If the rules have been internalized there is no tendency to read letter by letter.

Given the importance of the rule system, how do children learn the spelling patterns and conditional rules? By induction? By being told a verbalization of the rule? By practice with *contrasting* patterns, as recommended by Fries? Fries (1962) classified spelling patterns into three basic sets, as follows:

1. Monosyllabic words with the general shape of CVC
   a. (C)VC *rat, bat, cat* (initial contrast)
   b. C(V)C *bad, bid, bed* (medial contrast)
   c. CV(C) *bad, bag, ban* (final contrast)
   d. Digraphs *than, wish* (single phoneme represented by two letters)
   e. Consonant clusters *splint, cramp, brand**
   f. Double the last consonant if it is *f, s,* or *l;* when *k,* write *ck: back, fall, chess, cuff*

Fries comments that all the types of spelling patterns above belong to the same set.

They all use one of the five vowel letters in our alphabet with a single consonant letter (*top, pat; tip, pit*), or two consonant letters representing one consonant phoneme (*sh, ch, th, ng*), or two to five consonant letters representing a cluster of two to four consonant phonemes (*st-a-nd, str-a-nds, tw-e-lfths*). . . . The word-patterns represented by this very large set of spelling patterns are all single syllable words. But these syllables occur very frequently as parts of multi-syllable words. . . . This set of spelling-patterns is basic for all English spelling and must be responded to at high speed with practically no errors by those who would read with high efficiency. (p. 176 ff)

Fries goes on to warn that it is the *contrast* of one set of spelling patterns with other sets that relates spelling to sound in a rulelike way, not single letters and phonemes.

2. Monosyllabic words with the general shape of CVC vs. CVC*e,* e.g.: *can-cane, bid-bide, dot-dote, tub-tube, grad-grade.* This is another highly productive set of contrastive patterns.

3. Spelling patterns of more limited application:
   a. spelling patterns representing /i/ in contrast with those representing /ɛ/ *beat-bet, feed-fed*
   b. spelling pattern contrasts for /e/ *bat-bait, fly-flay*
   c. spelling pattern contrasts for /o/ and for the diphthong /aʊ/ *god-goad, prod-proud*

*According to Fries (p. 174), out of the more than 150 consonant clusters that appear frequently in modern English spelling, only three, *sp, st,* and *sk,* can occur both initially and finally in words. The reduction of information gained by knowledge of this conditional rule is an obvious processing economy as well as a neat contrastive relation.

The usefulness of internalizing these patterns so that they are automatically processed in "chunks"—units composed of many letters rather than
one—is unquestionable. Adult readers do it, as evidence in Chapter 7 demonstrated. How does the child learn the contrasts and generalize them?
Fries mainly emphasizes practice in a first stage which he terms "transfer
from auditory to visual sign for language signals." Principles which he recommends for instruction are repeated practice and drill, emphasis on contrastive features of the patterns, and pronunciation of only complete
words. His approach thus treats words as wholes, but the spelling pattern
approach, he believes, does "develop the connections between alphabetic
signs of reading and sound-patterns of talk."

How docs automatic abstraction of the "bundles of contrastive graphic
shapes" in writing come about and generalize over the common patterns?
Simply trying to impart the knowledge by verbal description and pointing
have not been found likely to result in automatic pickup. Two hypotheses
that seem reasonable are (1) that there must be abstraction of an invariant
pattern over many variable contexts by comparison with contrastive patterns; and (2) that a learning set gradually develops for finding regular
patterns in orthography. Should one teach verbal rules, such as "When
two vowels go walking, the first one is talking," or is there a better way?
Surely we can expect more transfer if the learner succeeds in making his
own inference. But will he do it?

Gibson, Farber, and Shepela (1967) attempted to develop a training
procedure aimed at providing opportunities for abstraction of a regular
pattern and for developing a learning set. They constructed a large number of problems that required the subject to sort positive from negative instances, like a simple concept-learning experiment. All the problems had
four positive instances, each of which contained a cluster of two letters in
an invariant position—initial, medial, or final (e.g., *qu, ea, ng*), or a separated pair (the marker *e* pattern, which occurred in five problems). The
other letters always varied. The child was given one problem at a time for
sorting, with one negative and one positive instance indicated to him when
the problem was presented. He was corrected when he was wrong. He
sorted for one problem four times, and then went on to another, whether
he had succeeded in a perfect sort or not, following a procedure much like
a discrimination learning-set experiment. He was not told the pronunciation of the word.

This training procedure was first tried on kindergarten children and first graders, giving them six problems a day for five consecutive days. The task was extremely hard for the kindergarten children. Only one out of 12 developed an indubitable learning set. This child could sort *all* the new problems correctly on the first sort by the fifth day. The task was somewhat easier for first-grade children; about half of a first-grade sample showed evidence of developing a learning set to abstract common patterns of orthography.

It was not clear whether these subjects had really attained a set to search for invariant structure over a series of items, or whether more specific habits had already been learned in first grade that helped on this task. A further experiment, therefore, compared success on the spelling pattern problems with success on analogous problems in which the elements were color chips instead of letters. Subjects for this experiment were first-grade and third-grade children, some given colors first and some given letters first. For the first-grade children, color and letter patterns were equally (and very) difficult; success on the color problems, however, transferred to the spelling patterns. For third graders, the letter patterns were much more easily picked up than the color patterns, and color problems were far more likely to be solved if they followed solution of letter problems than if they were given first.

It appears that a set to look for structure can be developed (albeit with difficulty) and can transfer to new problems, and that the ability to detect structure in letter patterns improves with age and schooling. It seems that this is more than specific learning, since it transferred to color patterns. The third graders easily succeeded in finding invariant spelling patterns. Following a task in which a child found them, he could pursue an analogous search for color patterns. Finding an economical structure has utility, and when these children had found it, they repeated their successful strategy with new material.

How could the first graders be assisted toward success in finding the structure to facilitate transfer to new cases? Lowenstein (1969) compared three procedures in an experiment with first graders presented as a "sort the mail" game. One group was given *no* special hints or help, as in the preceding experiments. One group was given *specific* help. When a problem was first presented, the experimenter said "You will be able to find your own mail, because all the cards will have *these two* letters on them." The pair of common letters was pointed out. This was repeated for each problem. A third group was told "You will be able to find your own mail because your cards will have the same two letters on them." But they were never told which letters. After two days of practice, all the subjects had a posttest set of new problems without any further instructions.

The group given specific help made very few errors during training, even on the first day. The group given no help made many, although some improvement occurred. The group given the general hint made many more errors to begin with than the children given specific help, but they improved steadily and on the posttest had a median of zero errors, whereas errors rose on the posttest to a median of 5.5 for the group that had received specific help. This was more than five times as many as they had made on Day 1. Although 70% of the subjects in the "specific" group made no errors on Day 2, only 20% made no errors on Day 3, the posttest. But in the group given the general instruction to look for an invariant letter pattern, 40% made no errors on Day 2, and 60% made none on Day 3. Response latencies confirmed these results. The specific group showed *no* change from Day 1 to Day 3, whereas the group given the general hint showed a steady and significant decrease in latency over the three days.

It may be concluded, then, that first-grade children can easily sort words on the basis of presence or absence of two specific letters that have been pointed out to them. But it is not this ability as such that leads to detecting common spelling patterns across items. There must be a search for an invariant pattern and discovery of such structure by the learner himself for transfer of this kind of abstraction to new problems. Subjects given no special instructions or hints may eventually accomplish this on their own— 20% of the subjects in the control group made no errors on Day 3 (the same percentage as the "specific" help group on Day 3). But it was clearly better to have attention directed to search for invariant features in the stimulus array, and finding them seemed to lead to repetition of the successful strategy and thus to consistently accelerated performance. This is perceptual learning, not just remembering something. Learning to abstract spelling patterns involves active participation by the scholar, not memorizing a verbal rule or simply being shown.*

Nevertheless, finding common patterns and generalizing the principle developed slowly in these first graders. It seemed possible that a task constructed so that the efficiency of using a common pattern was very evident might speed up finding and generalizing the principle. Gibson, Poag, and Rader (1972) gave second- and fifth-grade children a verbal discrimina-

*See the discussion of transfer by rule in Chapter 3.

tion task in which common spelling patterns could be used as a collative principle to learn the discrimination very economically. Differential reinforcement was given in the traditional manner as a subject pressed one of two keys arbitrarily designated as correct by the experimenter when a given word was projected on a small screen in front of him. There were two groups of subjects and two stages of learning (original learning and transfer). One group (E) saw words in Stage 1 which could be paired by spelling pattern (and by rhyme if they pronounced them). The words were *king* and *ring*, and *yarn* and *barn*. The same button was designated as correct for the two members of a rhyming pair, so a subject in this group had only two things to learn if he noted and used the spelling pattern. The other group (C) had four nonrhyming words (*nose, king, bell, yarn*) and so had to learn four arbitrary word-key-press relations. Stage 2 was the same for both groups and was similar to Group E's Stage 1. The words were *boat* and *coat*, and *cake* and *rake*. The subjects were run to a criterion of ten correct responses or stopped at the end of 60 trials. It was expected that the subjects who were presented with the collative principle in Stage 1 would be able to transfer it immediately in Stage 2 and would begin a criterion run by Trial 5, as soon as they had seen all four words.

Table 9-3 shows the percentage of subjects who began a criterion run by Trial 5 in both conditions and both stages. Looking at Stage 1, the fifth graders were significantly better than the second graders when the economical spelling pattern was present, but not when it was absent. In other words, they were not superior in simply learning four associations; they were superior because they used the economical information. The fifth graders were still superior to the second graders in Stage 2, no matter which Stage 1 condition had preceded it. The second graders did not learn to use a spelling pattern in Stage 1 when they were given the opportunity and transfer it to Stage 2. In fact, the same thing was true of fifth graders.

Table 9-3 Number and Percent of Subjects Solving the Word Tasks by Trial 5

Grade	Condition	Stage 1	Stage 2
2	E	3 or 20%	4 or 26.6%
	C	0 or 0%	2 or 13%
5	E	8 or 53%	9 or 60%
	C	1 or 6.6%	8 or 53%

Comparing Stage 1 and Stage 2, 53% of the fifth graders began a criterion run as soon as possible in Stage 1 and 60% did in Stage 2—a nonsignificant difference. One is forced to conclude that the child either applied the rule at once, in the training stage, or never did.

The fact that differential reinforcement in a traditional paired-associate task did not lead to pickup of useful pattern structure underlines once more what we have already said. The learner must discover the useful structure himself, with time, exposure, and active search all necessary contributors.

One further experiment appears, on the whole, to lead to the same unhelpful conclusion. Fletcher (1973) performed an elaborate study on transfer from alternative presentations of spelling patterns in initial reading, using computer-assisted instruction (see the section on the Stanford Computer Assisted Instructional Reading Program at the end of this chapter). First-grade children were given special training on spelling patterns, the training extending over eight days and followed by a transfer test. The children were already familiar with the computerized setup. There were four experimental training treatments: (1) B—practice with *both* initial and final spelling patterns (2- or 3-letter strings, such as *ca-, cla-; -ad, -and*); (2) I—practice with only initial units; (3) F—practice with only final units; (4) N—practice with neither (the spelling patterns used in training did not include any of those used in the final or initial units of the test words, although many of the same individual single letter-sound correspondences were used). All five vowels were included in the selected patterns. The patterns fitted into words of four types of configuration: CVC, CCVC, CVCC, and CCVCC. Exercises during training included copying (the display showed *an* and the child heard "Type *an* as in *can*"), recognition (the target pattern and two distractors were displayed and the child chose the appropriate segment to type when instructed, e.g., "Type *an* as in *began*"), and "building a word" (the display showed the target spelling pattern, two distractors, and a consonant or consonant cluster, such as *st*, and the child was instructed, e.g., "Type *stan*").

A child received training on half of the spelling patterns assigned him, and was finally tested on those plus the other half, containing all possible combinations of initial consonant and final consonant patterns in the set. In the criterion test, conducted by a live experimenter, the patterns were presented in whole configurations, half of them words and half of them pronounceable nonwords, and the child tried to read them aloud.

Results on the criterion test showed that training on the B and F treatments was more beneficial than either the I or N procedure. The B and F procedures were equally good, and the I procedure was as poor as the N procedure. The role of configuration of the monosyllable was tested separately for words and nonwords. In both cases performance was superior on the CVC and CVCC patterns as compared to the CCVC and CCVCC patterns. The two superior configurations did not differ from one another, nor did the two inferior ones. However, specific training on the I treatment showed some beneficial effect on nonwords of the CCVC type. Thus the prior practice with spelling patterns was most effective when it focused on the F patterns and the combined I and F patterns. The differences, however, are small; the percent of criterion words correctly read under the different conditions is: Both, 66%; Final, 63%; Initial, 58%; and Neither, 56%.

Results for words and nonwords on the criterion test was especially interesting for the question of generalization of pattern training to an item which could not have been learned specifically outside the training situation. Under all four treatments, real words were superior to nonwords. But the prediction was that this effect should have been *greater* under the N treatment. Actually the proportion of correct *words* greater was least here, the opposite of the prediction. The difference in favor of the N group is slight and could be due to differences in the selection of items for the four groups. But it seems that to the extent that there was generalization to the unfamiliar nonword items, the effect must have been attributable to the children's prior experience in reading, outside the experiment. It evidently had afforded some basis for generalization. This unexpected finding makes one wonder about the extent of the value of the experimental training on generalization of spelling patterns to novel examples. In any case, the ideal procedure for teaching generalizable knowledge of orthographic rules is still a matter of ignorance to us. Two inferences are plausible: one, that we have not yet achieved an adequate understanding of what it is that can be generalized in orthography; the other, that whatever it is, the child learns it on his own, and not by way of a set of planned exercises.

The problem of how to help a child learn to abstract spelling patterns is obviously in need of far more research, for not all children are successful in doing it spontaneously, even by the time they finish high school. The sorting task was a better vehicle for practice than discrimination learning, and a hint to look for a classifying principle helped. A demonstration followed by further search—essentially a lesson in transferring a strategy—

might be tried, as well as presentation of contrastive patterns together and presentation with redundant sound. It is a fact, however, that these patterns which are chunked so automatically by skilled readers are not salient for children when they begin to read. Perceptual learning and generalizing abstraction have to take place.

A small amount of research exists on using redundancy in various forms to point up (enhance the saliency of) the spelling patterns. Coloring common features or underlining them is a dubious practice unless it is carefully faded out, since the more salient redundant feature may win out and the desired one be ignored. Knafle (1971) reported that color and underlining aided "pattern responses" in a matching task (pointing to the one of two three-letter response choices that was more similar to the stimulus word), but there was no evidence that the subject abstracted anything. Making sound (pronunciation of the words containing the patterns) redundant with visual presentation is an obvious thing to do (and of course is done in school). Its effect is not known at present. Gibson, Poag, and Rader (1972) found that pairing pictures of objects with rhyming names was ineffective in the discrimination learning situation described above. While pronouncing the word for the child, or urging him to do it himself if he can, seems at least a harmless form of redundant presentation, it is not proven that it actually aids in abstracting the patterns. It even seems possible that by drawing attention to the words' meanings, the orthographic patterns might escape notice. The fact that faint signals are detected with greater accuracy in a vigilance task when they are transmitted redundantly (both visually and aurally) does not warrant any prediction about redundant visual-auditory presentation for pattern abstraction. The problem is clearly one for research. In the absence of further knowledge, it seems as if varied kinds of exposure, richly presented in different kinds of arrays and with different task requirements, could provide the most promising opportunities for the young learner to abstract the invariant patterns and optimize their transfer.

We might do well to recall William James' principle of abstraction by varying concomitants. *"What is associated now with one thing and now with another tends to become dissociated from either, and to grow into an object of abstract contemplation by the mind.* One might call this the *law of dissociation by varying concomitants"* (James, 1890, Vol. 1, p. 506). Embedding the spelling pattern in many varied contexts may not speed up original learning, but it should further transfer, and that is the ultimate goal.

Beyond the Word

We have been speaking of the word and its internal redundancy as the big hurdle for the child just beginning to read. We want him to find the correspondences between written words and spoken ones and learn to use, automatically and effortlessly, the economical regularities within the system. But in coping with this problem it is crucial never to lose sight of the goal of reading, to extract wanted information from discourse. And such information is seldom contained in a single word, except ones like *yes* and *no* which presuppose a preceding context without which they would make no sense. But sense there must be if the child is to get any reward from reading. We return now to our emphasis on a multilevel approach. A child must be presented with sentences and discourse at once, interwoven with practice in abstracting contrastive patterns and intraword redundancies. Nearly all reading programs take it as self-evident that sentences and stories must be presented as attractively as possible and at a level that can be grasped. We strive to lead the child as easily as possible to parallel processing of orthography and meaning.

While there are many children who have trouble just identifying words, and are thus bound to be poor at comprehension, there exists a group of children who can identify words well and quickly but still comprehend poorly, apparently because they treat the words as single units, unmodified by their context in phrases and clauses (Cromer, 1970). They are reading word by word and not processing orthography and meaning in parallel.

The earlier review of errors made it clear that dual processing does not come easily at first; the beginning reader attends to meaning or to graphic information but has trouble doing both at once. Questions arise, therefore, about how to provide material that will optimize the development of processing for both types of information. What type and size of units of discourse should be presented? How redundant should the text be? What kind of topical content is preferable? Should pictures be included in the text, and if they are to be, what should be their function? To what extent should the child be free to choose reading material and left to peruse it by himself, if he wants to? There is little experimental evidence available on any of these questions, but we can at least provoke thought about them.

Units of Discourse

If we are going to present the child with units of discourse larger than the word from the beginning, what length should they be? What level of complexity? It seems obvious that there must be units of sentence length at the very least, but must they be of the "Run, Dick, run" format? It has sometimes been proposed that the length of word and complexity of sentence structure in a primer should be at a level below the child's ability to produce words and sentences himself, since he is so enmeshed in the mechanics of decoding. The argument has also been made that the sentences should be very short because the decoding process is slow. If words are lost from short-term memory before the sentence is completed, its meaning cannot be extracted. There may be truth in these arguments, but they are speculative.

The opposite argument can equally well be pushed—that vocabulary and sentence structure should be modeled on the child's own stage of production and knowledge. The words should be familiar to him, but not "baby" words, and the sentence structure the kind he is using, neither oversimplified nor stilted, for him to comprehend the message optimally. A group of studies started by Strickland (1962) inquired about the appropriateness of children's spoken language for understanding the texts that they were reading. Strickland found that many of the oral sentence patterns used by children appeared in their readers, at least at the second and sixth grades, where she made the comparisons. Bormuth (1966) found that similarity of oral and written sentence structure enhanced comprehension, at least for poor readers. Ruddell (1964) tested the effects of congruence between written and spoken language patterns on comprehension more carefully. He compared fourth graders' understanding of passages made up of frequent oral patterns with the comprehension of infrequent oral patterns. Fourth graders understood the high-frequency patterns significantly more often. "These studies indicate a definite relationship between reading ease and the similarity of written material to the reader's spoken language" (Gammon, 1970, p. 3).

Certainly sentences of an agent-action-object structure are of minimal complexity, for children produce them before they are three years old (see Chapter 5). A study of the syntax produced in oral narration by kindergarten and elementary school children (O'Donnell, Griffin, and Norris, 1967) found that the word length of "minimal terminable syntactic units" (single independent predications together with any grammatically attached subordinate clauses) ranged from 5.2 to 10.1 among first graders, with a mean at 7.97. Mean word length increased with grade up to 9.80

in seventh grade. A number of the utterances of first graders contained sentence-combining transformations with one kernel sentence, usually in reduced form, embedded into another. Excluding mere conjunction (connection of main clauses with *and, but, so, or*), which occurs frequently in the narrative speech of grade schoolers (particularly with *and*), the mean number of sentence-combining transformations per unit utterance was .95 for first graders.

O'Donnell et al. analyzed these constructions, classifying them into nominal, adverbial, and coordinate constructions. Nominal constructions accounted for most, and among first graders included a variety of types: noun + noun (e.g., *north wind*), noun + adjective (e.g., *cold rain*), genitive forms (*man's coat*), relative clauses (e.g., *man who was wearing a coat*), prepositional phrases (e.g., *bird in a tree*), infinitives (e.g., *food to eat*) and participles or participial phrases (e.g., *the ant rolling the ball*). The noun + genitive form was most frequent. Nonheaded nominal constructions also occurred, the infinitive with subject most frequent and noun clause following. The grammatical function of these transformations most often affected the direct object (nearly five times as often as the subject). In the sentence "A hunter on his way hunting sees an apple tree," examples occur of a subject transformation, an object transformation, and a transformation on the object of a preposition.

Adverbial construction, especially adverbial clauses, occurred about six times per 100 unit utterances in first graders and increased rapidly up to seventh grade. Coordinate constructions (excluding coordination of main clauses) increased rapidly from kindergarten through seventh grade but occurred with moderate frequency in first grade, especially in predicates. The most frequent structural clausal pattern was subject-verb-object (e.g., "The ant found another ball").

The number of sentence-combining transformations increased with grade level, as did the word length of unit utterances, but an impressive finding of this report is that *all* the clausal patterns were used by at least some kindergarten children, and that there was a large increase from kindergarten to first grade. While hard empirical evidence is scarce, it makes sense to suppose that children, even when they are beginning to read, might well be presented with a variety of structural patterns including sentence-combining transformations. A study by Gammon (1970) of two reading series found that there were in fact a variety of structures, although they appear to be of limited complexity. Looking at children's first readers, one is commonly struck by the deviance of the sentences from the way anyone actually talks. If we want children to read flexibly and for meaning, it is surely reasonable to give them material that is like their own speech and that requires similar stress and intonation patterns.

Beyond the sentence, we know little about optimal size of units of discourse. Common sense tells us, however, that an interesting event requires more than one sentence for its description and a "story" is at least at the event level. A unit for one lesson should, reasonably, contain a complete episode, even if need be a short one.

Redundancy of Text

Cartcrctte and Jones (1963) have shown that children's initial readers are considerably more redundant than even simple adult texts. The measure of redundancy is related to difficulty and discriminates well between readers at different grade levels. Length of words and repetition of words contribute to redundancy. Children's first readers are highly redundant (short words and a small vocabulary with frequent repetition), while fifth-grade readers begin to approach the redundancy of average adult text. The question arises about the relation of the text's redundancy to the level of redundancy that children would choose for themselves.

Jones and Carterette (1963) sought to determine what level of redundancy is present in reading material that children prefer. Choices were taken from ratings by a wide sampling of children's librarians from all over the country, who judged on such bases as circulation and enjoyment in "story hours." Books were chosen at random from the top one-ninth at three levels. (Level 1 was kindergarten to grade 2 or 3; Level 3 was grades 2 or 3 to 5; and Level 5 was grades 4 to 6.) Level 1 was found to be slightly more redundant than the others. Word length gave no evidence of regularity, but sentence length showed regular growth. Redundancy at Level 1 was considerably less than that of first- or second-grade readers. Children appear, therefore, to prefer language that is less redundant than that presented in their readers. Whether a very high level of redundancy is optimal for learning is not thereby known, but it is at least questionable. Mean length of words appeared to vary randomly in children's free-reading choices, although it increased slowly and similarly in two graded series of readers (Carterette and Jones, 1964). Mean sentence length was similar in the two series of readers and grew slowly, but it was much greater in children's free-reading choices. These researchers suggest that there may be an undesirable restriction in word length in the basic reader and that reading books at Level 1 may be too redundant to be interesting.

Restriction in sentence length goes along with a restriction in grammatical forms. But as we have just seen, children's natural language at grade 1 is rich in patterns of linguistic structure and quite flexible in their use. This richness may not be congruent with basic readers at the beginning level.

Content in Children's Readers

That the content of the material in children's texts plays a role, or could play a role, in motivating even the beginning reader is generally taken for granted, certainly by us. A child must find that it "says something" worth knowing, something that has meaningful reference to his own life or stirs his imagination. Blom, Waite, and Zimet (1970) performed an analysis of the motivational content of children's primers. Three themes which accounted for 47% of the stories were coded as "real life with positive emotions," "active play," and "pets." They featured happy endings (if any) and were described as Pollyannaish and bland. Characters included in the stories were limited, most of them accounted for by children, mother and father, and animals. Older children were seldom included, so if the child reader were to identify with characters in the story, they would be age-identical or even younger children. In more than half the stories, only the primary family appeared.

An older study by Child, Potter, and Levine (1946) supports these findings. Their analysis of story types (animal stories, fairy stories, hero stories, and everyday stories) found the everyday stories to be by far the most preponderant, although they were examining third-grade stories. The Pollyanna quality was also noted by them.

A major defect of the readers from this point of view is what might be called their unrealistic optimism. . . . For children who have encountered failure in their everyday life, the easy attainment of goals such as nurturance and affiliation in the readers may be so unrealistic as to have little effect in strengthening their desire for such goals. . . . (p. 45)

A similar sort of unrealism was commented on in the discussion of infavoidance.*

*"Infavoidance" is Murray's term (see Murray, Barrett, Homburger, et al., 1938) for fears associated with self-consciousness, shyness, social embarrassment, and fear of competition.

While the content of these readers might do a great deal towards strengthening a desire for achievement in competitive success, there is very little about those children—perhaps the majority—who frequently experience failure in competition, and few suggestions about how such children can find some satisfactory way of adjusting to their failure. (Child et al., p. 45)

The Child et al. study was concerned with children's needs and motives as they are represented in and affected by the content of readers. This is relevant to the entire question of motivation for reading discussed earlier in this chapter. The potential "turning off" by the content of reading texts of black children, non-middle-class children, children from fatherless families, and children who are experiencing frustration or failure became a source of serious concern to many educators a few years ago. New readers began to appear with urban settings and characters of more than one ethnic background. Blom et al. (1970) made a content analysis of a multiethnic series and compared the results with those of the traditional series. Comparisons of theme and characters indicated that "the urban series contained the same emphasis as the standard series on Pollyannaish stories, with a somewhat greater emphasis on family-centered activities." Suburban settings still predominated; there were more urban settings than in the traditional series but fewer rural ones. However, more urban stories ended in failure than in the suburban stories (twice as many as ended in success), probably a dubious improvement.

Other multiethnic urban series have appeared since that study, with varied realization of the goals. Cultural values and attitudes can, and it seems do, appear in some of the multiethnic readers. A comparison of white and black six-year-old boys and their fathers in one series (Waite, 1968) found the black boy depicted as athletic, less intelligent, impulsive, distractible, and the object of humor, whereas the white boy was reflective, more intelligent, and socially secure. The fathers contrasted also in characteristic stereotyped ways. These are serious shortcomings that can be remedied and clearly must. Blom et al. also reported findings on first-grade children's own choices of books checked out from libraries. Their preferences were clearly discrepant from the contents of first-grade reading texts. Urban stories and stories about other environments were often chosen, in contrast to stories of children-only characters in suburban settings. If content exerts the motivational influence on the learning process for reading that we think it does, children should be allowed free choice of reading material as quickly as possible.

The Role of Pictures

Children's readers nearly always contain pictures. What is the function of the pictures as regards the child's learning to read? The child has looked at pictures and understood them for years before beginning to read. They interest him and make the book attractive. But if they give the same information as the text, might they not actually remove the incentive to discover the printed message? Will the child not be distracted by the picture from paying attention to the text itself?

Perhaps a picture presented along with a word might serve as a kind of mediating image to elicit the spoken word and facilitate forming of a meaningful association between the printed and the spoken one. Myrna Shure at Cornell University (unpublished ms.) ran a preliminary experiment on this issue. Children in the second term of kindergarten were given practice with three-letter common words (*cat, bed, dog,* etc.) on flash cards. In one group, the word on the card was accompanied by the appropriate picture. In another, it appeared alone. Training trials in which the experimenter pronounced the word as it was displayed to the child were alternated with test trials when the child was shown the word alone and asked to say what it was. The picture group made significantly more errors and took longer to reach criterion than the group without pictures. The pictorial redundancy appeared to be distracting rather than useful. Similar results were obtained by Samuels (1967) with the procedure outlined above, and in a classroom experiment with a story accompanied by an illustrative scene. Samuels (1970b) has reviewed other evidence confirming the failure of a picture to assist in learning a sight vocabulary. The picture tends to be used as a cue, and even with fading techniques it seems to have little value, although teachers sometimes report that a child recognizes a word (previously taught) faster if a picture accompanies it. Experimental evidence recently obtained by E. Garber (unpublished manuscripts) showed this to be a fact.

It has often been argued that illustrations are useful because they promote comprehension of what is being read. Samuels (1970b) reviewed a number of experiments on this issue, all with negative results. He found studies which reported that pictures do influence attitudes, however. But do they influence attitudes toward reading, by adding a source of aesthetic pleasure to the task? There seems to be little objective evidence, but children enjoy picture books. It seems as if this favorable attitude could serve some purpose in learning to read.

Children love comic strips and comic books, and at least one child we know taught himself to read with them. Why would he do this when the story was in the pictures? The answer may be that the story wasn't all in the pictures; it is (in a good comic strip) interwoven with the comments of the characters, often nonsense exclamations like "zowie" or "oops," which interest the child but are not specifically cued by the picture. A comic strip with no printed messages at all seldom survives. The text is important, as Hochberg (1968) pointed out. He also said that "picture-text amalgams are essentially teaching machines in that they convey information in a self-paced and self-reinforcing process" (p. 131). But this is only the ideal. Most comic strips are not. What makes the successful ones work? Except for Hochberg's preliminary work (1964, 1968), we know of no research on this really important problem. In a successful illustrated text, do the pictures contribute sequential or substantive information, or only a connotative setting for the story carried by the text? The question has not been answered, and so of course we cannot answer the question of whether, for learning, pictures should convey information in addition to the text, or whether they should only serve the incentive function of enhancing interest in the text. They could, for instance, pose a question that only reading the text will answer.

Early Reading Programs

There are literally hundreds of commercially published programs for teaching children to read. Representative types of these programs have been well described and evaluated by Chall (1967). Generally, the extant programs may be classified as whole-word programs, in which the emphasis is on reading for meaning, and decoding programs, which emphasize instruction in the correspondences between spelling and sound. The variations are wide in many of the programs, so that decoding, or phonics, programs may emphasize systematic phonics, meaning direct instruction on the correspondence system, while intrinsic phonics uses the story line as a basis for phonics instruction. Recently, so-called linguistic programs have called attention to the recurrent spelling-sound patterns: *cat, rat, sat,* etc., and used these for instruction directly and as the basis for stories. Also, linguistically based methods have tried to maintain natural sounds so that teachers are admonished not to use drills like *b* as in /*buh*/ since the sound /*buh*/ does not occur alone in English.

Chall's review concluded that phonics-based programs led to more efficient reading instruction. As might be expected, children taught by the whole-word, basal programs are at the beginning more skilled in comprehending text. But by the second or third grades specific training in decoding yields better techniques for reading new words as well as for comprehending text.

Today, classifying programs as basal or phonics appears to be academic. More and more, published programs are becoming eclectic—each has a bit of every technique to cover all bets, as it were. Also, the differences in the effects of programs are usually not very large. We would be well on the way toward solving the social problems of learning to read if all children could read as well as the norms of the less successful programs.

"Phonics" is an imprecisely defined term. Its origin is in the word "phonetic," though no program that we know of teaches children to perform phonetic analyses of their language. Phonics has become a blanket term to encompass instruction in correspondences between written and spoken languages, and, as we may expect, there are many such programs either as separate instructional packages—a much used piece of current jargon—or as components of programs that also purport to emphasize "reading for meaning."

Chall (1967) intentionally subtitled her book "The Great Debate," and when we realize that the debate has been going on since Colonial times (Mathews, 1966) there is no obvious cause for optimism. We have chosen three instructional programs in beginning reading for special attention. These are in various stages of development, so the assumptions, decisions, and data on evaluation are usually available. It seems to us that such programs are more informative to students of reading than completely worked-out and widely used programs, which at any rate are adequately described by Chall.

The Pittsburgh Program
The Learning Research and Development Center is now in the initial stages of working out its second reading program for children in grades 1 to 3 (Beck and Mitroff, 1972). After initial instruction by teachers, the program is designed to be self-paced and self-managed by the students. The New Primary Grades Reading System (NRS) "is an adaptive system that permits children to progress at different rates, that allows for different

routes to the mastery of objectives and that provides for children doing different things at different times in the same classroom" (p. 9). To these researchers, reading is "the perception and comprehension of written messages in a manner paralleling that of the corresponding spoken messages" (quoted from Carroll, 1964, p. 336). The implication is one that we have encountered before: Children have to master reading to the point where it is symbiotic on spoken language.

Generally, the program is eclectic, though the major emphasis is on code breaking, on making sounds from text. Sound-spelling relationships are taught directly and in isolation, so that in the first lesson children learn to reproduce the phonemes for *m, t, s,* hard *c,* and short *a.* The sequence of letter-sound correspondences to be taught may be rationalized in many ways. This program chooses letters from which many words can be constructed as well as widely separating visually and acoustically confusing elements. The difficulty faced by young children in segmenting phonemes has been covered (see Chapters 5 and 8). A critical part of the early teaching is to blend these isolated sounds into clusters or into words. Blending is taught as an "algorithm," although the process remains mysterious and artful. Basically, blending involves pronouncing the segments quickly so that the child recognizes the word. The Pittsburgh researchers claim that they are able to train children to synthesize *cat* from /kuh/ /ah/ /tuh/.

Also following the admonitions of linguists, word groups like *mat, fat,* and *rat* are presented. Through a teacher's guidance, a transfer word *sat* is taught by calling attention to the common VC terminal and pointing out the sound of the initial /s/. Following operant conditioning principles, the teacher may say /s/ and then fade out the prompt by mouthing the sound or by simply pointing to it.

When the child learns 11 symbol-sound correspondences and how to blend them, the instructional materials begin to include phrases, and later, sentences. The developers of this program find it "reasonable to engage a beginning learner in behaviors that are not totally comparable to the skilled performance" (p. 31). They do not, however, discuss the problems of unlearning behaviors whose components are incompatible with mature behavior.

After initial teacher instruction, the students work their way through the program via cassettes, workbooks, stories, games, etc. Frequent diagnostic testing tells the teacher whether the child can progress to the next level or should review the same or comparable materials. Teachers act mainly as guides and resources, though there are occasions for group instruction. Reading for meaning is introduced in stories which the group reads together when teachers can lead discussions around the story. Another method, using the cassettes and workbooks, is to color or circle pictures based on the printed captions.

It is really not fair to call the Pittsburgh program, at this point, an instructional scheme for teaching children to read. Rather, it is a detailed blueprint for constructing such a program. Except for the early commitment to phonics, the developers are prepared to take useful ideas without regard to orthodoxy. It will be to a great extent a program which the child will manage on his own. Given success or failure on a segment, he will be directed to the next experiences. Teachers are initially active and then become resources for individual children moving at their own paces. There is little room for individual decisions by teachers—the program is teacher-proof. The developers justify the strong and explicit constraints under which the teachers operate by the requirements to mesh teachers' activities with individual cassette or workbook instruction. There still remains the momentous task of choosing, trying out, revising, and sequencing the materials of instruction. Only then will we have the evaluative data by which to judge the program.

The Stanford Computer Assisted Instructional (CAI) Reading Program

For a host of reasons, special devices and procedures designed to facilitate teaching have not caught on. Films, filmstrips, audio tapes, gadgets for presenting programmed materials, TV, etc., have been trumpeted as another set of panaceas, but after initial enthusiasm they appear to be relegated to the rear shelves of the school's storeroom. Why? For one thing, they may have been oversold—the nature of education is such that no single approach or technique can possibly solve all of the problems. Second, the quality of the materials often leaves much to be desired. Children who are used to professionally produced, well narrated, dramatically colored films on TV may be excusably bored by the results of a hand-held camera, showing a black-and-white film, often silent, on eating habits among the Tonga. Most important, though, the so-called visual aids are not intrinsically related to the instructional programs. They are materials which teachers may choose to use, and we suspect that their value is in relation to the teacher's efforts to make the aids clearly applicable rather than an "add-on" whose usefulness is not clear to the students.

Programmed instruction should not be lumped with other audiovisual devices. Initially, hardware for presenting the programmed materials was part of the package, but with time simple workbooks and programmed tests have become available. The important questions have to do with the appropriate mix between programmed and other materials, the students for whom these techniques of presentation and reinforcement are indicated, the types of materials which lend themselves to such a format, the size of the unit, etc. We have the impression that the clarion call to program all instruction is past, but we think that for some children at some points in their education, programmed techniques may be useful.

The computer is the most recent addition to the technology of education. Compared to other devices, the computer *in theory* is light-years in advance of other educational devices. Its capacity for almost infinite memory, its flexibility and responsiveness to the learner make it the most enticing technological advance in education. Unfortunately, its use has not yet matched its promise for reasons that we will shortly detail. There are two large computer-assisted instructional programs now under development and evaluation: the Stanford system and the Plato system at the University of Illinois. It is premature to evaluate these systems. The development of software programs has been more difficult than anticipated. The systems are used not only for reading, but for mathematics at various levels, logic, statistics, mechanics, etc. As an example, we will describe Stanford's CAI program for initial reading.

Computers can be arranged for various degrees of freedom in the interaction or "dialogue" available between the computer and the student.

At the simplest interactional level are those systems that present a fixed, linear sequence of problems. Student errors may be corrected in a variety of ways but no real-time decisions are made for modifying the flow of instructional material as a function of the student's response history. Such systems have been termed "drill and practice." (Atkinson, 1968, p. 225)

At the other extreme of our scale characterizing student-system interactions are "dialogue" programs. Such programs are under investigation at several universities and industrial concerns, but to date progress has been extremely limited. The goal of the dialogue approach is to provide the richest possible student-system interaction where the student is free to construct natural-language responses, ask questions in an unrestricted mode, and in general exercise almost complete control over the sequence of learning events.

"Tutorial" programs lie between the above extremes of student-system interaction. Tutorial programs have the capability for real-time decision making and instructional branching contingent on a single response or on some subset of the student's response history. Such programs allow students to follow separate and diverse paths through the curriculum based on their particular performance records. The probability is high in a tutorial program that no two students will encounter exactly the same sequence of lesson materials. However, student responses are greatly restricted since they must be chosen from a prescribed set of responses, or constructed in such a manner that a relatively simple text analysis will be sufficient for their evaluation. The CAI Reading Program is tutorial in nature. (Atkinson, 1968, p. 226)

Initially, the Stanford CAI's hardware was elaborate. Each student station had a cathode ray tube, a light pen, typewriter, audio display, and slide projector. The more modest and adequate current student equipment includes a typewriter and an audio display. The schematic of the system maybe seen in Figure 9-5.

The program is an adjunct to the classroom at which the child spends 12 minutes per day. The programs are designed specifically for training in decoding, leaving the teacher to do in his own way the other aspects of teaching children to read. The purpose of the CAI segment is straightforward: to have the children associate sound with a graphic display. The assumption is that such learning involves a large number of paired-associate presentations. The program is divided into seven strands: 0. reading readiness; I. letter identification; II. sight word vocabulary; III. spelling patterns; IV. phonics; V. comprehension of categories; VI. comprehension of sentences.

Instruction is individualized, in that a child moves through a strand depending on his past performance. For children who do not attain criterion performance after several trials, the answer is provided and the next strand is taken up. A child may work simultaneously in several strands, but his progress in each strand is independent.

The actual exercises which a child goes through can best be seen from several exercises on the phonics program (Atkinson, Fletcher, Chetin, and Stauffer, 1970, pp. 26–27), illustrated in Figure 9-6.

It should be pointed out that in contrast to the Pittsburgh program, sounds are not presented in isolation. Other than teaching the alphabet, the syllable is the smallest unit. Further, in the Stanford program such decisions were made on the basis of prior research (e.g., Atkinson and Paulson, 1972). The overwhelming amount of work which goes into a program as modest as this one is obvious. If the child's response is correct he

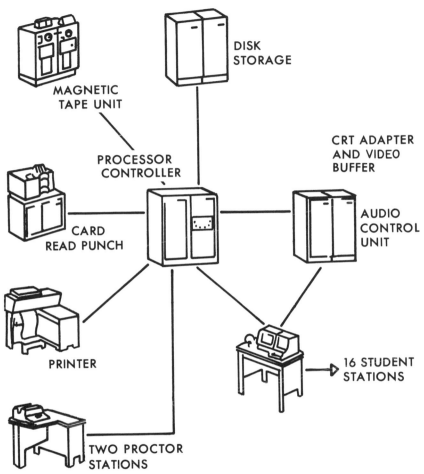

DISK STORAGE

MAGNETIC TAPE UNIT

CRT ADAPTER AND VIDEO BUFFER

PROCESSOR CONTROLLER

CARD READ PUNCH

AUDIO CONTROL UNIT

PRINTER

16 STUDENT STATIONS

TWO PROCTOR STATIONS

Figure 9-5.   System configuration for Stanford CAI system. From Atkinson, 1968, p. 226. Copyright 1968 by the American Psychological Association. Reprinted by permission.

Figure 9-6, Phonics exercises from the Stanford CAI Program. From Atkinson, Fletcher, Chetin, and Stauffer, 1970, p. 26.

Strand IV—Phonics. When the student has shown a mastery of a specified number of words in the spelling strand by completing a predetermined number of sections in that strand, he begins Strand IV with drill in phonics.

Again, we wish to emphasize that each strand is separate from every other strand although strands are related. For example, entry into Strand III is dependent on the student's progress in Strand II. Once a student enters a strand, he is allowed to proceed at a rate commensurate with his ability.

Exercises in the phonics strand concentrate on initial and final consonants and medial vowels. A departure is made, however, from traditional phonics exercises in that the students are never required to rehearse or identify consonant or vowel sounds in isolation. The smallest unit of presentation is a dyad, i.e., a single vowel-consonant or consonant-vowel combination.

The following exercises are used in Strand IV:

Final Consonant	Display on	
Exercise 1	the Printout	(Audio)
The program prints:	–IN –IT –IG	(Type /ɪG/ as in *fig.*)
The student responds by typing:	IG	
The program prints:	YES	
The program prints:	–IT –IN –IG	(Good. Type /ɪT/ as in *fit.*)
The student responds by typing:	IT	
The program prints:	YES	
The program prints:	–IG –IN –IT	(Type /ɪN/ as in *pumpkin.*)
The student responds by typing:	IN	
The program prints:	YES	(Fabulous.)

In exercise 2, the student types the full word. An example of Exercise 2 for the initial consonants is as follows:

	Display on	
Exercise 2	the Printout	(Audio)
The program prints:	DA– MA– HA–	
	—D	(Type *mad.*)
The student responds by typing:	MAD	
The program prints:	YES	(Great!)
The program prints:	HA– DA– MA–	
	—M	(Type *ham.*)
The student responds by typing:	MAM	
The program prints:	/ / / /HAM	(No. We wanted *ham.*)
The program prints:	DA– HA– MA–	
	—D	(Type *dad.*)
The student responds by typing:	DAD	
The program prints:	YES	(Good.)
The program prints:	MA– DA– HA–	
	—LF	(Type *half.*)
The student responds by typing:	HAT	
The program prints:	/ / /HALF	(No. We wanted *half.*)
The program prints:	HA– MA– DA–	
	—D	(Type *mad.*)
The student responds by typing:	MAD	

can go to the next exercise. If he makes an error, the computer program must be ready for that error and branch the learner to a remedial exercise. Should he make another error, another branch must have been anticipated and built into the program.

CAI seems to make many educators uncomfortable. "The process is depersonalized." "The child is locked into a booth." "Individuality among children will be stifled." "The computer will lead to technological unemployment of teachers." The Stanford researchers have addressed themselves seriously to these fears. The child is at the computer for about 12 minutes per day. An adult is present to help and answer questions. The program is highly individualized since each child's lesson is based on his past performance, both on the preceding question and on his performance on preceding days. The children seemed to like the procedure, or perhaps it's the break in routine that every child liked. Most important, it was those children who were doing poorly that appeared to prefer CAI. Sex differences (the usual finding that girls progress faster than boys) were not apparent.

Does the program work? The evaluation was limited to 50 first-grade children. The children were tested on the Stanford Achievement Test, the California Cooperative Primary Test, and the CAI Reading Project Test. The superiority of the CAI on almost every subtest is clear and impressive. The fact that the CAI children did better than the controls on tests like sentence comprehension may be due to the teachers' concentration on those aspects of reading, since the computer took care of the more mechanical parts of the instruction. Perhaps the most impressive evidence is that the computer-instructed children averaged from .4 to .7 years superiority in grade placement after only $5\frac{1}{2}$ months of CAI.

Ultimately the decision about the extension of CAI will be an economic one. "The cost of a daily 12-minute session per child is about forty cents" (Atkinson et al., 1970, p. 6). Compare this with the cost of a page or two in a workbook which costs one or two cents. True, the costs of CAI will be reduced when the computer is used in a time-sharing mode, where a large number of children work simultaneously on a variety of subject matters. In theory computer science is sophisticated enough for such uses, but the investment to adapt such a system to education has not yet become available. Further, the know-how for the dialogue mode compared to drill and tutorial is also available. But its adaptation to education has not advanced very far, and its development and operation costs would now be prohibitive.

Given the Stanford CAI program as it stands, there are a number of comments we can make about it. The decisions are often research based, that is, experimental mock-ups of the exercises are varied as the basis for final decisions. Opportunities for basic research on the process of reading are exploited (see the study by Fletcher, 1973). The choice of the syllable as the basic instructional unit seems sensible. Feedback to the child's response is immediate. Teachers can get immediate printouts of the progress of single students and of the class. On the other hand, reading seems to be thought of as a paired-associate learning process: "An effective way for these associations to become automatic is by repetitive presentations for short intensive drill periods with students given immediate knowledge of results after each of their responses" (Atkinson et al., 1970, p. 4). Orthographic patterns are presented but apparently not in ways that make it optimal for children to induce the rule-governed structure of English orthography (although none of us, so far, knows what the optimal way is). The philosophy seems to us to retain the notion that to learn to read is to learn a large set of spelling-sound associations. Perhaps the computer is wagging the conceptual dog.

The Project Literacy Multi-level Reading Program
Project Literacy was organized as a program of basic research on the process of reading. Much of that research is reported in this volume. For a number of reasons one of the authors (H. L.) decided to set up several first-grade classrooms for demonstration purposes. We wanted to try out our research findings under the complex, natural conditions that classrooms provide. Where we had no relevant research findings, we were prepared to extrapolate from our evolving theory of reading. And finally, we looked to the classrooms as sources of research hypotheses to be taken back and tested in the laboratory. Looking back on our activities, we inevitably note things that we would have done differently because our research findings were coming in at a rate faster than we could implement them and at the same time our theories about the nature of reading were changing. But an ongoing classroom has a certain amount of inertia that makes rapid adaptations difficult.

The first year was devoted exclusively to educating ourselves about the realities of reading instruction and searching for hypotheses. For these purposes, one first-grade classroom was continually observed by a psychologist and a linguist. A cooperative teacher was asked to carry on her classroom as she naturally would. In this case, the teacher happened to be using a popular basal reading series whose main emphasis was on word recognition and the extraction of meaning from the text. As researchers, we decided that adherence to any of the popular orthodoxies in reading would be self-defeating. We were prepared to use any methods to test our theories and to help the children learn to read as efficiently as possible.

By the start of the second year we were prepared to take over a classroom in which we would be responsible for instruction in reading. We developed the following guides for the development of instructional materials and the methods of teaching (Levin and Mitchell, 1969, pp. 3–5).

The guidelines   The seven points listed below set out the guidelines for the development of the instructional program.

1. A child must have certain preliminary skills before reading instruction is begun. There are two basic components to the preparation:

a. Understanding that reading is a means of communication, and that the written representation is a code for language.

b. Adequate discrimination skills, both visual and auditory.

It follows that it would be desirable to include an introduction to the basic notions of coding in the prereading phase. The main focus of such a program would be the demonstration of different means of coding in order to point up the fact that writing is a flexible and useful code for spoken language.

2. The competent reader has three kinds of information available to him as he reads:

a. Phonological (spelling-to-sound correspondences) and orthographic (spelling pattern) constraints.

b. Syntactic constraints (grammatical structure).

c. Semantic constraints (meaningfulness).

The beginning reader already has some of the skills required for reading as described here. Insofar as he can understand spoken English, he can utilize information gained from syntactic and semantic constraints. He has only to apply these to reading. For example, the grammatical structure of "He stopped his car at the red . . ." places great limitations on what follows. In this example, it is highly likely that the next word will be a noun. In addition, the meaning of these words constrains the remainder. It is probable that the next word will be *light,* and very improbable that it will be *justice.*

On the other hand, the beginners must learn to use spelling-to-sound correspondences; there is nothing in language behavior or other content previously acquired by the child that will transfer to this aspect of the reading task.

The curriculum will be designed to provide a balanced development in the use of the three kinds of information. At no time should the child learning to read fall into the use of one of these sources of information at the expense of the others. The reader must be flexible in using all sources in order to insure success in the various types of reading matter which require greater emphasis on one or another of the sources.

3. The beginning reader should be given simultaneous training in using all three types of information. This follows from the notion that when teaching a complex task it is preferable to start training on the task itself, or a close approximation to it, rather than giving training on each component skill independently and then integrating them.

One implication of this position is that there should be no separate spelling program or handwriting program per se, but that this instruction should be fully integrated into the reading program.

a. At any stage, training should be provided in several different contexts over a wide range of materials.

b. Because of the large individual differences in ability, it may be necessary to provide additional training for some students. This may be similar to the initial instruction, or it may involve the use of subroutines designed to provide specific instruction in using a particular type of information.

4. The child must learn to approach the reading task with the understanding that there is variability, that is, he should acquire a "set for diversity." Thus, for example, if more than one phoneme is represented by a single grapheme, the child should be introduced to both correspondences very early in training.

5. The child should encounter sentences from the very beginning of training, because the sentence is the minimal unit which (1) insures comprehension and (2) provides all three types of information. A differentiation model will be followed, that is, the complete sentence will be introduced first and then will be broken down into its component parts.

6. The relationship between reading and language must be made clear from the beginning, through natural intonation, emphasis on reading as a means of communication, and so forth.

7. The classroom should constitute a "literate environment." Exposure to language and reading-related activities should not be restricted to periods of formal instruction. The beginning reader should also be shown

what skillful reading is like, through frequent exposure to adult reading of material interesting to the child.

The curriculum should reflect the assumption that children come to reading instruction with rich language abilities which instruction should capitalize on. Moreover, beginning reading skill can be acquired not only through direct, formal instruction, but also through informal contact with various activities and materials in the classroom.

The use of story charts, class newspapers, displays, discussions, and other means of emphasizing communication should accompany direct instruction to advance the development of language and reading skills.

Our fundamental assumption was that the skilled reader's task is to extract information from the text and that he has available knowledge about the meaning and grammar of the text as well as the correspondences between writing and speaking. He uses these sources of information in parallel, sometimes emphasizing one or the other aspect depending on the nature of the task and his abilities. We made the assumption that so far as possible initial reading should provide the child with the sources of information available to the adult reader, although he might not exploit the various kinds of information with the same skill as the adult reader. Said another way, we wanted reading to approximate the mature model from the beginning. Also, teaching component parts of the reading skill raises the eventual problems of integrating the components into a smooth skill. We have seen in the analysis of errors that beginning readers use semantic, grammatical, and graphic information, so the task is not to emphasize one over the other but to reinforce the weak aspects of the skills and to put the skills together for simultaneous use, as does the skilled reader.

To start, we were not convinced that children understood what it meant to read. Did they understand that writing was a code for spoken language in certain systematic ways? We devised a series of "coding games" that seemed to us quite successful. The students devised light flashes or drum beats to send messages with the important inference that the sender and receiver must agree on the code. The permanence of writing was taught, each child devising a logogram for his name. The efficiency of the alphabet occurred naturally when a Jimmy and a Jerry saw that their logograms could be simplified on the basis of the common sound. Generally, the difficulty of memorizing 30 logograms, one for each child in the room, fell of its own weight. The coding game was tried with a number of first grades, including two classes in Harlem and as a series of prereading exercises in kindergartens. Our informal impressions are that the activities successfully taught the notion of alphabetic writing systems and, at a rudimentary level, the idea of correspondences between writing and speech.

The basic unit of instruction was the sentence. The sentence as a unit of instruction was suggested by Comenius in 1657 and first exploited by Farnham in Binghamton, New York, about 1870 (cited by Huey, 1908, pp. 272–273). Children made up sentences which the teachers wrote for them on the board or in workbooks. For the children who could read the sentences, well and good. For those who needed help on words or sentences, the teachers exploited the sentences for those purposes. The program was consciously opportunistic. During the first several weeks, the program differed little from basal programs with emphasis on word recognition and then on the meanings of the sentences. When the sentences became vehicles for teaching orthographic rules, for example, special books were written or sometimes commercial children's books were found useful. The instruction was organized from higher- to lower-order units. Sentences were analyzed into phrases, so that an exercise might use the following sentences.

John ran after the red cow.
Jane saw the blue fly.

Phrase structure was taught by presentations of groups of sentences.

John ran after the blue fly.
Jane saw the red cow.

Sound-spelling correspondences were introduced by the initial letters and sounds in *John* and *Jane*. In every case, the sentence was presented or created by the children, the teacher exploited some elements of the sentence, and then the sentence was put together. In that way, we believed that children would be able to use as much information in parallel as their skills permitted.

By the second year of our experiences we realized that teachers needed more guidance in a spelling-sound correspondence program. Again, we built the program around sentence materials, but the sentences were carefully chosen to provide instructional opportunities to teach correspondences. The program is reproduced in Figure 9-7 (Levin and Mitchell, 1969, pp. 95–100), and certain characteristics might profitably be pointed out. Contrasting forms were presented together: *mat mate*. Morphology

Figure 9-7.   Program of instruction for spelling-sound correspondences. From Levin and Mitchell, 1969, pp. 95–100.

Sequence

I Letter-Sound Correspondences	II Rationale	III Lesson Number
d m s a Letters stand for sounds. Here each letter stands for one sound. Letters, like sounds, occur in different positions of a word.	Letters chosen for: graphic contrast phonetic contrast productivity (high frequency in first grade words and combinability with concurrently presented inventory)	1. *d, s* with short *a* 2. *d, s, m* with short *a* 3. *d, m*
Order is significant. Not explicit: Vowels are phonetically and dis- tributionally different. E.g., only vowels fit in the frame *s–t*.	NB Working notions: word sentence beginning and end	
t	Regularity and productivity in previous pattern	4. *t*
i	Productivity	5. Short *i* with *d, s, m, t*
e as a marker for *a* and *i*	Productivity of pattern and concept	6. Long *a, i*
A letter can stand for more than one sound.	NB Medial *e* is not introduced early because it is not productive, especially in *eCe* pattern.	
Another letter may signal the appropriate sound.		
The marking letter does not stand for a sound itself.		
Morphological endings	Plurality and third singular present are represented by *s*.	7. Plurals, verb agreement
s in *sits, hats*	Teacher ignores *s/z* distinction in sound. Presented in context, e.g., 1. *mat*; 2. *mats*.	
n	Regularity and productivity, especially in final position and with marker *e* in VC*e* pattern.	9. *n* in initial position
sh A combination of two letters	Productivity NB *h* has not been introduced	10. *sh* in initial and final

Figure 9-7   (continued)

I Letter-Sound Correspondences	II Rationale	III Lesson Number
may stand for one sound.	alone. The combination *sh* does not occur with marker *e*.	position 8c. Discriminate between *sh* and *ch* 8d. *s* and *sh* 8e. *wh* and *sh*
Morphological *es*: *dishes, dashes*	Usefulness. This presents the other spelled form of plural and third singular present.	(See Lesson 7. *s* and *es* taught together.)
p	Productivity, especially with marker *e*. Review of earlier concepts. At this point, standards of mastery of old material are high. Regular new letters should be assimilated quickly.	11. *p* in initial position with short *a* 8a. *b* and *p* 8b. *f* and *p*
Morphological endings *ing, er*	Productive in forming disyllabic words.	12. *ed, ing*
Disyllabic words. Familiar letter-sound patterns occur in longer words.	Teacher only exemplifies this concept by presenting words. Children are expected not to read them but to recognize partial identity with familiar words.	13. Disyllabic words. Familiar patterns in longer words
o–oCe	Productivity	14. *o* in medial position 15. *o* contrast with *a, i* 16. Long *o*
ch, tch Pairs of this type are positional graphic variants of one sound.	Productivity (*tch* only with short vowels). At this point, present other positional variants, in monosyllabic words, e.g., mi*ss*, *si*t.	17. *ch* in initial position with short *a, i, o* 18. *ch* in initial position with long *a, i, o* 19. *tch* with short *a, i* 8c. *sh* and *ch* 8f. *wh* and *ch* 8j. *th* and *ch*
wh	Not productive in terms of this inventory, but important because of its occurrence in a small number of highly frequent words.	20. *wh* with short *a, o* 8e. *wh* and *sh* 8f. *wh* and *ch*

Figure 9-7   (continued)

I Letter-Sound Correspondences	II Rationale	III Lesson Number
		8g. *s* and *f* 8h. *th* and *f*
ss	Productivity	21. *ss* with short *a, i, o*
f, ff *u*	Productivity	22. *f* with short *u*
b	Productivity	23. *b* *b* and *d* *b* and *p*
h	Productivity	23. *h* 8a. *h* and *th* 8l. *h* and *f*
th (voiceless)	Not highly productive, but regular. NB Voiced *th* is not specifically taught, since it appears in common function words; *the* as in *bathe* is not presented.	23. *th* 8h. *th* and *f* 8n. *th* and *sh* 8j. *th* and *ch* 8k. *h* and *th*
y	Productivity in final position epsecially in the pattern VC, C, *y* and –VC, *y*. taffy pony daddy baby Bobby shady Sammy tiny	*
More disyllabic words	Long words, other than those ending in *y*, which begin with familiar patterns are presented. Children expected to identify stretches in addition to recognizing that they are familiar. chatter fantastic chipmunk battle chimney bottle	*
u, uCe	Productivity. Few words in expanded inventory require /yuw/ instead /uw/, e.g. *mute*. Teacher does not make a point of them.	24. Long *u*
ng	Productive	24. Long *u* with *ng*
More disyllabics	No distinction is pointed out between occurrence of /g/ in *finger* but not in *singer*.	*

Figure 9-7 (continued)

I Letter-Sound Correspondences	II Rationale	III Lesson Number
l in initial position only	Productive. Final *l* postponed because of effect on preceding vowels, e.g. *fall, pull.*	8l. *l* and r 8m. *l* and *w*
r in initial position only	Productive, but *r* postponed for same reason as *l.*	8l. *l* and *r*
Initial clusters of familiar letters with *l* and *r.* *sl, dr, tr, pr, pl, fr, fl, br, bl*	Productive	25. Consonant blends with *l, r*
		26. Blends: *p, f, b* with *l*
		27. *pl, fl, bl* with long *a, i, o, u*
		28. Blends with *r*
More disyllabics	Productive	*
e and *ee*	Short *e* is productive in the inventory at this point. Since *eCe* is not, *ee* is introduced as the long counterpart.	29. Short *e, ee*
Final consonant clusters *nt, st, sk, ft*	Productive, especially with *e.*	31. Final consonant clusters *nt, st, nd, ft*
w	Regular, *wa* ignored here.	32. *w* 8m. *l* and *w*
ck	Productive and regular	33. *ck*
c, k	Only "hard" /k/ value given, since /s/ and /j/ not productive. Taught together.	8n. *k* and *c* (visual) 8o. *k* and *g*
ke	Productive with long vowels.	34. *ke*
g	Only /g/ value. *ge,* and see Lesson 8o above.	
x	Presented in order to provide at least one value for each letter.	35. *x* in final position, *v* in initial position, *ve* in final position
v, ve *y* *z, zz* *qu* *j*		36. *y, z, zz, ze* *qu, j*

*Suggested in outline but not included in actual lessons.
Not included: Vowels before *l* and *r*; vowel digraphs (except *ee*); "soft" *c* and *g*; many uncommon correspondences, e.g. *ch* = /k/; derivational suffixes; many consonant clusters.

was part of the program. Common spelling patterns in initial and terr
positions were presented. Multisyllabic words were analyzed. Th
tributional variations of consonants and vowels were taught early.
erally, the program is a sophisticated one for providing first-grade le
with opportunities for inducing the orthographic rules of English.

A first-grade program of this type is very demanding on teach
pecially since so much new material had to be developed. We doubt that
the program would have been possible without the help of the research
staff. Besides the specific instructional procedures, books, workbooks, exercises, etc., we took every opportunity to make reading intrinsically rewarding to the children. Messages and notes were common means of communication. Students were exposed early to reading materials far in advance of their abilities but considerably more enticing than the usual
classroom fare. Interesting stories were tape recorded and children could
listen to the stories via tape recorders with the books before them and a
taped cue to turn the pages. The children especially liked to listen in
groups, each with his own earphones and book. Written labels and messages were prolific around the room. We found typewriters and printing
presses strongly motivating. Children copied their books on the typewriter
or made up stories or sometimes simply typed contrasting letters: *b* and *d*
were not uncommon.

In the end, after several years of cutting and fitting, we arrived at a program by which most first graders learned to read. As in many educational
experiences, we were more successful with middle-class than with lower-
class children. The program was theory based, at least as the theory and
research existed at that time. The program is not teacher-proof; quite the
opposite. Teachers were involved in the theory and the goals of the program and were encouraged to grasp any opportunity to achieve them.
Much was left to the judgment of teachers. Likewise, the researchers would
take any idea that made sense in terms of the goals of the program without
concern over whether we were poaching on the preserves of the whole-
word theory, phonics, linguistics, or any other religion.

It is fair to ask, "Is this better than other programs?" Frankly, we don't
know. It was a demonstration, not an experimental program, and even if
it were the latter we would be hard put to choose the appropriate control
groups. We are left with the modest claim that children learned to read
and that there are a host of methods and materials which teachers may exploit in any way they see fit. For our purposes, we would be most pleased to

see teachers be aware of the nature of reading and choose those methods and materials that make sense to them rather than be tyrannized by some prescription about how reading *must* be taught.

Summary

To learn to read is to learn a system of rules and strategies for extracting information from text. Cognitive learning of this sort is autoregulated, that is, what is learned are those strategies that extract information efficiently. The child's own curiosity is his best source of motivation. Many reading programs assume that reading is the formation of S-R associations for which external reinforcements are useful. So far as we can see, a program of external rewards and punishments cannot influence comprehension, for example, because the appropriate behavior must be emitted to be reinforced. Under certain circumstances external reinforcements may be useful in order to keep the child at the task long enough for intrinsic motivation to become operative.

Our problem in this chapter was what must be learned in the early stages of acquiring reading skill. Errors that children make provide insights about their strategies of reading. The most common errors are substitutions, that is, children invent words for those that are actually printed. About 90% of the substitution errors preserve the grammaticality and meaningfulness of the sentence to the point at which the error was committed. If subsequent reading with the substitution error yields nonsensical materials, the brighter children go back to correct the errors. There comes a point when children realize that their reading must relate to the graphic display. If the child cannot decode the word he says nothing. Later, his errors are constrained both by the graphic nature of the word and its meaning. The early reading strategy appears to take the following forms: (1) Substitute any word that makes sense (usually a word encountered earlier in the text); (2) inspect the graphic display and say nothing if you cannot decode the text; and (3) base the word read both on the graphic features and the sensibleness of the word in the sentence. It is difficult for beginning readers to handle both the graphic and the semantic information at the same time.

The issue of finding a single unit by which to teach reading seems to us a false one. The instruction should be multilevel so that the child can make use of sentences, words, syllables, letter clusters, etc., with particular attention to those levels with which the child is having trouble. The instructional units should always be placed into higher contexts to make use of the available redundant information. There is evidence that there must be instruction in intraword relations for generalization to new words to occur, though the best method for such analysis is not clear. There does appear to be some evidence that emphasis on relational spelling patterns and the rulelike internal structure of words are helpful. Readers continue to increase their mastery of spelling-sound correspondences through high school, long after formal schooling has been completed. It is important that children learn to notice structure within words, as good readers have been shown to do (see Chapter 7).

How are spelling patterns picked up? Simply telling children rules does not work. By the third grade, children appear to have developed some knowledge of structure which they can transfer to new items. Younger children can profit from general instructions to search for invariant patterns. But the learner must discover the useful structure himself, with time, exposure, and active search all necessary contributors.

Children's spontaneous oral language is more varied and complex than the grammatical forms that appear in their readers. Further, children seem to prefer less redundant materials than their readers offer. The context of children's readers can best be described as Pollyannaish, even the new readers built around ethnic themes. The meager experimental evidence regarding the relationship between pictures and word learning indicates the superiority of the word alone, but one should not hastily dismiss the aesthetic and semantic contribution of the illustrations to the text.

Finally, three reading programs under development were described: the University of Pittsburgh program, the Stanford Computer Assisted Reading Program, and the Project Literacy Multi-level Program.

10
The Transition to Skilled Reading

Learning to read goes on for many years, perhaps all one's life, as one's vocabulary and knowledge of the world continue to increase. The beginning of learning to read is necessarily heavily concerned with the mechanics of the process—with learning to decode, as some would say, although there is always more involved than that. By paying attention to the mechanics of the process, we refer to what might be termed the "surface" aspects: extraction of the graphic and orthographic information, moving the eyes in the right pattern, producing the correct phonetic pattern. That is not to say that comprehension is excluded. Children of course comprehend speech at this age, not only sentences, but speech of discourse length. In fact, Ramanauskas (1972) found that retarded children could better supply an appropriate word missing from a sentence (using a cloze procedure) when the sentence was embedded in the larger natural context of a paragraph. Children bring this comprehension of speech to the reading task, as their earliest errors of word substitution clearly show. But as they learn that the graphic information must be dealt with, the mechanics come in, and we see (and so does the child) that extracting all the relevant kinds of information at once is a problem, one that most children need time to master.

In examining the transition to skilled reading, we will consider how all aspects of the activity advance and, it is hoped, are put together: how orthography is produced in spelling, how subvocalization is reduced, how eye movement patterns develop, how syntactic information is used effectively, and finally, how comprehension of written text is developed.

Spelling and Reading

It is often taken for granted that spelling and reading are, if not the same process, simply reciprocal aspects of it. Perception and production of speech are generally considered reciprocal. To quote Carroll (1966), "The fact that in language learning, learning to understand speech and learning to speak are parallel processes argues for parallel teaching of reading and writing" (p. 579). It is hard to disagree with this, especially since we saw in Chapter 8 that children will take to writing quite spontaneously and progress to printing words and sentences, improving the quality of the product on their own. Some children even invented their own spelling systems, because they wanted to write.

But are reading and writing, or more particularly reading and spelling, truly reciprocal, merely two aspects of the same process? This seems to us doubtful. Rules for how to pronounce a word when it is read are not necessarily (or even very often) reversible, from the point of view of predictability. A child can learn all the spelling patterns (Fries, 1962) neatly summarized in contrastive sets, and know that an *e* added to *at* makes *ate* and thus the *a* is pronounced as a long vowel, but this knowledge doesn't tell him how to spell *eight*. Excellent readers are sometimes very bad spellers. The difference between reading and spelling is analogous to that between recognition and recall, acknowledged by psychologists to be different processes. Recognition is the easier process, in that it requires less information to distinguish and identify a display produced *for* one than to produce it oneself. A word can be recognized correctly without full information about its sp–ll–ng.

An overemphasis on phonics in teaching reading is apt to produce some poor spellers, especially if one-to-one letter-sound correspondence is emphasized. It is only too easy to furnish one's own examples of this source of error. That a pair (or a trio) of homophones should be spelled differently is a source of frustration and complaint by spelling reformists, but it must be remembered that different spellings for homophones disambiguate their meanings and enrich the written language, even if they do not appear to simplify it. It is our view that in the early transitional stages of learning to read, spelling accurately should not be given strong emphasis. It is better to read well and to write something that makes sense, even when the spelling leaves something to be desired. Frequently, in the long run, for a good reader spelling seems to take care of itself.

Verbal rules for spelling are often taught in transitional stages (rules about *i* before *e* except after *c*, for instance: *believe* vs. *receive*), and while this practice may improve spelling, there seems to be no evidence that it improves reading. Hanna, Hanna, Hodges, and Rudorf (1966) investigated the possibility of providing children with phonetic rules that would enable them to spell words they heard correctly. With the aid of a computer, they came out with a set of 200 rules that, used consistently, would yield accurate spelling of about 80% of English phonemes. But as Simon and Simon (1973) point out, words contain more than one phoneme, and they estimated that these rules alone could allow correct spelling of "only about one-half (49.87%) of the 17,009 most common English words."

The Simons stress that we can often recognize the correctness or incorrectness of spelling when we do not *recall* the correct spelling. A possible strategy, in that case, is to generate several possible spellings, write them out, and see if the correct one is recognized.* This is analogous, in a sense, to "sounding out" a word to see if it has a legal, known pronunciation and meaning. Diagrams of the two processes (see Figure 10-1) assume that we are equipped with two kinds of "generators," a spelling generator and a pronunciation generator. The heard word, as they put it, is decoded phoneme by phoneme, and recoded letter by letter, but recognized at the level of the whole word.

Both this procedure and the one proposed by Hanna et al. (1966), that is, direct phonetic spelling guided by their 200 rules, may be modified or supplemented by morphemic information. Morphemic components or words (roots, prefixes, suffixes, etc.) can be recognized as such and give access to spelling information. Since English spelling is actually a morphophonemic system (see Venezky, 1970b and Chapter 6), this is a useful strategy and saves us the labor of rote-learning thousands of individual spellings.

The Simons devised computer programs that simulated two of the proposed processes described above—the direct phonetic process plus rules, and their proposed generator test process—and tested the programs for their ability to predict spelling errors that had been actually committed by a sample of 50 pupils in a fourth-grade spelling course. The phonetic plus rule algorithm (from Hanna et al.) misspelled 26.6% of the time as compared to the children's 8.4% on a list of 30 new words (ones not yet studied in the class). The algorithm did no better with difficult words chosen from a higher grade level. Two of these, *indefinite* and *infinite,* were spelled *indefanate* and *infanate* by the algorithm; if it had been able to incorporate morphemic information and transformational relations (e.g., the embedded word *finite*) it would not have made the errors. The human misspellings were predominately mistaken phonetic spellings, with some errors due to incorrect use of morphemic information (e.g., *temperary* for *temporary*). The evidence appeared quite conclusive that teaching the algo-

*It is interesting that Sartre in his *The Psychology of Imagination* commented, "It is for this reason that the spelling of a word cannot be decided without writing it" (Sartre, 1966, p. 171).

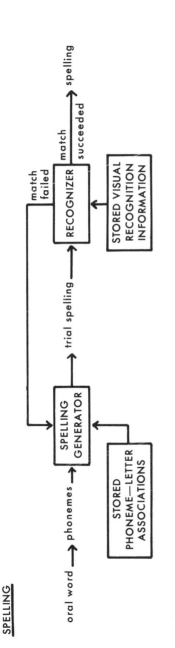

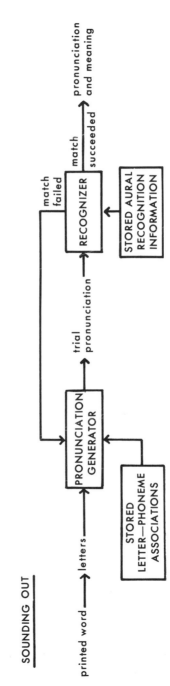

Figure 10-1. Diagrams of two possible processes for generating spellings. From Simon and Simon, 1973, p. 6. Copyright 1973, American Educational Research Association, Washington, D.C.

rithm to fourth-grade children would do little to help them spell words they did not already know how to spell.

The Simon program is also essentially phonetically and conditionally based, but it generates one or more spellings for each phoneme in a word and follows this generation of alternatives with a selection process to choose among them. The selection process applies tests drawn from word-recognition information, essentially sorting down a net until a match or a close approximation is found. Analysis of children's misspellings on such words as *knowledge* and *responsible* showed that the simulation program could be modified by simple changes to produce popular misspellings of the words. The authors concluded that a large part of the spelling behavior of fourth graders could be explained by hypothesizing their use of a phonetic generator combined with a recognition test when they were uncertain of a word's spelling. But their findings carry no implication, they asserted, about the most effective way to teach spelling. They suggested that the most valuable kind of phonetic experience for spelling under conditions of uncertainty may be generating possible alternative representations for testing by ensuing recognition and that spelling practice should be restricted to words within the children's current reading vocabularies to optimize the recognition test process. This view clearly implies that reading naturally precedes spelling, at least insofar as any kind of spelling drill is concerned. One might add to this proposition that spelling drill with strong attention to rules and emphasis on letters can lead to the "loss-of-meaning" or verbal satiation effect, which, although temporary, is still a kind of hindrance to comprehension. Comprehension—knowing a word's meaning as well as its context—is itself an aid to accurate spelling.

C. Chomsky (1970), following N. Chomsky (1970), emphasized the close underlying relation between phonology and spelling, which N. Chomsky described as being ideal for English (see Chapter 6). But how is knowledge of the underlying representations and relations achieved? We generally assume that as the child's speaking and reading vocabulary increases, the underlying relations are induced automatically; perhaps they are. C. Chomsky suggests that at some point after beginning reading, exercises can be given that will point up the relation between spelling, meaning, and phonology, making underlying relations easier of access by the learner. The child is taught that words have roots (underlying lexical representations) that can be transformed in many ways that result in different pronunciations of vowels within the word (e.g., *courage-courageous, relative-relation*). .Such transformations, often involving changing the accented syllable in the word, tell the reader how the vowel is to be pronounced. But they can serve a purpose for spelling, too. It is often hard to know what vowel to put before the *r* in an agentive transformation, in words such as *janitor* or *manager*. But knowing the adjectival spelling tells one at once (*janitorial, managerial*). A slurred-over, unstressed vowel, a "schwa," could often, from a phonetic point of view, be represented by almost any vowel, e.g., *competent,* from a phonetic point of view, could be spelled *compatent, compitent,* etc. But if one thinks of a transformation of the underlying lexical root that stresses the vowel (e.g., *compete*), it becomes quite clear what it has to be. The reduced schwa vowel sound is one of the most frequent sources of misspelling. It very often comes in the middle of the word or syllable, the part least attended to, and since it is not specified phonetically, it can only be specified by conditional relationships such as C. Chomsky describes.

"Another helpful exercise," writes C. Chomsky, "involves consonants which are silent in some words but pronounced in others" (e.g., *sign-signal, soften-soft*). The child could be given examples of words in which a consonant is not pronounced, she suggests, and "asked to think of related words in which the silent consonant is recovered phonetically" (1970, p. 305). She suggests that a good way to handle misspellings that come up in class is "to search with the child for a systematic reason why the word should be spelled the way it is" (pp. 307 ff). A good example is *medisin,* which "will lose the *s* and acquire a *c* if it is connected to *medical.*"

Obviously, the child's vocabulary must be up to tackling such rational exercises. But the case for using meaning and transformational relations of words to aid spelling seems a good one. The spelling system, according to the Chomskys' view, "leads the reader directly to the meaning-bearing items that he needs to identify, without requiring him to abstract away from superficial and irrelevant phonetic detail" (C. Chomsky, 1970, p. 294). This view of English orthography can have reality, it would seem, only for the mature reader, who

seeks and recognizes when he reads—not what are commonly called grapheme-phoneme correspondences, but rather the correspondence of written symbols to the abstract lexical spelling of words. Letters represent segments in lexical spelling, not sounds. . . . His task is facilitated by the fact that the orthography closely corresponds to this lexical representation. (p. 296)

In order to progress to more complex stages of reading, the child must abandon this early hypothesis, regularity of individual grapheme-phoneme correspondence, and come eventually to interpret written symbols as corresponding to more abstract lexical spellings. Normally he is able to make this transition unaided as he matures and gains experience both with the sound structure of his language and with reading. It may be, however, that the difficulty encountered by some poor readers is related to the fact that they have not made this crucial transition. (p. 297)

Teaching the child word relationships, extending his vocabulary, and showing him different ways of fitting the root of the word (transforming it) into various meaningful contexts may be a profitable way to teach spelling in the period of transition to skilled reading.

Subvocalization while Reading

At one time or another even the most skilled readers are aware of vocalizing while they are reading. Sometimes readers voluntarily read aloud, for instance, when they are savoring a poem or a memorable prose passage. Less obvious involvements of speech may be whispering or lip movements or feelings of tension around the lips or the larynx. Some readers report a stream of speech running through their heads, often annoying and difficult to turn off. Vocalizations while reading or performing other mental activities go by many names: subvocalization, subvocal speech, inner speech, implicit speech, silent speech, covert oral responses, etc. Many of these terms are used interchangeably, yet some have implicit theoretical connotations. For our purposes, we will choose the term "subvocalization" to stand for speech whose range goes from audible sound (e.g., whispering), to movements of speech musculature which must be highly amplified to be detected, to the extreme of speech so implicit that an investigator can make no physical observations. The important point is that the reader normally does not want to make sounds, but at some levels he does.

The study of subvocalization impinges on various persistent problems in psychology, such as Watson's (1930) dictum that "the term 'thinking' should cover all word behavior of whatever kind that goes on subvocally" (p. 243). The basic notion of the motor theory of consciousness influenced early research on subvocalization which persists to the present (see Sokolov, 1972 and McGuigan, 1970 for up-to-date summaries). Modern theorists in short-term memory concern themselves with the transformation of the input from visual to some auditory form. (See Gibson, 1971 for a review of relevant literature.) There is also extensive literature having to do with the subvocal accompaniments of problem solving (cf. Sokolov, 1972). None of these are really problems in reading. Subjects are asked to remember strings of letters or digits or to carry out problem-solving tasks of various difficulties or to search for targets which may be visually or acoustically confused. Since the tasks are not reading, the research adds little to understanding the reading process, so much literature on subvocalization is beyond the scope of a discussion of reading.

As we shall see in Chapter 12, subvocalization appears again in some theorists' explanations of the reading process. From their point of view one stage in reading is phonetic recoding, that is, the translation of text to sound or its surrogate, but we shall postpone that discussion of subvocalization to the point where we compare various theories of reading. In this section we shall concern ourselves with the conditions under which subvocalizations occur during reading, along with the age changes in this phenomenon and with the various experimental techniques which have been tried to reduce subvocalizations.

It seems strange, but it is nevertheless true, that it is next to impossible and perhaps also meaningless to give the rates at which texts are read. The difficulty or familiarity of the materials are obviously implicated. The purpose of the reading—casual scanning or remembering—have obvious effects. The rate of adult speech is around 170–200 words per minute. This is not too far off from casual reading (about 200–300 words per minute, according to Tinker, 1965). Subvocalization as a clinical problem is highly circumscribed. Remedial reading specialists attempt to eliminate subvocalization under conditions where the rate of reading simple materials is decreased because of conscious subvocalization. In other cases, readers deliberately subvocalize in order to slow their reading rates and concentrate on the text. Subvocalization is not only a mechanical device that slows the perusal of text but also adds the redundancy of another modality.

The implication seems to be that the reader translates into sound either motorically or auditorily every symbol that he encounters in the text. This may be true for readers who move their lips while reading, and one can see why remediation is called for in those cases, if only to counter the cultural stereotype that only semiliterate readers move their lips. Remember, though, that even skilled readers may move their lips, especially, we have observed, when reading a foreign language.

It seems futile to take a stand on the assertion that reading *always* involves subvocalization and that direct apprehension of the meaning of the text is impossible. The task requirements and individual differences are too diverse. Nevertheless, Huey's statement (1908) is characteristic:

The fact of inner speech forming a part of silent reading has not been disputed, so far as I am aware, by any one who has experimentally investigated the process of reading. . . . Purely visual reading is quite possible theoretically; and Secor, in a study made at Cornell University, found that some readers could read visually while whistling or doing other motor tasks that would hinder inner speech. . . . But although there is an occasional reader in whom the inner speech is not noticeable, and although it is a foreshortened and incomplete speech in most of us, yet it is perfectly certain that the inner hearing or pronunciation, or both, of what is read, is a constituent part of reading by far the most of people, as they ordinarily and actually read. (pp. 117–118)

Huey (1908) himself did a number of experiments in which his subjects, all adults, were instructed to read an interesting novel "the way you like to read," or to "say it all to themselves," or "to read aloud," or to think of "how it would sound" as they read. Most readers said that the pronunciation was "up in the head." Inner speech was a combination of auditory and motor elements, depending on the subject's usual mode of imagining. Subvocalizing was *not* reading aloud, which itself was 66% slower than reading silently. Subvocalization during reading is different from speech. Huey cited Dodge that subvocalization goes on during inspiration as well as expiration, the chest and larynx muscles are not operative, there is a slurring of words, only beginnings of words are pronounced, and in fastest reading certain words are not pronounced. From the experiences of these skilled introspectors, it is important to note that subvocalization differs markedly from oral reading and from complete language, even when it is inaudible. To equate these various processes would be a mistake. Also, the thinking on subvocalization lumps together actual motor components of speech with hearing the text. The conditions may be very different, but our information on this point is meager.

Treatment to Reduce Subvocalization
Hardyck and his coworkers (Hardyck, Petrinovich, and Ellsworth, 1966) reported a dramatic demonstration of the complete cessation of subvocalization among a group of 17 subjects chosen from a college class whose purpose was to give remedial instruction in reading. Many of the subjects did not realize that subvocalization was a problem in their reading disabilities. With subvocalization these students could read reasonably

simple fiction at the low level of 150 words per minute. Hardyck placed surface electrodes on the carotid cartilage, near the larynx, of the subjects so that muscle movement in the laryngeal area could be detected. The technique of measuring and recording muscle movement is called electromyography (EMG). The EMG signals were converted to audio signals which the readers could hear over earphones. The instructions were simple: Read so as to create no sounds over the phones. The sound was static-like noise. Subjects were asked to read simple materials, to stop reading, to read again, etc.

The results from a single session were unequivocal. "In all cases one session of the feedback was sufficient to produce complete cessation of vocalization" (p. 1468). A typical EMG tracing is presented in Figure 10-2. After this single clinical session there was no evidence of subvocalization after one month and even after three months. Although clear in itself, this demonstration led to questions which could be answered only by an experiment: What effects did the reduction of subvocalization have on the nature of reading? Was it related to the kinds of materials being read? Was there a generalized relaxation effect or was it due to the feedback from the laryngeal area itself?

In a subsequent experiment, Hardyck and Petrinovich (1967; 1970) worked with 18 freshmen students from a remedial English class. The reading materials were two essays judged by the English instructors to be similar in interest but to vary widely in difficulty of comprehension. One group read while EMG recordings were taken from the laryngeal area, the chin and lips, and the right forearm flexor. A second group was to keep the audio signal from the EMG off, as in the original study above. The control condition was the same as the feedback one except that the subjects had to keep off the acoustic signal generated by muscular activity in their forearms.

Congruent with other findings, as we shall see, EMG activity over all conditions increases with the difficulty of the task. Laryngeal and chin-lip EMGs were most responsive to difficulty level, the arm muscle least so. When laryngeal activity was diminished by the feedback condition, comprehension of the difficult passage suffered, and this effect was limited to laryngeal activity.

The authors took this evidence as confirming a mediation theory of comprehension, that grasping the meaning of a passage involves the motor aspects of subvocalization. However, if comprehension requires proprio-

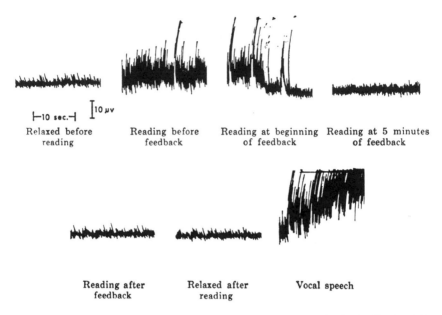

Figure 10-2. Tracing of laryngeal electromyograms. From Hardyck, Petrinovich, and Ellsworth, 1966, p. 1467. Copyright 1966 by the American Association for the Advancement of Science.

ceptive support from the speech musculature, why did comprehension on the easy passage also not differ? Since it seems an odd claim that comprehension is mediated by speech which supports the arbitrary symbol-sound-meaning relationships (Hardyck and Petrinovich, 1967), do the associations become active only when the subject is reading difficult material? What, then, is the mechanism for easily understood text which must also have the arbitrariness of the symbol-sound associations mediated by something, if not the feedback from subvocalizations? We think that what happened in this experiment is that when a subject had to divide his attention between understanding difficult text and keeping earphones silent, comprehension suffered. Evidently, readers of difficult prose were as successful as readers in the other conditions in keeping the tone off.

The dramatic demonstration of Hardyck et al. (1966) that brief training in reducing laryngeal EMGs had immediate and long-lasting effects on subvocalization, though at the cost of lowered comprehension of difficult text, has not gone unchallenged. McGuigan (1970) used standard operant conditioning techniques with six subjects who usually showed high-amplitude subvocalizations. The subjects were 7 to 19 years of age. There was no anal-

ysis by age; however, the individual curves look very similar. The operant program was designed for each subject, so the number of trials under
the various training conditions varied. Electrodes were attached to the
tongue, lips, and chin to get at speech-related musculature, and to the
neck, arms, and legs to measure the electrical potentials in other non-
speech-related musculature. When speech muscle activity while reading
reached a given point the subject heard an unpleasant tone. The subject's
task was to reduce the noise. None of the subjects discovered that the tone
was related to the amount of activity in his chin, for example. When they
were told about the relationships between the tone and chin or lip or
tongue activity, all of the subjects' EMGs decreased substantially. The
control electrodes, as on the legs, did not respond to the training procedure. The effects were clearly specific to the speech apparatus.

To this point, the results replicate Hardyck's, though the training procedures took more trials. However, the training effects were ephemeral.
From the first trial after the experimenters removed the tone, subvocalization returned to the pretest levels. There was no evidence that any of the
six subjects reduced subvocalization without external reinforcement. Incidentally, when subvocalization was lowered during training, reading
rate increased and there appeared to be no loss in comprehension.

To complicate the picture a bit more, Aarons (1971) found that small
groups of adults previously determined to be high or low subvocalizers
were responsive to feedback training and the reductions in subvocalization
lasted beyond the training trials. The reasons for the contradictory results
are not mysterious. When subjects are told that they can reduce their subvocalizations and become better readers, auditory feedback of speech
muscle activity has a rapid and persistent effect. McGuigan's contrary results seem due to the differences in instructions and the motivations of the
readers.

Subvocalization and the Difficulty of the Reading Task

A common observation among most skilled readers is that as the text
becomes difficult to understand, subvocalization increases. The research
on this problem requires independent appraisals of text difficulty in relation to the reader's ability. One useful method has been to study subvocalization while the subject is reading text in a language other than his
native one or while translating. Faaborg-Anderson and Edfeldt (1958)
found that among Danish and Swedish adults, EMGs of greater amplitude

were recorded when reading the nonnative language, especially if they were unaccustomed to reading foreign prose. From this preliminary study Edfeldt (1960) went on to one of the most careful studies of reading and subvocalization that exists in the literature.

Edfeldt, working in a medical setting, was able to use needle electrodes inserted directly into the speech musculature, in contrast with most researchers in this area, who have used surface electrodes which are prone to artifacts of surface muscle activity and to the loss of precision in the exact recording sites of the electrodes. Edfeldt's subjects were University of Stockholm students who read easy and difficult passages as well as text that was physically clear and text that was blurred. The amount of electrical activity in the speech muscles increased for difficult compared to easy selections, and clear prose was read with less subvocalizing than blurred print. Figure 10-3 gives an example of Edfeldt's EMG records. The amount of electrical activity becomes clearer when the EMGs are integrated over time.

Varying the difficulty levels of the prose is an obvious way to manipulate difficulty and to search for concomitant subvocalizations. Another task variation is to have subjects read while being distracted in one way or another (McGuigan and Rodier, 1968). College students read silently under the following conditions: no external stimulation; prose read to them simultaneously with their own silent reading; prose read backward; and noise. Surface electrodes were attached on the forearm, the chin, and near the tip of the tongue.

In general, EMGs of increased amplitudes occurred during the reading of prose—backward and forward—but not to noise. Also, these experimental conditions had little effect on the muscle potentials measured from the forearm. The effects are restricted to the speech mechanisms. The interpretation of these findings is straightforward. Under distracting conditions, subvocalizations serve to focus attention on the task of reading. It would be worthwhile to observe children doing homework to the accompaniment of the radio. Music should bother them little, whereas talk should increase subvocalization.

Sokolov's (1972) is the most elaborate program of research on subvocalization, but unfortunately for our purposes, he concentrated on problem solving and listening with only a small number of experiments on silent reading. In a number of experiments, his subjects translated English texts of varying difficulty into Russian. The Russian university students varied

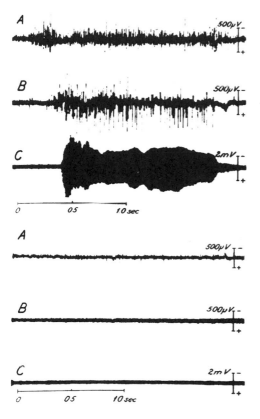

Figure 10-3. Electrical activity during reading. From Edfeldt, 1960, pp. 66–67. All rights reserved.

in ability: Some had studied English for one year, others were fifth-year students. A series of studies interfered with subvocalization by competing tasks: clamping the tongue between the teeth, enunciating the syllables la-la, and reciting a stanza from Pushkin's "The Snowstorm Covers the Sky with Darkness." Sokolov counted the number of semantic units correctly translated. Routine, mechanical tasks like clamping the tongue and reciting syllables had little effect. Reciting a poem interfered with speed and accuracy of translation for all students. Sokolov also carried out EMG studies on the translation task, with electrodes placed on the tongue and lower lip muscles. His subjects, again university students, read a control passage in Russian and two English prose pieces judged to differ in difficulty. There were wide individual differences in the rate of silent reading and the intensity of the electrical activity in the speech muscles. Since Sokolov

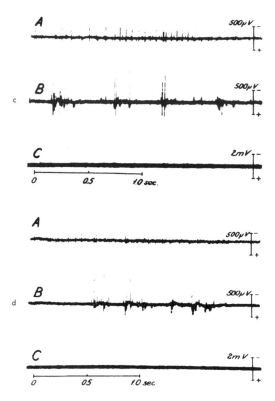

Figure. 10.3 (continued)

believes that thinking is inevitably attended by subvocalization, the wide individual differences are difficult for him to explain. Regarding the Russian passage for one student he writes, "When the same subject rereads the Russian text, the motor speech excitation is very weak (there even being moments when it disappears altogether)" (p. 210).

In contradistinction, repeated reading of the text with the instruction, "Reread it more attentively" or "Memorize it more accurately" results in an intensification of motor speech excitation as compared to the first reading of the text without instructions of this kind (p. 210).

As with other findings, the more difficult translations resulted in larger-amplitude EMGs, that is, in more electrical activity in the speech musculature. On the other hand, American students studying French showed no differences in lip and chin movements in reading the two languages (McGuigan, Keller, and Stanton, 1964).

Finally, it should be reiterated that efforts to reduce subvocalization on difficult materials led to loss of comprehension (Hardyck and Petrinovich, 1970). The various studies are consistent in showing that as the reading task becomes more difficult, by the nature of the prose or by introducing competing behaviors while reading, the rate of subvocalization increases. Sokolov implies that the instructions to the subjects are implicated. This body of research is neutral so far as the value of subvocalization in reading is concerned or whether all reading is accompanied by subvocalization.

The Developmental Course of Subvocalization
The hubbub of the first and second grades is due, it often seems, to the children reading to themselves. To some children private reading apparently means reading in full voice; other children whisper, some move their lips, and if we are to believe some of the research cited, every reader is producing some surrogate for sound detectable by microphones of amplified electropotentials of the speech musculature. Eduators have engaged in rousing debates about whether subvocalization during reading is "good" or "bad." Phrased that way, the question can only lead to more polemics. The research questions are at least answerable. Under what circumstances do children subvocalize while reading? What are the characteristics of the children who do or do not? What are the consequences for speed of reading and comprehension? Is subvocalization related to the task: to skim, to study, to memorize?

Edfeldt (1960, Chapter 6) wrote an excellent summary of the educational debates. Basically, some educators believe that subvocalization is the persistence of teaching children to read aloud. The obvious experiment would be to teach children to read silently from the beginning of instruction. The contrary point of view maintains that subvocalization permits children to get a "deeper" meaning of what they read because language is initially oral. Subvocalization indicates that the reader is thinking about what he is reading, a point of view with which Sokolov (1972) would agree.

There is an unfortunate dearth of data about the course of subvocalization as the child becomes a more skilled reader. One experiment involved children of elementary-school age reading materials which should have been difficult and other passages which were easy (McGuigan, Keller, and Stanton, 1964). The amplitude for chin and lip movements increased from the prereading to the reading period and then decreased during a postreading period. Unfortunately, the data are not divided for grade level, reading ability, or difficulty of the text. Selected subjects (average age 10 years) who originally showed high levels of subvocalization were retested after two and three years. By the second year, EMGs from the lips and chin reduced markedly, to the level of college students who were part of the original study (McGuigan and Bailey, 1969). Also, the occasional whispering of the original group which was loud enough to be tape recorded had completely disappeared over the two- to three-year period. Aarons (1971) quotes Crandell and McGuigan (1967) to the effect that subvocal activity decreased between 10 and 13 years.

Concluding Remarks and a Methodological Note
We have been concerned in this section with the conditions under which subvocalization takes place while reading. A broader question, which we shall reserve for Chapter 12 on theories of reading, asks whether reading can take place at all without some sort of articulation. For example, one encounters statements like ". . . the child, looking at the word, says something to himself, listens to himself, and then repeats what he has heard" (Conrad, 1972, p. 205). And later, "or do we make the speech sounds, listen to them and comprehend what it is that we have heard?" (p. 206). To anticipate our own point of view, vocalization may accompany reading, but it is not inevitable, and it depends on the text, on the reader's task, and on his skill.

"Subvocalization" is a term that covers various behaviors. At the extreme is reading aloud, which hardly qualifies as subvocalization but does provide unequivocal evidence that the reader is making sound when he reads. Various studies report no effect on comprehension when reading aloud (Conrad, 1971; Poulton and Brown, 1967; Rogers, 1937). At the next level are obviously observable whispering and lip and tongue movements while reading (cf. Flavell, 1970, for evidence of these behaviors while problem solving). Another behavioral task is to introduce a competing response to subvocalization (Sokolov, 1972; McGuigan and Rodier, 1968; Pintner, 1913). Highly practiced mechanical tasks, like repeating "la-la," have little effect on reading. Reciting poetry while reading creates a deficit in reading speed and comprehension (Sokolov, 1972). We interpret the latter finding as the effect of interference between two cognitively demanding tasks rather than the suppression of subvocalization.

Some indication of the validity of the EMG technique is given by the general finding that reading as well as other verbal tasks increase the amplitude of electrical activity *only* in the speech-related musculature. Reading words which included labial sounds gave larger-amplitude EMG readings from the lips than did nonlabial segments (Locke and Fehr, 1970). Also, McGuigan, Keller, and Stanton (1964) recorded faint vocalizations from a few of their child subjects, and these children gave wider-amplitude EMGs to a variety of tasks. In general, EMG techniques have contributed substantially to research on subvocalization while reading as well as on other mental tasks.

Eye Movements in Reading

The measurement of eye movements while reading, or while performing other visual tasks, was hailed as a lens into the private experience of reading. There is little wonder that from the turn of the century there have been numerous studies of eye movements related to many aspects of reading and characteristics of the reader. The implementation of eye movement recording has become increasingly complex, and the variables derived from these recordings have acquired their own terminology. It may be useful to describe some of the measuring devices and to define the variables most commonly referred to.

Hold a pencil vertically and move it in a smooth motion from left to right. Meanwhile, fixate on the eraser end of the pencil. The eye movement following the pencil end is smooth and linear and is called a *pursuit movement*. Next, look around the room. In turn, look at the window, door, desk, floor, chair, picture, etc. Your eyes are making a series of "hopping" motions. You pause to fixate on one object, then move to another. The length of time that you paused probably varied from object to object, and the size of the movement—the distance between the desk and chair, for example—may have varied. These eye movements are called saccadic, and a single movement from one point of fixation to another is called a *saccade*. The eye movements with which we are concerned in reading are saccadic movements whose purpose is to bring the fovea of the eye, the point of highest acuity, to rest on the letters (or words) that the reader wants to look at.

The saccadic movment may be analyzed into two basic components:

the movement itself and the pause, or fixation, which precedes and termi-
nates the movement. The saccade has been termed a ballistic movement
(Hochberg, 1970). The viewer voluntarily "throws" his eyes to some area,
at which point he may have to make minor adjustments to bring the desired
display into maximal clarity. During the saccade vision is not very acute,
although a bright flash can be detected while the eye is in motion (Volkmann, Schich, and Riggs, 1968). It was once thought that the reader is
virtually blind, during a saccadic movement but more recent evidence has
shown that vision for text, though reduced, is possible (Volkmann, 1962).

Besides saccadic movement and fixation pause, another ocular variable
in reading is the *regression movement,* which is a saccade to a previously per-
used part of the text.

Figure 10-4 demonstrates these most common eye movement measurements. Reader A makes five fixation pauses on this line. The saccades vary
in length. There are no regressions. The times for the pauses vary from 120
to 240 msec. There is a slight suggestion that the pauses are more dense at
the beginning and end of the line. The impression is that reader A read the
line smoothly from left to right. By comparison, reader B made more than
twice as many fixations of the same line. The saccades are obviously shorter. With few exceptions, more time is spent on each pause. Reader B shows
a considerable number of regressions. Notice that the reader jumps from
fixation point 1 to 2 and then back to 3 and 4. The saccade from 4 to 5 is
a long one, then a shorter eye movement to 6 followed by a complex series
of regressions to the left side of the line as though the reader were filling in
material that he missed. The longest fixation pause, almost a half second,
occurs at point 6, from which reader B initiates a complex pattern of
regressive eye movements. We will have occasion to return to this figure
when we discuss the eye movements of good and poor readers.

The Technology of Eye Movement Measurement
There have been a number of excellent reviews of the literature on eye
movements by Tinker (1946, 1958, 1965), and we shall make liberal use of
his work.

Techniques of eye movement recording have made many advances, but
the basic techniques remain the same. Investigators at first simply observed the number of saccades which the reader made. A system of mirrors
was arranged so that the investigator could see the reader's eyes and count
the number of movements. Or a telescope was set up to observe the eyes

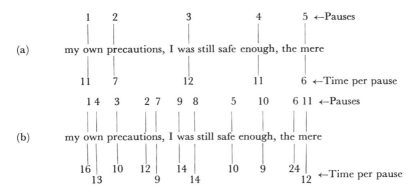

Figure 10-4.   Location of fixation pauses during reading (a) for a good adult reader; (b) for a poor adult reader. Numbers at the top of these lines show the sequence of the fixations; those at the bottom show the time taken for each fixation in fiftieths of a second. From Tinker, 1965, p. 61. © 1965 University of Minnesota.

from a distance. Sometimes a peephole in the reading material allowed the experimenter to count the saccades. The variables obtained by these procedures were simple, like the number of fixations per line.

The next generation attempted to record movements by devices attached directly to the eye (Ahrens, 1891). A marker attached to a cup on the eye would trace a path on a smoked drum. Coordination of this eye movement record with the text must have been very difficult.

Photographic techniques provided the major technological advance in eye movement recording. First a spot was placed on the cornea and the movement of this spot was photographed. Then a beam of light was directed into the reader's eyes and the reflection of this light from the cornea provided a record on photographic film, eventually moving picture film whose frame-by-frame exposure could be precisely counted. The text could be superimposed on the film. All modern techniques use the corneal reflection techniques in one form or another (e.g., Mackworth, 1968). Precision has been gained by using several beams of light reflected from different parts of the eye. The reflection may be picked up directly by a computer (McConkie and Rayner, 1973). However, the reflection methods require that the reader's head be immobilized. The artificiality makes one skeptical about generalizing to the normal, free head reading situation, although Tinker (1965) believes that the reader adapts easily to the demands of the measuring devices.

With the many technical advances in eye movement measurement, it is interesting (and a bit ironic) to note that all the basic information on how the eyes operate when reading was discovered with the early primitive apparatus and these facts remain trustworthy (see, e.g., Woodworth, 1938). The new apparatus, however, potentially opens new research problems, for example, controlling the exposure of text as a function of eye movements.

Eye Movements and Types of Material to Be Read

Across a variety of reading materials, about 6% of the time is spent in eye movements and 94% in fixation pauses. Tinker (1965, p. 70) has compared prose of varying difficulty including examination questions, and his results are given in Table 10-1. Pauses in reading are responsive to the difficulty of the text (see Table 10-2), so fixation pause time does not simply involve the pickup of text, but also thinking it.

Table 10-2 presents not only Tinker's findings, but data from two other studies, all of which show close similarities on this point: Pause duration is considerably affected by the content and requirements of the prose.

If we assume that reading foreign languages is at least a crude index to the difficulty of the task, the findings are congruent with the data in Table 10-2, Judd and Buswell (1922) found that for good third-year high school students, reading French and Latin was like labored reading of English. There were more and longer pauses per line and many more regressions.

Buswell (1926) found that in adding columns of figures, children who were not skilled at arithmetic showed chaotic eye movement patterns, whereas adults and children who were good adders exhibited brief and regular pauses, fixating one or two numerals at a time. An informative case in point is the reading of problems containing both words and numerals. The apparent difficulty in reading numerals may have less to do with the recognition of these symbols than with the ways that they are implicated in the overall difficulty of the task. Reading formulas is somewhat like reading words. If the formula is familiar and has a unitary character (H_2O), it will be fixated like a word, especially if the formula is in a context which facilitates its meaning (Rebert, 1932). Without context or if the reading involves analyzing the formula, each item may require a fixation. "As with numerals, eye movements in reading formulas are influenced by the task or purpose for which reading is done" (Tinker, 1965, p. 98).

Several recent studies, influenced by linguistic analyses, have related eye movements in reading sentences to the grammatical structure of those

Table 10-1   Percentage of Movement Time and Pause Time in Reading

Kind of Material Read in Various Line Widths	Percentage of Reading Time	
	Movements	Pauses
Very easy prose		
Silent reading (25-pica line)	9.6	90.4
Oral reading (25-pica line)	6.2	93.8
Easy narrative prose		
9-pica line	6.4	93.6
19-pica line	8.1	91.9
40-pica line	8.5	91.5
Hard scientific prose (25-pica line)	7.3	92.7
Algebra problems with formulas (20-pica line)	5.3	94.7
Easy speed of reading test (19-pica line)	7.9	92.1
Multiple-choice examination questions (25-pica line)	6.2	93.8
Overall mean	7.3	92.7

Source: Tinker, 1965, p. 69. © 1965 by University of Minnesota.

Table 10-2   Pause Duration in Reading

Material Read	Number of Readers	Mean in Milliseconds	Percentage of Variability
Tinker experiment			
Easy prose	77	217.0	12.9
Easy reading test	57	217.8	12.6
Scientific prose	77	230.8	12.2
Sisson experiment			
Easy narrative	60	226.6	12.2
Scientific prose	60	236.4	12.8
Frandsen experiment			
Scientific prose	66	243.4	10.4
True-false test items	66	270.6	17.4
Completion test items	66	323.6	25.8
Multiple-choice test items	66	281.2	14.9
Analogies test items	66	296.6	13.3
Wrong-word test items	66	298.6	12.7

Source: Tinker, 1965, p. 40. Original data from Tinker (1939), Sisson (1936), Frandsen (1934). © 1965 by University of Minnesota.

sentences (Wanat, 1971; Mehler, Bever, and Carey, 1967). These studies will be taken up in greater detail in the later section of this chapter concerning grammatical structure and reading.

Developmental Changes in Eye Movements

Tinker (1965) reported a remarkable similarity found by various researchers in the ways that eye movements change as the child grows older. Most eye movement behaviors have become stable by the fourth grade. Fixation frequency, the duration of pauses, and the number of regressions decrease markedly from the first to the fourth grades. There are small changes up to high school and an occasional finding that there are minor improvements during the high school years. For reading easy material, pauses lasting 240 to 250 msec are satisfactory, and these times are reached by the end of the fourth grade. The mechanical oculomotor aspects of reading reach an early level of competence so that later changes are attributable to attitude toward reading, the difficulty of the material, the ease of comprehension, etc. In other words, the increased efficiency of reading that comes with experience is not due to the mechanical, peripheral aspects of the reading process.

Good readers differ from their less skilled peers in almost all measures of eye movements. One can be a rapid reader by making fewer fixations or by pausing more briefly during the fixation. Pause duration appears to be the outstanding and least variable characteristic among skilled readers. Skilled readers are more adaptive to the nature of the material; their patterns of fixations and pauses are responsive to their comprehension of the materials they are reading (Walker, 1938). By implication, poor readers use the same oculomotor patterns regardless of the nature of the text.

The pattern of eye movements appears to be specific to reading and is not predictive of other visual tasks (Peterson, 1969). Third-grade children were tachistoscopically shown digits and letters so arranged that they could be read in various directions: left-to-right, diagonally, randomly, etc. Typically, they were read irregularly, each presentation showing a different pattern. There was a hint that children who were taught via phonics methods read the displays from left to right, but this was not a strong effect.

Peripheral Vision

Text falling on the fovea is seen most clearly. During a fixation pause, a reader has an area, not a point, of clear vision. This area of clear vision extends over seven to ten letter spaces. Movement or brightness contrast in the periphery can be detected. It is difficult to understand how peripheral vision aids the reading process, since the reader can detect little useful information besides interword spaces and the lengths and shapes of words. Hochberg (1970) makes peripheral vision an important source of the decision about where to move the eye during the next saccade, that is, to decide where the next fixation point will occur. The question is an important one which is implicated in theories of reading (see Chapter 7). An indirect test of Hochberg's theory involved second- and fifth-grade children reading text that had interword spaces filled with letterlike, meaningless symbols (Hochberg, Levin, and Frail, unpublished ms.). Older children were slowed in their reading by filled spaces more than the second graders. The finding was interpreted to mean that young children were reading word by word, whereas older children were using interword spaces, picked up peripherally, to move their eyes across units larger than single words.

Emphasis on the role of peripheral vision in reading is usually related to a theory of reading which explains the process as successive predictions about the nature of the text (e.g., Chapter 12; Dodge, 1907). Dearborn (1906) thought that a long fixation pause was followed by several briefer pauses, implying that the large pause permitted nonfoveal vision to guide the reading of the adjacent text. This assumption of a pause pattern marked by long-short-short-long has not been confirmed (Sisson, 1936).

A recent program of research by McConkie uses sophisticated electronic and computer methods to determine the nature of processing foveated and peripheral text (McConkie and Rayner, 1973). The subjects were skilled readers of high-school age. They read text exposed on a televisionlike screen while their eye movements were monitored. An area around the fixation point was clear print. Text on either side of the clear area was mutilated in various ways, for example, replacing each letter by an X. During a saccade, the text outside of the clear window was changed. There is a clear effect due to window size, that is, to the size of the area of clear, unmutilated text. This finding implies the reader's general use of peripheral vision (Poulton, 1962). Word shape information is not used further than nine spaces on each side of the fixation. Subjects picked up letter information ten or eleven characters from the fixation point. Word length affects reading farther into the periphery than does word shape or specific letter identification.

As part of McConkie's research program, Rayner (1974) has recently reported a study on the use of peripheral vision in reading which provides important information in an experimental situation that has many characteristics of reading normal discourse. The subjects were ten adults who read paragraphs displayed on a cathode ray tube. Eye movements were monitored, and in addition the experimenters controlled, by means of a computer, various aspects of the stimulus display. Rayner described the purpose of his research in this way:

> If a reader fixates on a certain character, are there certain areas in his periphery from which he acquires different types of information that are useful to him? More specifically, beyond the area of maximum visual acuity are there peripheral cues, such as word length, word shape, initial and final letters, etc., that enable a reader to process text more rapidly than if these cues were not available? This study investigated the extent to which two types of peripheral cues, (1) word shape and (2) initial and final letters, are used by skilled readers. (p. 30)

The procedure was ingenious and merits detailed description. In a sentence of the exposed paragraph a single word was selected as the critical word position. All sentences containing the target word were of the form subject + verb + object + prepositional phrase. In the initial display, the critical word could take various forms. For example, consider the sentence "The robbers guarded the — with their guns." The original word *palace* could be in the critical position. Another variation was to print the word *police* in this position, an alternative which preserved word length, outline, first and last letters, and yielded a perfectly reasonable sentence. Three additional word forms could appear in the critical position. One was a nonword that retained the first and last letters and word shape (*pcluce*); another retained only the first and last letters of the original word (*pyctce*); in the final variation, only word shape was the same as the original (*qcluec*).

When the reader's eyes crossed a preset boundary on the line containing the critical word, the computer either made no change, that is, retained the original word, or changed the other words back to the original, e.g., *palace*. The change occurred while the eyes were in saccadic motion so that most readers probably did not detect the change.

The basic assumption of the experiment is that if the peripheral and foveated information differ, the detection of the difference would result in longer fixations on the target word. The boundary locations varied from nine character spaces to the left of the first letter of the critical word to the fourth letter of the word itself. The subject could launch his saccade even farther to the left, but when his eye crossed the boundary, the word changed in all except the control conditions.

Two variables will be selected for discussion out of the rich data generated by this research: (1) the duration of the last fixation prior to crossing the boundary; and (2) the length of fixation on the critical word after the boundary was crossed and the word assumed its normal form. There are larger fixations before crossing the boundary for nonwords than for words, but this effect occurs only in the vicinity of the critical word itself, that is from one to four character spaces to the left of the word. This finding indicates that within approximately 1° of arc, the reader realizes that there is an oddity to the right of his fixation and the discrimination is between a word and nonword, since the various types of nonwords show no differences.

For fixation times on the critical words themselves, Rayner's data indicated that information about word shapes and about initial and terminal letters is picked up by the reader beginning about seven to twelve character spaces in the periphery, but recognizing the meaning of the word begins only about one to six character spaces to the right of the fixation point.

A detailed research program using this technique promises to yield new information about eye movements and reading for the first time in over half a century.

Training Eye Movements
Nowhere has the confusion between correlation and causality been more obvious than in the clinical implications drawn from the research on eye movements. Since good readers had long saccades, fewer fixations, fewer regressions, and shorter pauses, it was hypothesized that poor readers could be assisted by getting them to move their eyes in those ways. But to no avail. The eye movement patterns reflected efficient mastery of extracting information from text, not the other way around.

Grammatical Structure and Meaning

In this section we will review the evidence for the use of grammatical structure of sentences in reading. Most of the grammatical variation will concern the surface structure of sentences, especially immediate constituent analyses of sentences. Some research involves the concepts of deep structure of sentences. (The reader is referred to Chapter 4 for a discussion of the grammatical analyses of sentences.)

Orthographic rules describe the ways that letters are put together to form syllables, morphemes, and words (see Chapter 6). Grammar is a set of rules which organizes morphemes and words into acceptable sentences of a language (Chomsky, 1965). As such, grammar provides a complex set of invariant relations within language which the reader uses. Our theoretical notions about how the grammatical level interacts with words to facilitate reading will be the subject of a later section of this chapter. First, what are the facts?

Historical Note on the Eye-Voice Span (EVS)

Although various experimental methods will be discussed in this section, the eye-voice span (EVS) will be referred to most frequently, so descriptions of the methods of using it and their historical origins will be helpful. Besides, some of the early studies, though not ostensibly related to grammar and reading, may be interpreted in terms of the problem at hand.

In reading aloud, the EVS is the distance, usually measured in words, that the eyes are ahead of the voice. In order to read with normal intonation the reader must have information about the sentence which occurs to the right of the word he is actually reading aloud. The study of this span has a history going back to the turn of the century. Much of the research concerned the comparisons of good and poor readers and also age changes in the span. Quantz first reported the technique in 1897, and his method was elegantly simple. He covered the page at some predetermined point and asked his subject to report as much of the text in advance of his voice as he could. In one form or another, this is still the most common method: to have the subject read aloud and to remove the text by turning off the light, covering the lens of a projector, etc. A second method was to make a simultaneous record of the voice and of the eye movements, correlating both sets of measurements with the text. When one thinks of the state of instrumentation around 1920, the enormity of the task is staggering. Between Quantz (1897) and Buswell's classic monograph in 1920, there was little published work on the EVS. There was a rash of studies in the twenties and thirties and again little until 1960, when the EVS was used to explore another kind of problem, that is, the effects of the grammatical structure of the text on the nature of the EVS. We shall concentrate on the later studies, yet the early studies often could not ignore the effects of the nature of the text.

One consistent finding was that the EVS increases with age (Buswell, 1920; Tinker, 1965), and that it is readily affected by the difficulty of the reading material (Buswell, 1920; Anderson, 1937; Fairbanks, 1937; Stone, 1941). The more difficult the text, the shorter the EVS.

There was a flurry of concern about whether the position in the *line* affected the EVS. Both Buswell (1920) and Fairbanks (1937) found that position in the *sentence* affected the EVS, that it was longest in the beginning of the sentence and shortest at the end. We will have occasion to quarrel with the implications of this finding, but they asked the right question about the sentence rather than the typographic line. Buswell's interpretation of the nature of reading was sophisticated for 1920.

The fact that the EVS varies with the position in the sentence is of considerable significance. If the span varied only with the position within the line, as Quantz's study indicated, the determining factors would be entirely mechanical and would be governed by the printed form of the selection. The control of the span, in that case, would be a matter of the mechanics of book construction and would be independent of any teaching factor. But if the span varies with position in the sentence, it is evident that the content of meaning is recognized, and that the EVS is determined by thought units rather than by printed line units. Position in the line may be a minor factor . . . but the differences due to position in the sentence are much greater. (pp. 48, 50)

In his concentration on the meaningful sentence as an influence on the EVS, Buswell anticipates the emphasis on its grammatical determinants. He suggests that the EVS "allows the mind to grasp and interpret a large unit of *meaning* before the voice must express it" (p. 41).

The additional early research on the EVS may be summarized quickly. With good and poor readers selected by a standardized reading test, Buswell (1920) found that good readers had longer EVSs and read more rapidly. Using reading rate as the criterion for good and poor readers, the EVS is longer for good (fast) readers than for slow (poor) readers (Quantz, 1897; Morton, 1964a; Levin and Turner, 1968).

The Developmental Course of the Use of Grammatical Structure
In Chapters 6, 7, and 8 we pointed out that children learn at some point to use the orthographic structure of words—the grammar of words, if you

like—in reading. Knowledge of the invariants within words permits readers to form higher-order units which simplify the task of reading. We ask an analogous question in this section. At what point in their development do children learn that groups of words form units and that such units may also facilitate reading?

It is reasonable to infer from the older studies on eye movements and on the EVS that grammatical structure is used by older children and by more skilled readers. Eye movements become more efficient and EVSs longer with age. There seems to be no way to explain these findings without the implication that older readers are making use of higher-order invariants, except to suppose that they are still using small units but are moving their eyes across the text more rapidly. However, the limits on the speed of saccades and the large proportion of reading time spent on fixation pauses make this explanation unlikely. Most likely, the readers are making fewer and briefer pauses, and we may guess that the positions of the pauses are at least in part determined by the nature of the text. Unfortunately, the early research preceded the interaction between linguistics and psychology, and without clear specifications of the texts we can only speculate.

A direct test of the grammatical nature of sentences and reading involved ten children each from the second, fourth, sixth, eighth, and tenth grades and college undergraduates (Levin and Turner, 1968). Four types of sentences were used:

1. Active sentences in which each phrase contained two words.
2. Active sentences made up of three-word phrases.
3. Passive sentences made up of three-word phrases.
4. Active sentences composed of four-word phrases.

To take one example, a three-word-phrase active sentence might be "The big boy carrying two toys ran very fast to his home." An EVS procedure was used so that the light could be turned off at all possible between-word points in the first two phrases. In addition to the 48 test sentences, there were eight structureless word lists to provide a control for the effects of sentential structure in general.

Sentences were made up with enough phrase units so that there would always be at least ten words in the sentence beyond the light-out position. Starting with the sixth graders, each of the sentences was embedded in a "paragraph" of four unrelated sentences; for the second and fourth graders, the paragraphs contained two sentences. One set of sentences was made up with the vocabulary of a second-grade reader and was used for the second- and fourth-grade children; another set was made up with the vocabulary of a sixth grader and was used with the sixth-grade and all older subjects.

The subject was told to read at his normal rate or at the rate he would read a storybook out loud. The light was turned on and the subject began to read the exposed passage out loud. When the light went out, he was told to report all the words he had seen beyond the word he was saying when the text disappeared from view.

The most general finding demonstrates the effects of grammatical structure very convincingly. Across all ages and sentence types, the mean EVS for unstructured word lists is 2.19 words after the light-off position compared to an average of 3.91 words for sentences, a highly significant difference. This finding was replicated in another study with adults only, where the word lists yielded an EVS of 2.0 words (Levin and Kaplan, 1968). In other words, given no sentence structure, the EVS is short and surprisingly constant at about two words regardless of the reader's age or ability. So, in a general sense, the hypothesis about the effect of a grammatical structure is confirmed.

Yet the questions of the ages at which structure begins to be exploited and the effects of different kinds of sentence structure remain to be answered. The Levin and Turner study shows the average EVS tends to increase with age: second grade, 3.19 words; fourth, 4.41; sixth, 2.66*; eighth, 4.18; tenth, 2.95; adults, 5.02 words. The slow readers in the second grade had a mean span of 2.74 words, which was closest to the word list of 2.19, but still showed some use of grammatical structure. So even the youngest and poorest readers were making use of sentence structure in their reading.

Schlesinger (1968) hypothesized that the phrase is the unit of decoding in reading, that is, skilled readers chunk sentences into phrase units. He confirmed his prediction with Hebrew-speaking adults. Operationally, this prediction means that the reported EVSs extend to phrase boundaries. One purpose of the Levin and Turner (1968) study was to test this notion developmentally. In order to test whether there was a significant tendency

---

*The subjects were volunteers. For reasons that we do not understand, the data from the sixth-grade group were highly deviant. We suspect that the children did not take the task seriously. Therefore, this class was omitted from further analysis.

for subjects to read in phrase groupings, the number of times each subject read to the end of a phrase unit on each of the sentence types was recorded.* All age groups except the second graders ended their EVSs at phrase boundaries to an extent well beyond the chance level. Said another way, readers as early as the fourth grade chunked their oral reading in phrase units, but this tendency grew no stronger between the fourth grade and adulthood. Resnick (1970) found this effect stronger for adults, though also present in children. The second graders, we may infer, were still reading word by word, or at least in word groups that were not coincident with phrase breaks. It will be recalled that eye movement research showed that the patterns of eye movements in reading become adultlike at the fourth grade (Tinker, 1965).

In addition to the 492 times subjects read to phrase boundaries when the boundary was *not* at the end of the modal EVS, the reader changed the sentence structure or the last word 107 times in such a way as to make a phrase boundary. Thus, for example, if the final phrase was "next to the house," the subject might have read "next door."

There was an interesting interaction between the grade levels of the readers and the lengths of the phrases. The length of the EVS is about the same for the second graders irrespective of the phrase length. For fourth graders and older subjects, the EVS is longer for three-word than for two- or four-word phrases. A likely explanation for this finding is that if the light goes off on a two-word phrase, completing that phrase and the next one would give a maximum EVS of four words. Conversely, a light off in the four-word phrase would take the reader beyond his possible EVS if he completed both the target phrase and the succeeding one. Three-word phrases are optimal because completion of that phrase plus the next group of three words is still within the possible forward span.

Finally, this study replicated the findings on fast and slow readers. Reading speed was measured by the length of time (words per second) it took the subject to read to the light-off position. Fast readers had longer EVSs, a finding congruent with the research on eye movements and with the earlier experiments on the EVS. Also, fast readers were more likely to report EVSs ending at phrase boundaries than did slower readers. If we take reading speed to mean reading ability, better readers make more use of grammatical structure in their reading.

*See the original paper and Levin and Kaplan (1968) for the corrections applied to the number of expected EVSs which end at phrase boundaries.

Another EVS study including developmental comparisons was carried out for quite a different purpose: to learn whether the length of the EVS changes when the child is instructed to read (1) normally as though he were reading out loud to a friend; (2) carefully in preparation for questioning; and (3) right through for the general idea. The subjects included 15 pupils each from the second, fourth, ninth, and eleventh grades. The reading materials consisted of connected discourse from second-grade readers (for the younger subjects) or from tenth-grade books (for the upper two grades). The critical light-out position was always at the major constituent break, between the noun phrase and the verb phrase. Each child acted as his own control, reading passages with prior instructions under each of the three conditions (Levin and Cohn, 1968).

In general, as with the earlier study, the older children had longer EVSs. Instructions to read carefully resulted in the shortest EVS (3.69 words across all grade levels), normal reading next (3.97 words), and skimming, the longest (4.14 words). The instructions had the same effects in each of the four grades, indicating that in this study even second graders were able to respond to the task instructions. Faster readers had longer EVSs in all grades, but the rate of reading was not related to the three purposes for the reading. At all ages, the children did not increase their EVSs by reading faster but probably by shortening the duration of the fixation pauses and making fewer regressions. This is an inference from the data since we have no direct measures of eye movements, but the results fit well with Anderson's (1937) measurement of the eye movements of good and poor readers.

To summarize, the data indicate that children by the fourth grade are able to take advantage of grammatical structure in their reading, and improve in the use of structure with age. Good readers are more adept at using grammar to simplify the task of reading. Unfortunately, the developmental data came from a single method, the eye-voice span, but the findings are congruent with reasonable inferences made from studies of eye movements in reading. We turn next to evidence of the influences of grammar on reading by adults, where we will be able to explore some specific grammatical constructions as well as evidence from a variety of techniques.

Grammar and Reading among Adults
The simplest comparison to which we alluded in discussing the developmental course of the function of grammar is to compare grammatical

organization with no organization, that is, with a list of words bearing no interrelated meanings. Grammatical structure leads to longer EVSs in English (Levin and Turner, 1968; Levin and Kaplan, 1968; Lawson, 1961; Morton, 1964a), in Hebrew (Schlesinger, 1968), and in Japanese (Clark, 1972). Grammar also influences memory (e.g., Epstein, 1967) and perception of sentences (e.g., Tulving and Gold, 1963). Phrases act as units in reading (Levin and Turner, 1968; Levin and Kaplan, 1968; Schlesinger, 1968). A professional reader paused most often at surface phrase boundaries (Brown and Miron, 1971). Surface phrases appear to have unitary characteristics, the units formed perhaps by the stress contours of phrases and because phrases often communicate units of meaning. In fact, the expression that reading occurs in "meaning units" (e.g., Buswell, 1920) would today under the influence of modern linguistics be stated in terms of phrase structure of sentences. In the probe technique, latencies are longest across phrase boundaries (e.g., Blumenthal, 1967) and click studies indicate the psychological reality of phrases (e.g., Fodor and Bever, 1965).

To this point, the findings indicate that the constraints or interrelatedness of the elements within phrases are stronger than those across phrase boundaries, so we are led to question whether the degree of constraints—rather than simply their presence or absence—influences reading. Since there is considerable evidence that such intrasentence constraints exist, it is likely that readers are using them.

Morton's (1964a) adult subjects read eight separate passages of statistical approximations to English as well as a passage of connected prose. Lower-order approximations to English are essentially random word lists. As the approximations increase, e.g., at the fifth and sixth levels, the texts appear to have the grammatical and meaning qualities of normal English, or at least the readers begin to interpret them as such. There is a steady increase in speed of reading as the text approaches English, with actual text being read most rapidly. The EVS is also responsive to the closeness with which the text approximates English, with the first three approximations yielding EVSs of around 2.0 words, which it will be recalled was the finding for word lists (Levin and Turner, 1968; Levin and Kaplan, 1968).

The use of statistical approximations to English in research of this sort is somewhat dissatisfying because the assumption is made that as the approximations increase, the text is more constrained. But it is not clear what "constrained" means in this context. The text looks and sounds more like English so that the reader is able to impose meaning on the text, often idiosyncratically. However, the approach to grammar as a stochastic process which is determined (constrained?) from left to right has not proved useful. We prefer that the constraints be determined for actual English prose and that the effects of reading more or less constrained text be studied with real English sentences. The next several studies follow that model.

Two classes of sentences within which the constraints were known to be differently distributed were selected for study by Levin and Kaplan (1968). Clark (1965), in comparing active and passive sentences, had previously found that the latter part of passive sentences, consisting of the verb and the actor, is highly constrained by the first part, the object. This was not true for the corresponding parts of active sentences in which the latter part, the verb and the object, was relatively independent of the first part, the actor.

It was hypothesized by Levin and Kaplan, therefore, that if the EVS is sensitive to within-sentence constraints, the span should increase toward the middle of the passive form, but a corresponding increase should not occur in the active forms. Subjects were 18 college students. Four sentence types comprised the target sentence:
1. Active sentences composed of four-word phrases.
2. Passive sentences composed of four-word phrases.
3. Active sentences composed of five-word phrases.
4. Passive sentences composed of five-word phrases.
The sentences were constructed so that the first half of both active and passive sentences were structurally identical. For example,

Passive:

The cute chubby boy was slowly being wheeled by the maid along the narrow lane to the country store.

Active:

The brash tall man was certainly being loud at the meeting of the new group on the main campus.

Each sentence was embedded in a separate paragraph of either four or five unrelated sentences. EVS scores were obtained at various points starting after the third word and after every succeeding word up to the *by* phrase in the passives, and to the corresponding point in the active sentences which was a prepositional phrase. These points were called light-out positions or *critical positions*.

The paragraphs were exposed on a small ground-glass screen directly in front of the subject, who was positioned so that he could read the lines with minimal head movements. Following the report of the words he recalled after the critical position, he completed a recognition test containing words that had and had not appeared in the target sentence after the light-out position as a control for both guessing and for any tendency for a subject to be conservative in his report.

The EVS technique has occasionally been criticized as being simply a "guessing game" where the subject guesses at the words that were in the sentence after the light was turned off. In the recognition test, subjects reported words that had not actually been in the sentence at the minuscule rate of 1/1000, indicating that random guesses were not implicated in the procedure.

Figure 10-5 presents the EVS in words for the various critical positions in the five-word-phrase active and passive sentences. The data on the four-word phrases are similar, as are the data based on recognition compared to recall.

There are no differences among any of the critical positions in the active sentences. For the passive sentences, positions 1 through 6 do not differ from each other, but positions 7 and 8 are significantly different from positions 1 through 6. Comparing the two types of sentences, active and passive sentences do not differ for positions 1 through 6, but they do for positions 7 and 8. The results show that the EVS is longer for passive sentences at that point where the active and passive sentences begin to be differentially constrained. These findings support the major hypothesis that the size of the chunks which readers use in scanning sentences varies in accordance with intrasentence contingencies.

Though confirmatory, these findings, based on only two types of sentences—simple actives and passives—provide a slim base on which to make the generalization that those parts of sentences which are more highly constrained grammatically are read in larger units than less constrained sentence forms. Consequently, Levin, Grossman, Kaplan, and Yang (1972) tested the same hypothesis by comparing left and right embedded sentences. Left embedded (LE) sentences contain adjectival modifiers between the subject and the main verb of the sentence; right embedded (RE)

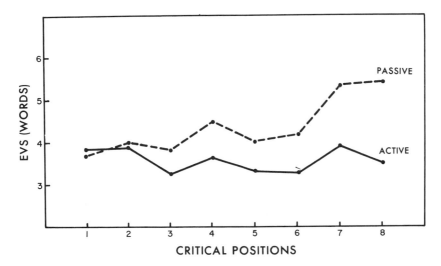

Figure 10-5.   Mean recall for words in critical positions during measurement of the eye-voice span. From Levin and Kaplan, 1970, p. 256. © 1970 by Basic Books, Inc., Publishers, N.Y.

sentences have the modifiers in the predicate, that is, in the verb phrase of the sentence. A simple LE sentence is, "The cake that she made won the prize." Rewritten as an RE sentence, it reads, "She made the cake that won the prize."

The constraint analysis for active and passive sentences (Clark, 1965) already existed when the research on the ways that these sentences were read was undertaken. For RE and LE sentences, the first step involved the determination of the intrasentence constraints. Once these were known, the research was analogous to the earlier study: the determination of the sizes of the EVSs at various points in RE and LE sentences (Levin et al., 1972).

A modified cloze procedure was used for the constraint analysis. In a standard cloze task (Taylor, 1953), single words typically are deleted from a text and subjects are asked to supply the missing word. Since we were interested in the *predictability* of *grammatical forms*, it was necessary to delete segments larger than single words and to estimate in this manner the number of different grammatical types found.

Sixty-eight undergraduate students served as subjects. There were demonstrable differences in the constraints in RE and LE sentences. In the cloze task, responses to RE frames were less variable. Embedded phrases after the main verb were more frequent than before it and were more constrained in form. Longer EVSs in RE than in LE sentences were therefore predicted.

Three experiments were performed, but we will report only one, since they tended to replicate each other. The procedure was the same as the active-passive study already described. Subjects were ten undergraduates. The critical positions were as follows:

LE:

Before he died/the gangster/that/the police/shot/closed/the/door/of the room near the kitchen.

RE:

After the meeting/the janitor/found/the magazine/that/the/woman/left/on the chair in the hall.

EVSs in the RE sentences were longer than in LE sentences, as expected. In fact, curves for RE and LE sentences began to diverge by the second critical position (see Figure 10-6). The left-embedded EVS shortened as the right-embedded EVS lengthened. These results taken together with the active-passive findings support the hypothesis that constraints within sentences determine the way in which the sentences are read.

While we know that children from the fourth grade on are able to take advantage of phrase structure in their reading, it is not clear that they are able to use intrasentence constraints in the way that we have just demonstrated that adults do. Generally, elementary school children have longer EVSs on passive than on active sentences, though the point of increase in span related to a specific part of the sentence is not clear (Levin and Turner, 1968). Another study found little evidence that elementary school children exploited the constraints either in active versus passive or LE versus RE sentences (Grossman, 1969). For one thing, these structures are late to develop in children's language (see Chapter 5). Nevertheless, it is a fruitful topic for future investigation.

Up to this point we have used a simple notion of grammar: that which describes the surface structure of a sentence. However, sentences which share a common surface structure may differ in their underlying, or deep structure, descriptions. The distinction is seen most clearly in ambiguous sentences. Using the common example, "Flying planes can be dangerous," the sentence may be interpreted to mean either that the act of flying or

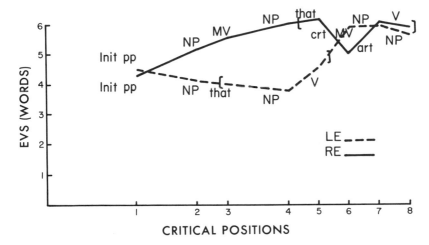

Figure 10-6.   Recall of critical positions during measurement of the eye-voice span in left-embedded and right-embedded sentences. From Levin, Grossman, Kaplan, and Yang, 1972, p. 37.

that planes which are flying in the air can be dangerous. The sentence can be understood only by reference to another level of analysis, now usually called "deep structure," which by way of transformational rules relates the ambiguous surface sentence to its underlying, unambiguous form (Chomsky, 1964). It is beyond the compass of this discussion to enter the arguments about the usefulness of postulating a deep structure level of analysis or the relationship between this level and meaning. We will show, however, that sentences with similar surface structures and differing deep structures are read differently.

Consider the two passive sentences:

(1) The ball was hit by the bat.

(2) The ball was hit by the park.

Sentence (1) has a straightforward underlying structure. It is a passive sentence in which *ball* is the object, *was hit* the passive form of the verb, and *bat,* the actor. Sentence (2) is considerably more complicated. The sentence is passive. The sentence contains two propositions: (2a) Someone hit the ball and (2b) Someone hit the ball in the vicinity of the park. At the surface level the sentences are identical except for one word. The agent of the action appears in (1); in (2) the agent is deleted and replaced by an adverb of place.

Two sets of sentences were developed with one member of a pair bearing the agent-present relationship and the other, the agent-deleted relationship (Wanat and Levin, 1968). An EVS study was performed on these sentences. The subjects were 30 university undergraduates who read each form of the sentences, but in different sessions and with many "filler" sentences. The procedure was identical to the previously described EVS studies. There were 16 test sentences (eight pairs). The light-out positions occurred at the beginning, middle, and end of the target sentences. The hypothesis was that sentences of type (1) would be easier to process than type (2) because the reader had more information to limit his interpretation in (1). This point will be taken up later when we discuss the function of grammatical structure in reading. Another way to interpret this hypothesis is that sentence (1) is less complex to understand than (2) because of the direct relation between the surface and deep structures. Said another way, the restriction of alternatives in (1) is greater than in (2) because of the closer congruence between an underlying passive construction that realizes the agent of action compared to one in which the agent is deleted and must be supplied by the reader.

When the light was turned out immediately prior to the critical word (agent or adverb), the mean EVS was 5.81 words for the agent-included sentences compared to 5.21 words for the agent-deleted passive sentences. The difference is statistically significant. When the light-out position was three words prior to the critical word, the mean EVS scores are in the same direction, though not statistically significant. Grammatical constraints may operate, as this experiment indicates, in ways that are more complicated than the direct, surface form of the sentences.

Grammatical Structure and Eye Movements
In another study, Wanat (1971) recorded the eye movements of adults reading the various types of sentences on which we have reported EVS data. First, it is interesting to consider the two types of passives discussed immediately above. The sentences differed not in forward fixations, but in regressive eye movements. In the agent-deleted passive sentences compared to the agent-present conditions, readers spent more time on regressive fixations and made more regressions. Further, a large number of regressions occurred after the adverb, and these regressions were directed back toward the area of the sentence in which the adverb occurred. It is as though the structure of the sentence led the reader to search for an agent

of action, and with the realization that the phrase was a locative rather than an agentive one, he reread it.

RE sentences, it will be recalled, were more constrained than LE sentences, and consequently EVS scores were longer for RE forms. The eye movement data confirmed these findings. There were no differences in the number of forward fixations in the LE and RE sentences, but the pause times, that is, the length of time spent on each fixation, were longer on the LE than on the RE sentences, and these longer times were spent specifically on the left embedded phrase. In both types of embeddings, most fixation time was allocated to the main verbs of the sentences, a finding which indirectly confirms Chafe's (1970) semantic analysis built around the main verb in the sentence and the role of the main verb in determining the complexity of the sentence (Fodor, Garrett, and Bever, 1968). Kolers (1970) found similar evidence for the importance of the main verb in reading. "If in fact, the second fifth of an independent clause contains the parts dealing with verbs, the data suggest that the perception of the relations a sentence expresses is more difficult to attain than the perception of the things being related" (p. 108).

The comparisons between EVS and eye movement patterns are not so neat between simple active and passive sentences as in the other sentence types described above. Generally, active sentences are read more smoothly —with fewer and briefer forward fixations and less regressions—than simple passive sentences, according to Wanat. The one exception is in the area of the by phrase which introduced the agent of action in passives and was a prepositional phrase denoting place in the actives. Examples are

(3) The ship was beached by the helper in the storm.

(4) The poet was writing in the studio of his home.

In the region of the *by* phrase there were fewer and briefer regressions in the passive than in the active sentences. This could account for the longer EVS around the agentive phrase in passives compared to actives in the same areas of the sentence.

Wanat's (1971) study was a carefully carried out study of eye movements related to grammatical structure of sentences. The lexicons used in the sentences were controlled and so far as possible the same words were used in sentences to be compared, though, because of the point of the study, the constituent structures of the sentences varied to allow certain

hypothesized comparisons. In general, there is a reasonable match between the findings of the EVS method and the patterns of eye movements.
That is, where the EVSs were long, the eye movements showed fewer fixations, briefer fixation pauses, and fewer regressions.

In an eye movement study not unrelated to those already discussed,
Mehler, Bever, and Carey (1967) observed the ways in which three
kinds of ambiguous statements were scanned:

Surface structure ambiguities

(1) They gave her dog candies. . . .

(2) They told her cat stories. . . .

Ambiguities at both the surface and deep structure levels

(1) They are surprising authors. . . .

(2) They are interesting farmers. . . .

At the deep structure only

(1) the shooting of the hunters . . .

(2) the punching of the sisters . . .

Subjects were 40 college students. Forward fixations only were recorded.
The most noticeable differences were mainly at the level of surface
structure. Constituent structure is more important than the specific lexical
item. The results may be summed up: "The rule is *fixate on the first half of
each constituent*" (p. 216). Wanat's (1971) criticism of this study is well
taken. There was a higher diversity of fixations than most studies have
shown. Forward fixations and regressions were not differentiated. This is
particularly important in the study of ambiguous sentences, where we
would expect large numbers of regressions to reveal and disambiguate the
sentences (cf. Wanat and Levin, 1968). Nevertheless, the study points to
an important problem that merits more investigation: the reading of
sentences including various sources of ambiguity.

Grammatical structure is a set of rules which facilitate the recognition
of the elements which make up that structure. This notion was tested
directly by Sawyer (1971), who exposed sentences, parts of which were
perfectly legible and parts of which were physically blurred. She was able
to create eight degrees of blur, so that if grammar was influential, the

blurred parts should be correctly recognized under more impoverished conditions when the grammar constrained that part of the sentence. Figure 10-7 shows the eight degrees of blur. Congruent with previous studies, the *by* + agent phrases in passive sentences were recognized under more blurred conditions than comparable prepositional phrases in active sentences. The comparison of agent-present and agent-deleted passives did not confirm earlier findings. *By* phrases introducing locatives were more easily recognized than *by* phrases introducing agents in simple passive sentences. Finally, readers were able to recognize the existence of right embeddings under poorer physical conditions than left embeddings. In general, using a different task than the EVS and eye movements, the interrelationship between grammar and reading was confirmed, though there is yet much to be learned about the effect of the nature of the task on the use of intrasentence grammatical forms.

How Does Grammatical Structure Work?

It is a popular current notion that grammatical structure influences reading by providing a basis for readers to make predictions about the ensuing text. We will have occasion to discuss this theory of reading in Chapter 12, where we compare various models of the reading process. In

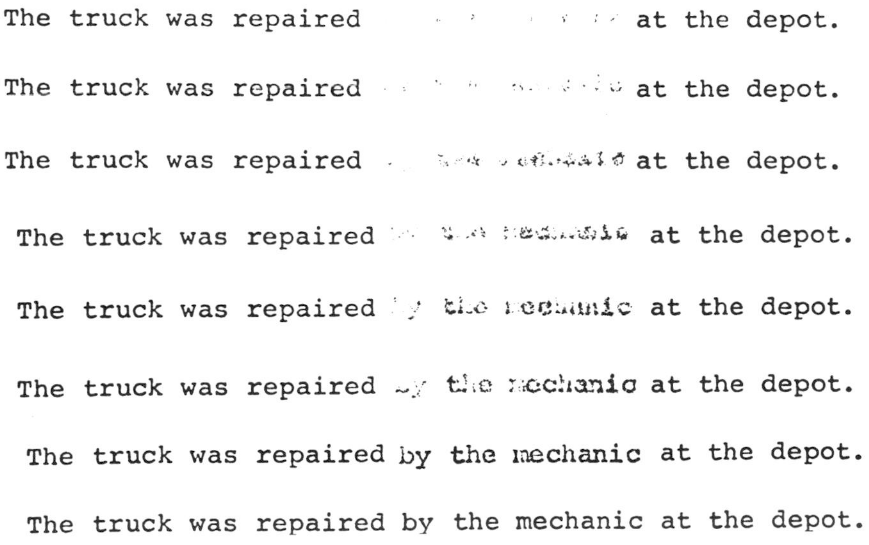

The truck was repaired   at the depot.

The truck was repaired   at the depot.

The truck was repaired   at the depot.

The truck was repaired   at the depot.

The truck was repaired   at the depot.

The truck was repaired   the mechanic at the depot.

The truck was repaired by the mechanic at the depot.

The truck was repaired by the mechanic at the depot.

Figure 10-7. Sentences with varied degrees of blur in *by* + agent phrases. From Sawyer, 1971, p. 19.

a sense this book is replete with examples of the efficacy of grammatical structure. To take an example, children just beginning to read make errors that preserve the grammaticality of the sentences (Weber, 1970), as do adults (Kolers, 1970). The functions of grammar in reading are ubiquitous. The question is, "How does grammar work?"

Written language may be analyzed into various levels: letters, letter clusters, syllables, morphemes, words, phrases, sentences, and discourse. A skilled reader takes advantage of the rules at the various levels, often in parallel. Grammar is an intermediate level encompassing the lower-level invariants. As such, grammar provides the *context* for the subsidiary units. The evidence is massive that context narrows the alternatives among the lower-order units. The contextual function of grammatical rules increases the efficiency of reading the subordinate units that these rules govern. The efficiency is realized by less attention to the units, implying reading in fewer fixations, briefer fixation pauses, and fewer regressions.

Context is efficient only if it is relevant to the identification of a word, and by definition grammar is relevant for the identification of words which form the grammatical structure in question. Besides the relevance of the context its length is also important, and independent contributions of the amount of context and its relevance for word identification are illustrated in Figure 10-8 (Tulving and Gold, 1963). Increasing the length of context narrows the range of possible alternatives (Aborn, Rubenstein, and Sterling, 1959). If we assume that the ends of sentences provide more grammatical context than the beginnings, we can see why reading errors decrease over the final three-fifths of sentences (Kolers, 1970) and why there are more correct guesses in a cloze procedure at the ends of sentences (Miller and Coleman, 1967).

Context and the length of exposure of the words are not additive in determining which part of speech the word represents (Tulving, Mandler, and Baumel, 1964). Though the authors do not speculate about the relationships between the presence of context and the length of exposure of the word for its correct identification, it seems reasonable to assume that the function is interactive. That is, grammatical context facilitates word identification, which in turn adds to the relevant context for successive word identifications. Morton (1964b) puts it well: "In other words, the presence of a context reduces the number of visual cues necessary for the correct identification of the word" (p. 176).

One could go on documenting the point that grammatical structure

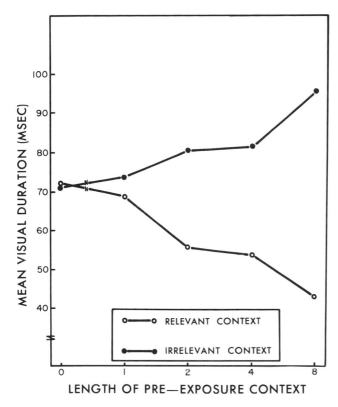

Figure 10-8.   The effect of length of preexposure context on word identification. From Tulving and Gold, 1963, p. 322. Copyright 1963 by the American Psychological Association. Reprinted by permission.

provides the context which facilitates a variety of reading-related behaviors. Levin, Ford, and Beckwith (1968) gave high school students the task of choosing the correct pronunciation for homographically spelled words, e.g., *sow*-/so/or/saU/, *present*-/présent/or/presént/. The pronunciation depends on the context of the homograph. The latency for reading the homograph was determined by preceding it with a synonym or with a grammatical cue as to its part of speech. Slides containing one word, context or target, were presented in sequential pairs. So one pair might be *pig-sow*, another, *to-sow*. The homograph was pronounced more rapidly when the preceding contextual word signaled its part of speech rather than its meaning. In both cases, the pronunciation was more rapid than when there was no relevant context. These results are best interpreted to mean that a normal two-word phrase yields more rapid pronunciations than when the context supplies meaning, but is not in the form in which it is usually said. The high school students found it easier to say the phrase "to présént" than the word sequence "gift présent."

To take one final example, third-grade children could use sentence structure to solve anagram puzzles (if they were given a hint) more quickly than children who had no grammatical structure available (Gibson, Tenney, and Sharabany, 1971).

In summary, our view of the many relationships of grammatical structure to reading is that grammar provides the context which increases the economy of processing the units making up the grammatical structure. Grammar also provides the relational framework for comprehending text, which we will now turn to.

Comprehending Text

Decoding vs. Comprehension

We referred earlier to the "mechanics" of the reading process, sometimes called decoding, that implicate attention to graphic and orthographic information, translation to speech sounds (whether vocal or subvocal), and moving the eyes over the text in the correct path. These mechanical processes must become smooth and automatic before attention can be strongly concentrated on the meaning to be extracted, for, as we have seen, the beginning reader in particular finds it hard to attend to all these activities at once. But suppose that the child has arrived at a stage of fast decoding. Does that insure that meaning will now be extracted without further effort? If that were so, the rate of scanning through words for a letter or word target should be positively related to reading achievement. But several experiments make it clear that this is not the case.

Katz and Wicklund (1971) examined word scanning rate for good and poor readers in the fifth grade. Sentences, of two, three, or five words in length were presented, with instructions to report whether or not a target word was presented. Half the time the target word was present, with each serial position in the sentence equally and randomly represented. Half the time a false target word which began with the same letter appeared in the same place. Each of the grammatical sentences was scrambled to produce a nongrammatical sentence as well, with targets inserted in the same fashion. Both good and poor readers took longer to scan a three-word sentence than a two-word sentence. There was no interaction between sentence length and reader ability. Grammaticality made no difference. It was concluded that good and poor readers did not differ in the ability to scan, transform, and match words—in other words, in the mechanics of the process. The same authors (1972) compared good and poor readers in grades 2 and 6 for the ability to scan a row of randomly selected target letters and again found no differences due to reader ability.

Leslie and Calfee (1971) carried out a visual search task with second-, fourth-, and sixth-grade students of high or low reading ability, as well as college students. They scanned a list of ten words, searching for a target word. Some of the lists contained no target. The major effect of grade level was a change in search rate, which increased steadily from second grade through college. But the main effect of reading level was not significant and entered into no interaction. To quote the authors' conclusion, "For retarded readers of the sort included in this experiment, the scanning process does not differentiate them from their more able peers" (p. 171).

While scanning can proceed without necessarily decoding verbally, something is developing from second grade to college in a word-search task of this type. But it is apparently a superficial skill that is not reflected in the differences between good and poor readers. It seems a fair guess that comprehension and segmentation into larger syntactically critical units such as phrases are involved in the difference, though there may still be a major difference at the level of the single word, dependent on the manner of processing it, that is, use of conditional rules and extraction of meaning. Extraction of meaning from printed words does not come automatically and instantly with ability to decode, as children's superior performance with pictures over words suggests.

Extracting Meaning from Words and Pictures
Gibson, Barron, and Garber (1972) performed an experiment in which children's (second-, fourth-, and sixth-grade) and adults' judgments of categorical identity were compared when they were shown pairs of words, pairs of pictures, and pairs composed of a word and a picture. Word pairs were printed in upper- and lowercase, and pictures of the same object (e.g., a cat) were portrayed from different angles, so that physical matches were not possible, the aim being for the subject to match on the basis of meaning. The children and the adults behaved differently, especially when the second-grade children were compared with the adults. The second-

grade children were faster at matching pairs of pictures that belonged to the same category, while the adults were faster at matching pairs of words. Furthermore, the picture-word pairs, which took the longest time to compare, showed a relative decrease in latency of decision from the second to the sixth grades. Presumably, as mechanical decoding gave way to comprehension, an abstract meaning common to both word and picture could be extracted from the word—neither an image nor a word, but abstract semantic features underlying and common to both.

Lynch and Rohwer (1971) compared learning of paired associates when the items were words, on the one hand, or pictures, on the other, sometimes giving a sentential connection between members of a pair. The subjects were sixth-grade students. Both associative and response learning measures proved to be influenced by the material, pictures being easier than words both to recognize as items previously presented and to enter into a meaningful association. This is one of many experiments showing that for children, pictures enter easily into learned relationships, but the situation appears to change with adults, especially when the relationships encompass events and rulelike structure.

Another experiment, by Matz and Rohwer (1971), is relevant in this connection. Rohwer (1967) had found that while children of high and low socioeconomic status did not differ in learning noun pairs, nevertheless black students of low socioeconomic status suffered from poor comprehension of printed text. Matz and Rohwer thought that pictures might be useful in "unitizing" ideas in text, that is, relating segments of text in a sequence of clauses and sentences. They accordingly prepared passages organized around a central theme, with sentences related sequentially to one another so as to build up an inferential pattern that would permit some simple but unstated predictions, knowledge inherent in the passage but not actually stated. There were four "levels" of inference depending on distance between the two sentences which were to be related (as more sentences had to be taken into account). Pictorial versions were also prepared, with pictures corresponding to sentences in the text presented cumulatively. Subjects were tested after one or the other mode of presentation with yes-no questions about the inferential knowledge, either with the original materials present or with them absent.

The subjects were black students of low socioeconomic status (SES) and high-SES white students in fourth grade. Having the materials present or not while answering the test questions did not affect performance, but all the other variables did. Errors increased as the level of the question went up, and the mode of presentation interacted significantly with SES. Figure 10-9 shows the results. Pictorial presentation resulted in fewer errors for the low-SES group. They performed quite as well as the high-SES group that was given verbal text, and better than that group when it was given pictorial text, but their test performance suffered with verbal presentation. This study suggests what the optimal use for pictures in a text might be: not a one-to-one pairing of word and picture, possibly leading to ignoring of the less salient word, but illustrations along with the text that group the ideas meaningfully, showing that the same organization can be applied to the text.

That failure to comprehend written text does not coincide with failure to extract meaning per se is corroborated in another experiment (Mackworth, 1973) in which children with reading difficulties were tested in a pictorial processing task. Children known to be poor readers were shown a fairly complex picture which was then withdrawn, and another presented

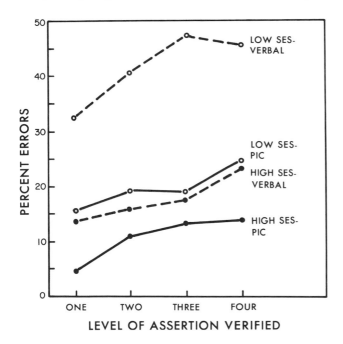

Figure 10-9. Inferences drawn from pictorial versus printed material by black and white fourth graders of different socioeconomic level. Data from Matz and Rohwer, 1971; graph from Frase, in Carroll and Freedle, 1972, p. 353.

which was the counterpart except for a single change in one area. The child was required to point to the area that was changed. The children tested ranged from kindergarten to sixth grade. While there was marked improvement from kindergarten through third grade, there was absolutely no difference between good and poor readers. Poor readers, however, took longer to match words with pictures.

Comprehension of Phrases, Sentences, and Discourse

Mackworth (1972) conducted another experiment with good and poor readers which he called the "missing word task." Children's ability to comprehend simple sentences was studied by asking them to search for a word missing from a sentence. The sentence appeared along the bottom of a slide display (e.g., "He could not carry the ———"). Above the sentence were two lists of three words well separated. One list consisted of nouns (e.g., *books, year, sky*), the other of verbs (e.g., *ran, threw, makes*). The missing word was either a noun or a verb. The arrangement was explained to the child beforehand, and illustrations and practice given. Eye movements were photographed and the time spent looking at the wrong group of words measured. Figure 10-10 shows the results for good and poor readers (assessed by an oral reading test). Good readers spent less than half as long looking at the wrong category as did poor readers. Perhaps the most interesting aspect of these data is the very large drop in time for both groups between grades 2 and 4. But the poor readers, with ample room for improvement, showed little change between fourth and sixth grades.

In Mackworth's task, it is possible that not only comprehension was at fault in the poor readers; they may have had problems at the more mechanical level as well. But other studies attest to the fact that there are poor readers who are perfectly good "decoders." They have learned the mechanical aspects of the task but are apparently processing the text word by word, not using contextual semantic relations and syntactic information. Cromer (1970) identifies one form of reading difficulty as failure to organize input of reading material into meaningful units. He separated a group of poor readers in a junior college into a "difference" group and a "deficit" group. The difference group had adequate intelligence and language and vocabulary skills but had difficulty comprehending, presumably because they were reading word by word rather than taking in phrases and larger units. The deficit group was poor in comprehension because of a specific deficiency in vocabulary. Cromer conducted an experiment with

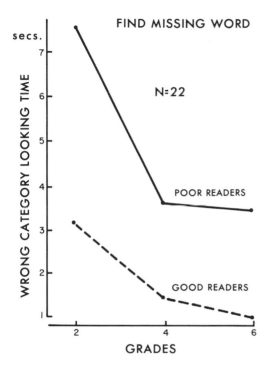

Figure 10-10. Comprehension measured by completion of sentences by good and poor readers. From Mackworth, 1972.

three groups of subjects, a difference group, a deficit group, and a group of good readers. A set of stories, each with a multiple-choice comprehension test, was chosen and presented in four different modes:

1. Regular sentences   *The cow jumped over the moon*
2. Single words   *The*
   cow
   jumped
   over
   the
   moon
3. Phrases   *The cow jumped   over the moon*
4. Fragmented groupings   *The cow   jumped over the   moon*

   It was reasoned that phrase grouping would facilitate comprehension for the poor readers in the difference group but not for the poor readers in the deficit group or for the good readers (who presumably already organized the text in meaningful units). When the material was presented word by word, the deficit poor readers and the good readers were expected to comprehend less well, while the difference group was not expected to be affected, since they were assumed to read this way normally.

When the number of questions answered correctly was compared for the four modes of presentation and the three groups of subjects, the poor readers overall answered fewer questions correctly than did the good readers. But the difference group of poor readers comprehended better on the phrase mode than they did on the other three modes, performing just as well as the good readers on that mode (good readers were best and equally good on sentences and phrases). The deficit poor readers, relative to their own low performance on regular sentence presentation, answered the most questions correctly on the single-word mode and were not helped by phrasing. Thus the difference poor readers, who were hypothesized to read poorly simply because they did not organize what they read for comprehension, were helped by presentation with meaningful grouping. Their performance was similar with regular sentence presentation and single-word presentation, lending credence to the notion that they typically read word by word.

It should be noted that these three groups of subjects did not differ on simple word identification (reading aloud the words in the single word presentation). They all had adequate word-naming skills. However, the deficit group took considerably longer to read the material aloud. This fact suggests that they were not only having trouble at the comprehension level but had not learned to use all the intraword redundancy either. This lack would contribute to a failure to deal adequately with units organized by meaning, simply by slowing them down. While intraword conditional redundancies must be mastered for skilled reading, this study implies that teaching solely by single word identification could be dangerous and lead to habits of reading word by word rather than by phrases and units grouped by meaning and linguistic structure. The multilevel approach again seems justified.

The same rationale that motivated the Cromer study was the basis for two further experiments with good and poor readers from the fifth grade. Oakan, Wiener, and Cromer (1971) hypothesized that adequate word identification was insufficient for comprehending written text. Subjects matched for age and IQ but varying in reading skill were given four types of presentation of a story, followed in each case by questions about the story. Two of the presentations were auditory. In one, a story was read aloud by a good reader and taped for the presentation. In the other, a story was read aloud by a poor reader and taped with all the hesitations, false starts, errors, omissions, etc., but with errors corrected by the experimenter. The two visual presentations were comparable to the auditory ones; one, a properly typed regular text, the other a typed rendering of the version given by a poor reader. Before the beginning of the experiment, the poor readers were trained to identify all the individual words contained in the stories.

The main finding of interest was that the good readers demonstrated their highest level of comprehension under the condition of good visual presentation, so the preliminary identification training was of little assistence to them. Getting meaning from printed text even when all the words are recognized is obviously not the same process as getting it from listening to proper speech, which the poor readers were quite able to do.

An experiment by Steiner, Wiener, and Cromer (1971) examined the effect of a kind of comprehension training on good and poor readers in fifth grade. The comprehension training, given on half the trials, consisted of reading aloud to the subject a paraphrased summary of a story he was afterward given to read. Presentation of the story appeared either properly arranged in paragraph style, or word by word on a roll of paper cranked along by the child after he read a word and was ready for the next. Test questions were answered after all the types of presentation. Error rates actually increased with comprehension training for the good readers, and there was no significant change for poor readers. With single-word presentation, the error rate decreased after comprehension training. Good readers made anticipation errors that made sense with this presentation and often identified whole phrases rather than single words, imposing organization on their output despite single-word presentation. The poor readers, in contrast, appeared to respond to these words "as isolated, unrelated items in a series" (p. 511).

We might refer back, at this point, to the discussion of organization as a cognitive strategy in Chapter 3. The studies cited there were concerned with strategies for remembering rather than for extracting meaning from text, but the two activities are interwoven in most schoolroom tasks by third grade at least. One of the papers (Smirnov, Istomina et al., 1969) described experiments which instructed young school children in extracting the main ideas from text, compiling a textual outline, and, as a second phase, using it for mnemonic purposes. Outlines of a narrative text or a story were compiled in group discussion and then independently by children from second through sixth grades, with steady improvement in extracting the main points of the text. The instructional techniques involved asking and answering questions about logical subjects and predicates of the text, gradually teaching the children to express the ideas in abbreviated and generalized form and with subordinate and superordinate organization. Analysis of the text and composition of an outline of a story was apparently possible even for the second-grade children after instruction, but they did not automatically use it as a mnemonic device, while the fourth- and sixth-grade children did. It is interesting that instruction was required in the reverse direction—decoding the outline later—for comprehension and good retention to result.

In short, the younger reader must learn to select the critical information in printed discourse, both when the information is well ordered and when it is not. He also has to become aware of the relations between sentences, often where they are considerably displaced from one another and where information from several assertions must be combined. Frase (1972) refers in his research to "levels of assertion." Level 1 is simply the assertion in the text in one sentence. A second level would require two sentences from the text, and so on up. These different levels of knowledge can generate new and true assertions that are not actually represented in the text. Frase and his colleagues prepared a simple story for children with a number of levels of assertion. The story was presented to children in second, fourth, fifth, and sixth grades, with the text always available. The children were to answer five questions by circling a *yes* or a *no*. There were three levels of assertion, the relationships being simple equivalences. For instance, "The small thing was red," a simple first-level assertion, was followed by "The red thing was a bag," another first-level assertion. The children were then presented with the second-level assertion "The small thing was a bag" (not actually represented in the text) and asked to decide whether it was true or false. The order of the sentences was varied as they were presented in the text, in one case organized by the two main concepts, in a second case organized by contrastive attributes, and in a third case scrambled. There was little difference in correct responses between the two types of organized passage, but a scrambled organization impaired performance, especially on the higher-level assertions. On the whole, performance on the question dropped about 20% when second-level assertions had to be processed (see Figure 10-11). City children performed considerably less well than suburban children; there was improvement with age in both these groups, for the suburban children principally on the higher-level assertions.

Frase ran a second similar experiment with city children in which he prompted the subjects, before reading, to pay attention to certain critical concepts, with consequent improvement. The reader at some point early in a text must make a decision about what is relevant, and the prompts, Frase thought, cued the children to do this. What are the critical cues in the text, and how does the reader learn to analyze the content for them? This question will be considered again in the following section on the use of grammatical structure in reading.

In concluding, it might be wise to pause and ask what comprehension is, preliminary to our discussion of learning from reading in the next chapter. Is it extracting the meaning of words, or of one word in relation to another—semantics? Is it perceiving syntax—subject, predicate, phrase structure? In a sentence such as "The butler did it," there are a subject and a predicate, an agent and an action that give syntactic information

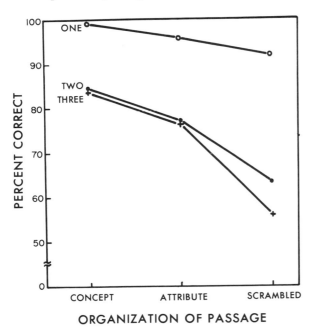

Figure 10-11. Effects of organization of text and level of assertion. From Frase, in Carroll and Freedle, 1972, p. 350.

necessary for comprehension. It also answers the question "*Who* did it," giving semantic information (animate, human, male, a servant, a butler). But we still don't know what the butler did. Now suppose we embed the sentence in a larger one: "The detectives suspected the gangster, but the butler did it." The sentence doesn't tell us exactly what he did, but nevertheless we infer that it was a crime, possibly murder. Much of the recent work on understanding sentences and sequences of sentences stresses the role of inferred knowledge (e.g., Bransford, Barclay, and Franks, 1972; Barclay, 1973; see also studies taken up in the following chapter). What is inferred is neither semantic information nor syntactic information that is directly given, but the role of inference in comprehension can hardly be overemphasized. Comprehending what is read at more than a superficial level is like thinking, a complex cognitive process.

Content and Comprehension

A few very obvious things about the content of material given children to read and the encouragement of comprehension might be pointed out. In the early stages of reading, as the last chapter stressed, the content should be of interest to the child and should be topically related to events within his scope of experience. It should be expressed in a linguistic style that has reality for him. But as children begin to master the mechanical problems and show evidence of comprehension of what is read as well, it seems important to broaden the scope of the content. Children enjoy stories about people in other lands, fairy tales, and make-believe animals—Pogo and Albert and the "swampland" animals are examples par excellence. Material that appeals to the imagination and arouses strong interest seems highly likely to spur efforts at comprehension.

But beyond arousing curiosity and interest, it begins to be important, even as the mechanics are getting smoothed out, to provide a broad variety of subject matter. Stories are fine for catching interest, but as maturing individuals and adults, we read for many other purposes than entertainment (more other purposes, actually), and strategies of reading when reading becomes optional vary with the purpose. It seems possible, as soon as a child begins to be competent in the basic mechanics of reading, to introduce gradually many different kinds of material: lists of people in the room, printed instructions for a fire drill, invitations to a birthday party composed by a child in the room and handed out to the others, simple instructions for making something (a puppet, for intance), a telephone book to look up names and numbers ("How many people in the telephone book have the same name as yours?"), directions for getting somewhere the children are all familiar with (or want to go to) and a map to apply them to. Obviously, lessons in geography and arithmetic are going to involve reading, so written material should be introduced (perhaps in small doses, at first) from areas in which reading will become a tool for learning.

In the last chapter we discussed children's oral language patterns and their fit (or lack of fit) with the language patterns in reading texts. It is still necessary to keep this relationship in mind during the transition to skilled reading. Comprehension is aided by familiar sentence structure, and it makes sense that the syntactic patterns children actually use (and perhaps those used by their parents in talking to them) are going to be the most familiar. Tatham (1970) prepared sentences of two levels of syntactic complexity and had second- and fourth-grade children read them. Their comprehension was measured by having them select from three alternative interpretations of the meaning of the sentence. Tatham concluded that comprehension was generally better where the written material coincided syntactically with frequent patterns of oral language. At some point in the child's education these patterns begin to diverge and written style may change materially from the spoken patterns, but when comprehension is still a problem some kind of match seems desirable.

Summary

This chapter considered a selection of problems in the transition to skilled reading. Reading, on the one hand, and spelling, on the other, correspond to the psychological processes of recognition and recall. Phonetic rules for spelling even a corpus of common words require a large set of rules, and it has been estimated that these rules alone would allow correct spelling of only about half of the 17,000 most common English words. We can often recognize whether a spelling is correct or incorrect when we do not recall the correct spelling. A possible strategy is to generate several possible spellings, write them out, and see if the correct one is recognized.

Under certain circumstances almost every reader subvocalizes while he is reading. The subvocalization can go from audible whispering to changes in the electrical potentials of the larynx, chin, lips, or tongue detectable only under conditions of very high amplification. The latter technique is called electromyography (EMG). Subvocalization may be troublesome enough to slow down reading to the rate of overt speech. Subvocalization may be reduced by converting the EMG signal to auditory form (which sounds like noise) and instructing the reader to keep the audio signal off. This technique appears to work quickly and to have long-lasting results provided the subjects understand the technique and are strongly motivated to improve their reading skills. For poor readers, reducing subvocalization lowers the comprehension of the text.

Subvocalization while reading interacts with the difficulty of understanding the text or with competing behaviors like listening to a story while trying to read. Children subvocalize more than adults, though little is known about the developmental course of subvocalization.

In reading, the eyes move in jumps called "saccades," whose purpose is to bring the fovea of the eye, the area of highest acuity, to rest on the portion of the text that the reader wants to look at. A reader may make forward saccades or regression movements to reread some portion of the text. About 6% of the time is spent in eye movements and 94% in fixation pauses. If the text is difficult, readers make more fixations, shorter saccadic movements, longer fixation pauses, and more regression movements.

Most eye movement behaviors have become stable by the fourth grade. Since the mechanical oculomotor aspects of reading reach an early level of competence, later changes in reading behavior are attributable to attitudes toward reading, the difficulty of the material, the ease of comprehension, etc. Skilled readers' eye movements are flexible and adapt to the nature of the material and of the task. An area of clear text beyond the foveated area facilitates reading, suggesting that peripheral vision is implicated in skilled reading, though we do not know precisely what information is available in the periphery nor how it is used by the reader. Semantic information is available only in the near periphery. Finally, the attempts to improve reading by teaching readers to move their eyes in the same ways that skilled readers do have proved useless.

The next section of the chapter concerned the influence of the grammar of sentences on reading. The most common technique used was the eye-voice span (EVS), the number of successive words a subject who is reading aloud can report after the text is removed. From the fourth grade on, the EVS is longer for sentences than for word lists, indicating that children start taking advantage of grammatical structure sometime between the second and fourth grades. There is a tendency starting with the fourth grade for reported EVS to end at phrase boundaries, especially for more skilled readers. Second graders do not yet chunk their reading in phrase units. Further, for adults, the EVS is longest on those parts of the sentences that are most highly constrained. The EVS is longest at the *by* + agent section of passive compared to active sentences and on right embedded (RE) as opposed to left embedded (LE) sentences. Passive sentences which have locative constructions with implied agents yield shorter EVSs than simple passives: *by (near) the park* compared to *by the bat*.

In general, eye movements confirm the EVS findings. The word *park* in the above example led to more regressions than the word *bat*. Fixation pauses were longer on LE than on RE sentences. We hypothesize that grammatical structure, by reducing the number of alternatives, provides the relevant context for the more efficient identification of the units—words and phrases—which make up the sentence.

When a child becomes a fast decoder, does that insure that meaning will now be extracted without further effort? Good and poor readers do not necessarily differ in the ability to transform a written word to speech, in other words, in the mechanics of reading. The ability to use larger units and to make inferences from the text is involved in skilled reading rather than simply the ability to decode, so that skilled decoders who have not learned to organize the text into higher-order groupings may still be poor readers, so far as comprehension is concerned. They may require assistance in developing the ability to learn from reading, the topic of the next chapter.

11
Learning from Reading

Learning to recognize words and learning to comprehend ideas from written text at the level of the phrase, the sentence, or a passage of discourse are not the same thing, as we saw in the previous chapter. Meaningful and syntactic relations between words provide a different level of information to the reader than do words alone. We know far less, in terms of basic research, at least, about factors that influence comprehension of sentences and longer passages of discourse in reading than we do about factors that influence recognition of individual words (see Chapter 7). Why should this be the case? Two reasons stand out. It is harder to define and segment into units the information contained in a passage of discourse; and second, we have made little progress toward a theory of comprehension, although a recent book (Carroll and Freedle, 1972) includes some promising attempts. We shall try to analyze the problem of learning from reading, calling attention to the questions that need answers as well as to the existing research.

What Is Involved in Learning from Reading

Extraction of Relevant Information
It seems fair to say that most of the older research on learning from reading simply looked at how much the subject remembered of what he had read, sometimes verbatim, sometimes in free recall, and sometimes answering questions. But it is obvious that learning something from what one reads involves far more than remembering. Rote memorizing is presumably a potential memorial process, but in recent years it has become clear that even memorizing serial lists or paired associates involves some organization, and is done most easily if some kind of meaningful structure is available and utilized by the learner. The need to extract meaning is even more essential when the person is reading a passage that carries a message—a statement about an event, a proposition that may or may not be true, an order for him to carry out, directions for how to find his destination, and so on. He must extract the information from the message, and furthermore he must select the relevant information, which is frequently embedded in a larger context that can overburden his memory and even confuse him (information about an entire subway system, for instance, when there is only one place

he wants to go). There are two aspects to extracting the relevant information: selecting the critical features and relations while filtering out the redundant or noisy portion, and comprehending the critical relations fully when they have been located. Knowing what is relevant is part of comprehension, but not all of it. Neither is it obvious to the young reader that there is economy for learning in passing lightly over things he doesn't need or want to know. He must be able to separate the wanted from the unwanted information, and then appropriately process what he has selected.

Assimilation to Prior Knowledge or Cognitive Structure

An individual's knowledge of the world as well as his theories about it (either naive or sophisticated) are constantly building up, but they do not consist of a jumble of unrelated bits of information. New information is entered in the system in some orderly way, and this is part of comprehending what one reads. This process is analogous to some extent to Piaget's concept of assimilation; new experience "nourishes" the schema, is assimilated to it, and the schema in turn accommodates to the new experience. We are not thinking now of sensory-motor schemata, however, but of knowledge that one gains from reading a book. Sir Frederick Bartlett (1932), in devising a theory of remembering based on free reproduction of meaningful passages of prose, emphasized that any new act of "perceiving and recognizing" was not apt to be retained as an individual and specific event, but was influenced by and assimilated to schemata, although he did not like the term "schema," considering that it suggested too static and unchanging a concept. "An organism," he wrote, "has somehow to acquire the capacity to turn round upon its own 'schemata' and to construct them afresh" (p. 206). A new fact, in any case, becomes part of an "organized mass of experience." It is doubtful that a truly isolated fact is understood by the reader in more than a superficial way, comparable, perhaps, to being able to answer a question on a quiz show. If the fact is new and is meaningful, it is more likely to change the existing structure of the individual's knowledge and is understood in this sense, or it increases the scope of the cognitive structure, perhaps shifting relations of superordinate and subordinate structure. If one were to read in the newspaper an article about a newly discovered animal which had many of the characteristics of mammals, but was covered with feathers, he should either disbelieve it, fail to comprehend it, or reorganize his system of knowledge about mammals. The history of science is a continuing story of assimilating new knowledge by revising the system of knowledge: Spectacular cases are the Copernican revolution, the theory of evolution, and the theory of relativity, all of which encompassed known facts but assimilated them with new ones to a fresh superordinate structure, but something similar happens in a humble fashion to all of us when we learn something new.

The idea has been framed in many other ways. Olson (1972, p. 141) remarked, for instance, that "language drags a context with it that forms the frame of reference for subsequent experience"; and language, as it evolves, "is not *free* from the perceived context; it comes to reflect a wider and wider context; the context is now the present plus the historical context, not just the immediate one" (p. 148). This becomes more and more manifest as a child grows older and more capable of fitting what he reads into a constantly expanding and differentiating cognitive structure. Carroll points out as well the importance of studying how the language user (reader, let us say) processes information "in order to assimilate or integrate it with his prior knowledge or cognitive structure" (1972a, p. 14).

Chafe (1972, pp. 50 ff) speaks in a somewhat different vein of "foregrounding" a semantic unit. Certain concepts are at the moment in the mind of the reader, in "sharp focus," which puts the new information in a semantic framework that permits comprehension. "To use another metaphor, we might think of what is going on in a discourse as if it described states and events unfolding on a stage. We could then say that at any particular point in the discourse there are certain things which are 'on stage.' It is whatever is on stage that I am calling foregrounded." Foregrounding is not the same thing as fitting new information into a whole system of knowledge, but is a necessary and more immediate preparation for comprehension, rather than a kind of ensuing digestion of the new information.

Remembering

To be sure, if anything is learned from reading we assume that it must be remembered for a time at least (until it is put to the use that made it worth learning, if no longer). But if the information extracted from the text has been organized into an individual's existing system of knowledge, it stands to reason that what is eventually recalled may come out in quite a different form from the input that the text displayed. As several studies have shown (e.g., Bransford and Franks, 1971; Sachs, 1967), the surface syntax of the text may be transformed in reproduction, while the semantic content is quite faithfully retained. The learner may be able to give a perfectly adequate paraphrase of the information in different words than the presentation. We are apt to be particularly convinced, in that case, that he understood what he read and really did learn something.

On the other hand, this aspect of the process of remembering gives rise to difficulties in performing research on learning from reading. What is to be measured? What can be counted if the words themselves cannot be specified exactly? This problem requires careful consideration and will be taken up in the sections below. The measure can be quite specific if a formula, for instance, is to be recalled. But there are many cases where it is important to consider whether learning resulted in going beyond the information displayed, in a creative fashion.

Making Inferences from Text

As long ago as 1917, Thorndike, in an article called "Reading as Reasoning," pointed out that understanding even rather simple text well enough to give sensible answers about the ideas it contained is an active process of selection and even inference, demanding an appreciation of the various concepts in relation to one another.

Understanding a paragraph is like solving a problem in mathematics. It consists in selecting the right elements of the situation and putting them together in the right relations, and also with the right amount of weight or influence or force for each. The mind is assailed as it were by every word in the paragraph. It must select, repress, soften, emphasize, correlate and organize, all under the influence of the right mental set of purpose or demand. (p. 329)

He examined errors made by pupils in answering questions about the content of paragraphs, such as the following:

John had two brothers who were both tall. Their names were Will and Fred. John's sister, who was short, was named Mary. John liked Fred better than either of the others. All of these children except Will had red hair. He had brown hair. (p. 329)

The question was, "Who had red hair?" One fifth of the children in grades 6, 7, and 8 thought that Will had red hair; about two-fifths of the children in grades 3, 4, and 5 did. Words like *except* and *although* often make trouble in reading, even when the pupil knows what the words mean. Thorndike thought that children often failed not because they were unable to remember facts and principles they had read, but because they had never understood them. He thought that silent reading to find answers to questions should replace oral reading, which he believed discouraged actively making judgments concerning what pupils were reading. He concluded, "Perhaps it is in their outside reading of stories and in their study of geography, history, and the like, that many school children really learn to read" (p. 332).

Making inferences from explicitly presented concepts and seeing implications are emphasized in several of the most recent theories of comprehension which we shall consider below. Olson, for example, stresses that "new knowledge can be derived from old by reading off the implications of a proposition. Once acquired, these skills are important tools for the child's further self-education" (1972, p. 164).

Applying Knowledge from Reading

The crux of learning from reading is the ability to use appropriately what we have learned. The need can be an instant one, such as following directions for making something, like a cake or a model airplane; repairing something, like changing a tire; operating a new device, like a camera or a tape recorder; wiring something; or simply following directions to a picnic spot. But transfer of the knowledge gained to a new situation is the really important achievement. Solving new geometry problems with the use of axioms and principles previously studied is the goal of the geometry student. Restructuring one's system of knowledge through reading is only adaptive as it serves the reader's purpose in dealing economically and appropriately with a new problem. We are back to inference and, of course, to transfer, which we considered in Chapter 3. Learning from reading is for most of us a major means for the generalization of knowledge to new situations.

Application of knowledge gained from a text nearly always requires more operations than reading and understanding the words on the page. It may require inference, as would solving the geometry problem. It may also require elaboration of the facts given, perhaps in the form of imagination. Consider one of the examples of a reading task presented in the introduction: following the instructions and the illustrations accompanying a dress pattern. The illustrations are not the same size as the pattern, and sequence of fitting the pieces together, supposing one has succeeded in cutting them correctly, requires envisaging the process. How to get that sleeve in the right place? Even the illustration does not make clear the total scheme of relations and actions that result in the right sleeve in the right armhole right-side out. Visual imagery is often useful in applying knowledge, but some abstract concepts like time do not lend themselves to visualization, and yet must enter into applying principles learned from reading. The length of fixation pauses provides further evidence that the reader does not simply recognize the text but also thinks about it (cf. Chapter 10).

Learning from reading is thus not a simple matter of remembering something and giving it back to the teacher verbatim when the examination comes up. The theories of reading comprehension that we shall describe below are attempts to handle this very complex problem.

Selective Extraction of Information

The Task Set

As Thorndike stated in the quotation above, the reader must select, repress, relate, and organize under the influence of a mental set— the purpose for which he is reading. The psychologists of the Würzburg school, under Külpe's leadership, emphasized the *Aufgabe* or task one set for himself and showed its importance in many experiments. There is the famous case of the subject who sat in the laboratory before a memory drum through 40 exposures of a list of nonsense syllables, and when asked to recall them, said "Oh, I didn't know I was supposed to learn them." "Incidental" learning, as we pointed out in Chapter 8, occurs with great frequency early in life, but it is not really purposeless. "School learning" is generally highly intentional and is often contrasted with incidental learning, but the reader may have subordinate covert goals of his own.

Postman and Senders (1946) compared intentional and so-called incidental learning under the influence of various instructions. Subjects (college students) were given a passage from a short story by Chekhov to read under six types of instruction:

1. The subjects were asked to read the selection for purposes of timing, simply to see how long it took.

2. The subjects were told to read the selection carefully because they would be tested for "general comprehension" of the material.

3. The subjects were told they were taking part in a memory experiment and would be tested for the "specific sequence of events in the story."

4. The subjects were told they would be tested for "details of content."

5. The subjects were told they would be tested for "details of wording."

6. The subjects were told they would be tested for "details of physical appearance." (Some errors, such as spelling and typing mistakes had been introduced for this purpose.)

The subjects read at their own speed, but there was a time limit of 90 seconds, which was quite sufficient.

All the subjects were tested three minutes later with a multiple-choice questionnaire of 50 questions. Ten of the questions examined general comprehension, ten tested memory for sequence of events in the story, ten tested details of content, ten tested details of wording, and ten tested memory for physical details. The questionnaires were scored for the number of items correctly recognized in each category of questions, each category corresponding to one of the sets of instructions, except for the nonspecific first set of instructions (the "incidental" condition). Results for the other sets were expressed relative to this one, which was assumed to represent incidental learning, without an explicit set. The scores did vary as a function of different instructions, different categories of question, and the interaction of the two. The explicit set influenced what was learned, but other things were learned too. "Covert" sets, the authors thought, could be demonstrated and varied in relation to the explicit set.

Under instruction 1, for instance, a covert set resulted in best answers for questions testing general comprehension of the material. Their general comprehension was as good, in fact, as that for the subjects given instruction 2. But the subjects with instruction 2 remembered more about the sequence of events, though less about details of wording and appearance. On the whole, with the more specific kinds of instruction, there was a trade-off of kinds of information. Details of physical appearance were remembered well under that instruction, for instance, but at the expense of all other details. But overall, general comprehension, a kind of "omnipresent set for understanding," an "urge to make experience coherent and meaningful," was not lost. Learning and memory, the authors concluded, are never restricted totally to those materials the student has been instructed to learn.* Incidental learning does not appear to be haphazard, but is rather a general set "to understand and structure the environment."

Man does not repress or throw out, therefore, all the experience that comes his way that fails to serve his immediate purpose. On the other hand, he is selective, and if he is given a specific learning task or sets himself one, he will adapt his strategies to gleaning the relevant information and contemplating its meaning in the light of what he wants to know. Good readers are most flexible in changing their reading techniques to

*T. A. Ryan (1970, p. 187) questioned the validity of the author's main conclusion as to the selective effect of instruction on what is learned, but this last conclusion appears to us to be justified.

suit the task. There is "learning to learn" in the development of cognitive strategies, as Chapter 3 tried to show. A child does not automatically set himself to search for relevant answers and come out with them, as one can see from Thorndike's example above. But to learn effectively from reading, selection of information is essential.

What Is Extracted?

The next question is, What is it that the reader must extract? What level or aspect of information is he interested in? Words contain many kinds of information: graphic, orthographic, phonological, syntactic, and semantic. But when we talk about learning from reading, we are seldom thinking about information at the level of a single word. The units of information are larger. They are statements about events, predications, propositions—units that contain semantic and syntactic relations. If we plan to do any research on learning from reading, these units must be countable. How big should they be? How do we decide what subordinate units they should contain?

Linguistic units can be defined by empirical methods, though one may have some reservations, in that case, about their intuitive validity. R. E. Johnson (1970) had college students divide a prose narrative (Bartlett's "War of the Ghosts," 1932) into "pause acceptibility" units. A pausal location was accepted as valid when one-half the sample of raters agreed on the pause. New groups of raters were presented with the passage with diagonal slashes separating the units defined by pauses and told to eliminate unimportant units. The number of times each unit was retained in the story was considered a measure of its "structural importance" as a linguistic unit. Other subjects were then given the passage to learn for recall, reading the story twice at their own pace. A "lenient criterion" of verbatim recall was used. Recall was measured after 15 minutes, 7 days, 21 days, with essentially the same results: The "structural importance" of the verbal units was positively related to their recall. The experiment was repeated a third time using paced presentation of the material (each linguistic unit was presented once, separately, by projection) and resulted in the same essential finding. The subjects apparently decided at once what was important, and recall was affected in relation to the "structural importance" of the unit. The only difficulty with this interesting finding is that we are still left wondering exactly what "structural importance" is.

Carroll (1972a), in considering "linguistic elements," defines them as any linguistic unit that has a meaning in the sense that "one or more rules or conventions can be specified as to the relation of that unit with a concept or class of experiences developed by members of the speech-community." Examples could be morphemes, grammatical constructions, etc., with either concrete or abstract meanings. But such units could be too small to convey to the reader the information intended by a passage of discourse, and Carroll suggests that the " 'total meaning' of an utterance has to do with the relation of a sentence or discourse to its total context" (p. 12). One must perceive the meaning of the smaller units, but in the light of the larger context.

No one would deny this eminently sensible conclusion. But we are still left with the problem of the unit, if anything is to be measured. Chafe (1972), in his essay "Discourse Structure and Human Knowledge," proposes a semantic unit consisting essentially of a verb and one or more nouns standing in some relation to the verb, such as agent, patient, beneficiary (cf. Fillmore, 1968). Some kind of semantic framework does seem essential in our units of discourse if we are to talk about learning from reading, and the people who have accepted and worked on the problem of discourse structure in the very recent past all seem to take this for granted. Simmons (1972), for instance, who described a network structure to represent the meaning content of natural language statements, used Fillmore's (1968) case grammar in his analysis. "A semantic structure," he asserted, "is *a system of unambiguous representations of meaning interconnected by logical relations*" (Simmons, 1972, p. 72).

What this boils down to, as far as we are concerned, is the need for a theory of comprehension in order to specify reasonable units that give us a tool to measure comprehension. Learning without comprehension is an empty exercise in which we have no interest. Let us turn, then, to this extraordinarily difficult problem.

Comprehension and Its Measurement

What Is Comprehension?
The question "What is comprehension?" may seem superfluous since we all have an intuitive notion of what the word means. We comprehend the meaning of a word, the meaning of a sentence, or the meaning of a passage of discourse when we apprehend the intention of the writer and succeed in relating his message to the larger context of our own system of knowledge.

Some writers would insist that comprehension requires that the reader "construct" the message from the information in the text and match it to some schematic component already present in his cognitive structure. If this were literally true, it is hard to see how we could extract any new information from what we read, but would anyone deny that we do? Surface syntactic structure may be transformed by the reader to fit some simpler underlying structure, but this would only be in the service of getting at the meaning. The meaning, in the final analysis, must relate to something in the world that the message generator can comment on, with the expectation that the reader has had some experience similar to his resulting in a common lexicon, common lexical features, and specifiable relations of the kind we discussed in the previous section on linguistic units—essentially a common semantic and grammatical notation for an event. But all these features can be recombined in innumerable ways to yield new information, and the reader is faced with the task of selecting the essential information, processing the units in some sort of sequence, and relating them logically.

Paul Kolers (1970) argues that a person who knows the language he is reading perceives the concepts that the words represent and not just the words themselves. He presented evidence for this idea in experiments with bilingual subjects (Kolers, 1966). He gave French-English bilinguals passages such as the following, as well as comparable passages in all English or all French:

> Son cheval, suivi by two hounds, en marchant d'un pas égal, made resound the earth. Drops of ice se collaient à son cloak. A wind strong soufflait. Un côté of the horizon s'éclaircet; et, in the whiteness de crépuscule, he saw des lapins sautillant au edge of their burrows. (p. 359)

After they had read the passages (with equal time for each one) they were tested for their understanding. The subjects were able to understand the mixed passages as well as the ones in a single language. They were also asked to read some of the mixed passages aloud, and their errors were observed. Errors of translation frequently occurred following a sequence of words in one of the two languages, either continuing in the language just read, or making a premature transition to the ensuing sequence in the other language. These errors suggested that the readers were treating the words in terms of their meanings and the context of the passage.

William James' comments on understanding in his classic description of the stream of thought are as applicable to reading as to thinking or speaking:

Now I believe that in all cases where the words are *understood*, the total idea may be and usually is present not only before and after the phrase has been spoken, but also whilst each separate word is uttered. It is the overtone, halo, or fringe of the word, *as spoken in that sentence*. It is never absent; no word in an understood sentence comes to consciousness as mere noise. We feel its meaning as it passes; and although our object differs from one moment to another as to its kernel or nucleus, yet it is *similar* throughout the entire segment of the stream. The same object is known everywhere, now from the point of view, if we may so call it, of this word, now from the point of view of that. And in our feeling of each word there chimes an echo or foretaste of every other. The consciousness of the "Idea" and that of the words are thus consubstantial. They are made of the same "mind-stuff," and form an unbroken stream. (William James, *Principles*, 1890, Vol. 1, pp. 281 ff.)

Present-day students of the reading process are still charmed by the insights in this quotation, but those who are concerned with research on how we learn from reading feel the need for a more highly specified model which will relate aspects of content of the text such as its stylistic readability and the complexity of the ideas, the reader's task, and some possible measurable outcomes in ways that will permit manipulation of variables in an experiment. Earlier theorizing about comprehension in reading concentrated on describing potential component skills, such as understanding the literal meaning of the writer, recognizing the writer's feeling or mood, comprehending the writer's "tone" and "attitude toward the reader," and recognizing the writer's intent (see I. A. Richards, 1929). With the advent of factor analysis, tests were constructed to measure a number of presumed component skills (as many as several hundred of them were listed by one writer or another, of course with much overlapping). Tests of component skills were administered to large samples of students, correlation matrices among the tests were obtained, and the principal factors (each different from the others, it is to be hoped) that accounted for variance within the matrix were analyzed out and given names.

The most recent large-scale study of this type was performed by Davis (1968), making use of a cross-validated "uniqueness" analysis in an attempt to identify the percentage of unique variance of each of the most important measurable skills of comprehension among mature readers. The subjects tested were twelfth-grade pupils in academic high schools. Eight tests were administered, containing sophisticated and very skillfully written items, such as the following item in a test called "Following the Structure of the Content."

Only the adult male cricket chirps. On a summer night, they sing by the thousand in unison, so that the forest seems to pulsate and the tiny unseen orchestra becomes its very voice.
"Its" (last line) refers to:
A. "adult male cricket"
B. "summer night"
C. "forest"
D. "tiny unseen orchestra" (p. 512)

Davis pointed out that intrinsic validity of the items was essential; that "this study stands or falls on the psychological insight that characterized the items used" (p. 513).

The Davis study identified five skills as having a unique contribution to reading comprehension, listed in order of the extent of the variance which they predicted: memory for word meanings; drawing inferences from the content; following the structure of a passage; recognizing a writer's purpose, attitude, tone, and mood; and finding answers to questions asked explicitly or in paraphrase. The first two skills accounted for a much higher percentage of the variance than the other three. This study points up the importance of knowledge of word meanings and what Davis (1944) earlier called "reasoning in reading" and makes clear the complexity of the concept of comprehension—that it is not a "unitary mental skill or operation," as Davis put it.

Factor analysis does not provide a very good handle for experimental research on the role played by factors potentially influencing comprehension. There was, in fact, a real dearth of research in this area until two recent approaches, information processing analysis and psycholinguistics, began to yield some new models of comprehension that hold promise for future progress. Psycholinguists and linguists have become interested in the analysis not only of the sentence, but of meaningful discourse in longer passages. The current revival of interest in semantics has been particularly influential and looks as though it will provide a way of measuring meaningful linguistic units, both in presented displays and in apprehension. Although these techniques are as yet young, a number of essays following one approach or the other (or both) have been collected in a volume by Carroll and Freedle (1972) which will be drawn on to provide illustrative models.

Models of Comprehension

We shall take up first a model of comprehension which is essentially an information processing, stage model that has been described and tested both by Chase and Clark (1972) and by Trabasso (1972). To quote Trabasso, comprehension

is viewed as a set of psychological processes consisting of a series of mental operations which process linguistic information from its receipt until an overt decision: Two main operations are noted: (1) *encoding* the information into internal representations and (2) *comparing* these representations. . . . Comprehension may be said to occur when the internal representations are matched. The overt response (True) is an end result of the act of comprehension. (Trabasso, 1972, p. 113)

Stage theories such as this one assume that the sequence of processes involved takes time, so experimental manipulation of the surface structure of a sentence, given a subject and a referential event to which it has to be matched, will affect the encoding and comparison processes in measurable ways and permit tests of the hypothesis.

Trabasso gives as an example a sentence verification task in which a subject is asked to compare a sentence (e.g., "The ball is red") with a picture. He is then shown a picture of a ball which is either red or blue. The sentence may also be phrased in other ways (e.g., "The ball is not red"). The processing time can be predicted as longer or shorter depending on the number of encoding, matching, recoding (e.g., negative to affirmative) operations required, and a breakdown in comprehension could occur with a missing component link in the sequence of stages.

To give a somewhat oversimplified account of the processing sequence, the subject first reads the sentence and "encodes" it in the form of an internal representation. If the sentence is expressed as a negation, the encoding may include "false" as a separate attribute. In stage 2, the picture is encoded in a similar form. The subject must then compare the two representations to see if they match, with the possibility that some recoding may be required. In a final stage, the result of the comparison emerges as a response ("true" or "false").

Chase and Clark (1972) reported a number of experiments in which a subject matched a sentence, such as "The cross is above the star," with a picture which might or might not correspond to the statement (e.g., ⁺). Sixteen different sentence-picture displays were presented. The subject looked first at the sentence, then at the picture, and made a true or false decision, which was timed. The latencies were analyzed for a test of predictions based on encoding, comparing, and recoding variables dependent on the various relations holding between the sentence and the picture.

Negative statements were assumed to require longer encoding processing than positive ones, for instance. "Above" and "below" were assumed to have special relations such that "not below" would be transformed at some stage to "above," though it is doubtful that this transformation took place. Chase and Clark concluded on the basis of their model and experiments that comprehension of both pictures and sentences are ultimately represented in the same mental symbolic system, in which there is, rather than a correspondence, semantic identity of an abstract meaning.

In addition to the recoding or transforming type of model described above, Trabasso described another form in which the process involved change in a "truth" index as contradictions were detected (e.g., changing the form of the assertion from the negative to positive), but encoding and comparison were still the essential processes. The models were applied to some other tasks (e.g., concept identification) as well as sentence verification, but on the whole the model seems to be restricted in applicability. The operations suggested do not appear to be easily generalizable to comprehending and learning from discourse, admittedly a very tough problem.

Consider now a very general model which has turned out, nevertheless, to be useful for the problem of measuring what has been learned (and remembered) in a prose passage of considerable length, as opposed to the very short sentences in the work described above. Dawes (1966), interested in the problem of how knowledge is acquired from reading, made the assumption that meaningful declarative statements assert set relations, in particular, set relations between a subject class and its predicate class. The relations were specifically identity, exclusion, inclusion, and disjunction. The set relations embody what is said in a passage and may be expressed in more than one way, so that memory for the relations need not be specific verbal units or even a particular grammatical structure. Dawes assumed that memory or distortion of meaningful material in a passage could be measured by testing recognition or recall of these set relations. Any two sets may have only one of these relations. Two sets have a "structured" relation when knowledge that an object is a member of one of these sets may yield knowledge of whether or not it is a member of the other (e.g., identity, a "nested" relation). Consider the statements "All men wear trousers" and "Some girls wear trousers." Knowing that someone is a man automatically yields that knowledge that he wears trousers, but knowing that someone is a girl does not. The first statement is structured (nested), but the second is disjunctive. A reader, Dawes thought, will try to optimize structure, essentially the same thing as reducing information but termed by Dawes "simplification." If a reader incorrectly remembers a disjunctive relation as a nested one, he has "overgeneralized" in an effort to increase semantic structure. Dawes predicted that errors of overgeneralization would predominate over errors of pseudodiscrimination (remembering a nested relation as disjunctive and thus weakening the structure). Dawes wrote two stories, the length of an average newspaper article. For example, one was a hypothetical sociopolitical problem involving several groups of people and their interrelations in such a way that half of ten relations among the groups were nested (structured) and half disjunctive. After reading a story the subjects, college students, were given questions to answer, each question having two versions between which he must choose: one an assertion of a disjunctive relation between two sets, and one an assertion of a nested relation. The subjects were asked to think about the issues as they read the story, as if they would have to vote on them.

A sample question of the types given the subjects was as follows: "Circle the correct alternative: (a) no rancher voted for construction of the canal; (b) not all but some ranchers voted for construction of the canal" (p. 80). Thus, each question consisted of one assertion of a nested relation (a) between two sets and one assertion of a disjunctive relation (b), and the subjects had to judge which assertion was the correct one.

Dawes found that recognition of the set relations tested was considerably higher than chance. Neither did accuracy decrease after a three-day interval, when the test was repeated. Errors of "simplification" (misrecognizing a disjunctive set relation as a nested one) were significantly greater than the opposite error, so the subjects did try to optimize structure. A second experiment with recall tests yielded essentially similar results. The subjects did recall basic relations, and when they were wrong the error tended to increase the structure in the material.

Another model of comprehension was developed by C. H. Frederiksen (1972) especially for the purpose of representing connected logical discourse in terms of a structural model, so that research on comprehension might achieve quantitative expression of outcomes. First comes the problem of the unit. The smallest element of semantic content Frederiksen identified as the *concept*. A second element of content was a *relation* (simple, compound, or nested) defined on two or more concepts. The relations, he asserted, can be classified in a number of ways, such as Fillmore's (1968) case relations or order relations. A third element of content is the *implication* defined on two or more propositions (i.e., the "if . . . then" relation). The fourth and most complex class of elements is referred to as a semantic *structure*, which is composed of systems of relations and implications. Such a structure is roughly of paragraph size.

These content units are utilized in various processing events, including input processes, production processes, verification, transformation, storage and retrieval, and output expressional processes, which may vary with the context of the task given the reader. Production processes may vary from simple production (veridical encoding of the text) to inferential production and elaborative production, the latter two yielding semantic elements not explicitly present in the text.

The hypotheses sketched above (presented by Frederiksen in much greater detail) were used to construct a model of a prose passage as a logical network, and a procedure was then developed for scoring an individual's protocol following some task involving presentation of the passage. The tasks were varied, with the purpose of examining the ensuing protocol for classes of semantic elements and inferred processes that described the subjects' cognitive operations—*how* they were extracting *what kind* of information. The tasks or "contexts" chosen were predicted to select different cognitive operations on the semantic context of the passage, so the nature and extent of specific production, selection, verification, and transformation processes ought to be influenced in concert with the instructions for the task.

The passage chosen was the sociopolitical essay invented by Dawes (see above), describing a conflict of interests between several groups on a hypothetical island. Subjects in three conditions, with varying instructions were all presented with the essay a number of times via a tape recording. In Condition A, the subjects were instructed that they were to recount in writing what they had heard, but not to attempt a verbatim reproduction. In Condition B, subjects were told they were participating in an investigation concerned with solving a problem using remembered heard material; they were given a specific problem involving the essay and told to think about it as they listened. They were supposed to generate as many alternative solutions as they could and also to remember all the information in the essay. In Condition C, subjects were given the problem, as in B, but nothing was said about remembering other information in the essay. Subjects in A and B recounted the story four times (after each exposure to the text). Subjects in C recounted it only after the fourth trial. All subjects were asked to give solutions to the problem after the memory reconstruction. Thus, Condition A was considered incidental problem solving, Condition C incidental memory, and Condition B intentional learning for both. The comprehension test used by Dawes was also administered, and one week later the subjects were asked to recall the passage again.

It was expected that production processes would vary with the three conditions and change with repeated exposure. Veridical processes were expected to decrease over time relative to inferential and elaborative productions, and veridical processes were expected to appear with lower frequency in Condition C, where only a problem set was given. Figure 11-1 shows the absolute and relative frequencies of the three types of production for the three conditions. As expected, Condition A subjects (recounting what they had heard) and B subjects (alternative solutions and memory) had significantly different frequencies of inferential productions after the first trial; Conditions A and B had significantly different frequencies of elaborative productions only on the first trial, and this type of production tended to decrease; Condition C (problem solving instruction only) subjects produced lower frequencies of veridical productions on both

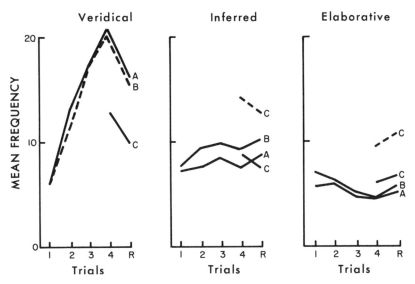

Figure 11-1. Variations in production processes (veridical, inferential, elaborative) with three conditions of exposure and repeated exposure. From C. H. Frederiksen in Carroll and Freedle, 1972, p. 229.

their recall trials than the other two groups of subjects; the three groups differed significantly in number of absolute inferential productions (solid lines in "inferred" chart); Condition C yielded more elaborative productions than the other two; and Condition C, given *only* the problem solving instructions, had a higher relative frequency of inferred productions.

As in the experiment of Dawes, the subjects tended to produce many more overgeneralizations than pseudodiscriminations, that is, these subjects also tended to "simplify" the structure when errors occurred, putting things into relation rather than fragmenting relations. The effect of instructions was very slight as regards this tendency.

On the basis of an elaborate correlation matrix, Frederiksen found that frequencies of producing veridical relations were predictable from reasoning for all the contexts he used. He concluded, "These results would appear to indicate that the generation of relational structures (other than those which are elaborative) in comprehending and remembering a text *necessarily* involves logical operations on the semantic context of the text," and ". . . the effect of the contexts was in part to induce generative reasoning processes" (p. 242).

While the subjects in Frederiksen's experiment listened to, rather than read, the passage, the conclusions are probably as applicable to reading as to listening, especially in the light of the agreement between his results and those of Dawes. Whatever comprehension is, it seems that learning at the level of comprehension involves more than recall of surface structure. It is also apparent that the adult learner, at least, is motivated by a search for structure.

Measuring Comprehension

As the studies cited in the preceding section make clear, measuring comprehension is not easy. Recall, either verbatim or free, does not suffice, and almost any measure raises questions of validity, reliability, and generalizability to any other material or task. Carroll (1972a) has an excellent classification and discussion of tests of comprehension to which the reader is referred. We shall confine ourselves here to a brief discussion of the kinds of tasks that may be used, relying chiefly on Carroll's classification and some examples.

The simplest measure of comprehension is merely to ask the reader if he understands, or how well he understands (classified by Carroll as *subjective report*). The reliability of a subjective report of understanding is highly fallible, of course, but as a quick estimate it seems to us to have its place, and considerable value. When either of us finishes writing a section of this book, the other reads it and provides an estimate of how easy it is to understand that is taken very seriously. T. V. Moore (1919) asked his subjects to press a key as soon as the meaning of a word he exposed came to them, and he was able to use the latency measure of subjective arrival of a meaning in a systematic way for experimental purposes. His subjects were highly trained adults, but this method would seem to deserve further exploration with children and with material varying along discourse parameters that could be systematically manipulated.

Reports of *truth* or *falsity* of a statement of a brief passage have been used with some frequency, but as Carroll points out, the statement may be probing the subject's previous knowledge, rather than his comprehension. Verification of a statement with an accompanying referent, such as a picture, avoids this particular difficulty (but requires that the picture be unambiguous). This technique was used in the experiments reported above by Trabasso (1972) and Chase and Clark (1972). Two statements could also be matched for equivalence, for instance grammatical transformations, or paraphrases. Construction of a good paraphrase (like an unambiguous picture) presents a problem. How close to semantic identity must a paraphrase come to be valid as an equivalent? Recognition of a paraphrase seems, intuitively, to be the essence of comprehension and might be used with success where the subject is asked to select the *best* of several paraphrases.

Following directions for performing a task has been used frequently, as Carroll points out, in intelligence tests and seems, again, an intuitively valid procedure and one with great generality. We are constantly having to comprehend and follow written instructions, ranging from following a cookbook recipe to filling out income tax forms. At varying levels of difficulty, following directions is feasible over a wide age range and depending on the task to be performed can be highly motivating (not the income tax, but perhaps a treasure hunt!).

Supplying missing words in sentences is an old task used in classic experiments on effects of set and other variables. It was once referred to by such terms as "skeleton words," but since its use by Taylor (1957) as a measure of readability it has frequently been termed the "cloze" procedure (see p. 369). The subject is simply given a passage with some blanks for missing words and asked to fill them in. Coleman and Miller (1968) performed an experiment using the cloze procedure to measure a reader's information gain from reading a passage and compared it with another procedure based on Shannon's "guessing game" technique. They were interested essentially in measuring how much *new* information a reader gained from a passage. College sophomores read and filled in a passage with 30 words deleted. Half the subjects had not read the passage before, while the other half had. The subjects who had not read the passage guessed 16.77 of the words correctly; the subjects who had read the passage filled in 18.62 correctly, an insignificant difference. The procedure was therefore not measuring information gain, but something the subjects already knew. With "bilateral constraint" (context on either side), reading the passage beforehand apparently adds little or no information. The second method presented a subject with a word and he then guessed the following word. If he guessed wrong, he was given the right word and tried to guess the next one. The measure was the number of correct guesses per hundred words. When the passage was completed, the subject went through the passage again, guessing each word. The difference in number of correct guesses on the two attempts was the measure of information gain. The mean information gain for a 100-word passage was 38.93 additional guesses per 100 words, so the method did appear to be measuring information gain, rather than mere guessing from context.

Coleman and Miller, using cloze scores as a measure of complexity, plotted information gain as measured by their second method to the calibrated complexity of 36 prose passages (see Figure 11-2). Judging from the obtained relationship, there appears to be an optimal level of redundancy (cloze difficulty) for information gain. This level fell at passages that were rated as suitable for fifth-grade students by a different measure of redundancy estimation. The curve falls for the easier passages because of a ceiling effect: there was insufficient opportunity for gain. Although the optimal level seems low for college students, it appears unreasonable to generalize unduly from the results, since there are certainly superior methods of study for yielding information gain than guessing at the ensuing word.

Coleman and Miller also used this measure of information gain for studying the effect of certain characteristics of the style of the text. Passages with a high percentage of abstract nouns and verb nominalizations (abstract nouns that are derived from verbs) had the effect of reducing information gain. Sentence length and clause length had only a low correlation

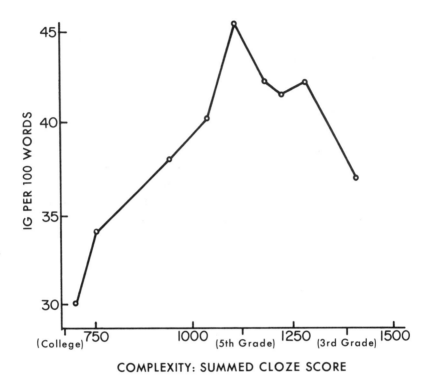

COMPLEXITY: SUMMED CLOZE SCORE

Figure 11-2. Information gain as a function of complexity measured by cloze scores. From Coleman and Miller, 1968, p. 377. Reprinted with permission of the authors and the International Reading Association.

with information gain, but number of kernels* per passage was significantly related: Passages containing few kernels were most efficient in transmitting information gain, by this measure. Completing a sentence when only a subject is given and an entire predicate must be supplied (not necessarily verbatim) comes closer to tapping comprehension of recalled material, and merges into the task of answering questions.

Answering questions based on a text previously studied or with the text itself present and available is a ubiquitous method. The questions can be in the form of sentences to be completed, multiple choices, and so on. In the latter case, the questions themselves often afford clues to the answer and "tip off" the subject. We have all heard anecdotes about the student who took the "true-false" final and passed with an A, although he had never attended the course. Recognition of material previously presented

*As defined by Coleman and Miller, kernels are "the simple units that are grammatically transformed to make more complex sentences" (p. 384).

for study can be influenced by "old" knowledge, common sense, style of wording, and other factors that may or may not get at comprehension but certainly not at learning from reading. Answering questions requiring an inference from what is being read or has been read is a good candidate and seems to be finding increasing favor as a measure of comprehension.

Reproduction or recall of a sentence or passage, either verbatim or by free paraphrase, has typically been the most frequently used task, under the assumption that the amount retained is a direct function of what was learned. Whether verbatim reproduction is a valid measure of comprehension is dubious; validity of recall by paraphrase would seem to depend on how the results are scored. Recent work, as we have seen, is progressing in the direction of defining semantic units and propositions that are meaningful, that need not be reproduced verbatim, and that can (though not easily) be extracted from a subject's recall protocol. Progress in the analysis of discourse may open up a new field for research on how (and what) people learn from reading, and in the final section on factors affecting comprehension and recall—learning from reading—it will become clear how useful such analyses can be for further research.

Factors Affecting Comprehension and Retention

In selecting wanted information from text, as the studies above show, the reader makes the best use he can of cues from sentence structure, sentence relations, and logical and semantic relations in the content. These are factors inherent in the text. Besides such factors, there are instructional devices explicitly designed to help the reader extract the essential ideas, such as sample questions for testing his understanding as he progresses through the text. And finally, there are the learning activities, more or less strategic, of the reader himself. While all these factors interact in normal reading behavior, there exists a fair amount of research directed at investigating the role of each of them, with some attempt at controlling the others. Much of this material, such as detailed analyses of programmed instruction is beyond the scope of this book, but some of it is appropriate for the kinds of problems we have been considering.

Factors Inherent in the Text

How material is written and presented in text—its style, what content is included, what is excluded in relation to the topic, and even physical features of presentation—make a difference in the ease of the reader's comprehension and consequently what he can learn. Let us consider first general *linguistic structure* or style, since the last chapter dealt intensively with syntactic features of sentences and the role they play in reading. At the level of the sentence, we know that reading behavior, that is, number and length of pauses, regressive eye movements, length of eye-voice span, and so on, is affected by several variants of sentence complexity. Some transformations of a sentence are more easily comprehended than others (Coleman, 1964), and some are learned more easily than others (Coleman, 1965). Rules for "readability" (e.g., Flesch, 1949)* can be restated in terms of specific grammatical transformations, such as a change from a sentence stated as a nominalization to an active-verb version containing two clauses. Coleman (1965) found that active-verb transformations were easier to learn than their nominalizations, active versions of a sentence easier than their passive versions, and nonembedded sentences easier than their embedded counterparts. The "simpler" version frequently resulted in a longer sentence, leading Coleman to conclude that readability is less affected by sentence length than by clause length. Coleman found no significant differences between adjectivalizations and counterpart sentences using adjectives.

Coleman's (1965) experiments used recall as a dependent variable in three cases (nominalizations, active-passive transformations, and adjectivalizations) and a cloze procedure (following one reading) for the embedded-nonembedded transformations. To what extent these measures reflect comprehensibility, or to what extent they would reflect "learnability" of material presented in passages of discourse length, is not clear, and Coleman refrains from overgeneralizing his results. He concluded that "some grammatical transformations of a sentence are more easily comprehended than others; and thus, other things being equal, a writer would be wise to choose the more easily comprehended transformation" (p. 340). He added, however, that "other things are frequently not equal."

Amount learned in a passage of 200-word length was related by Rubenstein and Aborn (1958) to readability and to the degree to which constituent words were predictable. Readability was measured by a Flesch count (Flesch, 1948) and by the Dale-Chall formula for predicting readability

---

*So-called Flesch counts of readability enjoyed great popularity about 25 years ago. An interesting article by Stevens and Stone (1947) supplied Flesch counts for a number of psychological authors with some surprising results. Koffka's Flesch count turned out to be lower (presumably more readable) than that of William James, the ideal of all psychological writers. Stevens and Stone discuss this curious result, which makes it plain that good style is more than "readability." Skillful use of vivid imagery, for instance, escapes statistical counts.

(Dale and Chall, 1948). Predictability was assessed by a procedure of giving subjects a word and asking them to guess the next, correcting them if they were wrong, to guess the next word, and so on until the passage was completed. Amount learned was obtained by instructing the subjects (college students) to memorize the passage, announcing to them the exact length of the study time, and afterward obtaining immediate recall with a measure approximating, as closely as possible, verbatim recall. The mean amount learned per minute of study time was taken as the learning score. Coefficients of correlation of the variables are presented in Table 11-1. The scores are all significantly related. The question still arises, however, how closely learning accomplished in this fashion, with exact time control and rather rigorous verbatim measurement, is related to comprehension.

What happens if the reader paces himself through the material, studying it as his own strategies dictate, and if learning is measured in some way other than by reproduction? Rothkopf (1972) questioned the validity of extrapolating from studies of the effects of meaningfulness, familiarity, complexity, and so forth on laboratory learning to learning from prose material on one's own. He pointed out that clear tests of the hypothesis that learning and reading ease are related are scarce, and that it is particularly difficult to find studies in which content is held constant while readability is varied. A study by Smith, Rothkopf, and Koether (1970) obtained data on learning for ten 1500-word passages closely matched for subject matter. The passages had been written by different authors and thus differed in structure and style. Various aspects of readability (see Table 11-2) were measured. A group of subjects read each of the passages and the amount they learned was evaluated by "stimulated" recall (short-answer questions) and by a free recall test. One content feature, the amount of irrelevant material not directly related to the instructional goal,

Table 11-1   Correlation between Readability, Predictability, and Amount Learned

	Dale-Chall Readability	Amount Learned	Predictability
Flesch Readability	.91	.61	.54
Dale-Chall Readability		.75	.60
Amount Learned			.73

Source: Rubenstein and Aborn, 1958, p. 30. Copyright 1958 by the American Psychological Association. Reprinted by permission.

varied and was measured. Amount learned was correlated with the various measured text properties. The correlations are presented in Table 11-2. On the whole, the stylistic features of the text usually considered as measures of readability did not predict learning very well. Average word length correlated —.50 with free recall, but the correlation of word length with answers to questions was only —.24, not very impressive. The most powerful predictor was the one content feature measured—the number of irrelevant or incidental facts contained. The same feature is visible in the paragraph quoted from Thorndike earlier (see p. 000) that resulted in so many erroneous answers. Rothkopf concluded that "sentence complexity and lexical factors such as frequency of use have *small* effects on what is learned by adults providing that inspection time is not limited" (p. 320).

Other aspects of style than the ones mentioned above have often been considered in manuals of style and guides for clear writing, and we have generally assumed that they promote comprehension, and thereby learning from reading. Use of "key" words, topical sentences at the beginning of a paragraph, and use of parallel structures in presenting closely linked information are examples of stylistic precepts, but we have found almost no research showing their influence on either understanding or learning. Freedle (1972) in discussing factors in comprehension points out the importance of knowing the *topic* in order to follow the gist of a spoken or written passage. He argues that the effectiveness of key words in an open-

Table 11-2 Correlations of Text Properties with Measures of Free and Stimulated Recall in Ten 1500–Word Passages Equated for Content

Text Property	Stimulated Recall	Free Recall
Reading ease (Flesch)	.28	.30
Average sentence length (words)	—.21	.03
Average word length (syllables per 100 words)	—.24	—.50
Number of technical terms	—.34	—.45
Frequency of technical terms	—.31	—.41
Type/token ratio of technical terms	.06	.08
Number of incidental facts	—.59	—.71

Source: Rothkopf, 1972, p. in Carroll and Freedle, 319. Original data from Smith et al., 1970.

ing statement varies with the size of the set of topical alternatives that might be discussed in the context. Key content words do not always signal a unique subject matter by themselves; Freedle inferred from his research that the number of words a subject had to hear (or read) to identify a topic depended on the potential number of alternative contexts. Presumably, any device that reduces the reader's uncertainty about the topic (or other aspects of the discourse) increases his chances of understanding. The fewer things a thing can be, the better our chance of identifying it. But here we can add something. If key words in a topic sentence of a paragraph do not sufficiently reduce the alternatives, there should have been a preceding preparatory context. Writers frequently take too much for granted in the "old knowledge" of their readers. They know what they are talking about and forget that they may need to lay the background (Chafe's (1972) term was "foregrounding"). One of the gravest sources of difficult comprehension for the reader in a badly written text is pronominalization without adequate foregrounding, and the greatest culprit is the word *it,* with unclear specification of the referent.

A pertinent question to ask at this point is whether a mature reader has a sense of what constitutes a paragraph and can appreciate a topical sentence so that it performs its proper role. Fortunately, a small amount of relevant research exists. Koen, Becker, and Young (1969) carried out experiments to assess the degree to which readers of several age groups could identify paragraph boundaries. They asked whether paragraphs were arbitrary semantic units or whether there might be some formal cues to paragraph boundaries. They changed the content words in a prose passage to nonsense "paralogs" (see "nonsense version" below) and had their subjects (elementary, junior high, high school, and college students) mark paragraph boundaries in both nonsense and English versions, with paragraph indentations removed. Morphological cues such as word endings that played a grammatical role (e.g., *ing, ed, s*) were retained, as was punctuation. Here are sample sentences from one passage:

English version
Sloths have no right to be living on the earth today; they would be fitting inhabitants of Mars, where a year is over six hundred days long.

Nonsense version
Smars have no mirt to be lewling on the kust retab; they would be tibbing nonetants of Ness, where a reat is over nus cantron tels dan. (p. 50)

For college students, interjudge consistency in marking paragraphs was quite high. In every case but one of the 11 passages, interjudge agreement was greater for English passages than for the nonsense verison (as high as 80% agreement). However, there was substantial agreement even on the nonsense passages, and a correlation of .71 between English and nonsense versions of the same passage, indicating correspondence of paragraph markers at common sentence junctures. Evidently both semantic features and formal markers—some sort of structural cues—contribute to perception of paragraph structure, but the authors concluded that there was an interactive, complex relation between the two.

Developmental comparisons revealed a regular increase in interjudge consistency as a function of increasing age and educational experience. The youngest age group (7–8 years old) evidently had no concept of the meaning of a paragraph and placed a rather high percentage of their paragraph markers within sentences. The correlations in the placing of paragraph markers between children and college students for English passages ranged from − .42 with the youngest group to .85 in the 14- to 16-year-old group. In the younger groups, the correlations were actually greater for the nonsense passages than for the English passages. The writer concluded that this difference is compatible with the notion that syntactic development is ahead of semantic development, but in view of our meager knowledge of the syntax of paragraph structure, one should be cautious about making the inference without replication and some attempt at manipulation of the formal structure.

Another study of paragraph analysis by Pfafflin (1967 and mimeo) investigated whether readers could identify first (topical) sentences of paragraphs and discriminate them from second sentences. She also asked whether position within the text was important, that is, whether the paragraph came at the beginning, middle, or end of an article. Adult subjects were asked to identify sentences selected from 22 articles as first and second sentences within a paragraph, and in another condition, to state whether the sentences showed links with other sentences. She found that these readers could indeed discriminate between first and second sentences of a paragraph at a level well above chance. The probability of a first sentence being identified correctly as first depended on the paragraph's position within the article. First sentences of first paragraphs were most readily identified. But the number of "linkages" perceived was greater in second sentences than in first sentences; and more were perceived in first sentences, the later the paragraphs appeared in the discourse. This finding regarding linkages is consonant with the notion of foregrounding. A linkage assumes some sort of introduction. An analysis of material underlined by the subjects as intersentence links showed a preponderance of constructions involving nouns and pronouns. A finer analysis using only words underlined by five or more subjects revealed two general types of intersentence links. They were devices for connecting sentences, such as intersentence conjunctions; or structures within the sentence, such as pronouns and relative and possessive adjectives without apparent referents, or nouns modified by the definite article.

Pfafflin's analysis shows that adult readers do possess a notion of discourse structure that enables them to judge what is acceptable style. Manipulations of discourse style relative to content potentially provide a method of studying how well subjects learn from different treatments of discourse style in relation to content. We turn now to some innovative experiments of this type.

McConkie (1973) and his students have undertaken a program of research on the memory for prose passages of considerable length. The chronological development of this program illustrates the problems considered earlier in the chapter that such research raises. What are the relevant units in the text? How are these units organized: hierarchically, in a network, etc.? What are the appropriate measures of memory and comprehension?

The first study (Kircher, 1971) prepared passages made up of sentences which judges had determined fell into related blocks. Subjects read either six related passages or mixed passages which contained a sentence from each of the six blocks. The college-student subjects read the block or mixed forms three times and wrote free recall versions after each reading. In both block and mixed conditions, recall of sentences rose significantly across the three trials, though the increases in the block version were considerably more substantial. Clustering of sentences occurred in the block passages but not in the mixed versions. In other words, when the prose was presented in a reasonably organized, meaningful structure, the readers remembered more and showed knowledge of the organization by the sentences they recalled together. Since there was no clustering in the recall of the mixed passages, any potential organization apparently was not recognized or used by the readers. Whether topic sentences come at the beginning or the end of the passage made absolutely no difference in recall. In this case, the topic sentence was simply the author's judgment about the idea under which the rest of the sentences in the passage might be subsumed.

In a second study (McConkie, 1973), again using a free recall model, the prose was given a time organization, that is, the college-student subjects heard versions which organized sets of events around time periods in the life of the hero of a story, e.g., when he went to college. This type of organization had little effect on the free recall of the prose, and the author states, ". . . what clustering there was appeared to be based largely *on semantic relationships among the units rather than the temporal sequence built into the passage*" (p. 4, italics ours).

The researchers decided that the next step was to use natural prose, retaining the complex, intricate, and often subtle semantic relationships. Two passages were divided into "idea units" which "were felt to be a meaningful piece of information . . . whether it consisted of a word, a definition or a phrase" (Meyer and McConkie, in press). The idea units were arranged hierarchically, very much like outlining the passage. This could be done with an interjudge reliability of 91.5%. Although various indices were derived from this organization of the prose passages, the two important ones for our purposes were the "hierarchy depth score," which was the unit's level in the hierarchy (main ideas stood at the top of the hierarchy), and the "units beneath score," which indicated how many items descended from a given unit in the hierarchy. Finally, each idea unit was rated for its importance to the message of the passage.

Sixty-nine adult subjects listened to the two passages three times and wrote a free recall version after each. Ideas which were high in the logical structure or had more ideas descend from them were recalled by more subjects. Where rated importance of the idea unit was related to recall, the relationship could be accounted for by the idea's position in the logical structure of the passage. If an idea was recalled, the idea logically above it was recalled 70% of the time (compared to an overall recall rate of 23%). Comparing across the three trials, idea units which were high in the logical hierarchy were most stable. Finally, in natural prose the influence of memory occured mainly on the first trial. That is, when the listener, or reader, got the meaning of the passage, repetitions added little to his recall.

The organization and unitizing of the experimental passages, though reliable, were intuitive. The authors later found that their organization agreed well with a scheme of discourse analysis being developed by a linguist (Grimes, 1972). Grimes' scheme is well summarized by Meyer (1973). Grimes' semantic grammar produces a tree structure whose nodes contain content words from the prose passage. Lines among the nodes show how the content is organized, and labels in the tree structure classify the relationships among nodes. From preliminary research, Meyer (1973) found that Grimes' discourse analysis removed some of the artifacts in the Meyer and McConkie study described above and predicted recall in a substantial fashion.

We seem to be at a promising point in the study of discourse and its recall and comprehension. Various schemes for the analysis of discourse are in early stages of development: those of Dawes (1966), Grimes (1972), Frederiksen (1972), Crothers (1972), and others. We expect progress in the area to be fast in the next decade.

It is pertinent to move from style to content at this point. Since concepts included in the content are often necessarily abstract and difficult, there is very little we can say about content and learning from reading that is not self-evident. If the content of a text is difficult, leaving style out of the picture, can anything be done to assist learning from reading the text? We have seen that one can eliminate irrelevant information, that is, stick to the point. One other device for improving the textual content if it is difficult is to provide examples and illustrations. It is unnecessary to cite evidence for the greater ease of comprehension of concrete than abstract material. Experiments abound, using nearly every dependent variable available, to show that abstract verbal material on almost any topic is harder to apprehend than concrete material. The obvious implication is not to be sparing with concrete examples. One can try to explain to a class the role of acoustic rehearsal in short-term memory and watch the words fall on deaf ears. But as soon as someone says, "Oh, you mean what you do when you look up a telephone number?" every face looks wise.

Sometimes concrete examples for very abstract ideas are hard to supply, and the message writer must rely heavily on paraphrase that makes use of the reader's old knowledge. Metaphorical paraphrase is a frequently used device, especially in science. In psychology, we can think of many examples (too many!): the telephone switchboard analogy for conceptualizing the nervous system; the plumbing analogy for some motivational conceptualizations and for ethological systems (e.g., terms like "well" and "drainage"); the digestive analogy for Piagetian concepts (e.g., "nourishment," "alimentation," and "assimilation"); "trees" and "nets" for psycholinguistic concepts. There is hardly any scientific concept or system of concepts that does not have its metaphor. Perhaps this is inescapable, considering that our fundamental source of knowledge is the world that we perceive—indeed our only source, unless we are willing to accept the notion of innate ideas.

Sometimes the message writer makes his concepts hard for the reader by inventing new terminology. Introducing new words may be essential, in order to avoid confusion with older connotations of a word that the writer wants to avoid because he is attempting to introduce a unique and novel viewpoint. He has a convenient device at his disposal, in this case a glossary. A glossary does not make the concepts more concrete, but it makes them easy for the reader to check and recheck until they at least become familiar. A well-known example of a psychologist who introduced many new terms and redefined many old ones was Tolman. In his book *Purposive Behavior in Animals and Men* (1932), he provided a glossary of new and redefined terms without which the book would have been unreadable. The definitions, wherever possible, were provided with concrete referents, as in the following:

Manipulanda. Manipulanda are the characters of objects which support (see Behavior supports) motor activity (manipulations). They derive in character from the independent physical character of the environmental object and from the response-organ make-up of the given organism. They are such properties of environmental objects as lengths, widths, weights, resistances, solidities, fluidities, etc. But they are these properties defined not as such, and in themselves, but in terms of the range and refinements of manipulations which they will support in the given organism. They are stand-on-able-nesses, pick-up-able-nesses, sit-in-able-nesses, etc., etc. (p. 448)

But "old knowledge," rather than concreteness, was also made use of:

Least effort, the principle of. This principle, which is found in numerous sciences under a variety of names, when applied to the study of behavior would assert that the final choices between alternative means-routes will always tend to occur in the direction of a minimum expenditure of physical energy.
The doctrine of the present treatise is that whereas this may ultimately be true for behavior, it has not yet been proved. At present all that can be done is to list, in each type of dimensional situation, the kind and degree of preference that have been experimentally shown. (p. 448)

Although some ideas are by their nature difficult to comprehend, style interacts with content, as we noted previously, and can be used to facilitate comprehension of content. Coleman (1964) achieved a 25.2% improvement in comprehension (answering questions after reading a long and difficult prose passage) by substitution of simpler transforms for some sentences. He thought the magnitude of improvement would vary with the reader and the material, but he concluded, ". . . still this improvement is heartening because the only changes made were in the grammatical frame of function morphemes: the content morphemes were not diluted to less technical synonyms" (p. 187).

Graphic devices have their role in clarifying both style and content. Illustrations, like examples, provide something concrete, or at least more concrete than a very abstract text. But illustrations themselves vary along a concrete-abstract dimension. A graph can be quite abstract and yet useful because of its redundancy with the text. It provides in visual form a representation of a verbal description or even a concept. The tree structures portrayed in Chapter 4, illustrating the way relations within a sentence can be represented visually, literally give the reader a picture of the structure. The practical value of nonpictorial graphic illustrations in scientific and socioscientific text is attested to by the persistent research effort of people trying to find a substitute for them for the blind.

Typographical features of the text are manipulated in newspapers and especially in advertising to catch the reader's attention and direct his gaze toward the critical part of the writer's message. Layout in newspaper and advertising design is a well-studied art, even more so by designers of books where the principles of layout are applicable. Variations in type, such as capitalization and italics, heavy print for headings, and so on, are a matter of course. Just how far their use can be carried and be of help to the student is a question for research.

Hershberger and Terry (1965) performed a study of the effect of typographical "cueing" in both conventional and programmed text on the amount learned by eighth-grade students. The text was a history lesson prepared for study in a number of versions. Three versions were prepared as conventional text, and three as programmed text with quiz sheets inserted at intervals within the lesson. The quiz sheets contained questions on what had been read (multiple-choice or completions) but no answers. If the student could not answer them, he was to turn back and seek out the answer. The principal variable was the typographical format. Each version of the text was prepared in three parallel formats. One contained no special typographical cues except those in the original version. A second version (simple typographical cueing) distinguished the essential from the "enrichment" content by color of the print. All "core" or essential content was printed in red, while the nonessential material, examples, etc., were printed in black. The third version (complex typographical cueing) distinguished five categories of rated textual importance by five variations in typography that combined underlining, caps versus lowercase, and color of type in various ways. New and unfamiliar keywords, for instance, were all in full caps printed in red. Familiar key words and statements were in lowercase, red, and underlined, and so on down to nonessential statements that were printed in black lowercase type.

The complex typographical cueing proved to be of no value in either programmed or conventional text. The test given after self-paced study included questions about both core content and nonessentials. The control groups (no typographical cueing) performed as well or better on both core and enrichment items as the complex-cued group. Simple typographical cueing (color of type) did yield a superior performance compared to both the other groups on the core content but not on the nonessential content, which was in fact inferior on amount learned. While both the programmed and the conventional text yielded significantly more learning for core items with simple cueing, the amount gained compared to normal text was not large (a gain from 15.62 to 16.56 questions correct with conventional text).

The programmed text that quizzed the subjects as they read along was superior to conventional text, no matter what the typography. Self-testing after a delay (reading a few pages) has value for learning under these circumstances. It does also when the learner tests himself spontaneously, as we saw in Chapter 3, where development of learning strategies was discussed. Including the quiz sheets increased the student's reading time appreciably (doubled it compared to the noncued format), so this device is not a case of getting something for nothing.

Devices for Enhancing Learning

The Hershberger and Terry experiment might well have been considered under this heading, for providing "quiz" or "adjunct" questions is one of the main devices for enhancing a student's learning without changing factors inherent in the text itself. A number of experiments making use of so-called adjunct questions have been performed, notably by Rothkopf and his colleagues. Rothkopf (1965, 1968, 1969) coined the term "mathemagenic" to describe "activities which give birth to learning" (1968, p. 116). These activities include attention, concentration, orientation, inspection behavior, problem solving, invention of mnemonic devices, and "other activities that resemble thinking." When the subject is learning from written materials, these activities have the function of translation, segmentation, and processing. Translation is the mechanical aspect of reading (scanning, decoding, etc.): segmentation divides the verbal material into units such as syntactic ones; and processing includes the other activities mentioned above.

A typical experiment deriving from this approach attempted to measure the effect of "test-like events" on poststudy test performance (Rothkopf, 1966, 1968; Rothkopf and Bisbicos, 1967). A special feature of the technique used was to separate the effect of direct, literal acquisition of information in response to test questions from "mathemagenic" activities produced in the subject's own behavior—essentially nonspecific transfer of training resulting from sponstaneous learning activities. Long prose passages with a heavy factual content were chosen (two chapters from Rachel Carson's book *The Sea Around Us*). A large number of short-answer questions was devised from the passage and divided into two subsets so that there was no direct transfer from answers to the questions of one set to questions of the other set. This relationship was verified by having subjects learn answers to all the questions in one set and then attempt to answer the questions of the other set. Since there was no direct transfer from this procedure, one set of questions could be used as adjunct questions during the study period and the other set used for a poststudy test to see if there was any general facilitation of learning.

An experiment was conducted as follows. Subjects (college students) read a long prose passage with two written questions interspersed after every three pages. There were three main conditions: an experimental group that had questions referring to what they were *about* to read; another that had questions referring to what they *had just read;* and a control group that had no interspersed questions. No knowledge of results other than that provided by the subject's own study was given. Following study, the subject took two tests. One measured the direct instructive effect of the adjunct questions themselves. The other administered the questions that the subject had *not* been exposed to, to see whether the interspersed questions had provided a general effect on study behavior.

Figure 11-3 shows a chart of the results on the poststudy test. The left

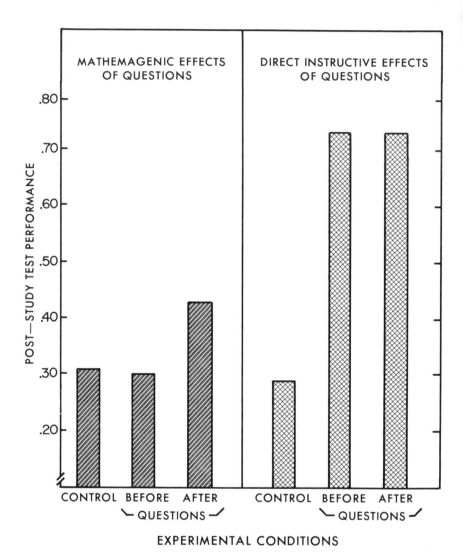

EXPERIMENTAL CONDITIONS

Figure 11-3. Results on a poststudy test comparing the effect of adjunct questions inserted during study before or after the relevant portions of text. Data from Rothkopf, 1966; figure from Rothkopf, 1968, p. 123.

half of the figure compares the results of the three groups on the test questions that were not included in the set of adjunct questions. The experimental group that had the questions following three pages of text performed significantly better than the other two groups, which did not differ. Thus only questions administered *after* the relevant portion of text "shape facilitating mathemagenic behaviors" (1968, p. 122). Both experimental groups performed better than the control group in the questions previously administered to them, as might be expected. Evidently, if the subject reads along knowing that questions are coming, but not exactly what ones, he adapts his behavior to picking up any facts that might be relevant, but if he knows the questions ahead, he limits his extraction of information to just what he needs and no more.

Biasing the experimental questions (Rothkopf and Bisbicos, 1967) was also shown to alter and limit a subject's learning. High school students took part in an experiment similar to the one just described. One group of subjects saw questions referring only to a measure like a distance or a date; another saw questions referring to common English words or technical words (e.g., *bathysphere*); and some subjects saw all types. The questions did have some biasing effect: For instance, questions about measures and names on the retention test were answered correctly more often by subjects who had been exposed to this type of question than by those who had been exposed to the other type (provided the adjunct questions had appeared after the relevant portion of text). But subjects who had been exposed to all types of questions performed just as well as the biased groups on both types of question.

The spacing of test questions in text appears to be another important variable. When there was no interval between presentation of material and a testlike event and the response belonged to a highly predictable conceptual category, the performance of the subjects was depressed (Rothkopf and Coke, 1963). It was hypothesized that the subject relied on short-term memory alone under these conditions and did not engage in active learning behaviors.

Another interesting question concerns the mode of presentation of the testlike event. Rothkopf and Bloom (1970) compared oral delivery of adjunct questions by the experimenter with written adjunct questions embedded in text. The oral question group scored higher on a criterion test (questions relevant to the text but different from the adjunct questions). The subjects were high school students. The subjects responded to the experimenter under the oral treatment and wrote an answer during the written question treatment. The interpersonal interaction was evidently effective, but the situation was not a common study one, since the subject was isolated in a booth and the material was slide-projected.

What about persistence of a subject's active learning behaviors (mathemagenic activities) when adjunct questions are administered, but omitted in certain portions of the text? Rothkopf (1968) reported results from an experiment where adjunct questions were included with portions of the text and omitted from others. Poststudy questions permitted evaluation of performances on the various portions of the text. Results from measures of both inspection time and learning showed that learning activities became less effective when questions were omitted; learning behaviors apparently degenerated without the external support.

One other experiment on the effect of adjunct questions will be cited, since the subjects were children (unlike the previously cited studies). Four age groups (grades 3 through 6) were compared (Farley and Eischens, 1971). Two passages of prose material were prepared. The content was the same for all four grades, but an easy version with short simple sentences was given the third and fourth grades. Grades 4, 5, and 6 had nine adjunct questions inserted in the first passage and six in the second (the principal test passage). A 25-question poststudy criterion test, with no items overlapping with the adjunct questions, was given immediately following the study period and once again a week later. The third grade was divided into eight groups, varying in the number of adjunct questions given them (0 to 9 in the first passage and 0 to 6 in the second). For the three older groups, performance on both poststudy tests was better when adjunct questions had been inserted in the study passages than when no adjunct questions had been administered. The pattern of results for the third grade was unclear. Only one group (with nine adjunct questions in the first passage and three in the second) was better than one other (not the group that received no adjunct questions at all). There was some indication that adjunct questions can be inserted with density too great to be of optimal value (see also Frase, 1969a).

Little has been said about the *type* of adjunct question interpolated during the reading of a passage. Obviously, what the subject is asked, or what he is told to do, could play an important role in what and how much he learns. Watts and Anderson (cited in Frase, 1972) found indications that questions which required the application of principles to new examples

yielded better posttest performance than questions which required identification of names. Application of knowledge to new examples is a time-
honored teaching method, for at least two good reasons: It calls attention
to the important principles, and it requires the student to test his comprehension.

A few devices for enhancing learning in addition to questions relating to
the text have been investigated. Kulhavy (1972) presented subjects with
prose material in which "testable units" were either underlined or deleted completely with black ink. These items were included in a criterion
test along with as many others which had not been cued in any way. The
deleted items appeared again elsewhere in the same paragraph, so that the
subjects had some basis for supplying the missing item other than guessing
from context. There were three types of instruction. Subjects in the *overt*
condition wrote the cued items (both underlined and deleted) on the bottom of the instruction page as they read. Subjects in the *covert* condition
were told to read the material and pay attention to the cued items. Control subjects read the unaltered passage. Only one group, the subjects who
received covert instructions and the text with underlined items, performed better than the others on the criterion recall test. Making the overt
response while reading apparently disrupted the reading process. Deletion of an item, even when the subject was not required to do anything
about it, did not increase his learning activities.

The effect of giving subjects a short title or theme for aiding them to
comprehend a prose passage was studied by Dooling and Lachman (1971)
and Dooling and Mullet (1973). Two short stories of 77 words were constructed, each having a familiar theme (e.g., Christopher Columbus
discovering America). Grasping the theme was made difficult by the choice
of words (e.g., instead of naming the three ships that made the voyage,
the passage referred to "three sturdy sisters"). Three versions of each passage were concocted: one in correct syntax with intact sentences; one with a
random phrase arrangement; and one with a random word arrangement.
The words were printed separately on individual cards. Half the subjects
were told the theme and half were not. Reading rate was paced by clicks,
one word every 1.5 seconds. After reading, the subjects were tested by free
recall or by a recognition test (whether a word had appeared in the text
or not).

Both foreknowledge of the theme and syntactic constraint increased the
amount recalled. With the recognition test, foreknowledge of the theme

made little difference in overall performance. However, if only words closely related to the theme were considered, more words were correctly recognized by the group that knew the theme, especially when the material had been presented in correct sentence order. Dooling and Mullet (1973) performed a similar experiment, presenting one group of subjects with the title before they read the passage, a second with the title after reading the passage, and not giving a third the title at all. Free recall after reading the passage was superior for the group given the title before reading the passage. The other two groups did not differ. To aid recall, the theme had to be available while the subject was reading, so improved comprehension while reading was probably the source of facilitation.

A motivational device for increasing rate of reading is to reward the reader for speed or accuracy. One study found that extrinsic rewards for speed increased reading rate 50% while maintaining the same level of postreading test performance (McConkie, Rayner, and Meyer, 1971).

Another study combined payoff conditions with various types of postreading questions (McConkie, Rayner, and Wilson, in press). Undergraduate students read six passages matched for readability. The experimental variations involved the types of questions following the passages so that each subject answered a series of only one type of question. The questions were:

1. Factual questions designed to test specific information explicitly mentioned in the text.

2. Number questions that tested retention of numerical information.

3. Structure questions, such as the point at which a particular topic was mentioned in the text and the relative amount of time devoted to the topic.

4. Higher-order questions A: The reader was asked to give a title and the author's main point.

5. Higher-order questions B: The reader gave a title, the main point, and answered three other questions that required inferences from the text.

6. Recognition questions in which the reader had to recognize whether a word or phrase had appeared in the text.

A seventh combined group received one question from each of the six types. The subject was told whether his answer was correct and in addition he was given points, later negotiable for money, for the speed at which he achieved a correct response. Following the sixth passage, all subjects received the same final test made up of five questions of each of the six types.

On the last passage, subjects reading for number information read more quickly than any of the other groups, whereas higher-order and combined questions led to the slowest reading. The groups did not differ in their final overall test performance in terms of number of questions answered correctly. It might be expected that after reading the first passage and its test questions, the students would read selectively for the type of information required in the test, since Rothkopf and Bisbicos (1967) found that adjunct questions produced learning consonant with the category of the question. However, in the present study the groups did not necessarily excel in answering questions on the type of information for which they had been reading. Interestingly, subjects who were reading in order to make inferences about the material adopted a strategy of noting factual details, perhaps planning to make inferences from the details at the point of the question, or because inferential questions provide very little guide for selective reading.

In a subsequent experiment the authors (McConkie et al., in press) tried to deemphasize speed by paying the subjects for correct answers regardless of speed. It is not surprising that they then read more slowly and received higher scores. There was no specific pattern of memory due to the nature of the questions. The slower rate permitted the readers to pick up more incidental information in addition to the types toward which the questions were pointing them.

The foregoing experiments have all attempted to influence the subjects' learning activities during reading. We return finally to the question posed first in Chapter 3: What cognitive strategies does a person employ spontaneously in reading, assuming that he wants to learn something? We can answer this pretty well by thinking about our own reading behavior. We look for key words, topic sentences, and summary sentences and perhaps underline them (when we own the book). We write key terms in the margins. We make outlines and take notes. Smirnov and Zinchenko (1969) reported a number of investigations of semantic grouping by school children during study. Smirnov had students ranging from the second grade up study and try to remember texts with differing structures and lengths. He found no conscious semantic grouping at all in second graders and little in pupils of grades 4 and 6. By eighth grade the pupils used a number of devices for remembering, with more purpose and awareness. Intelligent semantic grouping occurred earlier, he found, but not consciously. Active involvement and awareness of the economy of classifying by meaning is the process that matures. We have observed before the role of "consciousness raising" in phonological perception and in awareness of grammar. Something similar happens with comprehension of meaning as well. The child understands what is meant, but he does not know that he can do something deliberate and economical with this knowledge. As Smirnov put it, ". . . although it is within the capabilities of the school-children, semantic grouping has not yet become a technique for remembering. . . . Semantic grouping of ungrouped text is accomplished with exceptionally great difficulty and requires the help of the experimenter even for many older pupils" (p. 480).

Inference as an outcome of reading was referred to in the previous chapter in the discussion of development of comprehension in the transition from beginning to skilled reading. Frase's (1972) work was especially pertinent. Frase has performed similar experiments with adult readers, asking to what extent the reader goes beyond the information in the text. In addition to reading statements in the text, how often do readers combine these items of information in new and useful ways? Frase spoke of *levels of knowledge* as the outcome of combining processes. Level 1 would be only information given in the text. Level 2 required processing two sentences from the text to make an inference, and so on. In a typical experiment, a passage was constructed from which a number of levels of inferential statement could be generated, and the reader was tested after reading the passage by asking him to judge whether or not a statement followed from the passage.

Several passages were given subjects to read, with sentences typed above them. The subjects were asked to judge whether the sentences were valid conclusions while reading the passage. After completing all the passages, the material was removed and the subjects were asked to write down everything they could recall, including any inference they could generate. In some cases, recognition tests were given as well, including both valid and invalid assertions made by combining verbal classes in the text. Results on the recall test showed that many more first-level assertions (ones requiring only one sentence) were produced than assertions requiring an inference from two sentences, and the higher level of assertion, the fewer were cited in the recall protocols. The subjects were able to produce sentences that were in the text, but they generated very few higher-level assertions.

Two experiments studied the effect of having the subjects verify statements at different levels of complexity while reading. Both indicated that more of the text was recalled as the level of the statement to be verified increased, probably because more of the text had to be reviewed to verify a higher level of inference. But there was a strong trend to produce more statements from the text than inferential assertions, and the level of the statement to be verified during reading had little effect on this difference. Figure 11-4 illustrates both these trends. The scores for number of inferences recalled appear very low in light of the fact that subjects were exposed to them at the time of reading.

The method of testing could, of course, make a difference, and Frase found in other experiments that there was a difference between recognition and recall when subjects were asked to judge the validity of text assertions and inferential assertions, recognition being superior. Analysis of the

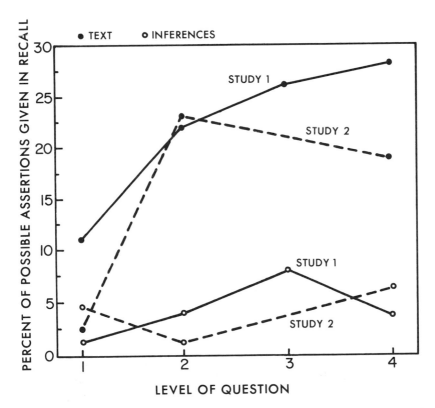

Figure 11-4.   Production of text and inferential assertions as a function of question level. Data from Frase, 1969b; figure from Frase, 1972, in Carroll and Freedle, p. 344.

textual items recalled shows that the problem (statement to be verified) did have an effect on recall, however, since the items recalled most frequently were components of the solution to a problem. Frase also investigated sentence order and its relation to inference and recall, depending on whether a good or poorly structured text was presented to the subject. Better structured text did result in better combination and judgment of assertions. Frase best summarizes his own findings:

It was also clear that organizing a text to facilitate linkages among related sentences was likely to influence higher-level learning outcomes. In general, readers infrequently produced sentences that went beyond the text, but if the structure was made apparent in some way, then *S*s produced as many (or more) higher level assertions as text assertions. (Frase, 1972, p. 348)

Thus not only the amount of knowledge a reader acquires but the kind of knowledge he acquires can be influenced by the structure of the text he must learn from. The better the structure of the text, the more likely the reader is to engage in learning activities that involve inference from the assertions presented.

Two types of potentially spontaneous learning activities that a reader may engage in have been described—classifying or semantic grouping, and inference from the textual assertions. A third type is equally important—adapting one's reading style to the difficulty of both the content and structural features of the text. Rothkopf (1972) has investigated the ability of the reader-learner to adapt his inspection activities to features of the text. Two versions of a lengthy passage about Thailand were constructed with the content essentially the same, but readability was varied by changing the average sentence length and the average number of syllables per word. Half the subjects read the first 10 of 19 paragraphs in the normal version and half read them in the difficult version. Half of each group was then switched to the other version, but half finished the passage in the same version it began with. Each paragraph was presented on a photographic slide and the subject's (self-paced) inspection time recorded for each slide. A test was administered after reading.

Figure 11-5 shows the results for rate of inspection. The normal (easy) passage for the first 10 paragraphs was inspected much faster than the difficult passage. Subjects were able to adapt themselves to the difficulty of the style by changing their reading speed. But when both groups were inspecting a normal passage (trials 11–19, right-hand panel), the subjects

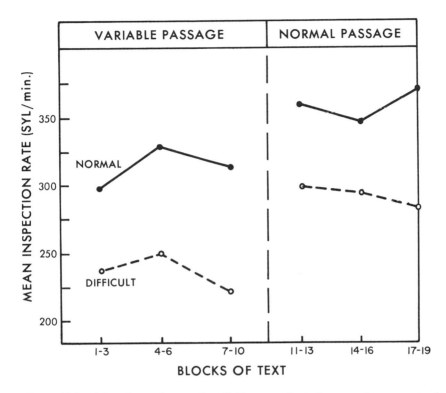

Figure 11-5.   Mean inspection rate in syllables per minute for successive segments of of text. The data in the lefthand panel are for two groups inspecting text of unequal difficulty. In the right-hand panel, both groups are inspecting the same text of average difficulty. From Rothkopf, in Carroll and Freedle, 1972, p. 323.

who started with the difficult passage, although decreasing their inspection time, did not reach the rate of those who began with the normal easier version. In other words, there was some tendency to persist in the rate, despite considerable adjustment. But these subjects, on the posttest, also had learned somewhat better than those who began with the normal easier form.

The adaptability of the reader will be emphasized again in the next chapter on theoretical models of the reading process. Skill in adjusting reading to content and style must interact as well with the reader's purpose, which is often that of learning, but by no means always.

Summary

One of the major purposes of a reader is to learn from the text. Learning from a text does not mean rote memory, or even the kind of verbal learning that has been studied in the laboratory in recent years. Many processes are involved. First, the reader must extract the relevant information—what he needs to know. What he has selected must then be assimilated to his previous knowledge and fitted into the system in a meaningful way. He is then in a position to remember it easily and retrieve it when it is wanted. Learning from reading often requires thinking and making inferences if true comprehension is the goal. And the essence of learning from what we have read is the ability to use the information on a new occasion and in a new context.

Selective extraction of information, the reader's first task, implies that he knows what he wants, has a "set," and is reading with an intention in mind. Instructions have been shown to influence what a reader learns, but he may pick up some incidental information, too, depending on how specific his set is. What the reader extracts, in terms of descriptive units, is hard to define. The problem of defining something like a unit of knowledge can only be coped with by arriving at an acceptable theory of comprehension.

Some recent theories of comprehension were discussed, chosen from their competitors because they have been tried out with experimentally manipulated variables. If we are to do research on learning from reading, we need a theory of comprehension that tells us what units to measure as dependent variables, as well as what independent variables to manipulate. Two types of models of comprehension are currently being developed, one deriving from information processing analysis and the other from discourse analysis—essentially a linguistic approach. Examples of both were given: Studies by Trabasso and Clark to illustrate an information processing approach, and those of Dawes and Frederiksen to illustrate models generated by analysis of connected logical discourse which, if they can be sufficiently refined and specified, offer great promise for research. Experiments deriving from each of the models were described.

Measurement of comprehension has been attempted in many ways, most of them related to the researcher's concept of the unit of information he should be interested in. The tasks used include subjective report, judgments of truth or falsity, following directions, supplying missing words, and recall, either verbatim or paraphrased, cued or noncued. All the measures require careful assessment of their validity as measures of comprehension.

The major and final section of the chapter was concerned with factors that affect comprehension and retention, particularly those that have the potential of facilitating learning from reading. These factors can be usefully divided into two broad classes: factors that are inherent in the text itself, and devices supplied by a programmer (instructional devices) or activities that the reader engages in for himself. Factors inherent in the text include linguistic style, earlier described as readability but more recently described in terms of linguistic concepts such as grammatical structure (e.g., use of one surface transformation rather than another). The structure of discourse beyond the sentence, such as paragraph structure, has been shown to be important for comprehension, but so far, studies of it are scarce, especially studies of passages of discourse longer than the paragraph. Those so far available agree, however, that while learning is affected by style of discourse in lengthy passages, semantic relations play a very heavy role.

Content—what is said—obviously plays a role in learnability. Some ideas are inherently more difficult than others, perhaps because of their abstractness. Concrete examples, illustrations, and metaphor should help, if we can extrapolate from laboratory learning, where imagery has been brought in as an aid to remembering. Typographical features of text also presumably help in directing the reader's attention to important ideas and concepts.

Instructional devices for enhancing learning, such as adjunct questions inserted at intervals in the text, have received considerable study, and it is clear that they can be helpful, with certain reservations. Facilitation by "test-like events" inserted during the reading process is most likely to result if the tests do not occur too frequently, and if they *follow* rather than precede the relevant material.

Learning from reading is also importantly (probably most importantly) influenced by sponteneous activities of the reader. These activities include classifying (semantic grouping); inference from statements given in the text; and adapting reading style and speed to the nature of the text—its relative difficulty of content and style—and to the reader's purpose. These strategies appear to characterize only a truly mature reader, and further study of how they are developed is needed.

12

Models of the Reading Process in the Mature Reader

Miss Marple gave her attention first to the main news on the front page. She did not linger long on that because it was equivalent to what she had already read this morning, though possibly couched in a slightly more dignified manner. She cast her eye down the table of contents. Articles, comments, science, sport; then she pursued her usual plan, turned the paper over and had a quick run down the births, marriages and deaths, after which she proposed to turn to the page given to correspondence, where she nearly always found something to enjoy; from that she passed on to the Court Circular, on which page today's news from the sale rooms could also be found. A short article on science was often placed there, but she did not propose to read that. It seldom made sense for her.

Agatha Christie
*Nemesis**

Can There Be a Single Model for Reading?

How Miss Marple reads the *London Times* may seem an odd way to begin a chapter on what a skilled reader does. But the description exemplifies, however quaintly, some of the chief points we want to make in this chapter. A skilled reader is very selective. Sometimes he skims, sometimes he skips, and sometimes he concentrates. He plans his strategy ahead, suiting it to his interests, to the material, and to his purpose, which may be entertainment, searching the want ads for a job, reading someone else's text while typing it, cramming for a quiz, or completing a *Double-Crostic*, to name but a few of a million or so possibilities. He doesn't read in the pure sense of performing a unique process composed of decoding and comprehending; he thinks, he remembers (often he forgets, quite deliberately), and he constantly relates what his eye is dwelling on to what came before, what will come next, and to his own experience. In other words, there is no single reading process.

If there is no single reading process, but instead many reading processes, there can be no single model for reading. Either one must construct many models, or instead take a different approach, seeking for some general principles that will apply, given the many variables of task and information to be considered. The latter strategy is the one we have adopted. It will be described later in the chapter, after presenting two types of model which are more orthodox and will serve to contrast with it. These two classes of model are information processing (stage) models, and models that emphasize analysis by synthesis (sometimes referred to as the "guessing-game" model).

Information Processing Models of Reading

We have made references to information processing analyses in earlier chapters. Speaking generally, an information processing analysis assumes that any cognitive task can be understood by analyzing it into stages that proceed in a fixed order over time, beginning with sensory input and ending with some sort of output or response. Feedback loops can be inserted at any point in the chain. These models are essentially a special class of theory and may be of varying degrees of complexity. The very model of an information processing model of reading is one proposed by J. Mackworth (1971, 1972), since it includes, broadly, many of the concepts used by information processing theories. Figure 12-1 is a diagram of Mackworth's model, the boxes indicating specific stages labeled according to the process assumed to be taking place and the arrows indicating the direction of the process which is always to some extent sequential (although a few things may be assumed to go on in parallel) and therefore can lead to inferences about processing time.

To summarize the model very briefly, a visual stimulus input during a single fixation pause is calculated to last approximately 250 msec, providing a *sensory visual trace* with parallel processing (not indicated in the diagram) of elements, whatever they may be, of the input. Recognition of the input results from matching it to a memory trace of the word and leads to an *iconic* image calculated to last for a second or longer. Meanwhile, recognition of the word, because of the way it has been learned, involves mediation of the *articulatory* system, and thus a match to an articulatory-neural representation. This matching, according to Mackworth, gives meaning to the written word. (However, in the adult reader the acoustic and articulatory activity may disappear, she believes.)

Words are *coded* from the iconic store into short-term memory by these verbal motor programs. Short-term memory may last for several seconds, but new input soon erases it. The content of short-term memory is stored in *long-term* memory, or else it is lost. Meaning is stored in long-term memory at all verbal levels (word, sentence, etc.), and predictions or expec-

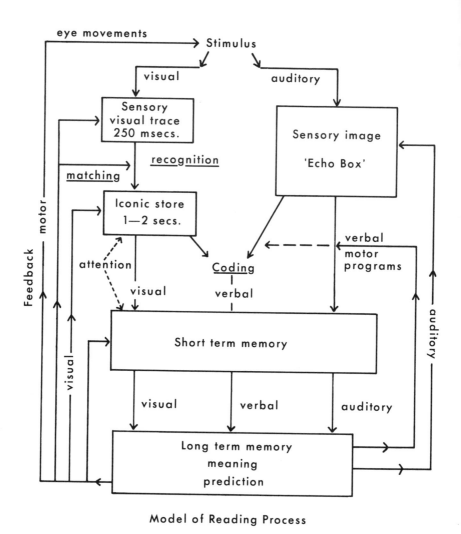

Model of Reading Process

Figure 12-1. An information processing model of the reading process. From Mackworth, 1971, p. 8–74.

tations of what will come next are aroused, providing feedback loops that may influence eye movements (new fixations) and the processing of succeeding information.

Mackworth (1972) summarizes research relating separately to the various stages in her diagram in some detail. However, the model is a very general one and does not seem to lend itself as well to specific predictions for research as some others do, so we shall describe two other models of the same class that have led their authors to rather specific predictions and experiments.

Rubenstein's Model of Word Recognition

In order to make specific predictions, a model must be limited to a very small segment of what we usually think of as the complete reading process. The Rubenstein model (Rubenstein, 1971; Rubenstein, Garfield, and Millikan, 1970; Rubenstein, Lewis, and Rubenstein, 1971a, b) is specifically a model of visual word recognition and does not pretend to be a model of the total reading process. It aims to take account of factors that are known to affect word recognition, such as word frequency, legality of orthography, phonology, homography, and so on (see Chapter 7).

The model involves four processes:

1. Quantization: ". . . the division of the stimulus into segments and the assignment of these segments to letters and phonemes" (Rubenstein et al., 1971b, p. 646).

2. Marking: A process occurring when a quantization output (e.g., *st* when a word such as *stab* was presented) distinguishes some subset of lexical entries as being in agreement with it. Lexical entries like *stab, stew,* and *stir* might be marked.

3. Comparison: Comparison of the subsequent quantization outputs with the marked entries. That is, the process continues with further quantizing and marking.

4. Selection: When the output "contains enough information to eliminate all marked entries but one, the search is over. If, however, more than one marked entry remains, these remaining marked entries would have to be compared against a third quantized output" (Rubenstein et al., 1971b, p. 646).

It will be noted that the central assumption of the model is that there *is* an internal lexicon with entries consisting of words (the possibility that the entries are morphemes is considered, but it would complicate the model considerably), and that this lexicon must be consulted in order to recognize a word. Word frequency is assumed to affect the order in which entries are marked, with the more frequently occurring entries marked earlier. Homographs have the advantage of multiple representation at the marking stage and so should have an advantage for early recognition.

A number of experiments were generated by this model and serve to flesh it out in more detail. The method used in all the experiments was to expose a string of letters before the subject with the requirement that he decide whether or not the display was an English word. He pressed a "yes" key if he thought it was a word and a "no" key if not. The latency of his decision was the dependent variable. The subject was not asked to identify the word before making his decision. In the first experiment (Rubenstein et al., 1970), the subjects were presented with half English words and half nonwords that followed English orthographic and phonological rules. The words and nonwords were four or five letters long and varied in homography, frequency, and abstractness-concreteness. Each homograph had two or more meanings (e.g., *bulb,* as in *light bulb* or *tulip bulb*). Mean accuracy of the judgments was over 95%, but latencies for deciding that a nonword was nonsense were long, considerably longer than the decision latency for any of the classes of real words. Reaction time decreased significantly with word frequency; it also decreased for homographs as distinguished from words with a single meaning, and the more meanings the homograph had, the lower the latency. This is an especially interesting finding, in view of the fact that the frequency count for the homographs included all the versions of meaning, so the word frequency did not go up as the number of meanings increased, suggesting that the meaning itself— the semantic information—was being accessed.

A further experiment (Rubenstein et al., 1971a) replicated the finding that deciding that a word was English rather than nonsense was faster when the word was a homograph rather than a nonhomograph. The experiment showed further that the meanings of the homograph had to be equiprobable for a significant effect to occur. This result led the authors to state in their model that lexical entries were marked in order of frequency of occurrence of the particular meaning covered by that entry. Where meanings are equipotential, the greater the likelihood would be that their entries would be present in the marked set simultaneously and thus yield redundant information for recognition.

Another experiment (Rubenstein et al., 1971b) sought to discover whether phonemic recoding (auditory or articulatory) occurred during word recognition. The same procedure was used as in the previous experiments, but besides the English words, the nonsense words were of three types. One type was legal, both phonologically and orthographically. A second type was illegal both orthographically and phonologically (e.g., *likj*). These nonsense strings were all constructed by placing an illegal consonant cluster in a final position. The third type consisted of orthographically illegal strings that the authors considered pronounceable (*gratf, lamg*), again constructed by placing an orthographically illegal cluster in final position. The major finding was that the legal nonwords required considerably longer for a decision than either type of illegal nonword (on the order of 100 msec). Thus deciding that an illegal nonword is nonsense does *not* require an exhaustive search through the lexicon, even when the illegality does not occur until the final cluster. The pronounceable but orthographically illegal nonwords yielded slightly longer latencies (a mean difference of 15 msec) than the words that were both orthographically and phonologically illegal, leading the authors to conclude that phonemic recoding did occur in the quantization stage. Walker (1973) confirmed the fact that increasing pronounceability increases the time required for categorizing a nonword as such.

Would homophonic nonsense words (ones that sound like real words but have incorrect spellings, such as *brane* for *brain*) increase latency as compared to legal nonhomophonic nonsense words? The authors thought that this would be the case, due to phonemic recoding and consequent false matches. Homophony was a significant variable, yielding a longer decision time. Sounding like a real word appeared to make a difference. Let us remember, however, what kind of decision the subject had to make ("Is it a word?"). With other types of judgment in word recognition experiments, it is not at all clear that acoustic or articulatory processes play a role (Gibson, Shurcliff, and Yonas, 1970; Baron, 1973; Baron and Thurston, 1973; see Chapter 7).

Real word homophones (*yoke, yolk*) were also compared to real word nonhomophones. Homophony increased latency. The fact that there was a similar sounding but orthographically inappropriate entry delayed recognition, causing the authors to conclude that "it is the phonemic form of the stimulus and of the representation in the internal lexicon that are compared to achieve the recognition of a word even when that word is presented visually" (Rubenstein et al., 1971b, p. 651).

There is one aspect of the data in these experiments that throws great doubt on the model. That is the fact that unpronounceable, orthographically illegal nonsense words actually required *longer* for a decision than did real English words (876 msec for illegal nonsense words versus 810 msec for reasonably high frequency words). If there is phonemic recoding at the quantization stage, why doesn't the subject realize instantly that the totally illegal string cannot possibly be a word and stop searching his lexicon? The authors state that

> to persist in the claim that the recognition of illegal nonsense words is accomplished during the quantization stage we must accept the notion that completing the quantization and detecting the illegality takes more time than the complete set of recognition stages. . . . (p. 654)

Now how can this be? In our opinion, it suggests that a mature reader faced with a word he is familiar with proceeds directly to higher-order structure or meaning and either does not "quantize" at all or does so at the same time. Even though "quantizing" might be slower with impossible words, discovery of illegality should terminate the process and eliminate lexical search, according to the Rubenstein model.

The same result with real, possible, and impossible word stems was found by Snodgrass and Jarvella (1972), using the same type of judgment. Thus a quantizing stage model, applied invariantly to any type of word or nonword display, loses credibility. However, results consonant with a two-stage model (processing for lawfulness, followed by lexical search) were found by Stanners, Forbach, and Headley (1971). They displayed only three-letter combinations: a real word (e.g., *sat*); a legal nonword of the CVC pattern (e.g., *sut*); and an illegal nonword, always a CCC pattern (e.g., *svt*). The initial and terminal consonants were the same for the three counterparts of each set. The judgment was the same as in the previous experiments. The mean latency for the CCC (illegal) patterns was much the fastest, words were next, and legal nonwords were slowest.

What could account for the discrepancy between these results and those of the other two experiments? It seems likely that the subjects in the Stanners et al. experiment adopted a different strategy, despite the fact that the judgment was the same ("Is it a word?"). The illegal strings in the Stanners et al. experiment contained no vowel at all. English spelling patterns for the syllable are always vocalic, built around the vowel (see Chapter 6). The subject would quickly notice that a sizable proportion of the displays were nonvocalic and would need only to glance at the middle letter to reject them. In the other two experiments, all the letter strings, including the illegal ones, contained a vocalic center (e.g., *crazj*, one of the illegal strings from Rubenstein et al., 1971b) and could not be so easily discarded. The point is that a string of letters arranged in word form potentially contains many kinds of information—orthographic, phonological, semantic, syntactic, morphological (the Snodgrass and Jarvella experiment attached prefixes and suffixes to the three classes of stems)— and the task determines what kinds get processed and in what order. We shall return to this point later in the chapter. Instructions determine the task (subjects were told to look for semantic information here), but the subject adapts to the task in his own way, using the most economical possible strategy. It was unnecessary for the subject to search for semantic information in the absence of a vowel. That he treated the CCC strings differently than the others is attested to by the fact that the frequency of initial and final consonants (in those places) affected the latencies of the words and the CVC patterns, but not the CCC patterns.

The experiment of Stanners et al. (1971) was replicated by Novik (1973), with a new twist. He included two classes of CCC patterns, one class forming meaningful initials (e.g., *LSD*). The meaningless CCC pattern had a much shorter latency than the CVC nonword pattern, but it was also slightly shorter than the patterns of all-consonant meaningful initials. Although they were not words, the meaningful initials possessed semantic markers, and the meaning did not pass entirely unheeded. Novik concluded that the subjects were able to analyze the meaning of the stimulus without first evaluating its phonological properties. However that may be, it is clear that what may appear to be small differences in the constitution of the verbal display can change the subject's strategy and rule out a model that affords no leeway for varying the processing.

Gough's Model

Gough (1972) calls his model "one second of reading," and the name is a precise fit. He follows the reader's processing of the information on the page from the beginning of an eye fixation to the emergence of a spoken word in literally split-second intervals. The word is uttered at the end of the second. The contents of each of a number of proposed stages of processing that occur in between the fixation and the utterance are specified in a very detailed table, at 100-msec intervals. "On the outside," as Gough puts it, "the Reader has rotated his eyes a few millimeters and he has begun to move his mouth. But on the inside, there has been a rapid succession of intricate events. Clearly, this succession could only be the product of a complex information processing system" (p. 341).

What these events are assumed to be is best described with reference to a diagram of Gough's model (Figure 12-2). The visual stimulus perceived by the reader is transformed first to an *icon,* which Gough assumes to be a "precategorical" visual image (composed of bars, curves, angles, etc.), capable of holding up to about 20 letter spaces. Its formation requires about 100 msec, and it will last about 250 msec, when new information will crowd it out. Letter recognition follows, within this 250-msec interval. Letters are identified one by one during this interval, serially from left to right, at a rate of about 10 to 20 msec per letter. Gough defends this assumption of serial processing of letters (reading letter by letter) with several arguments: that recognition latency increases steadily with word length in letters (Stewart, James, and Gough, 1969); and that deciding whether a given letter string is a word or not takes longer as the length of the string increases (Gough and Stewart, 1970). The assumption is counter to the generally accepted current view, for which we have provided evidence in earlier chapters, that the mature reader does not as a rule read letter by letter. Gough provides a scanner which can resort to pattern recognition routines for recognition of the letters, which are then deposited in a "character register."

How do the letters, after that, get "mapped onto entries in the mental lexicon"? Gough considers the specification of this mechanism as the fundamental problem of reading. Does the reader proceed directly to meaning? Does he make use of some orthographic rules to convert the characters to speech and then listen to himself? Gough considers and then discards both these possibilities in favor of the notion that characters are transposed into a string of "systematic phonemes" which are abstract entities related to phonetic segments by means of a system of phonological rules. These abstract entities are assumed to give direct access to the lexical representation which is, presumably, a word. Orthography (as argued by Chomsky) reflects this abstract representation, so things are dovetailing pretty neatly. A decoder with access to a code book is provided to take care of this process.

The abstract phonemic representation is now stored on a phonemic tape to await the next process, lexical search. A librarian with access to a lexicon takes care of this, using up another 100 msec or so. The latter calculation was arrived at by Rohrman and Gough (1967) in an experi-

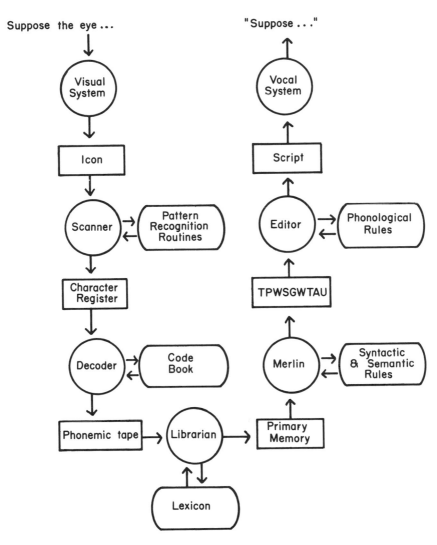

Figure 12-2. "One second of reading," an information processing model by Gough. From Gough, 1972, p. 345.

ment in which subjects were asked to make a decision as to whether two words were synonymous. Providing one of the words in advance reduced decision time by about 160 msec. The inference was that the time was saved because the search for meaning of one of the words had been eliminated. The words are understood, Gough assumes, serially, one at a time from left to right. This assumption is one of the more questionable ones underlying his model, since a large number of words have more than one meaning and require phrase or sentence context to disambiguate them. Consider the meaning of *light* in the following sentences:

The plane will light on the runway.
The cake was light as a feather.
Turn the light on.
It's time to light the fire.
The girl had light brown hair.

Gough is perfectly aware of this fact, of course, but thinks that disambiguation takes place only after lexical search. The lexical items (with the first meaning recovered) are then deposited temporarily in primary memory, one by one, already with word status including phonological, syntactic, and semantic information.

Primary memory, according to Gough, is the "working memory for sentence comprehension" and interacts somehow with the "comprehension device," a mysterious operator possessed of syntactic and semantic rules and dubbed "Merlin." By the time the reader has made three fixations (about 700 msec), enough words have gotten to the comprehension device to send them along for storage in a compartment labeled TPWSG-WTAU (the place where sentences go when they are understood). Phonological rules are applied after this by an editor, and the script emerges as an utterance, the process of getting the first word out taking up the last 300 msec. Gough has provided a detailed three-page chart following the words first fixated ("Suppose the eye . . .") all the way through the process, millisecond by millisecond, until the utterance of "suppose" emerges.

Gough's model is a bold and vulnerable one, in his mind susceptible of proof or disproof—at least, disproof. A child faced with learning to read is armed with most of the necessary equipment, he thinks, for assembling a primitive reading machine and needs to acquire only the scanner and the decoder that converts characters into systematic phonemes. The latter is the principal stumbling block. Gough thinks the child can only master the code through a kind of cryptanalysis, since the characters are converted into abstract systematic phonemes that we cannot teach him. He has to search for the abstract correspondences on his own, and the teacher can only provide him with the raw material, corresponding written and spoken messages. Slow decoding in early stages of reading may prevent comprehension because primary memory will not hold the words, coming one at a time, long enough. But guessing is bad, because it will hold up searching for the abstract correspondences. Gough's final statement is an apt characterization of his position.

In the model I have outlined, the Reader is not a guesser. From the outside, he appears to go from print to meaning as if by magic. But I have contended that this is an illusion, that he really plods through the sentence, letter by letter, word by word. He may not do so; but to show that he does not, his trick will have to be exposed. (p. 354)

We know all too well that his trick is not easy to expose, but we agree with Brewer (1972), who provided a discussion of the paper, that the model leaves largely unexplained the use of higher-order structures that is characteristic of the very economical behavior of the skilled reader. A major problem with the model is that it cannot handle the word superiority effect which has by now been thoroughly documented. An appeal to a lexicon will not do, because a reader's knowledge of word structure generalizes to nonwords with acceptable orthography and facilitates reading them (see Chapter 7). It seems to us, too, that it ignores comlpetely the flexibility of processing that characterizes the skilled reader, of which we shall have more to say.

Analysis-by-Synthesis Models

A contrasting type of theory of reading is "analysis by synthesis" which has been borrowed, though only in its general outlines, from a common theory of speech perception. Brown (1970), after reviewing an analysis-by-synthesis explanation of some reading experiments, points out the similarity between such a theory of reading and similar theories of speech perception:

The Levin* and Kaplan chapter concludes by developing a view of

*One of the authors of this book previously explained his research by an analysis-by-synthesis model but now finds that the principles which follow in this chapter subsume the same findings and are more powerful in explaining the same results.

reading as a process of hypothesis formation, directed data sampling and confirmation or disconfirmation. This is a view very like that found in the other chapters, and Levin and Kaplan anticipate my own reaction to these chapters when they say: "This model of reading, that is understanding written material, is in its important aspects applicable also to understanding spoken language." (p. 177)

Brown's reference to "other chapters" indicates the pervasiveness of this explanation of the process of reading.

In this section we shall describe the analysis-by-synthesis model as it was developed to explain speech perception, its adaptations by researchers on reading, and the problems we see in this theory of reading.

Analysis by synthesis was proposed by Halle and Stevens (1964; 1967) as a way to understand the comprehension of speech. The theory is excellently summarized by Neisser (1967, pp. 193 ff.) in a nontechnical fashion. In its simplest form, analysis by synthesis says that "one makes a hypothesis about the original message, applies rules to determine what the input would be like if the hypothesis were true, and checks to see whether the input is really like that" (Neisser, p. 194). In other words, the listener-reader, depending on prior information, hypothesizes what is to follow and checks his guess. In fact, the theory in the reading research community has been given the soubriquet that reading is a "psycholinguistic guessing game" (Goodman, 1967). The theory raises many questions, more of which have at least been faced in the speech than in the reading version of the theory.

1. On what basis are the predictions made: general context, meaning, the preceding grammatical structures, words, sounds (letters)?

2. How are the predictions checked? At what level of unit? In reading, how does the reader know where the confirmatory unit exists and so direct himself to it?

Halle and Stevens saw these problems, according to Neisser. If the speaker can select the units to be synthesized, from phonemes to the whole message, then he can reverse the process and use the mechanism to understand messages. The speaker apparently uses various-sized, hierarchically organized units in parallel, but is concerned mainly with "wholistic, gross properties of the input" and "makes use of contextual information" (Neisser, p. 195). One gets the impression that the analysis-by-synthesis model, at least in its popularized form, has the speaker operating at the level of the general meaning of the message.

Kenneth Goodman (1967) has written extensively on reading as a guessing and check process and has directed a research program on reading errors, or "miscues" as he calls them, based on his model of reading. He attempts to refute a position such as Gough's that the reader peruses the text letter by letter or word by word. Rather,

In place of this misconception, I offer this: Reading is a selective process. It involves partial use of available minimal language cues selected from perceptual input on the basis of the reader's expectations. As this partial information is processed, tentative decisions are made to be confirmed, rejected, or refined as reading progresses.

More simply stated, reading is a psycholinguistic guessing game. It involves an interaction between thought and language. Efficient reading does not result from precise perception and identification of all elements, but from skill in selecting the fewest, most productive cues necessary to produce guesses which are right the first time. The ability to anticipate that which has not been seen, of course, is vital in reading, just as the ability to anticipate what has not been heard is vital in listening. (p. 127)*

This point of view has led Goodman to put little emphasis on phonics training, since graphic cues are only one of many types of information that the reader uses to construct the message in the text. We reported earlier Goodman's (1965) study that children read identical words correctly more often when they are in meaningful context than the same words in isolation (see Chapter 9). One gets the impression that he is not bothered by a misreading, e.g., the substitution of a synonym, if the message is preserved.

Goodman's (1969) study of miscues in oral reading by second graders confirms our earlier generalization about reading errors (Chapter 9), that children as they become more experienced readers tend to pay more attention to the graphic nature of the text. Goodman also reported that semantic miscues predominated over grammatical ones, that is, in their guessing, these readers maintained the plot line of the text.

The questions we raise about Goodman's guessing game theory of reading apply in many instances to the other analysis-by-synthesis theories of reading discussed below.

1. On what basis does the reader make his predictions?

2. What is the nature of the predictions? Is the reader guessing succeeding letters, words, phrases, sentences, or the general plot or meaning of the text? Said another way, what units is he predicting?

3. How does he check his predictions? How does he know where to look

*From Goodman, 1967. Copyright © 1967 by the College Reading Association. Reprinted by permission of the College Reading Association and Kenneth Goodman.

in the subsequent, or perhaps preceding, text? What informs the reader where to focus his attention?

4. What constitutes a confirmation? What happens if he finds that he has guessed wrong?

In fairness to Goodman, he has developed a model in the form of an extraordinarily complicated flow diagram which takes up some of these points (1969, p. 147). For example, he states that if the prediction is not validated by subsequent syntactic and semantic information, the reader moves his eyes left and up the page. This bit of the flow diagram illustrates the broad nature of the theory and the details of some of the specific reading behaviors—in this example, the motor movements of the eyes.

Hochberg (1970), also an analysis-by-synthesis theorist of reading, comes to grips with one of the questions we raised above: Where do the eyes move next, after a prediction? Further, Hochberg tries to explain why more experienced readers have longer saccades than younger, less experienced readers. Here is the flavor of his writing as he lays out some of the problems to be explained:

> What makes it possible for the skilled reader to do with fewer fixations? For one thing, the skilled reader has acquired strong biases, or *guessing* tendencies. (p. 77, 78; italics ours)

> The experienced reader must treat each important cue, each distinctive visual feature of word or phrase, as confirmation or disconfirmation of some class of expectations and must respond with a set of expectations concerning what should follow the particular material he is reading. (pp. 78–79)

> The experienced reader must respond to the contents of one fixation by making plans as to where he will look next. At the very lowest level, he must pick up with his peripheral vision cues that tell him where regions of high informational value lie in the field. (p. 79)

Central to Hochberg's theory are the notions that the reader fixates on important cues and decides where the next important cues reside in the text so that he can move his eyes there. But he does not tell us how the reader locates important cues or points of high information. Further, he puts a heavy burden on peripheral vision. There is no doubt that the amount of text available to the reader in the periphery of his vision is important (see Chapter 10), but we are far from knowing precisely what characteristics of the text the reader can identify in the periphery, or how he uses whatever peripheral information he picks up. A recent study

(Rayner, 1974) indicated that readers do not pick up semantic information beyond at most six character spaces from their point of fixation.

Hochberg distinguishes between peripheral search guidance (PSG) and cognitive search guidance (CSG). PSG is low-acuity information picked up in the periphery which suggests to the reader where to move his eyes next to pick up potentially interesting information. This idea is interesting for visual search tasks other than reading, but it is difficult at this point in our knowledge to apply it to textual displays. CSG is a direct statement of the guessing game hypothesis: Previous information should provide the reader with hypotheses about where to look next. "I'm not talking about real or consciously reported hypotheses, but about *constructs*—the observer acts *as though* he had hypotheses" (p. 75).

Hochberg does address himself to the question "Where do we look next?" But the place of CSG is as unspecific as Goodman's theory, and it is hard to see what Hochberg gains in his theory by introducing this notion. Besides, there is no clue to how a reader behaves *as though* he had hypotheses, other than to mean that the process, insofar as it exists, is automatic and not consciously applied.

A final statement about the role of guessing in reading comes from an unexpected source. Luria, the famous Russian neuropsychologist, in discussing dyslexia, describes the process of normal reading as follows:

> The experienced reader ceases to extract individual letters or syllables. He quickly learns to recognize words "as individuals"; words are transformed into visual ideograms. Recognition of the meanings of words may occur with no reference to their sound structure. The experienced reader grabs only the general contour. . . . On the basis of this he guesses the meaning of the word as a whole. He is helped considerably in this process by the context of the word. In some cases the context may be such that the number of distinctive features required in the word itself for accurate recognition may be reduced to almost zero. (1970, p. 348)

In summary, to explain all reading by analysis by synthesis or any other single theory seems overly general at this point in our knowledge about reading. Certainly, the theory is too imprecise to account for all kinds of reading. At the same time, there may be occasions when the reader may have expectations about what is coming next, but this does not imply guessing and confirmation. We wonder then if the phenomenon is not the added efficiency of the identification of words (or other units) which results from knowing the context. Such alternatives to the analysis-by-synthesis explanations will be taken up later in this chapter.

Reading as an Adaptive Process

On Reading for a Purpose: Some Case Studies

It must now be clear that the foregoing models, however ingenious, do not seem to us to suffice as descriptions or to capture the essence of the business of reading. The reasons for their insufficiency vary, but one overrides all others, of such weight that it deserves to be mentioned again. No single model will serve to describe *the* reading process, because there are as many reading processes as there are people who read, things to be read, and goals to be served. Reading is as varied and adaptive an activity as perceiving, remembering, or thinking, since in fact it includes all these activities. To clinch this argument, several readers, different persons with different purposes, have described in the following pages what they think they do as they read different kinds of text. We begin with a rather general description and proceed to some more specific cases.

How a Young Scientist Reads

My background is technology: physics, computers, electronics. More than half of my reading is in one of these areas, but I will read almost anything put under my nose. Next to professional reading, I mostly read news and political writings, and my favorite entertainment literature is and always has been science fiction.

Science fiction is the easiest to read, of course, and I read something like a novel from beginning to end. Before I buy a book, I generally read a page or two at random to see if I like the feel of the author's writing (I do this with texts and professional books, too). In some cases when I'm buying entertainment literature and am in doubt about whether to buy a book, I'll read the last several pages of the book. Somewhat off the subject, I read entertainment literature very fast, but not skimming or skipping material unless I don't like it. In some cases, when I really like a passage, I'll read it several times before going on. I read my favorite books again about every two years, and when I read them again, I read continuously from beginning to end.

Any other material, I skim. I skim most in professional literature, because I don't like to get bogged down in extensive math unless I have to do the calculations or unless I want to do a derivation to see the relationship between concepts. I skim the material, looking mostly for conceptual statements and reading all the graphs and their headings. If my attention is drawn to a particular picture, then I rapidly read through the written material referencing it. If I don't comprehend, or if I enjoy the whole tone of the article, then I'll go back and read the article carefully from beginning to end, doing the math in my head when I can, and on paper otherwise. In journals, of course, my selection begins with reading abstracts. If the abstract looks interesting, I look at the pictures, generally skimming the material referencing it, etc. I didn't always read professional material this way; as an undergraduate, I tried to read physics texts continuously from beginning to end, a very time-wasteful method. Not only are many of the books indifferently written, but I got terrifically bogged down in detail. Thus, the way I read now developed slowly, over a period of years.

I read social material similarly to professional material. I also skim, perhaps more rapidly, since there are seldom mathematical relationships, and settle down to read from the beginning articles which really interest me. I cease doing this when the material becomes boring or poorly written (to my taste) and begin skimming again until I reach something interesting, at which point I start reading all the words. I should mention that when material is alternately boring and interesting, I tend to skip about, not reading with continuity. This is especially true of large texts, containing lots of subject matter.

Merrill asked, what is it that I'm doing when I'm skimming? I'm not sure I can say exactly, but I'll try. Sometimes I try to assimilate great clumps of words, even paragraphs at once, sort of in a gestalt fashion, so that I can get an approximate representation of basically what the author is trying to say in that material, and sometimes it's like running a tape reader by, keeping my eyes open for significant words or phrases, at which point I will stop, do a gestalt, and if that's interesting, read that material more slowly. Also, with respect to professional material again, I look for italicized words or phrases to see what the author thought was important.

David Pettijohn, MIT

Reading a Newspaper Columnist

Introspection on reading Art Buchwald's column entitled "Richard the Third (Modern Version)" in the *Boston Globe* of Thursday, May 10, 1973, when Watergate was at high tide. Over a first cup of coffee at 6:30AM

Started to read the column as part of a routine perusal of news and the Op-Ed page (page opposite the editorials, composed entirely of signed columns) which is part of my daily wake-up activity. Not the first thing I read—took in the Watergate stories on the front page first, noticed on the inside that someone, William Loeb, had urged upon Elliot Richardson the naming of Harvard's President Derek Bok as special prosecutor because of his perfect integrity.

Why did I read Buchwald at all? Unlike many people I don't, usually. Perhaps because the column conjoined Watergate, which fascinates me, and *Richard the Third,* a play I like (but as it turns out do not know very well). Read a couple of lines and suddenly remembered the request of Harry Levin and Eleanor Gibson for an introspective report on a reading experience. So decided to try.

The University of Michigan (my alma mater) included no courses on trained introspection so I wasn't quite sure how to go about it, but knew roughly that I should try to notice my process of reading while reading normally. The two seemed to interfere with one another and I found that what I did was read and make sporadic tallies, marking passages where I was aware of something about the process and then read again and set down what I thought the process was.

Noticed at once a tendency to be partially "telegraphic" in my report (as in omission of *I* in this sentence) as if introspection did not require fully social communication, but something more like inner speech. Will preserve this characteristic (it could also be laziness or the hour of the morning) though I cannot explain why the "partiality" of the telegraphese. *I* is often omitted but not always, and articles and prepositions and auxiliary verbs are almost always in place as they are not in the child's "telegraphic speech." I now think the occasional *I* omissions owe more to my preconception of what introspection involves than to the actual nature of inner speech. Probably a stylistic device to give the "flavor" of direct access to thought. Also of course *I* is usually redundant in an introspective report. But I stray from the task of introspection to the unassigned task of explanation.

Numbers on the Buchwald article designate tally points where I noticed something. Until "Ziegler: Bad news, My Lord. Dean has fled to Maryland; Magruder sings in Virginia, and the palace guard are confessing in chorus" I did not consciously take in anything. Everything before this seems to be obvious stuff: Ziegler is a duke, Biscayne a palace, etc. In Ziegler's speech at "1" I noticed "Dean has fled to Maryland" and vaguely thought it sounded more like *Macbeth* than *Richard the Third*. In "Magruder sings in Virginia" I noticed the verb *sings* especially. Probably because the criminal argot sense intended would have been an anachronism in a Shakespearean play. Don't think anything registered consciously about the palace guard.

2. "Zounds" reminded me that this word derives from "His wounds" (Christ's, that is). Just an odd fact.

3. Noticed "impeach thy motives." Don't think this is a correct modern use of *impeach* and one doesn't consult a dictionary while introspecting. Probably *impugn* is the right word but *impeach* suggests the present political case and the two words are phonemically identical at the start.

4. Noticed assignment to Erlichman and Haldeman of the title "baron" which is, of course, an English title suitable to *Richard the Third* but also, I believe, a German title suited to the "Germanic characteristics" of these two men.

5. The departure scene beginning at "Erlichman: My Lord, we must depart perforce" doesn't remind me of any in *Richard the Third* but rather to the departure to England, in *Hamlet*, of Rosencrantz and Guildenstern under instructions from King Claudius. Another German-sounding twosome.

6. The "ghosts" of McGovern and Muskie are surely from *Macbeth* (Banquo), not *Richard the Third*.

7. "Rebozo" gave me pause. Who is Rebozo? Nothing to do with Watergate as far as I know. But then I remembered there is a "Rebozo," a rich man, who is supposed to be Nixon's best friend or something.

8. "A horse! A horse!" etc. Unquestionably *Richard the Third*, but where is the Nixon parallel? I don't get it.

9. The "six crises" reverses the case being pure Nixon and not Richard at all.

10. Duchess of Mitchell again seems pure Nixon and not the play.

Overview: Clearly my conscious processing of this column was extremely selective. On some level I had to read the whole thing to pick out the points of analogy between the play and Richard Nixon but, not expecting to take a quiz on the contents (as I have not), I registered consciously what interested me—the parallels with the play. After all it was the suggestion of these in the title that led me to read the column in the first place. I did not think the parallels very strong or funny; in many cases there really were none and only the use of a vaguely archaic vocabulary and the royal setting suggested any. The parallels, I noticed in retrospect, were like those in the play *Macbird* (about Macbeth and President Johnson), not limited to the one Shakespearean play suggested but to a variety of Shakespeare's plays; but *Macbird* is much funnier. Last of all, oddly enough, I noticed the coincidence of first names—Richard—perhaps because names are expected to signify nothing. The general intent—to attack Nixon—was clear since Richard the Third was an ugly murderer, totally without scruple. I found that sympathetic enough but did not think the column as a whole very clever. As far as consciousness is concerned I seemed to be exclusively occupied with working over the content into a retainable capsule, a more abstract structure that throws most of the meaning away but is compact enough to hold in meaning.

The above is a certified true account of my introspection on reading Buchwald's column. However, one's introspection is limited by one's knowledge, and mine has proved to be pretty thin. Checking the text of *Richard the Third*, I find that there are in the play departures, ghosts, and a vengeful Margaret, if not a Martha, and one must suppose that Buchwald had these in mind rather than their more familiar counterparts in *Hamlet* and *Macbeth*. But you can only get from a reader what he has to give by way of comprehension; there are always lots of surprises in this process for an author.

Roger Brown, Harvard University

On Reading a Novel

The caption should really be "on reading a novelist," for I am thinking of only one, my absolute favorite of all time, Jane Austen. Her novels are not airport reading. They are for reading over and over, savoring every phrase, memorizing the best of them, and getting an ever deeper understanding of Jane's "sense for human comedy," as Whicher (1938) described her genius. She loves to laugh at people. Perhaps that is why critics generally consider *Pride and Prejudice* the best of her books, although it is not my favorite. As I read the book, for perhaps the twenty-fifth time, I consider what point she is trying to make in the similarities and differences between the characters of Elizabeth Bennet and her father. Mr. Bennet loves to laugh at human folly, even (perhaps especially) the folly of his wife and his own children. Consider this little vignette, or conversation between Mr. Bennet and his wife about his daughters, when an eligible young man moves into the neighborhood and Mrs. Bennet informs her husband that she intends the young man to choose one of their daughters for his wife:

> "They have none of them much to recommend them," replied he; "they are all silly and ignorant like other girls; but Lizzy has something more of quickness than her sisters."
> "Mr. Bennet, how can you abuse your own children in such a way? You take delight in vexing me. You have no compassion on my poor nerves."
> "You mistake me, my dear. I have a high respect for your nerves. They are my old friends. I have heard you mention them with consideration these twenty years at least."

Mr. Bennet carries his enjoyment of human folly to a rather unpleasant extreme. He expects Elizabeth to laugh with him, and she does, but her enjoyment is tempered with common sense and respect, as she tells Mr. Darcy in the following conversation:

> "Mr. Darcy is not to be laughed at!" cried Elizabeth. "That is an uncommon advantage, and uncommon I hope it will continue, for it would be a great loss to *me* to have many such acquaintances. I dearly love a laugh."
> "Miss Bingley," said he, "has given me credit for more than can be. The wisest and best of men, nay the wisest and best of their actions, may be rendered ridiculous by a person whose first object in life is a joke."
> "Certainly," replied Elizabeth—"there are such people, but I hope I am not one of *them*. I hope I never ridicule what is wise or good."

Elizabeth Bennet, Jane Austen's best-known heroine, may well represent Miss Austen's own way of perceiving human character and relationships. I wonder then, as I read, how we are to comprehend some of her other heroines? What about Fanny Price, the heroine of *Mansfield Park?* Fanny is a prude and a prig, a humble unprotesting sufferer who never laughs at anything. In fact, it occurs to me, no one in *Mansfield Park* laughs. Is this absence of laughter to provide a contrast with the other novels, perhaps? Then there is Catherine, the heroine of *Northanger Abbey,* who can laugh, but without comprehension. She is a simpleminded, ill-educated girl, a dimwit, and yet she is privileged to marry one of the most attractive young men in the novels, apparently just because he is loyal and responsible.

All of this, as we read the novels, is part of Jane Austen's sense for human comedy. Her settings are laid only for the sake of showing up the players and their personalities. The world never intrudes. All the novels were set during the Napoleonic wars, but we read on and on and the war is never mentioned. Sailors come and sailors go—from midshipmen to admirals—but we only see them in a drawing room. They win prize money in sea battles on men-of-war, but no one ever speaks of the war, except to express the hope that more of it will occur, so that more prizes and promotions will be available.

I think of all these things as I read Jane Austen, but I do not want to read her critics. I want to discover for myself what this sensitive and perceptive person is trying to tell me. Sometimes I only want to sink back and enjoy it and laugh myself.

Eleanor J. Gibson, Cornell University

Reading the Dictionary

Scholars have often wondered whether the concept of palingenesis is related to the meta-theory of developmental psychology.

My initial and vivid reaction to this sentence was that I did not know the meaning of the word *palingenesis,* and how central to understanding the sentence was this particular word. The sentence concerned a concept, so that *palingenesis* was in effect the "semantic headword" of the whole sentence. Is this the developmental psychological shibboleth "ontogeny recapitulates phylogeny"? *Palingenesis* is a noun, a concept functioning as the object of the preposition *of;* the phrase is adjectival, modifying *concept.* Were this prolonged discourse, my impulse would have been to read further giving the sentence the reading I assumed. If the succeeding text made sense, I am not sure that I would have looked up *palingenesis.* It would depend on what I was reading for, the time I had, etc. On the other hand, I am interested in philology—word origins—enjoy and collect dictionaries, so that unless I was skimming the text or under some pressure of time, I would likely look up the word, even in discourse.

Palingenesis. Genesis was no problem. *Palin,* though, was troublesome because I would be more sure of my interpretation if the spelling were *paleo,* so I could give it the reading *old* as in *paleontology.*

I realized that the choice of a dictionary was important. The word was long, technical, and not likely to be defined in the garden-variety desk dictionary. An unabridged volume was called for, and I had a choice between the Random House and Webster, both in my study. I chose Random House, which I generally prefer.

I opened the dictionary and landed first in the *R*s and, paying attention to the first letter, flipped back, landing in the *P*s, *Pa,* in fact. I found myself thinking over and over rhythmically, *PQR, PQR.* The page ended with the word *pantry* and my first impulse was to go farther when I realized that *l* precedes *n* in the alphabet. *LMN, LMN.* One page earlier did the trick. The headings were *palueotropical* and *palm.* Between them should lie *palingenesis.* Second column of the left-hand page—*pale;* first column of the right-hand page—*pali.* I was working with letter groups, usually four-letter chunks, as *pali.* The column ended with *palindrome.* I read the definition because several days ago, a colleague and I had a "tip-of-the-tongue" experience with that word. From *palindrome,* I read the words in order, without looking at the definitions, until *palingenesis.*

Palingenesis is an *n.* The first definition was only partially helpful: rebirth, regeneration. The second was marked *Biol.* and my thought was that this was it. "The development of an individual that reproduces the ancestral features (opposed to *ceneogenesis*)" (p. 1039). So my first guess about the meaning of the sentence was correct.

But I was left with two questions: (1) What is the origin of the prefix *palin,* and (2) what in the world was *ceneogenesis?* I was reminded of the many stories, probably apocryphal, about dictionaries leading one in a full, empty circle.

By reading the etymology, I learned that *palin* was from the NL out of of the Greek meaning "again." And since I was enjoying the task, I decided to look up *ceneogenesis.* I assumed the /si/ pronunciation. There were actually more page turnings than for *palingenesis,* but I might have guessed the meaning, just from the way the dictionary is set up. *Palingenesis* and *ceneogenesis* were contrasted, so I might have expected an antonym. *Ceno* is a learned borrowing from the Greek meaning "new," so that *ceneogenesis* means the "development of an individual which does not repeat the phylogeny of the race." I checked the pronunciation of the *e* in *ceno* and found I had been correct.

I had pronounced *palin* as /pa/ rather than /pae/ so I went back to check that. The pronunciation key told me that the *a* in *palin* is the /a/ in *act*. As I had thought. There is good reading, of its own kind, in dictionaries.

Harry Levin, Cornell University

On Reading a Poem

You have asked me how I read a poem. I take it you mean how do I as an individual come to understand a particular poem rather than how I think poems should be taught. But I shan't try to separate the two questions because I have been an amateur of poetry and a teacher of literature too long to be able to make useful distinctions between the two.

No theory without particulars. I will answer by talking about a poem of Emily Dickinson, of the "flood" year 1862, number 307 in Thomas Johnson's edition. (One can't get anywhere, of course, without the poet's own text accurately printed.) Poem 307* goes this way:

The One who could repeat the Summer day—
Were greater than itself—though He
Minutest of Mankind should be—

And He—could reproduce the Sun—
At period of going down—
The Lingering—and the Stain—I mean—

When Orient have been outgrown—
And Occident—become Unknown—
His Name—remain—

My first answer to your question is that Poem 307 must be read aloud as if it were a piece of music, directly and simply because the tone of

*Reprinted by permission of the publishers and the Trustees of Amherst College from Thomas H. Johnson (ed.), *The Poems of Emily Dickinson*, Cambridge, Mass.: The Belknap Press of Harvard University Press. Copyright 1951, 1955 by the President and Fellows of Harvard College.

the poem is colloquial, but also with a musician's awareness of the subtle, beautiful chiming of *Lingering, Stain, mean, Name,* and *remain.* As one reads the lines aloud, the mood of condition-contrary-to-fact or potentiality emerges, as well, so that the compressed last line comes to mean, "His, the painter's, name would remain, a long time." Thus one must read with some understanding of the syntax—and in Dickinson an exact sense of the words—in order to understand her short-hand economies. One must read also to discover, consciously or unconsciously, how the phrases and clauses, or the parts of the poem whatever they may be, work together to make an emotionally and intellectually satisfying whole. So that one regards the poem as a construct, quite as finely balanced and assembled as a 19th-century clipper ship or an Alexander Calder mobile of our own time. Seen in its two parts, the poet asserts: "The person who could film and reshow a summer day would be as great as the day itself; and [may mean *an,* or *if*] were he to paint the afterglow of the sunset, when east and west have gone dark, his name would last." The last line is plainly the rounding off of the construct, as it completes the sense of the second "if" statement after parenthetical phrases and clauses that create suspense. Part 2 is twice as long as Part 1. The exact sound reversal of *Name—(re)main* underlies the finality of the slant rhyme; and—one must still be reading aloud— one's ear with some help from the eye will record an inverted triangle pattern: the first line is five feet long, the next seven lines are four feet, and the last line concludes with two.

Since Dickinson believes that poets "tell all the truth but tell it slant," which is to say metaphorically, one will observe that the basic metaphor is embedded in the two key verbs: to "repeat the Summer day" and to "reproduce the Sun"—variants on the ancient poetic doctrine of "imitation" or of holding up the mirror to nature.

So far I have confined the questions mostly to the elements of the poem itself. But clearly, the more one has read of Dickinson's poetry, all 1775 poems, the better one is prepared to read a particular poem. Poem 307, the reader of Dickinson rather quickly recognizes, is one of many poems having to do with summer and with poetry itself. In Poem 569, she avers that she would not choose to be a painter, or a musician, or especially a poet—only to confess she would feel richly dowered *if* she had the "art to stun myself/with bolts of melody." So too in Poem 307 she dramatizes the difficult aim of the poet, to translate the beauty of the natural world into poetry. But Poem 308,* which is closely linked to 307 by time of composition and by subject, takes a different tone entirely:

I send Two Sunsets—
Day and I—in competition ran—
I finished Two—and several Stars—
While He—was making One—

His own was ampler—but as I
Was saying to a friend—
Mine—is the more convenient
To Carry in the Hand

Dickinson gives this verse the casual tone of a letter enclosing Poem 307 presumably; but she is witty and boastful rather than contemplative and wishful.

Still another kind of question, as difficult to answer as it is rewarding when properly answered, is what does one's knowledge of Dickinson's life add to one's feeling about the poem? For other Dickinson poems, much; for this poem, only a little, in that the reference to "Minutest of Mankind" is a glance by the poet at her own slight figure and small stature. This is of a piece in another poem with her observing her own "narrow hands" which are yet capable, she says, of "gathering Paradise." Still another possibly useful question may involve analogy or source. So, for Poem 308 and *her* sunset, which was more convenient to carry in her hand, she took her idea, it seems probable, from one of Davy Crockett's fabulous adventures on a frigid winter morning. Finding the January sun frozen fast in sweat on its axis at the top of Daybreak Hill, Crockett breaks it loose with the help of hot bear oil, and walks home whistling a tune and "introducin' people to the fresh daylight with a piece of sunrise in my pocket."

I suppose, finally, that in reading this concentrated small poem one may add still further to its dimensions by comparing it to poems in the ancient tradition of the "makers" who hope to achieve immortality in their verse. Or one can show, through this and other of her poems, that Dickinson as transcendentalist and romantic believes that the true poets possess divine power: to "repeat the Summer day" is the prerogative of a god. But it is in its particular images and metaphors, its subtle orchestration of sounds, its elegant structure, and its passionate aspiration that the poem moves me most.

Though Poem 307 is not one of the very best of Dickinson's poems, it is good and characteristic. It also embodies one of her most striking poetic traits—the serious pun, in the manner of Shakespeare, if we see and hear "reproduce . . . Sun" as "reproduce . . . son" (an old quibble in the history of poetry) though Dickinson may not have intended it or been conscious of it.

William M. Gibson, University of Wisconsin

If these little essays have not convinced our audience that mature readers read for a purpose, have their own styles of reading, and suit the style to the text that is being read, we despair of making our point that there are many reading processes, not one. It seems to us that these cases speak for themselves, and so we shall take the point for granted and go on, not to design a model, but to see if we can complete our study of reading by summing up what has gone before in a few concentrated generalizations. They have all been foreshadowed throughout the book. Now we shall try to state them.

Some Principles of Word Perception
Selective attention to features of words   It was proposed in Chapter 7 that a word can be thought of as embodying several kinds of information: graphic, orthographic, phonetic, semantic, morphological, and syntactic. These classes of information not only can be described separately; we intend to show, now, that they can be attended to independently as they have utility for the reader's task. Consider a word—SQUINT. It has graphic features that make it easily recognized, for the letters contain a variety of distinctive features and the sequence combines unique graphic shapes in an order that is not easily confusable. The print is uppercase, black on white. The orthographic pattern is highly redundant, since the word contains several constrained clusters. Its phonetic characteristics are apparent in the clusters too (especially *squ,* a tongue twister for native speakers of some other languages), and it can be neatly rhymed (e.g.,

splint). Semantically, it cannot be broken down into subordinate morphemes, but it can be characterized by lexical features: concrete, animate, potentially both human and subhuman, but only mammalian, having to do with the eyes, an abnormality, and so on. It has synonyms like *cross-eyed*, but no uniquely adequate one. The word is, in fact, a homograph with several related but different meanings. Syntactically, it can be a verb, *to squint*, or it can be a noun, *possessing a squint*. As an adjective, *squint-eyed*, it is possible but dubious.

All these kinds of information may be picked up at once, in parallel. But it is doubtful that they are ever all encoded so as to be memorable. The reader may process all these features of a word at some level, but it seems very likely that he assigns priorities, consciously or not, to one over another depending on their utility for his task. Processing different features of the same class—all the semantic ones, for instance—may be compatible. But trying to identify or encode for future reference several classes at once may not be compatible, and there is indeed evidence for independent processing of feature classes, with a hierarchy or priority for different laboratory tasks. There appears to be variable selection of features in relation to the task, with every class of features high in relevance for one task or another, although we are inclined to think that in real-life communication, the meaning of words is the class of feature most likely to be attended to.

Consider the evidence for selection and priority of processing classes of features (Gibson, 1971). Even graphic information is attended to, above all others, in certain tasks. In the preceding essay on looking up a word in the dictionary, the author noted that he flipped through the pages searching only for the *p* section, and then searched for *pa*, finally narrowing his search to the words beginning with *palin*. In laboratory search tasks, the graphic feature selected as a target tends to be optimally minimal. In scanning through a list of context letters for a single target letter, for instance, a practiced subject learns to detect only the smallest feature or set of features that will divide the target letter from the surrounding ones (Gibson and Yonas, 1966a; Neisser, Novik, and Lazar, 1963). If subjects are highly practiced in searching for a letter distinguishable from its context by possessing some feature like diagonality whereas that feature is absent from context letters, the rate of scan becomes very fast. But if the context or the target is changed, so that the minimal feature is no longer sufficiently distinguishing, scanning rate immediately slows down (Yonas,

1969; Schapiro, 1970). Despite long practice with the same context letters, the subject has not identified them sufficiently so as to recall them by name or even recognize them afterward (Schapiro, 1970).

While graphic features receive high priority in this task, phonetic features of the letters are virtually ignored. Exposing the subject to a voice pronouncing letter names that rhymed with the target letter's name produced no interference with the rate of scan, even with children (Gibson and Yonas, 1966b). Kaplan, Yonas, and Shurcliff (1966) compared the effect of high and low acoustic similarity of context letters to the target letter; the target was embedded among letters whose names rhymed with it (*b, v, d,* and so on), or among letters that sounded unlike it. In their experiment, acoustic similarity of letter names did not slow scanning rate at all, in contrast to a powerful effect of graphic similarity.

Subjects can search very swiftly for a word embedded in a list of other words in the scanning task (Neisser and Beller, 1965). The unity of the word appears to make it a superior target. But even in this case, the scanner appears to rely heavily on graphic and orthographic features, since semantic information that seemingly might be used to dissociate the target from its context is *not* used. Gibson, Tenney, and Zaslow (1971) had subjects search for a meaningful word belonging to a well-known category (e.g., an animal) embedded either in a list of words categorically related in another way (e.g., kinds of fruit) or in a list of words semantically unrelated. The subject was not given a specific target word for each list scanned, but was told to "look for the name of an animal." The contrast of meaningful categories between target and context did not facilitate the scan. Semantic features appear to have low priority as cues for fast scanning.

But even this priority can be shifted if the reader is searching for a target in connected prose rather than a list. Cohen (1970) had subjects read passages of prose, canceling targets that were visual (single graphemes), acoustic (phonemes), or semantic (words of a specified category). The targets were searched for singly, and also in all possible combinations. The acoustic targets (vowels or diphthongs) were represented in different spellings so they could not be identified visually as letters. The words were members of categories such as flowers, colors, clothing, etc. Two targets never occurred in the same word. Search was fastest for a semantically defined target, next fastest for a visual (letter) target, and slowest for an acoustic target. When two targets were to be sought at once, adding a semantic target to a letter or to a phonemic target increased search time only a little. A combination of visual and auditory targets or of all three types increased search time significantly. Evidently acoustic processing did not take place during letter search, since letter search was much faster than phonemic search. That semantic search (words) was fastest is not surprising in view of the contextual cues present to assist that search. Multiple search (combining two or more types of targets) increased the time by different amounts, suggesting that processing some combinations overlaps, but other combinations go on independently. Letter search was more compatible with semantic search than was phonemic search.

Visual (orthographic) similarity plays a role in learning lists of paired associates, far more than acoustic similarity. Allen (1970) found that words spelled similarly but with different pronunciation (e.g., *door* and *poor*) interfered more in learning verbal paired associates than rhyming words with different spellings (e.g., *door* and *pore*). We also know from innumerable experiments that meanings of words can be important in this kind of learning.

We know too that features frequently ignored in a scanning task can have top priority in other tasks. Phonetic features of a word, or especially of an alphanumeric character, have high priority for short-term memory (e.g., looking up a telephone number and remembering it just long enough to dial it). Conrad (1964) and others have shown in a number of experiments that acoustic similarity produces confusions in short-term memory even when the material is presented visually (Baddeley, 1966). Graphic and semantic confusions in short-term memory, on the other hand, are infrequent (Baddeley, 1966). Short-term memory is perhaps not a characteristic goal for very many reading tasks. But we read for sound inevitably when we read poetry, as the essay above on reading a poem emphasizes. Its author, in fact, wrote in a later postscript, " . . . the *feel* of poems is in reading them aloud, which no *print* can do for them. Shall I say it more emphatically?"

All the essays, no matter what the subject matter being considered by the writer, spoke of meaning and the frequent search for deeper meaning. A search for deep understanding (an author's feelings about a character, a poem's mood, a word's derivation) is seldom characteristic of laboratory tasks, but even in some of these, semantic features take priority. The importance of meaningful relations, organization, and categorizing typically comes out in experiments on long-term memory. As we saw in Chapter 3, a child's ability to use meaning and organization as deliberate strategies for remembering develops dramatically during his grade school years.

When the reader is looking primarily for meaning, other aspects of the text, like graphic ones, may be incompatible with his goal and be ignored or even get in his way. But meanings—different lexical features—seem to be compatibly processed, though we do not know whether this happens in parallel or in some strategic hierarchical organization.

The compatibility of looking for features of the same class is nicely illustrated by an experiment of Hyde and Jenkins (1969). In this experiment, the subjects were sometimes asked to do two tasks at once. They were presented with a list of words for later recall. In two conditions, subjects had to extract some graphic information about a word as it was presented: either estimate its length (number of letters) or detect the presence or absence of the letter *e*. Another group had to rate the word as it was presented for pleasantness or unpleasantness.

Compared to a control group with no second task, recall was greatly reduced for the first two groups, and so was the amount of organization in recall as measured by clustering of words in categories. But the task of rating words as pleasant or unpleasant did not reduce recall or organization in recall as compared with a control group that had no incidental task. When the subject was performing a second task that gave priority to *semantic* features of the word, neither recall nor its organization suffered. But when the second task required attention to a word's graphic features, like detecting *e*'s or estimating word length, the semantic pickup which is apparently vital to later recall of words was blocked.

The Hyde and Jenkins experiment suggests that features of the same class, like semantic features of all kinds, are picked up compatibly, while different feature classes are processed independently. The value of the word—pleasant or unpleasant—could apparently be assessed at the same time as pickup of semantic categories of the kind that operate in clustering.

An experiment by Calfee and Jameson (1971) provides independent evidence of compatibility of processing of a single class of information even when an incidental task is added to a primary one. Their subjects (college students) read passages of about 100 words from novels, with an ensuing test of comprehension. At the same time, they were required to tally all the occurrences of a given content word in the passage, or of words meaning the same thing as the target word. Rate of reading the text was slowed somewhat (depending on the number of targets to be sought for), but in neither case was comprehension of the passage affected.

Johnston and Jenkins (1971) performed an experiment parallel to the one by Hyde and Jenkins with two other incidental tasks, one requiring extraction of acoustic information (giving rhymes) and one semantic (providing a modifier). The subjects were presented with pairs of highly associated words in a sequential random order so that the members of any pair were never adjacent. The rhyming group was required to write down a rhyming word for each stimulus word as it was presented. The modifier group was required to write an adjective modifier for a noun stimulus, or an appropriate noun that could be modified if the stimulus was an adjective. Both the amount of free recall and the amount of associative clustering were greater for the modifier group than for the rhyming group. The modifier group in fact did not differ significantly in clustering from a control group that had no extra incidental task. Despite the relative lack of opportunity for rehearsal and organization, the kind of selective attention and effort expended in seeking appropriate modifiers was compatible with a tendency to organize recall semantically. Attending to acoustic features of the words was not.

That attending to physical features of a message, such as acoustic features of speech or graphic features of writing, is not compatible with optimal reception of the semantic contents of the message is in accord with common sense, and much more objective evidence could be produced (see, for instance, Martin and Strange, 1968). That different word features belonging to the same class are compatibly extracted at more or less the same time is an interesting but much shakier hypothesis. Compatibility does not necessarily imply parallel processing, however. It could equally well imply systematic search, following some well-organized pattern including all the major features of the class. Proponents of semantic processing via a hierarchy of lexical features would seem to entertain such an hypothesis (see, for instance, Collins and Quillian, 1972). The question whether there is a subjective lexicon that exists as an isolable, organized subsystem in memory, with its own properties, is of widespread interest at the present time (Miller, 1970, 1972; Conrad, in press), and current work is so far promising. The position that a word has isolable features of different classes that can be searched separately is thereby strengthened.

Nothing has been said so far about attention to syntactic features. Anyone who has edited or graded papers knows that this class of information can be singled out for attention: Subject and verb disagreements, inconsistent usage of tenses, split infinitives, etc., stand out like giants as one reads the first draft of a paper or thesis with a critical eye. Experimental demonstration of attention to syntax as a system of information in its own right is not lacking. Two studies of paragraph marking and analysis were described in Chapter 11 (see pp. 417 ff.). The study by Koen, Becker, and Young (1969) removed many of the semantic cues for paragraph boundaries by eliminating topical content; all the content words were given nonsense substitutes, but the function words, inflections, and punctuation remained. Interjudge agreement on paragraph boundaries was reduced by this device, but there was still substantial agreement on the nonsense passages, and a high correlation between English and nonsense versions indicated corresponding use of paragraph markers in the two. Syntactic information (including formal markers like punctuation) can therefore be attended to and used successfully on its own. The study by Pfafflin (1967) investigated cues for discriminating first from second sentences within a paragraph, and found that syntactic conventions like intersentence conjunction and structures within the sentence, such as use of pronouns and definite articles, enabled readers to make the judgment.

Convincing evidence can thus be found in controlled laboratory studies that there can be variable selection of features of words in relation to the task. Subjects can attend to the class of features having greatest utility for the task presented to them. But do readers do this on their own, when no experimenter is there to explain what the task is and give instructions?

Active strategies of the reader   The case studies above were chosen as examples of spontaneously varying strategies for dealing with different kinds of text. In Chapter 11, a number of experimental studies were described in which subjects were shown to use, more or less successfully, strategies such as inference in learning from reading connected discourse. We can summarize what we have so far uncovered or suspect as follows:

1. The mature reader exhibits flexibility of attentional strategies in reading for different types of information.

2. Strategies shift with characteristics of a text such as difficulty of concepts and style.

3. They shift with feedback (rate of gain of knowledge) as the reader progresses (e.g., he slows down under some circumstances, skims under others).

4. They shift with newness or oldness of information.

5. They shift with the reader's personal interests (he likes science fiction but doesn't like Jane Austen, or vice versa) and his educational objectives, and with instructions (his teacher said to prepare for a quiz on the history text).

The importance of active, flexible methods of attending while reading can hardly be doubted. How does success in reading for different kinds of information develop? A child still mastering the mechanics of reading can hardly be expected to show this flexibility. Perhaps it can be taught at a later stage, as the school and recreational facilities broaden the reading matter to include everything from dictionaries to craft instructions to science to poetry, and so on. It seems to us that exposure to such a broad diet is the basic vehicle for learning adaptive reading strategies, but explicit instruction may help (see, for instance, Wolf, King, and Huck, 1968, on teaching "critical reading").

Early research on reading for different purposes (Gray, 1917; Judd and Buswell, 1922) made use of eye movement photography to observe reading prose versus poetry, or reading casually versus reading with a serious intent to learn. Differences were found, but Judd and Buswell reported that some subjects exhibited no flexibility in adapting reading activity to a particular purpose. Other studies (see Tinker, 1958, and discussion in Chapter 10) confirm that oculomotor patterns reflect ease or difficulty of reading performance and degree of comprehension.

Smith (1967) studied the responses of good and poor readers when reading for different purposes. The subjects were high school students in twelfth grade. The two purposes compared were reading for details and reading for general impressions. Rather than taking objective physical measures such as eye movements, she employed an interview method. Two interviews were held with each subject. In one, the subjects were asked to read for details. In the other they were asked to read for general impressions. Following reading, in each interview they responded to eight questions, four requiring responses to details and four requiring general impressions, with the types of questions interspersed. Further questions probed their methods of reading for the two purposes and past experience in reading for different purposes. Descriptive classification schemes were developed for appraising the accuracy, appropriateness, and quality of the responses.

The findings reported were that good readers adjusted their procedures to the purposes of reading for details versus general impressions, while poor readers varied their procedures only slightly in the two cases. Good readers reported that they read every word for both purposes, but when reading for details, they mentally summarized them and reread factual material like names and dates. When reading for general impressions they stopped to evaluate ideas at the end of paragraphs or pages and if they reread, read whole sentences or paragraphs rather than single words. They were better able to hold their purpose in mind while reading. Both good and poor readers read with equal success for both purposes, as regarded correctness of responses, but good readers were more successful than poor readers in reading for details.

This type of research is hard to evaluate because of the qualitative nature of the responses. It seems clear, however, that the good readers had more insight into the techniques they were using, and varied them more as the assigned purposes differed. The majority of the subjects did not remember having been taught to read for different purposes. Those who thought they had received such instruction were able to give only generalized descriptions of reading and did not describe adjustment of reading procedures. In the interviews, none of the subjects referred to any purpose for reading other than the two they were asked to pursue. These results are somewhat discouraging as regards the role of school instruction in learning to read adaptively. Perhaps teaching techniques could be developed, as Smith recommends. Perhaps they develop in an individual spontaneously with breadth of the material read and a variety of purposes.

Reading for details versus reading for "general impressions" is not an easy contrast of motives to explain, but an experiment by Levin and Cohn found predicted differences in the eye-voice span* when subjects were instructed to read for details as opposed to reading for a general idea. Subjects from second, fourth, ninth, and eleventh grades were tested. They were selected at random, save for eliminating second graders who did not have a minimal second-grade reading ability. The reading material consisted of 22 short selections drawn from each of two grade levels (second and tenth grades). The elementary grades read second-grade material, while the upper grades read tenth-grade material. A selection consisted of a passage of six sentences of connected discourse. Both grade level and type of instructions had significant effects. The eye-voice span was longer for the older readers, and it was shorter, as predicted, when details were read for, rather than the general idea. The interaction between these two factors, however, was not significant. The subjects at all levels apparently read in smaller units, focusing more exclusively on each word, when reading for details, and read in longer units or groups of words when reading for the general idea.

A control condition with instructions to "read as you normally would" was also included in this experiment. A grade difference in general mode

*See Chapter 10 for a description of the technique of measuring the eye-voice span.

of reading was apparent in these results. In the two earlier grades, the spans for normal reading and for details were more similar, while the spans for normal reading and reading for the general idea were more similar in the two upper grades. The younger readers, in other words, probably tended more to read word by word normally.

In conclusion, we know that skilled readers are flexible and adaptive in their reading strategies as both the material read and the reader's purpose dictate. But we have as yet little knowledge of how this skill develops.

The economy principle and how it applies   In this final section on the basic psychology of reading, the intention is to epitomize in a few general statements some of the inferences drawn throughout the preceding chapters from the most reliable research and observations we could find. We have just emphasized in the paragraphs above the adaptiveness and flexibility of reading activities in relation to the reader's purpose, a frequent theme throughout the foregoing pages. Another recurrent theme in the book has been the trend toward economy of processing. The trend is an exceedingly prominent one in development, as we stressed in Chapter 2, and also in practicing a given skill or task. We will attempt to be more specific by stating two subprinciples, with some details about how they are exhibited in reading.

1. *The reader will direct his attention to processing textual material in the most economical way he can.* There is more than one way of doing this, as we have already seen. Four outstanding ways can be summarized.

a. The information relevant to the reader's purpose is selected for priority of attention. Kinds of information, selection of strategies, and growth toward adaptability and flexibility just described in the preceding section in turn relate back to the trend toward optimization of attention in the theory of perceptual development described in Chapter 2 and to the development of cognitive strategies treated in Chapter 3.

b. Information that is irrelevant, not wanted, of no utility for the task is ignored. This proposition was also considered in Chapter 2, and it came up again as we discussed switching of attention to different classes of features of words. It is possible for the skilled reader to concentrate on semantic or acoustic or other features of the information, and seemingly to discard the rest. Whether the rest is processed automatically without attention, whether it is in some way filtered out, or whether it is processed but not transferred to long-term memory has been the subject of much argument and remains an unsettled problem, but in any case potential information of no utility is generally discarded. To ask a homely question, who wants to fill his head with graphic or acoustic details, or even meaningful episodic information (Tulving and Donaldson, 1972), that is of no consequence to him? The evidence is strong that the skilled reader does not, any more than we take note of or remember trivial incidents in our daily lives. It is enlightening, indeed, to compare the flow of psychological processes in reading with their flow in living. Reading, when the stages of acquisition are sufficiently finished, is a kind of living.

c. The largest units appropriate for the task are processed. A reader can direct his attention to features of letters, to letters, to words, to phrases, and even to clauses as units. We might go farther, but it is unnecessary to push the point. We can agree with Huey:

We are brought back to the conclusion of Goldscheider and Muller that we read by phrases, words, or letters as may serve our purpose best. But we see, too, that the reader's acquirement of ease and power in reading comes through increasing ability to read in larger units. (Huey, 1968, p. 116)

Evidence for progressive processing in larger units was presented earlier (see Chapters 7 and 9). Events in life are generally perceived in large episodes, with subordinate events nested within them. Focusing attention on a momentary, fleeting occurrence is rare, though it sometimes happens, even in exaggerated form in an introspective novelist: for example, Proust's lengthy and vivid description in *Remembrance of Things Past* of a child's recollection of the taste of a *gateau* soaked in tea one afternoon of his childhood. Such a frozen second is as rare in perception and in recollection as it is in speech and, of course, writing. Fillmore's case grammar (see Chapter 4) reflects the eventlike nature of speech units, which like perceived occurrences come complete with agents, actions, recipients, objects, and locations. There is every reason to believe that we normally comprehend spoken language in such large structural units. There is also reason to suppose that we do so when we read. Larger units are economical, and for most purposes they are also more meaningful.

We could, indeed, speak of "idea units" as we did in Chapter 11. Such units, regardless of their size in syntactically expressed surface structure, are both economical and meaningful for comprehension and for learning. Size of a unit of either spoken or written language does not necessarily coincide with meaningfulness, since a word alone has meaning. But the greater coincidence of large units with life-size events and thoughts is correlated with economy as reflected in comprehension and in learning.

d. The *least* amount of information compatible with the reader's task is processed. This proposition may seem to be the inverse of the preceding one, but we do not think it contradicts it. As we have said repeatedly, tasks vary. A very small amount of information often suffices to accomplish the reader's purpose, and a clever reader tends to confine himself to extracting just that minimal amount of information. One might say he will accomplish his purpose in the cheapest way, except that the term "cheap" seems to cast unnecessary aspersions on what is really an adaptive strategy.

Suppose one needs to know a number—a quantity of something, a price, the length of time taken for a response—and remembers that it was buried on some page of a text he recently read. He skims through the text, reading not a word, simply scanning for a number till he finds it. Interestingly enough, research has shown that a reader scanning through a context of letters can (and does) find *any* number remarkably fast, clearly with the least possible knowledge of the letters of the context.

In Chapter 2 we described research showing that practice in a categorical discrimination task results in processing the minimal distinctive feature that permits the positive and negative set of stimuli to be discriminated (Yonas, 1969). In a same-different task, when letters can be discriminated on the basis of a graphic physical match alone, the subject will do so, with a very speedy reaction time; but when the letters are presented in different typography (upper- and lowercase), the subject has to go to a *name* match, and the necessity of verbal coding increases the cost, resulting in a longer reaction time (Posner, Boies, et al., 1969). But a name match can be faster than semantic processing, depending on the task and the reader's maturity. Word-word comparisons are shorter for both adults and second-grade children than picture-word matches, presumably because semantic processing must take place in the latter case. But the difference between the two decreases with age, in part because the adult has become more adept at processing words directly for meaning than the child (Gibson, Barron, and Garber, 1972). Adults reading silently to themselves bypass subvocalization and go directly to the abstract meaning for which the text is only a notation.* The articulatory and acoustic representation intervening is unnecessary, uneconomical, and is only processed when the going gets difficult or the "sound effects" are wanted.

---

*Meaningful sets of initials enjoy an advantage over meaningless letter strings in tachistoscopic identification (Gibson, Bishop, et al., 1964) and in same-different judgments (Henderson, in press). Naming would take an equivalent time in either case.

That processing for sound as opposed to meaning is faster for at least one task (short-term memory with a probe technique) was shown by Shulman (1970). The subjects listened to a list of ten words, and were then presented with a probe word, with the instruction to decide whether it, or one similar in sound or meaning had been in the list. The subjects were equally accurate in recognizing identical probes and homonyms, but less so with synonyms. Reaction times showed a longer intercept value for the synonym probe than for the homonym, so semantic encoding required more time than phonemic encoding, which was thus a less costly, more economical process for this task. But the instructions forced the subject to attend to both types of information. In other tasks, phonemic encoding may be bypassed, or meaning may be processed first (Moore, 1919), as task demands make appropriate. A strict stage model of reading, to be perfectly applicable, would thus have to be constructed for every task and every level of maturity.*

2. *Adaptive reading is characterized by continual reduction of information.* This second subprinciple can in turn be expanded in several ways.

a. Processing is reduced in proportion to the number of alternatives that *could* follow in the ensuing information as the reader proceeds through the text.

It has often been supposed (see the section on analysis-by-synthesis models in this chapter) that the reader predicts, forms hypotheses, or guesses what comes next. That he makes use of other information to the improvement of his efficiency is attested by any amount of evidence. Experiments with the eye-voice span (see Chapter 10), experiments on use of categorical information in anagram solution (see Chapter 3), and use of topical information and layout information in learning from reading (see Chapter 11) are but a few of the examples we could cite.

*After writing this section, a paper by LaBerge and Samuels (in press) was received which attempts to remedy this difficulty of previous models. Their model has the usual characteristics of a stage theory: visual input→feature detector→letter coding→spelling pattern coding→word coding→phonological coding→memory coding (including associations with the foregoing stages in visual, phonological, episodic, and semantic modes)→response. But *attention* sits at one side, detached, and can be focused on any of these processes, once they have become available through learning. They may all go on at once automatically, if they have been sufficiently practiced, but only one can be selected for attention. With enough practice, stages can be skipped, and the visual word code, for instance, elicit meaning "automatically." A visually presented word, according to the model, can take many alternative routes through the processing system toward its goal of activating meaning codes. This model is just as speculative as the others, but it has the virtue of being more realistic in recognizing the flexibility of reading processes.

But is the reader actually forming a hypothesis and then changing it, playing a guessing game, or predicting? Such descriptions imply either a phenomenology of reading activity which is certainly incorrect, or a metaphorical way of speaking which is not only unenlightening but obscures some underlying properties of all behavior that reading shares. In perception, in decision and choice, in solving problems, and in remembering, it has been demonstrated that reduction of alternatives renders the process not only more determinate, faster, and more efficient, but even more satisfying (Garner, 1962, 1972; Garner and Clement, 1963). If a subject has found in an anagram experiment that the completed anagrams formed sentences, and he has now got as far as "Sally helps Mom clean ———," there is hardly more than one solution possible. His uncertainty, the amount of work he has to do to decide on his solution, is reduced. The same thing takes place in reading. The reader does not merely guess at the word; studies using the eye-voice span have shown that the reader does not make mistakes when he uses foregoing structure to increase his span. He is reading, but something has narrowed the alternatives for decision and left him less work to do. Garner (1972), in discussing the facilitating effect of context on tachistoscopic word recognition (cf. Tulving and Gold, 1963), commented:

. . . it is likely that the context improves recognition accuracy by a mechanism which is not at all unique to the use of words as stimuli. Most likely, the context provides a smaller message set for the observer, and thus improves accuracy of recognition. (p. 278)

And further, in comparing verbal encoding with perceptual discrimination:

Words, of course, can be used as stimuli, but the factors governing the role of redundancy in improving discrimination of such stimuli are the same as for other types of stimulus material. (p. 279)

b. Alternatives are reduced by the application of rules and constraints, structural variables in the matter of the text, that are sometimes referred to as "redundancy."

There are rulelike structural variables in text, as well as in language in general, that specify what can occur. Knowledge of these rules is imperative, of course, for them to be operative, and presumably they must for the most part be learned. What and where are these rules and constraints? We have discussed them before, and they occur at many levels.

Uncertainty, to use Garner's term, is reduced at the level of the *word* by both the phonological and the orthographic rules of English (Garner,

1962, pp. 239 ff.). In Chapters 5, 6, and 7 these rules were discussed at length, and their effective operation was delineated for word recognition in Chapter 7. Rules for the structure of English monosyllables, though not as yet fully understood, are internalized and generalized to new words and nonwords, and knowledge of them has been shown by many methods (tachistoscopic identification, discrimination, detection in a confusable context, recognition with probe techniques, etc.) to facilitate reading the word. Knowledge of these rules does not generate hypotheses, in any known meaning of the term, for few readers (if any) could verbalize the rules. Redundancy of this type operates automatically in a skilled reader. Telling him two alternatives ahead of time, with nonredundant material, has the same effect on judgment as using redundant material and presenting the choices *after* exposure (Thompson and Massaro, 1973). The alternatives are reduced for him without foreknowledge or expectation of what is to come when acceptable orthography is present.

Uncertainty is also reduced beyond the level of the word within phrases, clauses, and sentences, as we saw in Chapter 10. It is unnecessary to summarize the evidence again, for the redundancy within a sentence provided by both grammar and meaning is obvious. The eventlike nature of the sentence, as well as surface rules of syntax, add to the reduction of possible alternatives. We live in a fairly predictable world—if one kicks a lamp it will fall over. This agent-action-object relation is reflected in the way we verbalize predications about events. We do not need to formulate predictions because they are generally perceptible in the "causal texture of the environment," as Tolman and Brunswik (1935) put it.

Passages of discourse beyond the sentence contain predications about longer episodes and events, but as we have seen in the very recent research on paragraphs and the studies making use of discourse analysis (see Chapter 11), thematic constraints and syntactic conventions exist even at this larger level and reduce the reader's alternatives and thus the amount of information he has to process.

c. Alternatives are reduced by using *old* information to comprehend *new* information.

The reader, as anyone would agree, uses his knowledge of the world, his stock of concepts, to comprehend what he reads. But he also uses knowledge contained in implications between sentences and within the sentence itself. Language has evolved in such a way that a subtle set of conventions provides a set of constraints within linguistic structure. Pfafflin's analysis of first and second sentences in paragraphs is a simple example of this. If the first sentence contains a proper name and describes an action, such as "William broke a glass," the second sentence need not mention the name again. "He apologized to his hostess" is perfectly comprehensible (even though we hadn't heard about a hostess before, the whole incident is comprehensible).

Chafe (1970) has written most convincingly about cooccurrence rules, such as the role of the verb in reducing uncertainty by providing constraints for the rest of the sentence. His discussion of the tightly interwoven structure of noun-verb relations is especially convincing, as is his position that "what lies behind universal constraints on the cooccurrence of semantic units" is "the nature of the knowledge which all human beings share" (Chafe, p. 83). Certain animate verbs can take animate objects but not inanimate ones; one cannot say "The noise frightened the chair." A similar constraint is that of a persistent state, such as tallness. One cannot combine it with a progressive tense (e.g., "He is being tall") or a past tense (unless the possessor of the state is dead). A verb of state will not be followed by an object (one cannot say "He sleeps the chair"), but it can be followed by a locative or a temporal phrase ("He slept in his chair during class"). Chafe's particular interest in noun-verb structures is accounted for in the following statement:

My assumption will be that the total human conceptual universe is dichotomized initially into two major areas. One, the area of the verb, embraces states, conditions, qualities and events; the other, the area of the noun, embraces "things" (both physical objects and reified abstractions). (p. 96)

Chafe draws many implications from these distinctions, always with semantic reference. A verb of state is accompanied by a noun which is its patient ("The dish was cracked"). A verb of action must have an agent ("Harriet cracked the dish"). One could go even farther along the lines of semantic constraints. Some verbs, like *push,* take a count noun as object; others, like *pour,* take mass nouns. These and many other semantic constraints, as well as one's systematized conceptual knowledge of things and events, limit what a sentence or a passage can say.

To say that the constraints provided by conceptual knowledge, semantic and syntactic structure, and phonological and orthographic rule systems provide a means of reducing alternatives and thereby increase the economy of the cognitive processes that occur in reading is not an explanation; but it is a verifiable statement of such generality that it has the status of a strong principle.

Summary

This chapter dealt with the question of models of the reading process in mature skilled readers. It will be evident by now that it is indeed a question whether looking for a model is a worthwhile enterprise. A model implies a paradigm, or a pattern to be closely followed. That any one model will suffice to typify the reading process is doubtful, but we described two classes of model, with examples, since they are currently much in style. Information processing models, one of the classes, are typically stage models, with a succession of events or encoding processes progressing from stimulus input at the beginning to a response output at the end. Different models may emphasize different encoding processes, but they all assume some hypothetical events moving along in a train of transformations, each occupying a fixed amount of time. Typically, research on these models seeks to estimate the time taken by the hypothesized events, and the experimental method always measures time to make one or another judgment. The models of Mackworth (1972), Rubenstein (1971), and Gough (1972) were chosen since they vary from one another but all exemplify the information processing approach.

The other class of model was referred to as "analysis by synthesis," a term borrowed from a theory of speech perception. This is essentially a constructionist model. The reader constructs the meaning for himself as his eyes move over the page, forms hypotheses about what is to follow, and pauses for a fixation occasionally to confirm what he has been predicting. This model is far looser than the information processing models that were described in detail and that require a fixed succession of processing stages. The emphasis here is on meaning. The principal proponent of this class of model is Goodman (1967), who in fact dubbed reading a "psycholinguistic guessing game." This model has not led to much research (save for Goodman's study of "miscues" or errors), since it is too vaguely specified to be checked. It does not specify, for example, how the reader knows when to confirm his guesses or where to look to do so. The fact that errors in oral reading are seldom nonsense might be predicted by any number of theories.

If we are dissatisfied with model building, must we eschew making any generalizations about what the mature reader is doing? By no means. We can make some firm generalizations about the skilled reading process which have the status of principles and as such tell us where the novice is heading and what we should look for in his behavior to see if he is getting there. The first thing to emphasize is that reading is an adaptive process. It is active and flexible, the processing strategies changing to meet the demands of the text and the purpose of the reader. Evidence was summarized to show that different features of a word can be and are attended to independently as they have utility for a task. The evidence for selection and priority of processing classes of features is not only available in laboratory experiments where the subject is at the mercy of the experimenter's instructions; but a selection of case studies was presented to show how different readers attend to information in different kinds of text (poetry, news, dictionaries, etc.) in highly variable ways. Laboratory studies confirm that readers read differently for different purposes, such as getting the gist or remembering details.

A second major principle is the trend toward increasing economy in the adult reader. This trend breaks down into two important subprinciples. One is that the reader will direct his attention to processing textual material in the most economical way that he can. This achievement is accomplished in four ways: (1) by selecting relevant information; (2) by ignoring irrelevant information; (3) by processing the largest units that are appropriate for the task; and (4) by processing the least amount of information compatible with the task.

The second subprinciple states that adaptive reading is characterized by continual reduction of information. The reduction is accomplished in three ways: (1) processing is reduced in proportion to the number of alternatives that could succeed; (2) alternatives are reduced by the application of rules and constraints which are structural variables in the text; and (3) alternatives are reduced by using old information, both conceptual and inferred from cooccurrence requirements in the text, to comprehend new information. Finally, we conclude that the reading process is rule governed and incapable of adequate description in simple terms.

III

Questions People Ask about Reading

What Is Dyslexia?*

"Dyslexia" has been variously defined in the literature, and authorities are unable to reach a consensus about what is meant by the term. Adams (1969) has pointed out the discrepancies and contradictions of many of the definitions of dyslexia that have been proposed. In part, as Applebee (1971) has noted, the disagreement is the result of three fields of inquiry with differing knowledge and interests—education, psychology, and medicine—carrying on their work with little communication. And in part the disagreement is the result of lack of knowledge concerning the etiology of dyslexia and the nature of the reading process.

We would like to offer a definition that is descriptive of the condition often referred to as dyslexia that is dealt with by parents, teachers, and reading specialists. Dyslexia is the condition of failure to master reading at a level normal for age when this failure is not the result of a generally debilitating disorder such as mental retardation, major brain injury, or severe emotional instability. To understand what dyslexia is, however, one must go beyond a descriptive definition. A full understanding of dyslexia must include knowledge of its possible etiology, as well as the cognitive and perceptual performance of dyslexic children that interferes in the normal reading process. It is the goal of this section to explore these aspects of dyslexia.

Many other terms have been used in the literature and in the schools to label the state of affairs of the otherwise normal child who is slow at mastering reading. Among these are "specific learning disability," "reading retardation," "word blindness," and "reading disorder." The problem of real significance, however, is understanding rather than naming, and no quarrel is made here over which name should be used.

The means for deciding whether or not a child is having trouble reading is, generally, through the use of standard reading tests. A rule of thumb seems to be: If a child falls one year or more below his expected grade placement in the primary grades and $1\frac{1}{2}$ years or more below his expected grade placement in the later grades, he has a significant reading problem (see HEW report, 1969). Of such children with significant reading problems, the number who are identified as dyslexic is disturbingly high. It has

*This section was coauthored by Nancy Rader.

been estimated that at least 15% of America's schoolchildren are dyslexic. The fact that dyslexia is so undesirable is largely a result of the importance of reading achievement in our educational system. In our schools children are expected to learn to read at a certain level depending upon their chronological age, and their general education is based on this expectation. If a child is not up to par in reading, he fails not only at reading, but generally at school achievement. This can have detrimental effects both on his personality and on his opportunities for future success.

The Etiology of Dyslexia

Using the term "dyslexia," or indeed any of the other common labels, does not imply that there is either a single behavioral syndrome or a single cause, historical or constitutional, of difficulty in learning to read. Rather, "dyslexia" should be thought of as a general term for a condition which can occur in otherwise normal children affecting different aspects of performance in different individuals and resulting from different causes. We will first take up the question of cause (in the sense of what it is that brought the condition about) and later take up the question of how performance is affected.

An analysis of the possible causes of dyslexia for an individual has been uncommon in the study of dyslexia. Rather, attempts have been made to find *the* cause of dyslexia, assuming the condition to result from a common cause in all individuals. Such use of the term is like trying to talk about a sore throat as a disorder with one unique cause, rather than a general condition that has many possible causes, such as flu, tonsillitis, or strep throat. This tendency is aggravated by the fact that different types of institutions which examine dyslexic children tend to attract only a particular type of dyslexic child, so that broad and incorrect generalizations about dyslexia result.

One particularly disturbing use of the term "dyslexia" has been as solely a neurologically determined phenomenon. This superficial diagnosis probably results from a tendency of a few clinical neurologists to assume that dyslexia is strictly a medical problem. The definition of dyslexia given by *Dorland's Illustrated Medical Dictionary* (1957, p. 419) is "an inability to read understandingly due to a central lesion." Parents and teachers who are given such a definition are inevitably in despair. This biased definition has been the cause of great confusion. Clinical neurologists have been acquainted, through war injuries of the brain, with a number of cases of *alexia*, that is, loss of an ability that was once present and well developed. There is no reason to conclude a priori that any child who has trouble learning to read must have specific brain injury. However, it seems that some dyslexic children, probably a very small percentage, do have subtle differences in brain functioning that are responsible for their reading problems; this case of "minimal brain dysfunction" will be discussed below.

After considering the possibilities and reviewing the literature, we have concluded that there are four broad causes for the appearance of dyslexia (for a somewhat similar analysis, see Bannatyne, 1971). These may be called: (1) communicative emotional deprivation; (2) cultural or educational deprivation; (3) minimal brain dysfunction; and (4) genetic makeup. These four causes may be grouped into two more general classes, intrinsic and extrinsic (cf. Applebee, 1971; see also Table 1). The distinction is useful because it emphasizes that one cannot blame all cases of dyslexia on either society and the school system or on physical causes. Extrinsic causes include those primarily outside the individual—his home background, the quality of instruction available to him, and the general cultural milieu surrounding him. Some of these variables may affect a whole community and others may differ for ethnic and economic groups in the population. Intrinsic variables or causes are specific to the individual and encompass unique combinations of abilities, as limited by organic and genetic factors. Such factors cross economic and cultural boundaries and are not the result of them, although they may interact with them. The causes of dyslexia are not only diverse, but frequently interact with other factors. For example, a child who senses early failure, for whatever reason, is highly likely to develop emotional reactions and an aversion to reading. Further, it should be emphasized that listing causes of dyslexia does not imply that any particular child will fall neatly under one type. If a child is having difficulty reading, it may be the result of a combination of these causes. Each of the four causes listed above will be discussed briefly.

Table 1 Classification of Causes of Dyslexia

Extrinsic Causes		Intrinsic Causes	
Communicative emotional deprivation	Cultural or educational deprivation	Minimal brain dysfunction	Genetically limited ability

Communicative Emotional Deprivation

Communicative emotional deprivation refers to the lack of proper stimulation for language acquisition in the social environment. That is, the environment may not permit language to be learned in ways that are required for normal reading. For example, there may be a poor mother-child relationship as a result of a disinterested, depressed, absent, or angry mother which results in poor verbal communication. Other abnormal family relationships could also be involved to the extent that they might result in a distortion of linguistic communication and hence language knowledge.

Through studying case histories of dyslexic children, Bannatyne (1971) concluded that early deprivation of normal communication between a mother and child can result in the child's not acquiring good language skills. If the child is spoken to infrequently or only angrily, and if his efforts to speak are not responded to at all or only negatively, it is likely that he will be deficient in language knowledge and his motivation to learn language-related tasks will be lowered.

We have seen earlier in this book how language knowledge is essential to the reading process. A child who is lacking in language knowledge will have difficulty learning to read. A study by Rabinovitch and Strassberg (1968) showed that good readers utilize syntactic structure better in a memory task than do poor readers, suggesting that at least some poor readers are deficient in syntactic knowledge or in the ability to utilize it adaptively.

Cultural or Educational Deprivation

Cultural or educational deprivation is the result of poverty in those experiences that are important for learning in school, and can lead to dyslexia. A rather specific example is that of the child who learns a dialect rather than the forms of language used in school and as a consequence has trouble learning to read (although evidence of this is inconclusive; see "Do Variations in Dialect Affect Learning to Read?"). More generally, a culturally deprived child's environment often does not provide the proper stimulation for learning to read. There is little opportunity to develop the prereading skills that have been described in Chapter 8. Books may be entirely lacking in the home, and the child may never have observed anyone reading and may never have been read to. Perhaps the most significant aspect of these children's problems is a lack of motivation to learn to read, reinforced by a lack of appropriate models in their home environment. It has been suggested that an impoverished environment also differs from one more culturally privileged in its lack of talk containing references to logical relationships, which are important in learning in the school situation (Bannatyne, 1971). Children from a culturally deprived environment seem to be unprepared to learn many abstractions that are characteristic of the school's culture.

The problems of the culturally deprived child are further aggravated by the likelihood that he attends inferior schools where he does not receive sufficient enriching or remedial attention. Or if these children do attend good schools, they are often unable to benefit from the instruction which is geared to the more privileged child, so they fall further and further behind their classmates. Programs such as Head Start were developed to correct this problem by offering the stimulation for learning to read missing in the child's environment and by preparing the child for school so that he could begin on a par with his classmates. However, such programs have been found to exert only a temporary stimulating effect, since the regular school instruction that follows remains ineffective in terms of the child's early background and unchanged home surroundings. Also, it may be that programs such as Head Start begin too late to make up for the lack of early rich language experiences.

The lack of an appropriate model in the classroom for the child to identify with is another type of educational deprivation which appears to be a significant problem for a large number of dyslexic children. We have pointed out earlier in this book that modeling is important in encouraging the child to learn to read. A teacher's inappropriate race or sex may seriously diminish effectiveness as a role model. In fact, it appears to be the case that the high ratio of dyslexic boys to girls in the schools of the United States is mainly the result of a high ratio of female to male teachers in the primary grades. As reported in the section "Are there Cross-National Differences in Reading Achievement?" the ratio of dyslexic boys to girls is almost reversed in a country such as Germany, where the ratio of male to female teachers in the primary grades is very high.

Minimal Brain Dysfunction
"Minimal brain dysfunction" (MBD) refers to subtle deviations in the functioning of the central nervous system which are not caused by major injury. Such deviations may be produced by biochemical irregularities,

perinatal brain insults, or injuries or illnesses sustained during the years critical for the development of the nervous system (see Clements, 1967). The abnormal functioning may result in various combinations of deficits in perception, conceptualization, language, memory, or control of attention which will interfere with the reading process. A child with minimal brain dysfunction may exhibit any or all of these cognitive deficits. It should be remembered that each child must be considered individually to determine which cognitive functions are being affected and how these interfere with his reading.

The diagnosis of the child with MBD is problematic, since there is no circumscribed set of factors which are always present and the connection between any particular factor and MBD is usually inferential and often disputed. Symptoms that are most commonly cited are perceptual deficits, motor incoordinations, an abnormal EEG, and abnormal reflexes. Clements (1966) lists as developmental variants associated with MBD frequent lags in developmental milestones, a generalized maturational lag, possible physical immaturity, reflex asymmetry, mild visual or hearing impairments, strabismus or nystagmus, incidence of left or mixed laterality, hyperkinesis and hypokinesis, general awkwardness, and impaired fine visual-motor coordination.

Of these symptoms of MBD, maturational lag and left or mixed laterality have been emphasized particularly as being responsible for the appearance of dyslexia (Critchley, 1968; de Hirsch, 1968; Money, 1966; Satz and Sparrow, 1970). More specifically, it is suggested that a lag in the maturation of the left hemisphere and a corresponding lag in the functional specialization of language results in dyslexia. Two studies have been carried out recently which add support to this hypothesis. Sparrow and Satz (1970) looked at differences in the manifestations of laterality between dyslexic children and normal readers. They found that while the dyslexic children did not differ from the normal readers on early-developing aspects of laterality (manual and visual), they differed on all late-developing measures of lateralization (e.g., lateral awareness and finger differentiation). Satz, Rardin, and Ross (1971) investigated the competence of various skills which are in ascendancy at different developmental ages. They found that young dyslexic children (ages 8–9) differed from normal readers of the same age on skills that are usually developed at this stage (e.g., some visual-motor integration tasks) but did not differ on skills which become proficient later. On the other hand, older dyslexic children (ages

11–12) showed a deficiency in skills which are normally well developed at their age (e.g., dichotic listening) when compared with normal readers, but did not differ from normal readers on the early-developing skills. It should be noted that the finding of a statistical difference in the rate of development between dyslexic children and normal readers does not imply that all dyslexic children show a maturational lag, nor that for those who do the cause is MBD, as it is defined here.

It is our opinion that only a small percentage of dyslexic children fall into the MBD category. A study by Owen, Adams, Forrest, Stolz, and Fisher (1971) found that of the 304 dyslexic children in their study, only four could be diagnosed definitively as neurologically impaired. Given the arguments over symptomatology, it is not clear exactly how many children in the general population should be considered as having dyslexia that is the result of MBD. Caution should be observed in categorizing any child as having minimal brain dysfunction.

Genetic Makeup
The genetic makeup of an individual may be responsible for his failure to learn to read competently. The genetic system could function to produce dyslexia either by determining a slower course of development for certain skills or by setting a limit on the level of ability that may be reached with respect to the skills necessary for learning to read. We mentioned that maturational lag is often used as an identifying symptom of MBD. However, we would like to suggest that there are normal differences in the rate of development of various skills, determined by the gene system, that need not be a sign of minimal brain dysfunction. (It is recognized that the genetic system, through faulty chemical production, for example, may bring about MBD; however, this would be a case of malfunction rather than normal variation in the rate of development.) Any lag in the development of the skills necessary for learning to read will produce a lag in mastering reading. Or a child's ability may be genetically limited, placing him at the low end of a normal distribution of language or perceptual skills. For example, some children will simply not have inherited enough language ability to learn to read competently; others may be slower than the average in learning to discriminate letters of the alphabet or in the ability to extract the higher-order structures of orthography that are needed to read well.

The evidence for genetically caused dyslexia, though not complete, is compelling. Geneticists have discovered the existence of regulator genes whose function can control the rate of development. Vandenberg (1966) has demonstrated that some language skills are based on the potential available in the genotype; and Bannatyne (1971) has described a group of dyslexic children who perform very poorly on such language-related tasks as the discrimination of sequences of sounds, the discrimination of similar speech sounds, and sound blending when attempting to read. In addition to evidence that certain language skills are inherited (and hence the lack of them as well), studies have examined the incidence of dyslexia or language-related disorders within families, siblings, and twins. Walker and Cole (1965) studied familial patterns of poor spelling ability and found that spelling disability was aggregated in families beyond chance at the .005 level of significance. A study carried out by Bakwin (1973) using 338 pairs of twins found that identical twins were alike in reading disability in 84% of the cases, but only 29% of fraternal twins were similar in this respect. An extensive research project by Owen et al. (1971) found that siblings of dyslexic children with high performance discrepancies (15 or more points higher in their performance IQ than in their verbal IQ) on the Wechsler Intelligence Scale for Children (WISC) exhibited many similarities of impairment with respect to reading and that the mothers of these children often had poor reading skills. Lenneberg (1967) reviewed a number of studies concerned with the inheritance of language ability. He found that studies of a variety of speech disorders (Huyck, 1940; Mussafia, 1960; Pfaendler, 1960) and studies of dyslexia (Drew, 1956; Hallgren, 1950) indicated the tendency of these disorders to run in families. A number of other reports cited by Lenneberg documented the familial occurrence of congenital language disability through published pedigrees (Luchsinger and Arnold, 1959; Arnold, 1961; Brewer, 1963). Lenneberg's conclusion is that "genetic transmission is relevant to language facilitation" (p. 265).

It has often been suggested that the inheritance of factors leading to dyslexia is sex-linked because of the high rate of occurrence of dyslexia in boys. However, this sex imbalance, while found in the United States, is not found in all countries (see the section "Are there Cross-National Differences in Reading Achievement?"). It appears that the sex imbalance is the result of some cultural factor such as the lack of a male model for boys, as we remarked earlier.

Where Do Dyslexic Children Fail?

Further understanding of dyslexia must come from consideration of where the dyslexic child fails in the reading process. What necessary language or cognitive and perceptual skills does he lack or what is he doing incorrectly that causes him to fail to learn to read competently? It is important to note that the set of factors contributing to reading failure may well be different for each child. Further, any set of factors will not necessarily correspond to a particular cause of dyslexia. For example, children whose dyslexia is the result of cultural-educational deprivation or communicative emotional deprivation may lack the same language skills and hence make the same pattern of mistakes while learning to read. Also, children whose dyslexia is the result of a particular cause, such as minimal brain dysfunction, may differ greatly with respect to the specific cognitive and perceptual skill or skills in which they are deficient.

Comparisons of the differences in skills of dyslexic children and normal readers have turned up a host of possibilities. The importance of motivation and good language skills has been discussed elsewhere in this book; certainly deficiencies in these areas will interfere with learning to read. Some proposed specific deficiencies in cognitive and perceptual skills that have received much attention will be discussed briefly below, namely, poor perceptual-motor coordination, deficient intermodal integration, reversals of letters or words, faulty serial ordering and temporal differentiation, and difficulties in sound segmentation.

Poor Perceptual-Motor Coordination

It has often been proposed that dyslexic children have difficulty learning to read because of a failure to coordinate their perceptual and motor systems. However, it is not at all clear how poor perceptual-motor coordination could interfere with the reading process; and there is no good evidence to date that in fact it does. The possibility seems highly unlikely when one considers that many people handicapped with cerebral palsy reach a high degree of literacy. A study by Nielsen and Ringe (1969) adds support to the conclusion that poor perceptual-motor coordination is not itself responsible for failure to master reading. Observing children in remedial reading classes, these investigators compared 20 nine- and ten-year-old dyslexic children with 20 normal readers, matched for age,

IQ, and socioeconomic background, on three standard tests of perceptual and perceptual-motor skills (the Frostig Test of Visual Perception, the Bender Visual Motor Gestalt Test, and the Goodenough Draw-a-Person Test). The results showed more similarity than difference in performance level between the two groups. Only one test, the Bender Gestalt Test, discriminated the groups significantly; the difference appeared to be due to the greater number of rotations found in the dyslexic children's drawings. The Bender Gestalt Test and one Frostig subtest are both designed to test perceptual-motor coordination, yet these two measures did not correlate significantly. The investigators concluded that impaired perceptual-motor functioning does not seem to be a necessary or an important correlate of dyslexia.

Perhaps the importance of perceptual-motor coordination to reading has been emphasized as a result of a methodological problem that has arisen in studies which have attempted to test the hypothesis that poor perceptual-motor coordination is responsible for failure to learn to read competently. Immature motor development, as we have mentioned, is associated with minimal brain dysfunction, one cause of dyslexia. Any study using a neuroclinical sample of dyslexic children is likely to discover that these dyslexic children have poor perceptual-motor development. However, presence of this symptom by no means indicates that the lack of good perceptual-motor coordination is itself responsible for the child's failure to learn to read. However, since poor perceptual-motor coordination can be a sign of MBD or, more generally, maturational lag, it may often go hand in hand with the lack of development of some other skill important for learning to read.

Deficient Intermodal Integration
The research on intermodal integration has been reviewed in Chapter 8 (pp. 246 ff.). We concluded that the research on intermodal integration does not support the general hypothesis that intermodal integration is a developmental skill uniquely related to reading. However, it was suggested that some process involved in pattern matching tasks both across and within modalities is similar to one required for initial reading success. This process may be the extraction of structure of patterned information—the relations between subordinate units, both over time and space and within and across modalities. The most relevant materials one could use to test

this notion would be those that simulate the type of materials that must be mastered in the reading process.

The patterned information with which beginning readers must deal is both visual-symbolic (the printed word) and auditory-verbal (the spoken word). An experiment that attempted to look at the integration of these two types of information by good and poor readers was carried out by Vellutino, Harding, and Phillips (1973), who used a code substitution task with both a visual-verbal condition and a visual-visual condition. The subjects were fourth, fifth, and sixth graders.

In the visual-verbal condition during training, pairs of novel geometric designs were matched with easily pronounceable bisyllabic nonsense words. The nonsense words were presented in both written and oral form concordantly. The child was told that each geometric design in a pair went with the syllable that was in the same position in the nonsense word. Then the child was given a transfer task where the same relationship between individual designs and syllables obtained, but now he was required to produce the new bisyllabic nonsense words that went with pairs of the geometric designs displayed in new combinations. Figure 1a gives some examples of the stimuli presented and responses required for the training and transfer tasks of the visual-verbal condition. The visual-visual condition was similarly a code substitution task, but now new designs rather than syllables of nonsense words were coded to the standard designs. In the training task, pairs of geometric designs (the standards) were matched with pairs of other geometric designs. The child was told that each design in the standard pair went with the design that was in the same position in the code pair. In the transfer task the child was required to choose from among five possibilities the pair of geometric designs that was the code for pairs made up of new combinations of the designs presented in the standard pairs of the training task. Figure 1b gives some examples of the stimuli presented and responses required for the training and transfer tasks of the visual-visual condition.

No difference was found between good and poor readers in the visual-visual condition. However, the good readers performed significantly better ($p < .01$) than did the poor readers in the visual-verbal condition. Even when verbal IQ was controlled for in an analysis of covariance, the difference was significant. This finding suggests that the ability to deal simultaneously with both types of information, visual and verbal, is important in learning to read.

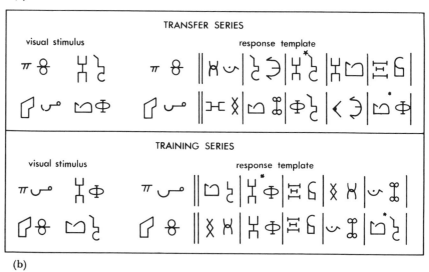

(a)

(b)

Figure 1. From Vellutino et al., 1973. (a) Visual-verbal condition. Stimuli and responses for the training and transfer series. (b) Visual-visual condition. Stimuli and response templates for the training and transfer series.

Reversals of Letters or Words

It has often been suggested that poor readers fail because of a tendency to reverse letters and words. Orton (1925; 1937) originally proposed that such faulty organization of letters and words was due to poorly established hemispheric dominance. Following his lead, many other investigators have taken up the study of the presence of such faulty organization in the dyslexic child (see Bender, 1957; Hermann, 1959; Silver and Hagin, 1960; Money, 1962; Anapolle, 1967; and Benton, 1962). Some evidence suggesting that letter reversals are not unique to the poor reader has been discussed in Chapter 8. In fact, as was noted, more than one-half of all kindergarten children reverse letters. This is only to be expected as a result of learning about object shape constancy in the environment by the developing child. Ilg and Ames (1950) reported that letter reversals tended to persist in normal children until eight or nine years of age. Shankweiler and Liberman (1972) found that single letter reversals accounted for only 10% of reading errors of very poor readers among third-grade children. With regard to word perception, it has been found that not many kindergarten children make word reversal errors, but many of them make permutation errors of letters within words. Shankweiler and Liberman (1972) found that this error in ordering letters in a word persists in poor readers at least into third grade. The confusion of ordering letters in words has been attributed to a more general deficit in organizing items sequentially. Whether this general deficit in serial ordering (including temporal sequencing) is present in dyslexic children and is responsible for their failure to learn to read is discussed in the following paragraphs.

Faulty Serial Ordering and Temporal Differentiation

As we have said, it has been suggested that some dyslexic children fail to learn to read because they are poor at serial ordering. The common feature of serial ordering tasks is that they all require responses to sequential elemental components, with each component bearing some definite relationship to other components of the sequence. In 1951, Lashley pointed out in a classic paper that language skills such as writing, speaking, typing, and reading are serially organized.

McLeod (1965) found that a large number of dyslexic children obtain low WISC Digit span scores. Bannatyne (1967), working with dyslexic boys from ages eight to eleven years found the "sequencing" score on the WISC (Digit Span, plus Picture Arrangement, plus Arithmetic) to be the main area of deficit.

Corkin (unpublished paper) attempted to test the deficient serial ordering hypothesis, that is, that marked reading disorders in children are attributable to a more general deficit in organizing items sequentially, independent of the symbolic nature of the reading process. She compared dyslexic children and normal readers from ages six to eleven years on both visual and auditory tasks free of verbal material. The children had to remember the correct serial positions of cubes as they were tapped by the experimenter and the order of digits presented orally. Significant differences ($p < .01$) were found between the dyslexic group and the normal readers in both tasks. She concluded that disturbances in reading may in part grow out of a general deficiency in serial organization. Further, it was pointed out that this could be due either to the ordering or to a mnemonic weakness. The fact that dyslexic children make permutation errors when reading words that are in front of them, a task requiring no memory, suggests that the ordering aspect is in fact an important one.

In considering what has been said about the normal reading process earlier in this book, it is easy to see how difficulties in ordering could cause difficulties in reading. If a child often makes permutation errors in his perception of letters in words and perhaps words in sentences, he will have difficulty perceiving the higher-order structures that obtain. The higher-order structures are the result of invariant events within orthography and phrasing. If these events are made variant by ordering errors, the higher-order structures necessary for good reading will not be discovered.

Perhaps related to poor serial ordering in many dyslexic children is a tendency to slow temporal differentiation of graphic items. Masking experiments by Stanley and Hall (1973) showed that a group of dyslexic children (without any apparent organic disorder) had significantly longer thresholds for separation and for identification of graphic items than a control group of average to good readers of the same age. For example, in one experiment single letters were presented for identification, followed by a masking field composed of a dot matrix. The interval between the letter and the mask began at 20 msec and was increased by steps of 20 msec until the child could identify the letter correctly. The dyslexic children required a significantly longer interstimulus interval between letter and mask to identify the letters. This requirement of a longer interval before masking to differentiate a graphic display is a typical developmental phenomenon which appears to persist in at least some dyslexic children.

Difficulties in Sound Segmentation

In Chapter 5 the nature of language was discussed, and it was pointed out that language can be analyzed into various linguistic segments—sentences, phrases, words, syllables, and phonemes. It has been suggested that dyslexic children may fail to learn to read because they have failed to differentiate the features of these segments, especially phonemes (Johnson and Myklebust, 1967). Phonemes are systematically represented in orthography by letters and letter clusters. If phonemes are not well differentiated, the child's task of learning to read becomes very difficult. He will find it difficult or impossible to discover the lawful relationships between the phonemic system and the orthographic system, as we considered in detail in Chapter 8. And this may, in fact, be the difficulty of some dyslexic children.

However, as Liberman (1971) points out, since the spoken language of many of these children is generally good, one cannot ascribe their difficulties with phonemic analysis and synthesis to poor auditory discrimination. Such difficulties with segmentation must involve something other than poor auditory perception, probably (as we suggested earlier) the child's difficulty in perceiving the physical, rather than the semantic and communicative, properties of language.

Summary

We have suggested that the causes of dyslexia may be extrinsic or intrinsic or an interaction of the two. Four possible causes of dyslexia were proposed. Two of these were extrinsic: communicative emotional deprivation and cultural-educational deprivation. The other two were intrinsic: minimal brain dysfunction and genetic makeup. It was suggested that motivation and good language skills are important in learning to read and that these can be limited by either extrinsic or intrinsic factors. Five main areas of research into the cognitive and perceptual skills of dyslexic children were discussed briefly: poor perceptual-motor coordination, deficient intersensory integration, reversals of letters and words, faulty serial ordering and temporal differentiation, and difficulties in sound segmentation. One picture of a dyslexic child that this research reveals is that of a child who fails to pick up the higher-order relations in the writing system, perhaps because of poor serial ordering ability, or who fails to relate higher-order relationships in orthography to those in his oral language, either because of faulty integration skills or because of poor differentiation of phonemes. However, we do not suggest that even this very general description would be appropriate for all dyslexic children, especially those whose failure to learn to read is the result of extrinsic factors.

No discussion of the remedial treatment of dyslexic children has been included in this discussion. The reason is, in part, because of the limited amount of knowledge concerning the deficiencies of dyslexic children related to the reading process, as we have indicated. But also, a discussion of remedial treatment would need to be at least as detailed and complex as a discussion of causes of dyslexia, of the role of motivational and language skills in learning to read, and of the possible deficient cognitive and perceptual skills of dyslexic children. We would like to stress that remedial help necessarily depends upon the problems of the individual child and that all aspects of his condition, both cause and deficiencies of performance, must be taken into consideration.

How Well Do Deaf Children Learn to Read?

The problem of deaf children learning to read is not, strictly speaking, a problem of reading per se, but of language development in general. Deaf children must not only acquire a communication system, but also must acquire the basic notion of language as a means of communication. Since our concern is with reading, we will concentrate on the more limited topic of reading by deaf children rather than on their language development. For those interested in the more general topic, there is a substantial literature (e.g., Lenneberg, 1967; Myklebust, 1964; Heider and Heider, 1940).* We will discuss two issues: (1) how well deaf children learn to read; and (2) whether their early communication training—oral or sign language—influences their ability to learn to read.

Average reading achievement for deaf children is not very encouraging. Table 2 shows the silent reading achievement of deaf students from $10\frac{1}{2}$ to $16\frac{1}{2}$ years (Furth, 1966). Furth takes minimal reading competence to be fourth-grade reading ability and shows that by midadolescence only 12% of the deaf subjects reach this level. Between the ages of 12 and 16, the deaf, in spite of intensive schooling, improve less than one grade level in their reading ability. Deaf students seem to reach a plateau at the fourth-grade level which in general is not improved by additional schooling, though it is not uncommon for deaf pupils to remain in school until they are 19 or 20 years old.

The profoundly deaf person who has been so since before the age of language learning may know quite a number of isolated words, but with rare

Table 2   Silent Reading Achievement of Deaf Pupils Compared to Grade Equivalent of Hearing Norms

Age	N	Mean Raw Score and Standard Deviation	Mean Grade Equivalent	Median Grade Equivalent	Percentage Scoring at Grade 4.9 or Above
$10\frac{1}{2}$–$11\frac{1}{2}$	654	12.6 (8.1)	2.7	2.6	1%
$11\frac{1}{2}$–$12\frac{1}{2}$	849	14.9 (8.5)	2.8	2.7	2%
$12\frac{1}{2}$–$13\frac{1}{2}$	797	17.6 (9.1)	3.1	3.1	6%
$13\frac{1}{2}$–$14\frac{1}{2}$	814	18.7 (9.3)	3.3	3.2	7%
$14\frac{1}{2}$–$15\frac{1}{2}$	1035	20.8 (9.3)	3.4	3.3	10%
$15\frac{1}{2}$–$16\frac{1}{2}$	1075	21.6 (9.5)	3.5	3.4	12%

Source: Furth, 1966, p. 14. Copyright © by Hans G. Furth.

*For an excellent recent review of the research on the education of deaf children see Bonzillian, Charrow, and Nelson (1973).

exceptions will he be able to form or comprehend sentences or paragraphs which approximate the complexity of Grade 4 reading level.

The linguistic deficiency of the deaf consists more precisely in their inability to handle linguistic ordering or structure. (Furth, 1966, p. 14)

How are deaf children taught to read? The two most widely used manuals (Hart, 1963; Streng, 1964) are similar in emphasizing that reading be taught in the context of language acquisition. Both rely on the "oral approach," about which we will have more to say shortly. Both authors agree that the deaf child must first know what language is and about the communicative function of language. Teachers are exhorted to give children rich language experiences and to put early emphasis on word meanings. The manuals recognize that words with concrete referents are easier to teach to deaf children. The manuals also put heavy emphasis on sentence frames:

Bill has a new————.
Mary has a new————, etc.

Myklebust (1964) points out that as a consequence the written compositions of deaf children contain many such common sentence frames or "carrier phrases," as he calls them.

Both Hart and Streng recognize that reading achievement is likely to be low:

The young deaf child looks at a sentence and picks out the words he readily recognizes. The words he is not able to handle may be: (1) words whose concepts are unknown; (2) words with abstract or multiple meanings; (3) words which provide the structural or syntactic form to the sentence. (Hart, 1963, p. 70)

Streng is even less sanguine than Furth about the reading skill that may be expected. "We know that deaf children plateau at about the second grade level and often do not achieve much beyond the sixth grade level" (p. 27).

In spite of the documented lack of success of this amorphous approach to teaching deaf children to read, Wood (1973), who surveyed educational practices in the early thirties and again within the past several years, found very little change.

We do not want to overdraw this picture of unsuccessful schooling among the deaf. Some deaf students achieve enough academic success to go to college, usually Gallaudet College in Washington, D.C., whose student body is deaf. Instruction makes use of both oral and sign language. Gibson, Shurcliff, and Yonas (1970) found that many of these students had learned the orthographic rules of English, although their knowledge over-all was not as complete as hearing students. Fry (1966) and Hirsh (1966) describe cases of excellent language abilities by some deaf people, though such exceptional behavior is likely to occur when there is some residual hearing or when the deaf person lost his hearing after language develop-ment had begun.

Since the turn of the century, educators of the deaf have debated the oral versus signing methods of communication and teaching. The contro-versy is still heated, though we suspect that in practice sensible com-promises and combinations of techniques are used by individual teachers. The arguments are obvious. If the deaf person learns to lip-read and to speak, he can join the speaking world. If he learns to communicate by sign language, his relationships are restricted to other deaf people. In theory, the oral method has much to recommend it. In practice, most deaf people do not learn to lip-read very well—a very difficult task—nor do they speak very understandably, and their school achievement is poor, as we have seen above. Early successes with the oral method may have accumulated because inadequate medical diagnosis at that time did not distinguish be-tween profoundly deaf people and those with some residual hearing. The latter group may well have profited from the oral methods.

Evidence is accumulating that the two approaches differ in their con-sequences for learning to read. Several studies compared the communi-cation skills of deaf children born to deaf parents with deaf children born to hearing parents. The former group was signed to from infancy; the second group received oral training in school. The linguistic nature of sign language is now being studied (e.g., Bellugi and Fischer, 1972). There are anecdotal accounts that deaf children who are exposed to signing from infancy develop their own signing language in a sequence similar to oral language by hearing children (Stuckles and Birch, 1966; Cicourel and Boes, 1972).

Vernon and Koh (1970) surveyed a number of studies with the con-clusion, "These studies all report superior linguistic and academic achieve-ment for children exposed to manual communication or combined manu-al-oral communication in preschool age years" (p. 527). In their own study the researchers compared deaf children of deaf parents with deaf children whose parents could hear and did not know sign language or finger spelling. The manual group exceeded the oral group on the Word Meaning and Phrase Meaning subtests of the Stanford Achievement Test by 1.2 to 1.6 grade years, and the differences between the two groups tended to increase with age. It should be noted, though, that the developmental rate of the deaf children was still considerably slower than hearing children. The manual children were superior to the comparison group in many other ways: More passed college entrance tests and their written language was judged to be better. The groups did not differ on their ability to lipread or in the intelligibility of their speech. The superiority of deaf children of deaf parents is especially noteworthy when we realize that deaf parents are less well educated and hold inferior jobs compared to the hearing parents of the other group.

In summary, deaf children rarely learn to read well, so that for most of them a fourth-grade reading level is their highest achievement. Reading seems to be the recognition of words that they know, usually words with concrete referents. The evidence is substantial that children who are signed to from infancy read better than students who are taught by the oral method. Perhaps early signing provides these children with general knowledge about language and communication which is learned later with greater difficulty.

Do Variations in Dialect Affect Learning to Read?*

Many researchers and polemicists have been exploring the possibility that learning to read may be more difficult for speakers of a nonstandard dialect. This notion probably grew from an implied analogy to foreign language learning. Speakers whose native language is not English presumably face some barriers in learning to read a language which they may be only beginning to understand and to speak. Perhaps, it is argued, the lower reading scores of dialect speakers reflect a similar process whereby features of that dialect interfere with learning to read. Though this hypothesis is intended to apply to dialects in general, most of the work and speculation actually done has been concerned with dialects spoken by black students (Black English). We will therefore confine our discussion to Black English.

Whereas foreign languages differ from each other in so many features that they are unintelligible to nonspeakers of the language, dialects differ in relatively few features. These differences may occur at several levels of the linguistic system. At the lowest levels we find phonological divergence. For example, in Black English /i/ and /e/ may show no contrast before consonants; e.g., *pin* and *pen* may be pronounced identically. Such phonological variations lead to different sets of homophones for Black English and standard English.

Morphological divergence between Black English and standard English often occurs in the affixes for tenses and possessives. In Black English the final /l/ may be dropped, producing future tense forms like "He go tomorrow." Past tense affixes may be affected by the tendency in Black English to simplify consonant clusters at the ends of words. Thus in Black English we may have *pass*, *fan*, and *raise* for the respective standard English *passed*, *fanned*, and *raised*. The possessive affix *s* may also be deleted in Black English, to yield forms like "Mildred book."

At the syntactic level differences between Black English and standard English may be more noticeable. For example, the deletion of the copula (the verb *to be*) in Black English may result in such forms as "He sick." Another variation appears in the forms for embedded questions. The Black English equivalent of "I asked if he liked me" is "I asked did he like me."

Finally, dialects may differ lexically when the vocabularies for the dialects differ or different meanings are assigned to the same lexical items. An example of a word found in Black English but not standard English is *shucking*, which means to assume a false submissive attitude toward authorities. The term *rapping* is now widely used in both dialects. Originally,

*This section was coauthored by Kathryn E. Yoselson.

however, *rapping* was used by blacks to mean pushing a line or giving a sales pitch. The implication is that one who raps is insincere about what he is saying. Standard English incorporated *rapping* but changed the meaning to signify the very opposite, that is, that the speaker is honest and sincere.

Many investigators have suggested that these kinds of differences between the rules of Black and standard English may cause reading problems:

Although the phoneme patterning of either group of children does not match the graphic representation in a direct one to one correspondence, some contend that the Black child has a more complicated task. In the early phases of reading, he must relate his speech to curriculum and instruction which do not consider variations from Standard English pronunciation. The Black child is baffled by this confusing and arbitrary relationship between unfamiliar sounds and symbols. Furthermore, the teacher who has a vague awareness of linguistic and cultural differences is often led to ambiguities as to whether a particular difficulty is a reading problem, a language problem, or simply a problem of misarticulation. (Melmed, 1971, pp. 1–2)

We shall refer to this viewpoint as the *linguistic interference hypothesis*.

Though there has been a good deal of speculation concerning how speaking a dialect may cause reading problems, there is little actual evidence bearing on the question. Many authorities have questioned the extent to which reading problems exist at all. They usually criticize the techniques for evaluating reading skills (Baratz, 1969; Melmed, 1971; Rystrom, 1972). Repetition tasks, for example, use standard English rules as the basis for judging whether or not the child has made an error. Thus a black child who drops the final consonant in a cluster receives a lower score. Similarly with discrimination tasks, the child in whose dialect *pin* and *pen* are homophones is at a disavdantage when judged by standard English criteria. Baratz (1969) demonstrated that speakers of standard English can be at a disadvantage in the same way simply by changing the criteria for correct pronunciation. When asked to repeat sentences in Black English, white students performed more poorly than blacks.

We have made the point many times in this book that learning to read is *not* tantamount to learning to pronounce standard English. Apparently many educators have not yet accepted this position, so that some investigators still feel compelled to admonish us to avoid this mistake. Shuy's (1969b) statement is typical:

Reading is a decoding of written language which reflects oral language. . . . All evidence seems to indicate that the child who reads "He walked up the street" as "He walk up the street" has learned to read rather well, well enough, in fact, to do what a good reader ought to do— to translate the printed page into his own language system. (pp. 1–2).

If cultural biases in measurement were the sole problem, then the whole furor over dialect and reading becomes a pseudo-issue which should disappear once the appropriate measures for evaluating reading skills have been devised. However, descriptions of the extent of the reading problem for blacks, particularly in the inner city schools, suggest that evaluation is only part of the problem. Blacks score below national norms in reading proficiency. The gap increases with grade level, so that at the end of elementary school blacks are lagging by two years (*New York Times*, December 3, 1968). Though it seems, then, that reading problems in fact exist, the sources of the problems are not clear. The linguistic interference hypothesis is only one of several explanations.

The earliest approach to gain popularity was proposed in its most extreme form by Bereiter and Engelman (1966). They maintained that Black English was not only different from standard English but was also inferior, illogical, and solely expressive in function. In their view, the black child is unable to form concepts, think logically, or use full sentences. All these alleged cognitive deficiencies were attributed to his "impoverished cultural and linguistic environment." This argument has been dubbed *cultural deficit hypothesis*. Bereiter and Engelman based this hypothesis on three kinds of data: (1) Bernstein's (1961) work on stylistic differences in the speech of the lower classes as compared with middle and upper classes; (2) their own data, mainly gleaned from interviews with students; and (3) Deutsch's Deprivation Index (Deutsch et al., 1968). Bernstein had argued that middle and upper classes tend to speak in a "formal" style which is abstract, analytic, and flexible. The lower classes, on the other hand, were said to use a "restricted" style which is descriptive, concrete, and incapable of making fine distinctions or communicating complicated information. Bereiter and Engelman applied this view of social class differences in linguistic style to black dialect, concluding that the language itself was logically deficient and therefore the way to improve reading and other scholastic skills was to teach students a "real" language—in other words, standard English. The instructional programs these authors developed indicate their view of the deficiencies of Black English, as well as what they accept as "logical forms." For example, "They mine" was considered an illogical form, though the only variation from standard English involves a superficial syntactic change, namely, deletion of the auxiliary. In their program for teaching standard English the correct answer to the question "where is the squirrel?" was restricted to the full form "The squirrel is in the tree." The child was not allowed to answer simply "In the tree," for this was only a fragment. It seems obvious that few of us speak standard English by these criteria. Bereiter and Engelman confused logic and simple syntactic variation, and seemed as well to demonstrate naiveté about syntactic processes in general. As Labov (1969, p. 21) wrote: "Given the data that Bereiter presents, we cannot conclude that the child has no grammar, but only that the investigator does not understand the rules of grammar."

Apart from data of the sort just described, Bereiter and Engelman point to the overall low level of verbal output obtained in interviews with black children to justify their claims. Labov argued that this "clamming up" is a function of the social constraints inherent in interview situations. The child feels that he is being judged and that the safest course of action is to do as little as possible. Labov has changed a speaker of monosyllables into a monologist simply by making a few adjustments, such as sitting on the floor, passing food, bringing in a friend of the child, and using taboo words. Once the situation is perceived by the child as nonthreatening, entirely different protocols are obtained.

Bereiter and Engelman's belief that Black English was linguistically inferior encouraged them to search further for the causes of this deficit. Thus they turned to Deutsch's (1968) explanation that blacks were culturally deprived in general. Deutsch composed a Deprivation Index consisting of several variables. If a child did not engage in such activities as visiting museums with his mother, he accumulated points indicating deprivation. Obviously, however, this is not evidence that there was little mother-child verbal interaction, and it ignores the possible importance of peer interaction in acquiring verbal skills. Thus several erroneous assumptions were made in supporting the proposed connection between cultural and linguistic deprivation.

In any case, the whole cultural deficit argument is at this point academic. Given that the view of Black English as a deficient dialect is based on misconceptions and inappropriate methodology, the need to explain such a deficit disappears. Black English is not an inferior dialect; neither is the black child deprived of verbal interaction. Quite the contrary. A good indication of the importance of the verbal mode is the existence of labels in Black English encoding various forms of verbal games, many of which do not appear in standard English: shucking, sounding, playing the dozens, loud talking, etc. (Abrahams and Gay, 1972b). Some of these terms refer quite specifically to the linguistic aspects of communication. For example, Abrahams and Gay describe "playing the dozens" as a *contest of word* in which opponents exchange insulting references to each other's family. Labov (1969, p. 11) also noted the dominant role of language in the black community:

> The view of the Negro speech community which we obtain from our work in the ghetto areas is precisely the opposite from that reported by Deutsch, Engelman, and Bereiter. We see a child bathed in verbal stimulation from morning to night. We see many speech events which depend upon the competitive exhibition of verbal skills: sounding, singing, toasting, rifting, louding—a whole range of activities in which the individual gains status through his use of language.

The cultural deficit hypothesis, then, was succeeded by the linguistic interference hypothesis. Black English, though not inferior to standard English, is different, and perhaps this difference can cause reading problems as well as mutual misunderstandings between teacher and pupil. As mentioned before, there is little experimental evidence on this question. A number of studies pursue the issue of just how "bidialectal" black students are, that is, how much productive and receptive control they have over printed or spoken standard English. Melmed (1971) found that black third graders were not as skilled as white students in production (in standard English) or in auditory discrimination of words which may be homonyms in Black English, such as *road* and *row*. Yet the fact that they were not totally bidialectal seemed to have had no effect on their reading ability. Their comprehension of written material was no different from that of white students. The errors that did occur were reduced when the homonyms were constrained by context. Data from a study by Rystrom (1970) further confirms the lack of relation between reading skill and the ability to discriminate sounds which are distinctive in standard English but not in Black English. Black subjects were trained to make this discrimination. Yet after training there was no improvement in their ability to translate graphic sequences into sound sequences.

So the evidence suggests that black students have receptive control (i.e., understand) written standard English, particularly if they are dealing with words in context rather than isolated lexical items. Others document the fact that even productive control of standard English exceeds that acknowledged and expected by many teachers and writers in the field. DeStefano

(1972) found that in a repetition task first graders responded in standard English 56% of the time. By fifth grade the percentage of standard English responses had increased to 70%. It could be that students were learning more standard English forms with age; it is also possible that they already knew most of the forms and were learning "style switching," that is, to use standard English in the appropriate contexts. Melmed's study with third graders showed them using standard English over 70% of the time. Goodman and Burke (undated) studied higher-order variations between standard English and Black English, finding that students from second to tenth grades produced very few nonstandard readings involving inflections, syntax, and vocabulary. When retelling stories in their own words, however, even students who had used *no* Black English forms in oral reading switched to Black English dialect.

Troike (1972) argues that a speaker's translation of standard English into Black English in repetition tasks is good evidence that the speaker already understands standard English. Direct imitation, on the other hand, could indicate lack of such understanding. Thus there may be no obvious relation between receptive and productive control of standard English. Troike also says that even young children are aware of dialectical variation as well as social constraints on its use. He recounts an anecdote in which a four-year-old girl in effect gave a lesson on dialect to her brother. In her family the parents' dialects varied so that the father pronounced the word for stream as *crick*, while the mother said *creek*. When the daughter heard her brother say *creek* to their father, she told him "Don't you know that you're supposed to say 'crick' to Daddy and 'creek' to Mommy?" (p. 308).

There is some evidence suggesting that it does take time for children to acquire standard English forms that are less obviously distinguished from the Black English equivalents. DeStefano (1972) found that it was quite easy to gain control of the standard English single negative in place of the Black English double negative. However, other differences were harder to learn, such as endings which are simplified in Black English (*ll* and *sks*, for example). At any age level, it might be expected that these harder forms would be more rarely produced by black students. Rosen and Ames (1972) found that subjects in a repetition task dropped the affixes for possessive and plural nouns, past tense, and third person singular agreement. This occurred more often when subjects were reading prose passages than when reading islolated sentences.

Though there may be no overall relationship between dialect and reading ability, we may still search for differences in the rules of standard and Black English which could cause interference for those particular cases. Let us examine some (not necessarily exclusive) possible sources of interference.

Labov (1967) suggests that "the most important [differences between standard English and nonstandard Black English] are those in which large scale phonological differences coincide with important grammatical differences," (p. 14) resulting in different sets of homonyms for the teacher and pupil. Previously mentioned are *l*-lessness and consonant cluster simplification. The phoneme /l/ is dropped before consonants or at the end of words. Homonyms not occurring in standard English may result, such as *toll-toe, help-hep,* and *fault-fought.* In consonant cluster simplification, final clusters may be reduced by dropping the final consonant. This affects both tense and plural markers, as well as producing homonyms such as *past-pass, six-sick, mend-men.* The condition of *r*-lessness is parallel to *l*-lessness, yielding homonym pairs like *sore-so, fort-fought,* and *Paris-pass.*

When such phonological changes affect grammatical affixes, it is hard to tell whether a response is a reflection of a grammatical or a phonological rule. Dropping *l*'s may coincide with the future tense in forms like "He drive next week." Dropping *r*'s may overlap environments involving copula deletion, as in "We late again." Consonant cluster simplification is most strongly confounded with tense affixes. Deletion of final /d/ and /t/ may yield such constructions as "I pass him on the right." Labov (1970) tried to assess whether subjects were more sensitive to the phonological or grammatical constraints in the realization of final consonants. The phonological constraint is that there is less deletion if the cluster is followed by a vowel; the morphemic constraint states that final consonants are less often dropped if they represent meaningful units. Subjects more responsive to the latter constraint seem to comprehend *-ed* as a past tense affix better than those for whom the phonological constraint was more salient. (Comprehension was assessed by having subjects read orally sentences like "When I passed by, I read the sign." From the subject's pronunciation of the second verb, one can infer the tense assigned to the first verb no matter how the first verb was pronounced.) Labov emphasized that there is no relation between overall reading ability and sensitivity to past tense affixes. Linguistic interference is confined to the particular domain that the morphological constraint involves.

Different sets of homonyms may cause confusion in communications between teacher and pupil. Piestrup (1973, p. 63) documents a case in which the Black English homonyms *win-wind* were the source of a misunderstanding. The teacher asked for sentences using the word *win*. One student offered, "The win' blew the hat off my frien' head." Such homonyms may create fewer problems in reading than in dialogues between teacher and pupil, particularly when such discussions are not set in contexts which could disambiguate the terms. A high percentage of such discussions are in fact metalinguistic—the teacher and pupil are discussing words, letters, and sounds. When talking about language itself, there is less opportunity to clarify by references to objects and events in the real world. Melmed (1971) cites some examples from a thesis by Henrie (1969). In one instance the student asked the teacher how to spell /ræt/. When she responded "*r-a-t*," the student said, "I don't mean rat mouse, I mean right now." During a typical exercise the teacher asked students to write *so* in a sentence and then read it. She specified that she didn't want the word meaning "to stitch," but "the other *so*." One student's answer was "I got a so' on my leg."

The extent to which different sets of homonyms may be problematic in the classroom has yet to be ascertained. Teachers who refuse to accept identical pronunciations of words which are homonyms only in Black English may create unnecessary difficulty for the student, even impeding his progress in reading. Gumperz (1972, p. 194) describes a teacher who drilled slow readers on the distinction between *pin* and *pen*. Piestrup (1973) observed a whole class of teachers who focused students' attention solely on such surface aspects of the language, thereby undermining their search for meaning in what they were reading. Instead these teachers produced a group of students who painfully and slowly sounded out the reading materials.

One might expect to find interference in cases where standard and Black English constructions are superficially similar though different in meaning (Stewart, 1969; Shuy, 1969). Due to the existence in Black English of copula deletion, a standard English phrase like "His eye's open" may be taken to mean "His eyes are open." Mistakes may also occur when the Black English speaker tries to "correct" to a standard English equivalent by choosing a superficially similar standard English construction. For example, "He be busy" may be changed to "He will be busy," even though the intended meaning is ongoing action. If this incorrect equivalence becomes established, it may affect the student's comprehension as well. Upon hearing "He will be busy," the student may interpret the verb as indicating ongoing rather than future action.

Difficulties may also occur for the situation in which forms are ambiguous for only one dialect. Smith (1969) discusses one such case. In Black English, the sentence "You know my sister plays the piano" is ambiguous; one reading of the sentence is, "You know my sister who plays the piano" (in standard English the subject relative pronoun would not be deleted). There is a technique in Black English for disambiguating such structures. To specify the reading which is equivalent to the standard English one, the redundant subject pronoun is inserted, yielding "You know my sister she plays the piano." Teachers may not only be unaware of the ambiguity, which exists only in Black English, but may also interpret sentences with the apparently redundant subject pronoun as incorrect.

A skill which might very well be affected by differences in Black and standard English is spelling. Most investigators seem to have ignored this aspect of verbal ability in their concentration on receptive control of standard English and on pronunciation. Fasold (1969) argues that conventional spelling is not so different from corresponding morphophonemic "spellings," and therefore conventional orthography should be suitable for speakers of Black English. One can often infer from the pronunciation of certain Black English forms that the speaker has in fact internalized a representation close to the conventional spelling. Stewart (1969) observes that Black English speakers may establish their own sound-spelling correspondences. For example, *th* is read as /f/ when not initial. Given the graphic form *with*, the student responds "wif." If he wants to write this word, he uses the same correspondence rule to produce the graphic form. An example from Piestrup amplifies this statement. When the teacher called for words ending in *th*, one student offered "cough." Apparently, the student had observed that many words he pronounced with a final /f/ corresponded to the standard Enligh spelling *th*. But in this case the correspondence rule was misapplied. Presumably this student would also spell *cough* with a final *th*. Of course, speakers of standard English are also subject to spelling errors, and one would not be surprised to see something like *coff* presented as the graphic form of this word. Yet given such errors, teachers would be more able to decipher them when they shared the same dialect as the student. It might take a very perceptive teacher to understand the error in a sentence like "I had a very bad couth."

It is also plausible that the general tendency of Black English to simplify the language (by such rules as consonant cluster simplification) would be more likely to cause difficulties in spelling than in reading. In the same way that "silent" endings may cause some trouble for speakers of standard English, this hindrance would be multiplied for Black English speakers, who encounter many more such cases. (Labov, 1970, observed that some children reduce final consonants to the point where syllables consist of a consonant followed by a vowel; these students have the most serious reading problems).

Most of these suggestions concerning how linguistic interference might cause reading problems or misunderstandings between teachers and pupils are speculative. Yet even if true, the sources of interference are very specific to the forms involved. It seems unlikely that such interferences could be the sole cause of the gap in reading ability between black and white students. There is a consensus that the teachers' attitudes toward dialect are a far more important determinant of reading achievement than the dialects themselves (Goodman and Burke, undated; Galvan and Troike, 1969; Labov, 1967; Piestrup, 1973; Shuy, 1969a; Venezky, 1970). The literature contains three positions about the effects of teachers' attitudes on black children's school achievement. One position is that no reading problem exists except in the eyes of the teacher who does not accept Black English; one must simply educate these teachers to recognize that students are responding correctly, though in dialect. A second view is that the attitude of teachers who consider Black English an inferior dialect is perceived by pupils and makes them hostile. Their motivation and attitudes toward school in general are affected. A third view holds that teachers' attitudes can affect their teaching techniques in ways that cause specific reading problems. We have already mentioned the evidence from Piestrup on how teachers may undermine attainment of reading comprehension by drilling the student on surface differences between Black and standard English. Students may abandon reading for meaning and begin simply to sound out text with little comprehension. Goodman and Burke (undated), who originally held that dialect per se did hinder reading, now agree that teachers' attitudes are more important. They concur with Piestrup in this criticism:

> Rejection or correction by the teacher of any dialect-based miscue moves the reader away from using his own lingusitic competence to get to meaning toward a closer correspondence to the teacher's expected response to the test. Word for word accuracy, in a narrow sense, becomes the goal, rather than meaning. (Goodman and Burke, p. 13)

They point out that teachers' concern with correcting Black English constructions may eventually produce "overcorrections" by the student, such as "smileded."

Fasold (1969) indicates how teachers may in effect give two conflicting sets of instructions to students. On the one hand, students may be told that one should pronounce a word like *basically* with three syllables. At the same time, the teacher may reject /tes/ as a correct pronunciation of *test*. Deletions consistent with the rules of standard English are sanctioned, while those appropriate only to Black English are rejected.

A number of authors attempt to attribute lack of success in reading to motivational factors unrelated to dialect. It has been argued that the usefulness of academic education is lower for blacks, and therefore they are less interested in acquiring the skills taught (Glazer, 1969; Epps, 1970; Abrahams and Gay, 1972a). Epps writes:

> If the child believes that academic skills have little value in the real world, that his future rewards depend on excellence in athletic and social skills, or his ability to influence people, he will tend to develop those skills he perceives as most relevant for his future success (while neglecting education skills). (p. 18)

Abrahams and Gay (1972a) add that teachers may be making a mistake when they try to get their pupils to emulate the "good" students. As Labov and Robins point out (1969), the leaders in the street culture, who have the highest prestige, are not likely to be the "good" students.

At one point there was some interest in whether the content of beginning readers had any effect on students' motivation in learning to read. Blom, Waite, and Zimet (1970) presented evidence that children do choose readers representing environments more relevent to their own situation over, say, rural settings. However, the use of dialect readers has no relation to the students' level of interest. More important, there is no evidence that changing the content of readers affects reading proficiency (with the possible exception of the citation by Blom et al. (1970) of Whipple's finding that use of multiethnic readers did increase some reading skills).

The teachers' ability to motivate students has also been cited as a factor influencing scholastic achievement. Piestrup studied a class of teachers she referred to as "Black Artful." The students of these teachers did not lag in reading proficiency. One way this group of teachers differed from others was in their high expectations for success in their pupils. The teachers exerted friendly pressure on their students to perform well. Similar results were obtained in one New York City school, where students' reading scores are above the national average (*New York Times*, May 28, 1973). Parents and teachers of these students expected and pressured them to do well.

At present there is some interest in assessing the role that conflict between the cultures of the teacher and student may play in causing misunderstandings detrimental to success in the classroom (Bauman, 1972; Abrahams and Gay, 1972a; Galvan and Troike, 1969; Gumperz, 1972; Labov, 1970). These authors present a *cultural interference hypothesis* that is similar but more encompassing than the linguistic interference hypothesis. Individuals from different cultures may misinterpret behaviors which have different meanings in the two cultures. Abrahams and Gay (1972a) write that it is necessary

to demonstrate what we have known for a long time, that there is a different cultural system operating among working class Blacks, and that it is simply a matter of getting beyond our stereotypic reactions to these differences so that we may begin to utilize these cultural perceptions in developing meaningful strategies for educating Blacks. (p. 68)

An example of a possible source of conflict is the interpretation of direct questioning. Abrahams and Gay note that this behavior occurs most frequently when the parent is angry with the child, though to the middle-class white teacher it is a perfectly appropriate pedagogical device. Gumperz (1972) similarly suggests that teaching style structured around questioning by the teacher, prohibition or interrruption of talking among students, etc., may be associated with the behavior of welfare workers. Thus the child may engage in willful noncooperation.

Another example of misinterpretation offered by Abrahams and Gay (1972a) concerns "voice overlap." In the black community, talking by the audience is a sign to the speaker that they are listening. For the white teacher, such behavior carries the opposite meaning. Lack of movement and silence are sure signs of boredom on the part of the black student; yet these very behaviors will be demanded and misread by teachers ignorant of their meaning for black students.

Piestrup's data support the notion that teachers' knowledge of cultural (and linguistic) differences can make them more effective in the classroom. Black Artful teachers not only understood the behavior of their students but could also behave similarly in the appropriate situations. In particular, they knew how to switch styles: Using standard English for most instruction and also demanding this of the students, yet they could also switch to Black English and accompanying appropriate behaviors to enter into social interactions with students. It has been suggested that such teachers provide excellent role models for students, who learn the rules for switching styles by observing their teachers.

Galvan and Troike (1969) describe training sessions designed to help teachers understand sources of cultural and linguistic interference. Though results are not yet available to assess the effect of this program on teaching, the investigators were most impressed with teachers' changes in attitudes toward dialects and cultural differences between blacks and whites. This observation compelled them to suggest that "teachers must be trained to take a sociolinguistic view, recognizing systematic social and cultural differences and the correlated linguistic modes for their expression" (p. 304).

In light of the available evidence, it seems that many of the suggestions offered by workers in this field for application by educators are useless. One approach has been to change texts in various ways. Some argue that first readers should be in Black English, to facilitate the students' ability to match the graphic forms to the spoken forms occurring in their own speech (Baratz, 1969; Shuy, 1969; Wolfram and Fasold, 1969). As Weber (1970) points out, however, even white students are confronted with a written style which is different from spoken language. No first grader produces sentences like "Quickly ran the fox." Yet these constructions appear to be no problem for them. The data already reported concerning the extent of black students' knowledge of standard English also suggest that converting readers to dialect would have little effect. The same applies to arguments made by those who feel blacks must be taught standard English orally, before even beginning to learn to read. Since students already have a high degree of control over standard English, this is a waste of time.

Other suggestions for changing texts assumed that a bidialectal approach in which both Black and standard English forms were included in the text might be beneficial. Some have proposed a "common core" approach, advising elimination from beginning readers any forms not common to both dialects. No evidence shows such readers to effect any improvement in reading proficiency. As mentioned before, the argument that changing the content of readers might improve reading skills is also unsupported by evidence.

On the other hand, the sorts of factors which do seem to affect learning to read are more difficult to implement in any simple way, namely, the teacher's knowledge and skill in switching styles, understanding cultural conflicts, and motivating students to perform academically. Piestrup's Black Artful teachers were not trained in any of these skills, but developed them independently. Though Galvan and Troike are optimistic that programs can be established to teach these skills and influence teachers attitudes, the success is yet to come.

Are There Cross-National Differences in Reading Achievement?*

Comparisons of literacy in different countries of the world have become of more and more interest as communication between cultures increases. UNESCO has initiated reports and conferences on the subject (cf. *UNESCO Handbook in Reading,* 1972), and newspaper reports about innovations such as Mao Tse-tung's decision to increase the phoneticization of Chinese writing are sure to arouse interest. What are the questions that we would like to have answered? The most obvious one is how the level of literacy compares from one country to another. But the answer to this question is really only interesting if we can compare populations that have had reasonably equivalent access to some formal education. A country that has no schools will have a low rate of literacy, a matter of great concern socially, to UNESCO for instance, but the fact is not informative for understanding the reading process. Furthermore, the definition of literacy varies from country to country, depending on the society's requirements (what might have been adequate literacy in the U.S. in 1850 would hardly do for filling out Income Tax Form 1040 today).

Psychologically, it is of interest to know whether literacy is related to the nature of the writing system; whether it is related only at early stages of learning to read, or also at mature stages; whether the methods of teaching reading are related to the writing system, and if so, how, or how they should be; the age at which instruction is begun and how it affects progress; cultural and motivational attitudes toward literacy and what their effect may be; whether comprehension of written material varies with the writing system, the language, and the educational system. Finally, it seems possible that there are universal factors that predict reading achievement across all languages.

Information for answering these questions is only recently becoming available. There are widespread biases that one often hears: for instance, that English has such irregular orthography that we must expect to have many retarded readers in English-speaking school systems, while Spanish is highly regular in letter-to-sound correspondence and so it is easy for Spanish children to learn to read; or that Chinese is incredibly difficult because one must memorize 42,000 separate ideographs, which to make matters worse are very complex and therefore hard to differentiate from one another. None of these statements has been based on hard knowledge. Some recent studies fortunately give us the beginning of a handle on the problem, especially Downing (1973) and Thorndike (1973).

*This section was coauthored by Ellen Garber.

Writing Systems

We will begin with a review of writing systems. These were already considered in Chapter 6, but we will summarize the material, trying where possible to relate it to ease of learning to read and methods of teaching. As we saw, writing systems can be classified into three major types: (1) alphabetic, each character representing a phoneme; (2) syllabic, each character representing a syllable; and (3) logographic, each character representing a morpheme, a meaningful unit. It is often taken for granted that the logographic system is the hardest to learn to read and the alphabetic the easiest (e.g., Goody, 1968). Unfortunately, little truly comparative work has been undertaken on the efficacy of the three codes.*

Chinese has the reputation of being a difficult language to learn to read. The reader, so it has been assumed, must commit to memory thousands of characters, each of which represents a different word in the language. The enormous memory load imposed on the would-be reader of Chinese is thought to be the main reason for the restricted literacy in China, since only the more intelligent people are capable of such a memory feat (Goody 1968). In addition, the extreme complexity of the characters (they vary from one to fifty-six strokes, with the average being about eleven strokes) and the lack of phonetic correspondence supposedly adds to the difficulty of learning to read Chinese.

However, the difference between learning to read English and Chinese may not be so great as is generally presumed. The logographs are made up of strokes, the closest counterparts to the letters of the alphabet (Wang, 1973). There are about 20 strokes in Chinese as compared to 26 letters in our alphabet. Both the order in which the strokes are written and their geometric orientation and position are important. Certain collections of strokes are called *radicals* (the Chinese radicals do not have a counterpart in other orthographies). The radicals are usually themselves characters with independent pronunciations, and approximately 80% of the Chinese characters are made up of a radical (signific) that gives the meaning plus a remainder (phonetic) that gives the sound. An example from Wang illustrates how this works: 日 is the radical for "sun" (prononced /ri/). This radical, when combined with the phonetic 尤 (pronounced /lóng/), results

---

*The early comparative work was concerned mainly with eye movements. The conclusions were that there was little difference in the basic processes involved regardless of the language (Gray, 1956).

in the character 昽, which is pronounced /lóng/ and means "morning sun." In order to look up a Chinese word in a dictionary, the reader first looks up the radical. In the case of "morning sun," the radical is "sun" 日. All the characters containing thes sun radical are listed underneath the sun radical according to the number of strokes in the phonetic remainder (in the example of morning sun, the phonetic remainder contains five strokes). There are at the present time 214 radicals in use. These radicals combine with 1700 phonetic units to form 80% to 90% of the logographs in common use (Leong, 1973 ; see also Chapter 6, p. 158). Thus there is a phonetic principle underlying many Chinese characters.

Chinese has also been criticized because the characters are so complex. In fact, in 1956 the Chinese government reduced thet number of strokes in many of the characters. However, Leong (1973) found the complexity of the logograph to be directly related to the ease of learning it. That is, the more complex logographs were found to be less confusing to children than the more simple ones. This is presumably because the more simple (fewer strokes) logographs have fewer features that can be used to distinguish them. It is not complexity of a grapheme that is important for learning, but its discriminability from the rest of the set.

Sakamoto and Makita (1973) also point out that logographs (in this case, the Japanese kanji) are not entirely arbitrary. The logograph can be divided into various radicals, and several kanji contain the same radical in a systematic way. They give the following example, using the radical water 氵: 池 = pond, 河 = river, 波 = wave, 海 = sea, and 泳 = swim (p. 450).

The recent claim of less than .1% reading disability in Japan (Makita, 1968) has focused attention on the syllabary as an easily learned writing system. In addition to the Japanese syllabaries there is the syllabary of the Cherokee Indians (Gray, 1956). This syllabary also resulted in a high level of literacy (90%) among its users (Walker, 1965; also cited in Gleitman and Rozin, 1973). Although Sakamoto and Makita (1973) and Muraishi (1972) present convincing evidence for the ease with which the Japanese hiragana syllabary is learned (a high proportion of children can read hiragana before they reach school age, in the sense of decoding the symbols to sound), it is not clear whether the high rate of literacy claimed is due to the writing system or to cultural factors. Assuming that the high level of literacy is attributable, at least in part, to the use of syllabaries, a brief description of the Japanese writing system follows (cf. Chapter 6).

Written Japanese has two syllabaries, hiragana and katakana, together called kana. They both consist of 46 monosyllabic symbols that have no meaning in isolation that is, are nonlogographic. In almost all cases the character has only one pronunciation. After the acquisition of the symbols plus a few other marks that give additional phonetic information, it is possible to write any word in the Japanese language simply by recombining the symbols. An example from Sakamoto and Makita (1973, p. 440) illustrates this.

ま	き	た	
/ma/	/ki/	/ta/	*Makita* (a person's name)
た	ま		
/ta/	/ma/		*ball*
た	き		
/ta/	/ki/		*waterfall*
き	た		
/ki/	/ta/		*north*
ま	き		
/ma/	/ki/		*firewood*
ま	た		
/ma/	/ta/		*again*

It is claimed that it takes children less than a year to master hiragana. Muraishi (1972) presented results showing that 88% of kindergarten children had acquired a knowledge of hiragana symbols in kindergarten. In the last half of the first grade katakana (used mainly for loan words) is introduced, and instruction with it is completed in the second grade. Also beginning in the first grade the child is introduced to kanji. Kanji are logographs originally borrowed from the Chinese. The transition from pure kana to the adult mixture of kana and kanji is accomplished gradually and is aided by the use of furigana. Furigana consists of writing the hiragana symbols above or to the right of the corresponding kanji. Gradually as the child progresses in school, the furigana translation is omitted. The final kanji-kana combination is approximately one-quarter kanji. It is claimed (Sakamoto and Makita, 1973) that this combination is read faster and more accurately than pure kana, and with more efficient eye movements (see Chapter 6). The kanji, which stand out in form from the kana, usually comprise the main ideas of the sentence, so that the main points of a sentence can be grasped quickly and easily.

Finally, Martin (1972) has observed that when English books are translated into Japanese, the translation is accomplished using one-third less pages than the original English text. He suggests that Japanese may be read more quickly than English. It is a common observation among educated Japanese that reading kanji is faster than reading hiragana.

Despite the apparent greater efficiency of reading kanji for the educated adult, there is reason to think that learning a syllabary is easy, because language segments naturally into the syllable as a phonetic unit, rather than into individual phonemes (see Chapters 5, 7, and 8; Gleitman and Rozin, 1973). But there is still something to be said for the logograph at an early stage of learning: It has direct semantic correspondence, and it is the meaning in language that children are aware of when they begin to read. Rozin, Poritsky, and Sotsky (1971) taught a group of inner city children with reading problems a limited number of Chinese characters with familiar meanings. The children were able to learn them and to read them combined in sentences, whereas an equal amount of time spent tutoring them in reading English was unproductive. The novelty of the task, rather than the direct mapping to meaning, may have been the reason for the success of the project.

Current trends to reform the writing system of Chinese in the effort to increase literacy in the People's Republic of China emphasize simplification of the characters (reduction of the number of strokes) and the introduction of a latinized phonetic alphabet coexisting with the written characters. But as Leong (1973) points out, the effect of doing so has often been the loss of the important combinatory property of the signific (radical) and the phonetic, sometimes even overlooking the root of the character. Latinization of the writing would surely have problems given the tonal qualities of the language, and Leong thinks it will be long in coming; meanwhile, "reading in Chinese may continue to utilize the inherent structural characteristics of the existing code for maximum information processing" (Leong, p. 400).

The alphabetic writing system makes use of a relatively small number of symbols that represent phonological elements and that can be combined in a variety of ways to form an infinite number of words. Goody (1968) claims that the invention of the alphabet was an important element in the development of political democracies, since it provided the populace with a writing system that could be easily learned, so that literacy was no longer restricted to a privileged few. However, among the alphabetic writing systems there is wide variation. For example, in Thai the choice of where to place the terminal punctuation is a matter of personal preference, and there are no clear boundaries between words. Arabic omits the vowels altogether except in beginners' books (Downing, 1973; Gray, 1956). Most importantly, the alphabetic systems differ markedly in the degree and the nature of grapheme-phoneme correspondence. We shall consider these differences in the following section, relating them when possible to reading achievement.

Orthography and Efficiency in Alphabetic Writing Systems

A high degree of one-to-one symbol-to-sound correspondence is thought to be an advantage to a child learning to read his native language. For instance, a series of reports by Hildreth on the acquisition of Arabic (1965), Armenian (1965), Greek (1968), and Russian (1968), all of which have fairly phonetic alphabets and consistent spellings, concludes that beginning readers are indeed helped by a "consistent alphabetic code." However, the validity of her conclusions is highly questionable in view of her evidence. In all four studies Hildreth apparently hunted about until she found a school that would allow her to observe classes. She then sat in on a class, and on the basis of one morning's observations, often in a language she did not understand, concluded that these children learned to read their languages more easily than English-speaking children learn to read theirs.

Whether this observation is true or not, it is questionable whether an initial advantage of a so-called regular orthography is maintained at more advanced reading levels. As a UNESCO expert put it, "It is important to note that the freedom of individual characters from ambiguity of phonemic reference does not imply a more efficient orthography. Whether or not the more economic orthography yields the more efficient reading is one of the research questions that remains unanswered" (Brimer, 1973, p. 21). Finnish, with an unusually small alphabet and a very consistent letter-to-sound mapping, is, according to Bloomfield (1942), "an almost perfect code." English, on the other hand, is very inconsistent in single letter-to-phoneme mapping, but it has structural redundancies of orthography that make it efficient when the reader knows them, and the morphophonemic nature of its orthography (see Chapter 6) gives it a further advantage. There is at present no reason to think that a mature reader is better off with Finnish; anecdote, indeed, has it the other way around.

In the following paragraphs, we will consider the orthography of various languages with alphabetic writing systems and relate them, where it is possible, to instructional methods and reading problems.

Finnish

Finnish, as we have said, is one of the most regular languages. According to Kyöstiö (1973), "Each phoneme always has the same letter irrespective of its place in a word. This feature enormously facilitates learning to read" (p. 308). The Finnish alphabet has 21 letters and one superscript. Children begin school at age 7 and reading instruction is begun at once. Finnish is generally taught by an alphabetic approach (Kysötiö, 1973; Nelville, 1972). Venezky, in an experiment reported in Chapter 8, found that although a high percentage of children could pronounce most words at the end of the first grade, the ability to pronounce words was not highly correlated with their reading comprehension. A good sound-to-symbol correspondence facilitates pronunciation, but merely "barking at the print" does not constitute reading. Reading is not considered a problem in Finland; however, larger cities have reading clinics, and there are also a few full-time reading specialists who go from school to school. Obviously reading problems do exist in Finland despite the official "nonproblem" attitude.

Spanish

Spanish is another language thought to have a good sound-to-symbol correspondence, and so, one might assume, is a relatively easy language to learn to read. However, DeBraslavsky (1972) is quick to point out that learning to read Spanish, at least in Argentina, is not simple. In the first place, she claims that the phoneme-grapheme correspondence has a one-to-one relationship in only nine cases (there are 29 graphemes and 24 phonemes). In addition, the definition of the "syllable frontier" is sometimes ambiguous. DeBraslavsky gives the example of the word *oso* that the child pronounces *o-so*, but in the written system he may see it as *os-o*. Finally, the numerous dialects create disparities between the spoken and the written language, thus removing any inherent sound-to-symbol advantage. There is no clear preference in Argentina for one teaching method over another, and apparently the level of reading achieved is often very unsatisfactory (DeBraslavsky, p. 275). Teachers currently receive no training in reading instruction, nor is there any university chair or institute specializing in reading research, although it is apparently badly needed. Although Argentina does recognize reading disability as a problem, it is dealt with at a medical level. There are no remedial resources available within the school system. Unfortunately, we have no good available source on learning to read in Spain.

Norwegian

Douglass (1969) writes that the number of children with reading difficulties in Norway is only a fraction of the number in the United States. He claims that only 5% to 6% of Norwegian children experience any real difficulty in learning to read. This number is reduced to half by age 10 to 11 as a result of an excellent remedial program. He points out that Norwegian is a phonetically regular language, and that this regularity is retained even in the dialects. The school system is highly centralized, with little variety in instructional method. Reading begins with instruction on the initial sounds of letters, proceeds quickly to a word approach, and soon becomes "eclectic." The basic method of word attack remains phonetic throughout school. There is little regard for individual differences and a total absence of the notion of failure. It simply isn't considered as a possibility. As in Finland, the children do not begin school until age 7.

Hebrew

Although Hebrew has a near perfect one-to-one symbol-sound relationship, written Hebrew words lack distinctive shape, the consonants resemble each other closely, and the vowels are very small diacritics written under the consonants (Feitelson, 1973). Thus the beginning reader must pay close attention to the minute details of the graphic display, a matter which was seriously neglected until methods of teaching reading in Israel were revised during the past decade.

Since the 1960s reading has been taught by a "sequential approach" in Israel. There are 22 consonants and nine vowels in Hebrew. The symbols are introduced gradually and immediately related to their sound values. At the same time the lessons are structured in such a way that the child deals with meaningful material from the beginning. The early stages of learning to read have now met with widespread success, but it is not clear that this progress has been matched by corresponding development at later levels (Feitelson, 1973). Since much of reading instruction is centered around the Old Testament, it is imperative that children obtain a high level of reading skill by the end of the first grade. The sequential approach is said to have accomplished this. Although extensive reading of the Bible alerts readers to the fact that passages can have more than one meaning, Feitelson worries that the emphasis on thorough reading may retard other reading skills. Basal readers in Israel are at present ungraded and the level of difficulty often taxing. The material is often pedantic. Whether the present approach transfers to flexible reading of varied material is in need of research.

Hindi

It has been estimated that 179 languages and 544 dialects are spoken in India (Oommen, 1973). Only Hindi, an official language of India, seems to have received any study as regards reading. Hindi is very regular in symbol-sound correspondence. The name of a grapheme and the phoneme it represents are said to be always the same. (That is, there is not a name for a grapheme that is different from the grapheme's sound, although for a stop consonant this hardly seems possible.) One source of difficulty is that the symbols are often similar in sound, sound and form, or form (Oommen, 1973). There are 14 vowels and 39 consonants in Hindi. The vowels have alternative symbols depending on their place in a word. In addition, when two or more consonants occur together, the form of the single letter changes (e.g., त + त becomes त्त). Rules for clusters vary, depending on such factors as position. Even though this adds to the number of symbols that must be discriminated, it may be helpful, since it signals the presence of a cluster. Children are first taught the letters and their sounds, and then taught to combine the sounds to form words. The emphasis is on rote learning of the sounds of the symbols. Ease of writing a symbol may determine its order of teaching. It is assumed that once the child has mastered the alphabet he can read. The emphasis in the lower grades is entirely on oral reading. Sound decoding rather than meaning is stressed. Even in later grades, the lesson is sounded out word by word. The following passage from Oommen illustrates India's methodological orientation. "Repeating the lesson by 'heart' is taken to be the mark of good reading. As one youngster queried, when asked to 'read' for some visitors, 'Teacher, with or without the book?' " (Oommen, 1973, p. 414). Efforts are being made to improve teaching, with reading for meaning getting a new emphasis, but training of teachers and provision of material for their instructional use are scant and inadequate at present. Literacy is low (by a 1961 census, only 34.5% of males and 13% of females were literate), but reading disability has not been recognized as an educational problem.

Swedish

In Sweden, children are not introduced to reading until age 7 or later, depending on the individual child. Positive experience and no risk of failure are considered of utmost importance. A variety of preparatory exercises for stimulating readiness are made use of (Malmquist, 1973). Sweden emphasizes the importance of good reading skills, and there is a relatively low level of reading disability. Swedish has a relatively simple phonetic correspondence, and the teaching methods take advantage of this, analyzing sounds within words. Although the phonic method is greatly valued as a means of teaching children to blend sounds into syllables and words, the meaning of what is read is stressed from the beginning. Every effort is made to "create a desire in the child to read." Concern for the individual child is very strong. There are many reading clinics and remedial classes, but no monthly grades are given, in order to prevent any climate of failure. A prominent goal in Sweden is the attainment of higher-level reading skills; that is, developing different reading skills to suit different types of reading tasks. Cross-national comparisons of reading comprehension (see below) suggest that this emphasis has paid off.

Russian

Russian enjoys a fairly regular sound-to-symbol correspondence, although the number of characters that mark the consonant phonemes are considerably fewer than the phonemes (Elkonin, 1973). The literacy rate in Russia is said to be almost 100% in the urban areas and not much lower in the rural areas (Hildreth, 1968). According to Hildreth, 98% of the first graders learn to read without difficulty. There are 33 graphemes in Russian plus a sign to indicate stress. The letter sounds are introduced one at a time in sequential lessons, and each letter sound is immediately used in syllables and words. The letters are not introduced in alphabetical order, but rather in a sequence that is considered optimal for learning and blending sounds. In addition, each lesson includes practice in reading simple sentences which contain the sounds that have been studied. If a word with an unfamiliar letter-sound is needed to complete a sentence, a small sketch is used instead.

Elkonin (1973) gives a definition of reading. If it is the generally accepted definition in the USSR, their literacy claims may be suspect. According to Elkonin, "Despite the fact that people often advance the comprehension of a word as a criterion of its correct reading, understanding is not an essential part of the process of reading. It is rather to be regarded as a facilitating or complicating factor." His formal definition of reading is as follows: "Reading is a creation of the sound form of the word on the basis of its graphic representation" (p. 552). In line with this definition, Elkonin has directed his research toward revealing to the child, before teaching reading, the "sound structure of spoken words" (see Chapter 8). Prereading auditory discrimination ("phonematic hearing") is thus a prominent feature of training for literacy in the USSR.

German

German, while not as regular in one-to-one correspondence as some languages, is more phonetically consistent than English (Biglmaier, 1973). Reading is not considered a serious problem since the illiteracy rate is below 1% of the population. As in the United States, there has been a great deal of controversy about the best method of teaching reading. Biglmaier's discussion of the reading primers indicates that a variety and mixture of methods are currently used. Several studies (Biglmaier, 1973; Preston, 1952) indicate that, at least in some aspects of reading achievement, German children are superior to their American counterparts. Biglmaier (1973) reported that German children can decode and understand words at the end of the second grade with an error rate reached by United States children only after the fourth grade. (It should be noted that he is comparing data collected in 1957 from German children with data compiled in 1932 on American children.) Preston (1952) claimed that there is a "greater incidence of word-recognition difficulties among pupils in the United States than among those in Germany." However, word recognition as used by Preston means the ability to pronounce a word and does not imply comprehension. In another study, Preston (1962) found American children to be generally superior to German children in reading comprehension at both the fourth- and sixth-grade levels.

Danish

Danish has an irregular orthography. Jansen (1973) claims that the rules that relate vowel graphemes to vowel phonemes would not be "easily understood by students below the university level" (p. 286). As a result no attempt is made to teach the children these rules. Teaching of reading is begun when children are between seven and eight years old. The methods employed to teach reading vary widely; but there is an emphasis on individualized instruction. A teacher stays with his class, normally through grade 7. Comprehension and communication are the goals of reading instruction. Although Denmark reports a high level of reading problems, this is probably due to the emphasis placed on the importance of reading skills. That is, many of the children who are diagnosed as needing remedial help would not be considered reading problems in other countries. Remedial help is provided on a large scale for adults and older pupils as well as in the early grades.

French

French is one of the most phonetically irregular languages. However, it has fewer sounds than English. It also makes use of diacritical marks to indicate the sound of certain vowels. Ruthman (1973) concludes that French,

> although not highly phonetic, is systematized, regular and consistent. The learner is able to identify the characteristics of the language, memorize its exceptions, make use of word derivations, and place more emphasis on syntax rather than on individual sounds for better reading comprehension. (p. 330)

Although these properties of the language may help the more advanced reader, it is doubtful whether they are of use to the beginning reader. A "synthetic" (phonetic) method seems to be the principal method of teaching. The high level of reading failure in France (25% of the children fail the first grade because they have not learned to read) would indicate that the children are not able to make use of the higher-order structure of French. But Ruthman reports that France's reading failures are usually blamed not on its orthography but on ill-trained teachers. Teachers in elementary schools do not hold degrees and have not attended a secondary school for university preparation. After they attend fifth grade, they enter a four-year course in a school of general education (Ruthman, 1973). They may then enter a four-year normal school, but no instruction is given in the teaching of reading.

English

The popular assumption is that English orthography is phonetically highly irregular, with the result that English is a difficult language to learn to read (Downing, 1973). Partly because the previous statement has acquired axiomatic status, and partly because the methodological problems are so overwhelming, no one has experimentally verified the difficulty of learning to read English as compared to other languages.

The much maligned English spelling system has been the subject of attempts at reform as far back as the 12th century (see Chapter 6). But recently some linguists have argued that at a deeper level English orthography is systematic, and that the morphemic information and transformational rules governing the orthography facilitate swift comprehension of written material by a skilled reader (Chomsky, 1970; Venezky, 1970). It is possible that although learning to read English is a difficult task, the final skill level attainable may be higher than if we were to increase the phonetic regularity of English spelling. Put another way, a good sound-to-symbol correspondence might facilitate the beginning reader at the expense of the more mature reader.

Children taught in the beginning with the initial teaching alphabet (ITA, an alphabet with 48 characters, each presumably phonetically in congruence with a phonemic element) make more spelling errors based on "phonemic logic." It is claimed that their experience of regularity of grapheme-phoneme relations in ITA leaves the students, after transition to traditional orthography, with "the sort of non-redundant 'skeletal' structure from which conventional English spellings can be readily developed" (Downing, 1973, p. 226). But can they? English orthography *is* redundant (see Chapters 6 and 7), and it is not simply phonemic but morphophonemic in nature.

In summary, it is not clear to what extent the orthographies of languages affect the acquisition or level of reading achievement. The lack of standardized reading tests in most countries, the variations in the total time spent on reading, and the variety of instructional methods used make valid comparisons difficult. However, it is clear that reading failures do occur even in countries with regular orthographies. It is also apparent that there is little connection between the phonetic regularity of correspondence in a language's orthography and the method by which reading is taught.

Educational Systems and Values

Among the countries considered above there are wide differences in the educational approach. In the Scandinavian countries the same teacher remains with a class for several years. Perhaps because the teacher is not under pressure to produce results in one year, there is less pressure placed on the child to read. Both Finland and Norway take it for granted that the child will learn to read, and there is little individual instruction. Sweden and Denmark take the attitude of waiting until the individual child is ready. The disastrous consequences for the child of an initially bad experience with reading are stressed.

This child-centered approach is also favored in Great Britain. Reading is individualized, and the needs of the particular child are considered of paramount importance. This approach is in contrast to the United States' curriculum-centered approach that emphasizes what has to be learned (Downing, 1972). Downing feels that this difference in educational orientation overshadows all other differences in the educational systems of the United States and Great Britain.

Within Great Britain there exist differences both in the instructional method used and the attitudes toward education. For example, a survey of the 1960s (cited in Goodacre, 1973) showed that more than half of the $5\frac{1}{2}$-year-old Scottish children had been taught phonetics as compared to 46% of the Welsh students and 29% of the English children. Another study reported by Goodacre revealed that Scottish parents showed more interest in their children's education than either English or Welsh parents. Incidentally, Scottish children were the best readers in this study.

In Japan, as well, parents are extremely interested in their children's education and place a great value upon educational achievement (Sakamoto and Makita, 1973). Most Japanese parents are aware of exactly what their children are reading in school. As noted earlier, Japan has a very low rate of reading failure.

In agreement with Gray (1956) and Lee (1972), we have found that most of the countries reviewed appear to rely on some mixture of the analytic and synthetic method of instruction. Contrary to Gray's perception of a growing trend to fit the method of instruction to the language, the relationship between the sound-to-symbol correspondence of the language and the instructional method used is no more apparent today than it was 20 years ago. Among the countries whose languages are fairly regularly (phonetically) spelled, some favor the synthetic approach and others have abandoned it completely. But if one compares the English-speaking countries taken as a whole with the other countries, there is a slight tendency for the synthetic methods of instruction to predominate in the more regularly spelled languages (Lee, 1972). But as Lee observed, there is no reason to believe that the controversy over teaching methods would disappear if English spelling were regularized.

It is difficult to substantiate Gray's (1956) finding that the teacher is an important variable, in the light of a recent cross-national study (Thorndike, 1973; see pp. 535 ff.). However, the admittedly low level of teacher competence in India (Oommen, 1973) and France (Ruthman, 1973) and the high level of reading problems in these two countries (Ruthman, 1973; Thorndike, 1973) point to the importance of the teacher's training.

Of the countries considered, six (France, Germany, India, Israel, Japan, and the United States) begin reading instruction at age 6, five (USSR, Denmark, Finland, Sweden, and Norway) at age 7, and two (Hong Kong and Great Britain) at age 5. There is a trend in Japan toward teaching the syllabaries before first grade. Except for the Japanese syllabary, there seems to be no obvious relationship between the difficulty of the language and the age at which reading instruction is begun.

American studies invariably report that girls are better readers than boys in the early years. However, the superiority of girls does not hold up across countries. In Japan, France, and the United States more boys are found in remedial classes (Downing, 1973), but in Germany, Nigeria, and India the girls are the more illiterate (Downing and Thackray, 1971). The results of studies in Great Britain show no consistent differences between the sexes. The evidence suggests that the differences are not due to innate differences between the sexes, but rather are the result of the different ways in which boys and girls are reared.

The primary finding that stands out in the Thorndike study (1973) is the importance of the students' home environment. This finding was present both within and between countries. In 15 countries reading achievement was positively correlated with the number of books in the home and the parents' socioeconomic status. This result indicates that if the parents read, the child will read. If reading is seen as a worthwhile, enjoyable pastime the child will be receptive to reading. The parents' reading habits as a motivational force for the child appear to be equal to or greater than considerations of writing systems, orthography, and methods of instruction.

Values of the parents, and of the culture transmitted through the parents, might be expected to be reflected in the content of material presented to children in readers. It is conceivable that this content has a motivational effect on the child, and thus, indirectly, on his ease and speed of acquiring reading skill. McClelland (1961) analyzed the content of children's primers, relating the level of need achievement, need affiliation, and power motives expressed in the stories to the countries' economic development, but these variables were not related by the author to achievement in reading in the countries studied.

A series of studies (Blom, Waite, and Zimet, 1970; Blom and Wiberg, 1973; Wiberg and Blom, 1970) analyzed the attitude contents of reading primers in various countries. Their original statement was that the content of primers exerts a powerful force on reading acquisition. More specifically, the authors hypothesized that the rather Pollyannaish, bland stories portrayed in American readers are detrimental to sustaining interest in beginning readers. While this hypothesis seems plausible and has been suggested by others, the authors provided no evidence to substantiate their views. Blom et al. did find significant differences in the attitude content of primers from the various countries and were able to relate these differences to the differences in national characteristics of children found by Lambert and Klineberg (cited in Wiberg and Blom, 1970). Unfortunately, they provided no evidence that the attitudinal content of the primers affected either the acquisition of reading or later reading achievement. In fact, the two later studies (Blom and Wiberg, 1973; Wiberg and Blom, 1970) make no mention of possible correlation between content of readers and acquisition, but stress the analysis of childrens' books as a means of understanding the societies that produced them.

Blom, Waite, and Zimet (1970) found that West Germany and Great Britain had more stories with successful outcomes than the United States. The higher number of successful outcomes was contributed by the higher number of girl activity stories in the former countries. Generally, studies report that American boys read more poorly than American girls; in Great Britain there is no clear difference (Downing and Thackray, 1971); and one study of Germany (Preston, 1962) shows German boys to be superior to girls. If girls identify more with girl's stories and boys with boy's stories, one might expect girls to be superior in Great Britain and West Germany rather than in the United States. That this is not the case suggests that the relationship of content to reading achievement is not straightforward. Nevertheless, this variable deserves research relating it directly to ease of learning to read, since the motivational variable seems intuitively so important.

Reading Comprehension in Fifteen Countries

A vast empirical study of reading comprehension in 15 countries, the International Study of Reading Comprehension, was undertaken by the International Education Association. Robert L. Thorndike, with the assistance of professional colleagues from all the countries studied, served as chairman of the committee. The 15 countries that participated were Belgium (Flemish speaking), Belgium (French speaking), Chile, England, Finland, Hungary, India, Iran, Israel, Italy, The Netherlands, New Zealand, Scotland, Sweden, and the United States.

Tremendous care was taken in the development of instruments for the study. The tests included three components: (1) a reading comprehension test; (2) a reading speed test; and (3) a test of word knowledge. A national center from each of the countries was invited to submit items to a central committee, which reviewed them, translated them into all the appropriate languages, and developed six tryout test forms for three populations; a ten-year-old age group, a fourteen-year-old age group, and students in the final year of secondary education (see Thorndike, 1973, for details of test construction). The test of word knowledge involved judging whether words of a pair were synonyms or antonyms, and proved, interestingly enough, to be the most difficult test to construct so as to be of comparable difficulty in all the languages; sometimes the items showed too little a spread of difficulty when translated, and sometimes too great, related to the fact that some languages have a much larger vocabulary than others.

In addition to the tests, questionnaires were prepared to be completed by the students tested, by a sample of teachers in each school, and by an administrative representative of the school. Information was sought on background variables such as socioeconomic status, reading resources in the home, parental interest and help, and number of siblings; teacher variables such as extent of training; and school variables such as size of class, availability of a library, and so on.

The populations of the 15 countries were compared for achievement on the tests, the national means having been converted into a type of standard score (see Thorndike, pp. 123 ff for the exact method of obtaining this score). The difference between the mean of each country and the general cross-national average was the basic datum. A positive score value thus reflected performance above the cross-national average, and a negative value performance below it. It is impossible to present the multiplicity of data, so we have included only reading comprehension scores, in Table 3.

Table 3   National Means for Reading Comprehension Expressed in Uniform Standard
Score Units

	Ten-Year-Olds	Fourteen-Year-Olds	Final Secondary
Belgium (Flemish)	0	−1	−1
Belgium (French)	0	2	2
Chile	−10	−12	−13
England	1	0	10
Finland	2	2	6
Hungary	−4	0	−3
India	−11	−21	−30
Iran	−16	−18	−28
Israel	−4	−3	0
Italy	3	3	−3
Netherlands	0	0	7
New Zealand		4	13
Scotland	1	2	11
Sweden	5	0	1
United States	−1	2	−5

Source: Thorndike, 1973, pp. 127, 128.

The main difference appearing in all the test results was that between
the so-called developing countries (Chile, India, and Iran) and the others.
The variation among the remaining 12 countries is not large, nor is it very
consistent across age levels. The largest differences appear at the highest
age level and reflect "not only the cumulative effects of any educational
experience but also the fairly wide range in selectivity operating in the different national programs" (Thorndike, p. 129). The highest level of
achievement at this age is found in England, New Zealand, and Scotland.
But only 20%, 13%, and 17% of the potential student population are still
in school, whereas in the United States, 75% are. Extent of variability is
different from country to country, but the causes for this are manifold and
not always clear. Variance was generally greatest in India, and lowest in
Sweden, where the sample appeared to be decidedly uniform. There were
also wide differences from country to country in amount of gain from the
youngest group tested to the oldest. The increment (see Thorndike, p.
145) was especially low in India and Iran, where progress in reading ability seemed to be very slow. Gains from the youngest to the oldest population were much higher and did not vary greatly in the European countries
and the United States, but again reflected the selectivity caused by the
proportion of students still remaining in school.

It is interesting to note that the nature of the orthography of the languages shows no relation to reading achievement as measured by the tests given. Three of the English-speaking populations (Scotland, New Zealand, and England) ranked consistently high, despite the presumed irregularity of English orthography. Dialects, it might be noted, differ widely in these countries. It is a pity that Japan, with a nonalphabetic writing system, could not have been included in the study, but on the whole the conclusion seems warranted that in countries where a public educational system has been in operation for some time, the nature of the orthography has very little to do with reading comprehension by the time a child is 10 to 14 years old.

The questionnaires given the students tell pretty much the same story from country to country. The two background variables that predicted reading achievement most effectively were the socioeconomic composite of factors (socioeconomic status, including father's occupation and father's and mother's education) and reading resources in the home (e.g., number of books, ownership of a dictionary, subscription to a daily paper). Active parental participation in teaching showed a negative relationship, as did number of siblings. It would seem that parental help tended to be given most often when a child was progressing slowly, when help was needed. Many detailed questions were included, such as hours spent watching television. The correlation with television watching for the youngest population was generally negative, but in the underdeveloped countries, taken overall, it was highly positive, probably because of its association with socioeconomic factors.

The results on school factors obtained from questionnaires given to teachers and administrators are quite disappointing. There was no consistent identification of school factors that made a difference, such as student/ teacher ratio, number of reading specialists available, or even teacher training. Whether the questionnaire results were for some reason unreliable (e.g., the relevant teachers did not happen to be the ones sampled) or whether a child's fate in ultimate reading comprehension is settled before he is ten years old by family and cultural factors beyond the school's control, we do not know.

Summary

To answer our last question (or try to), are there any universal factors that predict across nations, languages, and orthography progress in learning to

read? Economic status, parents' education, and especially reading resources in the home are the factors that consistently turn up. These factors
can operate on the child by way of his motivation and the learning environment provided him. From the existing evidence, it would seem that
reading comprehension is little affected by the writing system or the orthography, and that the mature reader attains the competence to abstract the
higher-order information as his exposure to the written code increases.
Cross-national studies tell us little about how he does this.

Rapid Reading: Whether, When, and How?

The average adult reads at an average speed of about 200 to 400 words per minute, usually nearer 200. But this figure is nothing more than an estimate. We are all aware that there are large individual differences in reading speed, and that the same individual may read slowly on some occasions and rapidly on others, for a great variety of reasons. The rate of output of printed matter appears to grow exponentially, and many people, to judge from the commercial success of courses designed to increase reading rate, feel the need to increase their speed. There are some basic facts about how fast one can read in the conventional sense. There are different definitions of what is meant by reading and different needs for information. Finally, there are a number of methods that have been tried to increase rate of processing written information. Let us consider these points in turn.

How fast *can* one read continuous text, assuming for the moment that all the information in the text is wanted? There is a *minimal* speed of reading below which the syntactical and meaningful relations within a sentence or a larger unit of discourse do not come through. Reading one word at a time, with pauses between, makes it nearly impossible to extract information beyond the word. The halting beginner of a foreign language is painfully aware of the need to speed up in order to get some sense from the text. But there is an upper limit too, beyond which comprehension is lost. One can scan for a graphic symbol or a word target very fast, but the scanner remembers almost nothing of what he saw except the target. It is possible to perceive a five-letter word exposed for only 1 msec, but that does not mean one could read 1000 words per second under any conditions. In reading the eyes must move from one fixation point to another, and there is a limit to what can be taken in during one fixation. The number of fixations per unit of time is limited for even the best reader, because of physiological "masking" effects; something exposed too soon before a target or too soon after it obliterates the target. The looker does not perceive it at all. To read the five-letter word with a 1-msec exposure, it must not be immediately preceded or followed by anything; an "icon" or image of it remains briefly accessible to the perceiver for processing; and besides, he is aided by his knowledge of English orthography which itself takes some processing time. By the time he has gotten the word "out" close to a second may have elapsed.

The facts of fixation and eye movement patterns were discussed in Chapter 10, but we shall review them briefly in the light of the present context. As the reader scans the text, his eyes move in jumps (saccades), pausing to fixate at frequent intervals, and no useful information is extracted during the movements themselves. Most of the time is spent during the pauses, which vary in number and in duration. A good reader (see Chapter 10) makes fewer fixation pauses per average line of text than a poor reader, but fewer than five is rare, since the extent of the material that can reach the fovea (area of clear focal vision) in one fixation is limited to about 10 spaces of average printed text. Pause time varies with the novelty, difficulty, and many other features of the text, as well as with the reader's skill and interest. A good reader does not pause as long as a poor reader, but even a good one may pause as long or longer than 250 msec. With three fixations and an average pause time of 250 msec, he would have spent nearly 1 second per line, not counting the time taken for moving his eyes. For difficult prose, pause durations average longer. If one estimated 10 words per average line, a good reader of easy material might, from such a crude estimate, read up to 800 words per minute. But this is not the whole story. Even a good reader makes regressions (goes back and looks again) as he reads. Moreover, as we saw in many previous chapters, reading is not merely decoding print, but involves extracting information. Comprehension takes time. As we saw in Chapter 10, average pause time decreases little, even for good readers, after the fourth grade or so. The increased efficiency of more mature readers does not, then, appear to be due to superior oculomotor mechanics, but to superiority at a deeper level of processing.

It has often been argued that peripheral vision (beyond the area of the fovea) is useful, especially to the skilled reader. But recent research by McConkie and Rayner (1973) and Rayner (1974), described in Chapter 10 makes it clear that little useful information is picked up more than 10 spaces from the fixation point. This fact is important in evaluating methods employed in speed reading courses, as we shall see. The facts about eye movements do not, in fact, tell us anything very positive about reading. What they do give us is some idea of the oculomotor limitations of the reading process if we assume that the reader is actually viewing all the text.

But is he? What is reading? Must one read every word to extract information from text? Perhaps not, but that depends on the nature of the text
and the purpose of the reader, points we have already discussed in great
detail. A favorite exhortation of professors, when they feel guilty about assigning excessive amounts of reading, is "Just read for the ideas." The implication is that one needn't read everything. But "getting the idea" implies comprehension—doing some planning and thinking. Suppose one
were assigned the poem of Emily Dickinson's quoted in Chapter 12 and
told to "read for the ideas." The assignment would not be completed very
rapidly. But there are, in fact, times when we do not want much of the
information in the text, and then we can scan it rapidly, or "skim" it.
Skill in skimming and knowing when to do so is undoubtedly valuable, is
tied in with the material and the reader's purpose, and can certainly be
learned, although it isn't perfectly clear what one does when one skims.

Over the years, many claims have been advanced about the promise
of various methods for increasing reading rate. One that achieved great
popularity in the 1940s was practice with a tachistoscope. The idea, although ill founded, was that practice in reading words and phrases exposed for increasingly shorter durations would automatically increase the
trainee's spontaneous rate of reading because the "span of apprehension"
would be increased. Careful research on the effects of such training showed
it to be without value (Goins, 1958; Tinker, 1965; Vernon, 1931). Other
experiments on the training of eye movements (Glock, 1949) using paced
exposure of lines of print were equally ineffective. To quote Tinker (1965),
who spent the major part of his life on research on reading and eye movements, "All well-designed experiments which have attempted to evaluate
the role of training eye movements to improve reading have failed to find
that such training is either necessary or desirable" (Tinker, 1965, p. 109).
The truth of the matter turns out to be that good readers move their eyes
efficiently, but drilling in "shaping" eye movements does not improve
reading. The cause of efficient eye movements is *knowing how to read well*.
One more quotation from Tinker is apt:

It was discovered early that the effective reader makes few fixations and
regressions in reading. This finding led to the devising of several techniques
for training eye movements. It was assumed that, if the poor reader was
trained to make fewer fixations and regressions per line, his reading would
automatically improve. Unfortunately, this presumes that external motor
factors are going to operate in bringing about the change in reading per-

formance rather than the more important central factors of perception, comprehension, and assimilation of material. (Tinker, 1969, p. 6)

Why should we belabor this point? One very good reason is that a flood of courses in "speed reading" are now being offered the reading public, at prices ranging from $75 to $250, that place heavy stress on eye movement training. Drilling the eye movements is not the entire curriculum, however, so let us try to describe a sample of the techniques used. A good source for the interested reader is a monograph by R. P. Carver (1971). Carver made a comprehensive study of the Evelyn Wood Dynamic Reading Program (which promises to triple one's rate of reading without loss of comprehension), after taking the course himself.* Carver is a trained psychologist whose research is concentrated on learning from reading.

What happens in such a course? It meets for eight weeks (once a week for $2\frac{1}{2}$ hours) and requires home practice. The principal tenets on which training methods were based came from observations made by Wood on a group of people who "could read over 1500 words per minute." To quote from her brochure, these people:

(a) Read *down* the page rather than from left to right.
(b) They read groups of words—or complete thoughts—rather than a word or two at a time.
(c) They rarely regressed—unlike the average reader, who frequently goes back to reread a phrase or even an entire paragraph. ("Evelyn Wood Reading Dynamics," pamphlet, p. 6)

The basic techniques of the course, as described by Carver, follow from these observations.

(a) read down pages instead of across them,
(b) read in thought patterns, whole concepts, and ideas instead of one word at a time,
(c) use the hand as a guiding pacer. (Carver, 1971, p. 13)

What does it mean to read "down pages" instead of across them? Presumably one looks at the center of a line and keeps moving down, the guiding hand proceeding ahead and preventing regressions. Do the reader's eye movements proceed in a straight vertical line down the page? If so, one could not expect him to see more than about seven letters per line, and not even that at a fast pace, for as we have seen, a single fixation can take in a span of at most ten letters, peripheral vision beyond this area is of little

*The reason for choosing this course for discussion, rather than one of the many others advertised in newspapers, is that descriptions of the curriculum were available and some evaluative research has been performed on it.

utility, and masking effects occur with a very rapid succession of exposures. Yet an instructor of Carver's warned the class that they must be sure they were "seeing both edges of the print as they read down the page." An instructor in a preview class that we attended ourselves said, "We always see every word on every page whether skimming with a preview of the material or not." Previewing the material before beginning was recommended, as was writing down "key words" and concentrating on recall.

To return briefly to the eye movements, it is patently impossible for the oculomotor system to permit the seeing of 1500 words per minute, no matter what the direction of scan or how fast the guiding hand proceeds ahead. What are the eye movements of graduate speed readers actually like? Eye movements of 41 trainees who had just completed the Reading Dynamics program were photographed by Dr. Stanford Taylor (1962). An analysis of the films did not reveal a vertical line of progression. According to Taylor, "An analysis of the graphs, however, indicates patterns that are very similar to those produced during skimming or scanning activities." The readers who showed greatest approximation to reading "dynamically" right down the center of the page had the poorest comprehension scores on a true-false posttest (actually less than 50% correct).

Thomas (1962) photographed the eye movements of a very highspeed reader (a professor holding a Ph.D.). Her mean fixation time was .32 sec, by no means fast, but she made many fewer fixations than the average reader. The pattern of fixations was extremely unusual. The eyes tended to move half-way down the center of the left-hand page (the book was open so that two pages were visible), then across to the center of the right-hand page, and straight upward, returning then to the top of the left-hand page. The pattern resembled a square, crossing the two pages. There were never any fixations in the lower third of a page. No comprehension test was given this subject, so it is not clear what she was really doing. That she was getting any information from the lower third of the page is impossible.

One further study of the eye movements of a "speed reader" might be mentioned (McLaughlin, 1969). McLaughlin recorded rate of reading and eye movements of one subject, reading varied kinds of material. Rate varied with the nature of the material, but fixation duration (about 250 msec) varied little, nor did the pattern of eye movements, which was described as typically "14 fixations distributed in a rough zig-zag down the page." There were sometimes regressions, then, to the top of the page. McLaughlin concluded that "speed reading" has limited usefulness, because of confused and sometimes fabricated recall, and that a speed reader's behavior is similar in nearly all respects to that of a normal reader. What, then, are speed readers doing that is different? McLaughlin concludes that the "essential objective difference between speed readers and other people is in their eye movement patterns" (p. 506). The speed reader goes up as well as down, and in zigzags, according to these reports. How does he combine the information he picks up to make any sense at all? McLaughlin quotes Neisser's (1967) statement that reading is "externally guided thinking" and applies this to the speed reader as follows:

This may be called the theory of parallel processing, because it suggests that seven or so different sentences can be built up at the same time in a reader's mind, just as parallel electric circuits within a single computer can perform different tasks simultaneously. Support for the theory is provided by the fact that, with training, it appears to be no great strain for a human being to search for even hundreds of items simultaneously, as do the employees of a news-clipping agency when looking for references to their clients. (McLaughlin, 1969, p. 507)

We might point out the dubiousness of this analogy, both to the computer and to the clipping agents (who are not trying to comprehend anything) and ask, as well, just how the speed reading courses teach parallel processing. McLaughlin himself points out that "it is probably fruitless to try to make a speed reader of someone who lacks high verbal intelligence." He also concludes that reading at high speed is principally useful for judging what may be ignored and what is informative and needs careful rereading.

McLaughlin's "parallel processing" analogy reminds us of an anecdote told by a professor of reading techniques on a television program. He had observed, he said, a phenomenally fast reader who claimed that she excelled in reading pages printed in double column fashion because she read one column with the left eye and one with the right. This is quite a trick, since we have only one brain. Even if it were split, the language processing center functions predominantly only on one side.

What about reading groups of words or "complete thoughts" rather than one word at a time? This is an achievement which one could hardly fail to find praiseworthy, and we have presented much evidence to the effect that mature readers do extract information in the largest units of which they are capable and that are suitable to their purposes. The text affords relations and rules to aid this kind of process—orthographic, syntactic, and semantic. But the question is, do the "reading dynamics" courses promote this kind of skill? Mechanical devices like scanning down the center of a page and following the hand seem irrelevant, whatever other purposes they may serve. Reading dynamics programs also advocate reduction of subvocalization, which is presumably circumvented by very fast scanning, but it is by no means clear that dropping out subvocalization aids the comprehension of poor readers, or even of good readers when the material is difficult (see Chapter 10). "Previewing" the material and extracting key words might indeed help, although there is remarkably little evidence to show that it does.

We are indebted to Peter Kump, National Director of Education for Evelyn Wood Reading Dynamics, for a summary of some ongoing research by Dorothy Hansen, a ph.D. candidate, who taught a course combining Evelyn Wood speed reading techniques with principles of language organization and discourse analysis. A control group matched on a test of reading ability beforehand was given a posttest, as was the experimental group exposed to the course. All the students were given 13 minutes to read a chapter. Afterward they took four tests: a free-recall test; concept-application questions; paraphrase questions; and verbatim-recall questions. The latter three kinds of questions were multiple-choice items. The experimental group remembered more on the open-ended free-recall test. The two groups did not differ on two of the multiple-choice tests, but the experimental group scored significantly *lower* on the paraphrase questions. This finding does not suggest that the dynamically trained group was aided in taking in "complete thoughts" as a result of the course.

A technique practiced in the Evelyn Wood course is something called "threading," which seems to sum up the essence of the learning program. The student proceeds down the page (using his hand as a pacer), reading only for the main idea, the gist of the material. Threading rate at the start of practice is several times as fast as full comprehension rate, but by constantly forcing an increase in the threading rate, comprehension rate supposedly improves. It is a limited comprehension, very rapid, and omits all concern with details. But (according to Carver) a goal of the course is for the threading rate automatically to become the comprehension rate. How this could happen is not clear, but it is clear that a large proportion of time in class is devoted to threading, often repeating a passage after writing notes on what was recalled from a first rapid "thread-through," frequently preceded by a "preview." Rereading passages at increasing rates following a preview is a typical method of the course and obviously would result in increased recall and probably comprehension as successive readings increased. But it is hard for a psychologist to see how this type of practice would lead eventually to full comprehension while reading at 1500 words a minute.

Some research has been devoted to specific evaluation of aspects of the Reading Dynamics program. The best known is a Ph.D. thesis by Liddle (1965), who compared two matched groups of university students before and after one group had taken a 12-week course (given by an experienced teacher and including study skills as well as practice in speed reading). Liddle constructed his own tests, writing multiple-choice items for two types of material, a novel and chapters from a sociology textbook. There were three types of multiple-choice questions—factual ones, ones requiring inference, and ones requiring "critical reflection." Reading rates were recorded. The comprehension tests had no time limit. The group that had had instruction did indeed read faster (more than five times faster) than the other group. On the comprehension tests, the practiced group had poorer comprehension scores than the control group for the fictional material on all three types of item. For the sociology material, the speed readers had somewhat higher scores on "critical reflection" items, but lower scores on factual and inference items. Critical reflection on sociological material, done at one's leisure, might be a reasonable accomplishment for a university student without reading the text. The results of this study indicate that very rapid reading does lead to a loss of factual details and, as a result, a loss of ability to draw inferences from them.

A more specific study was performed by Kluska (1971), using as subjects only graduates of a Reading Dynamics course. Kluska measured eye movements during a reading test when the hand was used as a pacer, and when it was not. The subjects were selected from a population of graduates of the Evelyn Wood Dynamic Reading course on the basis of strict criteria, such as having tripled their reading rate, having shown no more than a 5% loss in comprehension score, and having used their hand as a pacer during at least half their general reading since graduation from the course. Their eye movements were measured while they read selections from two reading tests. For one test the selections were short and the subjects crossed out an incongruous word in each passage; for the other, there was a longer passage to be read, followed by true-false and multiple-choice questions.

Results of Kluska's experiment showed that the subjects did indeed read at a faster rate when the hand was used as a pacer, especially on the longer passage, which was merely to be read without noting incongruities. There was no difference on the comprehension test associated with use of the hand. There was also no difference in duration of fixation. The "span of recognition" was found to be greater when the hand was used as a pacer. That is, the number of words taken in at each fixation was found to be greater, assuming that the reader was apprehending all the words despite fewer fixations. Although the hand, when used, moved regularly down the page, the eyes did not. According to Kluska, "under the hand condition the eye movements defy summarization." Reading rate was correlated positively with decrease in number of fixations, so hand pacing for these trained subjects was apparently effective (if one can infer a causal relation) in increasing reading rate. No correlations between any of the variables and comprehension were significant.

These results bring up the often-argued question of the relation between reading rate and comprehension. Some early studies indicated that faster readers showed better comprehension than slower readers, but of course such a finding does not imply that fast reading leads to superior comprehension. Over the years, innumerable studies relating rate and comprehension have come up with correlations ranging from $-.47$ to $+.96$ (Rankin, 1962). Many factors affect the correlation. To quote Rankin, "When the material is more difficult, when more critical thought processes are involved, and when the reader's purpose is more exacting, the relationship between reading rate and comprehension is minimal" (p. 5). Increasing one's rate of reading by learning to make use of orthographic, syntactic, and semantic structure in the text very likely does lead to both improved comprehension and faster rate, but mechanical pacers, including one's own hand, do not.

Some of Kluska's subjects, in responding to a questionnaire, professed that the use of the hand "heightened concentration," "led to greater reading involvement," and allowed for "idea rather than word orientation." A paper by Fischer (1969) attempted to evaluate the phonomenological impact of dynamic reading on its students. Her hypothesis was that "successful Dynamic Reading would require a relaxed openness to things as they appear, . . . to multiple events and personal feelings, . . . prereflective wanderings through an unfolding terrain" (p. 3). Students in Reading Dynamics classes were given two personality tests, both in the first week and the seventh week of the course. The tests were the Rokeach Dogmatism Scale, on which persons who score high are said to be closed to new ways of thinking and have less tolerance for ambiguity, and the Shostrom Personal Orientation Inventory, which is said to measure aspects of "self-actualization," characteristics of a person who is "more fully functioning and lives a more enriched life than the everage person" (Fischer, p. 5). Other tests, including reading and IQ tests were given as well, and intercorrelation matrices obtained for men and women separately. The results are too elaborate to summarize, but Fischer concluded that "openness to experience is a ground for Dynamic reading." It is not clear how this conclusion was arrived at, or exactly what it means, except that "Dynamic reading involves the reader's pleasure in allowing unreflected impressions (meanings) to come to him without worrying about the accuracy of his understanding, or the 'objective truth' of the words" (p. 11). Personal openness and flexibility did "seem to allow higher comprehension scores when reading at dynamic rates. However, the highest reading speeds are achieved by persons who are relatively less 'self-actualized' and 'open' " (Fischer, p. 23). Perhaps the moral of this study is that what the student gains from a Reading Dynamics course is related to certain characteristics of his own personality. The meaning of the data is very unclear, especially as regards the group of women studied. We doubt that Fischer's conclusion that Dynamic Reading is a special process which allows "a new relationship with printed expression" tells us anything helpful.

We have argued throughout this book that flexibility of reading style is of the greatest importance. The reader's purpose, the author's intention, and the style of the text are all factors to be adjusted to. Flexibility is not necessarily the rule, however, even in adult readers (Harris, 1968). Can it be achieved by increasing one's rate? The answer depends on what the reader wants to get from the material. All the available evidence leads to the conclusion that learning to read at very rapid rates does not increase comprehension—if anything, the opposite. But there are many occasions when skimming or scanning are appropriate, and if a reader finds it difficult to accommodate his rate to his purpose and the difficulty of the text, there is reason to think that practice, guided or self-instructed, can help. Many educators have emphasized, however, that variability in rate is not the cause of flexibility in reading styles, but a result of mature reading skill.

There is no magic route to reading speedily with good comprehension. We conclude with one last quotation from Tinker:

The best way to begin a program for increasing speed is first to remove causes of slow reading: too small a sight vocabulary; weakness in vocabulary knowledge and comprehension; word recognition difficulties; over-analysis; insufficient use of context; lack of phrasing; and vocalization. (1969, p. 7)

As to *whether* speed reading is possible, the answer depends on one's definition but most people can learn to read faster than they do, *when* they want to and consider it sufficient for their purposes. *How* they do it has no ready answer, because again it depends on definition. But no amount of practice can make us perceive what we do not look at.

How Can Parents Help Children with Reading?

One might ask if parents *should* help children with reading, since there was a strong bias on the part of many educators a decade or so ago that they should not. A number of parents were given to understand that they should keep hands off and leave the whole matter to the teacher, a trained expert. They might confuse the child, or put him off the whole subject by trying to teach him when he was unready, too immature. This is the kind of question that provokes moralizing and suggests the sententious tone of the Sunday newspaper supplement or perhaps the down-to-earth commonsense approach of Dr. Spock. For this reason we felt at first that it did not belong in a serious scientific discussion of the psychology of reading. But it is nevertheless one of the questions that parents most often ask teachers. We shall try, therefore, to provide reassurance and a few cautious conclusions. There *are* useful things that parents can do, and there are likewise potentially harmful things they should not do.

One conclusion that seems to be well justified is that what goes on in the child's home environment, especially before he goes to school, plays an enormous role in the progress he makes in later educational situations. It has even been suggested in a recent commissioned report (Jencks et al., 1972) that schools can do little to affect the different rates of development that result from varied early home backgrounds. A child who comes well prepared and ready to learn learns; a child who doesn't will profit much less from formal instruction, no matter who the teacher or what the methods of instruction. This is a gloomy conclusion that we are not pessimistic enough to accept. But one can heed it to the extent of thinking what kind of environment at home provides the richest soil for encouraging readiness (and eagerness) to learn.

We shall draw on Chapter 8, which was concerned with prereading skills, and Chapter 9, on beginning to read, for some hints. It was clear from the research of Lavine (1972) that middle-class children in a literate society have learned to discriminate writing from pictures by the age of three years, and have made much more progress in recognizing categorical features of writing and distinctive features of individual letters by the age of five years. How have they done this? Not by formal instruction of any kind, in most cases, since few could identify more than a letter or two by name. The learning was spontaneous. But children in a society that contained very few written displays were far behind in recognition of writing, although they could categorize pictures, even simplified line drawings, if they represented something in the child's environment. The inference is obvious that the mere presence of large amounts of print and writing in daily surroundings provokes perceptual learning that is painless and in-valuable as preparation for reading. It only has to be there for a child to get some advantage from it. Most homes in our culture provide this ma-terial in ample amounts in books, magazines, newspapers, and the dubious television set (the child could learn to ignore the print and just listen to the sound). But there are homes that provide few books or even magazines. A four-year-old child of our acquaintance was observed by his mother to choose some of his own books and carry them out of the house. When she inquired mildly where he was taking them, he said "to Ronnie, because he doesn't have a book." It was a fact that the only book in Ronnie's house was the telephone book, which is not, at an early age, very entertaining. Owning some books of his own seems to be especially important to a child. Having his own bookcase with his own books in it is a source of pride. It's fun to get new books for birthdays and other occasions, and to select a comic book in the drugstore for oneself (and far wholesomer than candy).

It was also clear from research reported in Chapter 8 that a very young child, given a writing tool and something to write on, will scribble spon-taneously and watch his production with great interest. Furthermore, if writing materials are easily available, a child will make use of them on his own. His interest in writing activity may occur in spurts and appear to lag in between, but such spontaneity is probably a good thing. The evidence available indicates that the quality of the scribbling matures by itself, gradually becoming linear and including more and more of the distinctive features of letters, such as contrasts of curves and straight lines, diagonals, and intersections, with "noisy" overlay disappearing. If there are letters and numbers available for copying, children make attempts to copy them and improve with time without correction or adult guidance. The child recognizes the better match himself and gets satisfaction from his improve-ment. It seems safe indeed to conclude that parents should make writing materials—pencil and paper, slates and chalk—readily available, in a place where the child can find them for himself and where he can sit quiet-ly and amuse himself with them. Mothers have been known to discourage this practice. One mother, when asked whether her son had ever shown any interest in learning to print or write, said, "Oh yes, but that was soon discouraged. He used to mess up the house, and once even wrote on the wall" (Durkin, 1966).

Another important point that came up in Chapter 8 was the difficulty young children have in analyzing words into component sounds. Their at-tention has always before been focused on the meaning of speech, not its phonetic aspects. Even though a child can produce speech accurately in accordance with the phonological rule system of his language by school age, he is unaware of phonology as an objective thing. Even though he will spontaneously give rhymes as associations in a free-association task or even a task constrained by the instruction "Tell me three words that will be easy to remember along with the word *blue*," he is not deliberately using rhyme as a strategy and is often apparently unaware that he is doing so (Tenney, 1973). When asked to give a rhyme or a word that "sounds like" another, with plenty of examples provided, he may be unable to. This lack of phonetic awareness can be a big stumbling block when he is trying to discover the relationships between sounds of words and their written counterparts.

When "consciousness raising" in this respect is called for, no unpleasant issue need be made of it, because all sorts of word games can be played in the family. It is probably far better to do this, making it purely a game, long before a teacher says that Tommy can't tell what sound or letter a word begins with. Rhyming games are excellent (see Chapter 8 for a description of "stinky pinky"—What's a large farm animal that says "oink"?). The idea of finding a rhyming combination gets over easily, and the child becomes more and more aware of the sounds without at the same time losing the meaning, which can easily happen with the sort of exercises given in school.

At five or six years a child is not too young to start playing a game like "I packed my trunk" or "Picnic" (another version of the same game). "I packed my trunk and in it I put an acorn." The next person adds a word beginning with *B*, repeating the *A* word first. Or a little simpler perhaps, "I'm thinking of something beginning with *A*. It's a juicy red fruit." (The sound rather than the letter name can be given.) Then each one takes a turn thinking of something beginning with *A*. These games are perfect for passing the time on a long car trip or when parents and children are doing something fairly dull together, like washing dishes. Naturally, one wants them to lighten the boredom and not produce it. Talking pig Latin, a secret language, is fun too, and helps teach sound segmentation.

Avoiding boredom and creating interest brings us to the all-important question of motivation. There are three really important "do's" here, and a couple of "don'ts." On the positive side, members of the family should provide good role models. When book-loving parents, grandparents, and siblings are frequently seen to be immersed in a book which they quite evidently enjoy reading, children cannot help perceiving that they are doing something interesting and want to do it too. Then comes the second point. The child will be curious about this absorbing pursuit and ask questions about it. When children ask "What does it say," or "Show me" or "How do you spell" something, they should be answered with encouragement. Parents who can't be bothered to answer such questions are killing curiosity, the spontaneous urge to learn that is the foundation of all adaptive behavior.

It might be objected that little children will find whatever a parent is reading to himself dull and incomprehensible. This is unlikely if an attempt is made to explain it to him. But in any case, there is an obvious answer to this—to read to the child books and stories that he is very interested in. Sometimes children want to hear the same story over and over, which may be tiresome for the parent. But it can be borne with and it seems to be profitable for the child. If the book is held so he can see it while he is read to, and if he begins to know the story "by heart," he may begin on his own to match up what he hears with what is on the page. Being read to brings other advantages, of course. It provides the best opportunity for discovering that books have something interesting and imaginative to say; it increases knowledge about other places and other people; and above all, it can increase a child's language skills. People do not always speak in complete sentences, and they are apt to talk to children in a rather limited vocabulary. But books need not do this.

What are the "don'ts" about motivation? They are pretty self-evident. Reading, word games, printing, and so on should not be forced on a child or formalized. They should be fun, not work. Most of all, when any of these activities are pursued, children should never be allowed to feel a sense of failure. If "stinky pinky" is too hard for a four-year-old, save it for a year until he can win a little success and reinforcement from it.

This little essay, compared to the rest of the book, is admittedly commonsense application of a few principles. Have we any evidence to show that they work? We do have some. Durkin (1966) published a monograph on children who read early. The monograph describes two studies of children in the first grade of the public school systems of Oakland, California, and New York City. As soon as the children entered first grade they were given a reading test, a list of 27 common words (*said, mother,* etc.) and some sentences made up from them. Children who could read previous to school instruction were located in this way, and their reading achievement was followed over a period of six years. A notable finding was that these children maintained their advantage over the other children all through this period, and a number of them were double promoted (skipped grades). It is thus a fallacy to suppose that learning to read at home will hinder a child's reading achievements in school.

In her New York City study, Durkin matched the early readers in each case with a child of similar IQ and background. The children in these groups varied widely in both IQ and socioeconomic status. She gave both groups of children various tests, such as the Bender Gestalt and the Minnesota Tests of Creative Thinking. The early readers and the nonearly readers were very similar as regards whatever traits were measured by these tests, although parents of the early readers often referred to them as "persistent" and as "pencil and paper kids." Where some important differences became apparent was in home interviews with the children's parents. When asked about interest shown in reading before entering school, 100% of the parents of early readers reported interest, whereas 73% of the parents of nonearly readers did. When asked about the source of the interest, parents of the two groups differed in frequency of mentioning the following factors:

	Percentage Answering "Yes"	
	Early Readers	Nonearly Readers
Availability of paper and pencil in home	83%	18%
Availability of reading materials in home	73%	14%
Availability of blackboard in home	57%	23%
Interest in the meaning of words	47%	9%

The most common age of expressing interest in reading was given as four years for both groups. As might be expected, more parents or siblings of early readers gave help when requested than did families of nonearly readers:

	Percentage Giving Help	
	Early	Nonearly
With printing	93%	73%
With identification of written words	91%	27%
With the meaning of words	77%	27%
With spelling	73%	27%
With sounds of letters	67%	27%

Mothers most often gave help, but siblings did fairly often, especially by "playing school."

The sequence with which interest and skills developed was very consistent within the group of early readers, usually developing from a prior interest in copying and writing. As Durkin put it, "Almost without exception the starting point of curiosity about written language was an interest in scribbling and drawing. From this developed interest in copying objects and letters of the alphabet. When a child was able to copy letters—and not all the children who had the interest developed the skill—his almost inevitable request was, 'Show me my name' " (p. 108).

Another important source of curiosity about words was being read to. Most parents felt that stories that were read over and over were most influential. The parents of the early readers also considered that the help they gave was in response to children's questions, and that it occurred intermittently. When parents of nonearly readers helped, it sometimes resulted from their own decision and ambitions rather than from the children's own questions and curiosity. "What is much more important [than socioeconomic status,] the research data indicated, is the presence of parents who spend time with their children; who read to them; who answer their questions and their requests for help; and who demonstrate in their own lives that reading is a rich source of relaxation, information, and contentment" (p. 136).

One more activity only indirectly related to reading should be mentioned—frequent linguistic interaction with children. To become fluent and expressive in his own speech, a child does not need tuition or instruction, but he needs ample opportunity to hear people speaking and to communicate with them directly. Richness of stimulation in a face-to-face communicative interaction appears to be the most important factor in language development (Cazden, 1966). Adequate language development, in turn, is essential for normal acquisition of reading skill. The average home provides this factor without any special effort, but it has often been said that the language milieu of children from low-income homes is likely to be impoverished. While a lot of talking may be going on (via the television set, for instance), conversation directed to the child may be too infrequent for him to participate actively. The Cornell Story Reading Program, established to study the effect of systematic story reading on the language development of young disadvantaged children, was followed up in a project directed by Macklin (1973). Children between 18 and 33 months of age and coming from very poor families were the experimental subjects. A comparable control group was also selected. Teenage readers from ninth grade, themselves from low-income families, were employed. They went every day after school to the homes of assigned children and read to them for 20 minutes each. A training program was held for the readers beforehand, explaining the goals of the project, and encouraging them to talk to the child while reading, to elicit active verbalization from the child, and to provide feedback to the child's productive speech—correction, expansion, extension, etc. The sessions began with talk about picture books, or sometimes toys, and progressed gradually to stories, always encouraging verbalization from the children. This activity continued for an eight-month period. Afterward, a nine-month followup program was conducted for children who were still available and not in nursery school or Head Start. This program attempted to get the mother to assume responsibility for daily reading to the child. A student visited the family for an hour each week, worked with the child in the mother's presence, discussed the mother's own reading to the child, and left books to be used during the coming week.

A series of tests was administered prior to the program, during the course of the program, and finally after 20 months. The tests were three indications of language development: average length of the child's utterance; expressive vocabulary; and receptive vocabulary. After three months in the program, the experimental children performed slightly (but not significantly) better than control children on two of the measures. After the third testing period, the experimental group exceeded the control group on all three measures. Although most of the differences were not significant, improvement showed up mainly in receptive vocabulary.

Interviews with mothers following the program revealed little difference between the experimental and the control group in attitudes toward the importance of reading to children, frequency of actually doing so, and ownership of books. Most of the children owned some books (not many), several none. Although nearly all the mothers agreed that reading was important, less than half the children in the experimental group had been read to during the week prior to the interview. The experimental group did not surpass the control group in this respect (if anything, the opposite). Perhaps the chief value of the program lay in the children's attitude toward it. Nearly all the mothers reported that the child enjoyed and looked forward to the reader's visit. It is difficult to evaluate a very young child's attitude toward reading, but the fact that it gave evident enjoyment is on the positive side. The mothers thought the program had increased interest in reading and ability to sit still and enjoy a quiet pursuit. In conclusion, the program did not appear to effect really significant improvement in language development—perhaps because it was not intense enough or long enough. The generally favorable attitudes toward the program by the mothers and the impressions of the children's increased interest in books and reading suggest that a stronger effort might be worthwhile, although pointing up once more that what goes on constantly in the child's own home surroundings is hard to offset.

We have said nothing about what parents can do to help children who are already in school and are not progressing. That is because the reasons for slow progress are multitudinous and vary with the school and especially with the child. There are no general precepts to apply, except not to badger the child and so increase his sense of failure, and to follow the teacher's recommendations. It is certainly unwise to purchase commercial products guaranteeing reading improvement. "Home learning" kits of various kinds are advertised like patent medicines, and the consumer would do well to be equally wary of them. The only magic in learning to read is the magic that the child supplies himself when a rich and responsive environment gives him the chance.

References

Aarons, L. Subvocalization: Aural and EMG feedback in reading. *Perceptual and Motor Skills*, 1971, *33*, 271–306.

Aborn, M., Rubenstein, H., and Sterling, T. D. Sources of contextual constraint upon words in sentences. *Journal of Experimental Psychology*, 1959, *57*, 171–180.

Abrahams, R. D., and Gay, G. Black culture in the classroom. In R. D. Abrahams and R. C. Troike (eds.), *Language and cultural diversity in American education*. Englewood Cliffs, N. J.: Prentice-Hall, 1972, pp. 67–84. (a)

Abrahams, R. D., and Gay, G. Talking Black in the classroom. In R. D. Abrahams and R. C. Troike (eds.), *Language and cultural diversity in American education*. Englewood Cliffs, N. J.: Prentice-Hall, 1972. pp. 200–209. (b)

Adams, R. Dyslexia: A discussion of its definition. *Journal of Learning Disabilities*, 1969, *2*, 616–633.

Addison, R. M., and Homme, L. E. The reinforcement event (RE) menu. *National Society for Programmed Instruction Journal*, 1965, *5*, 8–9.

Ahrens, A. *Untersuchungen ueber die Bewegung der Augen beim Schreiben*. Rostok, 1891.

Allen, D. Another look at formal similarity. *APA Proceedings*, 1970, 77–80.

Alleton, V. *L'Ecriture Chinoise* ("Que Sais-je?" no. 1374). Paris: Presses Universitaires de France, 1970.

Allport, G. W., and Vernon, P. E. *A study of values*. Boston: Houghton Mifflin, 1931.

Anapolle, L. Visual training and reading performance. *Journal of Reading*, 1967, *10*, 372–382.

Anderson, I. H. Eye-movements of good and poor readers. *Psychological Monographs*, 1937, *48*, 1–35.

Anglin, J. M. *The growth of word meanings*. Cambridge, Mass.: The MIT Press, 1970.

Anisfeld, M. A. A comment on "The role of grapheme-phoneme correspondence in the perception of words." *American Journal of Psychology*, 1964, *77*, 320–326.

Anisfeld, M. A., Barlow, J., and Frail, C. M. Distinctive features in the pluralization rules of English speakers. *Language and Speech*, 1968, *11*, 31–37.

Anisfeld, M. A., and Tucker, G. R. English pluralization rules of six-year-old children. *Child Development*, 1967, *38*, 1201–1217.

Appel, L. F., Cooper, R. G., McCarrell, N., Sims-Knight, J., Yussen, S. R., and Flavell, J. H. The developmental acquisition of the distinction between perceiving and memorizing. *Child Development*, 1972, *43*, 1365–1381.

Applebee, A. N. Research in reading retardation: Two critical problems. *Journal of Child Psychology and Psychiatry*, 1971, *12*, 91–113.

Arnold, G. E. The genetic background of developmental language disorders. *Folia Phoniatrica*, 1961, *13*, 246–254.

Ashton-Warner, S. *Teacher*. New York: Simon and Schuster, 1963.

Atkinson, R. C. The observing response in discrimination learning. *Journal of Experimental Psychology*, 1961, *62*, 253–262.

Atkinson, R. C. Computerized instruction and the learning process. *American Psychologist*, 1968, *23*, 225–239.

Atkinson, R. C., Fletcher, J. D., Chetin, H. C., and Stauffer, C. M. Instruction in initial reading under computer control: The Stanford project. Technical Report No. 158, August 13, 1970. Stanford University: Institute for Mathematical Studies in the Social Sciences.

Atkinson, R. C., and Paulson, J. A. An approach to the psychology of instruction. *Psychological Bulletin*, 1972, *78*, 49–61.

Ausubel, D. P. *Learning by discovery: Rationale and mystique*. Urbana: Bureau of Educational Research, University of Illinois, 1961.

Baddeley, A. D. Short term memory for word sequences as a function of acoustic, semantic, and formal similarity. *Quarterly Journal of Experimental Psychology*, 1966, *18*, 362–365.

Baker, K. E., and Feldman, H. Threshold-luminance for recognition in relation to frequency of prior exposure. *American Journal of Psychology*, 1956, *69*, 278–280.

Bakwin, H. Reading disability in twins. *Developmental Medicine and Child Neurology*, 1973, *15*, 184–187.

Ball, W., and Tronick, E. Infant responses to impending collision: Optical and real. *Science*, 1971, *171*, 818–820.

Bandura, A. *Principles of behavior modification*. New York: Holt, Rinehart and Winston, 1969.

Bandura, A., Grusec, J., and Menlove, F. Observational learning as a function of symbolization and incentive set. *Child Development*, 1966, *37*, 499–506.

Bannatyne, A. D. The etiology of dyslexia and the Color Phonics System. In *Proceedings of the Third Annual Conference of Association for Children with Learning Disabilities, Tulsa, Oklahoma*. San Rafael, Calif.: Academic Therapy Press, 1967. Pp. 67–79.

Bannatyne, A. D. *Language, reading, and learning disabilities*. Springfield, Ill.: Charles C. Thomas, 1971.

Baratz, J. C. Teaching reading in an urban Negro school system. In J.C. Baratz and R. Shuy (eds.), *Teaching Black children to read*. Washington, D.C.: Center for Applied Linguistics, 1969. Pp. 92–117.

Barclay, J. R. The role of comprehension in remembering sentences. *Cognitive Psychology*, 1973, *4*, 229–254.

Baron, J. Phonemic stage not necessary for reading. *Quarterly Journal of Experimental Psychology*, 1973, *25*, 241–246.

Baron, J., and Thurston, I. An analysis of the word-superiority effect. *Cognitive Psychology*, 1973, *4*, 207–228.

Barron, R. W., and Pittenger, J. B. The effect of orthographic structure and lexical meaning on *same-different* judgments. *Quarterly Journal of Experimental Psychology*, in press.

Bartlett, F. C. *Remembering*. Cambridge: The University Press, 1932.

Basso, K. H., and Anderson, N. A western Apache writing system: The symbols of Silas John. *Science*, 1973, *180*, 1013–1022.

Bauman, R. An ethnographic framework for the investigation of communicative behaviors. In R. D. Abrahams and R. C. Troike (eds.), *Language and cultural diversity in American education*. Englewood Cliffs, N. J.: Prentice-Hall, 1972. Pp. 154–165.

Beck, I. L., and Mitroff, D. D. The rationale and design of a primary grades reading system for an individualized classroom. University of Pittsburgh Learning Research and Development Center, 1972.

Bellugi, U. The acquisition of negation. Unpublished doctoral dissertation. Graduate School of Education, Harvard University, 1967.

Bellugi, U., and Fischer, S. A comparison of sign language and spoken language. *Cognition*, 1972, *1*, 173–200.

Bender, L. Specific reading disability as a maturational lag. *Bulletin of the Orton Society*, 1957, *7*, 9–18.

Benton, A. Dyslexia in relation to form perception and directional sense. In J. Money (ed.), *Reading disability: Progress and research needs in dyslexia*. Baltimore: The Johns Hopkins Press, 1962. Pp. 81–102.

Bereiter, C., and Engelmann, S. *Teaching disadvantaged children in the preschool*. Englewood Cliffs, N. J.: Prentice-Hall, 1966.

Berko, J. The child's learning of English morphology. *Word*, 1958, *14*, 150–177.

Berlyne, D. E. *Conflict, arousal and curiosity*. New York: McGraw-Hill, 1960.

Bernbach, H. A. The effect of labels on short-term memory for colors with nursery school children. *Psychonomic Science,* 1967, *7,* 149–150.

Bernstein, B. Aspects of language and learning in the genesis of the social process. *Journal of Child Psychology and Psychiatry,* 1961, *1,* 313–324.

Bever, T. G. The cognitive basis for linguistic structures. In J. R. Hayes (ed.), *Cognition and the development of language.* New York: John Wiley, 1970. Pp. 279–362.

Biemiller, A. J. The development of the use of graphic and contextual information as children learn to read. *Reading Research Quarterly,* 1970, *6,* 75–96.

Biemiller, A. J., and Levin, H. Studies of oral reading. II. Pronounceability. In *The analysis of reading skill: A program of basic and applied research.* Final report, Project No. 5–1213, Cornell University and U. S. Office of Education, 1968. Pp. 116–125.

Biglmaier, F. Germany. In J. Downing (ed.), *Comparative reading.* New York: Macmillan, 1973. Pp. 342–359.

Birch, H. G., and Belmont, L. Auditory-visual integration in normal and retarded readers. *American Journal of Orthopsychiatry,* 1964, *34,* 852–861.

Birch, H. G., and Belmont, L. Auditory-visual integration, intelligence and reading ability in school children. *Perceptual and Motor Skills,* 1965, *20,* 295–305.

Bishop, C. H. Transfer effects of word and letter training in reading. *Journal of Verbal Learning and Verbal Behavior,* 1964, *3,* 215–221.

Blank, M., and Bridger, W. H. Deficiencies in verbal labeling in retarded readers. *American Journal of Orthopsychiatry,* 1966, *36,* 840–847.

Blom, G. E., Waite, R. R., and Zimet, S. G. A motivational content analysis of children's primers. In H. Levin and J. P. Williams (eds.), *Basic studies on reading.* New York: Basic Books, 1970. Pp. 188–221.

Blom, G. E., and Wiberg, L. Attitude content in reading primers. In J. Downing (ed.), *Comparative reading.* New York: Macmillan, 1973. Pp. 85–104.

Bloom, L. *Language development: Form and function in emerging grammars.* Cambridge, Mass.: The MIT Press, 1970.

Bloom, L. One word at a time: The use of single word utterances before syntax. Paper presented at the Conference on Developmental Psycholinguistics. State University of Buffalo, August 2–6, 1971.

Bloom, R. D. Learning to read: An operant perspective. In F. B. Davis (ed.), *The literature of research in reading with emphasis on models.* New Brunswick, N. J.: Rutgers University, 1971. Section 7, pp. 3–20.

Bloomfield, L. *Language.* New York: Holt, Rinehart and Winston, 1933.

Bloomfield, L. Linguistics and reading. *Elementary English Review*, 1942, *19*, 125–130.

Bloomfield, L., and Barnhart, C. L. *Let's read*. Bronxville, N. Y.: Clarence L. Barnhart, Inc., 1963.

Blumenthal, A. L. Prompted recall of sentences. *Journal of Verbal Learning and Verbal Behavior*, 1967, *6*, 203–206.

Bolinger, D. L. Visual morphemes. *Language*, 1946, 333–340.

Bolinger, D. L. *Aspects of language*. New York: Harcourt, Brace & World, 1968.

Bonvillian, J., Charrow, Z., and Nelson, K. Psycholinguistics and educational implications of deafness. *Human Development*, 1973, *16*, 321–345.

Bormuth, J. R. Readability: A new approach. *Reading Research Quarterly*, 1966, *1*, 79–132.

Bowden, J. H. Learning to read. *Elementary School Teacher*, 1911, *12*, 21–33.

Bower, G. H. A multicomponent theory of the memory trace. In K. W. Spence and J. T. Spence (eds.), *The psychology of learning and motivation*. Vol. 1. New York: Academic Press, 1967. Pp. 230–325.

Boykin, A. W. Verbally expressed preference and complexity judgments as they relate to levels of performance in a problem solving situation. Unpublished doctoral dissertation. University of Michigan, 1972.

Braine, M. D. S. The ontogeny of English phrase structure: The first phase. *Language*, 1963, *39*, 1–13.

Bransford, J. D., Barclay, J. R., and Franks, J. J. Sentence memory: A constructive versus interpretive approach. *Cognitive Psychology*, 1972, *3*, 193–209.

Bransford, J. D., and Franks, J. J. The abstraction of linguistic ideas. *Cognitive Psychology*, 1971, *2*, 331–350.

Brennen, W. S., Ames, E. W., and Moore, R. W. Age differences in infants' attention to patterns of different complexities. *Science*, 1966, *151*, 354–356.

Brewer, W. F. Specific language disability: Review of the literature and a family study. Honors thesis. Harvard University. 1963.

Brewer, W. F. Is reading a letter-by-letter process? In J. F. Kavanagh and I. G. Mattingly (eds.), *Language by ear and by eye*. Cambridge, Mass.: The MIT Press, 1972. Pp. 359–365.

Brimer, M. A. Methodological problems of research. In J. Downing (ed.), *Comparative reading*. New York: Macmillan, 1973. Pp. 13–31.

Broerse, A. C., and Zwaan, E. M. The information value of initial letters in the identification of words. *Journal of Verbal Learning and Verbal Behavior*, 1966, *5*, 441–446.

Brown, E., and Miron, M. S. Lexical and syntactic predictors of the distribution of pause time in reading. *Journal of Verbal Learning and Verbal Behavior*, 1971, *10*, 658–667.

Brown, R. *Words and things*. Glencoe, Ill.: The Free Press, 1958.

Brown, R. Psychology and reading: Commentary on chapters 5 to 10. In H. Levin and J. P. Williams (eds.), *Basic studies on reading*. New York: Basic Books, 1970. Pp. 164–187.

Brown, R. *A first language: The early stages*. Cambridge, Mass.: Harvard University Press, 1973.

Brown, R., and Bellugi, U. Three processes in the child's acquisition of syntax. *Harvard Educational Review*, 1964, *34*, 133–151.

Brown, R., and Berko, J. Word association and the acquisition of grammar. *Child Development*, 1960, *31*, 1–14.

Brown, R., Cazden, C., and Bellugi-Klima, U. The child's grammar from I to III. In J. P. Hill (ed.), *The 1967 Minnesota symposium on child psychology*. Minneapolis: University of Minnesota Press, 1969. Pp. 28–73.

Broyler, C. R., Thorndike, E. L., and Woodyard, E. A second study of mental discipline in high school studies. *Journal of Educational Psychology*, 1927, *18*, 377–404.

Bruce, D. J. Analysis of word sounds by young children. *British Journal of Educational Psychology*, 1964, *34*, 158–169.

Bruner, J. S. *Toward a theory of instruction*. Cambridge, Mass.: Harvard University Press, Belknap Press, 1966.

Bruner, J. S., and O'Dowd, D. A note on the informativeness of parts of words. *Language and Speech*, 1958, *1*, 98–101.

Bryden, M. P. Auditory-visual and sequential-spatial matching in relation to reading ability. *Child Development*, 1972, *43*, 824–832.

Buswell, G. T. An experimental study of eye-voice span in reading. *Supplementary Educational Monographs*, No. 17. Chicago: University of Chicago, Dept. of Education, 1920.

Buswell, G. T. Diagnostic studies in arithmetic. *Supplementary Educational Monographs*, No. 30. Chicago: Dept. of Education, University of Chicago, 1926.

Butler, R. A. Discrimination learning by rhesus monkeys to visual exploration motivation. *Journal of Comparative and Physiological Psychology*, 1953, *46*, 95–98.

Butler, R. A. Investigative behavior. In A. N. Schrier, H. F. Harlow, and F. Stollnitz (eds.), *Behavior of nonhuman primates*. Vol. II. New York: Academic Press, 1965. Pp. 463–494.

Calfee, R. C. Diagnostic evaluation of visual, auditory and general language factors in pre-readers. Paper presented at meeting of the American Psychological Association, Honolulu, 1972.

Calfee, R. C., Chapman, R. S., and Venezky, R. L. How a child needs to think to learn to read. In L. W. Gregg (ed.), *Cognition in learning and memory*. New York: John Wiley, 1972. Pp. 139–182.

Calfee, R. C. and Jameson, P. *Visual search and reading*. Technical Report No. 157. Wisconsin Research and Development Center for Cognitive Learning, 1971.

Calfee, R. C., Venezky, R. L., and Chapman, R. S. *Pronunciation of synthetic words with predictable and unpredictable letter-sound correspondences*. Technical Report No. 71. Wisconsin Research and Development Center for Cognitive Learning, 1969.

Callaway, W. R., Jr. Modes of biological adaptation and their role in intellectual development. *PCD Monographs*, 1970, *1*, No. 1.

Carroll, J. B. The analysis of reading instruction: Perspectives from psychology and linguistics. In *Theories of learning and instruction*. Sixty-third Yearbook of the National Society for the Study of Education. Chicago: University of Chicago Press, 1964. Pp. 336–353.

Carroll, J. B. Some neglected relationships in reading and language learning. *Elementary English*, 1966, *43*, 577–582.

Carroll, J. B. Defining language comprehension: Some speculations. In J. B. Carroll and R. O. Freedle (eds.), *Language comprehension and the acquisition of knowledge*. Washington, D. C.: V. H. Winston, 1972. Pp. 1–30. (a)

Carroll, J. B. The case for ideographic writing. In J. F. Kavanagh and I. G. Mattingly (eds.), *Language by ear and by eye*. Cambridge, Mass.: The MIT Press, 1972. Pp. 103–109. (b)

Carroll, J. B., Davies, P., and Richman, B. *The American Heritage word frequency book*. New York: Houghton Mifflin, 1971.

Carroll, J. B., and Freedle, R. O. *Language comprehension and the acquisition of knowledge*. Washington, D.C.: V. H. Winston, 1972.

Carterette, E. C., and Jones, M. H. Redundancy in children's texts. *Science*, 1963, *140*, 1309–1311.

Carterette, E. C., and Jones, M. H. Statistical comparison of two series of graded readers. Technical Report No. 22. University of California at Los Angeles Communication Laboratory, 1964.

Caruso, J. L., and Resnick, L. B. Task structure and transfer in children's learning of double classification skills. *Child Development*, 1972, *43*, 1297–1308.

Carver, R. P. *Sense and nonsense in speed reading.* Silver Spring, Maryland: Revrac, 1971.

Cattell, J. M. Ueber die Zeit der Erkennung und Bennenung von Schriftzeichen, Bildern und Farben. *Philosophische Studien*, 1885, *2*, 635–650.

Cattell, J. M. The time it takes to see and name objects. *Mind*, 1886, *11*, 63–65.

Cattell, P. *The measurement of intelligence of infants and young children.* Rev. ed. New York: Psychological Corp., 1960.

Cazden, C. B. Subcultural differences in child language: An interdisciplinary review. *Merrill-Palmer Quarterly*, 1966, *12*, 185–220.

Chafe, W. L. *Meaning and the structure of language.* Chicago: University of Chicago Press, 1970.

Chafe, W. L. Discourse structure and human knowledge. In J. B. Carroll and R. O. Freedle (eds.), *Language comprehension and the acquisition of knowledge.* Washington, D.C.: V. H. Winston, 1972. Pp. 41–70.

Chall, J. S. *Learning to read: The great debate.* New York: McGraw-Hill, 1967.

Chall, J. S., Roswell, F. G., and Blumenthal, S. H. Auditory blending ability: A factor in success in beginning reading. *The Reading Teacher*, 1963, *17*, 113–118.

Chapanis, A. *Man-machine engineering.* Belmont, Calif.: Wadsworth, 1965.

Chapman, R. S. *Report on the February 1971 version of the Wisconsin basic prereading skill test.* Technical Report No. 187. Wisconsin Research and Development Center for Cognitive Learning, 1971.

Chase, W. G., and Clark, H. H. Mental operations in the comparison of sentences and pictures. In L. W. Gregg (ed.), *Cognition in learning and memory.* New York: John Wiley, 1972. Pp. 205–232.

Child, I. L., Potter, E. H., and Levine, E. M. *Children's textbooks and personality development: An exploration in the social psychology of education.* Psychological Monographs, 1946, *60*, No. 3.

Chomsky, C. *The acquisition of syntax in children from 5 to 10.* Cambridge, Mass.: The MIT Press, 1969.

Chomsky, C. Reading, writing and phonology. *Harvard Educational Review*, 1970, *40*, 287–309.

Chomsky, N. *Syntactic structures.* The Hague: Mouton, 1957.

Chomsky, N. *Aspects of the theory of syntax.* Cambridge, Mass.: The MIT Press, 1965.

Chomsky, N. *Language and mind.* New York: Harcourt, Brace & World, 1968.

Chomsky, N. Phonology and reading. In H. Levin and J. P. Williams (eds.), *Basic studies on reading.* New York: Basic Books, 1970. Pp. 1–18.

Chomsky, N., and Halle, M. *The sound pattern of English.* New York: Harper & Row, 1968.

Cicourel, A. V., and Boese, R. J. Sign language acquisition and the teaching of deaf children. In C. B. Cazden, V. P. John, and D. Hymes (eds.), *Functions of language in the classroom.* New York: Teachers College Press, 1972. Pp. 32–62.

Clare, D. A. A study of principles of integration in the perception of written verbal items. Unpublished doctoral dissertation. Department of Psychology, Cornell University, 1969.

Clark, E. What's in a word? On the child's acquisition of semantics in his first language. In T. Moore (ed.), *Cognitive development.* New York: Academic Press, 1973. Pp. 65–110.

Clark, H. H. Some structural properties of simple active and passive sentences. *Journal of Verbal Learning and Verbal Behavior,* 1965, *4,* 365–370.

Clark, H. H. The language-as-fixed effect fallacy: A critique of language statistics in psychological research. *Journal of Verbal Learning and Verbal Behavior,* 1973, *12,* 335–359.

Clark, L. A. The eye-voice span in reading Japanese. Unpublished paper, 1972.

Clay, M. M., and Imlach, R. H. Juncture, pitch and stress as reading behavior variables. *Journal of Verbal Learning and Verbal Behavior,* 1971, *10,* 133–139.

Clements, S. D. *Minimal brain dysfunction in children: Phase One.* NINDB Monogr. No. 3, Public Health Service Publ. No. 1415. Washington, D.C.: U.S. Department of Health, Education and Welfare, 1966.

Clements, S. D. *Some aspects of the characteristics, management and education of the child with minimal brain dysfunction.* Glen Ellyn, Ill.: West Suburban Assoc. for the Other Child, 1967.

Cohen, G. Search times for combinations of visual, phonemic, and semantic targets in reading prose. *Perception and Psychophysics,* 1970, *8,* 370–372.

Colegate, R. L., and Eriksen, C. W. Form of redundancy as a determinant of tachistoscopic word recognition. *Perception and Psychophysics,* 1972, *12,* 477–481.

Coleman, E. B. The comprehensibility of several grammatical transformations. *Journal of Applied Psychology,* 1964, *48,* 186–190.

Coleman, E. B. Learning of prose written in four grammatical transformations. *Journal of Applied Psychology,* 1965, *49,* 332–341.

Coleman, E. B., and Miller, G. R. A measure of information gained during prose learning. *Reading Research Quarterly,* 1968, *3,* 369–386.

Collins, A. M., and Quillian, M. R. Retrieval time from semantic memory. *Journal of Verbal Learning and Verbal Behavior*, 1969, *8*, 240–247.

Collins, A. M., and Quillian, M. R. Experiments on semantic memory and language comprehension. In L. W. Gregg (ed.), *Cognition in learning and memory*. New York: John Wiley, 1972. Pp. 117–137.

Conrad, C. Context effects in sentence comprehension: A study of the subjective lexicon. *Memory and Cognition*, in press.

Conrad, R. Acoustic confusions in immediate memory. *British Journal of Psychology*, 1964, *55*, 75–84.

Conrad, R. The effect of vocalizing on comprehension in the profoundly deaf. *British Journal of Psychology*, 1971, *62*, 147–150.

Conrad, R. Speech and reading. In J. F. Kavanagh and I. G. Mattingly (eds.), *Language by ear and by eye*. Cambridge, Mass.: The MIT Press, 1972. Pp. 205–240.

Copi, I. M. *Introduction to logic*. New York: Macmillan, 1961.

Corcoran, D. W. J., and Rouse, R. O. An aspect of perceptual organization involved in reading typed and handwritten words. *Quarterly Journal of Experimental Psychology*, 1970, *22*, 526–530.

Corkin, S. Developmental dyslexia. Unpublished manuscript, Department of Psychology, Massachusetts Institute of Technology.

Cramer, P. A developmental study of errors in memory. *Developmental Psychology*, 1972, *7*, 204–209.

Crandell, S., and McGuigan, F. J. A longitudinal study of covert oral behavior during silent reading. Paper presented at the 58th annual meeting of the Eastern Psychological Association, Boston, April, 1967.

Critchley, M. Developmental dyslexia. *Pediatric Clinics of North America*, 1968, *15*, 669–676.

Cromer, W. The difference model: A new explanation for some reading difficulties. *Journal of Education Psychology*, 1970, *61*, 471–483.

Crothers, E. J. Memory structure and the recall of discourse. In J. B. Carroll and R. O. Freedle (eds.), *Language comprehension and the acquisition of knowledge*. Washington, D.C.: V. H. Winston, 1972. pp. 247–283.

Dale, E., and Chall, J. S. A formula for predicting readability. *Educational Research Bulletin*, Ohio State University, 1948, *27*, 11–20 and 37–54.

Davis, F. B. Fundamental factors of comprehension in reading. *Psychometrika*, 1944, *9*, 185–197.

Davis, F. B. Research in comprehension in reading. *Reading Research Quarterly*, Summer, 1968, *3*, 499–545.

Davis, F. B. (ed.). The literature of research in reading with emphasis on models. Project No. Z: The literature search. Graduate School of Education, The State University, Rutgers, New Jersey. Project No. 0–9030, Contract No. OEC-0-70-4790 (508); 1972. See esp. Section 5, "Comprehensive and partial models related to the reading process," by J. J. Geyer.

Dawes, R. M. Memory and distortion of meaningful written material. *British Journal of Psychology*, 1966, *57*, 77–86.

Day, H. I., Berlyne, D. E., and Hunt, D. E. *Intrinsic motivation: A new direction in education.* Minneapolis: Winston Press, 1971.

Dearborn, W. F. *The psychology of reading.* New York: Columbia Univ. Contr. to Phil. and Psychol., Vol. 14, No. 1, 1906.

DeBraslavsky, B. P. Argentina. In J. Downing (ed.), *Comparative reading.* New York: Macmillan, 1973. Pp. 259–284.

DeHirsch, K. Specific dyslexia or strephosymbolia. In G. Natchez (ed.), *Children with reading problems: Classic and contemporary issues in reading disability.* New York: Basic Books, 1968. Pp. 97–113.

DeLaguna, G. A. *Speech: Its function and development.* New Haven: Yale University Press, 1927.

DeStefano, J. S. Social variation in language: Implications for teaching reading to Black ghetto children. In J. A. Figurel (ed.), *Better reading in urban schools.* Newark, Del.: International Reading Association, 1972. Pp. 18–24.

Deutsch, M. *The Disadvantaged child.* New York: Basic Books, 1967.

Deutsch, M., Katz, I., and Jensen, A. (eds.). *Social class, race, and psychological development.* New York: Holt, Rinehart and Winston, 1968.

Dodge, R. An experimental study of visual fixation. *Psychological Review Monograph Supplement*, 1907, *8*, No. 4.

Donaldson, M., and Wales, R. On the acquisition of some relational terms. In J. R. Hayes (ed.), *Cognition and the development of language.* New York: John Wiley, 1970. Pp. 235–268.

Dooling, D. J., and Lachman, R. Effects of comprehension on retention of prose. *Journal of Experimental Psychology*, 1971, *88*, 216–222.

Dooling, D. J., and Mullet, R. L. Locus of thematic effects in retention of prose. *Journal of Experimental Psychology*, 1973, *97*, 404–406.

Dorland's Illustrated Medical Dictionary. 23rd ed. Philadelphia: Saunders, 1957.

Douglass, M. P. Beginning reading in Norway. *Reading Teacher*, 1969, *23*, 17–22, cont. on 47.

Downing, J. A. *The initial teaching alphabet: Reading experiment.* Chicago: Scott, Foresman, 1965.

Downing, J. A. Reading in America as compared with Great Britain. Paper presented at the U.K.R.A., Edinburgh Conference Committee, 1972.

Downing, J. *Comparative reading.* New York: Macmillan, 1973.

Downing, J., and Thackray, D. *Reading readiness.* London: University of London Press, 1971.

Drew, A. L. A neurological appraisal of familial congenital word-blindness. *Brain*, 1956, *79*, 440–460.

Durkin, D. *Children who read early.* New York: Teachers College Press, 1966.

Edelman, G. The use of cues in word recognition. In *A basic research program on reading.* Final Report, Project No. 639. Cornell University and the U.S. Office of Education, 1963.

Edfeldt, A. W. *Silent speech and silent reading.* Chicago: University of Chicago Press, 1960.

Egeland, B., Braggins, J., and Powalski, J. Teaching children to discriminate letters of the alphabet through errorless discrimination training. Paper presented at meeting of the Society for Research in Child Development, Philadelphia, 1973.

Eimas, P. D., Sigueland, E. R., Jusczyk, P., and Vigorito, J. Speech perception in infants. *Science*, 1971, *171*, 303–306.

Elder, R. D. A comparison of the oral reading of groups of Scottish and American children. Unpublished doctoral dissertation. Department of Education, University of Michigan, 1966.

Elgin, S. H. *What is linguistics?* Englewood Cliffs, N. J.: Prentice-Hall, 1973.

Elkind, D. Piaget's theory of perceptual development: Its application to reading and special education. *Journal of Special Education*, 1967, *1*, 357–361.

Elkind, D., and Deblinger, J. A. Perceptual training and reading achievement in disadvantaged children. *Child Development*, 1969, *40*, 11–19.

Elkonin, D. B. The physiology of higher nervous activity and child psychology. In B. Simon (ed.), *Psychology in the Soviet Union.* Stanford: Stanford University Press, 1957. Pp. 47–68.

Elkonin, D. B. The psychology of mastering the elements of reading. In B. Simon and J.

Simon (eds.), *Educational psychology in the U.S.S.R.* London: Routledge & Kegan Paul, 1963. Pp. 165–179.

Elkonin, D. B. USSR. In J. Downing (ed.), *Comparative reading*. New York: Macmillan, 1973. Pp. 551–579.

Entwisle, D. R. Form class and children's word associations. *Journal of Verbal Learning and Verbal Behavior*, 1966, *5*, 558–565.

Entwisle, D. R. *Word associations of young children*. Baltimore: The Johns Hopkins Press, 1966.

Entwisle, D. R., Forsyth, D. F., and Muuss, R. The syntagmatic-paradigmatic shift in children's word associations. *Journal of Verbal Learning and Verbal Behavior*, 1964, *3*, 19–29.

Epps, E. G. Interpersonal relations and motivation: Implications for teachers of disadvantaged children. *The Journal of Negro Education*, 1970, *39*, 14–25.

Epstein, W. Some conditions of the influence of syntactical structure on learning: Grammatical transformations, learning instructions and chunking. *Journal of Verbal Learning and Verbal Behavior*, 1967, *6*, 415–419.

Erdmann, B., and Dodge, R. *Psychologische Untersuchungen über das Lesen auf experimenteller Grundlage*. Halle, 1898.

Ervin, S. M. Changes with age in the verbal determinants of word-association. *American Journal of Psychology*, 1961, *74*, 361–372.

Faaborg-Anderson, K., and Edfeldt, A. W. Electromyography of intrinsic and extrinsic laryngeal muscles during silent speech: Correlation with reading activity. *Acta Otolaryngologia*, 1958, *49*, 478–482.

Fairbanks, G. The relation between eye-movements and voice in oral reading of good and poor readers. *Psychological Monographs*, 1937, *48*, 78–107.

Farley, F. H., and Eischens, R. R. *Children's processing of prose: The effects of question arousal, text complexity, and learner strata on short- and long-term retention*. Technical Report No. 201. Wisconsin Research and Development Center for Cognitive Learning, 1971.

Fasold, R. Orthography in reading materials for Black English speaking children. In J. C. Baratz and R. Shuy (eds.), *Teaching Black children to read*. Washington, D.C.: Center for Applied Linguistics, 1969. Pp. 68–91.

Feitelson, D. Structuring the teaching of reading according to major features of the language and its script. *Elementary English*, 1965, *42*, 31–38.

Feitelson, D. The relationship between systems of writing and the teaching of reading. *Proceedings of the First World Congress on Reading*. Paris: UNESCO, 1966. Pp. 191–199.

Feitelson, D. Israel. In J. Downing (ed.), *Comparative reading*. New York: Macmillan, 1973. Pp. 426–439.

Felzen, E., and Anisfeld, M. A. Semantic and phonetic relations in the false recognition of words by third- and sixth-grade children. *Developmental Psychology*, 1970, *3*, 163–168.

Fernald, G. *Remedial techniques in basic school subjects*. New York: McGraw-Hill, 1943.

Fillenbaum, S. Words as feature complexes: False recognition of synonyms and antonyms. *Journal of Experimental Psychology*, 1969, *52*, 400–402.

Fillenbaum, S., and Rappaport, A. *Structures in the subjective lexicon*. New York: Academic Press, 1971.

Fillmore, C. J. The case for case. In E. Bach and R. T. Harms (eds.), *Universals in linguistic theory*. New York: Holt, Rinehart and Winston, 1968. Pp. 1–88.

Fischer, C. T. Relations among dynamic reading measures, Rokeach dogmatism, personal orientation inventory scales, Wonderlic Personnel Test, IQ, and reading experience protocols. Report to Diversified Education and Publishing Corporation, New York. Duquesne University, 1969.

Fitzgerald, J. A. Letters written outside the school by children of the 4th, 5th, and 6th grades: A study of vocabulary, spelling errors and situations. *University of Iowa Studies*, 1934, *9*, No. 1, 9–50.

Flavell, J. H. Developmental studies of mediated memory. In H. W. Reese and L. P. Lipsitt (eds.), *Advances in child development and behavior*. Vol. 5. New York: Academic Press, 1970. Pp. 181–211.

Flavell, J. H., Beach, D. H., and Chinsky, J. M. Spontaneous verbal rehearsal in a memory task as a function of age. *Child Development*, 1966, *37*, 283–299.

Flesch, R. F. A new readability yardstick. *Journal of Applied Psychology*, 1948, *32*, 221–223.

Flesch, R. F. *The art of readable writing*. New York: Harper, 1949.

Fletcher, J. D. *Transfer from alternative presentations of spelling patterns in initial reading*. Technical Report No. 216. Stanford University: Institute for Mathematical Studies in the Social Sciences, September, 1973.

Fletcher, J. D., and Atkinson, R. C. *An evaluation of the Stanford CAI program in initial reading (grades K through 3)*. Technical Report No. 168. Stanford University; Institute for Mathematical Studies in the Social Sciences, March 12, 1971.

Fodor, J. A., and Bever, T. G. The psychological reality of linguistic segments. *Journal of Verbal Learning and Verbal Behavior*, 1965, *4*, 414–420.

Fodor, J. A., Garrett, M., and Bever, T. G. Some syntactic determinants of sentential complexity. II. Verb structure. *Perception and Psychophysics*, 1968, *3*, 453–461.

Ford, B. Children's imitation of sentences which vary in pause and intonational pattern. Unpublished doctoral dissertation. Department of Human Development, Cornell University, 1970.

Foss, D. J., and Swinney, D. A. On the psychological reality of the phoneme: Perception, identification and consciousness. *Journal of Verbal Learning and Verbal Behavior*, 1973, *12*, 246–257.

Fraisse, P., and Blancheteaü, M. The influence of number of alternatives on the perceptual recognition threshold. *Quarterly Journal of Psychology*, 1962, *14*, 52–55.

Francis, H. Toward an explanation of the syntagmatic-paradigmatic shift. *Child Development*, 1972, *43*, 949–958.

Francis, W. N. *The structure of American English*. New York: Ronald Press, 1958.

Francis, W. N. *The English language: An introduction*. New York: Norton, 1965.

Francis, W. N. Linguistics and reading. In H. Levin and J. P. Williams (eds.), *Basic studies on reading*. New York: Basic Books, 1970. Pp. 43–56.

Frandsen, A. An eye-movement study of objective examination questions. *Genetic Psychology Monographs*, 1934, *16*, 79–138.

Frase, L. T. Structural analysis of the knowledge that results from thinking about text. *Journal of Educational Psychology*, 1969, *60*, Monograph Supplement 6. (a)

Frase, L. T. Paragraph organization of written materials: The influence of conceptual clustering upon the level and organization of recall. *Journal of Educational Psychology*, 1969, *60*, 394–401. (b)

Frase, L. T. Maintenance and control in the acquisition of knowledge from written materials. In J. B. Carroll and R. O. Freedle (eds.), *Language comprehension and the acquisition of knowledge*. Washington, D. C.: V. H. Winston, 1972. Pp. 337–357.

Frederiksen, C. H. Effects of task-induced cognitive operations on comprehension and memory processes. In J. B. Carroll and R. O. Freedle (eds.), *Language comprehension and the acquisition of knowledge*. Washington, D. C.: V. H. Winston, 1972. Pp. 211–245.

Freedle, R. Language users as fallible information-processors: Implications for measuring and modeling comprehension. In J. B. Carroll and R. O. Freedle (eds.), *Language comprehension and the acquisition of knowledge*. Washington, D. C.: V. H. Winston, 1972. Pp. 169–209.

Friedman, S. Newborn visual attention to repeated exposure of redundant vs. "novel" targets. *Perception and Psychophysics*, 1972, *12*, 291–294.

Fries, C. C. *The structure of English*. New York: Harcourt, Brace, 1952.

Fries, C. C. *Linguistics and reading*. New York: Holt, Rinehart and Winston, 1962.

Fry, D. B. The development of the phonological system in the normal and the deaf child. In F. Smith and G. A. Miller (eds.), *The genesis of language*. Cambridge, Mass.: The MIT Press, 1966. Pp. 187–206.

Furth, H. G. *Thinking without language*. New York: Free Press, 1966.

Galvan, M. M., and Troike, R. C. The East Texas dialect project: A pattern for education. In A. C. Aarons, B. Y. Gordon, and W. A. Stewart (eds.), *Linguistic-cultural difference and American education*, 1969, *7*, 29–31, 152.

Gammon, E. M. *A syntactical analysis of some first grade readers*. Technical Report No. 155. Stanford University: Institute for Mathematical Studies in the Social Sciences, June 22, 1970.

Garner, W. R. *Uncertainty and structure as psychological concepts*. New York: Wiley, 1962.

Garner, W. R. Information integration and form of encoding. In A. W. Melton and E. Martin (eds.), *Coding processes in human memory*. Washington, D. C.: V. H. Winston, 1972. Pp. 261–281.

Garner, W. R., and Clement, D. E. Goodness of pattern and pattern uncertainty. *Journal of Verbal Learning and Verbal Behavior*, 1963, *2*, 446–452.

Gelb, I. J. *A study of writing*. Chicago: University of Chicago Press, 1952.

Geschwind, N. Language and the brain. *Scientific American*, 1972, *226*, 76–83.

Gibson, E. J. A re-examination of generalization. *Psychological Review*, 1959, *66*, 340–342.

Gibson, E. J. *Principles of perceptual learning and development*. New York: Prentice-Hall, 1969.

Gibson, E. J. Perceptual learning and the theory of word perception. *Cognitive Psychology*, 1971, *2*, 351–368.

Gibson, E. J. Reading for some purpose. In J. F. Kavanagh and I. G. Mattingly (eds.), *Language by ear and by eye*. Cambridge, Mass.: The MIT Press, 1972. Pp. 3–19.

Gibson, E. J., Barron, R. W., and Garber, E. E. The developmental convergence of meaning for words and pictures. In Appendix to Final Report, Project No. 90046, Grant No. OEG-2–9–420446–1071 (010). Cornell University and U. S. Office of Education 1972. Pp. 12–26.

Gibson, E. J., Bishop, C., Schiff, W., and Smith, J. Comparison of meaningfulness and pronunciability as grouping principles in the perception and retention of verbal material. *Journal of Experimental Psychology*, 1964, *67*, 173–182.

Gibson, E. J., Farber, J., and Shepela, S. Test of a learning set procedure for the abstraction of spelling patterns. *Project Literacy Reports*, 1967, No. 8, 21–30.

Gibson, E. J., Gibson, J. J., Pick, A. D., and Osser, H. A developmental study of the discrimination of letter-like forms. *Journal of Comparative and Physiological Psychology*, 1962, *55*, 897–906.

Gibson, E. J., and Guinet, L. The perception of inflections in brief visual presentations of words. *Journal of Verbal Learning and Verbal Behavior*, 1971, *10*, 182–189.

Gibson, E. J., Osser, H., and Pick, A. A study in the development of grapheme-phoneme correspondences. *Journal of Verbal Learning and Verbal Behavior*, 1963, *2*, 142–146.

Gibson, E. J., Osser, H., Schiff, W., and Smith, J. An analysis of critical features of letters, tested by a confusion matrix. In *Final Report on A Basic Research Program on Reading*. Co-operative Research Project No. 639, Cornell University and U. S. Office of Education, 1963.

Gibson, E. J., Pick, A., Osser, H., and Hammond, M. The role of grapheme-phoneme correspondence in the perception of words. *American Journal of Psychology*, 1962, *75*, 554–570.

Gibson, E. J., Poag, M. K., and Rader, N. The effect of redundant rhyme and spelling patterns on a verbal discrimination task. In Appendix to Final Report, Project No. 90046, Grant No. OEG-2-9-420446-1071 (010), Cornell University and U. S. Office of Education, 1972. Pp. 1–11.

Gibson, E. J., Schapiro, F., and Yonas, A. Confusion matrices for graphic patterns obtained with a latency measure. In *The analysis of reading skill: A program of basic and applied research*. Final Report, Project No. 5–1213, Cornell University and U. S. Office of Education, 1968. Pp. 76–96.

Gibson, E. J., and Shepela, S. Some effects of redundant stimulus information on learning to identify letters. In *The analysis of reading skill: A program of basic and applied research*. Final Report, Project No. 5–1213, Cornell University and U. S. Office of Education, 1968. Pp. 63–75.

Gibson, E. J., Shurcliff, A., and Yonas, A. Utilization of spelling patterns by deaf and hearing subjects. In H. Levin and J. P. Williams (eds.), *Basic studies on reading*. New York: Basic Books, 1970. Pp. 57–73.

Gibson, E. J., Tenney, Y. J., Barron, R. W., and Zaslow, M. The effect of orthographic structure on letter search. *Perception and Psychophysics*, 1972, *11*, 183–186.

Gibson, E. J., Tenney, Y. J., and Sharabany, R. Is discovery of structure reinforcing? The role of semantic and syntactic structure in anagram solution. In *The relationship between perceptual development and the acquisition of reading skill*. Final Report, Project No. 90046, Grant No. OE G–2–9–420446–1071 (01), Cornell University and U. S. Office of Education, October, 1971. Pp. 48–64.

Gibson, E. J., Tenney, Y. J., and Zaslow, M. Is discovery of structure reinforcing? The effect of categorizable context on scanning for verbal targets. In Final Report, Research

Grant No. OEG-2-9-420446-1071(010), from U.S. Office of Education to Cornell University, 1971. Pp. 30-37.

Gibson, E. J., and Yonas, A. A developmental study of visual search behavior. *Perception and Psychophysics,* 1966, *1,* 169-171. (a)

Gibson, E. J., and Yonas, A. A developmental study of the effects of visual and auditory interference on a visual scanning task. *Psychonomic Science,* 1966, *5,* 163-164. (b)

Gibson, J. J. Observations on active touch. *Psychological Review,* 1962, *69,* 477-491.

Gibson, J. J., and Yonas, P. A new theory of scribbling and drawing in children. In *The analysis of reading skill.* Final Report, Project No. 5-1213, Cornell University and U.S. Office of Education, December, 1968. Pp. 355-370.

Gillooly, W. B. The influence of writing-system characteristics on learning to read. In F. B. Davis (ed.), *The literature of research in reading with emphasis on models.* Final Report to U.S. Office Education, 1971. Section 7, Pp. 7-21.

Ginsburg, H., Wheeler, M. E., and Tulis, E. A. The natural development of printing and related graphic activities. Mimeographed. Department of Human Development, Cornell University, 1970.

Glazer, N. Ethnic groups and education: Towards the tolerance of difference. *The Journal of Negro Education,* 1970, *39,* 171-176.

Gleason, H. A. *An introduction to descriptive linguistics.* Rev. ed. New York: Holt, Rinehart and Winston, 1961.

Gleitman, H., Gleitman, L. R., and Shipley, E. The emergence of the child as grammarian. *Cognition,* 1972, *1,* 137-164.

Gleitman, L. R., and Rozin, P. Teaching reading by use of a syllabary. *Reading Research Quarterly,* 1973, *8,* 447-483.

Glock, M. D. Effect upon eye movements and reading rate at the college level of three methods of training. *Journal of Educational Psychology,* 1949, *40,* 93-106.

Goins, J. T. Visual perceptual abilities and early reading progress. *Supplementary Educational Monographs,* No. 87. Chicago: Dept. of Education, University of Chicago, 1958.

Goldiamond, I., and Hawkins, W. F. Vexierversuch: The log relationship between word-frequency and recognition obtained in the absence of stimulus words. *Journal of Experimental Psychology,* 1958, *56,* 457-463.

Goldstein, M. J., and Ratliff, J. Relationship between frequency of usage and ease of recognition with response bias controlled. *Perceptual and Motor Skills,* 1961, *13,* 171-177.

Golinkoff, R. Children's discrimination of English spelling patterns with redundant auditory information. Paper presented to American Educational Research Association, February, 1974.

Gollin, E. S., and Shirk, E. J. A developmental study of oddity problem learning in young children. *Child Development*, 1966, *37*, 213–218.

Goodacre, E. Great Britain. In J. Downing (ed.), *Comparative Reading*. New York: Macmillan, 1973. Pp. 360–382.

Goodman, K. S. A linguistic study of cues and miscues in reading. *Elementary English*, 1965, *42*, 639–643.

Goodman, K. S. Reading: A psycholinguistic guessing game. *Journal of the Reading Specialist*, 1967, *6*, 126–135.

Goodman, K. S. A study of oral reading miscues that result in grammatical re-transformations. Final Report to U.S. Office of Education, June, 1969.

Goodman, K. S., and Burke, C. Theoretically based studies of patterns of miscues in oral reading performance. U.S. Office of Education Project 9–0375, undated.

Goody, J. (ed.). *Literacy in traditional societies*. London: Cambridge University Press, 1968.

Gough, P. B. One second of reading. In J. F. Kavanagh and I. G. Mattingly (eds.), *Language by ear and by eye*. Cambridge, Mass.: The MIT Press, 1972.

Gough, P. B., and Stewart, W. C. Word vs. non-word discrimination latency. Paper read at Midwestern Psychological Association meeting, 1970.

Gray, C. T. Types of reading ability as exhibited through tests and laboratory experiments. *Supplementary Educational Monographs*, No. 5. Chicago: Dept. of Education, University of Chicago, 1917.

Gray, W. S. *The teaching of reading and writing, an international survey*. Paris: UNESCO, 1956.

Greenberg, J. H. Some universals of grammar with particular reference to the order of meaningful elements. In J. H. Greenberg (ed.), *Universals of language*. Cambridge, Mass.: The MIT Press, 1962. Pp. 73–113.

Greene, J. *Psycholinguistics: Chomsky and psychology*. Baltimore: Penguin Books, 1972.

Gregg, L. W. *Cognition in learning and memory*. New York: John Wiley, 1972.

Grimes, J. E. The thread of discourse. Mimeographed. Department of Modern Languages and Linguistics, Cornell University, 1972.

Grossman, J. K. Constraints and the eye-voice span in right and left embedded sentences: A developmental study. Unpublished masters dissertation. Department of Human Development, Cornell University, 1969.

Gumperz, J. J. Verbal strategies in multilingual communication. In R. D. Abrahams and R. C. Troike (eds.), *Language and cultural diversity in American education.* Englewood Cliffs, N. J.: Prentice-Hall, 1972. pp. 184–196.

Hagen, J. W., and Moeller, T. *Cross-age tutoring.* Report No. 2. Ann Arbor: Developmental Program, Dept. of Psychology, University of Michigan, July, 1971.

Haith, M. M. Developmental changes in visual information processing and short-term visual memory. *Human Development,* 1971, *14,* 249–261.

Hall, R. A. *Sound and spelling in English.* New York: Chilton, 1961.

Halle, M. Some thoughts on spelling. In K. S. Goodman and J. T. Fleming (eds.), *Psycholinguistics and the teaching of reading.* Newark, Del.: International Reading Association, 1969. pp. 17–24.

Halle, M., and Stevens, K. N. Speech recognition: A model and a program for research. In J. A. Fodor and J. J. Katz (eds.), *The structure of language: Readings in the philosophy of language.* Englewood Cliffs, N. J.: Prentice-Hall, 1964. pp. 604–612.

Halle, M., and Stevens, K. N. Remarks on analysis by synthesis and distinctive features. In W. Wathen-Dunn and L. E. Woods (eds.), *Models for the perception of speech and visual form: Proceedings of a symposium.* Cambridge, Mass.: The MIT Press, 1967. Pp. 88–102.

Hallgren, B. Specific dyslexia (congenital word-blindness). *Acta Psychiatrica et Neurologica Scandinavica,* 1950, Suppl. 65.

Hanna, P. R., Hanna, J. S., Hodges, R. E., and Rudorf, E. H., Jr. *Phoneme-grapheme correspondences as cues to spelling improvement.* Washington, D.C.: U.S. Government Printing Office, 1966.

Hansen, D., and Rodgers, T. S. An exploration of psycholinguistic units in initial reading. In K. S. Goodman (ed.), *The psycholinguistic nature of the reading process.* Detroit: Wayne State University Press, 1968. pp. 59–102.

Hardyck, C. D., and Petrinovich, L. F. The functions of subvocal speech. *Project Literacy Reports* No. 8, Cornell University, 1967.

Hardyck, C. D., and Petrinovich, L. F. Subvocal speech and comprehension level as a function of the difficulty level of reading material *Journal of Verval Learning and Verbal Behavior,* 1970, *9,* 647–652.

Hardyck, C. D., Petrinovich, L. F., and Ellsworth, D. W. Feedback of speech muscle activity during silent reading: Rapid extinction. *Science,* 1966, *154,* 1467–1468.

Hardyck, C. D., Petrinovich, L. F., and Ellsworth, D. W. Note. *Science*, 1967, *157*, 581.

Harlow, H. F. Learning set and error factor theory. In S. Koch (ed.), *Psychology: A study of a science*. Vol. 2. New York: McGraw-Hill, 1959. Pp. 492–537.

Harlow, H. F., Harlow, M. K., and Meyer, D. R. Learning motivated by a manipulation drive. *Journal of Experimental Psychology*, 1950, *40*, 228–234.

Harris, A. J. Research on some aspects of comprehension: Rate flexibility and study skills. *Journal of Reading*, December, 1968, 205–210 and 258–260.

Hart, B. O. *Teaching reading to deaf children*. The Lexington School for the Deaf. Education Series. Book IV. Washington: Alexander Graham Bell Association for the Deaf, 1963.

Heider, F. K., and Heider, G. M. A comparison of sentence structure of deaf and hearing children. *Psychological Monographs*, 1940, *52*, 42–103.

Henderson, K. B. Research on teaching secondary school mathematics. In N. L. Gage (ed.), *Handbook of research on teaching*. Chicago: Rand McNally, 1963. Chapter 19, pp. 1007–1030.

Henderson, L. A word superiority effect without orthographic assistance. *Quarterly Journal of Experimental Psychology*, in press.

Hendrickson, L. N., and Muehl, S. The effect of attention and motor response pretraining on learning to discriminate B and D in kindergarten children. *Journal of Educational Psychology*, 1962, *53*, 236–241.

Hermann, K. *Reading disability*. Copenhagen: Munksgaard, 1959.

Hershberger, W. A., and Terry, D. F. Typographical cuing in conventional and programmed texts. *Journal of Applied Psychology*, 1965, *49*, 55–60.

Hershenson, M., and Haber, R. N. The role of meaning in the perception of briefly exposed words. *Canadian Journal of Psychology*, 1965, *19*, 42–46.

HEW report. *Reading disorders in the United States*. Arleigh B. Templeton (chairman). Report of the Secretary's (HEW) National Advisory Committee on Dyslexia and Related Reading Disorders. August, 1969.

Hildreth, G. Developmental sequences in name writing. *Child Development*, 1936, *7*, 291–303.

Hildreth, G. Lessons in Arabic. *The Reading Teacher*, 1965, *19*, 202–210.

Hildreth, G. Armenian children enjoy reading. *The Reading Teacher*, 1966, *19*, 443–445.

Hildreth, G. On first looking into a Greek primer. *The Reading Teacher*, 1968, *21*, 453–463.

Hilgard, E. R. *Theories of learning*. Second ed. New York: Appleton-Century-Crofts, 1956.

Hirsh, I. J. Teaching the deaf child to speak. In F. Smith and G. A. Miller (eds.), *The genesis of language*. Cambridge, Mass.: The MIT Press, 1966. Pp. 207–216.

Hochberg, J. Stimulus factors in literacy: Graphic communication, verbal and non-verbal. *Project Literacy Reports*, No. 1, Ithaca, N.Y.: 1964. Pp. 17–18.

Hochberg, J. Studies in reading. *Project Literacy Reports*, No. 9, Ithaca, N.Y.: 1968. Pp. 25–37.

Hochberg, J. Components of literacy: Speculations and exploratory research. In H. Levin and J. P. Williams (eds.), *Basic studies on reading*. New York: Basic Books, 1970. Pp. 74–89.

Hochberg, J., and Brooks, V. Pictorial recognition as an unlearned ability: A study of one child's performance. *American Journal of Psychology*, 1962, *75*, 624–628.

Hockett, C. F. *A course in modern linguistics*. New York: Macmillan, 1958.

Hockett, C. F. Where the tongue slips, there slip I. In *To honor Roman Jakobson*, Vol. II, *Janua Linguarum*, Series Major 32. The Hague: Mouton, 1967.

Hoffmann, J. Experimentell-psychologische Untersuchungen über Leseleistungen von Schulkindern. *Archiv für die gesamte Psychologie*, 1927, *58*, 325–388.

Holden, M. H., and MacGinitie, W. H. Children's conceptions of word boundaries in speech and print. *Journal of Educational Psychology*, 1972, *63*, 551–557.

Holt, G. L. Effect of reinforcement contingencies in increasing programmed reading and mathematics behaviors in first-grade children. *Journal of Experimental Child Psychology*, 1971, *12*, 362–369.

Horn, M. D. The thousand and three words most frequently used by kindergarten children. *Child Education*, 1926–1927a, *3*, 118–122.

Horowitz, L. M., White, M. A., and Attwood, D. W. Word fragments as aids to recall: The organization of a word. *Journal of Experimental Psychology*, 1968, *76*, 219–226.

House, B. J., and Zeaman, D. Learning sets from minimum stimuli in retardates. *Journal of Comparative and Physiological Psychology*, 1963, *56*, 735–739.

Howes, D., and Solomon, R. L. Visual duration threshold as a function of word probability. *Journal of Experimental Psychology*, 1951, *41*, 401–410.

Huey, E. B. *The psychology and pedagogy of reading*. New York: Macmillan, 1908. Republished by The MIT Press, Cambridge, Mass., 1968.

Hull, C. L. Quantitative aspects of the evolution of concepts. *Psychological Monographs*, 1920, *28*, No. 123.

Huttenlocher, J. Children's language: Word-phrase relationships. *Science,* 1964, *143,* 264–265.

Huyck, E. M. The hereditary factor in speech. *Journal of Speech and Hearing Disorders,* 1940, *5,* 295.

Hyde, T. S., and Jenkins, J. J. Differential effects of incidental tasks on the organization of recall of a list of highly associated words. *Journal of Experimental Psychology,* 1969, *82,* 472–481.

Ilg, F. L., and Ames, L. B. Developmental trends in reading behavior. *Journal of Genetic Psychology,* 1950, *76,* 291–312.

Inhelder, B., and Piaget, J. *The early growth of logic in the child.* New York: Norton, 1964.

Irwin, O. C. Infant speech consonant sounds according to the manner of articulation. *Journal of Speech Disorders,* 1947, *12,* 397–401.

Jacobs, P. I., and Vandeventer, M. The learning and transfer of double-classification skills by first-graders. *Child Development,* 1971, *42,* 149–159. (a)

Jacobs, P. I., and Vandeventer, M. The learning and transfer of double-classification skills: A replication and extension. *Journal of Experimental Child Psychology,* 1971, *12,* 140–157. (b)

Jacobs, R. A., and Rosenbaum, P. S. *English transformational grammar.* Waltham, Mass.: Blaisdell, 1968.

Jakobson, R. *Child language, aphasia and phonological universals.* The Hague: Mouton, 1968.

Jakobson, R., Fant, C. G. M., and Halle, M. *Preliminaries to speech analysis: The distinctive features and their correlates.* Cambridge, Mass.: The MIT Press, 1963.

Jakobson, R., and Halle, M. *Fundamentals of language.* The Hague: Mouton, 1956.

James, C. T., and Smith, D. E. Sequential dependencies in letter search. *Journal of Experimental Psychology,* 1970, *85,* 56–60.

James, W. *Principles of psychology.* New York: Holt, 1890.

Jansen, M. Denmark. In J. Downing (ed.), *Comparative reading.* New York: Macmillan, 1973. Pp. 285–307.

Jarvella, R. J., and Sinnott, J. Contextual constraints on noun distributions to some English verbs by children and adults. *Journal of Verbal Learning and Verbal Behavior,* 1972, *11,* 47–53.

Jeffrey, W. E., and Samuels, S. J. Effect of method of reading training on initial learning and transfer. *Journal of Verbal Learning and Verbal Behavior,* 1967, *6,* 354–358.

Jencks, C., Smith, M., Ucland, H., Bane, M. J., Cohen, D., Ginitis, H., Heyns, B., and Michelson, S. *Inequality: A reassessment of the effect of family and schooling in America.* New York: Basic Books, 1972.

Jenkins, J. J., and Palermo, D. S. Mediation processes and the acquisition of linguistic structure. In U. Bellugi and R. Brown (eds.), *The acquisition of language. Monographs of the Society for Research in Child Development,* 1964, *29*(1), 141–169.

Jensen, A. R. Spelling errors and the serial-position effect. *Journal of Educational Psychology,* 1962, *53,* 105–109.

Johnson, D. D. *An investigation of sex differences in reading in four English-speaking nations.* Technical Report No. 209. Wisconsin Research and Development Center, 1972.

Johnson, D., and Myklebust, H. *Learning disabilities.* New York: Grune & Stratton, 1967.

Johnson, R. A., and Zara, R. C. The influence of word meaningfulness on visual duration threshold at various frequency levels. *Journal of General Psychology,* 1964, *70,* 235–239.

Johnson, R. C., Frinke, G., and Martin, L. Meaningfulness, frequency, and affective character of words as related to visual duration threshold. *Canadian Journal of Psychology,* 1961, *15,* 199–204.

Johnson, R. C., Thomson, C. W., and Frinke, G. Word values, word frequency, and visual duration thresholds. *Psychological Review,* 1960, *67,* 332–342.

Johnson, R. E. Recall of prose as a function of the structural importance of the linguistic units. *Journal of Verbal Learning and Verbal Behavior,* 1970, *9,* 12–20.

Johnson, R. J. The effect of training in letter names on success in beginning reading for children of differing abilities. Paper presented at American Educational Research Convention, Anaheim, Calif., 1970.

Johnson, S. C. Hierarchical clustering schemes. *Psychometrika,* 1967, *32,* 241–254.

Johnston, C. D., and Jenkins, J. J. Two more incidental tasks that differentially affect associative clustering in recall. *Journal of Experimental Psychology,* 1971, *89,* 92–95.

Jones, M. H., and Carterette, E. C. Redundancy in children's free-reading choices. *Journal of Verbal Learning and Verbal Behavior,* 1963, *2,* 489–493.

Judd, C. H. The relation of special training to general intelligence. *Educational Review,* 1908, *36,* 28–42.

Judd, C. H., and Buswell, G. Silent reading: A study of the various types. *Supplementary Educational Monographs,* No. 23. Chicago: University of Chicago Press, 1922.

Kaplan, G., Yonas, A., and Shurcliff, A. Visual and acoustic confusability in a visual search task. *Perception and Psychophysics*, 1966, *1*, 172–174.

Karpova, S. N. Awareness of the word composition of speech in the preschool child. *Voprosy Psikhologii*, 1955, *1*, No. 4, 43–55. Translated by Peter W. Carey.

Katz, J. J., and Fodor, J. A. The structure of semantic theory. *Language*, 1963, *39*, 170–210.

Katz, L., and Wicklund, D. A. Word scanning rate for good and poor readers. *Journal of Educational Psychology*, 1971, *62*, 138–140.

Katz, L., and Wicklund, D. A. Letter scanning rate for good and poor readers in grades two and six. *Journal of Educational Psychology*, 1972, *63*, 363–367.

Keeney, T. J., Canizzo, S. R., and Flavell, J. H. Spontaneous and induced verbal rehearsal in a recall task. *Child Development*, 1967, *38*, 953–966.

Keeney, T. J., Jenkins, J. R., and Jenkins, J. J. Identification of absolute and relational properties in the three-stimulus (ABB) configuration. *Child Development*, 1960, *40*, 1223–1231.

King-Ellison, P., and Jenkins, J. J. The durational threshold of visual recognition as a function of word-frequency. *American Journal of Psychology*, 1954, *67*, 700–703.

Kingsley, P. R., and Hagen, J. W. Induced vs. spontaneous rehearsal in short-term memory in nursery school children. *Developmental Psychology*, 1969, *1*, 40–46.

Kircher, M. C. The effects of presentation order and repetition on the free recall of prose. Unpublished masters dissertation. Department of Education, Cornell University, 1971.

Kluska, E. J. The function of the hand as a pacer in reading dynamics. Unpublished masters dissertation. Department of Psychology, Xavier University, 1971.

Knafle, J. D. Word perception: An experiment with cues in the development of unit-forming principles. Unpublished doctoral dissertation. Department of Education, University of Pennsylvania, 1971.

Koen, K., Becker, A., and Young, R. The psychological reality of the paragraph. *Journal of Verbal Learning and Verbal Behavior*, 1969, *8*, 49–53.

Kolers, P. A. Reading and talking bilingually. *American Journal of Psychology*, 1966, *79*, 357–376.

Kolers, P. A. Three stages of reading. In H. Levin and J. P. Williams (eds.), *Basic studies on reading*. New York: Basic Books, 1970. Pp. 90–118.

Kolers, P. A., and Katzman, M. T. Naming sequentially presented letters and words. *Language and Speech*, 1966, *9*, 84–95.

Kristofferson, A. B. Word recognition, meaningfulness, and familiarity. *Perceptual Motor Skills*, 1957, *7*, 219–220.

Krueger, L. E. Search time in a redundant visual display. *Journal of Experimental Psychology*, 1970, *83*, 391–399.

Kuhn, D. Mechanisms of change in the development of cognitive structures. *Child Development*, 1972, *43*, 833–844.

Kulhavy, R. W. Effects of embedding orienting stimuli in a prose passage. *Psychonomic Science*, 1972, *28*, 213–214.

Kyöstiö, O. K. Finland. In J. Downing (ed.), *Comparative reading*. New York: Macmillan, 1973. Pp. 308–318.

LaBerge, D., and Samuels, S. J. Toward a theory of automatic information processing in reading. *Cognitive Psychology*, in press.

Labov, W. Some sources of reading problems for Negro speakers of nonstandard English. In A. Frazier (ed.), *New directions in elementary English*. Champaign, Ill.: National Council of Teachers of English, 1967. Pp. 140–167.

Labov, W. The logic of nonstandard English. Georgetown University Monograph Series on Language and Linguistics, 1969, *22*.

Labov, W. The reading of the -ed suffix. In H. Levin and J. P. Williams (eds.), *Basic studies on reading*. New York: Basic Books, 1970. Pp. 222–245.

Labov, W., and Robins, C. A note on the relation of reading failure to peer-group status in urban ghettos. *The Teachers College Record*, 1969, *70*, 395–406.

Langacker, R. W. *Language and its structure*. Second ed. New York: Harcourt Brace Jovanovich, 1973.

Lashley, K. S. The mechanism of vision: XV. Preliminary studies of the rat's capacity for detail vision. *Journal of Genetic Psychology*, 1938, *18*, 123–193.

Lashley, K. S. The problem of serial order in behavior. In L. A. Jeffress (ed.), *Cerebral mechanisms in behavior*. New York: John Wiley, 1951. Pp. 112–136.

Lavine, L. O. The development of perception of writing in pre-reading children: A cross-cultural study. Unpublished doctoral dissertation. Department of Human Development, Cornell University, 1972.

Lawson, E. A note on the influence of different orders of approximations to the English language upon the eye-voice span. *Quarterly Journal of Experimental Psychology*, 1961, *13*, 53–55.

Lee, W. R. *Spelling irregularity and reading difficulty in English.* London: NFER in England and Wales, 1960.

Lefton, L. A. Guessing and the order of approximation effect. *Journal of Experimental Psychology*, in press.

Lefton, L. A., Spragins, A. B., and Byrnes, J. English orthography: Relation to reading experience. *Bulletin of the Psychonomic Society*, in press.

Legrün, A. Wie und was "schreiben" Kindergarten-zöglinge? *Zeitschrift für pädagogische Psychologie*, 1932, *33*, 322–331.

Lehman, E. B. Selective strategies in children's attention to task-relevant information. *Child Development*, 1972, *43*, 197–209.

Lenneberg, E. H. *Biological foundations of language.* New York: John Wiley, 1967.

Leong, C. K. Hong Kong. In J. Downing (ed.), *Comparative reading.* New York: Macmillan, 1973. Pp. 383–402.

Leopold, W. F. *Speech development of a bilingual child: A linguist's record.* four vols. Evanston, Ill.: Northwestern University Press, 1939, 1947, 1949(a), 1949(b).

Lepper, M. R., Greene, D., and Nisbett, R. E. Undermining children's intrinsic interest with extrinsic reward: A test of the "overjustification" hypothesis. *Journal of Personality and Social Psychology*, 1973, *28*, 129–137.

Leslie, R., and Calfee, R. C. Visual search through word lists as a function of grade level, reading ability, and target repetition. *Perception and Psychophysics*, 1971, *10*, 169–171.

Levin, H., Baum, E., and Bostwick, S. The learning of variable grapheme-phoneme correspondences: Comparison of English and Spanish speakers. In *A basic research program on reading.* Final report, Project No. 639, Cornell University and U.S. Office of Education, 1963.

Levin, H., and Cohn, J. A. Studies of oral reading: XII. Effects of instructions on the eye-voice span. In H. Levin, E. J. Gibson, and J. J. Gibson (eds.), *The analysis of reading skill.* Final report, Project No. 5–1213, Contract No. OE6–10–156, Cornell University and U.S. Office of Education, 1968. Pp. 254–283.

Levin, H., Ford, B. L., and Beckwith, M. Homographs in grammatical frames. In H. Levin, E. J. Gibson, and J. J. Gibson (eds.), *The analysis of reading skill.* Final report, Project No. 5–1213, from Cornell University to the U.S. Office of Education, December, 1968. Pp. 157–167.

Levin, H., Grossman, J., Kaplan, E., and Yang, R. Constraints and the eye-voice span in right and left embedded sentences. *Language and Speech*, 1972, *15*, 30–39.

Levin, H., and Kaplan, E. L. Eye-voice span (EVS) within active and passive sentences. *Language and Speech*, 1968, *11*, 251–258.

Levin, H., and Kaplan, E. L. Grammatical structure and reading. In H. Levin and J. P. Williams (eds.), *Basic studies on reading*. New York: Basic Books, 1970. Pp. 119–133.

Levin, H., and Mitchell, J. R. *Project Literacy: Continuing Activities*. Final report from Cornell University to U.S. Office of Education, Project No. 50537, September, 1969.

Levin, H., and Turner, A. Sentence structure and the eye-voice span. In H. Levin, E. J. Gibson, and J. J. Gibson (eds.), *The analysis of reading skill*. Final report Project No. 5–1213, from Cornell University to U.S. Office of Education, December, 1968.

Levin, H., and Watson, J. The learning of variable grapheme-to-phoneme correspondences. In *A basic research program on reading*. Final report, Project No. 639, Cornell University and U.S. Office of Education, 1963. (a)

Levin, H., and Watson, J. The learning of variable grapheme-to-phoneme correspondences: Variations in the initial consonant position. In *A basic research program on reading*. Final report, Project No. 639, Cornell University and U.S. Office of Education, 1963. (b)

Levin, H., Watson, J. S., and Feldman, M. Writing as pretraining for association learning. In *A basic research program on reading*. Final report, Project No. 639, Cornell University and U.S. Office of Education, 1963.

Liberman, I. Y. Basic research in speech and lateralization of language: Some implications for reading disability. *Status Report on Speech Research*, Haskins Laboratories, January–June, 1971.

Liberman, I. Y. Segmentation of the spoken word and reading acquisition. Paper presented to the Society for Research in Child Development, Philadelphia, March 31, 1973.

Liddle, W. *An investigation of the Wood Reading Dynamics Method*. Ann Arbor, Michigan: University Microfilms, 1965, No. 66–5559.

Lippitt, P., and Lippitt, R. Cross-age helpers. *NEA Journal*, March, 1968.

Lippman, M. Z. Correlates of contrast word associations: Developmental trends. *Journal of Verbal Learning and Verbal Behavior*, 1971, *10*, 392–399.

Lipsitt, L. P., and Serunian, S. A. Oddity problem learning in young children. *Child Development*, 1963, *34*, 201–206.

Locke, J. L., and Fehr, F. S. Young children's use of the speech code in learning. *Journal of Experimental Child Psychology*, 1970, *10*, 367–373.

Lott, D., and Smith, F. Knowledge of intraword redundancy by beginning readers. *Psychonomic Science*, 1970, *19*, 343–344.

Lowenstein, A. M. Effects of instructions on the abstraction of spelling patterns. Unpublished masters dissertation. Department of Human Development, Cornell University, 1969.

Luchsinger, R., and Arnold, G. E. *Lehrbuch der Stimm- und Sprachheilkunde.* Second ed. Vienna: Springer, 1959.

Luria, A. R. *Traumatic aphasia.* The Hague: Mouton, 1970.

Luria, A. R., and Vinogradova, O. S. An objective investigation of the dynamics of semantic systems. *British Journal of Psychology,* 1959, *50,* 89–105.

Lynch, S., and Rohwer, W. D. Effects of verbal and pictorial elaborations on associative learning and response learning in a children's paired-associate task. *Journal of Educational Psychology,* 1971, *62,* 339–344.

Lyons, J. *Noam Chomsky.* New York: Viking Press, 1970.

Maccoby, E. E. Selective auditory attention in children. In L. P. Lipsitt and C. C. Spiker (eds.), *Advances in child development and behavior,* Vol. 3. New York: Academic Press, 1967. Pp. 99–124.

MacKay, D. G. The structure of words and syllables: Evidence from errors in speech. *Cognitive Psychology,* 1972, *3,* 210–227.

Macklin, E. D. Evaluation of a program designed to affect the language development of young disadvantaged children. Unpublished doctoral dissertation. Department of Human Development, Cornell University, September, 1973.

Mackworth, J. F. Some models of the reading process: Learners and skilled readers. In M. Kling, E. B. Davis, and J. J. Geyer (eds.), *The literature of research in reading with emphasis on models.* Project No. 2: The literature search. Contract No. OEC-0-70-4790(508), Project No. 0-9030. Cornell University and U.S. Office of Education, 1971.

Mackworth, J. F. Some models of the reading process: learners and skilled readers. *Reading Research Quarterly,* 1972, *7,* 701–733.

Mackworth, N. H. The wide-angle reflection eye camera for visual choice and pupil size. *Perception and Psychophysics,* 1968, *3,* 32–34.

Mackworth, N. H. Verbal and pictorial comprehension by children with reading or speech disorders. Paper presented at the Twentieth International Congress of Psychology, Tokyo, 1972.

Mackworth, N. H., and Bruner, J. S. How adults and children search and recognize pictures. *Human Development,* 1970, *13,* 149–177.

Makita, K. The rarity of reading disability in Japanese children. *American Journal of Orthopsychiatry,* 1968, *38,* 599–614.

Malmquist, E. Sweden. In J. Downing (ed.), *Comparative reading*. New York: Macmillan, 1973. Pp. 466–487.

Marchbanks, G., and Levin, H. Cues by which children recognize words. *Journal of Educational Psychology*, 1965, *56*, 57–61.

Marsh, G., and Sherman, M. *Transfer from word components to words and vice versa in beginning reading*. Southwest Regional Laboratory for Educational Research and Development, March, 1970.

Martin, J. G. Rhythmic (hierarchical) versus serial structure in speech and other behavior. *Psychological Review*, 1972, *79*, 487–509.

Martin, J. G., and Strange, W. The perception of hesitation in spontaneous speech. *Perception and Psychophysics*, 1968, *3*, 427–438.

Martin, S. E. Nonalphabetic writing systems: Some observations. In J. F. Kavanagh and I. G. Mattingly (eds.), *Language by ear and by eye*. Cambridge, Mass.: The MIT Press, 1972. Pp. 81–102.

Mathews, M. *Teaching to read historically considered*. Chicago: University of Chicago Press, 1966.

Mattingly, I. G. Reading, the linguistic process, and linguistic awareness. In J. F. Kavanagh and I. G. Mattingly (eds.), *Language by ear and by eye*. Cambridge, Mass.: The MIT Press, 1972. Pp. 131–147.

Matz, R. D., and Rohwer, W. D., Jr. Visual elaboration and comprehension of text. Paper presented at Annual Meeting of the American Educational Research Association, New York, 1971.

Mayzner, M., and Tresselt, M. Anagram solution times: A function of word transition probabilities. *Journal of Experimental Psychology*, 1962, *63*, 510–513.

McCaffrey, A. Speech perception in infancy. Unpublished doctoral dissertation. Department of Human Development, Cornell University, 1971.

McCall, R. B., and Melson, W. H. Amount of short-term familiarization and the response to auditory discrepancies. *Child Development*, 1970, *41*, 861–869.

McCarthy, D. Language development in children. In L. Carmichael (ed.), *Manual of Child Psychology*. Second ed. New York: John Wiley, 1954. Pp. 476–581.

McClelland, D. C. *The achieving society*. Princeton, N. J.: Van Nostrand, 1961.

McConkie, G. W. The study of organization and recall with prose. Paper presented to the American Educational Research Association, New Orleans, 1973.

McConkie, G. W., and Rayner, K. The span of the effective stimulus during fixations in reading. Paper presented to the American Educational Research Association, New Orleans, 1973.

McConkie, G. W., Rayner, K., and Meyer, B. J. Manipulating reading strategies through payoff conditions. Unpublished manuscript. Department of Education, Cornell University, 1971.

McConkie, G. W., Rayner, K., and Wilson, S. J. Experimental manipulation of reading strategies. *Journal of Educational Psychology*, in press.

McCracken, G., and Walcutt, C. C. *Basic Reading: 1–1*. Philadelphia: Lippincott, 1963.

McGinnies, E. M., Comer, P. B., and Lacey, O. L. Visual recognition thresholds as a function of word length and word frequency. *Journal of Experimental Psychology*, 1952, *44*, 65–69.

McGuigan, F. J. Feedback of speech muscle activity during silent reading: Two comments. *Science*, 1967, *157*, 579–580.

McGuigan, F. J. Covert oral behavior during the silent performance of language tasks. *Psychological Bulletin*, 1970, *74*, 309–326.

McGuigan, F. J. External auditory feedback from covert oral behavior during silent reading. *Psychonomic Science*, 1971, *25*, 212–214.

McGuigan, F. J., and Bailey, S. C. Longitudinal study of covert oral behavior during silent reading. *Perceptual and Motor Skills*, 1969, *28*, 170.

McGuigan, F. J., Keller, B., and Stanton, E. Covert language responses during silent reading. *Journal of Educational Psychology*, 1964, *55*, 339–343.

McGuigan, F. J., and Rodier, W. I. Effects of auditory stimulation on covert oral behavior during silent reading. *Journal of Experimental Psychology*, 1968, *76*, 649–655.

McLaughlin, G. H. Reading at "impossible" speeds. *Journal of Reading*, 1969, *12*, 449–454 and 502–510.

McLeod, J. A comparison of WISC sub-test scores of pre-adolescent successful and unsuccessful readers. *Australian Journal of Psychology*, 1965, *17*, No. 3, 220–228.

McNamara, W. G., Patterson, D. G., and Tinker, M. A. The influence of size of type on speed of reading in the elementary grades. *The Sight-Saving Review*, 1953, *23*, 28–33.

McNeill, D. A. Study of word association. *Journal of Verbal Learning and Verbal Behavior*, 1966, *5*, 548–557. (a)

McNeill, D. A. Developmental psycholinguistics. In F. Smith and G. A. Miller (eds.), *The genesis of language: A psycholinguistic approach*. Cambridge, Mass.: The MIT Press, 1966. Pp. 15–84. (b)

McNeill, D. A. *The acquisition of language*. New York: Harper & Row, 1970.

McNeill, D. A. and Lindig, K. The perceptual reality of phonemes, syllables, words and sentences. *Journal of Verbal Learning and Verbal Behavior*, 1973, *12*, 419–430.

McNeill, D. A. and McNeill, N. B. What does a child mean when he says "no"? In E. M. Zale (ed.), *Language and language behavior*. New York: Appleton-Century-Crofts, 1968. Pp. 51–62.

Meacham, J. A. The development of memory abilities in the individual and society. *Human Development*, 1972, *15*, 205–228.

Mednick, S. A., and Lehtinen, L. E. Stimulus generalization as a function of age in children. *Journal of Experimental Psychology*, 1957, *53*, 180–183.

Mehler, J., Bever, T. G., and Carey, P. What we look at when we read. *Perception and Psychophysics* 1967, 2, 213–218.

Melmed, P. J. Black English phonology: The question of reading interference. *Monographs of the Language-Behavior Research Laboratory*, 1971, *1*.

Meltzer, N. S., and Herse, R. The boundaries of written words as seen by first graders. *Journal of Reading Behavior*, 1969, *1*, 3–14.

Menyuk, P. Children's learning and production of grammatical and nongrammatical phonological sequences. *Child Development*, 1968, *39*, 849–859.

Menyuk, P. *Sentences children use*. Cambridge, Mass.: The MIT Press, 1969.

Menyuk, P. *The acquisition and development of language*. Englewood Cliffs, N. J.: Prentice-Hall, 1971.

Messer, S. Implicit phonology in children. *Journal of Verbal Learning and Verbal Behavior*, 1967, *6*, 609–613.

Mewhort, D. J. Sequential redundancy and letter spacing as determinants of tachistoscopic recognition. *Canadian Journal of Psychology*, 1966, *20*, 435–444.

Meyer, B. J. F. Structure of prose: Identification and effects on memory. Paper presented at the Fourth Annual Invitational, Interdisciplinary Meeting on Structural Learning, Philadelphia, April, 1973.

Meyer, B. J. F., and McConkie, G. W. What is recalled after hearing a passage. *Journal of Educational Psychology*, in press.

Miller, G. A. Psychology as a means of promoting human welfare. *American Psychologist*, 1969, *24*, 1063–1075. (a)

Miller, G. A. A psychological method to investigate verbal concepts. *Journal of Mathematical Psychology*, 1969, *6*, 169–191. (b)

Miller, G. A. English verbs of motion: A case study in semantics and lexical memory. In A. W. Melton and E. Martin (eds.), *Coding processes in human memory*. Washington, D.C.: V. H. Winston, 1972. Pp. 335–372.

Miller, G. A., Bruner, J. S., and Postman, L. Familiarity of letter sequences and tachistoscopic identification. *Journal of General Psychology*, 1954, *50*, 129–139.

Miller, G. A., Heise, G. A., and Lichten, W. The intelligibility of speech as a function of the context of the test materials. *Journal of Experimental Psychology*, 1941, *41*, 329–335.

Miller, G. R., and Coleman, E. B. A set of thirty-six prose passages calibrated for complexity. *Journal of Verbal Learning and Verbal Behavior*, 1967, *6*, 851–854.

Miller, W., and Ervin, S. The development of grammar in child language. In U. Bellugi and R. Brown (eds.), The acquisition of language. *Monographs of the Society for Research in Child Development*, 1964, *29*, No. 92, 9–34.

Minuchin, P. Correlates of curiosity and exploratory behavior in preschool disadvantaged children. *Child Development*, 1971, *42*, 939–950.

Miskin, M., and Forgays, D. G. Word recognition as a function of retinal locus. *Journal of Experimental Psychology*, 1952, *43*, 43–48.

Moely, B. M., Olson, F. S., Halwes, T. G., and Flavell, J. B. Production deficiency in young children's clustered recall. *Developmental Psychology*, 1969, *1*, 26–34.

Money, J. (ed.). *Progress and research needs in dyslexia*. Baltimore: The Johns Hopkins Press, 1962.

Money, J. On learning and not learning to read. In J. Money (ed.), *The disabled reader: Education of the dyslexic child*. Baltimore: The Johns Hopkins Press, 1966. Pp. 21–40.

Moore, O. K., and Anderson, A. R. The responsive environments project. In R. D. Hess and R. M. Bear (eds.), *Early education*. Chicago: Aldine, 1968. Pp. 171–189.

Moore, T. V. Image and meaning in memory and perception. *Psychological Monographs*, 1919, *27*, No. 2.

Moorhouse, A. C. *The triumph of the alphabet*. New York: Schuman, 1953.

Morehead, D. M. Processing of phonological sequences by young children and adults. *Child Development*, 1971, *42*, 279–289.

Morton, J. The effects of context upon speed of reading, eye movements and the eye-voice span. *Quarterly Journal of Experimental Psychology*, 1964, *16*, 340–354. (a)

Morton, J. The effects of context upon the visual duration thresholds for words. *British Journal of Psychology*, 1964, *55*, 165–180. (b)

Muehl, S., and Kremenak, S. Ability to match information within and between auditory and visual sense modalities and subsequent reading achievement. *Journal of Educational Psychology*, 1966, *57*, 230–239.

Müller, G. E., and Pilzecker, A. Experimentelle Beiträge zur Lehre von Gedächtniss. *Zeitschrift für Psychologie*, 1900, Erg. 1.

Muraishi, S. Acquisition of reading Japanese syllabic characters in pre-school children in Japan. Paper presented at Twentieth International Congress of Psychology, Tokyo, 1972.

Murray, H. A., Jr., Barrett, W. G., Hombuger, E., and others. *Explorations in personality*. New York: Oxford University Press, 1938.

Mussafia, M. Le role de l'hérédité dans les troubles du langage. *Folia Phoniatrica*, 1960, *12*, 94–100.

Myklebust, H. R. *The psychology of deafness*. New York: Grune & Stratton, 1964.

Neimark, E., Slotnick, N. S., and Ulrich, T. Development of memorization strategies. *Developmental Psychology*, 1971, *5*, 427–432.

Neisser, U. Decision-time without reaction-time: Experiments in visual scanning. *American Journal of Psychology*, 1963, *76*, 376–385.

Neisser, U. Visual search. *Scientific American*, 1964, *210*, 94–102.

Neisser, U. *Cognitive psychology*. New York: Appleton-Century-Crofts, 1967.

Neisser, U. Selective reading: A method for the study of visual attention. Paper presented at Nineteenth International Congress of Psychology, London, 1969.

Neisser, U., and Beller, H. K. Searching through word lists. *British Journal of Psychology*, 1965, *56*, 349–358.

Neisser, U., Novick, R., and Lazar, R. Searching for ten targets simultaneously. *Perceptual and Motor Skills*, 1963, *17*, 955–961.

Nelson, D. L., Peebles, J., and Pancotto, F. Phonetic similarity as opposed to information structure as a determinant of word encoding. *Journal of Experimental Psychology*, 1970, *86*, 117–119.

Nelson, T. O. Spelling-pronunciation integration: Determinant of bimodal recall. *Journal of Verbal Learning and Verbal Behavior*, 1969, *8*, 118–122.

Neville, M. H. Reading in the first school: A comparison with Finland. *Reading*, 1972, *6*, 18–22.

Newbigging, P. L. The perceptual redintegration of frequent and infrequent words. *Canadian Journal of Psychology*, 1961, *15*, 123–132.

Newfield, M. U., and Schlanger, B. B. The acquisition of English morphology by normal and educable mentally retarded children. *Journal of Speech and Hearing Research*, 1968, *11*, 693–706.

Newman, E. B. Speed of reading when the span of letters is restricted. *American Journal of Psychology*, 1966, *79*, 272–278.

Nielsen, H. H., and Ringe, K. Visuo-perceptive and visuo-motor performance of children with reading disabilities. *Scandinavian Journal of Psychology*, 1969, *10*, 225–231.

Noble, C. E. An analysis of meaning. *Psychological Review*, 1952, *59*, 421–430.

Nodine, C. F., and Evans, J. D. Eye movements of prereaders containing letters of high and low confusability. *Perception and Psychophysics*, 1969, *6*, 39–41.

Nodine, C. F., and Lang, N. J. The development of visual scanning strategies for differentiating words. *Developmental Psychology*, 1971, *5*, 221–232.

Nodine, C. F., and Simmons, F. Processing distinctive features in the differentiation of letter-like symbols. *Journal of Experimental Psychology*, in press.

Nodine, C. F., and Stuerle, N. L. Development of perceptual and cognitive strategies for differentiating graphemes. *Journal of Experimental Psychology*, in press.

Novik, N. Parallel processing in a non-word classification task. Paper presented at Eastern Psychological Association, Washington, D.C., 1973.

Novik, N., and Katz, L. High-speed visual scanning of words and non-words. *Journal of Experimental Psychology*, 1971, *91*, 350–353.

Oakan, R., Wiener, M., and Cromer, W. Identification, organization, and reading comprehension for good and poor readers. *Journal of Educational Psychology*, 1971, *62*, 71–78.

O'Connor, J. D., and Tooley, O. M. The perceptibility of certain word boundaries. In D. Abercrombie et al. (eds.), *In honour of Daniel Jones*. London: Longmans, Green, 1964. Pp. 171–176.

Odom, R. D., McIntyre, C. W., and Neale, G. S. The influence of cognitive style on perceptual learning. *Child Development*, 1971, *42*, 883–891.

O'Donnell, R. C., Griffin, W. J., and Norris, R. C. Syntax of kindergarten and elementary school children: A transformational analysis. Research Report No. 8. Champaign, Ill.: National Council of Teachers of English, 1967.

Ohnmacht, D. D. The effects of letter-knowledge on achievement in reading in the first grade. Paper presented at American Educational Research Association meeting, Los Angeles, 1969.

Oléron, P., and Danset, A. Donnés sur l'appréhension des mots. Le role de diverses parties des mots et leur identification. *Psychologie Française*, 1963, *8*, 28–35.

Olson, D. R. Language use for communicating, instructing, and thinking. In J. B. Carroll and R. O. Freedle (eds.), *Language comprehension and the acquisition of knowledge*. Washington,

D.C.: V. H. Winston, 1972. Pp. 139–167.

Oomen, C. India. In J. Downing (ed.), *Comparative reading*. New York: Macmillan, 1973. Pp. 403–425.

Orbach, J. Retinal locus as a factor in recognition of visually perceived words. *American Journal of Psychology*, 1953, *65*, 555–572.

Orton, S. Word-blindness in school children. *Archives of Neurology and Psychiatry*, 1925, *14*, 381–615.

Orton, S. *Reading, writing and speech problems in children*. London: Chapman and Hall, 1937.

Owen, F. W., Adams, P. A., Forrest, T., Stolz, L. M., and Fisher, S. Learning disorders in children: Sibling studies. *Monographs of the SRCD*, 1971, *36*, No. 4.

Paivio, A., and O'Neill, B. J. Visual recognition thresholds and word meaning. *Perception and Psychophysics*, 1970, *8*, 273–275.

Palermo, D. S. Characteristics of word association responses obtained from children in grades one through four. *Developmental Psychology*, 1971, *5*, 118–123.

Parker, R. K., Rieff, M. L., and Sperr, S. J. Teaching multiple classification to young children. *Child Development*, 1971, *42*, 1779–1789.

Paterson, D. G., and Tinker, M. A. *How to make type readable*. New York: Harper & Brothers, 1940.

Perfetti, C. A. Psycho-semantics: Some cognitive aspects of structural meaning. *Psychological Bulletin*, 1972, *78*, 241–259.

Peterson, R. P. Patterns of eye movements in rapid symbol identification and their relation to reading achievement. *Perceptual and Motor Skills*, 1969, *28*, 307–310.

Pfaendler, U. Les vices de la parole dans l'optique du généticien. *Aktuelle Probleme der Phoniatrie und Logopaedie*, 1960, *1*, 35–40.

Pfafflin, S. M. Some psychological studies of sentence interconnections in written English prose. *Psychonomic Bulletin*, 1967, *1*, 17.

Pfafflin, S. M. Paragraph analysis. Bell Labs., Murray Hill, N. J. Mimeographed.

Piaget, J. *The origins of intelligence in children*. International Universities Press, 1952. Reprinted by Norton, New York, 1963.

Piaget, J. Cognitive development in children. The Piaget papers. In R. E. Ripple and V. N. Rockcastel (eds.), *Piaget rediscovered, a report of the conference on cognitive studies and curriculum development*. Ithaca: School of Education, Cornell University, 1964. Pp. 6–40.

Piaget, J. Piaget's theory. In P. H. Mussen (ed.), *Carmichael's manual of child psychology*. Vol. 1. Third ed. New York: John Wiley, 1970. Pp. 703–732.

Piaget, J., and Inhelder, B. *The child's conception of space*. New York: Humanities Press, 1956.

Pick, A. D. Improvement of visual and tactual form discrimination. *Journal of Experimental Psychology*, 1965, *69*, 331–339.

Pick, A. D. Some basic perceptual processes in reading. *Young Children*, 1970, *25*, 162–181.

Pick, A. D., Christy, M. D., and Frankel, G. W. A developmental study of visual selective attention. *Journal of Experimental Child Psychology*, 1972, *14*, 165–175.

Pierce, J. Some sources of artifact in studies of tachistoscopic perception of words. *Journal of Experimental Psychology*, 1963, *66*, 363–370.

Piestrup, A. M. Black dialect interference and accommodation of reading instruction in first grade. *Monographs of the Language-Behavior Research Laboratory*, 1973, *4*.

Pillsbury, W. B. The reading of words: A study in apperception. *American Journal of Psychology*, 1897, *8*, 315–393.

Pintner, R. Inner speech silent reading. *Psychological Review*, 1913, *20*, 129–153.

Posner, M. I., Boies, S. J., Eichelman, W. H., and Taylor, R. L. Retention of visual and name codes of single letters. *Journal of Experimental Psychology Monographs*, 1969, *79*, No. 1, Part 2.

Postman, L., and Adis-Castro, G. Psychological methods in the study of word recognition. *Science*, 1957, *125*, 193–194.

Postman, L., Bruner, J. S., and McGinnies, E. Personal values as selective factors in perception. *Journal of Abnormal Social Psychology*, 1948, *43*, 142–155.

Postman, L., and Rosenzweig, M. R. Practice and transfer in the visual and auditory recognition of verbal stimuli. *American Journal of Psychology*, 1956, *69*, 209–226.

Postman, L., and Senders, V. Incidental learning and generality of set. *Journal of Experimental Psychology*, 1946, *36*, 153–165.

Poulton, E. C. Peripheral vision, refractoriness and eye movements in fast oral reading. *British Journal of Psychology*, 1962, *53*, 409–419.

Poulton, E. C., and Brown, C. H. Memory after reading aloud and reading silently. *British Journal of Psychology*, 1967, *58*, 210–222.

Preston, R. C. Comparison of word-recognition skill in German and in American children. *Elementary School Journal*, 1952, *53*, 443–446.

Preston, R. C. Reading achievement of German and American children. *School and Society*, 1962, *90*, 350–354.

Quantz, J. O. *Problems in the psychology of reading.* New York: Macmillan, 1897.

Rabinovitch, M. S., and Strassberg, R. Syntax and retention in good and poor readers. *The Canadian Psychologist*, 1968, *9*, No. 2, 142–153.

Ramananskas, S. Contextual constraints beyond a sentence on cloze responses of mentally retarded children. *American Journal of Mental Deficiency*, 1972, *77*, 338–345.

Rankin, E. F. The relationship between reading rate and comprehension. *Eleventh Yearbook of the National Reading Conference*, 1962, 1–5.

Rayner, K. The perceptual span and peripheral cues in reading. Unpublished doctoral dissertation. Department of Education, Cornell University, 1974.

Read, C. Pre-school children's knowledge of English phonology. *Harvard Educational Review*, 1971, *41*, 1–34.

Rebert, G. N. A laboratory study in the reading of familiar formulas. *Journal of Educational Psychology*, 1932, *23*, 192–203.

Rees, H. J., and Israel, H. E. An investigation of the establishment and operation of mental sets. In J. J. Gibson (ed.), Studies in psychology from Smith College. *Psychological Monographs*, 1935, *46*,

Reicher, G. M. Perceptual recognition as a function of meaningfulness of stimulus material. *Journal of Experimental Psychology*, 1969, *81*, 275–280.

Resnick, L. B. *Design of an early learning curriculum.* Pittsburgh: Learning Research and Development Center, University of Pittsburgh, December, 1967.

Resnick, L. B. Relations between perceptual and syntactic control in oral reading. *Journal of Educational Psychology*, 1970, *61*, 382–385.

Restle, F., and Brown, E. R. Serial pattern learning. *Journal of Experimental Psychology*, 1970, *83*, 120–125.

Rice, U. M., and DiVesta, F. J. A developmental study of semantic and phonetic generalization in paired-associate learning. *Child Development*, 1965, *36*, 721–730.

Richards, I. A. *Practical criticism.* New York: Harcourt, Brace & World, 1929.

Riegel, K. F., and Riegel, R. M. Prediction of word-recognition thresholds on the basis of stimulus-parameters. *Language and Speech*, 1961, *4*, 157–170.

Riess, B. F. Genetic changes in semantic conditioning. *Journal of Experimental Psychology*, 1946, *36*, 143–152.

Rinsland, H. D. *A basic vocabulary of elementary school children.* New York: Macmillan, 1945.

Rogers, M. V. Comprehension in oral and silent reading. *Journal of General Psychology*, 1937, *17*, 394–397.

Rohrman, N. L., and Gough, P. B. Forewarning, meaning, and semantic decision latency. *Psychonomic Science*, 1967, *9*, 217–218.

Rohwer, W. D., Jr. Social class differences in the role of linguistic structures in paired-associate learning: Elaboration and learning proficiency. Final report. U.S.O.E. Basic Research Project No. 5–0605, Contract OE6–10–273, University of California at Berkeley and U.S. Office of Education, 1967.

Rosen, C. L. An experimental study of visual perceptual training and reading achievement in first grade. *Perceptual and Motor Skills*, 1966, *22*, 979–986.

Rosen, C. L., and Ames, W. S. Influence of nonstandard dialect on oral reading behavior of fourth grade Black children under two stimuli conditions. In R. D. Abrahams and R. C. Troike (eds.), *Language and cultural diversity in American education*. Englewood Cliffs, N.J.: Prentice-Hall, 1972. Pp. 305–310.

Rosen, C. L. and Ohnmacht, F. Perception, readiness, and reading achievement in first grade. In *Perception and Reading: Proceedings of the 12th Annual Convention of the International Reading Association*. Newark, Del.: 1968. Pp. 33–39.

Rosenzweig, M. R. Intelligibilité, visibilité et fréquence des mots. *Cahiers d'Études de radio-télévision*, 1956, *12*, 283–289.

Rosenzweig, M. R., and Postman, L. Frequency of usage and the perception of words. *Science*, 1958, *127*, 263–266.

Rosinski, R. R., and Wheeler, K. E. Children's use of orthographic structure in word discrimination. *Psychonomic Science*, 1972, *26*, 97–98.

Rosner, J. *The design board program*. Learning Research and Development Center, University of Pittsburgh, 1971/7. (a)

Rosner, J. *Phonic analysis training and beginning reading skills*. Learning Research and Development Center, University of Pittsburgh, 1971/19. (b)

Rosner, J. *The development and validation of an individualized perceptual skills curriculum*. Learning Research and Development Center, University of Pittsburgh, 1972.

Rosner, J., and Simon, D. The auditory analysis test: An initial report. *Journal of Learning Disabilities*, 1971, *4*, 384–392.

Ross, D. Effect on learning of psychological attachment to a film model. *American Journal of Mental Deficiency*, 1970, *74*, 701–707. (a)

Ross, D. Incidental learning of number concepts in small group games. *American Journal of Mental Deficiency*, 1970, *74*, 718–725. (b)

Rothkopf, E. Z. Some theoretical and experimental approaches to problems in written instruction. In J. D. Krumboltz (ed.), *Learning and the educational process*. Chicago: Rand McNally, 1965. Pp. 193–221.

Rothkopf, E. Z. Learning from written instructive materials: An exploration of the control of inspection behavior by test-like events. *American Educational Research Journal*, 1966, *3*, 241–249.

Rothkopf, E. Z. Two scientific approaches to the management of instruction. In R. M. Gagne and W. J. Gephart (eds.), *Learning research and school subjects*. Itasco, Ill.: Peacock, 1968. Pp. 107–132.

Rothkopf, E. Z. Concerning parallels between adaptive processes in thinking and self-instruction. In J. F. Voss (ed.), *Approaches to thought*. Columbus: Merrill, 1969. Pp. 299–316.

Rothkopf, E. Z. Incidental memory for location of information in text. *Journal of Verbal Learning and Verbal Behavior*, 1971, *10*, 608–613.

Rothkopf, E. Z. Structural text features and the control of processes in learning from written materials. In J. B. Carroll and R. O. Freedle (eds.), *Language comprehension and the acquisition of knowledge*. Washington, D.C.: V. H. Winston, 1972. Pp. 315–335.

Rothkopf, E. Z., and Bisbicos, E. E. Selective facilitative effects of interspersed questions on learning from written materials. *Journal of Educational Psychology*, 1967, *58*, 56–61.

Rothkopf, E. Z., and Bloom, R. D. Effects of interpersonal interaction on the instructional value of adjunct questions in learning from written material. *Journal of Educational Psychology*, 1970, *61*, 417–422.

Rohtkopf, E. Z., and Coke, E. U. Repetition interval and rehearsal method in learning equivalences from written sentences. *Journal of Verbal Learning and Verbal Behavior*, 1963, *2*, 406–416.

Rozin, P., Poritsky, S., and Sotsky, R. American children with reading problems can easily learn to read English represented by Chinese characters. *Science*, 1971, *171*, 1264–1267.

Rubenstein, H. An overview of psycholinguistics. Mimeo. Department of Psychology, Lehigh University, Bethlehem, Pa., 1971. To appear in *Current trends in linguistics*, Vol. 12. The Hague: Mouton.

Rubenstein, H., and Aborn, M. Learning, prediction, and readability. *Journal of Applied Psychology*, 1958, *42*, 28–32.

Rubenstein, H., Garfield, L., and Millikan, J. A. Homographic entries in the internal lexicon. *Journal of Verbal Learning and Verbal Behavior*, 1970, *9*, 487–494.

Rubenstein, H., Lewis, S. S., and Rubenstein, M. A. Homographic entries in the internal lexicon: Effects of systematicity and relative frequency of meanings. *Journal of Verbal Learning and Verbal Behavior,* 1971, *10,* 57–62. (a)

Rubenstein, H., Lewis, S. S., and Rubenstein, M. A. Evidence for phonemic recoding in visual word recognition. *Journal of Verbal Learning and Verbal Behavior,* 1971, *10,* 645–657. (b)

Ruddell, R. B. The effect of the similarity of oral and written patterns of language structure on reading comprehension. *Elementary English,* 1964, *42,* 403–410.

Ruthman, P. France. In J. Downing (ed.), *Comparative reading.* New York: Macmillan, 1973. Pp. 319–341.

Ryan, T. A. *Intentional behavior.* New York: Ronald Press, 1970.

Rystrom, R. Teaching remedial reading to Black children: Some results. *The Journal of Negro Education,* 1972, *41,* 352–360.

Sachs, J. Recognition memory for syntactic and semantic aspects of connected discourse. *Perception and Psychophysics,* 1967, *2,* 437–442.

Safren, M. A. Associations, sets, and the solution of word problems. *Journal of Experimental Psychology,* 1962, *64,* 40–45.

Sakamoto, T. On reading skills of vertical versus horizontal sentences. Unpublished paper read at Third Annual Congress of Japanese Association of Educational Psychology, 1961.

Sakamoto, T., and Makita, K. Japan. In J. Downing (ed.), *Comparative reading.* New York: Macmillan, 1973. Pp. 440–465.

Samuels, S. J. Attentional process in reading: The effect of pictures on the acquisition of reading responses. *Journal of Educational Psychology,* 1967, *58,* 337–342.

Samuels, S. J. Word associations and the recognition of flashed words. Mimeographed report, Project No. 6-8774, Minneapolis: University of Minnesota, 1968. (a)

Samuels, S. J. Relationship between formal intralist similarity and the von Restorff effect. *Journal of Educational Psychology,* 1968, *59,* 432–437. (b)

Samuels, S. J. An experimental program for teaching letter names of the alphabet. Project No. 9-F-009. Washington, D.C.: U.S. Office of Education, 1970. (a)

Samuels, S. J. Effects of pictures on learning to read, comprehension, and attitudes. *Review of Educational Research,* 1970, *40,* 397–408. (b)

Samuels, S. J. Modes of word recognition. In H. Singer and R. Ruddell (eds.), *Theoretical models and processes in reading*. Newark: International Reading Association, 1970. Pp. 23–37. (c)

Samuels, S. J. Attention and visual memory in reading acquisition. Research Report No. 26, Project No. 332189, University of Minnesota and U.S. Office of Education, 1971.

Samuels, S. J. The effect of letter-name knowledge on learning to read. *American Educational Research Journal*, 1972, *1*, 65–74.

Sanford, E. C. The relative legibility of the small letters. *American Journal of Psychology*, 1888, *1*, 402–435.

Sartre, J. P. *The psychology of imagination*. Tr. by Bernard Frechtman. New York: Washington Square Press, 1966.

Satz, P., Rardin, D., and Ross, J. An evaluation of a theory of specific developmental dyslexia. *Child Development*, 1971, *42*, 2009–2021.

Satz, P., and Sparrow, S. Specific developmental dyslexia: A theoretical formulation. In D. J. Bakker and P. Satz (eds.), *Specific reading disability*. Rotterdam: Rotterdam University Press, 1970. Pp. 17–40.

Savin, H. B. What the child knows about speech when he starts to learn to read. In J. F. Kavanagh and I. G. Mattingly (eds.), *Language by ear and by eye*. Cambridge, Mass.: The MIT Press, 1972. Pp. 319–326.

Savin, H. B., and Bever, T. G. The nonperceptual reality of the phoneme. *Journal of Verbal Learning and Verbal Behavior*, 1970, *9*, 295–302.

Sawyer, D. J. Intra-sentence grammatical constraints in readers' sampling of the visual display. Unpublished doctoral dissertation. Department of Education, Cornell University, 1971.

Schapiro, F. Information extraction and filtering during perceptual learning in visual search. Unpublished doctoral dissertation. Department of Psychology, Cornell University, 1970.

Schlesinger, I. M. *Sentence structure and the reading process*. The Hague: Mouton, 1968.

Schlesinger, I. M. The production of utterances and language acquisition. In D. I. Slobin (ed.), *The ontogenesis of grammar*. New York: Academic Press, 1971. Pp. 63–101.

Schlosberg, H. Time relations in serial visual perception. *Canadian Psychologist*, 1965, *6a*, 161–172.

Scribner, S., and Cole, M. Effects of constrained recall training on children's performance in a verbal memory task. *Child Development*, 1972, *43*, 845–857.

Shaffer, L. H., and Hardwick, J. Reading and typing. *Quarterly Journal of Experimental Psychology*, 1969, *21*, 381–383.

Shankweiler, D. Developmental dyslexia: A critique and review of recent evidence. *Cortex*, 1964, *1*, 53–62.

Shankweiler, D., and Liberman, I. Y. Misreading: A search for causes. In J. F. Kavanagh and I. G. Mattingly (eds.), *Language by ear and by eye*. Cambridge, Mass.: The MIT Press, 1972. Pp. 293–317.

Shaw, G. B. *Androcles and the Lion*. Alphabet ed. Harmondsworth, Middlesex: Penguin, 1962.

Shen, E. An analysis of eye movements in the reading of Chinese. *Journal of Experimental Psychology*, 1927, *10*, 158–183.

Shulman, H. G. Encoding and retention of semantic and phonemic information in short-term memory. *Journal of Verbal Learning and Verbal Behavior*, 1970, *9*, 499–508.

Shulman, L., and Keislar, E. *Learning by discovery*. Chicago: Rand McNally, 1966.

Shuy, R. W. A linguistic background for developing beginning reading materials for Black children. In J. C. Baratz and R. Shuy (eds.), *Teaching Black children to read*. Washington, D.C.: Center for Applied Linguistics, 1969. Pp. 117–137. (a)

Shuy, R. W. Whatever happened to the way kids talk? Lecture presented to National Conference on the Language Arts, Washington, D.C., 1969. (b)

Silberman, H. F. *Exploratory research on a beginning reading program*. Santa Monica, Calif.: System Development Corporation, 1964.

Silver, A., and Hagin, R. Specific reading disability, delineation of the syndrome and relationship to cerebral dominance. *Comprehensive Psychiatry*, 1960, *1*, 126–134.

Simmons, R. F. Some semantic structures for representing English meanings. In J. B. Carroll and R. O. Freedle (eds.), *Language comprehension and the acquisition of knowledge*. Washington, D.C.: V. H. Winston, 1972. Pp. 71–97.

Simon, D. P., and Simon, H. A. Alternative uses of phonemic information in spelling. *Review of Educational Research*, 1973, Vol. 43(1), 115–137.

Sinclair de-Zwart, H. *Acquisition du langage et développement de la pensée*. Paris: Dunod, 1967.

Sinclair de-Zwart, H. Developmental psycholinguistics. In D. Elkind and J. H. Flavell (eds.), *Studies in cognitive development*. New York: Oxford University Press, 1969. Pp. 315–366.

Sisson, E. D. The role of habit in eye-movements of reading. Unpublished doctoral dissertation. University of Minnesota, 1936.

Skailand, D. B. A comparison of four language units in teaching beginning reading. Paper read to American Educational Research Association, New York, 1971.

Skinner, B. F. *Verbal behavior.* New York: Appleton-Century-Crofts, 1957.

Slobin, D. I. Grammatical transformations and sentence comprehension in childhood and adulthood. *Journal of Verbal Learning and Verbal Behavior,* 1966, *5,* 219–227.

Slobin, D. I. (ed.). *The ontogenesis of language.* New York: Academic Press, 1971.

Slobin, D. I. *Psycholinguistics.* Glenview, Ill.: Scott, Foresman, 1971.

Slobin, D. I., and Welsh, C. A. Elicited imitation as a research tool in developmental psycholinguistics. In C. A. Ferguson and D. I. Slobin (eds.), *Readings on child language acquisition.* New York: Holt, Rinehart and Winston, in press.

Smirnov, A. A., Istomina, Z. M., Mal'Tseva, K. P., and Samokhralova, V. I. The development of logical memorization techniques in the preschool and young school child. *Soviet Psychology,* 1971–1972, *10,* 178–195.

Smirnov, A. A., and Zinchenko, P. I. Problems in the psychology of memory. In M. Cole and I. Maltzman (eds.), *A handbook of contemporary Soviet psychology.* New York: Basic Books. 1969. Pp. 452–502.

Smith, E. E., and Haviland, S. E. Why words are perceived more accurately than nonwords: Inference vs. unitization. *Journal of Experimental Psychology,* 1972, *92,* 59–64.

Smith, F. Familiarity of configuration vs. discriminability of features in the visual identification of words. *Psychonomic Science,* 1969, *14,* 261–262. (a)

Smith, F. The use of featural dependencies across letters in the visual identification of words. *Journal of Verbal Learning and Verbal Behavior,* 1969, *8,* 215–218. (b)

Smith, F., Lott, D., and Cronnell, B. The effect of type size and case alternation on word identification. *American Journal of Psychology,* 1969, *82,* 248–253.

Smith, H. K. The responses of good and poor readers when asked to read for different purposes. *Reading Research Quarterly,* 1967, *3,* 53–83.

Smith, M. E. An investigation of the development of the sentence and the extent of vocabulary in young children. *University of Iowa Studies on Child Welfare,* 1926, *3,* No. 5.

Smith, M. E., Rothkopf, R. Z., and Koether, M. The evaluation of instructional text: Relating properties of free recall protocols to text properties. Paper presented to American Educational Research Association, Washington, D.C., 1970.

Smith, R. B. Interrelatedness of certain deviant grammatical structures in Negro nonstandard dialects. *Journal of English Linguistics,* 1969, *3,* 82–88.

Smock, C. D., and Kanfer, F. H. Response bias and perception. *Journal of Experimental Psychology*, 1961, *62*, 158–163.

Snodgrass, J. G., and Jarvella, R. J. Some linguistic determinants of word classification times. *Psychonomic Science*, 1972, *27*, 220–222.

Snow, K. A detailed analysis of the articulation responses of normal first grade children. *Journal of Speech and Hearing Research*, 1963, *6*, 277–290.

Sokolov, A. N. *Inner speech and thought.* New York: Plenum Press, 1972.

Solberg, M. The acquisition of Quechua. Unpublished doctoral dissertation. Department of Human Development, Cornell University, 1971.

Solomon, R. L., and Howes, D. H. Word frequency, personal values, and visual duration thresholds. *Psychological Review*, 1951, *58*, 256–270.

Solomon, R. L., and Postman, L. Frequency of usage as a determinant of recognition thresholds for words. *Journal of Experimental Psychology* 1952, *43*, 195–201.

Sparrow, S., and Satz, P. Dyslexia, laterality and neuropsychological development. In D. J. Bakker and P. Satz (eds.), *Specific reading disability.* Rotterdam: Rotterdam University Press, 1970. Pp. 41–61.

Spitz, H. H., Goettler, D. R., and Webreck, C. A. Effects of two types of redundancy on visual digit span performance of retardates and varying aged normals. *Developmental Psychology*, 1972, *6*, 92–103.

Spoehr, K. T., and Smith, E. E. The role of syllables in perceptual processing. *Cognitive Psychology*, 1973, *5*, 71–89.

Sprague, R. L. Effects of differential training on tachistoscopic recognition thresholds. *Journal of Experimental Psychology*, 1959, *58*, 227–231.

Spreen, O., Borkowski, J. G., and Benton, A. L. Auditory word recognition as a function of meaningfulness, abstractness and phonetic structure. *Journal of Verbal Learning and Verbal Behavior*, 1967, *6*, 101–104.

Staats, A. W. *Learning, language, and cognition.* New York; Holt, Rinehart and Winston, 1968.

Staats, A. W., and Butterfield, W. H. Treatment of nonreading in a culturally deprived juvenile delinquent: An application of reinforcement principles. *Child Development*, 1965, *4*, 925–942.

Staats, A. W., and Staats, C. K. A comparison of the development of speech and reading behavior with implications for research. *Child Development*, 1962, *33*, 831–846.

Staats, A. W., and Staats, C. K. *Complex human behavior: A systematic extension of learning principles.* New York: Holt, Rinehart and Winston, 1963.

Staats, A. W., Staats, C. K., Schutz, R. E., and Wolf, M. The conditioning of textual responses using "extrinsic" reinforcers. *Journal of Experimental Analysis of Behavior*, 1962, *5*, 33–40.

Staats, C. K., Staats, A., and Schutz, R. E. The effects of discrimination pretraining on textual behavior. *Journal of Educational Psychology*, 1962, *53*, 32–37.

Stanley, G., and Hall, R. Short-term visual information processing in dyslexics. *Child Development*, 1973, *44*, 841–844.

Stanners, R. F., Forbach, G. B., and Headley, D. B. Decision and search processes in word-nonword classification. *Journal of Experimental Psychology*, 1971, *90*, 45–50.

Starch, D. *Advertising*. Chicago: Scott, Foresman, 1914.

Steiner, R., Wiener, M., and Cromer, W. Comprehension training and identification for poor and good readers. *Journal of Educational Psychology*, 1971, *62*, 506–513.

Sterritt, G. M., Martin, V. E., and Rudnick, M. Sequential pattern perception and reading. In *Proceedings of the 13th Annual Convention of the International Reading Association*. Newark, Del.: 1969. Pp. 61–71.

Stevens, S. S., and Stone, G. Psychological writing, easy and hard. *American Psychologist*, 1947, *2*, 230–235.

Stewart, M. L., James, C. T., and Gough, P. B. Word recognition latency as a function of word length. Paper read to Midwestern Psychological Association, 1969.

Stewart, W. A. On the use of Negro dialect in the teaching of reading. In J. C. Baratz and R. Shuy (eds.), *Teaching Black children to read*. Washington, D.C.: Center for Applied Linguistics, 1969. Pp. 156–219.

Stone, L. C. Reading reactions for varied types of subject matter: An analytical study of eye movements of college freshmen. *Journal of Experimental Education*, 1941, *10*, 64–77.

Streng, A. *Reading for deaf children*. Washington, D.C.: Alexander Graham Bell Association for the Deaf, 1964.

Strickland, R. G. The language of elementary school children: Its relationship to the language of reading textbooks and the quality of reading by selected children. *Bulletin of the School of Education, Indiana University*, 1962, *38*, No. 4, 1–131.

Stuckles, E. R., and Birch, J. W. The influence of early manual communication on the linguistic development of deaf children. *American Annals of the Deaf*, 1966, *111*, 452–462 and 499–503.

Tatham, S. M. Reading comprehension of materials written with select oral language patterns: A study at grades two and four. *Reading Research Quarterly*, 1970, *5*, No. 3, 402–426.

Taylor, A. M., and Whitely, S. E. Overt verbalization and the continued production of effective elaborations by EMR children. Research Report No. 38, Project No. 332189, Grant No. OE-09-332189-4533(032), University of Minnesota, Minneapolis, 1972.

Taylor, J. A. Meaning, frequency, and visual duration threshold. *Journal of Experimental Psychology*, 1958, *55*, 329–334.

Taylor, S. E. An evaluation of forty-one trainees who had recently completed the "Reading Dynamics" program. *Eleventh Yearbook of the National Reading Conference*, 1962, 41–55.

Taylor, W. L. Cloze procedure: A new tool for measuring readability. *Journalism Quarterly*, 1953, *30*, 415.

Taylor, W. L. "Cloze" readability scores as indices of individual differences in comprehension and aptitude. *Journal of Applied Psychology*, 1957, *41*, 19–26.

Tenney, Y. J. Development of cognitive organization in children. Unpublished doctoral dissertation. Department of Psychology, Cornell University, 1973.

Tenny, Y. J. The child's conception of organization in recall. *Journal of Experimental Child Psychology*, in press.

Thomas, E. L. Eye movements in speed reading. In R. G. Stauffer (ed.), *Speed reading: Practices and procedures*. Vol. 10. Newark, Del.: University of Delaware, Reading Study Center, 1962. Pp. 104–114.

Thomas, H. Children's tachistoscopic recognition of words and pseudowords varying in pronounceability and consonant-vowel sequence. *Journal of Experimental Psychology*, 1968, *77*, 511–513.

Thompson, M. C., and Massaro, D. W. Visual information and redundancy in reading. *Journal of Experimental Psychology*, 1973, *98*, 49–54.

Thorndike, E. L. *Educational psychology*. Vol. II. *The psychology of learning*. New York: Teachers College, Columbia Universtiy, 1913.

Thorndike, E. L. Reading as reasoning: A study of mistakes in paragraph reading. *Journal of Educational Psychology*, 1917, *8*, 323–332..

Thorndike, E. L. Mental discipline in high school studies; A communication and a reply. *Journal of Educational Psychology*, 1924, *15*, 1–22 and 83–98.

Thorndike, E. L., and Lorge, I. *The teacher's wordbook of 30,000 words*. New York: Bureau of Publications, Teachers College, Columbia University, 1944.

Thorndike, E. L., and Woodworth, R. S. The influence of improvement in one mental function upon the efficiency of other functions. (I); II. The estimation of magnitudes; III. Functions involving attention, observation and discrimination. *Psychological Review*, 1901, *8*, 247–261, 384–395, and 553–564.

Thorndike, R. L. *Reading comprehension: Education in fifteen countries.* New York: John Wiley, 1973.

Tinker, M. A. Reliability and validity of eye-movement measures of reading. *Journal of Experimental Psychology*, 1939, *19*, 732–746.

Tinker, M. A. The study of eye movements in reading. *Psychological Bulletin*, 1946, *43*, 93–120.

Tinker, M. A. Prolonged reading tasks in visual research. *Journal of Applied Psychology*, 1955, *39*, 444–446.

Tinker, M. A. Recent studies of eye-movements in reading. *Psychological Bulletin*, 1958, *55*, 215–231.

Tinker, M. A. *Bases for effective reading.* Minneapolis: University of Minnesota Press, 1965.

Tolman, E. C. *Purposive behavior in animals and men.* New York: Century, 1932.

Tolman, E. C. and Brunswick, E. The organism and the causal texture of the environment. *Psychological Review*, 1935, *42*, 43–77.

Trabasso, T. Mental operations in language comprehension. In J. Carroll and R. O. Fredle (eds.), *Language comprehension and the acquisition of knowledge.* Washington, D.C.: V. H. Winston, 1972. Pp. 113–137.

Trager, G. L., and Bloch, B. The syllabic phonemes of English. *Language*, 1941, *17*, 223–246.

Troike, R. C. Receptive bidialectalism: Implications for second-dialect teaching. In R.D. Abrahams and R.C. Troike (eds.), *Language and cultural diversity in American education.* Englewood Cliffs, N. J.: Prentice-Hall, 1972. Pp. 305–310.

Tulving, E., and Donaldson, W. (eds.). *Organization of memory.* New York: Academic Press, 1972.

Tulving, E., and Gold, C. Stimulus information and contextual information as determinants of tachistoscopic recognition of words. *Journal of Experimental Psychology*, 1963, *66*, 319–327.

Tulving, E., Mandler, G., and Baumal, R. Interaction of two sources of information in tachistoscopic word recognition. *Canadian Journal of Psychology*, 1964, *18*, 62–71.

Turner, E. A., and Rommetveit, R. The acquisition of sentence voice and reversibility. *Child Development*, 1967, *38*, 649–660.

UNESCO Handbook in Reading. Paris: UNESCO, 1972.

Vandenberg, S. G. Human behavior genetics: Present status and suggestions for future research. *Merrill-Palmer Quarterly of Behavior and Development*, 1966, *15*, 121–154.

Vande Voort, L., Senf, G. M., and Benton, A. L. Development of audiovisual integration in normal and retarded readers. *Child Development*, 1972, *43*, 1260–1272.

Vellutino, F. R., Harding, C. J., and Phillips, F. Differential transfer in poor and normal readers. *Journal of Genetic Psychology*, 1973, in press.

Velten, H. V. The growth of phonemic and lexical patterns in infant language. *Language*, 1943, *19*, 281–292.

Velezky, R. L. English orthography: Its graphical structure and its relation to sound. *Reading Research Quarterly*, 1967, *2*, 75–106.

Venezky, R. L. *The structure of English orthogarphy*. The Hague: Mouton, 1970. (a)

Venezky, R. L. Regularity in reading and spelling. In H. Levin and J. P. Williams (eds.), *Basic studies on reading*. New York: Basic Books, 1970. Pp. 30–42. (b)

Venezky, R. L. Principles for the design of practical writing systems. *Anthropological Linguistics*, 1970, *12*, 256–270. (c)

Venezky, R. L. Nonstandard language and reading. *Elementary English*, 1970, *47*, 334–345. (d)

Venezky, R. L. *The prereading skills program*. Madison: Wisconsin Research and Development Center for Cognitive Learning, 1971. (a)

Venezky, R. L. *Letter naming and learning to read*. Wisconsin Research and Development Center for Cognitive Learning, Theoretical Paper No. 31, 1971. (b)

Venezky, R. L. *Language and cognition in reading*. Wisconsin Research and Development Center for Cognitive Learning, Technical Report No. 188, 1972. (a)

Venezky, R. L. *The letter-sound generalizations of first, second, and third grade Finnish children*. Wisconsin Research and Development Center for Cognitive Learning, Technical Report No. 219, 1972. (b)

Venezky, R. L., Chapman, R. S., and Calfee, R. C. *The development of letter-sound generalizations from second through sixth grade*. Wisconsin Research and Development Center for Cognitive Learning, Technical Report No. 231, 1972.

Venezky, R. L., and Johnson, D. *The development of two letter-sound patterns in grades 1–3*. Wisconsin Research and Development Center for Cognitive Learning, Technical Report No. 189, 1972.

Venezky, R. L., and Shiloah, Y. The learning of picture-sound associations by Israeli kindergartners. Mimeographed, 1972.

Venezky, R. L., Shiloah, Y., and Calfee, R. *Studies of prereading skills in Israel.* Wisconsin Research and Development Center for Cognitive Learning, Technical Report No. 227, 1972.

Vernon, M. D. *The experimental study of reading.* Cambridge: Cambridge University Press, 1931.

Vernon, M., and Koh, S. D. Early manual communication and deaf children's achievement. *American Annals of the Deaf,* 1970, *115,* 527–535.

Vernon, M., and Koh, S. D. Effects of oral preschool compared to early manual communication on education and communication in deaf children. *American Annals of the Deaf,* 1971, *116,* 569–574.

Volkmann, F. C. Vision during voluntary saccadic eye movements. *Journal of the Optical Society of America,* 1962, *52,* 571–578.

Volkmann, F. C., and Pufall, P. B. Adjustments of visual tilt as a function of age. *Perception and Psychophysics,* 1972, *11,* 187–192.

Volkmann, F. C., Schich, A. M. L., and Riggs, L. A. Time course of visual inhibition during voluntary saccades. *Journal of the Optical Society of America,* 1968, *58,* 562–569.

Vurpillot, E. The development of scanning strategies and their relation to visual differentiation. *Journal of Experimental Child Psychology,* 1968, *6,* 622–650.

Vygotsky, L. S. *Thought and language.* Edited and translated by E. Hanfmann and G. Vakar. Cambridge, Mass., and New York: The MIT Press and John Wiley, 1962.

Wagner, J. Experimentelle Beiträge zur Psychologie des Lesens. *Zeitschrift für Psychologie,* 1918, *80,* 1–75.

Waite, R. R. Further attempts to integrate and urbanize first-grade reading textbooks. *Journal of Negro Education,* Winter, 1968, 62–69.

Walker, J. H. Pronounceability effects on word-nonword encoding in categorization and recognition tasks. *Journal of Experimental Psychology,* 1973, *99,* 318–322.

Walker, L., and Cole, E. M. Familial patterns of expression of specific reading disability in a population sample. Part 1: Prevalence, distribution and persistence. Bulletin of the Orton Society, 1965, *15,* 12–24.

Walker, R. Y. A qualitative study of eye movements of good readers. *American Journal of Psychology,* 1938, *51,* 472–481.

Walker, W. Cherokee Primer. Tahlequak, Oklahoma; Carnegie Corporation Cross-cultural Education Project of the University of Chicago, 1965.

Wallach, M. A. Perceptual recognition of approximations to English in relation to spelling achievement. *Journal of Educational Psychology*, 1963, *54*, 57–62.

Walsh, L. *Read Japanese today*. Rutland, Vt.: Charles E. Tuttle, 1969.

Wanat, S. F. *Linguistic structure and visual attention in reading*. Newark, Del.: The International Reading Association Research Reports, 1971.

Wanat, S. F. and Levin, H. The eye-voice span: Reading efficiency and syntactic predictability. In H. Levin, E. J. Gibson, and J. J. Gibson, *The analysis of reading skill*. Final Report No. 5–1213, from Cornell University to the U.S. Office of Education, December, 1968. Pp. 237–253.

Wang, W. S-Y. The Chinese language. *Scientific American*, 1973, *228*, 50–63.

Wardhaugh, R. *Reading: A linguistic perspective*. New York: Harcourt, Brace & World, 1969.

Warren, R. M. Identification times for phonemic components of graded complexity and for spelling of speech. *Perception and Psychophysics*, 1971, *9*, 345–349.

Watson, J. B. *Behaviorism*. Chicago: University of Chicago Press, 1930.

Watson, J. S. The development and generalization of "contingency awareness" in early infancy: Some hypotheses. *Merrill-Palmer Quarterly of Behavior and Development*, 1966, *12*, 123–135.

Weber, R. M. The study of oral reading errors: A survey of the literature. *Reading Research Quarterly*, 1968, *4*, 96–119.

Weber, R. M. First graders' use of grammatical context in reading. In H. Levin and J. P. Williams (eds.), *Basic studies on reading*. New York: Basic Books, 1970. Pp. 147–163. (a)

Weber, R. M. Some reservations on the significance of dialect in the acquisition of reading. In J. A. Figurel (ed.), *Reading goals for the disadvantaged*. Newark, Del.: International Reading Association, 1970. Pp. 124–131. (b)

Webster's New World Dictionary of the American Language. College ed. New York: World, 1958.

Webster's Third New York International Dictionary. Unabridged. New York: G. & C. Merriam, 1966.

Weir, R. H. *Language in the crib*. The Hague: Mouton, 1962.

Werner, H. *The comparative psychology of mental development*. New York: Science Editions, 1961. Reprinted after original edition in 1948.

Westman, A. S. A developmental study of the ability to perceive and utilize categorical structure. Unpublished doctoral dissertation. Department of Psychology, Cornell University, 1971.

Wheeler, D. D. Processes in word recognition. *Cognitive Psychology*, 1970, *1*, 59–85.

Wheeler, M. E. Untutored acquisition of writing skill. Unpublished doctoral dissertation, Department of Human Development, Cornell University, 1971.

Whicher, G. F. *This was a poet*. Ann Arbor: University of Michigan Press, 1957. Original printing C. Scribner's, 1938.

Whorf, B. L. Linguistics as an exact science. In J. B. Carroll (ed.), *Language, thought and reality*. Cambridge, Mass.: The MIT Press, 1956. Pp. 220–232.

Wiberg, J. L., and Blom, G. E. A cross national study of attitude content in reading primers. *International Journal of Psychology*, 1970, *5*, 109–122.

Wilder, L. *Analysis training: Failure to replicate Elkonin*. Technical Report No. 202, Wisconsin Research and Development Center for Cognitive Learning, 1972.

Williams, J. P. Training kindergarten children to discriminate letterlike forms. *American Education Research Journal*, 1969, *6*, 501–514.

Willows, D. M., Reading between the lines: A study of selective attention in good and poor readers. *Child Development*, June, 1974.

Willows, D. M., and McKinnon, G. E. Selective reading: Attention to the "unattended" lines. *Canadian Journal of Psychology*, 1973, *27*, No. 3, 292–304.

Winnick, W. A., and Kressel, K. Tachistoscopic recognition thresholds, paired-associate learning, and free recall as a function of abstractness-concreteness and word frequency. *Journal of Experimental Psychology*, 1965, *70*, 163–168.

Wispe, L. G., and Drambarean, N. C. Physiological need, word frequency, and visual duration thresholds. *Journal of Experimental Psychology*, 1953, *46*, 25–31.

Wolf, W., King, M. L., and Huck, C. S. Teaching critical reading to elementary school children. *Reading Research Quarterly*, 1968, *3*, 435–498.

Wolfe, L. S. An experimental study of reversals in reading. *American Journal of Psychology*, 1939, *52*, 533–561.

Wolfram, W. A., and Fasold, R. S. Toward reading materials for speakers of Black English: Three linguistically appropriate passages. In J. C. Baratz and R. Shuy (eds.), *Teaching Black children to read*. Washington, D.C.: Center for Applied Linguistics, 1969. Pp. 138–155.

Wood, M. W. Teaching reading to deaf children. Unpublished doctoral dissertation. School of Education, University of Pennsylvania, 1973.

Woodrow, H., and Lowell, F. Children's association frequency tables. *Psychological Monographs*, 1916, *22*, No. 97.

Woodworth, R. S. Vision and localization during eye movements. *Psychological Bulletin*, 1906, *3*, 68–70.

Woodworth, R. S. *Experimental psychology*. New York: Holt, 1938.

Wyckoff, L. B., Jr. The role of observing responses in discrimination learning. Part I. *Psychological Review*, 1952, *59*, 431–442.

Yonas, A. The acquisition of information-processing strategies in a time-dependent task. Unpublished doctoral dissertation. Department of Psychology, Cornell University, 1969.

Zachrisson, R. Four hundred years of English spelling reform. *Studia Nephilologica*, 1931, *4*, 1–69.

Zaporozhets, A. V. The development of perception in the preschool child. In P. H. Mussen (ed.), *European research in child development*. Monographs of the Society for Research in Child Development, 1965, *30*, Ser. No. 100. Pp. 82–101.

Zaporozhets, A. V., and Elkonin, D. B. (eds.). *The psychology of preschool children*. Cambridge, Mass.: The MIT Press, 1971.

Zaslow, M. The effect of orthographic structure on letter search: A reexamination. Senior honors thesis. Department of Psychology, Cornell University, 1972.

Zeitler, J. Tachistoskopische Versuche über das Lesen. *Wundt's Philosophische Studien*, 1900, *16*, 380–463.

Zettersten, A. *A statistical study of the graphic system of present-day American English*. Lund, Sweden: Studentlitteratur, 1969.

Zhurova, L. E. The development of analysis of words into their sounds by preschool children. *Soviet Psychology and Psychiatry*, 1963/64, *2*, 17–27.

Zimmerman, B. J., and Bell, J. A. Observer verbalization and abstraction in vicarious rule learning, generalization, and retention. *Developmental Psychology*, 1972, *7*, 227–231.

Zinchenko. V. P., Van, C.-T., and Tarkanov, V. V. The formation and development of perceptual activity. *Soviet Psychology and Psychiatry*, 1963, *2*, 3–12.

Zyve, C. I. Conversation among children. *Teachers College Record*, 1927, *29*, 46–61.

Subject Index

Author Index